U.S. ARMY SPECIAL OPERATIONS IN AFGHANISTAN

COVER PHOTO CREDITS

FRONT COVER:
Top Left: SSG Dean Will (18B, ODA 2025) during an early-morning arms-cache raid in a village in rural eastern Afghanistan along the Pakistan border. (Photo copyright © Paul Avallone, Green Beret from 1978–2004.)

Top Right: Special Forces soldiers and a Marine Corps contingent maintain security as a medical evacuation helicopter lands to evacuate wounded Coalition personnel after a combat action south of Camp Blessing, Afghanistan. (Photo courtesy of U.S. Army.)

Bottom Left: SF 18D and sniper SSG John Cain, with AF Tac-P SGT Frank Lofton spotting, maintains sniper overwatch following a successful raid on an opium-processing lab in Nangarhar Province in late 2002. (Photo copyright © Paul Avallone, Green Beret from 1978–2004.)

Bottom Right: Soldiers of the 3rd Special Forces Group drive their Humvee through a river on the way to the Daychopan region of Afghanistan. (Photo by SGT Horace Murray, courtesy of U.S. Army.)

BACK COVER:
Seen through a night-vision device, a soldier of the 3rd Special Forces Group maintains security from a fortified position during a direct fire attack on Bagram Air Field, Afghanistan. (Photo by Spc. Thomas Bray, courtesy of U.S. Army.)

U.S. ARMY SPECIAL OPERATIONS IN AFGHANISTAN

Charles H. Briscoe
Richard L. Kiper
James A. Schroder
Kalev I. Sepp

PALADIN PRESS • BOULDER, COLORADO

U.S. Army Special Operations in Afghanistan
by Charles H. Briscoe, Richard L. Kiper, James A. Schroder,
Kalev I. Sepp

Publisher's foreword copyright © 2006 by Paladin Press

ISBN 10: 1-58160-510-2
ISBN 13: 978-1-58160-510-5

Printed in the United States of America

Published by Paladin Press, a division of
Paladin Enterprises, Inc.
Gunbarrel Tech Center
7077 Winchester Circle
Boulder, Colorado 80301 USA
+1.303.443.7250

Direct inquiries and/or orders to the above address.

The figures that appear in this book are credited as follows:

U.S. government photos: chapter 1, figures 3, 8, 9, 10, 11, and 12.

CIA photos: chapter 1, figures 1 and 2; chapter 2, figures 4, 24, 25, 27, 28, and 31; chapter 3, figures 2, 19, and 52; and chapter 5, figure 5.

Joint Combat Camera Center: chapter 1, figure 6; chapter 2, figures 6, 12, 15, 30, and 36; chapter 3, figures 7, 8, 13, 15, 24, 59, 66, and 69.

U.S. Army Special Operations Command History Office: chapter 1, figures 4, 5, and 7; chapter 2, figures 1, 3-5, 7-11, 13, 14, 15-22, 26, 29-35, 39-60; chapter 3, figures 1-5, 8-12, 14, 16-18, 20-23, 25-58, 60-68, 70, 73-75; chapter 4, figures 1-34; and chapter 5, figures 1-4, 6-31.

Combat Studies Institute (CSI) Press publications cover a variety of military history topics. The views expressed in this CSI Press publication are those of the authors and not necessarily those of the Department of the Army or the Department of Defense.

A full list of CSI/CGSC Press publications, many of them available for downloading, can be found at <http:www.cgsc.army.mil/csi>.

PUBLISHER'S FOREWORD

This book is reprinted "as is" by Paladin Press from the original work created by U.S. Army Special Operations Command (USASOC) under the title *Weapon of Choice–ARSOF in Afghanistan* for distribution to the United States Army Special Operations soldiers. It is the first time this book has been available to the general public.

Some digital photographs and illustrations in this text appear blurry, as they do in the original work. While Paladin Press has made every effort to create the best possible presentation of this book, we decided that the information is of such historical significance that the inclusion of some photos of less than perfect appearance should not prevent or delay its publication and distribution.

> *We will find these people and they will suffer the consequence of taking on this nation. We will do what it takes. No one is going to diminish the spirit of this country.*
> *President George W. Bush*
> *September 11, 2001*

U.S. Army Special Operations Forces were committed to Afghanistan almost immediately following the September 11, 2001, attacks on the United States by the terrorist organization al-Qaeda. For years, al-Qaeda, with the knowledge and support of Afghanistan's ruling body, the Taliban, had operated terrorist training camps there. The first order of business for the U.S. military was to hit the enemy hard and fast, destroying al-Qaeda's visible infrastructure and many of its personnel, and severely limiting the terrorist's capability, at least for a while, to carry out further attacks.

This book chronicles the "boots on the ground" actions taken by USASOC from September 11, 2001, until May 15, 2002. Most of the actions documented here were carried out by junior officers and NCOs. The USASOC historians who conducted interviews with special operations personnel are themselves former Special Forces soldiers. Their tasks were to sanitize classified accounts of the war in Afghanistan and to provide a snapshot of the campaign waged by USASOC in a format that is easily understood. They have included the mistakes, frustrations, and failures along with the successes. Rather than an armchair historian's overall strategic view of the campaign 10 years later, it is a contemporary account of what individuals and small teams did on a day-to-day basis to rid Afghanistan of the Taliban, assist the Afghan people, and begin the work of rebuilding the infrastructure of the country.

What makes this work so significant is that much of the information presented within its pages was collected at the time the individual operations and battles took place. LTG R. Doug Brown, the commander of U.S. Army Special Operations Command at the time, directed that the history of the actions of USASOC troops should be captured *as they were fighting the war*. This entailed the deployment to Afghanistan of the USASOC Command History Team, which included the authors and two active duty Special Forces soldiers (MAJ David Beech and CW3 William Bill Bryant) in conjunction with 126th Military History Detachment covering Civil Affairs.

Richard Kiper, one of the authors and a former Special Forces officer with a Ph.D. in history, recounted how the team dressed in boots and cargo pants, a Kevlar vest, and a carbine for action in Afghanistan. A tape recorder, cameras, and many pens completed their working gear. On arrival at their headquarters in Bagram, the team split up; half of them worked between Bagram and Kabul, while the others went to Kandahar. They interviewed special operations soldiers who were conducting widely varying assignments: Rangers (light infantry trained to seize airfields), Psychological Operations (TV and radio broadcasts, leaflets, etc.), Special Operations Aviation (helicopters), Civil Affairs (providing humanitarian assistance to the locals), and Special Forces (Green Berets). "They were just phenomenal," Kiper later said when asked his overall impression of the troops.

The mission of the USASOC Command History Team was clear: to write an account of what Army special operations soldiers did in Afghanistan to defeat the Taliban and help the people of Afghanistan rebuild their country, as seen through the eyes of the soldiers who were actually there at the time, and to make the book easy for American readers to understand. This outstanding book, the first of its kind for the historians at USASOC, is the result.

About Afghanistan

Located in southern Asia between Iran, Pakistan, China, and some of the former Soviet satellite countries, Afghanistan was formed in 1747 when the Pashtun tribes were unified under Ahmad Shah Durrani. This landlocked country, which is slightly smaller than Texas, has endured occupations by both Britain and the Soviet Union. From 1996 to 2001, most of the country, with the exception of parts held by the Northern Alliance, was under the control of the radical Pakistani-backed Taliban.

By most standards, Afghanistan is a forbidding place: cold in winter, hot in summer. There is a shortage of drinking water, causing most of the population to live in varying degrees of dehydration. Mountainous terrain, with peaks up to 17,000 feet, makes travel difficult, and it is not uncommon to see vehicles imported from countries such as Pakistan stripped down and carried in pieces over the mountain passes by camel. Wheat and other crops can be grown in some of the more arable valleys, but with water controlled by war lords many farmers are tempted to go for the big money and plant poppies, which are used in the production of heroin.

This geographical environment alone has contributed to the defeat of every foreign military force that tried to dominate Afghanistan. But, in addition, the population is made up of many separate factions: tribal, subtribal, religious (mainly between the majority Sunni Muslims and the minority Shi'a Muslims). There are three major languages spoken and thirty minor languages. This cultural patchwork makes it difficult for outsiders to interact with, and gain the support and cooperation of, the indigenous population as a whole without appearing to either favor or ignore one local group over another. Arms and ammunition caches are still scattered around the countryside, left over from the Soviet occupation, when the individual factions put aside their tribal differences and united to oppose the invaders. The *mujahideen*, as these freedom fighters came to be known, also received weapons and other military assistance from the West.

It is this harsh environment into which USASOC forces deployed after the September 11 attacks, and in which they continue to operate today. As the following pages attest, they have performed—and continue to perform—their vital but delicate mission with bravery, skill, and honor.

FOREWORD

This extensive account of U.S. Army Special Operations soldiers and their actions in Afghanistan is an important contribution to understanding how these unique individuals removed the *Taliban* from power and destroyed *al-Qaeda* and *Taliban* strongholds in Afghanistan as well as part of the US global war on terrorism. The originating idea, research, and writing that went into it are strictly the product of U.S. Army Special Operations Command and its assigned authors.

The Combat Studies Institute (CSI), Fort Leavenworth, Kansas, is pleased to have been selected to provide the technical editing and production assistance required to produce this novel work. The editing section of CSI's Research and Publication Team has faithfully produced the thoughts, ideas, and sentiments of the original authors.

Lawyn C. Edwards
Colonel, Aviation
Director, Combat Studies

USSOCOM Foreword

October 1, 2003

The contributions of Army Special Operations to free an oppressed people and deny sanctuary for global terrorism were absolutely critical to the success of Operation ENDURING FREEDOM. Army Special Operations spearheaded our Nation's first response to the terrible attacks of September 11, 2001. Their story is one of courage, dedication, and honor. *Weapon of Choice* tells the Army Special Operations story -- from the daring infiltration of Special Forces "A" teams through the treacherous mountain passes by our 160th Special Operations Aviation Regiment, to the heroism in Operation ANACONDA, to the courageous night parachute jump by our Rangers, and the phenomenal work done by our Civil Affairs, Psychological Operations and support Soldiers. Our success, along with our talented Joint and Coalition partners, overwhelmed the enemy and freed a Nation.

Small numbers of men and women of Army Special Operations made the difference in Operation ENDURING FREEDOM. The quality of these great Americans made the difficult missions seem routine -- the impossible missions possible. The unique skills, bravery, and harrowing exploits were the foundation of success in Afghanistan.

The lessons derived from today's battlefield will better prepare us for tomorrow. *Weapon of Choice* will help tell the story of Afghanistan. As the battle in the Global War on Terrorism continues, America can be justifiably proud of Army Special Operations' contributions. Special Operations forces will remain at the forefront in the war. The very freedom of our great Nation depends on our collective efforts. If our past is any measure, we are in great hands.

Bryan D. Brown
General, U.S. Army
Commander

i

USASOC FOREWORD

October 1, 2003

This current operations history of Army Special Operations Forces in Operation ENDURING FREEDOM-Afghanistan (OEF-Afghanistan) explains what our soldiers accomplished during the "First Round" of America's Global War on Terrorism (GWOT). <u>Weapon of Choice</u> is the command's first published history for the general public. Since the successful toppling of the Taliban regime in Afghanistan was directly attributable to mid-level ARSOF leaders (Majors and below) and the operational teams, well-documented soldiers' stories are used to describe and explain how missions were accomplished. Vital roles of staff elements and support agencies have been included because three-fourths of "the USASOC Force" enables the operators at the "tip of the spear" to fight the war.

While not all solutions applied to the challenges of war strictly followed doctrine, they worked the majority of the time. Disciplined, highly motivated, and innovative professionals best describe the soldiers in Army special operations units at all levels. Their success in the unconventional warfare and foreign internal defense environment of Afghanistan validated the critical selection process and the extensive training of Special Forces, Rangers, Special Operations Aviation, Civil Affairs, Psychological Operations, and Special Operations Support Command soldiers to work in today's joint and coalition war arena.

<u>Weapon of Choice</u> is the first book in the USASOC-sponsored ARSOF History series. This book is timely operational history because it illustrates the caliber of today's special operations soldiers and explains what they really did in combat for every reader. And it also benefits "the Force" and America's other armed forces by providing quality information applicable to all levels of command and staff. Since warfighting is not "all sunshine and roses," there were injuries and fine soldiers were lost in this "First Round" of GWOT. Rest assured that these warriors did not die in vain. God bless America.

Philip R. Kensinger, Jr.
Lieutenant General, U.S. Army
Commanding Officer

Contents

Chapter   *Page*

USSOCOM Foreword...i

USASOC Foreword iii

Figures viii

Acknowledgments xiii

Introduction xv

1. Prelude to Terror 1

2. Awakening the Giant 33

    "Subdue Without Fighting": JPOTF, MacDill Air Force Base, Florida 47

    Developing the SOF Campaign at SOCCENT, Tampa, Florida.................... 50

    Top Draft Choices: 10th SFG, Fort Carson, CO, and 7th SFG, Fort Bragg, NC ... 51

    5th SFG = CJSOTF-North, Fort Campbell, Kentucky................................... 52

    Standing Up JSOTFs in Tampa and Fort Campbell 54

    Committed to Middle East Exercises.. 57

    3rd SFG Prepares for the Horn of Africa at Fort Bragg............................. 58

    Thinking Ahead: Senior Liaison Officers for Resistance Leaders 59

    Civil Affairs to Islamabad, Pakistan.. 60

    Of Vital Importance: PSYOP.. 62

    Site Coordination With the Uzbeks at Karshi Kanabad 64

    Uncorking the Bottled Airlift.. 66

    All Credit Cards Accepted at K2 Gas Station.. 68

    Air Campaign and CSAR Go Hand in Hand 68

    Making Camp Freedom a Fully Operational Base: K2, Uzbekistan............ 70

    Northern Air Campaign CSAR = MH-47Es 71

    Building Camp Freedom at Double Time 72

    The Universal Morale Booster at K2—Hot Food.. 73

    Special Forces: CSAR Personnel Recovery and UW Preparation............. 74

    Real Estate and Security at K2 74

    Task Force Dagger = JSOTF-North at K2 74

    Hot-Wiring the "Snake": Rearranging JSOTF-North Communications 75

    Building the JOC Inside the "Snake": TF Dagger's JOC............................ 77

    Staff "Battle Captain": The Combat Operations "Pulse Monitor" 78

    Different Intelligence Concerns for Air Planners 78

    JSOTF-North Growing Pains at K2 79

    We Don't Fail 80

    DAPs Set the Stage for UW in Afghanistan 82

3. Toppling the *Taliban* in Afghanistan, 19 October-7 December 2001 93

    Jumping Into the Dark: Seizing Rhino, 19 October 2001 109

    Tactical PSYOP for Rhino.. 113

    Showing American Power 115

    "Look, We Have to Get the Special Forces Teams Into Afghanistan!"...... 117

    On Horseback With Dostum 122

    ODA 595 Begins Bombing *Taliban* Defenses 125

    Aerial Resupply From the Receiver 127

    Aerial Resupply by SOCEUR.. 129

    A "Bump" and Missiles in the Abyss 132

500 Afghans Can Die, But Not One American Can Be Injured 134

AAA = A Bad Night in the Hindu Kush 134

Getting a Handle on the Air Threat 138

Fostering Faith and Providing Solace 138

AAA Payback Time 139

Bastogne in Afghanistan 140

"Little Birds" of Prey 141

High Desert Rat Patrol 143

The Great Communications Terminus 145

Resupply From 10,000 Feet 146

PSYOP = Hard, Steady Work 147

A Supportive Populace 150

Getting PSYOP on the Ground in Afghanistan 151

Have Tools Will Travel 151

Mr. President 153

A Significant Meeting With an Unusual Man 154

The Battle of Tarin Kowt 155

SOCCENT to Mazar-e-Sharif 158

Al-Qaeda Uprising—Qala-i-Jangi—24-29 November 158

ODA 583 Meets Gul Agha Sherzai 165

The Fight at Tahk-te-pol 167

Fighting at Arghastan Bridge 169

Plans Versus Reality 171

The Karzai Way to Kandahar 172

Charge to the Airport and Back Again 174

Attacking the Arghendab Bridge With Karzai 175

Who Dares, Wins 178

Death From Above 179

Another Reaction to Kandahar's Fall 182

CA and Humanitarian Relief 183

CA Teams on the Ground 184

Tactical PSYOP to Mazar-e-Sharif 185

Emergency Casualty Evacuation at K2 187

4. The Campaign in Transition, 8 December 2001-28 February 2002 203

Old Glory Flies Again in Kabul 211

Tora Bora 213

One Army 216

The Answer is Out There 219

A New Twist on an Old Idea 220

Chokepoint 225

"60 Minutes II" 227

High-Altitude Rescue of a Marine CH-53 229

Taking Down *al-Qaeda* at the Mir Wais Hospital 232

The Raid at Hazer Qadam 235

SR Eyes on Target 241

From EMT to Special Forces Force Multiplier 244

Politics, War, and Rapport 248

Chapter	Page

GTMO Bound 250
CA Liaison Work 251
CJSOTF-West 253
End of Mission—Aerial Resupply in Afghanistan 253
"We're Going for Sure This Time" 255
Be Prepared for SSE 256
Native Pashto and Dari Speaker Seeking PSYOP Assignment 257
Keep on Trucking 260
Rescue at 10,000 Feet 261
Date Drop at Khowst 263
ODA 394: The Next Mission 265

5. The New War 275
Entering the Valley 282
Field Expedient Triage 285
Disaster and Frustration 285
Combat Multipliers 287
D-Day ANACONDA From the Viewpoint of Force Multipliers 288
ARSOF in Direct Support 292
On Again-Off Again 293
With the Aussies 295
Forty-Five Seconds Too Long 296
Never Leave a Fallen Comrade 299
Against All Odds 302
Joining the Fight on Takur Ghar 309
ODA 394 Climbs the "Whale" 319
Integrating Civil Affairs 328
Ambush at 80 Knots 330
Trail of Caches 332
Establishing CJSOTF-Afghanistan 335
Communications at Bagram 337
High Desert Automation Management 338
"Good Morrrrning, Afghannnnistan" 340
A Disaster Provides a Catalyst 342
The Communications Handoff 344
Better Communications 344
CJSOTF-Afghanistan and the Joint Air Component 345
CJSOTF-Afghanistan and "Zulu Time" 345
Command Guidance and VTCs 346
Rebuilding the Kabul Military Academy 347
Another View of the Kabul Military Academy Task 349
"Chiclets" and PSYOP Teams in Kandahar 350
Their Lucky Day 353
Dealing With Cryptographic Compromise 355
Caves and Graves 356
Vietnam-Style A Camp at Orgun-e 358
A National Army for Afghanistan 358
Observations and Reflections 369

    Preparation for War 370

    Driving the *Taliban* From Power: ARSOF in the Supported Role 376

    Transition and Combat Operations 383

    The CJSOTF-Afghanistan Era Begins 389

  Glossary 393

  About the Contributors 399

  Index 401

Figures

Chapter 1

1. Regional Map and Selected Cities in the Country 1
2. Regional Location Map and Neighboring Countries 3
3. Jimmy Carter 11
4. Soviet Tank Carcass 12
5. Abandoned MiG at Mazar 15
6. Hamad Karzai 18
7. Afghan Children 20
8. Madeleine Albright 22
9. Bill Richardson 22
10. William Cohen 24
11. GEN Henry Shelton 24
12. George Tenet 26

Chapter 2

1. Extensive Mountainous Terrain 34
2. Pakistan Government Building 35
3. Tribal Factions, Regions, and Leaders 36
4. Map Depicting the Ethnic and Linguistic Diversity of Afghanistan 37
5. BG McClure, COL Volckmann, and COL Bank 39
6. Defense Secretary Rumsfeld Names the Operational Efforts 40
7. LTG Bryan D. Brown Encourages Soldiers 42
8. Helicopter View of Karshi Kanabad (K2) Air Base, Uzbekistan 45
9. The 528th Support Battalion Kept the Water Flowing 45
10. The 112th Signal Battalion Established the JSOTF-North Communications Links 45
11. The 528th Support Battalion Soldiers Prepared for Base Camp Construction 45
12. C-17 Globemaster III Taking Off From K2 to Make Humanitarian Food Drops 46
13. Commando Solo Airborne Broadcasting Platform 46
14. "Drive Out the Foreign Terrorists" Leaflet Dropped During the Air Campaign 46
15. 75th Rangers Night Parachute Assault on Objective Rhino 47
16. MH-47E Helicopters Taxi for Preflight Checks Before Night Missions 47
17. 160th SOAR—Loaded and Ready for Night Operations 47
18. Resistance is Futile; Assistance Works Better 48
19. "Reassurance" Leaflets in Multiple Languages 48
20. Leaflet Messages Directed at the Civilian Population 49
21. Leaflet Appealing to Afghan Nationalism 50
22. 4th POG Printing Presses Regularly Operated Overtime 50
23. SOCCENT Map Dividing Afghanistan Geographically 54

24. Afghanistan 55
25. LAN Connectivity to the K2 "Snake" 56
26. Amman, Jordan 58
27. The Central Command's Horn of Africa Region 59
28. TF Dagger Commander COL Mulholland Gives GEN Myers (CJCS) an Update at K2 59
29. U.S. Army Civil Affairs and Psychological Operations Command Shoulder Patch 60
30. Islamabad in Relation to Afghanistan 61
31. PSYOP Themes Centered on Accepting Coalition Assistance 63
32. Karshi Kanabad (K2), Uzbekistan 64
33. K2, Uzbekistan 65
34. Uzbek Guards—The Bottom of the Bureaucratic Ladder 66
35. K2 Buildup With Backlog of Accumulating Supplies and Equipment 67
36. 160th Special Operations Aviation Regiment (SOAR) 67
37. Refueling a Soviet Mi-17 at K2 68
38. Night Stalker View of the C-130P Trailing Refuel Lines and Probe Basket 69
39. Trail Aircraft View of MH-47E Refueling 69
40. MH-47E Hooked Up for Aerial Refueling 69
41. 112th Signal Battalion Satellite Antennas 70
42. K2 Buildup 70
43. MH-47E Landing at K2 70
44. MH-60L DAPs 71
45. Aircraft Maintenance Was a Crucial Factor for Success 71
46. 528th SOSB Initial Logistics Chaos 72
47. K2 Cantonment Area 72
48. COL Frank Kisner and COL John Mulholland 75
49. TF Dagger Logo 75
50. The Support Battalion Needs Communications to Provide Support 76
51. 112th Signal Battalion Unit Insignia and Beret Flash 76
52. Dry for the Moment 77
53. JSOTF-North Commander COL Mulholland With Secretary of Defense Rumsfeld 80
54. Antennas, Power, and Cabling Installed First 81
55. Initial Signal Links to K2 81
56. MH-60L DAP. Winter Operations in High Mountainous Terrain Posed Major Challenges 82
57. Identifying the Good Guys From the Bad Guys 84
58. Preflight Check Included Attaching Glint Tape to Identify "Friendlies" 84

Chapter 3

1. LTG Bryan D. Brown, USASOC Commander 93
2. Kabul, Afghanistan's National Capital 94
3. General Abdul Rashid Dostum 95
4. Refueling the MC-130P Tanker Was a Major Task 96
5. View of an Impacting Smart Bomb 97
6. General Shariff and Supporters 97
7. 75th Rangers Combat Parachute Assault on Objective Rhino 98
8. A Soviet-Made Mi-17 Utility Helicopter Flown by Contract Pilots 99
9. An MH-47E Deploying Defensive Measures 100
10. Ismail Khan 100
11. Special Forces Teams Use Satellite Links for Communications 101

12.   A Special Forces Soldier Employing a Laser Designator to Mark Targets 101
13.   Lethal AH-6 "Little Bird" Conducts a Night Raid 103
14.   Loading Nonstandard Tactical Vehicles Aboard an MH-47E 104
15.   U.S. Air Force AC-130 Spectre Gunship Firing at Night 105
16.   D Company, 109th Maintenance Battalion, ARNG, Reinforces the 160th SOAR 106
17.   Hamad Karzai Poses With Special Forces Soldiers 106
18.   Masirah Island Off the Coast of Oman 108
19.   Masirah Airfield 108
20.   Shoulder Scroll of the 3rd Battalion, 75th Ranger Regiment 110
21.   Receiving Mission Orders Before Departure 110
22.   75th Rangers Prepare for an Airborne Assault 110
23.   Rangers Preparing to Seize Objective Rhino 111
24.   Parachute Assault on Objective Rhino 112
25.   Rangers Clearing Objective Cobalt 112
26.   75th Ranger Calling Card 114
27.   U.S. Navy P-3C Orion Aircraft 116
28.   75th Rangers Rehearsing a Fast Rope Infiltration from a 160th SOAR MH-60K 118
29.   Patriotism Abounds at All Hours 119
30.   High Mountain Terrain Obstructed the Route 119
31.   MH-47E Clearing the "Bear" at Night 120
32.   Dostum Travels in a More Traditional Way 123
33.   Pack Mules and Rucksacks—A Good Combination for ODA 595 124
34.   Mobility Issues Were Overcome by an Old-Fashioned Solution 124
35.   ODA 595's Second Echelon Moves to Link Up With Dostum's Main Body of Fighters 124
36.   An American Special Forces Soldier on His Afghan Horse 125
37.   A Middle-Aged Afghan Man 126
38.   JDAM Strikes Were a Morale Booster for Dostum 127
39.   Western Versus Cordura Saddles 129
40.   GEN Holland and BG Fuller With COL Mulholland 129
41.   Units Worked Very Long Hours to Support Resupply Demands 130
42.   Bodyguards for the Special Forces Team 134
43.   General Dostum Sharing a Meal With Special Forces Personnel 134
44.   An MH-47E Deploying Flares During a AAA Threat 136
45.   Night Stalker Crew Chief 137
46.   75th Rangers Conducting Long-Range Armed Reconnaissance 140
47.   75th Rangers Awaiting MC-130s 141
48.   An AH-6 "Little Bird" Armed for Night Raids 142
49.   75th Ranger Hide Site 144
50.   75th Ranger Night Movement Under NVGs 144
51.   Unexpected, But Welcome, Resupply Bundles 147
52.   The Modular Print System (MPS) at Bagram Air Base 147
53.   Reward Leaflet 148
54.   CA Personnel Give Transistor Radios to Afghans 149
55.   4th POG Leaflet With Radio Broadcast Frequencies 149
56.   Diego Garcia in the Indian Ocean 150
57.   The 109th Aviation Maintenance Battalion (AVIM) Provided Quality Support 152
58.   Hamad Karzai 153

59. Afghan Leader With a PSYOP Leaflet..154
60. Preparations Under Way to Reestablish Control Over the Prison.................160
61. AC-130 20mm Gatling Guns (Vulcan)..164
62. Gul Agha Sherzai...165
63. Location and Importance..168
64. Deploying Forces..168
65. Battle of the Arghastan Bridge..170
66. One of the Major Objectives of the Southern Offensive 171
67. Training New Karzai "Recruits" for Combat 173
68. A U.S. Air Force A-10 Warthog CAS Aircraft 174
69. Actions at the Arghendab Bridge...176
70. The Kandahar Welcoming Committee..179
71. A Mission-Ready JDAM 180
72. JDAM Components 181
73. President George W. Bush 181
74. President Bush and Hamid Karzai 182
75. Inventory and Accountability Were a Constant Part of Humanitarian Aid..........184
76. CA Collar Insignia and the USACAPOC Shoulder Patch............................185
77. A Casualty Evacuation Kit on an MH-47 Chinook 188
78 CA Always Fostering Goodwill and Demonstrating Compassion..................188

Chapter 4

1. American Colors Unfurled at the U.S. Embassy in Kabul...............................203
2. Preparing for *al-Qaeda* 204
3. Under New Management 205
4. Sand Table for DA SSE Raid Preparations 205
5. Afghan Children 207
6. The Camp Abel Motor Pool in Bagram 208
7. Post-Mission Discussions Among ARSOF Personnel 210
8. Kabul Sprawl and Majestic Mountains...212
9. U.S. Embassy Cornerstone and a Solemn Ceremony 212
10. Two Northern Afghan Leaders..213
11. Cave Searches Locate Weapons and Munitions Caches 214
12. Mobile Cave Operations...214
13. The 19th SFG Beret Flash With Special Forces Crest.................................217
14. A 5/19th SFG Soldier Establishing Communications in Afghanistan.............217
15. The 112th Signal Battalion Successfully Improvised at Kandahar Air Base...........220
16. Bamian Buddha Site After the *Taliban* Destroyed it on 11 March 2001 221
17. Autoclaves Inside Herat Hospital 222
18. A Typical Classroom in a Bamian School 223
19. CA Teams Examine the Condition of a Community Well.............................223
20. Impromptu "Contract Negotiations" With Village Leaders...........................224
21. Salang Tunnel and Road Conditions..224
22. Friendship Bridge 225
23. Making Friends and Influencing People 225
24. Ground Mobility Vehicles (GMVs) Ready for Action..................................236
25. A/1/5 SFG Uses an "Up" Armored HMMWV GMV..................................237

26. Elements of the Kelly Force Aboard a Marine Corps CH-53 238
27. Weapons Captured During a Hazer Qadam Raid 240
28. ODA 514 Conducts SR in Mountains of Southern Afghanistan 242
29. PSYOP Leaflet Warning About Unexploded Ordnance 245
30. PSYOP Loudspeaker HMMWVs Traveling in Pairs 246
31. Broadcasting Music Outside an Afghan Village 246
32. People Long Remember the Good Others Do for Them and Their Children 247
33. Airdropped Bundles Created Logistics Challenges for the Teams 254
34. MC-130Ps Fly a "Racetrack" to Remain Available for Refueling 262
35. Recruiting "Runway Maintenance Specialists" From the Local Population 265

Chapter 5

1. Marching Was the "First Step" in Building a National Army 275
2. Equipment Issue is the First, and Sometimes Last, Official Act for Some Army Recruits 276
3. ANA Officers Course Begins at Kabul Military Academy 279
4. Terrain Models for Officer Tactical Training 280
5. Focused View of Paktia Province 280
6. Bagram Air Base Becomes the "Center of the Universe" 281
7. Coalition View of Operation ANACONDA 284
8. Objective Remington in the Shah-i-Khot Valley 291
9. Babulkhel Damage Assessment 291
10. Serkhankhal Aftermath 291
11. Millions of 4th POG Leaflets Emphasized Hopelessness and Encouraged Surrender 293
12. AH-64 Apache Attack Helicopter 294
13. Two-Wheeled LZs Became Routine for 160th SOAR MH-47E Pilots 296
14. The Impossible Becomes Inevitable 300
15. The Unlikely Becomes Fact 300
16. The Harsh Terrain of Takur Ghar 310
17. Mountains and "Whales" 316
18. Typical Special Forces Base Camp Area in Afghanistan 320
19. General Haidar at Rest 323
20. General Haidar on the Move 323
21. Humanitarian Aid Arrives 328
22. Good Wells are Vital to Life in Afghanistan 329
23. Destroyed DshK Antiaircraft Weapon System in the Shah-i-Khot Valley 333
24. Cave Caches Produced a Surprising Variety of Items 334
25. Cave Caches Were Commonly Uncovered in Sweeps of Shah-i-Khot Valley 335
26. SOMS-B Broadcasts the News 340
27. The "Scope of Work" Was Immense 348
28. Local Leaders Help Decide What Comes Next 350
29. One of America's Favorite Pastimes Appeals to Others as Well 351
30. Deliveries Were Always a Significant Priority 352
31. Special Forces Medics Conduct Triage of Afghan Wounded 354
32. Special Forces Medics Stabilize the Wounded 355

Acknowledgments

Weapon of Choice is a history of the Army special operations forces in Afghanistan from 11 September 2001 to 15 May 2002, during America's global war on terrorism (GWOT). Lieutenant General R. Doug Brown, commander, U.S. Army Special Operations Command (USASOC), directed and personally sponsored this initial effort "to capture the current operations history of the Army special operations soldiers as they fought the war in Afghanistan." Writing an unclassified, well-documented history of current operations was a first for the command and staff of USASOC as well as for the supported headquarters, U.S. Central Command (CENTCOM); U.S. Special Operations Command (USSOCOM); Joint Special Operations Command (JSOC); and Special Operations Command, CENTCOM (SOCCENT). The "learning curve" was steep for all parties, but the final results—a special edition of *Special Warfare* magazine, "ARSOF in Afghanistan," and this book, *Weapon of Choice*—demonstrate what can be accomplished.

Appropriate thanks are due a myriad of people whose encouragement, assistance "above and beyond," and constant support made this timely history possible. Within the USASOC history community are Dr. Cherilyn Walley, USASOC historian, and Dr. Kenn Finlayson, U.S. Army John F. Kennedy Special Warfare Center and School (SWCS) historian, who read, commented on, and edited *Weapon of Choice* and who proofread the final manuscript; Mr. Earl J. Moniz, resident "computer wizard," who physically organized and compiled all of the written material into a manuscript, scanned photographs and leaflets into the text, and designed the cover for *Weapon of Choice*; LTC Robert Jones, a mobilized U.S. Army Reserve (USAR) historian, who "commanded" and tended to the administrative needs of the 126th and 45th Military History Detachments (MHDs), facilitating the 126th's overseas deployment and personally coordinating their activities in Afghanistan; Ms. Monet McKinzie, archives technician, who performed innumerable administrative tasks to assist the historians; Ms. Cyn Hayden, USASOC archivist, who helped the contract historians; and Mr. Erdie Picart, archives technician, who ensured the physical security of classified material; the 126th MHD, Army National Guard (ARNG), Boston, Massachusetts—MAJ Paul Landry, SFC Daniel Moriarty, SSG Patrick Jennings, and SGT Landon Mavrelis—for covering civil affairs (CA) activities during Operation ENDURING FREEDOM (OEF), Afghanistan; and the USAR 45th MHD, Atlanta, Georgia, for covering psychological operations (PSYOP) in OEF at Fort Bragg, North Carolina.

There are many on the USASOC, U.S. Army Special Forces Command (USASFC), U.S. Army Civil Affairs and Psychological Operations Command (USACAPOC), and SWCS staffs who deserve special mention. From USASOC: COLs Ives Fontaine and Charles Cleveland, Chiefs of Staff, the major proponents of the project; Mr. Charles Pimble, Secretary of the General Staff; Ms. Connie Wicker; Ms. Jane Sutherlin and Ms. Karen Glass, Acquisition and Contracting; COL Steve Schrum, Mr. John Green, Ms. Sally Hurt, Mr. Dan Brand, Mr. John Watkins, Mr. Ed Nelson, and Ms. Sarah Fields, Deputy Chief of Staff, Intelligence; COL Philip McGhee, LTC Christopher White, Ms. Susan Ritter, Ms. Rose Reid, and Ms. Robin Jones, Deputy Chief of Staff for Resource Management; Mr. Dorsey Mellott, MSG Charles Koonce, and Ms. Shelley Marné, Deputy Chief of Staff for Information Management; COL Randy Cochran, Deputy Chief of Staff, Special Operations Aviation; Mr. Randall Wilkie of the Army Compartmented Element; LTC Jack Ziegler, MAJ Robert Cairns (manuscript reader), MAJ Andrew Nichols, and Ms. Sally Smith, Deputy Chief of Staff for Operations and Plans (DCSOPS); MAJ John T. Corley and MAJ Eric Patterson, TDY to DCSOPS for Project Insight; and Major Robert Hardy, SFC T. Dennis, and SSG J. Simon, HHC, USASOC. From USASFC: COL Manny Diemer, Deputy Commander; COL John Knie, Chief of Staff; Mr. James Hargraves (manuscript reader) and Mr. Chris Crain of the G3; and MAJ Jim Rosenberry and MSG Charles Hopkins of the G1. From USACAPOC: LTC Christopher Leyda, G3, and MAJ David Fox and SFC G. Doles, CENTCOM desk. From SWCS: COL Richard Helfer, Chief of Staff; MAJ Brian Banks, Staff Judge Advocate (manuscript reader); COL Andy Anderson; Major David Beech; CW3 William Bryant; and Mr. Jerry Steelman, editor, *Special Warfare* magazine, Department of Training and Doctrine. To all the soldiers and airmen of USASOC who contributed their time, personal photos, and records to the USASOC history team, thanks for being true professionals.

Within the U.S. Special Operations Command (USSOCOM), Tampa, Florida, thanks go to Mr. Kirk Moeller for the practicalities of "how to get contract personnel into the theater of operations" and points of contact in Afghanistan. In the USSOCOM History Office, Dr. John Partin, Command Historian; Ms. Gaea Levy, archivist; and the USSOCOM historians who worked in Afghanistan—COL Richard Stewart, LTC Thomas Searle, and MAJ Matt Dawson, CJSOTF-Afghanistan—for meeting the USASOC team in Qatar and getting it to Bagram to begin work. At JSOC, COL Andrew Milani, Mr. Steve Cage, and Mr. James Kelliher (manuscript readers); Mr. Mario Forestier; and Mr. D.J. Friederichs. At SOCCENT headquarters in Tampa and overseas in Qatar, we appreciate the help from the J3 section that arranged the USASOC trip to Afghanistan.

Special thanks go to Carol Rippey and Tad Sifeis, Armed Forces Information Service, Alexandria, Virginia, for providing electronic copies of the *Early Bird* covering September 2001-May 2002. These proved invaluable to the history writers.

Thank you to Mark Boyatt of SYTEX, Inc., Fayetteville, North Carolina, for providing three outstanding retired Army special operations personnel with advanced academic credentials and the requisite experience to serve as contract historians for this project.

Finally, accolades are due for Dr. W. Glenn Robertson, Combat Studies Institute (CSI), Fort Leavenworth, Kansas, and editors Patricia H. Whitten who edited and laid the book out and Robin D. Kern who assisted with layout and worked on the covers, Research and Publication Team, CSI, for producing a quality *Weapon of Choice*.

While all authors sincerely appreciate the help rendered by everyone mentioned above, errors of fact and identification, and the nonattributable observations and reflections section in *Weapon of Choice* are my responsibility as senior writer and editor.—Dr. Chuck Briscoe

Introduction

The purpose of this book is to share Army special operations soldier stories with the general American public to show them what various elements accomplished during the war to drive the *Taliban* from power and to destroy *al-Qaeda* and *Taliban* strongholds in Afghanistan as part of the global war on terrorism. The purpose of the book is not to resolve Army special operations doctrinal issues, to clarify or update military definitions, or to be the "definitive" history of the continuing unconventional war in Afghanistan. The purpose is to demonstrate how the war to drive the *Taliban* from power, help the Afghan people, and assist the Afghan Interim Authority (AIA) rebuild the country afterward was successfully accomplished by majors, captains, warrant officers, and sergeants on tactical teams and aircrews at the lowest levels. If Army special operations forces (ARSOF) operations and the operational employment of teams in Afghanistan by various Joint Special Operaions Task Forces (JSOTFs) create doctrinal debate, the appropriate venue within which to resolve those issues is at the U.S. Army Special Warfare Center and School. Combat operations in Afghanistan remain classified by the U.S. Central Command (CENTCOM). This is a carefully "sanitized" rendering of selected combat operations, and used pseudonyms for military personnel in the grade of lieutenant colonel and below (unless the individuals had received so much media exposure that this simple security measure would be meaningless). Likewise, the "eyes" of ARSOF personnel below the grade of colonel have been "blacked-out" in the photos for operational security (OPSEC) reasons. Chapter introductions and the vignettes have been written so that individuals with little previous knowledge of the military can understand and appreciate the contributions of the small Army special operations units that succeeded in driving the *Taliban* from power in Afghanistan.

The selected historical vignettes tell the ARSOF story. Many of these soldier stories demonstrate the capabilities of special operations forces (SOF)-unique equipment, while others point out the skills and bravery of the soldiers and aviators. The strength of ARSOF resides in its highly trained, very motivated soldiers. While technology plays a part in ARSOF, the soldiers make the difference. There has been a conscious effort to ensure that the stories of all ARSOF elements are presented. Thus, to provide a fair representative sampling of different activities within the security constraints, not all interviews became vignettes. One hundred-percent coverage of all participating teams was impossible. The examples selected were the best of those available to demonstrate a capability, illustrate an activity, or clarify a combat mission. The sensitive classified parts have been sanitized based on specific security rules, hence special forces elements do not always mean special forces teams, and pseudonyms are used predominantly. A limited-access U.S. Army Special Operations Command (USSOCOM) classified annex of sources will contain true names and specify documents and briefings to corroborate the material included. The controlled classified annex will not be available to researchers who do not have the appropriate security clearances and a clear "need to know."

This historical project is not intended to be the definitive study of the war in Afghanistan. It is a "snapshot" of the war from 11 September 2001 until the middle of May 2002. Since the published word promotes analysis and provokes discussion, the first official account of this successful unconventional war should come from Army Special Operations because they spearheaded the ground campaign that forced the *Taliban* from power in Afghanistan. The vignettes are based primarily on recorded interviews, after-action reports, personal notes of participants, and tactical operations center (TOC) logs. Open secondary sources were also used, but for this operations history, the recorded interviews of soldiers from tactical teams to various JSOTF and Special Operations Command Central (SOCCENT) staff personnel proved to be the most valuable. Where minor differences were found between accounts by a tactical team and head-quarters records and cross-referencing corroborated data provided by the "team on the ground," that was adopted. In the interest of producing a timely product while the war was still "fresh," discrepancies that could not be resolved satisfactorily were handled by the project director who evaluated importance, relevance, and whether they contributed to or confused the issue.

This is a current history of war. The decision to have professional historians with ARSOF experience capture the history of current operations in Afghanistan is proof that the book is not intended to be a public relations piece. War and combat have never been "all sunshine and roses." Just as campaign plans and units orders tend to "go to the winds" once the fighting starts, reluctant and ill-prepared leaders are replaced, confusion and incomplete information are relegated to the "fog of war," and recollections from the headquarters afterward as to what really happened on the ground tend to dominate after-the-battle reports. The writing team—composed of retired ARSOF veterans—understood those "given" elements. When everything goes according to plan, professional soldiers consider it an anomaly. Thus, to reach 95-percent objectivity, the writing team veterans kept the following sports adage in mind: "It's easy to fool the fans, but you can't fool the players." While observations and reflections are included, complete analysis can be done only when the ARSOF mission in Afghanistan is concluded.

Chapter 1

Prelude to Terror

Oh, East is East, and West is West,
and never the two shall meet,
Till Earth and Sky stand presently at
God's great Judgment Seat;
But there is neither East nor West,
Border, nor Breed, nor Birth,
When two strong men stand face to face,
tho' they come from the ends of the earth.[1]

On 11 September 2001, two strong men from the ends of the earth stood face to face—President of the United States George W. Bush and Osama bin Laden, leader of the *al-Qaeda* terrorist network. Although they had never met, both stood at the epicenter of one of the most cataclysmic events ever to strike the United States. These two men embodied the clash between Western liberalism and eastern Islamic fundamentalism. One culture valued freedom, equal rights, and religious tolerance. The other culture epitomized hatred—especially for the United States and Israel—suppression of women, demonization of any religion other than Islam, and strict adherence to a radical form of Islam that embraced terrorism and equated death in the *jihad* (holy war) against perceived enemies as glorious martyrdom. Although Americans had encountered Muslim fanaticism in 1993 with the bombing at the World Trade Center and again in 1998 when bin Laden terrorists attacked U.S. embassies in Kenya and Tanzania, most failed to understand the vicious nature of a man who viewed "hostility towards America [as] a religious duty."[2] On that September morning, the extent of that hostility was brought home to millions of Americans in a flaming shower of glass, metal, and death.

Figure 1. Regional map and selected cities in the country.

Even after the events of 1993 and 1998, Afghanistan had little relevance to most Americans as they went about their daily lives. What was unfolding there, however, suddenly would dominate the news, the stock market, the airlines, and the very security of the United States. Only soldiers, diplomats, historians, and oil pipeline executives expressed any interest in or knowledge of that far-away Third-World country. Few Americans understood why the United States would be drawn into a conflict with religious overtones that seemed so distant and so confusing. While the United States was not at war with Afghanistan and had no interest in attacking, occupying, or intervening in that country, *al-Qaeda*, with the support of the *Taliban*, saw the world differently.

To better understand this most recent war in Afghanistan, a summarized history of the region is provided. What should become very apparent are three constants: perpetual internal fighting between tribal ethnic groups, the dominance of Islam in society, and intervention by external actors using this discord to achieve influence in the country. Afghan leaders, in turn, have sought to take advantage of power plays, whether they were made by regional actors or international superpowers engaged in Cold War or more powerful warlords. To Westerners, internal alliances seem to "shift with the wind." The limited number of large cities makes them critical control points in the country. The dominant ethnic group has controlled the population centers. Thus, the significance of their capture or control in 2001 can be related to past wars and internal tribal fighting. Mountains, among the highest in the world, have always dictated the natural flow of traffic in and out of this landlocked country. Throughout this story, historical references will be made to show links between the present war and past conflicts.

Foreign invasion is an integral part of Afghanistan's history. Alexander the Great invaded the region between 330 and 327 A.D. In the seventh century, Arab Muslims, after conquering Iran, moved east and reached Kandahar around 700 A.D. By 715, Mohammad Bin Oasim had overrun the entire area and begun to convert the populace to Sunni Islam. From the Ghaznavid capital at Ghazni, Yamin ad-Dawlah Mahmud, of Turkish descent, led his military forces through Afghanistan, Pakistan, and parts of India during the first half of the 10th century. His conquests assured the domination of Sunni Islam throughout the region. Various Turkish rulers would rule Afghanistan until 1221 when, from the North, Genghis Khan crossed into present-day Afghanistan and destroyed the city of Balkh. Fifty years later Marco Polo would comment on the ruins of the town. Although his Mongol horde was halted just north of Kabul, Genghis Khan quickly regrouped and proceeded to devastate the area. The destruction was so complete that one historian has referred to Genghis Khan as "the atom bomb of his day."[3] But what the Mongols could not destroy was Islam, and by 1295, the descendants of Genghis Khan were Muslim.[4]

In the late 1300s, the warrior Tamerlane (Timur the Lame) moved south from his home near Samarkand in present-day Uzbekistan to incorporate Afghanistan into his Timurid Empire. Tamerlane's interest in conquest rather than administration prompted the empire's dissolution after his death in 1405. Although his immediate successors established Herat as a cultural center, they were unable to control the competition for power. For the next three centuries, turmoil characterized what would become Afghanistan. Babur (Zahiruddin Muhammad), a descendant of Tamerlane and Genghis Khan, founded the Moghul Dynasty that captured Kabul in 1504 and extended his rule throughout India. Simultaneously, the Persian Safavid Empire seized territory around Kandahar, and Uzbeks attempted to gain control over Herat.

Figure 2. Regional location map and neighboring countries.

Native Pashtun tribes attacked what they perceived to be foreign invaders, but disunity precluded large gains. Competition, lack of unity, and weakness were ingredients that enabled the Persian, Nadir Shar, to control the region with military might.[5]

Seeking to overthrow the weak Persian ruler and eliminate the Turks from Persia, Nadir embarked on a successful campaign that not only recovered land lost to Turkey but also dealt with his Pashtun enemies at Herat, Farah, and Kandahar. Because Nadir admired the Pashtun fighting skills, he relocated them in the southwestern part of Afghanistan, the center of their power to this day. His suspicion of those closest led many to be executed, and his son was blinded before Nadir was assassinated in 1747.[6]

Nadir had incorporated into his army a body of cavalry commanded by Ahmad Shah, a Pashtun. After Nadir's death, Ahmad and his men fled the Persian camp, stealing the treasury that Nadir had used to bribe potential enemies. They arrived at Kandahar where a *loya jirga* (council) convened to select a tribal leader. Undoubtedly, Ahmad Shah's powerful cavalry force influenced the *loya jirga's* decision. Ahmad Shah, as the leader of the most powerful Pashtun tribe, became Ahmad Shah Durrani (Pearl of Pearls) and quickly seized Ghazni and Kabul. After military expeditions into India, Ahmad returned to quell revolts in Herat and southwest Pakistan. Then, a difficulty that would plague Afghanistan into the 21st century surfaced. "No Pashtun likes to be ruled by another," observed historian Louis Dupree, "particularly someone from another tribe, subtribe, or section."[7] By 1752, Ahmad had subdued the northern regions surrounding Konduz, Khanabad, Balkh, and Bamian to bring the Turkmen, Uzbek, Tajik, and Hazara tribesmen under his control. While he had succeeded in uniting the numerous regional tribes, their loyalty "was not transferred from their own leaders and kin to the concept of nation." Nevertheless, after his death in 1773, Ahmad Shah Durrani was called Ahmad Shah Baba, the father of Afghanistan, Baba being "father." By 1800, however, tribal rivalries had plunged the once-united country into civil war, and with civil war came foreign intervention.[8]

3

The 19th century was the great period of empire for England, France, and Russia when all competed in what Rudyard Kipling described as "the Great Game" in his epic, *Kim*. With imperialism and power expansion as the guiding principles, each empire sought to dominate and influence the Indian subcontinent. Since the 1600s, England and France had competed for India's lucrative commerce. That competition quickly turned political. By 1763, British influence was dominant. While Napoleon Bonaparte's dreams of using Persia to counter British and Russian influence in East Asia died at Waterloo in 1815, the czarist dream of a warm-water port found new life. The Russian defeat of a Persian army in 1807 prompted a defense treaty between the British and Shah Shuja Mirza, the Afghan ruler in Kabul, in 1809 and with the Persians in 1814. Suspicious of Afghan intentions toward India, the British later stationed a sizable force in northwest India.[9]

Following the overthrow of Shah Shuja in 1809 and his successor in 1818, Afghanistan disintegrated into tribal warfare. Different factions controlled the population centers of Kabul, Kandahar, and Herat as well as the Kashmir and Peshawar regions. Dost Mohammad Khan eventually achieved a measure of dominance in 1826 in the areas of Kabul and Ghazni. Balkh was lost to northern invaders, and Shuja, even with British assistance, failed to regain Kandahar in 1833. In the meantime, the Russians had been exerting influence on the Persians. In 1837, a Persian army with Russian officers accompanying it advanced on Herat. The Persian advance and the presence of a Russian commercial agent in Kabul caused Great Britain to demand that Dost Mohammad renounce contacts with Persia and Russia, expel the Russian agent from Kabul, and recognize the Indian Sikh conquest of Peshawar. When a strongly worded British note made the capture of Herat into a threat to India, the Persian army was withdrawn and the Russian agent recalled. The Governor General of India, Lord Auckland, was determined that Shuja, whom he believed he could control, should rule in Kabul and Kandahar. The "Great Game" overshadowed the diplomatic and military maneuvering between Russia and Britain where Afghanistan was the playing field.[10]

On 26 April 1839, an invading British army occupied Kandahar, took Ghazni on 22 July, and reached Kabul on 6 August. When Dost Mohammad fled, the British installed Shuja on the throne. British soldiers moved to garrisoned Bamian, Jalalabad, and Charikar. An uneasy peace settled upon a region ruled by an unpopular Afghan puppet supported by English bayonets. The remainder of the country was controlled by tribal leaders, mostly Pashtun.[11]

British envoy William Macnaghten unsuccessfully attempted to negotiate with the other Afghan leaders to form alliances with Shah Shuja who remained in power only while the British occupied the country. Macnaghten's murder by Dost Mohammad's son, coupled with successful Afghan attacks against the British garrison and the diplomatic residency in Kabul, led to the final abandonment of the city in January 1842. Of 16,500 British soldiers, families, Sepoy infantry and cavalry, and camp followers who left together from Kabul, there were only 123 Europeans and about 2,000 Sepoys who survived the Afghan attacks and the harsh winter trek. On 5 April, Shah Shuja was assassinated. The British garrison at Ghazni surrendered, but those at Kandahar and Qalat withdrew safely. Tribal anarchy plagued Afghanistan until Dost Mohammad returned in 1843 to fight 20 years to wrest control of the eastern region from rival warlords.[12]

The Persians took advantage of the chaotic conditions to occupy Herat in October 1856. When the British declared war, the Persians withdrew. It would not be until Herat was captured by Dost Mohammad in 1863 that most of present-day Afghanistan would be consolidated under his control. In the meantime, concerned that British intervention in Afghanistan threatened their interests, the Russians steadily pushed southward, reaching the Amu Darya River in 1869, the present-day border between Uzbekistan and Afghanistan. Four years later, in 1873, an Anglo-Russian Convention established the Amu Darya as the boundary between Afghanistan and Russia.[13]

Following the cycle of Afghan strongmen, warfare erupted throughout the country when Dost Mohammad died in 1863. For six years his sons fought a fratricidal war until Sher Ali Khan succeeded in becoming ruler in Kabul. Again, the Persians took advantage of the family discord to occupy southeastern Afghanistan. Great Britain had long been concerned about any Russian expansion toward the Mediterranean. While the Crimean War of 1853 led to limits being placed on Russian expansion into Europe and Turkey, the British became alarmed by subsequent Russo-Turkish wars and Russian intentions. The Treaty of San Stefano that ended the war was viewed so unfavorably by Great Britain that Prime Minister Benjamin Disraeli threatened Russia with war if it were not revised. Fortunately, the 1878 Congress of Berlin alleviated British tension, but suspicions of Russian expansion remained strong.

Unfortunately for Afghanistan, the Russians sent an uninvited diplomatic mission in summer 1878 to Kabul. When they were slow to withdraw after formal protest, the British sent forces into Afghanistan in November 1878 to precipitate what is called the Second Anglo-Afghan War. Sher Ali Khan unsuccessfully solicited Russian assistance and died in Mazar-e-Sharif.[14]

The inability of the Afghan tribes to unite against the British and Sher Ali's death led to the Treaty of Gandamak on 26 May 1879. A disturbing aspect of the fighting had been that the British were unable to distinguish friendly Afghans from enemy tribesmen. Although they had been defeated and the treaty had, in reality, imposed British rule of Afghanistan from Kabul and control of foreign affairs, the Afghan tribes could not be controlled. Native troops from Herat revolted. The British garrison fought desperately in Kabul, and another British force was defeated near Kandahar. British retaliation left more than 1,000 Afghans dead.

This combination of calamities culminated in another British withdrawal, and Abdur Rahman Khan became ruler in Kabul. He ruthlessly put down numerous tribal revolts, forcibly relocated the dissident Pashtuns from the south to the north, relieved tax burdens on non-Pashtuns, named provincial governors without regard to tribal affiliation, and raised an army that would be loyal to him. During his reign, Sir Mortimer Durand crafted the Durand Line to serve as either an international boundary or a demarcation line between Indian and Afghan influence, depending on the views of those nations at any specific time in history. Rather than settling differences, the line became the stimulus for future fighting between Afghanistan and British-controlled India and later between Afghanistan and Pakistan. The British also delineated the Afghan borders with India and China in the extreme northeast part of the country, although the Chinese did not officially recognize the demarcation until 1964. After Abdur Rahman's death in 1901, Afghanistan enjoyed the first peaceful transfer of power in history.

The country was united as never before, and a geographic area to serve as a buffer between Russia and British India had been defined. During the reign of Abdur Rahman's son, Habibullah, at the 1907 Anglo-Russian Convention, Russia conceded that Afghanistan was outside its sphere of influence. Habibullah Khan did not agree to the convention, but the Russians and British imposed it anyway.[15]

As World War I engulfed Europe, the Turks and Germans pressured Habibullah to join them in an attack on British India. Habibullah's response was to approach the British with an offer. If Great Britain would relinquish control of Afghan foreign policy, he would stall the Central Powers in the region. The threat relieved, British control over Afghan foreign policy continued. Then, Habibullah was mysteriously assassinated—by whom has never been determined.[16]

Although several of Habibullah's sons and his brother claimed succession, his third son, Amanullah, who controlled the treasury and the army, gained most Afghan tribes' loyalty. His reign as emir brought significant change to Afghanistan. As British troops withdrew to fight in the Great War, the Afghan tribes began launching small raids against British border posts. Sensing weakness, in May 1918, Amanullah used his army in several attacks. This precipitated the Third Anglo-Afghan War. After the initial setbacks, the British rallied and countered with air attacks against Kabul and Jalalabad. After a month of fighting, negotiations were sought. The Treaty of Rawalpindi, signed 8 August 1919, ended Great Britain's 40-year control of Afghan foreign policy but did not stop tribal attacks on British border posts.[17]

After the Bolshevik Revolution, the Reds had brutally oppressed Muslims during their consolidation of power in the southern regions. Amanullah wanted to stabilize the situation on his northern frontier and to play off his northern neighbor against the British to his east. In 1921, Russia and Afghanistan signed a Treaty of Friendship—the first treaty signed by the Afghans since regaining control of their foreign policy. The Soviets considered the treaty a diplomatic strike against a European power that opposed the rise of a communist state. The treaty provided the Kabul government with money, airplanes, and technicians. Telephone lines were established between Kabul and Mazar-e-Sharif as well as between Herat and Kandahar. Despite the treaty, Soviet troops occupied an island in the Amu Darya River in 1925, forcing Afghan forces to withdraw. The issue was settled peacefully by a Pact of Neutrality and Non-aggression, recognizing the borders as previously established, affirming nonaggression, and resolving that neither would become involved in the internal affairs of the other. The "Great Game" continued as the British responded with an ambiguous treaty with Afghanistan that failed to resolve the disputes over the status of Pashtun people sitting astride the Afghan-Indian border. However, the British Secretary of State for Foreign Affairs declared that Afghanistan was "within the British sphere of political influence."[18]

Emir Amanullah kept a wary eye on the Soviets while twisting the British lion's tail with his anti-Great Britain speeches at public events that English diplomats attended. While walking the diplomatic tightrope between the two regional powers, Amanullah also dealt with the Afghan tribal leaders who saw their power being eroded. Revolts continued to be a common response as Pashtun leaders near Khowst rebelled against his reforms. The British and the Afghans blamed each other for stirring rebellion, but as Afghan historian Louis Dupree observed, "In the frontier areas trouble does not need to be stirred up; it is constantly whirling in the air waiting to light."[19]

Further alienating the traditional tribesmen were Amanullah's social reforms. Intent on bringing the country into the modern era, he sought to impose education for women, to abolish the requirement for women to be veiled, to eliminate government subsidies for tribal chiefs, and to reform the army. Religious leaders declared many of his reform ideas to be anti-Islamic and pointed to photographs of Amanullah's wife, regarded as Afghanistan's queen, taken during their European tour, unveiled and with bare shoulders. As the reforms posed threats to both religious leaders and tribal chiefs, revolt became widespread. In January 1929, Amanullah abdicated. Following another period of tribal warfare, a *loya jirga* (grand council) proclaimed one who advocated reasonable reforms to be emir. Nevertheless, he was assassinated in 1933.

Muhammad Zahir Shah became king in 1933 and reigned until 1973. Afghanistan joined the League of Nations and received official diplomatic recognition from the United States in 1934.[20] Being very aware of the "Great Game" and distrustful of Russia and Great Britain, Zahir Shah turned to Germany for technical and economic assistance. Lufthansa scheduled regular flights between Kabul and Berlin. The United States acquired oil exploration rights in Afghanistan but relinquished them as Europe became embroiled in World War II. Except for some minor frontier skirmishes, Afghanistan, which declared its neutrality on 17 August 1940, remained relatively at peace while much of the world was engulfed in war. Two significant regional postwar political changes that impacted Afghanistan heavily were Indian independence and the separation of Muslim Pakistan from Hindu India. Vastly separated into an eastern and a western Pakistan, the newly created country refused to adjust the Durand Line of 1893. Thus, the Pashtun region was divided between West Pakistan and its northern Muslim neighbor. In retaliation for cross-border attacks, the Pakistanis cut off oil shipments to Afghanistan in 1950. With the British Empire in the process of collapsing, testy Pakistani relations, and western influence prevailing in Iran, the Soviets seized the opportunity to reestablish friendly relations with Afghanistan.[21]

In need of oil and anxious to obtain money for internal improvements, Zahir Shah looked north. The Soviets gladly provided both. One of the more impressive engineering achievements was a highway with a 2-mile-long tunnel through the Salang Pass about 60 miles northwest of Kabul. Diplomatically, the two nations renewed the 1931 Pact of Neutrality and Nonaggression and signed a major trade agreement in 1956. As Cold War tensions heightened, the United States sought to improve relations throughout the region to counter perceived Soviet expansion. U.S. foreign aid funded an airport in Kandahar and a major irrigation project along the Helmand River in southern Afghanistan; however, military aid was not forthcoming. While Pakistan was invited to join the Southeast Asia Treaty Organization (SEATO) in 1955, Pakistan-Afghanistan differences over the Pashtun region and the level of Soviet aid made membership in the regional defense organization moot. The Soviets were quite willing to provide the desired military aid.

The U.S. Joint Chiefs of Staff (JCS) concluded that "Afghanistan is of little or no strategic importance to the United States" and that "it would be desirable for Afghanistan to remain neutral." The National Security Council adopted a similar position. Officially, then, Afghanistan remained neutral as the United States became more active in the "Great Game."[22]

Reminiscent of Amanullah's unsuccessful social reforms to modernize Afghani society were the bold efforts of Prime Minister Daoud Khan to end the isolation of women. In 1959,

7

the wives and daughters of government officials were allowed on a reviewing stand with their faces uncovered. This supposedly violated two Muslim religious traditions—women wearing a veil and women remaining apart from men in public. Before this episode, the Zahir Shah government had sanctioned working without a veil for the stewardesses on Ariana Afghan Airlines because it was impractical. Females were also permitted to work as radio announcers, and young women could work in a pottery factory. These exceptions were nothing compared to the upheaval caused by the women's public appearance on the reviewing stand.

Mullahs, many of whom were illiterate, protested vehemently, but when challenged to cite specific passages from the Koran to support their position, they could not. While those who spoke openly against the government were arrested, they were soon released. Some recanted their positions; others did not.[23] Two explanations can be given for the mullahs' views. Some mullahs sincerely believed an Islamic woman played a very minor role in society, which Westerners would consider sexual discrimination. Additionally, any social measure that touched on religion diminished the power of the mullah. Education could lead to serious questioning by the people, and the people might question mullahs who could neither read nor reason.

Politically, the period from 1953 to 1973 was one of tension between liberalism and fundamentalism, nationalism and tribalism, and monarchy and democracy. Islam established by Mohammad Bin Oasim and interpreted by the mullahs had been an inherent part of Afghan society since 715. Daoud's attempts to wrench Afghanistan from its feudal state into modernity produced mixed results. Although some women obtained liberties not previously available, they were freedoms generally limited to women in large cities. Modernized infrastructure came only by accepting aid from a nation that had once been a threat. Taxation to support the efforts of a central government caused antigovernment riots in Kandahar. Because Afghanistan had been a country created geographically with little regard for cultural lines, it was constantly plagued with conflicts along its southern border with Pakistan over the artificial boundary that split Pashtuns who considered the dividing line irrelevant. Border crossing closures prompted clashes between nomads seeking to move animals back and forth between grazing areas as they had for centuries and Pakistani border guards who considered such movements to threaten national stability. The Pakistani actions compelled the Afghans to seek economic relief from Russia.

This new development prompted the National Security Council to reassess its position. The decision was made to adopt a more active role in the region: "The United States should try to resolve the Afghan dispute with Pakistan and encourage Afghanistan to minimize its reliance upon the Communist bloc . . . and to look to the United States . . . for military training and assistance."[24] U.S. government efforts, however, proved to be too little, too late.

In 1963, Prime Minister Daoud, whom many Afghans blamed for Pakistan's problems, stepped down in a surprise move. Two weeks later, the new prime minister, Muhammad Yousuf, formed a committee to draft a new constitution and sought to resolve differences with Pakistan. Instigated by the Shah of Iran, envoys from Pakistan and Afghanistan met in Tehran, and on 29 May 1963, diplomatic relations were reestablished.

Demonstrating its neutral, nonaligned status, Afghanistan did not seek advice for drafting its new constitution from the United States but instead, sought guidance from France, which had 15 constitutions since 1789. After the document was drafted, the king called for a *loya jirga* to convene in September 1964 to review it. Elected delegates countrywide attended. This was no small feat since the literacy rate was about 5 percent. Election details were disseminated primarily by radio. After deliberations, the *loya jirga* submitted the 128-article constitution to the king. On 1 October 1963, Muhammad Zahir Shah approved the document. It declared Afghanistan to be "a constitutional monarchy" having an elected bicameral parliament and that "Islam is the sacred religion." With no tradition of democracy, only approximately 16 percent of the eligible voters turned out for the first election. Still, four women were elected to the parliament.[25]

For the next decade, Afghanistan vacillated between monarchy and democracy. Political parties were forbidden. Newspapers were allowed but were closely controlled. Parliament was ineffective. The four female members were defeated in the 1969 elections. Drought and famine brought misery to the population. During King Zahir's visit to Europe in 1973, former Prime Minister Daoud initiated a coup and abolished the monarchy. Within two years, he approved a new constitution that created a one-party government overseen by a president. In an attempt to reduce Soviet influence, President Daoud sought aid from India, Iran, and the United States and removed Russian military advisers from many units. He also improved relations with Pakistan. Daoud's actions infuriated Communists in Afghanistan. On 27 April 1978, the reactions turned violent as Afghan armored units and MiG-21s attacked the presidential palace. The next day Daoud was killed. Nur Mohammed Taraki became president, and the People's Democratic Party of Afghanistan—the Communist Party—took control of the country.[26]

President Taraki's programs included cleansing Islam of "bad traditions, superstition, and erroneous belief." He redesigned the Afghan flag, eliminating the color green (the color of Islam), and made the dominant color red to resemble the flag of the Soviet Union. Loan payments, gender equality, female education opportunities, and land reform were dictated by government decrees. The rural villagers considered these Taraki reforms to be anathema because they overturned the traditional ways of social life. Faced by numerous antigovernment uprisings and increased desertions from the army, the president responded by signing a Treaty of Friendship and Good Neighborliness with the Soviet Union and invited Russian military advisers to help suppress the rebels. In February 1979, U.S. Ambassador Adolph Dubs was kidnapped in Kabul, presumably by a Maoist extremist group, and killed during the rescue attempt.

The U.S. government, absorbed by the Shah of Iran's overthrow and the return of Ayatollah Khomeini, considered Afghanistan a lower priority. In Herat in March 1979, after rebels killed nearly 100 Soviet advisers and their families, more than 5,000 Afghans died when government forces, equipped with substantial quantities of new Russian weapons and armored vehicles, recaptured the city. Traditional Afghan factional infighting erupted in the Communist Party. President Taraki was murdered on 14 September 1979 by his Prime Minister Hafizullah Amin, who seized power.[27]

Infighting quickly flared into full-scale civil war. Amid a growing apprehension that Russian communists were dominating Afghanistan, the intelligentsia and well to do fled the country. The Afghan armed forces, whose officers had been trained in the Soviet Union, fell apart.

9

Soviet newspaper, *Pravda*, announced that the Soviet leadership could not "remain indifferent" to a civil war "in direct proximity to us." The Russians responded by sending an infusion of advisers to shore up the collapsing ground forces and experienced pilots to fly combat missions against the antigovernment rebels. In October 1979, Soviet-advised forces moved into Paktia Province. Rebel forces retreated, but when government troops withdrew, they returned. Shortly afterward, U.S. intelligence reported heightened Soviet military activity as reservists were called up, bridging equipment was centralized, and an army headquarters was established near the Amu Darya River. In early December, a reinforced airborne regiment sent to Bagram earlier quickly moved to secure the Salang Tunnel and Kabul International Airport.[28]

On the night of 27 December 1979, Soviet troops assaulted Darulaman Palace in Kabul and killed President Amin. Soviet leaders attempted to explain their actions using the pretext that "We are responding to an appeal from the Afghan leadership to repel outside aggression." General Secretary Leonid Brezhnev had invoked Article 51 of the United Nations (UN) charter that guaranteed "the inherent right of individual or collective self-defense if an armed attack occurs against a Member of the United Nations." Afghan communists claimed that Soviet assistance was necessary to defend themselves against attacks by the United States, Pakistan, and China. Then, in a clumsy attempt to justify their actions, the Soviets proffered former deputy premier Babrak Karmal as the new president. Karmal broadcast a message to the Afghan people on the Radio Kabul frequency that "the torture machine of Amin . . . has been broken" and to declare a *jihad* "for true democratic justice, as respect for the holy Islamic religion." The newly touted president did not mention that he was actually broadcasting from Termez, Uzbekistan. During another broadcast, Karmal claimed that he had requested military assistance from the Soviets.

Careful scrutiny of the invasion timetable of events revealed how inept the Soviets were in their attempts to legitimize the heavy-handed actions. The individuals whom the Soviets claimed had elected Karmal were in prison during the supposed election; announcements that first Amin and then later, Karmal had requested intervention contradicted each other; the propaganda apparatus did not explain why Amin—if he had requested military intervention—was killed and replaced by Karmal; and there were no explanations as to why Karmal did not appear in public in Kabul until 1 January 1980. Efforts to portray Amin as a Central Intelligence Agency (CIA) agent had no credence based on his supposed request for a massive Soviet invasion.[29]

Russian scholar Robert Baumann writes, "The motives for a large-scale Soviet military intervention were the subject of exhaustive comment and speculation." Documents released in the 1990s prove that Taraki and Amin did ask for military intervention at least 16 times between 14 April and 17 December 1979. Soviet military advisers in Kabul, however, had advised against such intervention. Although the real reasons for the Soviet intervention may never be known, a 31 December 1979 article in *Pravda* provided as good an explanation as any to date. The article spoke of holes in the "strategic arc." The perception that there were holes in Afghanistan that needed to be plugged may explain why the Soviet army's nightmare began.[30]

Reaction in the U.S. government was outrage. President Jimmy Carter blocked sales of grain and high-technology equipment to Russia and boycotted American participation in the

1980 summer Olympics in Moscow. More ominously, he declined to submit the Strategic Arms Limitation Treaty II (SALT II) to Congress for ratification. Signed in Vienna on 18 June 1979, SALT II would have limited U.S. and Russian strategic nuclear offensive weapons. In his State of the Union Address of 21 January 1980, the president enunciated a sweeping foreign policy declaration that became labeled the "Carter Doctrine." Specifically alluding to the Soviet invasion, Carter made clear that "An attempt by any outside force to gain control of the Persian Gulf region will be regarded as an assault on the vital interests of the United States of America, and such an assault will be repelled by any means necessary, including military force."[31]

Figure 3. Jimmy Carter.

International reaction was decidedly unfavorable as well. The UN General Assembly voted 104 to 18 to "deplore the recent armed intervention in Afghanistan" and called for the "immediate, unconditional, and total withdrawal of foreign troops from Afghanistan." Although voting with the Soviet Union, Fidel Castro was concerned about the implications that the invasion had for Cuba's future sovereignty. Would Cuba be the next object of Soviet military intervention? Iran was pointedly critical of the invasion of its Islamic neighbor.

A history of tensions with Pakistan concerned U.S. government officials. Remembering the 1959 cooperative security agreement, President Carter's initiative to establish a "regional security framework" that involved Pakistan, the provision of a $400-million aid package that was substantially greater than previous years, and a visit by Deputy Secretary of State Warren Christopher and National Security Adviser Zbigniew Brzezinski all raised the level of Soviet hostility toward Afghanistan's southern neighbor. Concurrent overflights, cross-border incursions, and threats raised concerns about stronger Soviet military action.[32]

The Soviets did not withdraw and soon learned that the Afghans were willing to ignore most ethnic and tribal differences temporarily and unite against a foreign invader. The mullahs' (religious teachers) call for *jihad* against the Soviets was presented as a spiritual obligation to the 99-percent Muslim population. To fight and even die in a holy war against Communist *kafirs* (infidels) was a duty that rallied support, not to support an Afghan central government but to oppose an invading army. The freedom fighters came to be known as the *mujahideen*—the soldiers of God.

Although united by a military objective, the *mujahideen* fighting groups could not agree on a common political objective. The Islamic Alliance for the Liberation of Afghanistan, an alliance of six parties created in January 1980, began to fall apart in March. Led by Gulbuddin Hekmatyar, the anti-Western Party of Islam gained prominence in the Kandahar area. Mullah Omar soon joined Hekmatyar, but rather than seeking the company of other factions, the Party of Islam seemed to be more intent on establishing an Islamic theocratic state than in removing the foreign invaders. The Islamic Alliance wanted a country ruled by a *loya jirga* but with a very clear Islamic focus. By the mid-1980s, the Party of Islam, with a primarily Pashtun membership, had spread its influence into the provinces near Kabul. Although the Party of Islam cooperated with other *mujahideen* groups, a RAND study's conclusion was not encouraging: "Many of the political parties seem to be expending most of their energy bickering and fighting each other and are rife with corruption and nepotism. In the opinion of many *mujahideen* field commanders, the political factions at present represent more of an obstacle to effective resistance than an asset."[33]

Afghan military forces in Kandahar, Kabul, and Herat had initially opposed the invading 40th Soviet Army, but three battalions in Jalalabad had deserted en masse. By summer 1980, only one-third of the old Afghan army supported the Soviets and their puppet government. Karmal pleaded for an end to "factionalism," affirming his government's support of Islam. But he also made it clear that "eternal friendship and solidarity with the Leninist Communist Party of the USSR" was a key tenet of his regime. Factionalism in the Afghan army units was so severe that occasionally elements fired on each other. Defections, desertions, and sabotage destroyed Soviet trust. Somewhat more effective than the army were government militia units created in the tribal areas. By paying off tribal leaders, the government sought to secure a region against rival *mujahideen* tribes. Occasionally, these efforts backfired when "loyalists" switched sides and took the government-supplied equipment with them.[34]

In January 1980, Soviet forces occupied Farah and Herat to guard against incursions from Iran. A motorized rifle division moved into Mazar-e-Sharif. In March 1980, another motorized rifle division secured control of Konar Province, north of Jalalabad. In June, however, disaster struck when the *mujahideen* ambushed and annihilated a motorized rifle battalion on the road between Gardez and Khowst. With only a few helicopters in Afghanistan, the Soviet supply convoys were extremely vulnerable. This also meant that attacking or pursuing the *mujahideen* in mountainous areas was difficult. By mid-1981, the number of helicopters had increased fivefold—from 60 to 300—and by the end of the year, 130 jet fighters were in Afghanistan. Realizing that tanks were largely ineffective in what had become a guerrilla war, Soviet tanks were reduced from nearly 1,000 to 300 that same year.

Figure 4. Soviet tank carcass.

With few exceptions, conventional division- and brigade-size offensive operations were the norm. Many of these were directed at guarding supply routes. Exceptions occurred toward the end of 1980 when heliborne troops conducted raids in the Panjshir Valley north of Kabul and in Lowgar Province south of the capital. Still, the Soviets were unable to dominate any region permanently. In the Panjshir, their limited success was due in no small measure to *mujahideen* leader Ahmad Shah Massoud, "the Lion of the Panjshir," who organized his troops into defense, mobile strike, and reaction forces. In the vicinity of Herat, resistance units of the Islamic Society of Afghanistan, commanded by Ismail Khan, enjoyed some success. By February 1982, however, Soviet forces had inflicted significant casualties on these guerrilla forces.[35]

Mujahideen leaders, having recognized that their elements could not stand toe to toe with Russian military forces, focused on attacking Soviet residential areas and assassinating officials in Kabul, Kandahar, and Herat. The Soviets often retaliated with brutal efficiency to cleanse the cities and nearby villages of rebel forces and sympathizers. A successful attack on Bagram Air Base in April 1982 that destroyed 23 aircraft prompted a major Soviet offensive into the Panjshir Valley. The *mujahideen* captured nine tanks and killed 300 to 400 Russian soldiers in this engagement, but the guerrilla and civilian casualties were twice that number. The "Lion of Panjshir," Ahmad Shah Massoud (war leader of another Party of Islam), withdrew into the mountains. Shortly thereafter, the Soviet military left the valley in a wake of destruction, razing villages, burning crops, and blowing up irrigation systems. Guerrillas in the south, supplied from Pakistan, attacked Soviet garrisons in Khowst and surrounding villages. In the north, kidnapping Soviet technicians in Mazar-e-Sharif triggered large-scale Soviet and Afghan army operations in the region.[36]

Soviet conventional forces faced a major counterinsurgency situation for which they were doctrinally unprepared. The *mujahideen* did not mass to facilitate destruction by Soviet artillery. The Russians established control in specific areas only as long as large formations maintained an active presence. Once they withdrew, the area reverted to guerrilla control. In essence, the Soviets faced many of the problems that the British had faced previously. Unlike the British, however, the Soviets gained the upper hand with air power. They quickly learned that, although the guerrillas could choose the time and place to ambush convoys, helicopters could put ground forces on the high ground along convoy routes. If the convoys were attacked, the massive firepower of tactical aircraft could be called on the attacking forces. Although limited by terrain, weather, and aircraft performance limits, helicopters were able to deliver supplies to remote garrisons, thus avoiding defiles that channeled ground convoys for ground ambush. In 1983, the Soviet garrisons in Bamian, Ghazni, Gardez, and Khowst were resupplied entirely by airdrops and helicopters. The *mujahideen* resorted to using conventional ground weapons, like the ZPU-1 and 12.7 millimeter (mm) DshK machine gun, to shoot down 20 helicopters a year. In 1983, the *mujahideen* first acquired SA-7 (surface-to-air) missiles from Pakistani arms dealers. Three years later they began to receive British Blowpipe antiaircraft missiles.[37]

In 1986, several Congressmen recommended funds to supply the *mujahideen* with U.S. Stinger antiaircraft missiles. Exactly when the American shipments commenced remains cloudy; they possibly began as early as July 1985 but not later than September 1986. The CIA shipped 300 in 1986 and 700 in 1987. According to CIA officer Vincent Cannistraro, "The Stingers neutralized Soviet air power and marked a strategic turning point in the war." Soviet aircraft losses averaged one a day for the initial 90 days when Stingers were first employed. In 1987, 270 aircraft were shot down.[38]

The rigidity of Soviet military leaders delayed tactical and systemic changes that could have reduced aircraft and crew member losses. A system that discouraged initiative or deviation from established procedure caused casualties. Initially, pilots stuck to the flight route, even if it meant flying through confirmed enemy air defense zones. All training emphasized a doctrinal approach to flight operations with no room for innovation if situations changed. As one analyst noted, "The learning curve seems to have been quite lengthy." Rather than gathering the tactical lessons learned in Afghanistan and disseminating them to all units, changes were made based on individual pilot or unit recommendations. Pilots adapted to survive. They flew higher, did more night operations, dropped flares during takeoff and before landing, and learned the value of false helicopter insertions. They also began dropping bombs from higher altitudes, which significantly reduced accuracy. With the greater air defense threat, especially from Stingers and other antiaircraft missiles, Soviet air operations became less frequent and less effective.[39]

In 1983, ground tactical operations shrank to battalion- and regimental-size efforts instead of the previous division-size operations. Part of the rationale behind the smaller-scale operations was a cease-fire in the Panjshir Valley arranged by Massoud. Although this initiative infuriated Hekmatyar (the leader of the original Party of Islam centered about Kandahar), who regarded Massoud's act as a betrayal, it gave the "Lion of Panjshir" time to rebuild his depleted forces and to reestablish a supply network in the valley. At the same time, the Soviets shifted their forces and gained free use of the highway between Kabul and Konduz. Another part of the rationale was the Soviets' desire to get more Afghan army units into the battle. This started in fall 1983. Afghan army brigades started fighting the *mujahideen* in Paktia and Paktia Province. The Russians wanted a strong national Afghan army to provide stability to the country when their forces withdrew. Although the operations in Paktia and Paktia Province showed improvement in effectiveness, the Afghan army could not match the *mujahideen* on the battlefield.[40]

Mujahideen ground and rocket attacks against Kabul caused renewed Soviet large-scale offensives into the Panjshir and Konar valleys. Over the next several years, bold guerrilla attacks against Soviet and Afghan forces in Khowst, fierce fighting with mujahideen in Kandahar and Herat and the surrounding areas, and the destruction of 20 MiG-21s at Shindand Air Base convinced the Soviets and the Karmal government that a short war with a decisive victory over the guerrillas was not possible. Despite success in several regions, the *mujahideen* were unable to achieve decisive long-term results either, for several reasons: their inability and/or unwillingness to coordinate activities and operations among themelves; their inability to capitalize on war supply sources in Pakistan; or their inability to get the most from modern technology because of the high illiteracy rate among the Afghans.

The warfare was extremely brutal: both sides killed prisoners, Afghan officials were assassinated, civilians died in terrorist attacks, villages were destroyed, populations were displaced in reprisal, and mines were airdropped by the thousands. At least 5 million Afghans fled to Iran and Pakistan, most settling in refugee camps. Karmal and the Soviets realized that something had to be done quickly to break the developing stalemate in the war.[41]

On 29 March 1985, President Babrak Karmal called for "major socio-political work among the people and the need to raise the social awareness of the masses." To foster this effort, Babrak wanted the *loya jirgas* to elect local councils. After the broadcast, the *mujahideen* threatened to kill anyone who attended a meeting. Having discovered that an imposed military solution had not worked, the Soviets recognized that they needed a different approach—one that would garner support for the government and reduce guerrilla support. Incorporating key religious tenets from the 1964 constitution, the Afghan Revolutionary Council adopted a

Figure 5. Abandoned MiG at Mazar.

provisional constitution that guaranteed "respect, observance, and preservation of Islam as a sacred religion." Seizing on the importance of Islam in Afghanistan, the Soviets and Karmal agreed to establish religious schools and to improve conditions for women. The Afghan president also tried to gain support from the mullahs by providing them with extra food allowances and money to repair existing mosques and to build new ones.

The Russians managed to "retool" this idea by sending 16,000 to 20,000 Afghan children to schools in Warsaw Pact countries to be educated. This blatant effort to indoctrinate Afghan youth caused international outrage. Destroying the bases of support for the *mujahideen* posed the classic dilemma—identifying the insurgents and isolating them from the general population. The Soviet solution was to drive everyone from the villages, destroy the crops and irrigation systems, and mine the farmland. Although these tactics separated the guerrillas from their support system and deprived the *mujahideen* of local intelligence, the refugee numbers in the cities greatly increased, as did the insurgents in the urban areas, and resolve in the anti-Soviet factions was strengthened.

Militarily, the Soviet strategy was to employ large garrisons to control the cities and infrastructure, to man series of outposts at critical points along supply routes, and to launch combat operations against the *mujahideen* from well-protected base camps. Paratrooper, heliborne assault, and *Spetsnaz* (special operations) units concentrated on securing the high ground along major transportation routes and ambushing *mujahideen* forces at water points, the favored routes through defiles, and along well-traveled paths or roads. Although successful initially, the guerrillas countered these efforts by doing more reconnaissance. Using local intelligence, they often were able to ambush the ambushers. Over time, the effectiveness of the military counterinsurgency effort diminished considerably.[42]

15

On 11 March 1985, Mikhail Gorbachev became General Secretary of the Communist Party in the Soviet Union. During the Communist Party congress in 1986, the new General Secretary characterized Afghanistan as Russia's "bleeding wound." Although Communist leaders like Fidel Castro were invited to the congress, President Karmal was conspicuously absent. At a Politburo meeting on 13 November 1986, Gorbachev made it clear that he was dissatisfied with the military situation in Afghanistan, that he had little faith in Karmal, and that the war had to be ended "in the course of one year—at maximum two years." The military situation could not be fixed quickly, but Karmal was replaceable. After the Central Committee of the People's Democratic Party of Afghanistan met on 4 May 1987, "the resignation of comrade Babrak Karmal on health grounds" was announced. Mohammad Najibullah, head of the secret police, was named as Karmal's successor. Gorbachev's determination to staunch the "bleeding wound" became quite evident when he directed a limited withdrawal of Soviet military forces from Afghanistan on 28 July 1987.

Mujahideen ambushes of convoys, patrols, and outposts and ground and rocket attacks against Soviet garrisons and airfields, however, continued. Fighting was particularly heavy in and around Kandahar. Thousands of mines were laid, the city was devastated, and nearby villages were destroyed. In 1987, the State Department cited Kandahar as "the scene of . . . the heaviest concentration of combat of the war." When Soviet forces withdrew, the Afghan population was one-eighth of what it had been in 1979.[43]

In a dramatic reversal of the expansionist policy promulgated by his three predecessors—Leonid Brezhnev, Yuri Andropov, and Konstantine Chernenko—Gorbachev announced on 8 February 1988 that beginning 15 May, all Soviet forces would be withdrawn from Afghanistan in 10 months. On 14 April, in a ceremony in Geneva, Soviet, Afghan, Pakistani, and U.S. representatives signed five accords associated with the Soviet troop withdrawals to be completed by 15 February 1989. The United States and the Soviet Union pledged not to interfere in the internal affairs of Pakistan and Afghanistan. Noticeably absent was representation from the *mujahideen*.[44]

While some Soviet military advisers remained behind, the 40th Army completed its withdrawal from Afghanistan as prescribed on 15 February 1989. It left behind at least 13,833 dead Soviets. A journalist writing in *Izvestiia* summed up the difficulties the Soviets had faced in Afghanistan: "The foreign intervention stirred patriotism, and the appearance of 'infidels' spawned religious intolerance. On such a field, even a tie would have been miraculous."[45]

Although the infidels had been expelled, peace did not come to Afghanistan. While President Najibullah was attempting to establish a government in Kabul, the two largest ethnic factions turned on each other. Massoud led the Tajiks and their party, the *Jamait-i-Islami* (Islamic Society). Abdul Haq led the Pashtun *Hizb-i-Islami* (Party of Islam). Massoud's battleground had been the Panjshir Valley, while Haq's had been Kabul. (Although this Party of Islam had the same name as that of Hekmatyar, the two parties were different.) Pakistan's president had other concerns.

From relative safety across the border, President Zia ul-Haq of Pakistan had long opposed the growing Soviet presence to his north. Zia was concerned about the large number of Pashtun refugees that fled into Pakistan's frontier provinces. In 1984, he had condoned the creation of the seven-party Islamic Unity of Afghan *mujahideen* in Peshawar. This multiple-party group included factions led by Hekmatyar, Massoud, and Haq. President Zia and Hekmatyar shared the same fundamentalist Islamic dream of imposing Islamic theocratic governments in the region. With the announced withdrawal of Russian troops, a group of anti-Soviet Afghans who were friendly with Zia formed an Afghan Interim Government (AIG) headed by Sibghatollah Mojadeddi to take control when the Soviet puppet government fell. Even after Zia's death in a suspicious plane crash 17 August 1988, the U.S. government supported Hekmatyar because he was considered the best alternative to the communist-controlled Najibullah government in Kabul.

The political situation in Afghanistan was very unstable during the Soviet withdrawal. Najibullah had to mediate for tribal factions who were killing each other. Haq was sneaking into Kabul regularly to meet with dissidents he had met during the height of the Soviet occupation. He covered his covert meetings with rocket attacks on the city. In 1989, Pakistan cut all aid to Haq and diverted the resources to Massoud who had a more audacious plan for seizing Kabul. The city, however, would not fall until 1992.[46]

Mujahideen commanded by Abdul Qadir, Haq's brother, attempted to seize Jalalabad in March 1988. The Soviets left behind tanks, artillery, and ammunition for the Afghan army; left more than 200 aircraft; and supplied $300 million monthly in aid to Najibullah's government. Infighting among the *mujahideen* leaders led to uncoordinated attacks, and a combination of tactical ineptness and superior firepower cost the guerrillas more than 3,000 fighters at Jalalabad. That military disaster split the AIG alliance apart. In July, Hekmatyar's men ambushed a group of Massoud's fighters. Massoud retaliated, capturing Hekmatyar's responsible commander and hanging him. This caused Hekmatyar to withdraw from the alliance. While the United States was preparing for war against Iraq, the Soviet Union was disintegrating. The *mujahideen* forces successfully attacked Afghan government troops at Kandahar, Khowst, and Herat, but they suffered heavy casualties in a direct assault on Kabul. Khowst fell in 1990.[47]

In northern Afghanistan, Uzbek warlord Rashid Dostum, who had previously led pro-Soviet forces, united with Najibullah's Afghan army to fight the *mujahideen* when the Russians withdrew. However, in February 1992, Dostum changed sides and aligned with Massoud, and their combined forces captured Mazar-e-Sharif. In April 1992, the two forces reached Bagram. Fearing the imminent collapse of his government, Najibullah sought refuge in a UN compound in Kabul where he remained in asylum until September 1996. When Najibullah abandoned the government, the Afghan army disintegrated. Former Afghan army soldiers joined the advance of Dostum and Massoud toward Kabul from the north. Hekmatyar raced toward the capital from the south to beat his rivals to the prize. Although Hekmatyar's lead elements got into Kabul, the better-organized northern forces forced Hekmatyar's men from the city and seized control of the government buildings.

Sibghatollah Mojadeddi assumed the presidency, but Burhannudin Rabbani replaced him in June 1992. Rabbani was Tajik, as were Massoud and Ismail Khan who had fought the Russians near Herat. Suddenly, the minority Tajiks, supported by the Uzbek, Dostum, controlled the government and Kabul. Pashtun leader Hekmatyar, after surrounding the city, responded by rocketing the capital. Estimates of Afghans killed in 1993 varied from 2,000 to 30,000.[48]

The expression "you can't tell the players without a scorecard" aptly fit the alliance shifts among the ethnic groups in Afghanistan in the 1990s. Pashtuns controlled Kandahar, Dostum controlled Bagram, and Dostum and Massoud fought for control of Konduz. Ismail Khan, with support from Iran, controlled Herat. In 1994, Dostum, who had been ignored in all government decisions (possibly because he was Uzbek), aligned with the Pashtun, Hekmatyar, to attack the Tajik Rabbani government. Massoud had an opportunity and seized Konduz. Then he swung about and forced the Dostum-Hekmatyar alliance away from Kabul. As ethnic infighting intensified among the *mujahideen* warlords, a new group was added to the Afghan scorecard.[49]

In spring 1994, local *mujahideen* kidnapped and raped two girls near Kandahar. From that brutal crime would spring a popular movement that was directly involved in the events of 11 September 2001 and against whom U.S. and coalition forces would fight in Afghanistan. Mohammad Omar, a *talib* (religious student) and former member of the Soviet resistance in Kandahar, gathered 30 fellow *Taliban* (religious students) to free the girls. The rescue was successful, the *mujahideen* commander was hanged, and the *Taliban* movement was born. The *Taliban* goal, based on a 1996 interview with Omar, was to protect women and the poor and to punish those who were guilty of crimes. "We are fighting against Muslims who have gone wrong," Omar declared. Hamad Karzai, who was named president of Afghanistan in December 2001, initially believed that "the *Taliban* are good honest people . . . and were my friends from the *jihad* against the Soviets." Karzai willingly provided support. The *Taliban* grew in strength as many young men who had been *educated* in the refugee *madrasas* (Islamic schools) of Pakistan joined the cause.[50]

Figure 6. Hamad Karzai.

Pakistan was willing to supply more than just men who were educated in Islamic fundamentalism. President Benazir Bhutto, who had become president after Zia's death, had two major objectives vis-à-vis Afghanistan. One objective was to find a regime that was friendly

18

to Pakistan—support for Hekmatyar. The other was to establish a secure trade route through Afghanistan to the former Soviet republics. Fighting around Kabul had closed the eastern route north from Peshawar. Bhutto quickly focused on the western route north from Quetta. Pakistani envoys initiated discussions with Ismail Khan and Dostum to allow convoys to use the western highway. But Spin Boldak, a critical border town, was garrisoned by Hekmatyar's forces. On 12 October 1994, 200 *Taliban* fighters with Pakistani support defeated the garrison and captured 18,000 rifles and artillery pieces and a large quantity of ammunition. On 29 October, a Pakistani convoy bound for Turkmenistan departed Quetta. Near Kandahar, three local commanders halted the convoy and demanded a cut of the goods. The Pakistanis asked the *Taliban* to help. On 3 November, *Taliban* soldiers rescued the convoy, killing one of the local commanders. The *Taliban* force immediately moved to capture Kandahar. On 5 November 1994, the city was taken, along with tanks, artillery, six MiG-21s, and six helicopters. It was rumored that Pakistani advisers had been involved in the fighting. Many of the *Taliban* soldiers had been refugees in Pakistan and had been taught a strict interpretation of Islam that required total acceptance of the Koran and advocated eliminating the corrupting influence of the West. By December 1994, *Taliban* ranks in Kandahar had swollen to 12,000 as the populace embraced the fledgling movement as a better alternative to the corrupt regime. In the midst of these activities, President Bhutto denied any involvement with the *Taliban*.[51]

Historian Ahmed Rashid, who has studied Afghanistan extensively, described the young men who comprised the *Taliban*.

> These boys were a world apart from the Mujaheddin whom I had got to know during the 1980s—men who could recount their tribal and clan lineages, remembered their abandoned farms and valleys with nostalgia, and recounted legends and stories from Afghan history. These boys were from a generation who had never seen their country at peace. They had no memories of their tribes, their elders, or their neighborhoods. . . . They admired war because it was the only occupation they could possibly adapt to. Their simple belief in a messianic, puritan Islam drummed into them by simple village mullahs was the only prop they could hold on to and which gave their lives some meaning.[52]

These young men had lived in segregated refugee camps, having no contact with women. Fundamentalist mullahs taught them that women would distract them from their service to Allah. Adopting a strict interpretation of the Koran, they locked away the women, forbidding them to participate in normal society. To the *Taliban*, television, motion pictures, cameras, and music were corruptions that Islamic law forbade. Within days after the *Taliban* seized Kandahar, the women had disappeared from the streets, and the physical signs of Western influence had been eradicated.[53]

By January 1995, the *Taliban* had established control of the three provinces that bordered Kandahar and Kandahar Province—Helmand, Zabol, and Oruzgan provinces—through bribery or military power. In a series of lightning moves, the *Taliban* seized Ghazni and were within 35 miles of Kabul by 2 February. Hekmatyar's forces around the capital, facing the two armies of Rabbani and Massoud coming from the north, fled east toward Jalalabad when *Taliban* forces appeared from the south.[54]

Figure 7. Afghan children.

Massoud also had a problem in Kabul. The Shi'a Moslem Hazaras—the minority Shi'a represented 15 percent of the population—held the southern part of the capital and resisted Massoud's dominance. In March 1995, the "Lion of Panjshir" had launched a large-scale attack against the Hazaras. The commander, Abdul Mazari, sought help from the *Taliban*. Shortly afterward, he mysteriously was found dead—the possibility that the *Taliban* pushed Mazari from a helicopter remains unconfirmed. Mazari's demise angered the Hazaras (19 percent of Afghanistan's population) and the Shi'a Iran communities. Undeterred, Massoud and his better-trained troops ejected both the Hazaras and *Taliban* from Kabul by mid-March.[55]

In the meantime, the *Taliban* seized the western provinces of Nimroz and Farah. At Shindand, they encountered not only Ismail Khan's forces but also Tajiks airlifted from Kabul by Massoud and Afghan government tactical aircraft. The *Taliban* lost 3,000 fighters there, and by the end of May, they had been driven back almost to their Kandahar stronghold. Then, from Pakistan, 25,000 new volunteers were sent forward. The *Taliban* counterattacked; Khan's army disintegrated; and on 5 September 1995, the *Taliban* entered Herat. Ismail Khan fled to Iran.[56]

Mullah Omar became head of the *Taliban* officially on 3 April 1996 when the Kandahar leaders proclaimed him "Commander of the Faithful." The next day, Mullah Omar appeared in the city wearing Mohammad's cloak. This act signified that Omar believed that he was not just the leader of the *Taliban* but of all Muslims as well.[57]

20

By late spring 1996, the *Taliban* had regrouped and was showering rockets into Kabul. Massoud, Dostum, and Hekmatyar belatedly joined forces. The *Taliban* took Jalalabad on 5 September, captured Bagram shortly thereafter, and entered Kabul on 27 September 1996. Rabbani and the three warlords fled. Hekmatyar escaped to Iran. *Taliban* fighters took Najibullah from the UN compound and tortured and killed him. They hung his body from a light pole for all to see. As they had done in Kandahar and Herat, the *Taliban* forced women off the streets, eliminated them from the workplace, and imposed the wearing of the burqa. Particularly destructive was banning women from the educational and medical professions. Television, music, movies, games, and kites were prohibited. Men without beards were arrested. Theocratic totalitarianism, under the guise of Islam, was being imposed.[58]

The *Taliban* pursued Dostum and Massoud as they withdrew. Dostum managed to thwart the *Taliban* by blocking the Salang Tunnel. On 18 October, Massoud retook Bagram, but by the end of January 1997, a *Taliban* counterattack recaptured the air base. Then the *Taliban* shifted focus, and major elements were launched north from Kabul and Herat. General Abdul Malik, one of Dostum's commanders, defected to the *Taliban* with 4,000 men and marched toward Mazar-e-Sharif. As Dostum fled to Termez on the Uzbekistan border, *Taliban* forces took Mazar on 24 May 1997. That proved sufficient for Pakistan, Saudi Arabia, and the United Arab Emirates to recognize the *Taliban* as the government of Afghanistan.

The residents of Mazar-e-Sharif, however, did not recognize the *Taliban*, and on 28 May, they revolted. Six hundred *Taliban* were killed, another 1,000 were captured, and the 10 top leaders were killed or captured. Malik switched sides again and took control of four northern provinces, killing thousands more *Taliban*. Massoud, with Russian logistics backing, also counterattacked and, by the end of July 1997, had inflicted heavy losses—about 6,600 *Taliban* killed, wounded, or captured as well as 250 killed and 550 captured Pakistani fighters. In the aftermath of the success, Rabbani and others formed a United Islamic and National Front for the Salvation of Afghanistan, later to be called the Northern Alliance. Infighting severely limited its effectiveness.[59]

Massoud's counteroffensive recaptured Bagram. As they retreated toward Kabul, *Taliban* forces poisoned wells and destroyed crops. In September, the *Taliban* in Konduz attacked toward Mazar. Fighting erupted between Malik's troops and those still loyal to Dostum. As Malik fled to Turkmenistan, Dostum returned from Turkey to drive back the *Taliban* threat. As Dostum forced the *Taliban* back toward Konduz, entire villages were destroyed, and their inhabitants were murdered as they withdrew. UN investigators examined the mass graves but in an atmosphere of mutual recriminations could not determine responsibility. The *Taliban* ordered the UN out of the country, directed the nongovernmental organizations (NGOs) doing humanitarian assistance to desist providing aid to women, and arrested journalists for taking photographs of women. This brought humanitarian assistance to the people in Afghanistan to a virtual standstill.[60]

The official U.S. position on the civil war initially was neutral. Economically, a peace held promise for the American-built gas pipeline across Afghanistan to connect Turkmenistan to Pakistan. Despite its antipathy toward Iran, the U.S. government was reluctant to support the anti-Iranian *Taliban*. Increased evidence of *Taliban* atrocities led Secretary of State Madeleine

Albright to declare in November 1997: "We are opposed to the *Taliban* because of the opposition to human rights and their despicable treatment of women and children and great lack of respect for human dignity." U.S. Ambassador to the UN Bill Richardson traveled to Afghanistan in April 1998 to arrange a meeting between the *Taliban* and UN officials to discuss the plight of women. After Richardson left the country, Omar withdrew his pledge.[61] Within months, diplomacy was shelved as internal fighting flared up again in Afghanistan, and the U.S. government redirected its attention on international terrorism in Africa.

Figure 8. Madeleine Albright.

Figure 9. Bill Richardson.

While Western diplomats argued over courses of action, the anti-*Taliban* Uzbeks and Hazaras battled each other. The *Taliban* monitored the progress while further tightening down their reign of oppression. Windows had to be blackened so that women could not be seen from outside. Newborn children could only have names from an approved list. Public executions and open amputations for criminal activity became commonplace. The *Taliban* closed all NGO offices on 28 July 1998. Then, with financial support from Saudi Arabia and Pakistan, the *Taliban* launched a major offensive north from Herat, capturing Mazar-e-Sharif in August and forcing Dostum to flee the country after 1,400 soldiers were killed. Afterward, the *Taliban* engaged in a "killing frenzy" resulting in at least 6,000 people dead. Thousands more were imprisoned in the Mazar-e-Sharif fortress and in Sheberghan. Prisoners were delivered to the two sites in packed overseas shipping containers. In the midst of the frenzy, *Taliban* soldiers also killed 13 Iranian diplomats, almost causing a war with Iran. On 13 September, Bamian fell to the *Taliban*. Five days later, *Taliban* gunners desecrated the 2,000-year-old Buddha statues carved in the nearby rock cliffs by using them for target practice. (In March 2001, the 36- and 53-meter-tall Buddhas would be totally destroyed to the distress of the world community.) In September 1998, Saudi Arabia withdrew its financial support after Mullah Omar insulted the king's nephew with regard to Osama bin Laden. The UN Security Council castigated the *Taliban* on 8 December for their actions (Resolution 1214). Only Pakistan abstained on the resolution.[62] In the meantime, Washington was responding to more terrorist attacks on U.S. government posts and its military serving overseas.

It had taken a string of terrorist bombings in 1998, 1999, and 2000 to promulgate a "full-court press" by U.S. intelligence agencies to uncover those responsible. The dust had long since settled on the truck bomb that exploded beneath the World Trade Center in New York City at midday, 26 February 1993, killing six and injuring another 1,000 at a cost of $300 million. Then, the U.S. embassies in Nairobi, Kenya, and Dar es Salaam, Tanzania, were destroyed by terrorist bombs on 7 August 1998. The following year, 19 military servicemen died when another explosive-filled truck was detonated alongside the Khobar Towers housing complex in Saudi Arabia. In December 1999, a plot to bomb Los Angeles International Airport was foiled. Less than a year later, on 12 October 2000, a bomb-laden terrorist speedboat attacked the USS *Cole* in Yemen's harbor, killing 17 American sailors and wounding 39. Intelligence agencies linked Osama bin Laden and his *al-Qaeda* terrorist network to the incidents. In February 1998, before the Khobar Towers bombing, bin Laden had declared: "To kill the Americans and their allies—civilian and military—is an individual duty for every Muslim."[63] Few were familiar with Osama bin Laden at the time, and those who were tracking him did not realize at the time that his rhetoric had already been transformed into reality.

Bin Laden was born in 1955 or 1957 to a Yemeni father and Saudi Arabian mother. At King Abdul Aziz University in Jeddah, Saudi Arabia, he pursued both business administration and Islamic studies. Having inherited tremendous wealth, Osama bin Laden began in the early 1980s to finance construction projects for the *mujahideen* in Afghanistan. He quickly branched into supporting military operations against the Soviets using troops, approximately half of whom were Saudis, who were trained in his camps. After returning to Saudi Arabia, bin Laden was expelled in 1994 for statements against the regime. Bin Laden was next tracked to Khartoum, Sudan, when the Sudanese government asked him to leave in 1996. He settled in Jalalabad until the *Taliban* threatened the city. Sometime after relocating to Kandahar, Osama bin Laden met Mullah Omar.

From Kandahar on 23 August 1996, bin Laden issued his Declaration of War Against the Americans Occupying the Land of the Two Holy Places. Angered that Saudi Arabia let the United States launch attacks against Iraq in 1990, he condemned them for permitting U.S. military forces to be stationed on the Arab peninsula where the holy sites of Mecca and Medina are located, attacked Israel for its "occupation of Palestine," and declared war against the United States as an occupier of Muslim lands. In 1998, Osama bin Laden formed the *al-Qaeda* and created an umbrella organization for Islamic extremists called the International Islamic Front for Holy War Against Jews and Crusaders. During an interview with ABC News in December 1998, bin Laden made clear his anti-America views. "Hostility toward America is a religious duty," he declared, "and we hope to be rewarded for it by God."[64]

The response to the 7 August 1998 embassy bombings came less than two weeks later when U.S. cruise missiles slammed into terrorist training sites near Khowst and in Sudan on 20 August 1998. Afterward, President Bill Clinton, Secretary of Defense William Cohen, and Secretary Albright all emphasized that the United States was not fighting Islam but warned that international terrorists could not "escape the long arm of justice." Two days later, President Clinton revised Executive Order 12947, issued in 1995, to add Osama bin Laden to a list of terrorists whose assets in the United States would be frozen. The *Taliban*'s funds had been frozen by Executive Order 13129 on 4 July 1999. Clinton further allowed intelligence agents to use lethal force for self-defense, to preempt possible terrorist attacks, and to focus on bin Laden's associates. Secretary Cohen ordered two submarines armed with Tomahawk cruise missiles to the Persian Gulf. National Security Adviser Sandy Berger and Secretary Albright queried Chairman, Joint Chiefs of Staff (CJCS) General (GEN) Henry Shelton about using small Special Forces ground teams to attack bin Laden. News reports said that Shelton thought the idea was naïve. The State Department's Counterterrorism Reward Program raised the reward for information leading to bin Laden's arrest to $5 million.[65]

Figure 10. William Cohen.

Figure 11. GEN Henry Shelton.

American actions did not intimidate or deter the *Taliban* or bin Laden. As the *Taliban* recruited and rearmed, Massoud recaptured Bamian in April 1999. Three weeks later, the *Taliban* drove Massoud's forces from the city. Having garnered 250 opposition leaders and their families, the *Taliban* fighters herded the captives into houses and set them afire, killing all of them. On the diplomatic front, the *Taliban* offered to exchange bin Laden for U.S. recognition of their regime. State Department officials spoke directly with Mullah Omar and established a February 1999 deadline to deliver bin Laden to U.S. authorities. Omar refused after declaring bin Laden to be his guest. Shortly afterward, bin Laden departed Kandahar amid reports of growing dissension between him and the *Taliban*. Albright warned the Pakistanis that their country was becoming more and more isolated in the region because of their refusal to act decisively against the *Taliban*. The growing isolation was true because the murder of the Iranian diplomats in Mazar in August 1998 had so infuriated Iran against the *Taliban* and Pakistan that relations between Iran and the United States had begun to improve.[66] Another major issue was the *Taliban*'s attitude about the drug trade, a blatant contradiction of Muslim theocracy.

While Afghans died in civil war, opium dealers thrived. The U.S. State Department had labeled Afghanistan an international conduit for drugs as early as 1996. Although drugs are not permitted under Islamic law, growing poppies to convert into opium was permitted freely. "Opium is permissible because it is consumed by *kafirs* in the West and not by Muslims or Afghans," argued the *Taliban*'s antidrug force commander.[67] The reality was that opium consumption helped finance the fighting necessary for the *Taliban* to gain control of the country. From 1995 to 1997, during much of the fighting to consolidate power (gaining control of the Afghan cities), opium production increased 25 percent. The UN attempted to negotiate with the *Taliban*, promising aid to grow substitute crops if they would eliminate the drug trade. That effort ended when the *Taliban* ordered the UN to leave Afghanistan in 1998. Government customs revenues and agricultural taxes for poppy propagation went directly into the *Taliban* treasury—a box kept under Mullah Omar's bed. Afghan opium accounted for 72 percent of the world's supply in 2000.[68]

When the elusive bin Laden was discovered residing south of Jalalabad on 4 July 1999, ABC News had just reported that Saudi Arabian and Persian Gulf businessmen were financing his terrorist activities. The Saudis arrested one banker on charges of funneling $2 million to bin Laden. This prompted President Clinton to issue Executive Order 13129. On 9 July, the *Taliban* acknowledged that bin Laden was in Afghanistan.[69]

Pakistani Prime Minister Nawaz Sharif was meeting with President Clinton when Afghanistan admitted that bin Laden was living there. Although the president angrily addressed the lack of Pakistani cooperation in apprehending bin Laden and pointedly told Sharif that he would send a communiqué outlining Pakistan's suggested role, that topic was not a part of the message. Sharif did agree to withdraw Pakistani military forces from Kashmir—at the time the critical concern to the United States because India and Pakistan possessed nuclear weapons.[70] The internecine war in Afghanistan and bin Laden were overshadowed by the threat of regional nuclear war.

Although there was fighting in the first half of 1999, it was sporadic. A major three-prong offensive that *Taliban* forces launched from Kabul signaled the resumption of full-blown combat on 28 July. For the first time this major *Taliban* effort combined tanks, artillery, and organized infantry. Bagram fell on 31 July, and other cities quickly followed, including a key point along Massoud's supply line to Tajikistan. From the Shomali plain north of Kabul the *Taliban* drove the refugees—numbers varied from 55,000 to 250,000—toward the capital. In their wake was devastation—burned villages, destroyed crops, slaughtered livestock, and uncounted numbers of dead villagers. Massoud struck back, killing more than 1,000 *Taliban* fighters, including Arabs and Pakistanis. When he quickly closed on Kabul and Bagram, Mullah Omar sought help from Pakistan; 2,000 more *madrassa* students volunteered. On 24 August, Omar survived an assassination attempt by unknown persons when a fuel truck was detonated near his house in Kandahar. Those responsible never sought recognition.[71] With Afghan assistance to capture bin Laden seemingly out of the question, the U.S. government sought alternate approaches.

Having prevented nuclear war between India and Pakistan, Washington redirected its priorities toward capturing bin Laden. Having concluded that Pakistan offered the best avenue to that end, President Clinton lifted some trade sanctions in September. The following month Prime Minister Sharif's brother met with several Persian Gulf states' envoys to apprise them of Pakistan's intent to demand bin Laden's extradition from Afghanistan. The Pakistan army chief of intelligence met with Mullah Omar to insist that the *Taliban* stop training Pakistanis who he considered threats to his nation's stability. A few days later Omar made an official statement denouncing terrorism.[72]

To complicate matters, on 12 October 1999, Pakistan army General Pervez Musharraf orchestrated a military coup that overthrew the democratically elected Sharif. Musharraf, supported by former Prime Minister Benazir Bhutto, pledged to reduce tensions along the Indian border while warning India not to take advantage of the situation in Pakistan. As for Afghanistan, Musharraf vowed to "continue our efforts to achieve a just and peaceful solution. . . ." The U.S. government was disappointed that the general did not set a date to return to democracy.

During his visit to Pakistan in March 2000, President Clinton reiterated that the United States supported "an orderly restoration of democratic civilian rule" and was adamantly opposed to regional terrorism. Musharraf promised to work with the *Taliban* to resolve the problem of bin Laden. The following month, Under Secretary of State Thomas Pickering warned the Pakistani chief of intelligence not "to put [his country] in the position" of supporting people "that are our enemies." In May, Pickering reiterated that same message to the *Taliban* deputy foreign minister. Mullah Omar responded that the change in leadership was an internal Pakistani matter.[73]

The deteriorating situation in Afghanistan once again became a discussion topic in the UN Security Council. On 22 October 1999, the Council belatedly condemned the *Taliban* for the 1999 summer offensive; called for the extradiction of bin Laden, an end to drug trafficking, and the restoration of human rights; and castigated the leaders for the Iranian diplomats killed in 1998. CIA Director George Tenet told a Senate Select Committee in February 2000 that bin Laden "is still the foremost among these terrorists" and that "he wants to strike further blows against America." The *Taliban*, following the typical summer campaign cycle, launched another offensive in July 2000 that concentrated on Massoud's headquarters in Taloqan. On 5 September, the city fell. Massoud was pushed back into the Panjshir valley from

Figure 12. George Tenet.

where he made an unsuccessful attempt to retake Taloqan. While Massoud and Dostum had met in March 1999 in Termez allegedly to plan joint operations, the "Lion of Panjshir" appeared to be battling the *Taliban* alone, despite Dostum's assertion on 1 October to the contrary.

By early 2001, with Massoud controlling only portions of the two northeastern provinces, Badakhshan and Takhar, neighboring countries began giving recognition of the dominant *Taliban* regime and Tajikistan. Uzbekistan President Islam Karimov stated that Russian troops would not be allowed into his country to move against the *Taliban*. He also made it clear that Uzbekistan would avoid any border confrontations with the *Taliban*. In October 2000, Karimov, who previously declared the *Taliban* to be the "main source of fanaticism and extremism in the region," stated a willingness to accept it as the government of Afghanistan if "the people of Afghanistan trust it."

What the change reflected was the growing influence of the terrorist Islamic Movement of Uzbekistan (IMU). Trained in bin Laden's camps, IMU leaders made the creation of an Islamic state within Uzbekistan a major goal. Improved relations with the *Taliban* would potentially allow the Uzbeks to focus on destroying the IMU as well as eliminating an excuse for Russian intervention.[74]

In January 2001, the trial of four men accused of bombing the U.S. Embassies in Kenya and Tanzania began in New York. Among 22 suspects, also indicted was Osama bin Laden, in absentia. On 18 May 2001, a jury convicted the four and sentenced them on 18 October 2001 to life imprisonment without parole. Thirteen of the men indicted, including bin Laden, remained at large. In Afghanistan, the *Taliban* continued to consolidate its repressive hold on most of the country. On 9 September 2001, two assassins, posing as journalists filming a documentary, struck Afghan resistance leader Ahmad Shah Massoud. They detonated a video camera packed with explosives. One assassin was killed in the explosion, and bodyguards killed the other. The "Lion of Panjshir" died en route to the hospital. Shortly after the act, bin Laden released a video interview to the world press in which he stated, "It's time to penetrate America and Israel and hit them where it hurts the most."[75]

26

Two days later, the people of the United States were painfully aware that Osama bin Laden's threat had been a promise.

Notes

1. Rudyard, Kipling, *The Works of Rudyard Kipling* (Roslyn, NY: Black's Readers Service Co., nd), 85.

2. Rahimullah Yusufzai, "Wrath of God," *Time* (11 January 1999), <www.time.com/time/asia/magazine/1999/990111/osama1.html>.

3. Louis Dupree, *Afghanistan* (Princeton, NJ: Princeton University Press, 1973), 316.

4. Ahmed Rashid, *Taliban: Militant Islam, Oil and Fundamentalism in Central Asia* (New Haven, CT: Yale Nota Bene, 2001), 9; "Political History of Afghanistan," <www.afghan-info.com/Afghistory.htm>, 2; "Arab Rule of Pakistan," <www.geocities.com/pak_history/arab/html>.

5. "The Islamic World to 1600: The Mongol Invasions (The Timurid Empire)," www.ucalgary.ca/applied_history/tutor/islam/Mongols/timurid.html; "Babur," http://encarta.msn.com/index/conciseindex/51/051a1000.htm.

6. Dupree, 329-32.

7. Ibid., 332, 35.

8. "Nadir Shah," <www.encyclopedia.com/html/n/nadirs1ha.asp>; *Afghanistan: A Country Study*, Richard F. Nyrop and Donald M. Seekins, eds. (Washington, DC: Department of the Army, 1986), 19.

9. Dupree, 363-64. In 1935, Persia would be renamed Iran.

10. Ibid., 365, 369-76; *Afghanistan: A Country Study*, 23-27.

11. Stephen Tanner, *Afghanistan: A Military History From Alexander the Great to the Fall of the Taliban* (New York: DeCapo Press, 2002), 143; Dupree, 379.

12. Ibid., 389, 394, 405; Tanner, 201.

13. Ibid.; *Afghanistan: A Country Study*, 30.

14. The fighting of 1839-42 is considered to be the First Anglo-Afghan War. See Dupree, 406; Tanner, 203; "Berlin, Congress of," "Crimean War," "Eastern Question," "Russo-Turkish Wars," "San Stefano, Treaty of," *The Columbia Encyclopedia*, Sixth Edition, 2001, <www.bartleby.com>.

15. "Abdur Rahman Khan, amir of Afghanistan," <www.avsands.com/abdur-armir-av.htm>; Dupree, 417-29, 433; Tanner, 215-19. The convention also divided Persia into two areas of influence—the Russians in the north and the British in the south. This division was the "legal" justification for the Russian and British occupation of Iran after World War II.

16. Dupree, 434-35.

17. Tanner, 218-19; "Third Anglo-Afghan War, 1919," <www.regiments.org/milhist/wars/20thcent/19afghan.htm>; Dupree, 444.

18. *Afghanistan: A Country Study*, 43-44; Dupree, 446; Ludwig W. Adamec, *Afghanistan, 1900-1923: A Diplomatic History* (Berkeley, CA: University of California Press, 1967), 163; "History," <http://crick.fmed.uniba.sk/~zahin/hist.html>.

19. Dupree, 449.

20. *Afghanistan: A Country Study*, 44-50.

21. Dupree, 478-80; Tanner, 225; "Iran," <www.encyclopedia.com/html/section/iran_history.asp>.

22. Tanner, 225-27; *Afghanistan: A Country Study*, 56, 59; Index of Declassified Documents, No. 33A (1979), No. 377A (1978).

23. Dupree, 532-33.

24. Declassified Documents Quarterly Catalog, 5, No. 1 (1979), No. 448.

25. Ibid., 565-66, 594; Articles 1 and 2, "Constitution of Afghanistan," as quoted in Ibid., 574; *Afghanistan: A Country Study*, 62-64.

26. Ibid., 69-73.

27. Ibid., 231-33; Tanner, 232; "Adolph Dubs," <http://politicalgraveyard.com/bio/duane-dudkin.html>, #RLI-OM57AK; *Afghanistan: A Country Study*, 234, 239; Afghanistan Online: "Biography (Noor Mohammad Taraki)," <www.afghan-web.com/bios/yest/taraki.html>. Various sources will give different dates for Taraki's death. Another date mentioned is 10 October. Scott R. McMichael, *Stumbling Bear: Soviet Military Performance in Afghanistan* (London: Brassey's, 1991), 27.

28. Anthony Hyman, *Afghanistan Under Soviet Domination, 1964-1983* (New York: St. Martin's Press, 1982), 101, 111, 115; *Pravda*, 1 June 1979, 5; Joseph C. Collins, *The Soviet Invasion of Afghanistan: A Study in the Use of Force in Soviet Foreign Policy* (Lexington, MA: D.C. Heath and Co., 1986), 69; McMichael, 5.

29. Ibid., 78-79; U.S. Department of State, *Soviet Invasion of Afghanistan*, 1, as quoted in Collins, 78, 101; *Afghanistan: A Country Study*, 242; "Charter of the United Nations," <www1.umn.edu/humanrts/instree/chapter7.html>; Douglas A. Borer, *Superpowers Defeated: Vietnam and Afghanistan Compared* (London: Frank Cass, 1999), 133.

30. Robert F. Baumann, *Russian-Soviet Unconventional Wars in the Caucasus, Central Asia, and Afghanistan*, Leavenworth Paper Number 20 (Fort Leavenworth, KS: Combat Studies Institute, 1993), 132-133; *Pravda*, 31 December 1979, 4. The article credits National Security Adviser Zbigniew Brzezinski with coining the term "strategic arc." Brzezinski actually used the term "arc of crisis." See Zbigniew Brzezinski, *Power and Principle: Memoirs of the National Security Adviser, 1977-81* (New York: Farrar, Straus, Giroux, 1983), 446.

31. Ibid., 431-34; "Treaty Between the United States of America and the Union of Soviet Socialist Republics on the Limitation of Strategic Offensive Arms," <www.state.gov/www/global/arms/treaties/salt2-1.html>; "State of the Union Address," 21 January 1980, <www.jimmycarterlibrary.org/documents/speeches/su80jec.phtml>.

32. *The New York Times*, 15 January 1980, 8; Robert Rand, "Cuba Continues to Take an Ambiguous Stand on Soviet Actions in Afghanistan," *Radio Liberty Research Bulletin*, RL 56-80 (6 February 1980), np; Collins, 92; Brzezinski, 448; "Pakistan: The United States Alliance," <http://lcweb2.loc.gov/cgi-bin/query/r?frd/cstdy:@field (DOCID+pk0149)>.

33. Rashid, 19; Mark Urban, *War in Afghanistan* (New York: St. Martin's Press, 1988), 59; *Afghanistan: A Country Study*, 336; McMichael, 26; Alexander Alexiev, *Inside the Soviet Army in Afghanistan* (Santa Monica, CA: RAND, 1988).

34. Tanner, 243-44; *The New York Times*, 19 August 1981, 3; McMichael, 45-47, 49-50. The Afghan army numbered approximately 90,000 when the Soviets invaded. It would fluctuate between 25,000 and 40,000 during the Soviet occupation.

35. Urban, 60-61,67-68, 70, 72, 96; McMichael, 15. Massoud was assassinated on 9 September 2001 by pro-*Taliban* Arabs who wounded three other Northern Alliance officials in the same attack.

36. Urban, 80-81, 101-105, 116; Tanner, 252.

37. Baumann, 153; McMichael, 85.

38. "Afghanistan: Lessons From the Last War," <www.gwu.edu/~nsarchiv/NSAEBB/ NSAEBB57/essay. html>; "Cold War Postscript: Legacy of Afghanistan Haunts Both Cold War Superpowers," *CNN*, 7 March 1999, <www.clw.org/atop/media/cnn030799.html>; Ken Silverstein, "Stingers, Stingers, Who's Got the Stingers?" *Slate*, 2 October 2001, <www.globalsecurity.org/org/news/2001/011002-attack03.htm>; McMichael, 90; Tanner, 267. It must be noted that exact losses are impossible to obtain. One study by Aaron Karp in *Armed Forces Journal* notes that aircraft losses after 1986 were from 438 to 547.

39. McMichael, 91, 93-95.

40. Tanner, 258-59; Urban, 134; Mohammad Yahya Nawroz and Lester Grau, *The Soviet War in Afghanistan: History and Harbinger of Future War?* (Fort Leavenworth, KS: Foreign Military Studies Office, 1995), <http://call. army.mil/fmso/FMSOPUBS/issues/waraf.htm>.

41. *Afghanistan: A Country Study*, 316-323; Urban, 138, 157.

42. Kabul Radio, 20 March 1985, as quoted in Urban, 165-67; Baumann, 171; McMichael, 66, 71; *Afghanistan: A Country Study*, 265.

43. CPSU CC Politburo Transcript (excerpt), "Meeting of CC CPSU Politburo," 13 November 1986, <http://cwihp.si.edu/cwihplib.nsf>; Mikhail S. Gorbachev, Speech to the Twenty-Seventh Congress of the Central Party of the Soviet Union, 6 March 1986; Kabul Radio, 4 May 1986, as quoted in Urban, 196, 200; Robert D. Kaplan, *Soldiers of God: With Islamic Warriors in Afghanistan and Pakistan* (New York: Vintage Books, 2001), 186-87.

44. *The Soviet Withdrawal From Afghanistan*, Amin Saikal and William Maley, eds. (Cambridge, MA: Cambridge University Press, 1989), 16; "Afghanistan," <www.state.gov/r/pa/ei/bgn/5380/htm>.

45. McMichael, 145f. This is an official figure. Anecdotal reports are that the figure is much higher. A. Bovin, "A Difficult Decade," *Izvestiia*, 23 December 1988, as quoted in Baumann, 177.

46. Kaplan, 41, 168, 170, 173, 176; Urban, 16; Michael Griffin, *Reaping the Whirlwind: The Taliban Movement in Afghanistan* (London: Pluto Press, 2001), 131; "Herbert Marion Wassom," Arlington National Cemetery Website, <www.arlingtoncemetery.com/hnwassom.htm>. Also killed in the crash were U.S. Ambassador to Pakistan Arnold Raphel and Brigadier General Herbert Wassom, chief, U.S. Military Group, Pakistan. The *Taliban* killed Abdul Haq following a battle on 26 October 2001.

47. Tanner, 271-75.

48. "Inside the *Taliban*: Rashid Dostum," <http://abcnews.go.com/sections/world/DailyNews/*taliban*_profiles. html>; Griffin, 24-25; Tanner, 277-78.

49. Ibid.; Griffin, 28.

50. Ibid., 35; John F. Burns and Steve LeVine, "How Afghans' Stern Rulers Took Hold," *New York Times International*, 31 December 1996, A1; Kaplan, 234-35.

51. Rashid, 27-29; Tanner, 279-80; Kaplan, 236; *The Nation*, 18 February 1995, and *Dawn* (Pakistan), 18 March 1995, as quoted in Rashid, 29.

52. Rashid, 32-33.

53. Ibid.

54. Ibid., 33; Griffin, 42.

55. The Hazaras, the majority of whom are Shi'a, had close ties to Iran, which is 89 percent Shi'a. See "Iran," <www.countrywatch.com>; "Afghanistan," <www.countrywatch.com>; Rashid, 35.

56. Ibid., 39-40.

57. Ibid., 42. Omar's title has not been accepted by Muslims outside of Afghanistan. Robert Marquand, "The Reclusive Ruler Who Runs the *Taliban*," <www.csmonitor.com/2001/1010/p1s4-wosc.html>.

58. Ibid., 49-51. On 26 September 2002, the *Associated Press* reported that Hekmatyar and *Taliban* fugitives had formed the Islamic Martyrs Brigade specifically to attack Americans. The report also stated that Hekmatyar was receiving aid from Iran. "Former U.S. Ally Declares War on American Troops in Afghanistan," *Associated Press*, 26 September 2002.

59. Griffin, 52-53, 96-97, 111; Rashid, 53, 58, 61.

60. Ibid., 62-65.

61. Ibid., 45-46, 71; Reuters, 18 November 1997, as quoted in Rashid, 65. The antagonism between the two nations was twofold. The Iranians regarded the *Taliban*'s view of Islam as un-Islamic. Much of that view is because the *Taliban* is primarily Sunni Muslim and the Iranians are Shi'a Muslims. Furthermore, the Hazaras in Afghanistan are mostly Shi'a, while the rival Pashtun, who comprise most of the *Taliban*, are Sunni. See "Politics-Iran/Afghanistan: Tehran Stares Down the *Taliban*," <www.oneworld.org/ips2/aug98/03_58_008.html> and "*Taliban* Threatens Retaliation if Iran Strikes," <http://europe.cnn.com/WORLD/MEAST/9809/15/iran.afghan.tensions.02/>.

62. Rashid, 70, 72, 78; Michael Winchester, "Inside Story: Afghanistan," *Asiaweek* (6 November 1998), <www.pathfinder.com/asiaweek/98/1106/nat_7-2_ismazar.html>; Griffin, 192-93, 138-39; "Photos Document Destruction of Afghan Buddhas," 12 March 2001, <www.cnn.com/2001/WORLD/asiapcf/central/03/12/afghan.buddha.02/index.html>.

63. "Terrorist Attacks on Americans" <www.infoplease.com/spot/terrorism6.html>; "Strike One—Khobar Towers, Strike Two—TWA 800, Strike Three . . . ," <http://members.aol.com/bardonia2/towers.htm>; "Text of *Fatwah* Urging *Jihad* Against Americans," *Al-Quds al-`Arabi*, 23 February 1998, <www.ict.org.il/articles/fatwah.htm>.

64. Rashid, 131-33; "Al-Qa`ida (The Base)," <www.intellnet.org/documents/ 200/060/269.html>; "Osama bin Laden," <www.adl.org/terrorism_america/bin_1.asp>; "Terror Suspect: An Interview With Osama bin Laden," 22 December 1998, <www.abcnews.go.com/sections/world/DailyNews/transcript_binladen1_981228.html>; "Declaration of War Against the Americans Occupying the Land of the Holy Places," <www.outpost-of-freedom.com/opf980830a.htm>.

65. "U.S. Missiles Pound Targets in Afghanistan, Sudan," 21 August 1988, <www.cnn.com/US/9808/20/us.strikes.02/>; "Executive Order, 22 August 1998," <www.fas.org/irp/offdocs/eo-980822.htm>; Bob Woodward and Vernon Loeb, "CIA's Covert War on Bin Laden," <www.washingtonpost.com/ac2/wp-dyn/A28094-2001Sep13?language=printer>; Barton Gellman, "Broad Effort Launched After '98 Attacks," <www.washingtonpost.com/ac2/wp-dyn?A6725-2001Dec18?language=printer>; U.S. Department of State, "Reward Offer: Osama bin Laden and Mohammad Atef," <http://usinfo.state.gov/topical/pol/terror/98110401.htm>; Presidential Documents, "Blocking Property and Prohibiting Transactions With the *Taliban*, Executive Order 13129 of July 4, 1999," Federal Register 64, Number 129, 7 July 1999.

66. Griffin, 221, 215; Rashid, 78, 140, 180, 205.

67. Robin Raphel, Testimony to the Senate Foreign Relations Subcommittee on the Near East and South Asia, 11 May 1996; Rashid, 118.

68. Ibid., 119, 123-124; Bureau of South Asian Affairs, U.S. Department of State, "The *Taliban* and the Afghan Drug Trade," <www.state.gov/www/regions/sa/facts_taliban_drugs.html>.

69. David Phinney, "Bankrolled for New Terrorist Attack," <http://abcnews.go.com/sections/world/DailyNews/ binladen990707.html>; Reuters, 9 July 1999, cited in Griffin, 224.

70. Bruce Riedel, "American Diplomacy and the 1999 Kargil Summit at Blair House," Center for the Advanced Study of India Policy Paper Series 2002, <www.sas.upenn.edu/casi/reports/RiedelPaper051302.htm>.

71. Griffin, 227-29.

72. Ibid., 232-33; "Army Chief: Pakistan Coup Launched 'as Last Resort,'" 13 October 1999, <www.cnn.com/ ASIANOW/south/9910/12/pakistan.06>.

73. "General Pervez Musharraf's Address to the Nation," 17 October 1999, <www.fas.Org/news/Pakistan/1999/991017-mushraf_speech.htm>; "World Reacts Cautiously to Pakistan Coup Leader's Speech," 19 October 1999, <http://europe.cnn.com/ASIANOW/South/9910/18/Pakistan.reax/>; *Frontier Post* (Peshawar, Pakistan), 13 October 1999, as cited in Griffin, 237; "Background Press Briefing by a Senior Administration Official on the President's Meetings in Pakistan," The White House Office of the Press Secretary, 25 March 2000, <http://usembassy.state.gov/islamabad/wwwhp077.html>; Gellman, "Broad Efforts Launched After '98 Attacks."

74. "Statement by the President of the Security Council," UN, 22 October 1999, <http://srch0.un.org/plweb-i/fastweb?state_id=1031234529&view=scdocs&docrank>; Senate Select Committee on Intelligence, *Current and Projected National Security Threats to the United States*, 106th Congress, 2d Session, 2 February 2000, 12; Griffin, 248-49; Justin Burke, "Tashkent Interested in Settlement in Afghanistan Regardless of Political Leadership—Uzbek President," *Uzbekistan Daily Digest*, 13 October 2000, <www.eurasianet.net/resource/uzbekistan/hypermail/200010/0021.htm>; U.S. Department of State, *Fact Sheet: Islamic Movement of Uzbekistan*, 15 September 2000, <http://usinfo.state.gov/topical/pol/terror/00091511.htm>; Pauline Jones Luong, "A Dangerous Balancing Act: Karimov, Putin, and the *Taliban*," Program on New Approaches to Russian Security Policy Memo 166, November 2000, <www.csis.org/ruseura/ponars/index.htm>; "Uzbekistan to Recognize *Taliban* Control," *Associated Press*, 13 October 2000, <www.bangla2000.com/News/Archive/International/10-14-2000/news_detail12.shtm>; "Moscow Prepared to Consider Military Means to Stop *Taliban*," *Uzbekistan in the News*, 23 March 2000, <www.cu-online.com/~k_a/uzbekistan/news.htm>; Abraham Rein, "Dostum Denies Helping Uzbek Authorities Crack Down on Islamic Militants," *Uzbekistan Daily Digest*, 3 October 2000, <www.eurasianet.org/resource/uzbekistan/hypermail/200010/0004.html>.

75. "Embassy Bombing Trial Under Way in New York," 3 January 2001, <www.cnn.com/2001/LAW/01/03/embassy.bombings>; "Four Embassy Bombers Get Life," 21 October 2001, <www.cnn.com/2001/LAW/10/19/embassy.bombings/index.html>; "The Murder of Massoud," <http://members.aol.com/_ht_a/mbeve10258/Assassination.html?mtbrand=AOL_US>; "Osama bin Laden: Profile," <www.adl.org/terrorism_america/bin_1.asp>.

Chapter 2

Awakening the Giant

*War is not merely an act of policy but a true political
instrument, a continuation of political intercourse,
carried on with other means. The political object
is the goal, war is the means of reaching it, and means
can never be considered in isolation from their purpose.*[1]

Taliban, al-Qaeda, Osama bin Laden. As the rays of the early morning sun reflected from the twin towers of the World Trade Center on 11 September 2001 (9/11), few Americans had heard those names. Within hours, however, few Americans would not recognize those names. Not since 1941 had a foreign power directly attacked the United States. Just as one generation of Americans can recall where it was on 7 December 1941 when Pearl Harbor was bombed and another remembers 22 November 1963—the day President John F. Kennedy was assassinated—so, too, will another generation of Americans recall where it was on the morning of 9/11.

President George W. Bush characterized the 9/11 attacks as "acts of mass murder" and pledged "to find those responsible and bring them to justice." Unequivocally, he declared that the attacks were "acts of war." Within 24 hours, intelligence reports had linked bin Laden to the attacks, and congressmen and military officials were calling for retaliation.[2] While Secretary of State Colin Powell mounted a diplomatic offensive to garner support for U.S. offensive action, Secretary of Defense Donald Rumsfeld prepared an order to mobilize reservists and members of the National Guard. Deputy Secretary of Defense Paul Wolfowitz announced that the military was "entering into a campaign against terrorism."[3] On 14 September 2001, the U.S. Congress approved a joint resolution that authorized "the use of United States armed forces against those responsible for the recent attacks launched against the United States."[4] Islamic extremist Osama bin Laden had become America's "public enemy number 1" and the focus of an unprecedented worldwide manhunt with Afghanistan the center of attention.[5]

Having been regarded as a "backwater" country by U.S. government departments and agencies, designating Afghanistan as a top priority after 9/11 did not yield instant gratification, even with America's vast information resources and technology. The geography and demography posed significant challenges to operations in Afghanistan. Mountains that rise to almost 17,000 feet cover two-thirds of the country, and high desert plateau dominates the rest. Only 15 percent of the land can support agriculture. There are three major languages and 30 minor languages spoken. Religious divisions between the majority Sunni Muslims and minority Shi'a Muslims are further complicated by different tribal cultures and historic rivalries. Centuries of oppression, 80-percent illiteracy, famine conditions as a result of seven years of drought, and general lack of infrastructure would hamper diplomatic and military options designed to destroy the *al-Qaeda* terrorists and drive the *Taliban* from power.[6] Of no small import were the millions of unmarked land mines strewn all over the country during the 10-year Soviet occupation.

Figure 1. Extensive mountainous terrain.

History also had made Afghanistan a difficult battleground. Whether it was involved in the "Great Game" played by Russia and Great Britain or a newer regional power version that involved the Russians, Iranians, and Americans, Afghanistan had been a geopolitical pawn for more than a century. Its neighbor, nuclear-armed Pakistan, could not be ignored nor could that nation's nuclear-armed rival to the east, India. Within Afghanistan, perpetual ethnic infighting, tension between the extreme fundamentalists and the more moderate branches of Islam, primary loyalty to ethnic regional warlords rather than to a nation, a common willingness to sell military service to the highest bidder, and a tradition of violent overthrows of any "national" governments were legacies that U.S. diplomats and soldiers could not disregard.

"We will rally the world," declared the president, and Powell immediately launched a diplomatic offensive to garner the support of the UN and the North Atlantic Treaty Organization (NATO). "We're building a strong coalition to go after these perpetrators," Powell told reporters. Within days, U.S.government officials had received words of support from Russia, China, NATO, and the European Union. The tangible evidence was the commitment of British, Australian, and New Zealand military forces to join America in the fight against terrorism. Iran's position was questionable, but British Foreign Secretary Jack Straw obtained a pledge that the Persians would not interfere with the coalition's efforts. On 22 September 2001, the United Arab Emirates severed all diplomatic ties with the *Taliban*, and three days later, Saudi Arabia followed suit. Pakistan refused to break diplomatic ties with the *Taliban* regime.[7] Coalition support of the war on international terrorism proved invaluable.

American relations with Pakistan had always been and would continue to be extremely delicate. Although the United States had a long history with Pakistan that included surrogate support of the *mujahideen*, the Pakistanis provided recruits and equipment and recognized the *Taliban* government. President Bush and British Prime Minister Tony Blair, a leading figure among the leaders of the growing coalition, knew that Pakistani cooperation would be critical. The day after the attacks on the United States, President Musharraf had pledged his "unstinted cooperation." Powell provided Musharraf with a list of exactly what support the United

34

States wanted. The sometimes violent internal reactions to Musarraf's commitment indicated how tenuous his power was, especially after the *Taliban* had threatened invasion if the United States was permitted to launch attacks against Afghanistan from Pakistan. A strong diplomatic push from State Department officials convinced Pakistan to send envoys to meet with Mullah Omar to urge him to turn bin Laden over to the United States. A similar demand from the UN followed. On 21 September, the *Taliban* rejected the UN demand and a week later informed Pakistan that it would not surrender bin Laden. As the only country maintaining diplomatic relations with the *Taliban*, Musharraf did not want Pakistan to become an international pariah. At the same time, U.S. government officials needed to exploit that link to convey messages to the *Taliban* and quietly urged the Pakistanis to maintain ties. The United States prevailed until the war was well on its way. On 22 November 2001, Pakistan ordered all *Taliban* diplomats out of the country, and the embassy closed.[8]

Figure 2. Pakistan government building.

Equally as important as creating a coalition of nations to fight the *al-Qaeda* and drive the *Taliban* from power was creating an alliance among the anti-*Taliban* factions in Afghanistan. Former Soviet Army Lieutenant Igor Lisinenko, a wounded Afghanistan veteran, warned, "the Afghans will stop fighting each other and join together to fight you." American diplomats, mindful of the Soviet experience, began weaving their way through the maze of tribal, subtribal, factional, and religious relationships that had characterized Afghanistan for centuries. In Washington, a representative of the Northern Alliance living in exile met with U.S. officials who recognized the importance of building a strong relationship. Defense Secretary Rumsfeld understood that the Northern Alliance could "be useful in a variety of ways." To avoid offending Pashtuns who were not well represented in the Northern Alliance, Rumsfeld reminded officials that ties had to be forged with "tribes in the south." An alliance that included all Afghan tribes was critical to dispelling the appearance of favoritism, that a foreign power was supporting one group, or that another foreign army was invading Afghanistan. In the forefront of every major military decision was the political goal of providing the Afghans with the environment and

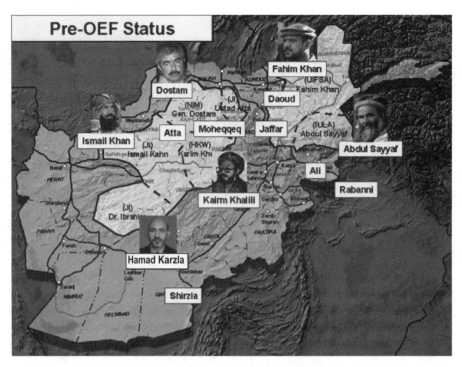

Figure 3. Tribal factions, regions, and leaders.

opportunity to establish a stable government after the *Taliban* was forced from power. Powell made that clear in a late September 2001 pronouncement: "We are interested in a multiethnic Afghanistan."[9]

Ironically, just as Leonid Brezhnev had done in 1980 to justify the Soviet invasion of Afghanistan, Secretary Powell invoked Article 51 of the UN Charter—"the inherent right of individual or collective self-defense"—to establish secure footing for additional coalition support.[10] The difference in September 2001 was that the community of nations saw through the Soviet chimera of foreign invasion while the rubble of the World Trade Center towers provided glaring evidence to UN diplomats in New York. Calmly, systematically, and methodically, U.S. government leaders were "dotting the i's" and "crossing the t's."

"Dead or Alive" was the order issued at the Pentagon on 17 September 2001. That was how badly the president wanted bin Laden brought to justice.[11] This was no idle threat. Two days earlier at Camp David, President Bush met with his national security team to review options for responding to the terrorist attacks. CIA Director George Tenet proposed a plan to capitalize on the Northern Alliance's opposition to the *Taliban*. U.S. ground forces would link up with those fighters to attack terrorist supporters in and around cities of northern Afghanistan. According to the president, Rumsfeld "understood the utility of having the CIA involved" and "quickly grasped" the essence of the plan "to mate up our assets with the Northern Alliance troops." Then the Chairman, Joint Chiefs of Staff (CJCS), GEN Henry Shelton presented three military options. The first two consisted of cruise missile and manned bomber attacks; the third combined cruise missile and manned bomber attacks with placing American "boots on the ground"—inserting Army Special Forces troops.[12]

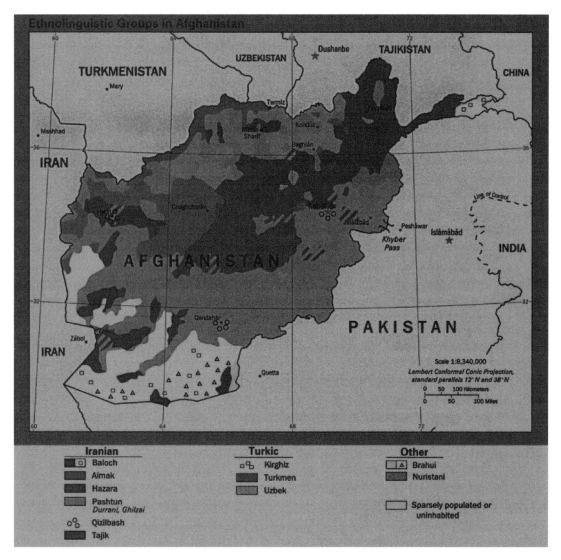

Figure 4. Map depicting the ethnic and linguistic diversity of Afghanistan.

President Bush ordered development of Shelton's third option. According to National Security Adviser Condoleeza Rice afterward, "Probably the most important conclusion that he [Bush] came to was that this military action . . . had to look different from what the United States had been doing over the past ten years or so. It could not just be an air campaign. It could not just be a cruise missile campaign. There had to be boots on the ground. We had to have a ground presence to demonstrate our seriousness. Probably that insight governed more of what we did than anything else."[13] As the American news media bandied about on courses of action, Russian veterans of Afghanistan shared their experience and opinions.

Prussian military theorist Carl von Clausewitz lectured statesmen and commanders that "the most far-reaching act of judgment" that they "have to make is to establish . . . the kind of war on which they are embarking; neither mistaking it for, nor trying to turn it into, something that is alien to its nature." Russian military analyst Aleksandr Golts, who studied Soviet involvement in Afghanistan, concluded that Soviet leaders failed to heed Clausewitz's warning: "Our armed forces came prepared for the Cold War, for general battle, and they were completely ineffective." Lieutenant General (LTG) Boris Gromov, who had commanded the Soviet 40th Army, agreed with Golts: "For the Americans, introducing land forces would not lead to anything good," he predicted. Other Soviet officers speculated on the value of committing American ground forces to fight in Afghanistan and what they would encounter. A ground war would be "useless" warned General Makmut Goryeev. Former infantry battalion commander Ruslan Auslev predicted, "The American army will meet with fanatical resistance." GEN Tommy Franks, who commanded the U.S. Central Command (CENTCOM), knew full well the history of Soviet involvement in Afghanistan and made it clear that he did not intend to repeat those mistakes. "The Soviets introduced 650,000 troops," he said. "We took that as instructive, as a way not to do it."[14]

It would not be done that way. On 15 September 2001, when President Bush, as Commander in Chief of the U.S. Armed Forces, told "everybody who wears the uniform to get ready," *Washington Post* reporters had already speculated that Special Forces were "certain to be at the center of the action."[15] Rumsfeld acknowledged that when the war against terrorism began, "a lot of the effort . . . will be special operations." Army Secretary Thomas White seconded that acknowledgment. He warned America's adversaries "to watch carefully, for you are about to see our finest hour."[16] At a joint session of Congress on 20 September, Bush spoke passionately about grief, anger, resolution, and justice. "The *Taliban* is committing murder," he declared, and as "heirs of the murderous ideologies of the 20th century . . . they will follow that path all the way to where it ends in history's unmarked grave of discarded lies."[17] U.S. Army Special Operations Forces (ARSOF) would push the *Taliban* into that grave.

Some background history is necessary to better understand who and what constitutes the ARSOF today. ARSOF traces its heritage to the very foundations of America. During the French and Indian wars in the 1750s, Major (MAJ) Robert Rogers led his rangers on daring raids deep into French territory. Brigadier General (BG) Francis Marion, the "Swamp Fox," attacked unsuspecting British troops in the Southern colonies during the Revolution using unconventional tactics far different from those that European armies experienced. Union and Confederate raiders, on land and at sea, harassed rear areas, destroyed rail lines, cut telegraph lines, and disrupted sea commerce during the Civil War. During World War II, the U.S.-Canada 1st Special Service Force, "Darby's Rangers," and "Merrill's Marauders" achieved results far out of proportion to their numbers in North Africa, Italy, France, and Burma. Having realized the need to gather intelligence and conduct operations behind enemy lines, Major General (MG) William J. Donovan created the Office of Strategic Services (OSS) to conduct raids and train partisans for guerrilla operations in Europe and Asia. In 1952, the dedicated efforts of Colonel (COL) Aaron Bank, BG Robert McClure, and COL Russell Volckmann resulted in the formation of the Army Special Forces and the transformation of the Army's Psychological Warfare School into the Special Warfare Center. Training concentrated on infiltration techniques, foreign languages, small-unit tactics, intelligence collection, and counterinsurgency operations. In September 1961, the Special Forces adopted the Green Beret as their official headgear. From

1956 until 1971, Army Special Forces served in the Republic of Vietnam and earned a heroic reputation in American military history.

Figure 5. BG McClure, COL Volckmann, and COL Bank.

In 1980, less than a year after the debacle of Desert One in Iran, Army Chief of Staff GEN Edward Meyer directed the enhancement of the ARSOF's capabilities. Two years later, the 1st Special Operations Command (SOCOM) was activated to coordinate the training, equipping, and organizing of the Army's SFGs, Ranger battalions, Civil Affairs Battalion (CAB), and Psychological Operations Group (POG). This was the beginning of a major Army effort to broaden special operations capabilities—an effort that resulted in a third Ranger battalion and a regimental headquarters, the 3rd SFG, the 160th Special Operations Aviation Regiment (SOAR), and the 528th Special Operations Support and 112th Special Operations Signal Battalions. In 1989, the U.S. Army consolidated 1st SOCOM, the U.S. Army John F. Kennedy Special Warfare Center and School (SWCS), and the Reserve Special Operations Command under a major command—the U.S. Army Special Operations Command (USASOC). USASOC became the Army component of the U.S. Special Operations Command (USSOCOM) that was activated in 1987.[18] As one would expect, ARSOF trains and conducts operations worldwide year-round, having done so since its inception.

Thus, USASOC forces were conducting scheduled training exercises in the United States and overseas when America came under attack on 9/11. Small elements from the Special Operations Support Command (SOSCOM) headquarters and the signal and support battalions were in the Middle East for Exercise EARLY VICTOR, supporting the 5th SFG and preparing for Exercise FOAL EAGLE in Korea. The 5th SFG was also preparing for Exercise DESERT SPRING in the Persian Gulf region. One battalion of the 3rd SFG was training in Africa. Ranger companies were conducting small-unit training, including standard parachute assaults. Unit staff officers were planning for the cycle of spring 2002 exercises. The commander of the 9th PSYOP Battalion was at the Joint Readiness Training Center (JRTC) in Arkansas, and other PSYOP soldiers were preparing to deploy to the Middle East for the annual BRIGHT STAR exercise. Aircraft from the 160th Special Operations Aviation Regiment (SOAR) were supporting in the Persian Gulf region and at JRTC, and staff planners were attending an exercise conference in New Mexico. The headquarters staffs at Fort Bragg, North Carolina, were going about their daily routine. For ARSOF soldiers, it was just another day.

Within hours of the 3,052 Americans being murdered at the World Trade Center in New York; at the Pentagon in Washington, DC; and in a Pennsylvania field, the posture of the U.S. military changed to full alert, and preparations for war began—threat and defense conditions had been raised to the highest levels based on the multiple terrorist attacks. CENTCOM, whose area of responsibility (AOR) spanned the Middle East and Eurasia, cancelled all official travel in the region, and the U.S. European Command (EUCOM) cancelled all regional exercises. U.S. intelligence agencies focused maximum effort on identifying the perpetrators of the attacks and heading off follow-up assaults. Federal buildings and U.S. defense installations quickly instituted stringent access procedures to inspect vehicles and to verify the identity of all personnel seeking entrance. The thorough implementation of these increased security measures initially resulted in lengthy waits at entry checkpoints and traffic backups that affected both the installations and the surrounding civilian communities. Within a 10-mile radius of Fort Bragg, there were major traffic delays. USASOC soldiers were issued weapons and ammunition and joined other Fort Bragg soldiers to close access roads, install traffic barriers, stretch concertina wire, and guard family housing areas and headquarters. Although all soldiers receive some basic infantry skills training, many found themselves on guard duty, having never performed that role. In several support units, noncommissioned officers (NCOs) with previous infantry experience taught their troops how to walk a guard post, to challenge anyone who approached them, and what to do when faced by a perceived threat. "Force Protection" had real meaning, and unit commanders scrutinized security measures to protect soldiers and their families, units, and installations. Shortages of critical equipment were sent directly to Department of the Army. The "lock down" at Fort Bragg, home of USASOC and the 82nd Airborne Division, "America's Guard of Honor," pulled national media reporters like a magnet.

The *Washington Post* had speculated on 15 September that Special Forces would be at the center of America's response. While individual National Guardsmen and Army reservists were being mobilized openly and tight security measures were being followed at U.S. military installations nationwide, CENTCOM and its regional special operations headquarters—the Special Operations Command Central (SOCCENT)—were summoning operations and logistics planners to Tampa, Florida, from USASOC to develop plans to retaliate against the terrorists. Less than a week after 9/11, Defense Secretary Rumsfeld gave the battle against terrorism a name—Operation ENDURING FREEDOM (OEF).[19] By 5 October, commanders had decided on possible courses of action. Staffs worked to prepare documents necessary to implement any of the courses of action being considered so that when the JCS made decisions, the implementing commands of CENTCOM, SOCCENT, and USSOCOM could issue warning orders, operation orders, supporting plans, and overseas deployment orders. As it turned out, Rumsfeld personally set the date to begin infiltrations into Afghanistan.

Figure 6. Defense Secretary Rumsfeld names the operational efforts.

The JCS designated CENTCOM as the supported combatant command. CENTCOM was to "fight the war," and Franks was in charge. All other defense commands would furnish what CENTCOM requested. That headquarters implemented the guidance of President Bush. SOC-CENT rapidly became the focus for military operations. Franks' mission was to destroy the *al-Qaeda* terrorist organization and its infrastructure and then to provide military support to humanitarian operations. To accomplish these tasks, the CENTCOM combatant commander had to build a force that allowed for credible military options, conduct initial combat operations and establish the conditions for follow-on operations, build coalition military support and execute decisive combat operations, prevent the reemergence of terrorism, and provide support to humanitarian relief efforts. The SOCCENT commander, Rear Admiral (RADM) Bert Calland, recognized that his command had to get SOF with their unique capabilities into Afghanistan to destroy *al-Qaeda*.

SOF across the spectrum would be needed. Since unconventional warfare (UW) would be a major part, Army Special Forces, those with the most training and experience, would be supported by Psychological Operations (PSYOP) and Civil Affairs (CA) elements. Since PSYOP would support all aspects of the CENTCOM war campaign, Franks established a Joint Psychological Operations Task Force (JPOTF) to coordinate PSYOP efforts. With winter approaching, the Afghan people's needs had to be considered. Humanitarian assistance would be a major undertaking. That meant Army CA would have a major role. As during the war against Iraq (Operation DESERT STORM), U.S. air power would play a major role in combat operations.

With the potential of aircraft being shot down during the air campaign, Calland established the Joint Special Operations Task Force–North (JSOTF-North) to recover downed aircrews. Anticipating that ground operations, humanitarian assistance, and UW would follow initial air attacks, the 5th SFG was tasked to serve as the JSOTF-North. Since an SFG doctrinally would direct only the ARSOF assigned to a joint task force (JTF), the 5th SFG had not trained for this expanded role and did not have the personnel and equipment necessary to perform as a joint field headquarters. Considerable augmentation from the other military services was required, more equipment was needed to accommodate different requirements of the other services, and a "cram course" on joint staff functions facilitated the rapid transition to a JSOTF headquarters. In late December 2001, Calland established JSOTF-South to integrate coalition forces with American SOF conducting direct action (DA) and special reconnaissance (SR) missions in southern Afghanistan. This JTF was built around the headquarters of Naval Special Warfare Group One (NSWG-1). Together, these two JTFs would maintain pressure on *al-Qaeda* and *Taliban* forces throughout Afghanistan. Rather than deploy his SOCCENT headquarters to a staging base near Afghanistan, Calland established his base in a Persian Gulf country to maintain theaterwide situational awareness. "My job is AOR wide," the rear admiral said.[20]

As the supported combatant command, many headquarters assisted CENTCOM. The U.S. European Command (EUCOM) and its Special Operations Command, Europe (SOCEUR) immediately began planning the logistics support required for any military operation in Afghanistan. The Special Operations Command, U.S. Joint Forces Command (SOCJFCOM) sent training teams to the 3rd and 5th SFGs to help staffs identify other service augmentees, to coach JTF operations procedures, and to provide experienced joint staff officers to facilitate the necessary rapid standup of the JSOTF headquarters. In addition to the military, numerous U.S.

government departments and activities were called on to support the war, and soldiers were called on to coordinate with those staff elements.[21]

The primary USASOC mission was to provide ARSOF to fight and support the war effort. COL Phillip McGhee, the USASOC Deputy Chief of Staff for Resource Management (DCSRM), met daily with the Deputy Chief of Staff for Operations and Plans (DCSOPS), Deputy Chief of Staff for Logistics (DCSLOG), and Deputy Chief of Staff for Force Development and Integration (DCSFDI) under the direction of the Chief of Staff, U.S. Army, to brainstorm requirements and funding; to provide additional equipment and vehicles to deploying ARSOF units; to identify the training, instructors, and facilities needed to produce more ARSOF soldiers faster; to increase flying hours for the 160th SOAR; and to identify internal sources of funding for immediate needs while the Defense Emergency Response Fund (DERF) was appropriated to fund the war in Afghanistan.

The DCSRM staff, major subordinate commands (MSCs), and major subordinate units (MSUs) began daily meetings on 9 October 2001 to discuss plans to finance the war, what requirements had funding priority, reporting systems, and the approved use of DERF funds from USSOCOM. LTG Bryan D. Brown's guidance on DERF funds for Operations NOBLE EAGLE and ENDURING FREEDOM was very specific: "Along with this funding comes the responsibility to comply with guidelines related to spending and accounting for expenditure of these dollars. . . . My guidance to you is succinct—Do What's Right! I will personally review selected DERF expenditures on a weekly basis." Needless to say, the $69 million DERF appropriation did not expire on 30 September 2001, but the fiscal year (FY) end close for FY 01 was a success.[22]

Figure 7. LTG Bryan D. Brown encourages soldiers.

Training soldiers to fill the ARSOF ranks is the primary mission of the U.S. Army John F. Kennedy Special Warfare Center and School (SWCS). Without war pending, this is a difficult task. Two sobering realities are that units scheduled for deployment are filled to full strength, and during war, casualties have to be replaced. Thus, reconstituting SF detachments would severely impact the SF training cadres.

With the prospect of a lengthy special operations campaign, manpower was critical. Special operations soldiers cannot be mass-produced quickly. Enlisted soldiers who volunteer for SF duty, on average, have been in the Army for four years. Officers must have three and one-half years of service. The individual training necessary to produce an SF soldier requires approximately six months. All SF-qualified soldiers then undergo four to six months of language training. Many then attend advanced training in underwater operations or military freefall parachuting. Special operations aviators must have three to four years' flying experience before volunteering for the 160th SOAR. The pilots and air crewmen undergo six months of intensive training to attain basic mission qualification status. Then they must have one and one-half to two years of SOF flight operations experience before they are considered fully mission qualified to fly all special operations missions. On 2 December 2001, the U.S. Army directed all soldiers with military occupational specialties (MOSs) of SF, special operations aviation, and other aviation specialties to be retained on active duty involuntarily. This directive resulted in one officer, 13 warrant officers, and 983 enlisted soldiers being retained on active duty beyond the date they otherwise would be eligible to retire, resign, or be released from their enlistments.[23]

While Department of the Army instituted "stop loss" to freeze retirements, resignations, and end-of-enlistment releases of SF-qualified personnel and ARSOF aviators, SWCS developed a plan to continue training SF-qualified personnel with a reduced military cadre. SWCS mobilized U.S. Army Reserve (USAR) and Army National Guard (ARNG) augmentees; prepared to hire contractors as instructors; evaluated the impact of shortened courses of instruction; and made contingency plans for additional housing, classrooms, and transportation for an increased student load. The plan, fortunately, did not have to be implemented fully. Several CA officers' courses were conducted to meet critical needs in the Army Reserve units. Because of a shortage of SF soldiers, the U.S. Army Recruiting Command increased its efforts and initiated a program to recruit for SF "off the street," just as they do for Army Rangers.

Mobilizing Army reservists, National Guardsmen, ARNG SFGs and aviation maintenance units, and USAR PSYOP and CA units was a major task for USASOC and its subordinate commands, the U.S. Army Special Forces Command (USASFC); the U.S. Army Civil Affairs and Psychological Operations Command (USACAPOC); and the U.S. Army John F. Kennedy Special Warfare Center and School (SWCS). The SWCS accelerated initial training programs for ARNG SF soldiers and increased refresher training class sizes. USASOC used USAR training battalions to qualify approximately 300 CA soldiers in their MOSs. In addition, USASOC exercised an approved contingency plan to activate 36 USAR CA instructors. That decision enabled SWCS to double the number of CA and PSYOP enlisted soldiers the school could train. The quality of training that Army special operations soldiers received had prepared them well for the rigors and dangers of combat.[24]

ARSOF staff and unit training with conventional Army forces had to be reduced during the war buildup. Normally, ARSOF train at the Joint Readiness Training Center (JRTC), Fort

Polk, Louisiana, and the National Training Center (NTC), Fort Irwin, California. The special operations group and battalion staffs are rotated regularly through the Battle Command Training Program (BCTP) at Fort Leavenworth, Kansas. These realistic training experiences give commanders and staffs the opportunity to "fight" their units in a variety of environments, getting performance feedback that will enable the leaders to capitalize on the experience and improve their capabilities under combat conditions. Overseas deployment orders caused the rescheduling of one JRTC exercise and the cancellation of another. Three BCTP exercises were cancelled; one was conducted but with reduced numbers. No exercises were scheduled for the NTC.[25]

In addition to field exercises in the United States, the ARSOF regularly trains with foreign militaries. Thirteen JCS-scheduled annual overseas exercises to increase military-to-military contact and train at unit level were cancelled because of the terrorist attacks. The Joint Combined Exchange Training (JCET) program differs from the JCS overseas training exercises in that its purpose is to familiarize American SOF with how their counterparts in other countries operate. According to former Department of Defense (DOD) spokesman Ken Bacon, JCETs allow American SOF "to build up relationships with the military in other nations." Twenty-one exchanges were cancelled because of the attacks.[26] While these invaluable foreign exchanges could not be supported, responsibilities and obligations associated with mobilizing USAR and ARNG units filled those voids.

USASOC, as do most other Army commands, has a mobilization table of distribution and allowances (TDA) that allows the headquarters in wartime to augment its staff with USAR and ARNG officers, warrant officers, and NCOs. On 14 September 2001, President Bush authorized the activation of 10,000 USAR and ARNG personnel. From those numbers and based on the TDA, six personnel reported to serve on the USASOC and subordinate command staffs on 23 September, and another 98 arrived over the next few months. USASOC also mobilized the two ARNG SFGs, one PSYOP company, one CAB, one aviation maintenance company, a transportation company, a quartermaster company, an ordnance company (attached to the 528th Special Operations Support Battalion [SOSB]), and two military history detachments from September 2001 through April 2002. The mobilization had some problems. Some individuals were mobilized before the USAR units that were to in-process the soldiers had been mobilized. Highly motivated USAR and ARNG soldiers reported to USASOC headquarters, but they could not be put to work until they had been officially brought onto active duty. There were staff issues concerning responsibilities and standing operating procedures (SOPs) to administer the individual and unit federal service activations. These problems were resolved as the command settled into a war posture.[27] All that became reality within three weeks of 9/11.

On 8 October 2001, President Bush announced to the American people in a nationally televised address that during the previous night U.S.-led airstrikes struck targets near Kabul and Kandahar.[28] However, to wage a military campaign effectively in the remoteness of Afghanistan, the use of regional bases was critical. Secretary of State Powell, the CJCS during Operation DESERT STORM, clearly recognized that need and, in particular, the critical value of Uzbekistan: "Uzbekistan was [the country] of greatest interest to us . . . because it was a direct line of supply down into the area of the Northern Alliance." Powell's focused diplomatic efforts paid off when the Uzbeks granted airspace clearance and permitted coalition support and search-and-rescue forces to be based at Karshi Kanabad. With permission granted, U.S. Air Force cargo planes began to shuttle ARSOF nonstop into Karshi Kanabad (later known as K2) from European bases. Elements of the 528th SOSB, 112th Signal Battalion, and 160th SOAR preceded the advance parties of the 4th Psychological Operations Group (POG), the 96th CAB, and the 5th SFG. The 5th SFG was the nucleus of JSOTF-North that initially provided command and control for combat search and air rescue operations in northern Afghanistan.[29]

Figure 8. Helicopter view of Karshi Kanabad (K2) Air Base, Uzbekistan.

Critical to conducting any military operations is establishing a command and control center, communications network, and logistics base. While the 528th SOSB valiantly labored to convert half of a former Soviet airfield into a usable American facility, the 112th Signal Battalion established critical communications.

Figure 9. The 528th Support Battalion kept the water flowing.

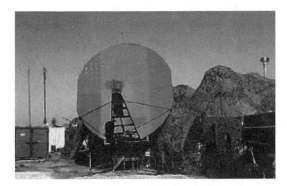

Figure 10. The 112th Signal Battalion established the JSOTF-North communications links.

Figure 11. The 528th Support Battalion soldiers prepared for base camp construction.

Within JSOTF-North headquarters, the 160th SOAR staff coordinated combat search and air rescue missions with Joint Special Operations Air Component Command (JSOACC) planners and with 5th SFG for future combat missions. State Department spokesman Richard Boucher said that envoys were in contact "with the whole gamut of Afghan factions, including the Northern Alliance," and Defense Secretary Rumsfeld had stated on "Meet the Press" that the United States was attempting to find ways to assist antiterrorist forces.[30] CA detachments prepared plans to provide

Figure 12. C-17 Globemaster III taking off from K2 to make humanitarian food drops.

blankets and food to displaced persons within Afghanistan as soon as the tactical situation stabilized. Concerned that winter would exacerbate survival problems for Afghan villagers who had already faced seven years of famine, U.S. Air Force C-17s began airdropping food on 7 October.

Two days later, EC-130 Commando Solo aircraft broadcast radio messages that emphasized an international mission to free the Afghan people from oppressive, fundamental Islamic, *Taliban* rule. Some messages the Product Development Company (8th Psychological Operations Battalion), JPOTF, prepared were pointed directly at the Afghan populace, urging them to "Drive out the Foreign Terrorists."[31] These ARSOF precombat activities and the air

Figure 13. Commando Solo airborne broadcasting platform.

campaign were preparing the way for ground combat operations.

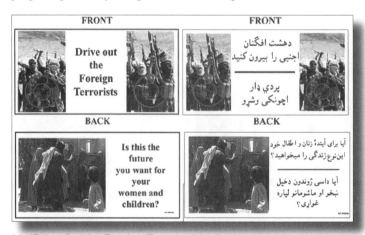

Figure 14. "Drive Out the Foreign Terrorists" leaflet dropped during the air campaign.

46

During the night of 19 October 2001, the ground war began when nearly 200 Rangers parachute assaulted into Afghanistan from MC-130s, and two operational detachment As (ODAs) from the 5th SFG were inserted into the mountains of northern Afghanistan by 160th SOAR MH-47E helicopters. Those well-orchestrated multiple night combat operations put American "boots on the ground" to launch the ground campaign to root out and destroy the *al-Qaeda* and *Taliban* and establish a viable multiethnic government in Afghanistan. War as an instrument of U.S. policy had begun.

Figure 15. 75th Rangers night parachute assault on Objective Rhino.

Figure 16. MH-47E helicopters taxi for preflight checks before night missions.

Figure 17. 160th SOAR—loaded and ready for night operations.

Since it was the efforts of individual ARSOF soldiers and detachments on the ground that made the ground campaign to drive the *Taliban* from power and successfully provide an environment in which a multiethnic government could be established, the story of the war can be presented most interestingly in a chronological series of "soldier stories." The first group describes initial preparations for war in the United States by PSYOP and SF staff personnel and two SFGs—the 5th at Fort Campbell, Kentucky, and the 3rd at Fort Bragg—with support from the Special Operations Command of the Joint Forces Command, Norfolk, Virginia. These stories are based primarily on recorded interviews with participants.

"Subdue Without Fighting": JPOTF, MacDill Air Force Base, Florida

"To win one hundred victories in one hundred battles is not the acme of skill. To subdue the enemy without fighting is the acme of skill."[32] So spoke ancient Chinese philosopher Sun Tzu around 500 B.C. Rare is the war in which no fighting occurs, but many are the wars in which PSYOP is employed to minimize the degree of fighting. The war in Afghanistan was but the latest war in which PSYOP was used to convince the *Taliban*, the *al-Qaeda*, and its people that resistance to coalition forces was not only futile but also detrimental to the future welfare of the nation. Coordinating that PSYOP effort was the Joint Psychological Operations Task Force (JPOTF) located at the U.S. Central Command (CENTCOM), MacDill Air Force Base, Florida. The JPOTF commander was Lieutenant Colonel (LTC) Sam Halstedt (pseudonym), commander of the 8th Psychological Operations Battalion (POB), 4th Psychological Operations Group (POG), U.S. Army Special Operations Command (USASOC).

Figure 18. Resistance is futile; assistance works better.

Figure 19. "Reassurance" leaflets in multiple languages.

Few soldiers outside the PSYOP military specialty had heard of a JPOTF. A unified combatant command can create such a task force "as a separate functional component of the combatant commander." When established, the JPOTF normally is under the theater commander's operational control. Tactical PSYOP units are then attached to ground maneuver commanders. The mission of a JPOTF is to provide "PSYOP support to the overall joint or combined operation at the operational and tactical levels." To do that, it coordinates requirements with the defense service components based on mission requirements. The command becomes joint when members of several services form the organization.[33]

Following doctrinal guidelines, in September 2001, CENTCOM, the combatant command, established a JPOTF, the nucleus of which was the 8th POB staff. The JPOTF mission was to

48

conduct operational and tactical PSYOP to isolate terrorists from their support systems and to strengthen resolve between the allies and the people of Afghanistan to eliminate those terrorists. The 8th POB formed the nucleus of the JPOTF because of its war trace alignment with CENTCOM, just as other PSYOP battalions are aligned with other regional combatant commanders.[34]

Halstedt was an experienced soldier. During Operation DESERT STORM in 1991, he commanded a Special Forces ODA and served in the 75th Ranger Regiment. He knew how to plan and how to get things done, and he also knew that because PSYOP attracted great interest at DOD level, everything the JPOTF did would be subject to media scrutiny. But Halstedt had a mission, and defining the scope of that mission was his first task. He knew that PSYOP must support the overall war campaign plan. The more the JPOTF and the PSYOP soldiers on the ground could influence enemy soldiers to surrender, the less fighting Special Forces and conventional soldiers would have to face. Halstedt also knew that support from the populace was key. His plan, therefore, had to include the people.

Figure 20. Leaflet messages directed at the civilian population.

On 14 September 2001, Halstedt and a staff of four reported to CENTCOM headquarters. Based on careful examination of the region and the culture, the JPOTF cadre, military planners, and civilian experts developed several themes. The first objective was to produce anti-*Taliban* and anti-*al-Qaeda* material that would persuade the Afghan people to reject their legitimacy. Simultaneously, the planners proposed themes to demonstrate that the coalition forces were there to assist the people in overthrowing their oppressors and to provide humanitarian aid. The group also knew that at some point in the ground campaign the coalition forces would sponsor reconstruction efforts and that some form of legitimate government would need to be created. It was critical for the Afghan people to understand that the government would be of their choosing, not the United States' or any other members of the coalition.

With these themes and objectives in mind and having coordinated their plan with the overall campaign plan, Halstedt forwarded the proposed CENTCOM PSYOP plan to the Pentagon for approval. Military officials in the Office of the Joint Chiefs of Staff (OJCS) reviewed it and then sent it to the Office of the Secretary of Defense (OSD). At OSD, the Assistant Secretary of Defense for Special Operations and Low-Intensity Conflict (ASD-SO/LIC) and the Under Secretary of Defense for Policy (USD-P) reviewed and approved the draft. OJCS then gave

CENTCOM approval to implement the plan. As the war in Afghanistan progressed, the approval process for PSYOP products would be modified. During the first month of the war, all PSYOP products were approved at OSD, but beginning in November 2001, Franks, as combatant commander, CENTCOM, assumed that authority.

Figure 21. Leaflet appealing to Afghan nationalism.

While the approval process was under way, the JPOTF began to fill its staff. From the initial 120 from 8th POB, it grew to 313 personnel. About one-third of the staff was reservists activated for Operation ENDURING FREEDOM (OEF). The JPOTF coordinated with Air Force personnel who advised on using the EC-130 Commando Solo aircraft. One U.S. Navy officer coordinated PSYOP support for maritime operations. Because the preponderance of PSYOP assets was Army, the staff was predominantly Army personnel. Two coalition liaison officers coordinated PSYOP support to military forces from other nations.

Figure 22. 4th POG printing presses regularly operated overtime.

Although SOCCENT tactically controls SOF for the CENTCOM commander and PSYOP units are SOF, the combatant command, CENTCOM, directly controlled the JPOTF. The JPOTF commanded all PSYOP forces, but JSOTF-North would eventually tactically control them. While the leaders understood these organizational lines, the funding for the PSYOP units was unclear. The issue of whether USSOCOM funded the sustainment costs of deployed SOF had to be resolved. Funding issues, like foreign repairs of printing presses, were overcome.

Developing the SOF Campaign at SOCCENT, Tampa, Florida

Designated the "supported" headquarters for the war against Afghanistan, CENTCOM asked MG Geoffrey Lambert, USASFC, to provide several staff officers to prepare the SOF campaign.

Lambert chose two officers and two NCOs to assist SOCCENT in developing its regional counterterrorist plan. This plan was intended to "look beyond" the near-term deployment of SOF to the region for action in Afghanistan to formulate concepts for subsequent activities. COL Manuel "Manny" Diemer, Lambert's chief of staff and the team leader, was accompanied by CPT Paul Colter (pseudonym), a former 3rd SFG officer who had worked in the CENT-COM AOR.[35]

When the SF command team arrived at SOCCENT headquarters in Tampa, Diemer was surprised to find his colleague, COL Mike Findlay, at work there also. Findlay, the special operations commander from the Joint Forces Command, Norfolk, Virginia, had a task much like his. "I'm here to give staff guidance and training to the SOCCENT staff," Findlay told him. Diemer soon discovered why they needed additional support. COL Eric Stanhagen, deputy commander, SOCCENT, told Diemer in their first meeting that "We've put all our J5 (the regional contingency planners) guys into our J3"—that is, the planning cell was disbanded and the personnel moved into the current operations section. The headquarters had become focused on "the tactical war in Afghanistan," Diemer relayed to MG Lambert; "There is no special ops strategy for the whole region." Lambert directed Diemer to help the SOCCENT staff expand its efforts into a long-range theaterwide plan.[36]

Twenty-four hours later, Diemer and his team produced a doctrinally correct "classic seven-phase unconventional warfare plan" outlined on yellow legal pads.[37] In particular, the plan included Lambert's concept of "operationalized engagement" to ensure that the noncombat exercises in the region were integrated into CENTCOM's counterterrorist and counternarcotics campaigns. Shortly afterward, LTC Darrin Matteson (pseudonym), from the SOCCENT Special Plans Office, presented the new plan to Franks, the warfighting general of the theater, and his principal staff in a formal briefing. Matteson explained how this proposed UW plan was "synchronized with the CENTCOM four-phase plan" to remove the *Taliban* government from power in Afghanistan. Diemer remembered that Franks did not ask a single question during the briefing, which he later learned was "a first" for the CENTCOM commander. At the end of the presentation, Franks said to Matteson, "I understand everything you said . . . I understand all the acronyms . . . your plan is approved." Diemer flew back to Fort Bragg the next day to "gear up" USASFC's resources to make the SOCCENT campaign plan into reality.

Top Draft Choices: 10th SFG, Fort Carson, CO, and 7th SFG, Fort Bragg, NC

COL John Mulholland knew his group needed augmentation to be able to function as the JSOTF directing UW operations across northern Afghanistan, and one Special Forces company especially needed select personnel to get it to full strength before deployment. When he asked for help from USASFC, COL Diemer recommended two 10th SFG officers that he had served with in the Balkans. For the position of JSOTF-North operations officer, Diemer chose LTC Matt Rhinehart (pseudonym).[38] Rhinehart was deputy commander, 10th SFG, based at Fort Carson. While he had not yet been a battalion commander, Rhinehart was "well known and well respected" in the SOF community for his performance as commander of the 10th SFG support company in Bosnia during the NATO intervention. Diemer felt he was "the right guy" for the J3 position.[39]

At Fort Bragg, LTC Marcus Steinmann (pseudonym) was working temporarily in the SWCS Battle Lab, waiting to begin his study at the U.S. Army War College, Carlisle Barracks,

Pennsylvania, in summer 2002. The former special warfare training battalion commander was Diemer's pick to lead the Army Special Operations Task Force (ARSOTF) of JSOTF-North. Steinmann had impressed Diemer when he was the J3 operations officer for the Combined Joint Special Operations Task Force (CJSOTF)-Bosnia, and Diemer knew he could readily command all of the Army special operations troops in Afghanistan as a part of the larger JTF.[40] As it turned out, both 10th SFG officers served admirably on Mulholland's JSOTF-North staff. Their experience in Bosnia proved most helpful in preparing for the land campaign in Afghanistan.[41]

On the morning of 11 September 2001 Chief Warrant Officer (CWO) Vincent "Vince" Garvey (pseudonym) was receiving his parachute at Green Ramp, one of the runway accesses at Pope Air Force Base, directly adjacent to Fort Bragg.[42] As a member of the 7th SFG that is focused on Latin America, his company was preparing to board an Air Force transport plane to make a training jump on Fort Bragg.[43] One of the company's master sergeants asked the jumpers if they had heard the news about New York City. Garvey ran to his parked pickup, pulled the truck alongside the parachute-laden soldiers, and turned up the volume on his radio. The Special Forces troopers listened in stunned silence to the news broadcasts. The jump was cancelled, and Garvey and the rest of the company went back to their barracks anticipating orders to fight somewhere in the world.[44] Orders came soon but only for a few 7th SFG soldiers on 28 September. CWO Will Sherman (pseudonym), the operations officer for B Company, 2nd Battalion, 7th SFG, told Garvey that he had been handpicked—"by-name selected," in the reverse-order jargon of the military—to join A Company, 1st Battalion, 5th SFG, that was scheduled to leave for CENTCOM's theater of operations. Three other sergeants from 7th SFG accompanied Garvey but for other assignments. The desired qualifications set for those three sergeants were exceptional: school-trained Special Forces sniper or close-quarter battle specialists or former service in one of several select special operations units. Garvey was the only member from the 7th SFG augmentee group who met all of the prerequisites.[45]

5th SFG = CJSOTF-North, Fort Campbell, Kentucky

As COL Mulholland watched the televised reports of the terrorist attacks on 9/11, he realized his 5th SFG "would be players" in whatever retaliatory action the United States undertook. Based at Fort Campbell, the 5th SFG was trained and equipped to fight in the deserts of the Middle East and Southwest Asia. They had done field exercises in Egypt, Jordan, Kuwait, and around the Persian Gulf region. When Osama bin Laden and his *al-Qaeda* organization emerged as the 9/11 culprits and their connection to the *Taliban* government was established, Mulholland felt "it was apparent we'd be going into Afghanistan." His immediate problem was what he considered an "information deficit." Before 9/11, neither his unit nor SOCCENT in Tampa had any operational interest in Afghanistan.[46] SOCCENT was responsible for planning and conducting all special operations in the CENTCOM theater of operations. Mulholland was certain that his boss, MG Lambert at USASFC, would soon place the 5th SFG at the disposal of RADM Bert Calland, the SOCCENT commander, as part of the "expedition to Afghanistan," as it was initially called.[47]

By 14 September 2001, the organization of the Afghanistan expedition SOF had not been established. Doctrinally, in wartime, SOCCENT was to turn its headquarters into a JSOTF headquarters to direct the attached SOF units from the Army, Navy, and Air Force in combat. The 5th SFG would become a subordinate component of the JSOTF, called the Army Special

Operations Task Force (ARSOTF), managing the Army elements of the task force.[48] "Initially, the JSOTF in the north (eventually Karshi Kanabad, or K2, in Uzbekistan) was to be sourced and structured for combat search and rescue (CSAR). Thus, an Air Force officer was to be in charge. However, since K2 was to be converted into a base that would also support UW operations, the differences in Army combat service support and structure or "size, weight, and cube" had to be factored, otherwise disruptions to the air movement schedules could have delayed combat operations for weeks or months. LTG Brown, the USASOC commander, agreed that K2 should be built not only for current CSAR operations but also to support a fluid transition to follow-on combat operations. Brown convinced the SOCCENT planners that Mulholland should be put in charge, said MG Lambert.[49]

Despite COL Mulholland telling the SOCCENT staff that his unit lacked the staff and equipment to perform all of the doctrinal duties expected of a theater-level JSOTF, it became moot with LTG Brown's recommendation. In Tampa, RADM Calland regarded his command responsibilities as "AOR-wide," meaning SOCCENT had to oversee special operations not only in Afghanistan but also throughout the CENTCOM theater AOR that covered all the Middle East and Central and Southwest Asia. "What made sense," Calland recalled, "was multiple JSOTFs." He directed the creation of several subordinate task forces to prosecute the coming campaign.[50] That afternoon, U.S. Navy Captain (Capt) Randy Goodman, SOCCENT's J3 operations officer, responded to Mulholland's query about the JSOTF by simply saying, "You're it." The 5th SFG headquarters had been "tagged" to command all SOF that would fight inside Afghanistan—at least for the time being.[51]

For the help he now needed for his unique mission, Mulholland turned to COL Mike Findlay, Special Operations Command, U.S. Joint Forces Command (SOCJFCOM), Norfolk. Findlay immediately dispatched a joint training team to Fort Campbell to train the group staff on how to function as a JSOTF and provided computer hardware on loan to install a secure local area network (LAN). Having taken command only two months earlier and with no experience in setting up a JSOTF base, Mulholland welcomed the JFCOM help.[52]

In the absence of planning guidance from SOCCENT, Mulholland put four A detachments (ODAs) into the 5th SFG's isolation facility (ISOFAC). While the Special Forces A teams did not know what their missions might be, inside the closely guarded ISOFAC, they could openly study the available classified data to learn more about the geography, the population, the culture, their enemies, and their possible allies in Afghanistan—the *Taliban* resistance elements.[53] The teams quickly discovered that there were no maps of Afghanistan available in normal U.S. Army stocks. Being resourceful, they called various defense organizations, including the Land Information Warfare Activity, from which they obtained old Soviet-era military maps they could use for tactical planning.[54] After his Pentagon briefing, MG Lambert, the Army Special Forces commander, told LTC Carl Hooper (pseudonym) at the 5th SFG ISOFAC to "Climb on the tanks and trucks and hang on when the dam breaks and the Northern Alliance sweeps into Kabul."[55]

To prepare for future operations, the 5th SFG staff analyzed the ethnic and geographic makeup of Afghanistan and divided the Texas-sized country into five major sectors. It later reduced this number to three and, finally, to two. The northern sector included the vast Hindu Kush mountain range, itself the size of Kentucky, and all lands to the north and northwest. The southern sector was the area south of the Kush, which also had formidable chains of mountains

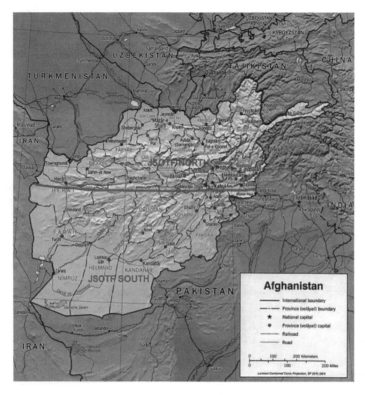

Figure 23. SOCCENT map dividing Afghanistan geographically.

as well as arid high deserts. When Mulholland proposed this north-south division during a telephone call to the SOCCENT J3 (operations officer), Navy Capt Goodman told him that his command was now designated JSOTF-North. Mulholland was to focus solely on the northern half of Afghanistan, above the east-west highway between Herat and Kabul, which ran roughly along the 34th parallel. When Mulholland asked who was going to run special operations in the other half of the country, he was told that SOCCENT intended to form a second task force, JSOTF-South, from the headquarters of NSWG-1, San Diego, California. Eventually, elements of U.S. Navy Sea-Air-Land (SEAL) teams would be assigned to that JSOTF to work with anti-*Taliban* resistance forces in southern Afghanistan. Mulholland knew that the Navy SEALs, while adept at lightning-fast raids, were not trained to advise local resistance forces in conducting UW that might last months or even years. He predicted then that the 5th SFG was going to "end up doing UW across the country."[56]

Standing Up JSOTFs in Tampa and Fort Campbell

LTC Warren Richards (pseudonym), SOCJFCOM operations officer, was on a training exercise in Hungary when the United States was attacked. Subsequent erratic flight schedules delayed his return to Norfolk for two weeks. While Richards was stuck in Hungary, Mulholland, 5th SFG commander, learned that he had to form a Joint Special Operations Task Force (JSOTF) to control

54

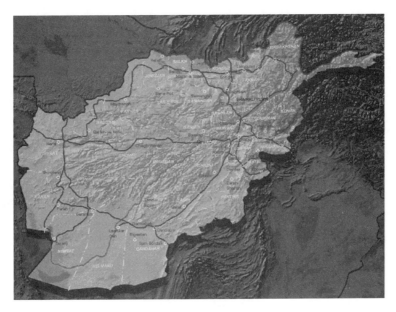

Figure 24. Afghanistan.

SOF operations against the *Taliban* and *al-Qaeda* in northern Afghanistan. U.S. Special Operations Command (USSOCOM) had never directed an SFG to be prepared to assume that mission.

While SOCJFCOM's mission had been to "facilitate joint integration . . . to enhance SOF effectiveness" and to be "prepared to form a JSOTF to conduct special operations," it had an inherent task to train prospective commanders and staffs of new JSOTFs.[57] Shortly after reaching Norfolk, Richards and four soldiers left for USASOC headquarters, Fort Bragg, to assist that staff in meeting the 5th SFG's mission requirements as a JSOTF. From his experience as a Special Forces officer and as a SOCJFCOM trainer, Richards knew that the 5th SFG headquarters would need help in three areas.

One of the problems it would encounter was the lack of local area network (LAN) equipment it would need to function as a JSOTF. Thus, identifying the specific requirements and requisitioning the necessary equipment became a top priority. Richards, the USASOC information management staff, and experts from the 112th Signal Battalion identified and resourced equipment for the LAN for $500,000.

A second shortcoming was personnel. To function as a JSOTF, an SFG headquarters staff would require an additional 120 people. Those people can come from a variety of sources, but unless the "drafted" soldiers have trained with that particular JSOTF, basic issues such as SOPs and familiarity with the staff principals would delay actions. The unit staff also had to integrate the new augmentees into its everyday functions. Joint staff training, therefore, was the third problem that faced the group.[58]

While Richards' team was at Fort Bragg, retired Special Forces COL Dave Rasmussen and eight SOCJFCOM soldiers were working with SOCCENT headquarters in Tampa. RADM

Figure 25. LAN connectivity to the K2 "Snake."

Calland had called COL Findlay earlier, asking for assistance in converting his headquarters from a peacetime to a wartime footing. Rasmussen ascertained that "they had a problem" in that key SOCCENT staff positions were predominantly filled by Navy SEALs who had little experience with other service operations and staff procedures. Since Calland's guidance from CENTCOM was contained in a PowerPoint briefing, his staff struggled to develop a plan to employ SOF troops. Rasmussen was concerned that the SOCCENT staff was more focused on getting into the theater than in preparing plans or requesting additional personnel to meet their staffing requirements. The best Rasmussen and his trainers could do was to develop a phased implementation plan that supported CENTCOM guidance before accompanying the staff into the theater. The former Special Forces colonel and 12 trainers from SOCJFCOM departed the Persian Gulf staging base in early December, quite frustrated with the situation.[59]

It was a different story for a third SOCJFCOM group at Fort Campbell. For two weeks, LTC Jack Walters (pseudonym), chief observer trainer, and 11 other staff members conducted seminars to educate the 5th SFG staff on the intricacies of JSOTF functioning. Walters used his considerable Special Forces experience as a commander and staff officer to advise the staff on the additional functions a joint headquarters would require. The staff quickly realized that, in addition to performing the wartime functions of a group headquarters it would also be the communications hub for the attached joint subordinate units, arrange the logistics support for the other service units, and coordinate all planning for joint operations.

Communications were a major problem because most of the message traffic had to be conducted over a classified LAN, and there were insufficient terminals in the 5th SFG's staff sections for adequate coordination. More hardware quickly resolved this problem. Findlay and his officers emphasized to Mulholland that internal staff communications were only part of the problem he faced. While an SFG commander controls his own communications, a JSOTF commander does not. Findlay stressed that external communications requirements could overwhelm the 5th SFG's signal staff. One problem was video teleconferences (VTCs) because higher-level commanders and staffs commonly use them, but VTCs are a practice that could be virtually unknown to an SFG commander.

The staff was also responsible for long-range planning, but that function often became secondary because of the press of the new day-to-day operational business. Still, Mulholland would have to focus on ARSOF tactical operations and, as the JSOTF commander, develop and execute the special operations campaign. COL Findlay was especially concerned about long-range planning. The commander "cannot be the guy to do the coordination between current and future operations," he warned. To do both required a J3 staff with more personnel than those authorized in the SFG S3 section. Unfortunately, SOCCENT used all 120 augmentees to fill its battle staff. None were available for the 5th SFG or NSWG-1.

Another outstanding problem was security classifications on potential operations in Afghanistan. Soldiers in ODAs have Secret clearances, but they were not authorized access to Focal Point information. Operations in Afghanistan were classified under the focal point system. Special Forces soldiers who had to conduct those operations were not authorized to have the vital information they needed for planning. A similar problem was the level of security classification on messages from higher headquarters to COL Mulholland. Most messages were classified Top Secret. This time, it was the limited number of personnel with Top Secret clearances in the Special Forces battalions that severely limited access to information. Again, this meant that the soldiers in the ODAs were not authorized the necessary information. With no solution coming from higher headquarters, Mulholland determined that the restrictions the classification process imposed were unrealistic and would endanger his soldiers' safety. He decided that the ODAs had a "need to know" and directed that they receive all necessary information.[60]

Richards, Walters, and Findlay realized that "Mulholland was way over-tasked." In response, Findlay recommended to RADM Calland that he designate the 5th SFG the Army Special Operations Task Force (ARSOTF) and that SOCCENT either be the JSOTF or that he establish a JSOTF from other assets. The SOCCENT commander elected to continue with the 5th SFG as a JSOTF. While the designation ensured that the 5th SFG would receive special operations air assets and improve its position in the joint environment, both Mulholland and Richards knew that the 5th SFG could not, because it had never been a long-term JSOTF, function as such without experienced joint staff help.[61]

That experienced help came in the form of Richards, Walters, and 13 others from SOCJF-COM. Richards deployed to Afghanistan with the 5th SFG advance party in early October to help establish the JSOTF. The other SOCJFCOM soldiers arrived with the main body. COL Mulholland used the SOCJFCOM personnel as his J2, J3, J4, assistant J6, and chief of the joint planning group. They also assisted the rest of the nascent JSOTF-North staff with its functional areas. Without standing up a separate ARSOTF, the JSOTF staff was responsible for isolating all Special Forces detachments to be inserted, for resupplying those detachments, for controlling subordinate unit communications, and for tracking the movements and tactical operations of those detachments in the combat zone 24 hours a day.

Committed to Middle East Exercises

For the 2nd Battalion, 5th SFG, the 9/11 attacks prompted an immediate cancellation of its scheduled Middle East exercise. However, within 24 hours, the cancel order was rescinded, and the exercise was "back on." Thus, on 16 September, the initial elements of the 2nd Battalion, less one Special

Forces company, departed Fort Campbell for a regional air base to participate in Exercise BRIGHT STAR. At its forward operating base (FOB), the 2nd Battalion headquarters staff organized a small Combined Joint Special Operations Task Force (CJSOTF) to support the U.S. (joint) and allied (combined) units. LTC Don Forsythe (pseudonym) was in charge, and his executive officer, MAJ Jeffrey Solis (pseudonym), directed FOB operations and commanded the Army units in the task force.[62]

For Exercise EARLY VICTOR, Forsythe's CJSOTF directed the operations of two Special Forces companies, a Navy SEAL platoon, an element of Air Force special operations transport aircraft, a 160th SOAR Army helicopter unit, and a company of Army Rangers.[63] The allied elements in the task force were Jordanian ranger and special forces companies and observer teams from Yemen, Egypt, and Kuwait. Forsythe's mission was to conduct combined special reconnaissance (SR) and direct action (DA) missions—violent, rapidly executed raids. Practicing combined SR and DA missions in a Middle East environment proved prescient in late October when reports of 5th SFG's ODAs being inserted in Afghanistan after the initial air campaign were received. By the time EARLY VICTOR ended on 26 October, LTC Forsythe and MAJ Solis felt that the 2nd Battalion staff, with its Special Forces Operational Detachments B (ODBs) and ODAs, was combat ready. They were anxious to join the 5th SFG's fight in Afghanistan.[64]

The next stop for the "2nd of the 5th" was Al-Jafr Air Base in southern Jordan to await further orders from the SOCCENT forward element in Qatar. LTC Forsythe was told to be ready for several possible missions. His battalion might be sent to Masirah Island, near Oman, or to Yemen or Qatar to be the CENTCOM theater crisis response element (CRE) or to serve as the headquarters for other units serving as a theater CRE. Solis was convinced that they would be moved to a base in Pakistan and from there into Afghanistan. As trained and most recently practiced in EARLY VICTOR, Forsythe and his staff planned to commit the 15 Special Forces ODAs first and then the three Special Forces company headquarters (ODBs) for regional command and control while the battalion base (FOB) initially remained outside the "denied area." The battalion intelligence staff provided daily updates from the war zone and distributed information on Afghan culture; the country's terrain, weather, infrastructure, and politics; and some history on British and Soviet interventions while they waited for orders.[65]

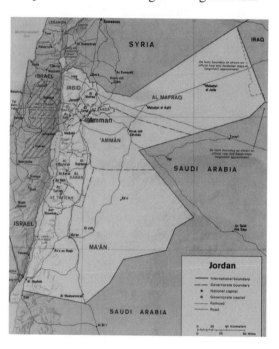

Figure 26. Amman, Jordan.

3rd SFG Prepares for the Horn of Africa at Fort Bragg

In the wake of 9/11, COL Mark Phelan, commander, 3rd SFG, Fort Bragg, flew to Special Operations Command Central (SOCCENT) headquarters in Tampa to receive planning

58

guidance for future operations. He anticipated that the coming war would eventually expand to attack terrorist bases outside of Afghanistan, and his 3rd SFG would be assigned to SOCCENT to deal with those in eastern Africa. U.S. Navy Capt Randy Goodman, the SOCCENT J3 operations officer, told Phelan that intelligence reports indicated that some of the *al-Qaeda* were leaving Afghanistan for Somalia and some of the neighboring countries. Since there were no war plans on the shelf for counterterrorist action in that region, Goodman granted Phelan "mission planning authority" to support deployment to the Horn of Africa. Phelan briefed his initial concept for this mission to the principal staff

Figure 27. The Central Command's Horn of Africa region.

officers at U.S. Central Command (CENTCOM) and received their approval. He intended to rotate his 1st and 2nd battalions in the theater every 30 days. CENTCOM directed the 3rd Battalion to complete Exercise FOCUS RELIEF in Nigeria. When that battalion returned in December to Fort Bragg, it would recover and then backfill shortages in the other two battalions moving in and out of the Horn of Africa.[66]

While the 3rd SFG staff refined this plan to carry Operation ENDURING FREEDOM (OEF) to eastern Africa in fall 2001, COL Phelan alternated his 1st and 2nd battalions to Camp Pickett, Virginia, where they rehearsed the daily tasks they would need to perform as forward perating bases (FOBs) once they arrived in the war zone. In particular, they practiced round-the-clock communications with isolated units dispersed over a wide area. The 3rd Battalion in Nigeria was already operating as an FOB and would have two months' experience when it returned in December.[67]

Thinking Ahead: Senior Liaison Officers for Resistance Leaders

The 5th SFG had identified only two key resistance leaders in northern Afghanistan and none in the south based on initial intelligence briefings. It had learned little more than the names—Fahim Khan of the Northern Alliance and Rashid Dostum. These were the highest-ranking military commanders, and it was assumed that each had considerable political influence. In the UN, a delegate from Fahim Khan's faction had been accepted officially as the political representative for Afghanistan. Detailed personal information about Fahim Khan and Rashid Dostum—ethnicity and education; personalities and backgrounds; the size of their forces; and the tactical state of their soldiers, weapons, and equipment—was not yet fully available.[68]

Despite that limitation, COL Mulholland chose to build his UW campaign around those two Afghan leaders. He believed that "it was going to be important to put a senior level of leadership" with Dostum and Fahim Khan "to help influence the political battlefield as well as the military." He felt that he could accomplish

Figure 28. TF Dagger Commander COL Mulholland gives GEN Myers (CJCS) an update at K2.

59

this by using two of his three lieutenant colonel battalion commanders as liaison officers to the two Afghan warlords. Mulholland recounted that battalion commanders provided a more senior presence with these significant Afghan leaders. In addition, they were to establish sectors of responsibility.[69] He contended that this arrangement would provide the Afghan generals "with an extra level of experience and expertise" and "disseminate the command and control dilemma."[70]

As the campaign progressed, the planning staffs anticipated that a Pashtun counterpart to Dostum and Fahim Khan would emerge to rally resistance in the south. If that happened, Mulholland would have a third battalion commander to send to that leader. While this concept fragmented the three battalion staffs and gave initial command and control of nine Special Forces companies and their ODAs directly to him, Mulholland considered it to be necessary to accomplish the assigned mission. It also allowed him to fill JSOTF-North staff vacancies.[71]

Civil Affairs to Islamabad, Pakistan

In his remarks to the State Department on 4 October 2001, President Bush declared that "we are friends of the Afghan people," pledging $320 million for humanitarian aid. He emphasized that the United States was not alone in this effort: "We will work with the UN agencies such as the World Food Program and work with private volunteer organizations to make sure this assistance gets to the people."[72] Three nights later, the commander of the 96th Civil Affairs Battalion (CAB) knocked on MAJ Matt DiJurnigan's (pseudonym) door and told him, "Pack your bags." This former marine and Army enlisted soldier, and DESERT STORM infantry company commander suddenly found himself a "first responder" to the president's pledge.[73]

On 9 October, DiJurnigan was in Tampa at the U.S. Central Command (CENTCOM) as the 96th CAB liaison officer in the civil-military operations cell in the J5 section. As the liaison officer to CENTCOM, he was familiar with the headquarters, the civil-military operations staff, and his normal duties. What he had not expected was his assignment on 12 October to the CENTCOM liaison cell at the U.S. Embassy in Islamabad, Pakistan. DiJurnigan's mission was to determine whether there was a need to establish a civil-military operations center (CMOC) in Pakistan to implement the president's desires.

A CMOC serves as the primary interface between the U.S. Armed Forces and the local population, humanitarian organizations, nongovernmental organizations (NGOs), international organizations, the UN, multinational forces, and other U.S. government agencies. Basically, the CMOC can help prioritize humanitarian support and ensure that civilian organizations do not attempt to begin relief efforts in areas where there is active combat.[74] To accurately assess whether a CMOC was required, DiJurnigan met first with the Department for International Development in London to determine the level of assistance for CA that Great Britain would provide. Then, in Islamabad, DiJurnigan met with BG Ronald Sams, the chief of the CENTCOM liaison cell; the director of the UN Office for Coordination of Humanitarian Affairs–Afghanistan; the UN Joint Logistics Cell; United Nations International Children's Emergency Fund (UNICEF) representatives; the head of the UN Mine Committee, and the five UN regional

Civil Affairs

Figure 29. U.S. Army Civil Affairs and Psychological Operations Command shoulder patch.

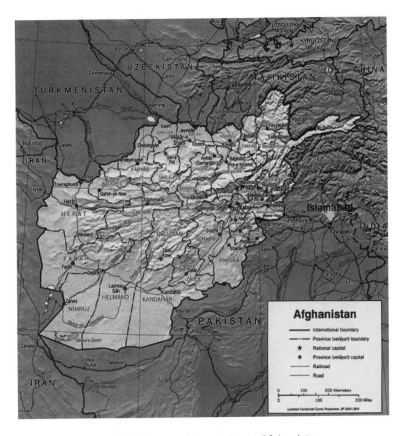

Figure 30. Islamabad in relation to Afghanistan.

coordinators created for Afghanistan. After meeting with these officials and representatives from numerous NGOs, DiJurnigan concluded that a CMOC was not necessary and recommended against its establishment. In his view, the humanitarian relief effort was "mature," and military coordination of the effort was unnecessary. He recommended, instead, that a military CA cell be collocated with the UN Joint Logistics Cell that channeled all humanitarian assistance into Afghanistan. Ideally, all aid organizations would coordinate their efforts through the international cell that could balance requests for support and information with available resources and receive early notice of potential new donors. Unfortunately, many NGOs elected to operate independently, thus minimizing the advantages of the UN cell.

In late October 2001, DiJurnigan was the only American CA officer working on humanitarian assistance issues with the help of three British soldiers. This severely limited his ability to coordinate with the multitude of NGOs arriving in theater. DiJurnigan realized that his initial recommendation against a CMOC might have been premature and requested a civil affairs team (CAT) from his battalion. On Thanksgiving Day 2001, Captain (CPT) Marty Cavanaugh (pseudonym), with three members of CAT-A46, arrived in Islamabad from D Company, 96th CAB.[75] The team quickly began developing new contacts and exploiting those contacts that DiJurnigan had made. Their "full court press" to meet with as many NGOs as possible opened significant lines of communication that later paid great benefits.

Of Vital Importance: PSYOP

In 1951, Secretary of the Army Frank Pace wrote, "The psychological warfare program" is of "vital importance to national security and defense."[76] The level of importance was quite evident as the 4th Psychological Operations Group (POG) began planning for PSYOP missions in Afghanistan shortly after the 9/11 terrorist attacks. The group was to provide operational- and tactical-level PSYOP to undermine the terrorists and to separate them from their support systems. While the 4th POG had teams constantly deployed in the CENTCOM region, none had been focused on Afghanistan. That changed overnight, and within weeks of the September attacks, PSYOP teams were ready to move into the region in support of Operation ENDURING FREEDOM (OEF).

The 8th PSYOP Battalion had already established a Joint Psychological Operations Task Force (JPOTF) for all PSYOP within the CENTCOM area of operations. But elements of the 4th POG, as well as mobilized Reserve units, provided tactical PSYOP forces to augment special operations forces (SOF) and conventional forces worldwide in support of OEF. These PSYOP forces initially deployed not only to forward staging bases to support ground operations in Afghanistan but also to Guantanamo Bay to help debrief captured terrorists and to the Philippines to support OEF-Philippines and the U.S. Embassy.

As stated before, all PSYOP plans and programs required policy-level approval from the Assistant Secretary of Defense for Special Operations and Low-Intensity Conflict (ASD-SO/LIC) and the Under Secretary of Defense for Policy (USD-P). Once the overarching plans and programs had been approved, a prototype of every individual PSYOP product went to the CENTCOM commander for approval. Then, the specific product was sent to ASD-SO/LIC for policy review for final approval before being released for dissemination.[77] In the case of radio programs, the product was sent into theater by satellite communications for local broadcast. When printed products received final approval, they could be printed at Fort Bragg or transmitted digitally via satellite to a forward-deployed print facility for production. Because of the immense size of the PSYOP requirement for OEF, approximately 136 USAR soldiers—printing specialists, staff augmentees, and a tactical PSYOP company—were mobilized.

Critical to PSYOP planning was analysis of the target audience by civilian analysts in the regionally oriented Strategic Studies Detachments in the Research and Analysis Division of the 4th POG staff. These sociocultural experts, most of whom had Ph.D.s, had extensive research resources and contact networks to help them develop themes and a specific focus within the target audience. For example, dedicated *al-Qaeda* or *Taliban* members might not be affected by a PSYOP campaign, whereas villagers who had suffered at the hands of a repressive regime were viable targets. Included in the supporting PSYOP plan that the JPOTF developed were a number of themes—encourage support for the Partnership of Nations forces, undermine the *Taliban/al-Qaeda*, emphasize the inevitability of *Taliban/al-Qaeda* defeat, rally support for the Afghan Interim Authority (AIA), promote the capture of Osama bin Laden and other *al-Qaeda* leaders by offering rewards, and strengthen Afghan-U.S. friendship. Once the plan and themes had been completed and approved, specific products were developed. The entire process drew heavily on the knowledge, analytical acuity, and cultural empathy of Ph.D.-level area experts as well as military PSYOP specialists.

Figure 31. PSYOP themes centered on accepting coalition assistance.

Within two weeks after 9/11, two PSYOP liaison officers were sent to the 5th SFG at Fort Campbell. They were soon followed by tactical PSYOP elements, a deployable print production center (DPPC), and a satellite downlink for radio programs. And the 8th PSYOP Battalion had established a "bare bones" JPOTF command element at CENTCOM headquarters in Tampa.

DOD PSYOP resources were limited, and the Army had the only comprehensive military PSYOP capability, so it naturally got "the lion's share" of the work involved in executing a PSYOP plan. An adequate supply of native linguists was a constant challenge, given the tactical requirements overseas. To keep the huge volume of translation as well as broadcasting work manageable, contract linguists were hired to augment those Pashto and Dari speakers in the 4th POG. Air Force capabilities were limited but included important EC-130 aircraft broadcast platforms (Commando Solo) and the means to deliver leaflets on target. The Navy had but one shipboard and one land-based system, neither of which were available for OEF.[78] Still, in the first months of the war, more than 75 million leaflets were dropped from B-52 bombers and C-130 transport aircraft. Commando Solo Air Force EC-130 PSYOP aircraft broadcast more than 3,000 hours of radio programs.[79]

The preceding historical vignettes revealed how the special operations commands, AR-SOF units, commanders, staff personnel, and soldiers responded and prepared for America's global war on terrorism, beginning in Afghanistan. The reader should have gotten a sense of how enormous the mission of combating terrorism worldwide was, the impact of that enormity on the various headquarters and subsequent overseas JSOTFs, the complexity of the problems in Afghanistan, the limited information that was initially available to military planners, the administrative burden, and the frustrations the field commanders and fighting elements faced. Equally significant were the proactive, "can-do" stances of ARSOF leaders at all levels; the resourcefulness, flexibility, and adaptability that were common denominators among all SOF soldiers; and the ARSOF community's commitment to ensuring that those elements deploying overseas got the highest priority for resources and training.

The following stories address the next phase of the operation—the overseas deployment of ARSOF forces into Karshi Kanabad (K2) Air Base and the establishment of the JSOTF-North headquarters and the American operating base called Stronghold Freedom.

Site Coordination With the Uzbeks at Karshi Kanabad

Before the first meal had been cooked, the first tent erected, or the first aircraft launched, an advance echelon (ADVON) had preceded the main body of troops. This ADVON of specifically chosen personnel normally arrives early to establish rapport with foreign government officials and local inhabitants. This small element makes necessary arrangements to efficiently receive the main body of soldiers and equipment, usually arriving by aircraft for a military operation. The initial ADVON to K2 Air Base, a former Soviet installation in Uzbekistan, consisted of a three-man team from Fort Campbell and an 11-person SOCCENT element from Tampa. It was to evaluate what eventually became Stronghold Freedom, most commonly referred to as "K2." Its mission was to assess the logistics and operational facilities of the base and to coordinate with local officials to build an infrastructure that would support approximately 3,500 people.

According to Staff Sergeant (SSG) James Willet (pseudonym), the 2nd Battalion, 160th SOAR logistics NCO, an "old hand" with ADVON duty, the Uzbek air base commander at K2 was not really happy to have Americans on his base.[80] He was worried about their personal safety and about possible retribution from the Islamic Movement of Uzbekistan (IMU), a militant terrorist group based across the border in Afghanistan. Willet said, "It was weird and kind of eerie being one of only ten Americans, and constantly watched by Uzbek soldiers. When I left high school it [Uzbekistan] was still Russia, and I had never heard of Uzbekistan."[81]

Figure 32. Karshi Karnabad (K2), Uzbekistan.

Once settled, SSG Willet made initial contact with the air base commander, an Uzbek Air Force lieutenant colonel, through an interpreter and quickly developed positive rapport, despite the wide disparity in ranks. Willet explained that the ADVON traveled light and that he needed to buy supplies and rent equipment. Concerned about their good relationship, the Americans did not want to exploit the Uzbek commander's generosity. It took some convincing before he was granted permission and escorted by an Uzbek pilot. Willet and his interpreter were driven to the open-air market in the village. Dressed in khaki trousers and a sports shirt, and carrying an M-9 automatic, the 6-foot, blonde-haired, blue-eyed American was "head and shoulders" above everyone in the Asian crowd as he moved among the vendors' stalls. Feeling very conspicuous and surrounded, Willet was glad that the Uzbek colonel had insisted on the escort. After making his purchases in *soms*, the local currency, the trio returned without incident. Until the evening, that is, when Willet realized his visit to the market had made him a television celebrity on the local news. The Americans had truly arrived.

Figure 33. K2, Uzbekistan.

Over the course of the next few days, Lieutenant Commander (Lt Cdr) Millender (pseudonym) from SOCCENT met with the military commander and other local Uzbek officials, negotiating as much space as possible for the incoming American forces. However, it was the Uzbek commander of the Joint Chiefs of Staff, General Kasymov, who ultimately decided the boundaries. Kasymov marched to the western edge of an unused taxiway, stopped, and decreed, "From this point that way is yours; nothing more!"[82] This, as the Americans quickly discovered, was how everything was accomplished in Uzbekistan. Operating in a slow, bureaucratic manner, all officials had to call their superiors for final approval. It was only after Uzbekistan President Islam Karimov had personally given Defense Secretary Rumsfeld permission to use the air base for search-and-rescue missions that the main body of U.S. forces was allowed to arrive.[83] Colonels became primary action officers for getting things done in this former Soviet republic.

While diplomatic negotiations continued, the rest of the ADVON began setting up the tactical operations center (TOC) in the only building allotted, an old Soviet-era structure with paint peeling off the walls and broken windows. While the building had only a few separate rooms and was poorly ventilated, it became the central resourcing point for the ADVON party. U.S. Air Force CPT Paul West (pseudonym) conducted a survey of the taxiways and runway to accommodate

65

Figure 34. Uzbeck guards—the bottom of the bureaucratic ladder.

the arrival, unloading, refueling, and departure of C-17 jet transport aircraft.[84] He also reviewed U.S. military air traffic control procedures with the Uzbek air traffic control officials to ensure that they fully understood the differences. MAJ Kyle Killinger (pseudonym), a contracting officer from SOCCENT, arranged for fuel deliveries (aircraft and heating), building materials, supplies, and laborers with local businesses and government officials.[85] The future economic benefit was not lost on any of the Uzbek hierarchy or the local population; these visitors would help the local economy. SSG Willet's rapport with the air base commander enabled him to wrangle seven aircraft bunkers for incoming helicopters and airplanes to better divide the available real estate. A force protection assessment evaluated the airfield's security and prioritized needed improvements, especially to the old earthen berm around the aircraft bunkers. The daily coordination meeting between Millender and the Uzbek colonel in charge of base logistics mandated nightly progress reports from the entire ADVON. On 2 October 2001, the worst sandstorm in 50 years hammered K2. With more storms predicted, acquiring temporary troop shelters escalated to the top priority. The Uzbeks provided 19 general purpose burlap tents.

Uncorking the Bottled Airlift

Meanwhile, the delay in obtaining diplomatic country overflight clearances and basing rights caused a bottleneck in the strategic airflow of troops, equipment, and supplies into the theater of operations. Transport aircraft packed airfield aprons and taxiways at Morone, Spain; Sigonella, Sicily; and Incirlik, Turkey. To complicate the air movement, the U.S. Air Force C-17 Globemaster III was the only heavy-lift jet aircraft permitted to use K2 Air Base. This meant that loads carried by the largest Air Force jet transport, the C-5B Galaxy, had to be "downloaded" and split up to fit the much smaller C-17s. Caught in the bottleneck was an Air Force theater airlift control element (TALCE) at Morone, Spain. When that 50-person detachment arrived with none of its aircraft unloading equipment late on 3 October, it was unprepared for the gush of backed-up airplanes.

66

Figure 35. K2 buildup with backlog of accumulating supplies and equipment.

When Secretary Rumsfeld was granted permission to use K2 for "search-and-rescue operations" finally on 5 October, the physical effect on the airplanes backed up from Spain to Turkey was like uncorking a champagne bottle.[86] Limited ramp and taxiway parking space turned an orderly, carefully prioritized, and orchestrated flow of airplanes into a hodgepodge. In an effort to free clogged European air bases for follow-on traffic, airplanes were launched as quickly as possible, merely shifting the traffic jam to the unprepared K2 Air Base and overwhelming its air traffic control capabilities. This was made worse by the limited cargo offloading equipment available. With a C-17 arriving every 2 hours by 6 October, the base population exploded from 100 personnel to more than 2,000 in a week. The resulting command and control situation could only be described as "utter chaos"![87]

Figure 36. 160th Special Operations Aviation Regiment (SOAR).

All Credit Cards Accepted at K2 Gas Station

The early arrival of the forward arming and refueling point (FARP) section of the 2nd Battalion, 160th SOAR, alleviated the long delays associated with the Uzbeks refueling all U.S. aircraft. In addition to seven fuel handlers and an ammunition handler, the FARP had three heavy expanded mobility tactical truck (HEMTT, pronounced "hemmit" by the soldiers) tankers, each capable of carrying 2,550 gallons of fuel. The FARP team leader, Sergeant First Class (SFC) Douglas Steverson, seeing how long it took the Uzbeks to refuel the C-130P air tankers, started refueling all aircraft with his HEMTTs.[88] The FARP team tirelessly pumped fuel to all U.S. and coalition aircraft that landed at K2—120,000 gallons of fuel the first month. When the Americans began to exceed the contract for 30,000 gallons of fuel a day, Uzbek officials at the fuel farm became alarmed about their reserves. These fears were alleviated when C-17s began flying fuel stocks into K2 to support the UW campaign. Then the 528th SOSB set up a contingency fuel point of six 10,000-gallon bladders to support the refueling operation. The Uzbek hosts were happy, and the JSOTF-North staff moved on to other problems.

Figure 37. Refueling a Soviet Mi-17 at K2.

Air Campaign and CSAR Go Hand in Hand

COL Frank Kisner, with the Air Force Special Operations Command (AFSOC) staff, arrived aboard two MC-130P tanker aircraft from the 9th Special Operations Squadron (SOS) shortly before the first C-17s began landing. Kisner directed his pure Air Force staff from the 16th Special Operations Wing (SOW) to establish a JSOTF headquarters and to begin planning for the personnel recovery mission—recovering downed aircrews in Afghanistan. The 16th SOW colonel took command of the JSOTF and became the senior American envoy to the Uzbek government officials. Kisner controlled everything at K2 and named the base "Camp Freedom." His top priority was to conduct full mission profile rehearsals of aerial refueling before the CENTCOM air campaign began.

Figure 38. Night Stalker view of the C-130P trailing refuel lines and probe basket.

Figure 39. Trail aircraft view of MH-47E refueling.

Figure 40. MH-47E hooked up for aerial refueling.

Making Camp Freedom a Fully Operational Base: K2, Uzbekistan

The key to command, control, and operations is communications. Thirty-five soldiers from A Company, 112th Signal Battalion, were quite surprised when they arrived shortly after dark on 6 October. Because their C-17 aircrew had warned them to be prepared for a hostile environment, they donned full combat gear and stood with their weapons at the ready, expecting the worst when the aircraft ramp was dropped. Then, instead of a hostile environment, the

Figure 41. 112th Signal Battalion satellite antennas.

"charged-up," battle-ready soldiers faced a female Air Force captain, the JSOTF chief of personnel, CPT Childs (pseudonym), and Air Force MAJ Victor Mercado (pseudonym), the chief of communications.[89] The surprised troops were welcomed to Camp Freedom and then ushered to a customs tent for in-processing. This was the standard procedure for most of the early chalks. For some unknown reason, neither the C-17 aircrews nor the inbound troops ever received the truth about the real threat at K2.

The personnel who would establish the SOCCENT Joint Special Operations Air Component (JSOAC) headquarters, the command element responsible for the CSAR mission, followed the signalers. When MAJ Wes McKellar (pseudonym), D Company, 2nd Battalion, 160th SOAR, arrived, he remarked, "You know you've won the Cold War when you walk out the back of a C-17 carrying an American flag, loaded weapons, and have Soviet helicopters flying CAP [overhead air cover]."[90]

Figure 42. K2 buildup.

Figure 43. MH-47E landing at K2.

LTC James Brinks (pseudonym), commander, 2nd Battalion, 160th SOAR, had been tasked to command the JSOAC. Having an Army aviator in charge of a JSOAC in combat was a first.[91] With no experience in the battalion, MAJ Mark Henderson (pseudonym), the operations officer (S3), had his hands full.[92] Thus, in the first few days, during the simultaneous "standup" of JSOTF-North and the JSOAC, the 160th SOAR officers and NCOs worked for both staffs to support the personnel recovery mission that had to be in place to begin the air campaign. Learning curves were steep, but being ready to perform the personnel recovery mission drove the collective effort. Within days, SOF air assets to

Figure 44. MH-60L DAPs.

support the mission included two MC-130P tankers from 9th SOS, a number of special tactics squadron (STS) teams from the 23rd STS, a joint Army-Air Force staff, and four MH-47E Chinooks and two MH-60L Direct Action Penetrators (DAPs) from 160th SOAR. When the strategic bombing campaign was moved up to begin on the evening of 7 October, the urgency became acute. The JSOTF and JSOAC had to be ready to support the air campaign despite the disorderly airflow.

Northern Air Campaign
CSAR = MH-47Es

The compressed time line drove the 160th SOAR "helicopter buildup" teams, the D Company mechanics, the maintenance test pilots, and the B Company crew members to attack the aircraft like "ants on a Twinkie." Despite the fatigue and jet lag from the long journey, the buildup crews performed exceptionally well. Quality control NCOs who certified every completed maintenance task found only three minor errors during the night helicopter buildups. MH-60L

Figure 45. Aircraft maintenance was a crucial factor for success.

DAP crewmen and mechanics unloaded their helicopter gunships to prevent damage when it became evident that the Air Force TALCE and C-17 loadmasters were unfamiliar with these aircraft. Thus, within 24 hours, the JSOAC had an immediate reaction force.

When the rest of the helicopters arrived the next day, the mechanics and aircrews had to forego their rest and subsist on short catnaps until all four Chinooks and the two DAPs had been built up, test flown, and made mission ready. Within 48 hours, the entire Army helicopter fleet had been made ready for war. Exhausted maintenance crews fell asleep alongside helicopters on the guano-covered floors of concrete bunkers. When they awoke the next day, they were covered with dust and debris from a sandstorm.

The 160th SOAR MH-47E Chinook and MH-60L DAP Black Hawk pilots and aircrews spent the first week in Uzbekistan rehearsing combat search and rescue (CSAR) scenarios. LTC Brinks, the JSOAC commander, believed that it was imperative that his staff, the 160th SOAR enlisted planners, and the aircrews could seamlessly exercise their mission responsibilities.[93] He knew from experience during Operation DESERT STORM that time was the critical element in successfully recovering a downed pilot or aircrew in northern Afghanistan. His acceptable standard was to launch a rescue within an hour of notification, and it was met.

Building Camp Freedom at Double Time

The Air Force TALCE unloaded C-17 aircraft as fast as it could, dumping cargo pallets anywhere and everywhere. Just as the flood of arriving personnel and equipment threatened to overwhelm the infrastructure and resources of the Uzbek base, soldiers from the 528th Special Operations Support Battalion (SOSB) arrived. COL Kisner's first words when he met MAJ Charles Mahoney (pseudonym), A Company commander, were, "Boy, am I glad to see you.[94] We have some problems." After receiving a quick rundown, Mahoney, remembering the

Figure 46. 528th SOSB initial logistics chaos.

capabilities of the Air Force base support packages, did a quick triage of the K2 maelstrom and dispatched teams to provide urgent care in the critical areas.

Military theorist Baron Antoine Henri de Jomini defined logistics as "the art of moving armies."[95] Since reactivation in 1987, the 528th SOSB had become quite skilled in providing outstanding logistics support worldwide to special operations soldiers. Although operations security (OPSEC) considerations limited details as to where they were going, the U.S. Special Operations Command (USSOCOM) in Tampa had tasked them to establish a ration point and a warehouse for repair

Figure 47. K2 cantonment area.

parts; to provide office supplies and cold-weather clothing for SOF overseas; and to establish a fuel point. Shortly before receiving medical, veterinary, and mortuary services attachments, the leaders were told that they were going to K2, Uzbekistan; a small element would go to Oman;

and there would be no conventional support units to assist the 528th SOSB in country.[96] The number of aircraft determined the final numbers and exactly what equipment would go. The battalion staff and company leaders made last-minute adjustments to ensure that all assigned missions could be performed. "Though we had little or no guidance, we had lots of experience," remarked First Lieutenant (1LT) Michael Bridgewater (pseudonym).[97] Thus, the 528th SOSB was prepared when it arrived.

Throughout Camp Freedom, the 528th SOSB's junior leaders took charge of unspecified tasks and, with little or no guidance, restored a semblance of order to the chaos. As cargo was dumped on the flight line, SSG Celeste Holmes (pseudonym) directed her crew to separate everything into the appropriate logistics classes, from class I to class IX.[98] These soldiers were used to taking the initiative, thinking on their feet, and taking responsibility for their actions. The sergeants decided what was needed, and their decisions enabled the unit to operate independently in theater for two weeks without resupply. They understood the importance of their mission to the national effort to combat terrorism worldwide. Although the 528th SOSB's mission was to support the Army special operations units, its "can do" attitude and reputation for never turning away soldiers who needed support spread rapidly. Instructed by their company commander to provide as much support as possible, the supply section had a daunting task. Some Air Force elements arrived at K2 without basic subsistence gear like sleeping bags and cold-weather clothing. They had assumed that these items would be issued "in country." The JSOTF-North and JSOAC staffs quickly demolished the office supplies. SSG Holmes said, "We wouldn't turn away a shooter at the warehouse," except for toilet paper, which became a treasured commodity as the camp population rapidly grew.[99] The true measure of mission accomplishment was this comment by SSG Timothy Matthews (pseudonym), 3rd Battalion, 4th POG: "The 528th is a class act."[100]

The Universal Morale Booster at K2—Hot Food

SSG Mark Parsons (pseudonym), a 528th SOSB food service specialist, had been on joint exercises and was familiar with what the Air Force brought.[101] Parsons found his dining facility equipment among the scattered pallets and set to work. Unforeseen problems were the fuel-contaminated soil, trash dumps everywhere, abandoned Soviet equipment relics, and snakes. The emergence of a cobra from a temporary latrine area got everyone's attention. Still, SSG Parsons had a mess hall operating in one week instead of the anticipated three weeks. Hot "real" food boosted camp morale 100 percent. That single meal per day was the highlight of some very long days as well as a welcome relief from the constant diet of meals, ready to eat (MREs).

A combat soldier's most valuable tools are his weapon and his ammunition. The 528th SOSB's soldiers quickly learned that their most valuable items were the lumber and forklift that had accompanied them from Fort Bragg. The foresight of carrying plywood, 2-x-4 lumber, and other construction material paid big dividends for A Company. These building materials were quickly turned into tent floors and walls to enclose latrines. The forklift moved pallets of equipment that arrived daily on U.S. Air Force aircraft, the sea/land containers that became a warehouse, and mountains of abandoned Soviet equipment and trash to clear space to accommodate the growing numbers of SOF personnel at Camp Freedom. The forklift operator became one of the most sought-after soldiers on the encampment by anyone who needed something moved.

Special Forces: CSAR Personnel Recovery and UW Preparation

MAJ Steven Broderick (pseudonym), commander, B Company, 3rd Battalion, 5th SFG, arrived during the night of 7 October with ODB 580. Master Sergeant (MSG) Bowdler (pseudonym) from the 5th SFG advance party met the 18 Special Forces soldiers, got them through customs, and got the group bunked down for the night in a few medium-size general purpose tents. Their main tasks were to establish an isolation facility (ISOFAC) for the ODAs preparing for future combat missions and to provide force protection at K2 and in the local area. Restrictions imposed by the Uzbeks made any force protection measures outside K2 Air Base impossible. The Special Forces soldiers spent several days erecting 18 tents; setting up cots, tables, and chairs; and installing fuel oil heaters to create an ISOFAC. Long working hours became the norm as more and more ODAs kept arriving at K2. Although Broderick's ODB had never set up or operated an ISOFAC, the NCOs applied their experience and SOPs to provide a working operation in record time.[102] SFC Kevin Anderson (pseudonym) coordinated the use of local marksmanship ranges with the Uzbek military to assist the ODAs in isolation.[103] COL Kisner's JSOTF staff was concentrated on the CSAR mission of the air campaign. Getting the ISOFAC ready to accommodate the additional ODAs involved in the UW campaign was a subsequent Army Special Forces mission, and MAJ Broderick's ODB 580 was expected to "carry that ball" alone.[104]

Broderick and his ODB 580 isolated the first 11 Special Forces teams (ODAs) going into Afghanistan. Missions and insertion times differed between ODAs, and there were constant adjustments based on contact with Northern Alliance combat leaders, weather, and intelligence factors. MAJ Broderick and his operations sergeant, Sergeant Major (SGM) Manuel Victoro (pseudonym), kept the teams attuned to the constant mission changes by attending briefings in the JSOTF and JSOAC.[105] They restricted access to the ISOFAC to reduce rumors and divert uncoordinated conflicting information from the teams. Broderick discovered COL Mulholland's key concerns during the JSOTF commander's premission back briefs for each ODA. Sharing these insights with the ODA commanders reduced mission assignment turbulence that accompanied unsatisfactory premission briefs to the commander and focused planning better.[106]

Real Estate and Security at K2

As more personnel arrived daily and tried to get established, conflicting priorities caused considerable friction between services and units. The responsibility for real estate management changed hands several times in the first week, eventually settling on the JSOTF-North logistics officer (J4), U.S. Air Force LTC Richard Shaw (pseudonym).[107] Despite demands for more space and prime locations, General Kasymov had set limits—end of Uzbek discussion. Air Force COL Richard Parker, a civil engineer, stepped forward to address base design and the necessary infrastructure to support 3,500 troops.

Base security was solved when the 1st Battalion, 87th Infantry, 10th Mountain Division, landed. The infantrymen quickly built checkpoints and fighting positions using the earth berm that encircled the camp. A few weeks afterward, the Uzbeks agreed to expand the security zone, and a second berm was built to provide more force protection.

Task Force Dagger = JSOTF-North at K2

Command relationships were initially "sketchy" until the 5th SFG headquarters and main body arrived on 10 October. The confusion about JSOTF command was cleared up. The relationships were clarified, and the Army and Air Force staffs were united as a JSOTF-North team when COL Kisner, at the initial joint staff meeting, turned to COL Mulholland and said, "Boss, what are your orders?" Thus, in this most professional and gentlemanly manner, Mulholland assumed command, and Kisner became his deputy. JSOTF-North became Task Force (TF) Dagger, and with Kisner's concurrence, the K2 base was renamed "Stronghold Freedom," the initials "S" and "F" connecting it to Special Forces. With command and control established, Army LTC Warren Richards, SOCJFCOM, shifted his focus from base security and force protection to making the operations staff more effective.[108] This prompted collocation of the JSOTF and JSOAC command centers into a long series of interconnected tents across the taxiway from the ISOFAC. The resulting "Snake" turned the established communications lines upside down.

Figure 48. COL Frank Kisner
and COL Mulholland.

Figure 49. TF Dagger logo.

Hot-Wiring the "Snake": Rearranging JSOTF-North Communications

The 112th signalers, 5th SFG, and Air Force communications personnel scrambled fast to accommodate the rearrangement while supporting the CSAR mission and anticipating the UW campaign. MSG Don Sullivan (pseudonym), the 5th SFG communications chief, and MAJ Derrick Jacobi (pseudonym), the 5th SFG signal officer, accompanied COL Mulholland from Fort Campbell.[109] Their initial mission was to provide communications for the two SF ODAs that were on "strip alert" at K2, ready to take off by helicopter at a moment's notice to search for and rescue any U.S. Air Force aircrews that had bailed out of their aircraft during the air campaign while bombing targets, dispersing propaganda leaflets, or dropping humanitarian relief in Afghanistan.

MAJ Jacobi had been made the JSOTF-North communications and electronics staff officer (J6) responsible for continuous and reliable telecommunications. His principal assistant was MSG Sullivan, a former chef and top-notch tennis player with an undergraduate degree in medieval history and Islamic studies. Why the entire 5th SFG staff was going to Uzbekistan to set up a base for two ODAs was a mystery to Sullivan, despite having the same security clearances as the principal commanders and staff officers and having helped design the networks for the operation. His "need to know" did not extend beyond the initial planning for CSAR.[110] Whatever the reason, Sullivan focused on his key task—ensuring that the 5th SFG commander always "got the information he needed to do his job."[111]

That meant rapidly integrating the established Air Force and 112th Signal Battalion communications array to best support the JSOTF-North headquarters without losing voice and digital message connectivity because the JSOAC was already coordinating flights of MC-130P tankers and 160th SOAR helicopters to perform the CSAR mission. The 5th SFG soldiers built their "tent city" operations center first, setting up work tables, desks, and chairs and hanging wall charts and maps in the principal staff areas. The 5th SFG's communications section then shifted half of the Air Force network setup from its principal location in several abandoned buildings on the opposite end of the runway.

Figure 50. The support battalion needs communications to provide support.

Then MAJ Jacobi's communications section established the network systems and tactical communications links and brought them operationally "on-line." Having completed this, they took the Air Force communications "off-line" and walked together with them, helping to carry wiring harnesses, equipment, and other connectors down the runway to new workstations in the Snake. Next, they were "logged back in" through the digital network "cloud." The other half of the network then followed, with all its hardware and cables being incorporated in the eight-section "temper tent" that was the joint operations center (JOC) for the JSOTF headquarters.[112] Thus, operational communications were never lost, despite the rapid relocation of equipment and personnel. With the 112th Signalers and the Air Force

Figure 51. 112th Signal Battalion unit insignia and beret flash.

communications element helping, the joint base station was completed in less than 48 hours. "We went from dirt to a functional J6 in thirty-six hours—bottom line—it worked," reported MAJ Jacobi.[113]

Shortly after COL Mulholland arrived at K2, CPT Steve Marks (pseudonym), commander, A Company, 112th Signal Battalion, was tasked to be fully mission capable to support future missions by 13 October. Marks, having successfully led his unit during Operations JOINT ENDEAVOR and JOINT GUARDIAN, was determined not to be the weak link in supporting those missions. The 112th Signalers met the challenge and established a secure video teleconferencing (VTC) link from the theater back to the United States. At the height of combat operations, A Company was conducting 10 to 14 VTCs a day.[114] These conferences enabled the TF Dagger and JSOAC commanders to provide real-time reports, to recommend future operations, and to receive guidance directly from CENTCOM's leaders in Tampa. First Sergeant (1SG) Martin Masterson (pseudonym) summed up the unit's performance: "We don't fail; we just don't fail."[115]

Building the JOC Inside the "Snake": TF Dagger's JOC

After three false starts, CPT Carlos Hernandez (pseudonym) had been told that the 5th SFG intelligence section would leave for Central Asia on 8 October.[116] This time it did, and Hernandez and the intelligence staff landed at K2 in the predawn darkness of 10 October. The staff had been cramming on Afghanistan since 9/11. Before then, the former 82nd Airborne Division infantry platoon leader only knew that it was "a mountainous country with lots of snow in the winter" in the CENTCOM region. Since then, his section had been searching classified and public data bases for information on Afghanistan and had talked with analysts at the Defense Intelligence Agency, seeking background material on several Afghan warlords in the Northern Alliance; namely, Rashid Dostum, Mohammad Atta, Fahim Khan, Ishmail Khan, and others. To their dismay, there were no personality data bases available or any information about any subordinate leaders. Copies of *The Bear Went Over the Mountain* and *The Other Side of the Mountain*, books on the Soviet war in Afghanistan in the 1980s, were circulated among the staff.[117]

Along with the intelligence he needed to collect and analyze, CPT Hernandez was also focused on setting up his S2 "shop" in the JSOTF headquarters. En route to Uzbekistan, he chanced to meet MSG Jason Bennington (pseudonym), a 5th SFG staff NCO during a refueling stop at Sigonella, Sicily. Bennington was returning from the site survey of the former Soviet air base at K2.[118] Elements of the Air Force Special Operations Command (AFSOC) and the 528th SOSB were already there, Bennington reported. Air Force aircraft and Army helicopters were at the airfield, ready to conduct search-and-rescue missions in support

Figure 52. Dry for the moment.

of the bombing campaign that had begun on 7 October. On a hand-drawn sketch of the airfield, Bennington pointed to a spot next to the runway and said, "Here's the space for the JSOTF." The Uzbeks had granted the Americans use of abandoned parts of the active air base. Since the Air Force had already occupied the only building, the 5th SFG staff would have to create their task force headquarters with tents.[119]

The "space for the JSOTF" that Bennington had pointed out turned out to be a narrow strip of land about 200 feet long and 100 feet wide between a taxiway and several old concrete aircraft bunkers. Twenty large tents were assembled and then erected in a row, mostly end to end, creating what became known as the "Snake." Shortly after the tents were set up, a heavy rain began to fall, and the downpour lasted for 10 days. That was when Hernandez remembered one of the "lessons learned" from the Kosovo deployments: "Never set up tents next to a runway or the adjacent taxiways because they are designed to allow water to drain naturally off their surfaces into adjacent fields." To make matters worse at K2, the dirt security berms that surrounded the base prevented natural runoff. There was no other location big enough (and more importantly available) to go. Within days the water was ankle deep in the JOC. Computer servers, cables, and electrical wiring soon filled the folding tables used as desks. Throughout the rainstorm, Special Forces engineers continued to elevate the wooden flooring in the Snake. Although the temperatures were surprisingly mild, the rain threatened to shut down the JSOTF headquarters just as the UW campaign was ready to "kick off."[120]

The JSOAC was charged with the CSAR mission. On 12 October, Mulholland told LTC Brinks, the JSOAC commander, that six Special Forces ODAs would be infiltrated into Afghanistan within 48 hours.

Staff "Battle Captain": The Combat Operations "Pulse Monitor"

While the J3, LTC Warren Richards, an augmentee from the Special Operations Command, U.S. Joint Forces Command (SOCJFCOM), Norfolk, directed daily operations and activities in the JOC, the staff "battle captains" were responsible for maintaining constant situational awareness. CPT Mason Arquette (pseudonym) learned his new duties as he performed them.[121] The most important task for the tall, lean West Pointer was to keep COL Mulholland and the J3 up to date on "everything of note" that the task force was doing. It was the "everything of note" that kept Arquette scrambling because that grew each day as the UW campaign evolved. At the regularly scheduled morning and evening briefings, "Battle Captain" Arquette formally presented this information, including the availability of transport and combat aircraft (Air Force and Army); the exact number of personnel assigned to CJSOTF-North, where they were, and what they were doing; summaries of all classified message traffic in and out of the JSOTF; and a myriad of other issues facing a tactical commander in wartime who had also served as the senior American military officer in Uzbekistan and as Stronghold Freedom commander.[122]

For most of the 5th SFG staff officers and their commander (COL Mulholland took command of the 5th SFG two months before 9/11), serving as the nucleus of a special operations task force that was evolving into a joint headquarters JSOTF was "a challenge a minute." Integrating staff from the other services and USAR and ARNG augmentees was a constant process, especially when some services rotated personnel after 45 to 90 days in country. Despite not having had the opportunity to practice group-level operations in the field or having participated in a large-scale UW exercise since Mulholland's arrival, the 5th SFG staff under the tutelage of several experienced JFCOM officers fought the war well.[123]

The daily pace in the JOC was relentless. Arquette, a parachute infantry officer before joining the Special Forces, worked 18- to 20-hour days the first week. With the arrival of another staff captain, his duties were pared to just the "Day Battle Captain." This reduced the work shift to only 14 to 15 hours a day—12 hours on duty and an hour of transition with the "Night Battle Captain" before and after each shift change. There were no days off for Arquette or for anyone serving on the CJSOTF-North staff, which is typical during war.[124] On 13 October, just three days after arriving at K2, JSOTF-North issued the mission order to the Special Forces ODA that would initiate the UW campaign in Afghanistan.[125]

Different Intelligence Concerns for Air Planners

Night helicopter infiltrations in the high mountains of northern Afghanistan in winter posed major challenges for the JSOAC, both for air rescue (personnel recovery) during the air campaign and for inserting Special Forces for the anticipated UW campaign. Density altitude had reduced helicopter loads, and the first barrier was the 12,000-foot altitude of the best crossing points in the 18,000-foot mountains between K2 and Afghanistan. Helicopter aerial refuels from MC-130P tankers were required for missions from the north. The issues were maximum loads and getting through the 12,000-foot passes. MH-47Es would dump fuel to increase lift as they climbed for the crossing points on the "Bear." Of concern was the number of refuels per mission as the escorting MH-60L Black Hawk DAPs needed to refuel more often than the MH-47E Chinooks. The enemy antiaircraft threat was another matter.

Getting a complete threat picture from CENTCOM had been LTC Brinks' biggest problem. Intelligence had been provided in generalities, detailing the different types of "triple A"—antiaircraft artillery, or AAA—but without locations. The biggest fear was surface-to-air missiles (SAMs). CPT Jason Mills (pseudonym), the 2nd Battalion intelligence officer, and SFC Brandon Carr (pseudonym), his intelligence analyst, had collected everything available from the 160th SOAR headquarters before departing Fort Campbell.[126] Mills also got CWO Erick Jefferson (pseudonym), the 160th SOAR intelligence technician, attached to his section.[127] Based on what they had brought, Mills, Jefferson, and Carr prepared an intelligence picture of the battlefield. Current photo imagery, critical to selecting helicopter landing zones (LZs) and selecting routes, was unavailable. Secure data retrieval from the states was delayed when SCAMPI, the "nickname" for a portable secure compartmented information facility, was down, but once operational, Jefferson and Carr collated reams of raw data, analyzed it, and developed a comprehensive enemy order of battle picture.[128]

JSOTF-North Growing Pains at K2

Another problem 5th SFG faced as the JSOTF was the influx of units ordered into theater without their corresponding headquarters. For example, both CA and PSYOP units arrived and reported to the JSOTF. By doctrine, however, a joint civil-military operations task force would normally command CA units, and a joint PSYOP task force would command PSYOP units. A JTF usually would command both. However, none of these commands had been established in the Afghanistan theater. Although those units were invaluable in conducting the campaign, directing them placed an additional burden on an already overburdened staff.[129]

Within the JSOTF, COL Mulholland soon recognized that he was short the expertise to coordinate fire support and to plan aviation operations. LTC Richards borrowed a captain and staff sergeant from the 10th Mountain Division to plan fire support. He implored the Air Force 16th Special Operations Wing (SOW) to provide someone to assist in planning fixed-wing aviation missions and a planner from the 160th SOAR for rotary-wing operations. The problem of liaison and planning was solved when the Joint Special Operations Air Component (JSOAC) collocated with the JSOTF.

The staff was also saddled with base operations functions—sanitation, billeting, feeding, and security. Eventually, about 40 individuals were added to the 5th SFG staff to assist in accomplishing all its assigned missions. Many of those soldiers came from the 20th SFG—an ARNG group.

LTC Walters departed the JSOTF headquarters in mid-November, and LTC Richards left in December. Because of the professionalism and dedication of the 5th SFG soldiers and the assistance of the SOCJFCOM training team, by then, the JSOTF was performing its assigned responsibilities admirably. This is due in no small measure to the professionalism of all involved.

Figure 53. JSOTF-North commander COL Mulholland
with Secretary of Defense Rumsfeld.

Nevertheless, there were areas identified that needed to be resolved. Among those areas was determining whether SFGs should be prepared to become JSOTFs. Second, all levels of command must understand that a JSOTF is not a Special Forces operating base with a "J" for "joint" inserted in front of it. The SFG must be trained, equipped, and organized to perform the mission. The higher headquarters must ensure that the additional personnel required for the group to perform that mission are not only identified but also that those personnel are integrated into training exercises. The group staff must be prepared to accept the additional burdens of functioning as a joint headquarters with all the added responsibilities. Finally, the group must have the equipment—particularly communications equipment—essential to facilitating its increased span of control.[130] These are lessons that would not die after the SOCJFCOM staff left the theater. The same soldiers would soon find themselves providing the same training and advice to other SFGs as they prepared to deploy to Afghanistan to accept the JSOTF mission from 5th SFG.

We Don't Fail

On 21 September 2001, 10 days after the terrorist attacks on the United States, A Company, 112th Signal Battalion, received a U.S. Central Command (CENTCOM) deployment order to provide communications support to the JSOTF being established at K2, Uzbekistan, in support of Operation ENDURING FREEDOM.[131] On 4 October, 37 soldiers deployed to the theater. They arrived on 6 October and reported to the JSOTF J6.[132]

The 112th Signal Battalion was capable of deploying rapidly to establish the long-haul links to communicate from deployed special operations forces (SOF) to headquarters in Europe and the continental United States and to embassies in neighboring countries. Although this was a combat mission, it was a typical mission practiced numerous times on exercises both in the continental United States and abroad. Those exercises also led the company to develop standard communications deployment packages that minimized last-minute predeployment planning.

Figure 54. Antennas, power, and cabling installed first.

Figure 55. Initial signal links to K2.

An initial difficulty at K2 was determining where to set up. This was a critical decision because a guiding principle is that once communications have been established, the equipment should not be moved. There were only about 100 people on the ground when the company arrived in theater, and there was little knowledge of what other units would arrive or when. Additionally, available real estate was littered with trash and discarded Russian equipment, and the soil was contaminated with oil. Some difficulties developed among the communicators from different headquarters, and real estate allocators as units began to move into the base. A critical concern was that systems that processed Top Secret information be located near the Secure Compartmented Information Facility (SCIF). Not having the facility established early on led to equipment being moved and communications interrupted contrary to standard procedures.

The company deployed with one superhigh-frequency satellite hub, a tactical telephone switch, a data services team, one SCAMPI node to provide secure and nonsecure networking plus data services and secure telephones, equipment for secure video teleconferencing (VTC), and three Special Operations Communication Assemblage (SOCA) teams to provide tactical satellite (TACSAT) communications. They also took about 200 personal computers. Within 48 hours, the company had installed communications to support the Joint Special Operations Air Component (JSOAC) that had already been established. Real estate allocation difficulties that required some equipment to be moved and minor technical problems resulted in the SCAMPI not being reestablished for about four days. Normally, some of these problems are resolved in a predeployment communications exercise. Under the given conditions, however, being able to troubleshoot problems before hand was not possible.[133] The company also deployed two SOCA teams to embassies and one team to provide communications between a Special Forces detachment at Mazar-e Sharif and its headquarters.

After approximately 100 days, A Company at K2 was replaced by a conventional Army signal battalion. That, though, did not end the unit's involvement in the war against terrorism. In March 2002, the second platoon of B Company deployed to Bagram, Afghanistan, to provide communications to the JSOTF being established at that location. Second Lieutenant (2LT) Tom Washington (pseudonym), a former enlisted Special Forces soldier, and his platoon immediately appropriated space in a dirt field near the perimeter and went to work. Within 48 hours, as did A Company, Washington completed the links between the JSOTF and the higher headquarters. In his words, "that was possible only because incredible guys are running these systems." The next month, soldiers from first platoon, B Company, established communications in Kabul between 1st Battalion, 3rd SFG, and the JSOTF. The platoon also deployed three SOCA teams to support forward operating bases (FOBs) in Khowst, Kandahar, and Shkin.[134]

DAPs Set the Stage for UW in Afghanistan

LTC Brinks, the JSOAC commander, had been told on 12 October to begin planning air infiltrations into Afghanistan.[135] This order expanded his mission from CSAR support to inserting Special Forces teams into Afghanistan to advise and assist anti-*Taliban* leaders in conducting UW. Coordinated through diplomatic and military channels, the first ARSOF aviation mission was to insert an eight-man pilot team at night south of Mazar-e-Sharif to establish contact with General Dostum.

CWO Roger Charles (pseudonym), the MH-60L Direct Action Penetrator (DAP) flight leader, received the mission. Originally deployed to Uzbekistan to provide armed escorts to MH-47Es performing air rescue of downed aircrews in northern Afghanistan for the air campaign, the DAP would demonstrate what it was designed to do—conduct independent long-range penetrations into hostile environments to insert special reconnaissance (SR) teams. Although the DAP had weapon systems and the 160th SOAR relied heavily on the cover of darkness for protection, CWO Charles' main concern was the incomplete antiaircraft artillery (AAA) threat picture in Afghanistan.[136] Overhead cover of the helicopter mission by Air Force combat air patrol fighters was not an option. Thus, in an abandoned Soviet concrete building, the JSOAC staff worked feverishly to collect data from alternate sources because the SCAMPI system (secure intelligence reachback) was temporarily down and access was restricted to national intelligence sources.

CWO Charles' second concern was weather that potentially was an even greater threat than the enemy. Poor visibility masked terrain, and a 10,000-plus-foot mountain range controlled access to Afghanistan from K2. Sand or dust storms constantly obscured the high desert plains beyond them. Visibility routinely dropped to less than one-eighth of a mile in the plains region. When the dust storms slammed into the mountains, visibility limitations reached as high as 10,000 feet, and the associated air turbulence was lethal.

Figure 56. MH-60L DAP. Winter operations in high mountainous terrain posed major challenges.

Adhering to Night Stalker tradition, "Alone and unafraid," the 160th DAP pilots prepared their insertion plan with the information available and what the pilot team could tell them. On 14 October, Charles did the mission brief in an old Soviet aircraft bunker where the crews slept because there was more room than in the JSOAC building. The two DAP crews, the Chinook crew carrying emergency contingency fuel, the MC-130P tanker crew providing primary fuel by aerial refuel, and the JSOAC staff principals received the mission briefing huddled in a small circle around a map of the area of operations. The flight route was long, requiring two aerial refuels. The plan was simple but had several key elements for success; fuel and weather headed the list. Barring poor weather, the mission could be executed the next night. However, CENTCOM bumped the mission several days for diplomatic considerations, weather, and reservations. Finally, on the night of 16 October, the execute order was given.[137]

Under the cover of darkness, a flight of DAPs, configured more like Black Hawk assault helicopters with their armor stripped off, and an MH-47E Chinook took off from K2 headed to the south and Afghanistan. The two DAPs rendezvoused with an Air Force MC-130P Hercules tanker orbiting above southeastern Uzbekistan to refuel. After the DAPs had refueled from the tanker, the MH-47E Chinook helicopter returned to K2. It would meet the returning DAPs at the scheduled border-crossing time in the morning darkness. They were carrying an internal fuel bladder to refuel the DAPs on the ground if needed.

Shortly after the DAP flight crossed the border just east of Termiz, Uzbekistan, around midnight, it hit an unforecasted sandstorm in the northern plains where earlier satellite imagery had shown clear weather. Undeterred, CWO Charles led his flight onward as visibility shrank to less than one-half mile. While the pilots could see stars above through their night vision goggles (NVG), providing the illusion of a possible escape, the sandstorm rose to 10,000 feet. The helicopter's forward-looking infrared radar (FLIR) helped the pilots maintain proper obstacle clearance altitude, especially as the flight reentered mountainous terrain to the south of Mazar-e-Sharif. Relying on instruments, the pilots adroitly flew their helicopters "nap of the earth" (NOE), following the terrain down steep valleys and then climbing the rugged terrain before they broke out of the sandstorm at approximately 8,000 feet mean sea level (MSL). When the weather cleared, the moonless night challenged even the latest-generation NVG as the pilots flew into the central mountain region. They were looking for landing zone (LZ) Albatross, a cleared plateau in the bottom of a canyon, close to General Dostum's headquarters.[138]

After flying for two and one-half hours, the DAPs neared their objective. Expecting the LZ to be marked with some lights, CWO Charles was slightly taken aback when he discovered the landing area surrounded by more than 100 armed Afghans carrying AK-47s and rocket-propelled grenade (RPG) launchers. Just before takeoff, SSG Michael Stark (pseudonym), the crew chief on the lead DAP, had put an infrared chemical light on the right shoulders of the pilot team to track the ground force once they disembarked the helicopters.[139] This was to help identify the U.S. personnel among the Northern Alliance forces in the event something went wrong on the ground. En route to the LZ, the pilot team had radioed Dostum's forces and had been assured that everything was looking good. Still, prudence dictated caution.

Thus, CWO Charles in the lead DAP landed first in the dusty LZ, while the second DAP circled overhead maintaining visual contact with the other aircraft. After circling the area twice, the second DAP landed behind the first. Once both helicopters were on the ground, the pilot

Figure 57. Identifying the good guys from the bad guys.

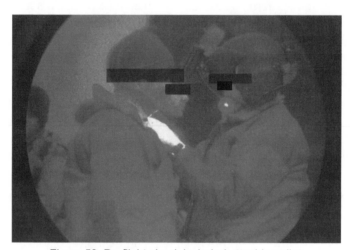

Figure 58. Preflight check included attaching glint
tape to identify friendlies on the night battlefield.

team pulled their equipment off the aircraft, gave the aircrews a "thumbs up," and disappeared into the crowd of Northern Alliance troops. While the DAP crew chiefs manned miniguns on each side of the helicopter, a young Afghan boy filmed the whole activity with an 8-millimeter (mm) movie camera. The threat of being shot down had been greatest when the helicopters flared on short final approach to the LZ. It seemed unlikely that they would have been attacked on the ground in a group of people. Confident that the team had found its contacts, Charles gave the order for the DAPs to depart.

Tactics dictated that the DAPs return on a different route, but the sandstorm dominating the northern plains had not abated and visibility had deteriorated even more as the pilots flew to their 0400 refuel rendezvous point. A unique phenomena associated with flying in a sandstorm is the ability to see lights below clearly. Thus, DAP aircrew members reported seeing obvious lights going on near populated areas to mark their flight path as they flew over. It seemed that people on the ground were signaling or tracking their advance in the middle of the night. This primitive tactic was later discovered to have been developed by the *mujahideen* to track Soviet helicopters. Like clockwork, the DAP flight crossed the border and hit the 9th Special Operations Squadron (SOS) MC-130P tanker on schedule. Once refueled, the Chinook with emergency fuel joined the two Black Hawks for the return flight to K2 as the tanker sped away. The 9th SOS tanker crews quickly established a reputation with the 160th SOAR for always being at the right place at the right time to refuel the ARSOF helicopters.

Unbeknown to many, this mission paved the way for the UW campaign in Afghanistan. It was a historic night. Army special operations aviation had achieved Night Stalker standards—time on target, plus or minus 30 seconds at night—under extreme weather conditions with aerial refuels and penetrated some of the highest and most rugged mountains in the world to deliver a team, on time and on target.

COL Kisner, deputy JSOTF commander, asked CWO Charles to carry an American flag on this first combat mission into Afghanistan. Charles said that "he would be honored." What he did not know was that Kisner planned to present the flag to the president. Afterward, Charles wrote a letter to accompany the flag, assuring the Commander in Chief that his orders had been executed with honor and dedicated to the nation. So it was with great pride that TF Dagger and the Night Stalkers sent President Bush the flag and letter as tokens of appreciation for his leadership.[140]

Organizing two joint special operations tactical headquarters—JSOTF-North or TF Dagger and the JSOAC—in the midst of establishing a joint FOB in Uzbekistan was a significant accomplishment. More important, these fledgling joint tactical staffs met the CENTCOM mission for CSAR in northern Afghanistan before the air campaign date was moved forward and conducted a successful long-range helicopter penetration deep into Afghanistan to insert a team responsible for coordinating the UW campaign with anti-*Taliban* war leaders. This was all done in less than two weeks.

Success must be attributed to the junior special operations leaders and soldiers who accepted responsibility for the myriad tasks that needed to be accomplished. They often learned as they did and persevered in the face of obstacles. Another critical element was the maturity and flexibility of the SOF leaders who responded professionally to new command arrangements, who took mission changes in stride, and who had confidence in their subordinates' ability to get the job done well and on time, regardless of the difficulty.

The preceding stories describe some of the preparations for the war on terrorism by ARSOF stationed throughout the United States; the movement of troops overseas into combat; standing up Stronghold Freedom at K2, Uzbekistan; and initial combat missions. These should have conveyed the quality of the soldiers in ARSOF, the wide spectrum of ARSOF capabilities, the different components of ARSOF—Special Forces, PSYOP, CA, aviation, Rangers, signal, and support—the importance of USAR and ARNG units and individual augmentees to ARSOF, and what is involved in training Army soldiers for SOF assignments.

Having set the stage for the UW campaign in Afghanistan with the final story about the DAP long-range penetration to General Dostum's mountain redoubt near Mazar-e-Sharif, the soldier stories in the next chapter will chronologically cover the war that leads to the *Taliban* government's collapse in late November 2001.

Notes

1.   Carl von Clausewitz, *On War*, Michael Howard and Peter Paret, ed. and trans. (Princeton, NJ: Princeton University Press, 1976), 87.

2.   Rowan Scarborough, "Military Officers Seek Swift, Deadly Response," *Washington Times*, 12 September 2001, 1; Dan Eggen and Vernon Loeb, "U.S. Intelligence Points to Bin Laden Network," *Washington Post*, 12 September 2001, 1; eMedilMillWorks Inc., "President Bush's Remarks," *Washington Post*, 12 September 2001, 2; Bob Woodward and Dan Balz, "'We Will Rally the World,'" *Washington Post*, 28 January 2002, A01.

3.   Thom Shanker and Eric Schmitt, "Rumsfeld Asks Call-Up of Reserves, as Many as 50,000," *New York Times*, 14 September 2001; Rowan Scarborough, "U.S. Plans War on Terrorists, Not Infrastructure," *Washington Times*, 14 September 2001, 13.

4.   David Von Drehle, "Senate Approves Use of Forces; Military Patrols Cities and Ports," *Washington Post*, 15 September 2001, 1; Associated Press, "Text of Joint Resolution," *Washington Post*, 15 September 2001, 4.

5.   Eggen and Loeb, 1.

6.   "Afghanistan Online," <www.afghan-web.org>; "Country Watch—Afghanistan," <www.countrywatch. com>.

7.   "A New World Order," *Christian Science Monitor* (14 September 2001), 1; President Bush's address to the nation, 12 September 2001; *FRONTLINE*, "Campaign Against Terror: Chronology," <www.pbs.org/wgbh/pages/ frontline/shows/ campaign/etc/cron.html>; "British Join in Anti-Terror War," Editorial Number 0-09464; "Coalition Support Grows," Editorial Number 0-09474; and "Australia Helps Fight Terrorists," Editorial Number 0-09480, The United States Government's International Broadcasting Bureau, <www.voa.gov>; *FRONTLINE*, "Campaign Against Terror."

8.   Dan Balz and Bob Woodward, "A Day to Speak of Anger and Grief," *Washington Post*, 30 January 2002, A01; Ben Barber, "*Taliban* Threatens to Invade Pakistan," *Washington Times*, 16 September 2001, 1; Molly Moore and Pamela Constable, "*Taliban* Asks Clerics to Rule on Surrender of Bin Laden," *Washington Post*, 18 September 2001, 1; Rajiv Chandrasekaran, "*Taliban* Rejects U.S. Demand, Vows a 'Showdown of Might,'" *Washington Post*, 22 September 2001, 1; Susan B. Glasser and Kamran Khan, "Pakistan Closes *Taliban*'s Last Embassy," *Washington Post*, 23 November 2001, 33; "Interview with Richard Armitage," *FRONTLINE*, <www.pbs.org/wgbh/pages/ frontline/shows/campaign/interviews/armitage.html>; *FRONTLINE*, "Campaign Against Terror."

9.   Michael R. Gordon and Eric Schmitt, "Groups Could Help Find Bin Laden and Assist American Attacks," *New York Times*, 24 September 2001, 1; Maura Reynolds, "Soviet Vets Warn U.S. of Perils in Afghanistan," *Los Angeles Times*, 19 September 2001, 1; *FRONTLINE*, "Campaign Against Terror."

10.   Nicholas Kralev, "U.S. Can Strike Without U.N. Nod," *Washington Times*, 27 September 2001, 17; "Charter of the United Nations," <www1.umn.edu/humanrts/instree/chapter 7.html>.

11.   Dan Balz, "Bush Warns of Casualties of War," *Washington Post*, 18 September 2001, 1.

12.   Bob Woodward and Dan Balz, "At Camp David, Advise and Consent," *Washington Post*, 31 January 2002, A01.

13.   *FRONTLINE*, "Campaign Against Terror."

14.   Clausewitz, 88; Susan Glasser, "Soviet Generals War of 'Sea of Bloodshed,'" *Washington Post*, 19 September 2001, 13; *FRONTLINE*, "Campaign Against Terror."

15.   Elaine Sciolino, "Bush Tells the Military to 'Get Ready'; Broader Spy Powers Gaining Support," *New York Times*, 16 September 2001, 1; Dana Priest, "Special Forces May Play Key Role," *Washington Post*, 15 September 2001, 5.

16.   Michael R. Gordon, Eric Schmitt, and Thom Shanker, "Scarcity of Afghan Targets Leads U.S. to Revise Strategy," *New York Times*, 19 September 2001; Rowan Scarborough, "Pentagon Prepares Variety of Responses," *Washington Times*, 21 September 2001, 1; Anne Plummer, "Army Secretary Vows U.S. Adversaries About to See 'Our Finest Hour,'" *Inside the Army*, 17 September 2001, 1.

17.   "Transcript of President Bush's Address," <www.cnn.com/2001/US/09/20/gen.bush.transcript/>.

18.   U.S. Army Special Operations Command (USASOC), *Sine Pari: The Story of Army Special Operations*, Historical Monograph #1 (Fort Bragg, NC: USASOC, 1997), 2-8; USASOC, *Standing Up the MACOM: The U.S. Army Special Operations Command, 1987-92*, Historical Monograph #8 (Fort Bragg, NC: USASOC, 1996), 11-13.

19.   Elizabeth Becker, "Renaming an Operation to Fit the Mood," *New York Times*, 26 September 2001. Initially, the operation was named INFINITE JUSTICE. Muslim countries, however, objected to the name because, in their opinion, only Allah could dispense infinite justice.

20. RADM Bert Calland, Commander, Special Operations Command, U.S. Central Command, interview with Kalev Sepp, 3 May 2002, As Sayliyah, Qatar, transcript, USASOC Classified Archives, Fort Bragg, North Carolina.

21. BG Les Fuller, Special Operations Command, Europe, interview with Richard Kiper, 15 April 2002, Fort Bragg, notes, USASOC Classified Archives, Fort Bragg; CPT James Saxon (pseudonym), 5th Special Forces Group, interview with Richard Kiper, 10 July 2002, Fort Campbell, Kentucky, notes, USASOC Classified Archives, Fort Bragg; "Front-Row Seat," *The Joint Journal* (March/April 2002), 3.

22. Headquarters, Department of the Army (HQDA), USASOC, CG letter, Subject: Defense Emergency Response Fund (DERF) Guidance, 22 October 2001.

23. HQDA, DAPE-MPE, message, Subject: Suspension of Voluntary Separation of Officers and Enlisted Soldiers From the Active Army (Stop Loss) in Selected Specialties, 021635Z Dec 2001; USASOC Military Personnel Division, Office of the Deputy Chief of Staff for Personnel, e-mail, 3 October 2002, 1217 and 1534 (hours), USASOC Classified Archives, Fort Bragg; Memorandum for Record, Richard Kiper and U.S. Army John F. Kennedy Special Warfare Center and School (SWCS), Directorate of Training and Doctrine and Special Operations Proponency Office, 10 October 2002, USASOC Classified Archives, Fort Bragg.

24. LTC Ralph Washington (pseudonym), SWCS, interview with Richard Kiper, 20 August 2002, Fort Bragg, transcript, USASOC Classified Archives, Fort Bragg; COL Scott Faught, Deputy Assistant Commandant for Reserve Affairs, SWCS, interview with Richard Kiper, 27 September 2002, Fort Bragg, notes, USASOC Classified Archives, Fort Bragg, hereafter cited as Faught interview.

25. USASOC Unit Training Division, Office of the Deputy Chief of Staff for Operations, e-mail, Subject: SOF in OEF History Project, 30 September 2002, USASOC Classified Archives, Fort Bragg.

26. "Special Operations Command Central (SOCCENT)," <www.globalsecurity.org/military/agency/dod/soccent.htm>; "Special Operations Forces," JCET, <www.ciponline.org/facts/sof.htm>; HQ, USASOC, message, 29 October 2002, Subject: JCS/JCET.

27. CPT Geoff Morris (pseudonym), Office of the Deputy Chief of Staff for Personnel, USASOC, interview with Richard Kiper, 27 September 2002, Fort Bragg, notes, USASOC Classified Archives, Fort Bragg; Faught interview; Steve Vogel and Matthew Mosk, "Area Reserve Forces Wait Anxiously to Be Called Up," *Washington Post*, 15 September 2001, 5.

28. Patrick E. Tyler, "U.S. and Britain Strike Afghanistan, Aiming at Bases and Terrorist Camps; Bush Warns '*Taliban* Will Pay a Price,'" *New York Times*, 8 October 2001, 1; Peter Baker, "Kabul and Kandahar Hit in Attacks Through Night," *Washington Post,* 8 October 2001, 1.

29. C.J. Chivers, "2d Wave of Troops Arrives in Uzbekistan," *New York Times*, 8 October 2001; U.S. Army Special Operations Command Crisis Response Cell briefing, 092000Z Oct 2001; "The Islamic Movement of Uzbekistan," Editorial Number 0-09473, The United States Government's International Broadcasting Bureau, <www.ibb.gov>; *FRONTLINE*, "Campaign Against Terror."

30. Rowan Scarborough, "Northern Alliance Gets Help From U.S.," *Washington Times*, 28 September 2001, 1; Michael R. Gordon and David E. Sanger, "Bush Approves Covert Aid for *Taliban* Forces," *New York Times*, 1 October 2001, 1.

31. U.S. Army Center for Military History, "Afghan War Chronology," 25 April 2002; Andrea Stone, "USA's Airborne Message: *Taliban*, 'You Are Condemned,'" *USA Today,* 17 October 2001, 10; MAJ Larry Paulson (pseudonym), 4th Psychological Operations (PSYOP) Group, interview with Richard Kiper, 3 April 2002, Fort Bragg, tape recording and notes, USASOC Classified Archives, Fort Bragg. The back of the leaflet had a picture of a man whipping a woman. The message read: "Is this the future you want for your women and children?"

32. Sun Tzu, *The Art of War*, Samuel B. Griffith, trans. (London: Oxford University Press, 1963), 77.

33. U.S. Army Field Manual (FM) 3-05.30, *Psychological Operations* (Washington, DC: U.S. Government Printing Office [GPO], 2000), 5-1 and 5-2.

34. LTC Sam Halstedt (pseudonym), 8th PSYOP Battalion, interview with Richard Kiper, 1 November 2002, Fort Bragg, tape recording and notes, USASOC Classified Archives, Fort Bragg.

35. Paul Colter and Darrin Matteson are pseudonyms. Manuel A. Diemer, 28 May 2002, Fort Bragg, interview with Kalev Sepp, transcripts at USASOC Classified Archives, Fort Bragg, hereafter cited as Diemer interview.

36. Ibid.

37. Copies are stored in the classified section, USASOC Classified Archives, Fort Bragg.

38. Marcus Steinmann and Matt Rhinehart are pseudonyms.

39. Diemer interview.

40. Diemer interview. MG Geoffrey Lambert had the authority to send Rhinehart to join Mulholland's 5th SFG since Rhinehart was serving in his command. As per regulations, Lambert had to formally ask MG Jerry Boykin, commander, SWCS, to provide Steinmann to 5th SFG. Boykin gladly granted the request.

41. Diemer interview.

42. Vincent Garvey, Will Sherman, Jon West, and Harry Sims are pseudonyms.

43. Vincent Garvey (pseudonym), interview with Kalev Sepp, 20 September 2002, tape recordings, USASOC Classified Archives, Fort Bragg.

44. Ibid.

45. Ibid.

46. SOCCENT is pronounced "SOCK-cent."

47. COL John F. Mulholland, 12 July 2002, Fort Campbell, interview with Charles Briscoe, transcripts and tapes at USASOC Classified Archives, Fort Bragg, hereafter cited as Mulholland interview.

48. JSOTF is pronounced "juh-SO-tiff," and ARSOTF is pronounced "ARE-so-tiff."

49. MG Geoffrey C. Lambert, 29 April 2003, Fort Bragg, e-mail note to Charles Briscoe, USASOC Classified Archives, Fort Bragg.

50. RADM Bert Calland, 3 May 2002, As Sayliyah, Qatar, interview with Matthew Dawson, tapes at USSOCOM Command Historian's Archives, MacDill Air Force Base (AFB), Florida.

51. The rank of U.S. Navy captain is equivalent to a U.S. Army colonel. Mulholland interview.

52. Concurrently, COL Mulholland prepared a joint manning document (JMD) for SOCCENT's approval to support his request for additional personnel to augment his headquarters and combat units, and to meet the additional responsibilities of serving as a JSOTF. SOCCENT rejected his JMD "five or six times," without providing him the planning guidance he needed to properly prepare the document. "It was absolute agony," remembered Mulholland. Mulholland interview.

53. ISOFAC is pronounced "EYE-so-fak."

54. Mulholland credited MSG Morton Chase (pseudonym) with eventually obtaining the high-quality, 1:100,000-scale topographic maps used by all the 5th SFG teams that entered Afghanistan. Mulholland interview.

55. MG Geoffrey C. Lambert, 29 April 2003, Fort Bragg, note to Charles Briscoe, USASOC Classified Archives, Fort Bragg.

56. Mulholland interview.

57. "Special Operations Command Joint Forces Command (SOCJFCOM)," <www.globalsecurity.org/ military/agency/dod/ socjfcom.htm>.

58. LTC Warren Richards (pseudonym), SOCJFCOM, interview with Kalev Sepp and Richard Kiper, 29 May 2002, Fort Bragg, tape recording and notes, USASOC Classified Archives, Fort Bragg, hereafter cited as Richards interview.

59. Retired COL Dave Rasmussen (pseudonym), SOCJFCOM, interview with Kalev Sepp, 19 July 2002, Norfolk, Virginia, notes, USASOC Classified Archives, Fort Bragg, hereafter cited as Rasmussen interview.

60. COL Mike Findlay, SOCJFCOM, interview with Charles Briscoe, 19 July 2002, Norfolk, tape recording and notes, USASOC Classified Archives, Fort Bragg; Rasmussen interview.

61. LTC Jack Walters (pseudonym), SOCJFCOM, interview with Richard Kiper, 19 July 2002, Norfolk, tape recording and notes, USASOC Classified Archives, Fort Bragg, hereafter cited as Walters interview; LTC Warren Richards (pseudonym), SOCJFCOM, briefing to Charles Briscoe, Richard Kiper, Kalev Sepp, and James Schroder, 19 July 2002, Norfolk, notes, USASOC Classified Archives, Fort Bragg.

62. Jeffrey Solis and Don Forsythe are pseudonyms.

63. The participating units were the Air Force 6th Special Operations Squadron, the Army 3rd Battalion, 160th Special Operations Aviation Regiment (SOAR), and A Company, 2nd Battalion, 75th Ranger Infantry Regiment. MAJ Jeffrey Solis (pseudonym), interview with Kalev Sepp, 24 April 2002, Fort Campbell, transcripts and tapes, USASOC Classified Archives, Fort Bragg, hereafter cited as Solis interview.

64. Solis interview.

65. Ibid.

66. COL Mark Phelan, 18 July 2002, Fort Bragg, interview with Kalev Sepp, transcripts and tapes, USASOC Classified Archives, Fort Bragg.

67. Ibid.

68. Mulholland interview.

69. COL Mulholland informed his battalion commanders of his concept for their employment at separate times. LTC Carl Hooper (pseudonym) called Mulholland from SOCCENT headquarters in Tampa, Florida, on 26

September 2001 and recommended that a liaison officer from 5th SFG be sent to the Northern Alliance. Mulholland concurred. LTC Marc Bell (pseudonym), after leaving Fort Campbell on 4 October 2001, was informed of this concept at the JSOTF-North base at Karshi Kanabad (K2) in mid-October. LTC Don Forsythe (pseudonym), who left for Jordan with his battalion on 16 September 2001, learned of the concept from a JSOTF-North staff officer in mid-November, two days after arriving at K2. LTC Carl Hooper, 10 December 2002, Fort Campbell; Bell, 6 December 2002, MacDill AFB; and LTC Don Forsythe, 6 December 2002, Fort Polk, Louisiana, telephonic interviews with Kalev Sepp; Mulholland interview.

70. COL John F. Mulholland, "Commanders' Conference Presentation," May 2002, Fort Bragg, videotape, USASOC Classified Archives, Fort Bragg. COL Mulholland also indicated that he felt the lieutenant colonels were not necessary to help him and his task force staff direct the A detachments in Afghanistan, asking rhetorically, "did they [the A detachments] need a battalion commander be put on top of them?" Battalion headquarters were recreated in late November, although each of them was assigned a mix of A and B detachments from all three battalions. Mulholland interview.

71. Ibid.

72. "Transcript: Bush Says U.S. Giving Millions More in Food Aid to Afghan People," U.S. Department of State International Information Programs, 4 October 2001, <http://usinfo.state.gov/regional/nea/sasia/afghan/text20011004bush.htm>.

73. MAJ Matt DiJurnigan (pseudonym), C Company, 96th Civil Affairs Battalion, interview with Richard Kiper, 4 November 2002, Fort Bragg, tape recording and notes, USASOC Classified Archives, Fort Bragg.

74. FM 41-10, *Civil Affairs Operations* (Washington, DC: GPO, 2000), H-1 - H-3.

75. Marty Cavanaugh is a pseudonym.

76. DA, Office of the Secretary of the Army, Subject: Importance of Army-Wide Support of the Psychological Warfare Programs, 2 February 1951, Record Group 319, National Archives.

77. Dr. Darren Curtis (pseudonym), Strategic Studies Detachment, 4th Psychological Operations Group, interview by Richard Kiper, 15 April 2002, Fort Bragg, transcript, USASOC Classified Archives, Fort Bragg.

78. Andrea Stone, "Soldiers Deploy on Mental Terrain," *USA Today*, 3 October 2001, 7.

79. Keith B. Richburg and William Branigin, "U.S. Bombs Aid Rebels in North; Propaganda Campaign Intensifies," *Washington Post*, 8 November 2001, 13. Totals as of 17 October 2002 were 84,215,894 leaflets disseminated, 6,873:39 hours broadcast by SOMS-B and Commando Solo, 538 different radio scripts, and 7,670 radios distributed.

80. SSG James Willet (pseudonym), HHC, 2nd Battalion, 160th SOAR, interview with James Schroder, 25 March 2002, Fort Campbell, tape recording and notes, USASOC Classified Archives, Fort Bragg.

81. Ibid.

82. "Secretary Rumsfeld Press Conference With President of Uzbekistan," News Transcript, <http://www.defenselink.mil/news/Oct2001/t10082001_t1005uz.html>, hereafter cited as "Rumsfeld Press Conference.

83. Ibid.

84. Paul West is a pseudonym.

85. Kyle Killinger is a pseudonym.

86. Rumsfeld Press Conference.

87. Harkin interview.

88. SFC Douglas Steverson (pseudonym), HHC, 2nd Battalion, 160th SOAR, interview with Charles Briscoe, 25 March 2002, Fort Campbell, tape recording and notes, USASOC Classified Archives, Fort Bragg.

89. Childs and Victor Mercado are pseudonyms.

90. MAJ Wes McKellar (pseudonym), Commander, D Company, 2nd Battalion, 160th SOAR, interview with Charles Briscoe, 24 April 02, Fort Campbell, tape recording and notes, USASOC Classified Archives, Fort Bragg.

91. LTC James Brinks (pseudonym), Commander, 2nd Battalion, 160th SOAR, interview with James Schroder, 27 March 2002, Fort Campbell, tape recording and notes, USASOC Classified Archives, Fort Bragg.

92. Mark Henderson is a pseudonym.

93. James Brinks is a pseudonym.

94. MAJ Charles Mahoney (pseudonym), Commander, A Company, 528th Special Operations Support Battalion (SOSB), interview by Richard Kiper, Kalev Sepp, and James Schroder, 19 March 2002, Fort Bragg, hereafter cited as Mahoney interview.

95. Antoine Henri de Jomini, *The Art of War* (Navato, CA: Presidio Press, 1992), 69.

96. "After Action Review for Operation Enduring Freedom" (Fort Bragg, NC: Alpha Forward Support Company, 528th Support Battalion, 13 March 2002), 1.

97. 1LT Michael Bridgewater (pseudonym), A Company, 528th SOSB, interview with Richard Kiper, 6 March 2002, Fort Bragg, tape recording and notes, USASOC Classified Archives, Fort Bragg, hereafter cited as Bridgewater interview.

98. SSG Celeste Holmes (pseudonym), Headquarters (HQ) and Main Support Company, 528th SOSB, interview with Richard Kiper, 19 March 2002, Fort Bragg, tape recording and notes, USASOC Classified Archives, Fort Bragg.

99. Ibid.

100. SSG Timothy Matthews (pseudonym), HQ and Service Company, 3rd Battalion, 4th PSYOP Group, interview with Richard Kiper, 4 April 2002, Fort Bragg, tape recording and notes, USASOC Classified Archives, Fort Bragg.

101. Mark Parsons is a pseudonym.

102. MAJ Steven Broderick (pseudonym), Commander, B Company, 3rd Battalion, 5th Special Forces Group (Airborne), interview with Kalev Sepp, 21 March 2002, Fort Campbell, tape recording and notes, USASOC Classified Archives, Fort Bragg, hereafter cited as Broderick interview.

103. Kevin Anderson is a pseudonym.

104. Broderick interview.

105. Manuel Victoro is a pseudonym.

106. Broderick interview.

107. Richard Shaw is a pseudonym; Mahoney interview.

108. Warren Richards is a pseudonym; SOCJFCOM facilitates the joint integration of SOF elements and trains special operations commanders and their staffs to function as a theater joint special operations task force.

109. Don Sullivan and Derrick Jacobi are pseudonyms.

110. Sullivan was not notified that A detachments had moved into the 5th SFG's isolation facility (ISOFAC) at Fort Campbell on 19 September 2001, even though it was his duty to provide those teams with critical information for their communications plans such as what radios, frequencies, codes, and call signs they would use. He discovered this the day after the teams' isolation began, when he was contacted to provide the data. Don Sullivan (pseudonym), 24 April 2002, Fort Campbell, interview with Kalev Sepp, transcripts and tapes, USASOC Classified Archives, Fort Bragg, hereafter cited as Sullivan interview.

111. Sullivan interview.

112. "Temper tent" was slang for temperature-controlled tent, a modular internally framed wall tent that could accept larger vinyl tubes that carried either heated or cooled air from blowers into the tent's interior.

113. Sullivan interview.

114. 1SG Martin Masterson (pseudonym), A Company, 112th Signal Battalion, interview with Richard Kiper, 19 March 2002, Fort Bragg, tape recording and notes, USASOC Classified Archives, Fort Bragg.

115. Ibid.

116. Carlos Hernandez and Jason Bennington are pseudonyms.

117. CPT Carlos Hernandez, 24 April 2002, Fort Campbell, interview with Kalev Sepp, transcripts and tapes, USASOC Classified Archives, Fort Bragg, hereafter cited as Hernandez interview.

118. MSG Jason Bennington was the brother of MAJ Del Bennington, also serving in 5th SFG.

119. Hernandez interview.

120. Ibid.

121. Mason Arquette is a pseudonym.

122. CPT Mason Arquette, 26 April 2002, Fort Campbell, interview with Kalev Sepp, transcripts and tapes, USASOC Classified Archives, Fort Bragg.

123. Ibid.

124. Ibid.

125. Sullivan interview.

126. CPT Jason Mills (pseudonym), HHC, 2nd Battalion, 160th SOAR, interview with James Schroder, 26 April 2002, Fort Campbell, tape recording and notes, USASOC Classified Archives, Fort Bragg.

127. CWO Erick Jefferson (pseudonym), HHC, 160th SOAR, interview with James Schroder, 12 July 2002, Fort Campbell, tape recording and notes, USASOC Classified Archives, Fort Bragg.

128. SCAMPI includes deployable systems and tactical gateways that allow SOF organizations to obtain voice, data, and video teleconferencing (VTC) of all classification levels while deployed anywhere in the world to support SOF missions. See <http://www.sotech-kmi.com/printarticle.cfm?DocID=119> accessed 2 Jan 04.

129. FM 3-05.30, 5-1 and 5-2; FM 41-10, 4-5.

130. Richards interview; Walters interview; "Joint Special Operations Insights," Special Operations Forces Joint Training Team, June 2002.

131. U.S. Central Command Deployment Order, 19 September 2001.

132. Briefing by CPT Sam Mitchell (pseudonym), January 2002, USASOC, Fort Bragg.

133. CPT Steve Marks (pseudonym), A Company, 112th Signal Battalion, interview with Richard Kiper, 19 March 2002, Fort Bragg, tape recording and notes, USASOC Classified Archives, Fort Bragg.

134. 2LT Tom Washington (pseudonym), 2nd Platoon, B Company, 112th Signal Battalion, interview with Richard Kiper, 6 May 2002, Bagram, Afghanistan, tape recording and notes, USASOC Classified Archives, Fort Bragg.

135. Brinks is a pseudonym.

136. Roger Charles (pseudonym), DAP Flight Lead, D Company, 1st Battalion, 160th SOAR, interview with James Schroder 22 April 2002, Fort Campbell, tape recording and notes, USASOC Classified Archives, Fort Bragg, hereafter cited as Charles interview.

137. Ibid.

138. Ibid.

139. Michael Stark is a pseudonym.

140. Charles interview.

Chapter 3

Toppling the *Taliban* in Afghanistan
19 October - 7 December 2001

War should be carried on like a monsoon;
one changeless determination of every particle
towards the one unalterable aim.[1]

When the war in Afghanistan accelerated ahead of the estimates the U.S. Central Command (CENTCOM) staff prepared, it was not a surprise to Army special operations commanders. After GEN Charles R. Holland, the U.S. Special Operations Command (USSOCOM) combatant commander, and others in the Pentagon had been briefed on the seven classic phases of unconventional warfare (UW), MG Geoffrey Lambert, the U.S. Army Special Forces Command (USASFC) commander, cautioned that each faction in the Northern Alliance had distinct capabilities and strengths, which meant that they would not progress into the fight in linear fashion. LTG Bryan D. Brown, the U.S. Army Special Operations Command (USASOC) commander, included a slide in the briefing that explained that the Northern Alliance factions were in different phases of development and that a slow phase-by-phase model for buildup did not really fit reality on the ground. Lambert felt strongly that the war would have a "velocity and momentum of its own." GEN Holland agreed to explain to the Chairman, Joint Chiefs of Staff (CJCS) the unknown velocity and momentum of the Northern Alliance forces.[2]

Figure 1. LTG Bryan D. Brown, USASOC commander.

The initial concept called for reconnaissance units and Army Special Forces teams to fly into Afghanistan in October and November 2001.[3] The supposedly beleaguered Afghan Northern Alliance forces would weather the winter much like a "Valley Forge" experience. The CENTCOM planners envisioned that Special Forces ODAs would spend those cold, snowy months in the high valleys of the rugged Hindu Kush drilling a loose collection of warrior bands into a well-trained, battle-ready, well-equipped army.

If there were bands of resistance fighters ready and anxious to do battle, the Special Forces soldiers would assist them in attacks against the *Taliban* army as soon as practicable. To these ends, the Special Operations Command of CENTCOM had directed COL John Mulholland to use his 5th Special Forces Group (SFG) staff as the nucleus of the JSOTF-North headquarters and to carry out this effort with his operational Special Forces detachments. Mulholland hoped that one, possibly two, northern towns might be taken from the enemy before the cold weather brought the traditional winter hiatus from military operations.[4]

Around April or May 2002, this new, Special Forces-trained, anti-*Taliban* army was to begin a spring offensive to secure the northern tier of Afghan cities. It was also to open roads into Pakistan and Uzbekistan to receive supplies, particularly humanitarian aid, and possibly to facilitate U.S. combat divisions' entrance into Afghanistan. Then, perhaps later that year, a general offensive toward Kabul could be launched. Operations in the southern region around Kandahar were thought to be problematic. Strong anti-*Taliban* leaders had not yet been identified among the

Figure 2. Kabul, Afghanistan's national capital.

94

ethnic Pashtuns who constituted the majority of the Afghan population south of Kabul. However, events would soon move faster than the initial time line estimations by the CENTCOM staff.[5]

By the middle of September 2001, the 5th SFG staff learned that intelligence sources had identified two key leaders of the anti-*Taliban* resistance forces.[6] One was Mohammed Fahim Khan, the military successor to assassinated senior resistance commander Ahmad Shah Massoud, the "Lion of Panjshir," who operated in the northeast corner of Afghanistan. Before his murder, Massoud led a confederation of primarily Panjshir Valley Afghan Tajiks called the Northern Alliance.[7] Several other groups, formed and defined by ethnicity and sometimes by tribe, were aligned with Massoud and then with Fahim Khan. While Pashtun Afghans make up most of the population in the southern half of Afghanistan, they constitute less than 10 percent of the inhabitants north of Kabul. Massoud had been recognized as an exceptionally capable, charismatic leader and was the only resistance leader with wide popular support. His death, just two days before the 9/11 attacks in the United States, left the viability of the Northern Alliance in doubt in the minds of American leaders.

The other leader, General Rashid Dostum, an ethnic Uzbek who led the Junbush-e-Millie, the largest single military corps in the north, was of particular concern to COL Mulholland because he planned to send a Special Forces ODA to live with and advise him and his Afghan fighters through the winter. His loosely associated amalgam of resistance elements of Uzbek, Tajik, and Hazara Afghans was thought to number between 10,000 and 15,000 fighters. Their opponents, the *Taliban* armed forces, were thought to number as many as 40,000. Dostum was based in the Dari-a-Souf Valley in the mountains south of Mazar-e-Sharif.

General Dostum had served in the Red Army before joining the Afghan armed forces of the Soviet puppet regime that strongman Mohammed Najibullah led.[8] He then changed sides to fight with the anti-Soviet *mujahideen* against Najibullah, who was ousted by rebel forces. Najibullah was later taken from the UN compound where he had sought refuge and executed by the *Taliban*. During the continuing civil war, Dostum was reported to have initially supported the *Taliban* and then opposed them. In reprisal for a 1997 *Taliban* attack against Mazar-e-Sharif, the center of his political and military power in northern Afghanistan, Dostum allegedly ordered the execution of captured *Taliban*. When the *Taliban* drove Dostum and his army out of Mazar-e-Sharif the following year, reprisals were taken in return against those captured fighters from Dostum's forces.[9] Although many of the allegations were never substantiated, a Special Forces captain remarked, "No one [the Afghan leaders] here is clean."[10] COL Mulholland told his detachments to be prepared for the worst.[11]

Figure 3. General Abdul Rashid Dostum.

After two days of waiting for the weather to clear, the first two SF detachments were inserted into Afghanistan on the night of 19 October 2001 by specially configured MH-47E Chinook helicopters. The 2nd Battalion, 160th Special Operations Aviation Regiment (SOAR) aircrews flew the teams through steep walled valleys choked with dust storms that rose 2 miles into the night sky, over mountain ranges higher than any the Night Stalkers had ever flown, and did aerial refueling from Air Force MC-130P tankers en route. The 160th SOAR pilots pushed their helicopters to the limits of aircraft design performance. The weather conditions were so bad that the two MH-60L Black Hawk DAP helicopters flying armed escort for the MH-47E Chinook flight were forced to turn back to Karshi Kanabad (K2). Relying almost exclusively on the advanced multimode radar systems to avoid the rugged mountainous terrain, the Chinook pilots pressed on through the blinding dust to deliver the two Special Forces teams to landing zones (LZs) deep in Afghanistan.

The 12 men of Special Forces ODA 595 (Five-Nine-Five) stepped off the back ramp of their Chinook helicopter at 0200 on 20 October into a tiny cultivated plot in the mountain-walled Dari-a-Souf Valley about 50 miles south of Mazar-e-Sharif. Guides had appeared from the darkness to take them to one of General Dostum's camps. The SF team met the Afghan leader at sunrise. Within hours of that meeting, half the team, to its complete surprise, was riding on horseback to Dostum's command post. The next day, ODA 595 started guiding "smart" bombs dropped from a B-52 Stratofortress bomber circling overhead on the *Taliban* front-line positions.

Figure 4. Refueling the MC-130P tanker was a major task.

In northeast Afghanistan, in the mountains above the Panjshir Valley, the Special Forces ODA 555 (the "Triple Nickel") had also landed in the darkness of 20 October and been taken by guides to meet General Shariff, one of Fahim Khan's field commanders.[12] Like Five-Nine-Five, within 24 hours, the Special Forces soldiers traveled to the long-stalemated front lines and were directing the aerial bombardment of *Taliban* defensive fighting bunkers and trenches around the abandoned Soviet air base at Bagram. For the past three years, these entrenchments between the imposing mountain ranges guarded the northern end of the broad Shomali Plain that runs between them, thus serving as the first line of protection for the Afghan capital city of Kabul only 25 miles away.

Figure 5.
View of an impacting smart bomb.

Figure 6. General Shariff and supporters.

At exactly the same time the Special Forces teams were being surreptitiously flown into northern Afghanistan, almost 200 Army Rangers parachute assaulted on a landing strip in the southern Afghan desert to publicly demonstrate that the American military could put "boots on the ground" deep inside enemy territory at will. The airfield, code-named Objective Rhino, was first blasted by Air Force AC-130 gunships and then overwhelmed in minutes by several platoons of Rangers from the 3rd Battalion, 75th Ranger Regiment. Two Rangers were injured in the night parachute assault, and one *Taliban* guard at the site was killed.[13] Army photographers with night-vision cameras videotaped the parachute assault and the extraction of the Ranger force by MC-

97

130 aircraft. Within hours of the successful night combat operation, a combat camera team had done a first edit of the raw footage of the raid and electronically delivered the reduced footage to a product development team of the 3rd Psychological Operations Battalion (POB) at Fort Bragg. This team edited and transmitted a finished video clip to the Pentagon in time for Secretary of Defense Donald Rumsfeld to show it the following day during his noon press conference and in time for it to be integrated into the American "news cycle."[14] Concurrently, another night raid took place to the north of Objective Rhino, which was not filmed.[15] That same night, after a second successful parachute assault to seize an airfield, two Rangers died in

Figure 7. 75th Rangers combat parachute assault on Objective Rhino.

an accidental helicopter crash in Pakistan during supporting operations. These soldiers were the first ARSOF casualties in the U.S. military campaign against the *Taliban* in Afghanistan.[16]

More Special Forces ODAs were inserted into northern Afghanistan as the JSOTF-North headquarters learned of more anti-*Taliban* resistance groups that were capable of taking the offensive. Contentious relationships among the various resistance chiefs, especially Dostum and Fahim Khan, required the JSOTF to "balance" teams between the factions to preclude the perception by the ethnic groups that any were "more favored" by the Americans. To assuage Fahim Khan's displeasure when he learned that his old rival Dostum had U.S. advisers, COL Mulholland dispatched Special Forces teams to bolster two of Khan's allies. On 23 October, Special Forces ODA 585 was inserted by MH-47E Chinooks into the Callocutta region near Konduz to support Burillah Khan. Weather delayed ODA 534 until 4 November when it was also inserted by MH-47E helicopters into the Dari-a-Balkh Valley to work with Afghan Tajik General Atta Mohammed, the head of the Jaamat-e-Islami militia who was at times a confederate and other times a rival of Dostum.[17]

With the belief that, politically, more senior, experienced Special Forces officers were necessary to advise the most important Afghan resistance leaders, COL Mulholland planned to use his battalion commanders in that role. During the night of 24 October, he dispatched a Special Forces lieutenant colonel and several staff members to the Bagram area to advise and assist General Bismullah Khan, the senior Northern Alliance military commander operating in the Shomali Plains region. A week later, on 2 November, another Special Forces battalion commander was provided to Dostum as a senior adviser as well to help coordinate his offensive with Atta as they marched north toward Mazar-e-Sharif.[18]

Despite constant aerial bombardment, the *Taliban* army remained a potent military force, and it moved to counter the resistance forces' advances. The 26 October attempt by long-time anti-*Taliban* leader Abdul Haq to infiltrate overland into Afghanistan to help the fighting ended in *Taliban* soldiers capturing him and immediately executing him by decapitation.[19] About the same time, a "*jihad* brigade" of 5,000 to 10,000 Pakistanis, incited by mullahs calling for a crusade against the invading American "infidels," reportedly entered Afghanistan.[20] In the north and center of Afghanistan, some anti-*Taliban* warlords continued to mobilize fighters and mass those troops for a general offensive. Others pressed their attacks against the *Taliban*, aided by Special Forces soldiers directing airstrikes onto the enemy positions.[21]

More Special Forces teams made the harrowing long night flights into the mountains of the Hindu Kush. Flying in normal conditions near sea level, the 160th SOAR MH-47E Chinooks could easily carry 40 or more American soldiers loaded with packs, ammunition, and weapons. But to fly over the 2-mile-high mountains of Afghanistan, the Night Stalkers had to send two "stripped" medium cargo helicopters to deliver a single detachment. The 10 men

Figure 8. A Soviet-made Mi-17 utility helicopter flown by contract pilots.

of Special Forces ODA 553 slated to go to Yakawlang, near Bamian in the center of the country, were split between two Chinooks to reduce the helicopter loads in the low-density altitude conditions. On 8 November, ODA 586 and ODA 594 flew together on MH-47Es to a way station near the Afghanistan-Tajikistan border. At daybreak the next morning, the Special Forces soldiers of Five-Eight-Six were flown to Konduz aboard a Russian-made Mi-17 helicopter flown by contract pilots to join General Daoud Khan at Farkhar. Mi-17s also shuttled ODA 594 into the Panjshir Valley to reinforce the Triple Nickel (ODA 555) as its anti-*Taliban* forces prepared for an offensive against Bagram and Kabul. While the powerful, rugged, old Russian helicopters could fly higher altitudes than the American rotary-wing aircraft, they could only fly during daylight in good weather, and the flight oxygen systems were primitive and barely adequate.[22]

Even the cover of darkness did not fully protect the aircrews of the 2nd Battalion, 160th SOAR, as they transported the Special Forces ODAs into Afghanistan. *Taliban* soldiers and *al-Qaeda* fighters frequently fired at the black Chinooks as they flew nap of the earth (NOE), hugging the terrain as they flew down the mountain valleys and skimmed the ridges and mountain crests. The ambushers positioned themselves in the mountain valleys where they suspected the Americans would fly and waited for the sound of the helicopter rotor blades. The MH-47 Chinook, larger than a Greyhound bus, offered a big target to gunners on the ground. Often, during a night sortie—a round trip from K2 into Afghanistan and back—the MH-47E Chinook pilots would weave through barrages of bullets and rocket-propelled grenades (RPGs) and dodge shoulder-fired antiaircraft missiles.

On 2 November, ODA Five-Five-Three landed in freezing darkness to support General Kareem Kahlili, the 65-year-old senior Hazara military commander in the Bamian region. The Shiite Muslim Hazaras had been viciously persecuted by the *Taliban*, and they were eager for retribution. Like all ODAs across Afghanistan, the Special Forces team at Bamian made it clear to their new allies that Americans would not tolerate reprisals for past killings, particularly murdering prisoners. This was a big concern for the Special Forces troops who worked alongside pro-Iranian General Mohammed Mohaqqeq. Mohaqqeq, leader of 3,000 Hazara Hezb-e-Wahadat fighters, had volunteered his troops to hunt down the fleeing *Taliban* mercenaries. He also wanted to negotiate with Dostum and Atta for a fair share of the post-*Taliban*

99

Figure 9. An MH-47E deploying defensive measures.

political power in northern Afghanistan.[23] There would be no such contest in the far west of the country, as ODA 554 discovered when it joined General Ismail Khan during his offensive to seize Herat from the *Taliban* on 11 November. Ismail Khan was the single most powerful military and political figure in that vast region along the Iranian border, and thus, he was key to ODA Five-Five-Four's mission to establish a humanitarian relief base at the Herat airfield.[24]

Figure 10. Ismail Khan.

Augmented by the combination of American guided aerial bombing, humanitarian aid, and other assistance that included air-dropped weapons and ammunition, the anti-*Taliban* forces began to gain the initiative.[25] Some warlords like Dostum were independent and aggressive while others responded slowly, despite prompting by their new American Special Forces advisers. While 160th SOAR's Chinooks continued to be the only viable means of infiltrating SOF soldiers into Afghanistan, the supplies and equipment that the SF teams advising the anti-*Taliban* forces needed could be delivered by U.S. Air Force MC-130 Combat Talon transports controlled by the Special Operations Command, Europe (SOCEUR).[26] BG Les Fuller, commander, SOCEUR, directed the procurement and packing of supplies and equipment in Germany and their shipment by Air Force cargo jets to Incirlik Air Base, Turkey. There, parachute bundles—packed with items as diverse as satellite radios, horse feed, and saddles to fit the larger American Special Forces soldiers—were loaded on the dull grey, four-engine, turboprop Combat Talons. The Air Force special operations aircrews then flew the 14-hour round trip down into mountainous valleys to drop their cargo by parachute in the middle of the night onto drop zones as small as a football field.[27] The MC-130s made these supply and equipment airdrops to the isolated Special Forces teams and continued to deliver humanitarian food rations all over Afghanistan. At Bamian, ODA Five-Five-Three witnessed the largest single night drop of rations of the Afghan war when Air Force C-17 Globemaster III jet transports scattered 110 tons of yellow-wrapped vegetarian meals over the airfield from 10,000 feet above ground level (AGL).[28]

The Special Forces teams and their Afghan militia-type forces each developed distinctive "battle rhythms" to keep continuous pressure on the *Taliban* armies. The Special Forces ODAs, many of which had been augmented with Air Force special tactics airmen who were specially trained to direct tactical airstrikes and guide smart bombs, split apart into several three- and four-man teams. This permitted the ODAs to cover more of the mountainous battlefields in their regions and to use their close-air-support (CAS) teams in shifts to keep bombs falling and airstrikes on the *Taliban* around the clock.[29] Each of the smaller CAS teams carried a targeting laser and satellite-linked global positioning devices to guide smart bombs precisely to their targets.

Figure 11. Special Forces teams use satellite links for communications in northern Afghanistan.

Figure 12. A Special Forces soldier employing a laser designator to mark targets for close air support.

Dividing the ODAs to capitalize on the CAS capability proved to be a major combat multiplier for the small SOF teams. Against the Bagram Airfield defenses, the Triple Nickel directed B-52 heavy bomber flights to drop swaths of 500-pound bombs onto the *Taliban* trench lines, a technique referred to during Operation DESERT STORM in 1991 as "carpet bombing" because of the breadth of devastation that resulted. In the Dari-a-Souf and Balkh valleys, SF ODAs 595 and 534 blasted *Taliban* bunkers, artillery emplacements, and tanks with airstrikes while their Afghan allies prepared for an early afternoon ground attack. Using this *modus operandi*, they attacked and if they were successful in forcing the *Taliban* to retreat, there normally would not be sufficient daylight remaining for the *Taliban* to mount an effective counterattack. In this way, they fought their way through successive *Taliban* defensive lines. On 9 November, the forces of Dostum and Atta broke out of the Balkh Valley and, via the Tangi Pass, swept down into the city of Mazar-e-Sharif. On the outskirts of the city, several hundred defiant Pakistani *Taliban* fighters barricaded themselves in a former girls' school and swore to "fight to the death." When the Pakistanis gunned down a party of mullahs seeking to negotiate a surrender, anti-*Taliban* troops prepared to assault the school compound. ODA 595 guided smart bombs directly into the barricaded building, eliminating all of the fanatical defenders.[30] Shortly afterward, another 3,000 *Taliban* soldiers surrendered.[31]

On 10 November, as the victor of the battle of Balkh Valley, General Rashid Dostum made Mazar-e-Sharif the first major Afghan city liberated from the *Taliban*.[32] When a struggle for political control of the city arose, the Army Special Forces advisers brokered a transitional power-sharing agreement between Dostum, Atta, and Mohaqqeq. Having negotiated deals among contesting factions in Bosnia, the Special Forces officers brokered an accord based on dividing municipal functions and responsibilities instead of city sections. CENTCOM commander GEN Tommy Franks sent RADM Bert Calland, a U.S. Navy SEAL, and the senior special operations officer in SOCCENT to monitor the implementation of the accord and to oversee the humanitarian relief effort.

Considerable infrastructure repair had to be done to support expanded humanitarian aid and reconstruction. Outside the city, the Special Forces engineers arranged and supervised the local repair of the bomb-cratered runway at the airport. They showed local Afghan workers how to fill the bomb craters and artillery shell holes with a mix of riverbed gravel and tar accumulated from burning old tires. To foster stable conditions in Mazar-e-Sharif, JSOTF-North sent a four-man civil affairs team (CAT) from the 96th Civil Affairs Battalion (CAB) from K2. CAT-A33 made field assessments to identify those projects that merited immediate funding to support the "reconstruction of a civic fabric."[33] CAT-A32 was attached to a Special Forces ODA in the vicinity of Bagram. CAT-A33 and CAT-A32 coordinated their relief efforts with the international volunteer organizations struggling to deliver private assistance and foreign government aid to needy Afghans.[34] Tactical PSYOP Team (TPT) 922 used its loudspeakers to play music and broadcast anti-*Taliban* messages to the largely illiterate population throughout the city. It also passed out information leaflets to the Afghan populace and posted handbills in central locations.[35]

On 10 November 2001, the date of the first major victory at Mazar-e-Sharif, CENTCOM had more than 50,000 American servicemen and women in its theater of operations, one that extended from the Red Sea to the Indian Ocean.[36] Of those personnel, approximately half were aboard U.S. naval vessels in the Arabian Sea, 3,000-plus were in Oman, and almost 2,000 were in Uzbekistan at Stronghold Freedom on K2 Air Base. In the skies over the CENTCOM area of responsibility (AOR), there were 400 Air Force and Navy combat aircraft, including those patrolling "no-fly" zones over Iraq, flying sorties almost every day. In the United Arab Emirates, Kuwait, Yemen, and Jordan, 5th SFG units conducted maneuvers and trained the special operations forces of those countries. These military exercises, planned and coordinated more than one year before the 9/11 attacks, were considered essential to shore up the counterterrorist capabilities of friendly countries in the region. The American Special Forces teams were eager to "get in the Afghan fight" and were prepared to move to Uzbekistan as soon as they finished their training obligations. In Afghanistan, Defense Secretary Rumsfeld only admitted that an unspecified number of U.S. troops were at "four locations" somewhere in a vast area the size of Texas.[37] On the ground, the UW campaign to topple the *Taliban* regime was being directed by about 130 U.S. Army Special Forces, CA, and PSYOP soldiers and a handful of Air Force special tactics airstrike controllers.[38]

With the 10 November fall of Mazar-e-Sharif, the second largest city in Afghanistan, others fell in rapid succession to the growing anti-*Taliban* forces. The towns of Bamian in the central region, Taloquan in the north, and Herat in the west surrendered within days, and Konduz was besieged.[39] Then, on 12 and 13 November, Northern Alliance forces, most of which rode standing, jam-packed in large Ginga (brand name) cargo trucks, literally drove from the trench lines at Bagram into the hastily abandoned capital of Kabul in less than 24 hours.[40] The following day, 14 November, Jalalabad fell, essentially closing the Khyber Pass access route to the *Taliban* and their Pakistani supporters.[41] Just before Thanksgiving, the *Taliban* forces at Konduz capitulated after being threatened with annihilation by "angels of death"—the devastating AC-130 Spectre gunships that had rained down carpets of explosive shells without warning in the night—and the "death rays"—the target lasers—Army Special Forces used to guide smart bombs to their targets. Broadcasts in the local dialects accelerated surrender.[42]

In the midst of the constant aerial bombardment, hundreds of thousands of propaganda leaflets were dropped in special air-delivery bombs. Thus, when the U.S. warplanes came, *Taliban* fighters did not know whether they were going to be bombed or showered with paper. PSYOP units had designed the leaflets and printed them on their own massive presses at Fort Bragg for overseas shipment and distribution by "leaflet bombs" over Afghanistan. The PSYOP cells also produced radio programs with popular Dari and Pashto music—Afghan "greatest hits," as the PSYOP teams referred to them—intermixed with anti-*Taliban* and anti-*al-Qaeda* messages. They recorded these programs on mini discs, which were transmitted to Afghan listeners by airborne radio broadcast stations inside Air Force special operations EC-130 Commando Solo aircraft orbiting over the population centers in regular circuits over the country.[43]

As the offensive continued to gain momentum, coalition forces joined the U.S. effort in Afghanistan. One hundred British Royal Marines were met by U.S. Special Forces and other British troops when they landed at Bagram airfield on 15 November.[44] Pakistan, the only country to maintain diplomatic relations with the *Taliban* regime, closed the Afghan Embassy in Islamabad on 22 November.[45] Deft U.S. diplomatic negotiations had garnered forward bases for American and coalition forces in Pakistan, Uzbekistan, and later Tajikistan while simultaneously isolating the *Taliban* from its outside sources of money, personnel, and aid.[46]

MH-60L Direct Action Penetrator (DAP) helicopters from the 160th SOAR, when not providing armed escort to the MH-47Es inserting Special Forces ODAs, prowled Afghanistan hunting for, and then attacking, *Taliban* antiaircraft gun positions and truck-mounted systems that shifted about trying to ambush and shoot down the lumbering Chinooks. To extend the helicopters' range without aerial refueling and to expand area coverage by these roving helicopter prowlers, Army Rangers and Air

Figure 13. Lethal AH-6 "Little Bird" conducts a night raid.

Force special tactics airmen did a "mini Rhino-like" night parachute assault on 13 November to seize another desert airfield. Conducting a low-altitude combat parachute jump in total darkness directly on the airstrip, code-named Bastogne, the Rangers cleared the area for four small AH-6 helicopters called "Little Birds" by the 160th SOAR aviators. These Little Birds quickly flew off to attack a *Taliban* compound with rockets and machine gun fire, then returned to the airstrip to rearm and refuel for a second raid against another target. Before sunrise, the Army Rangers and the 160th SOAR's Little Birds were long gone from Bastogne. Within days, more Little Bird attack helicopter raids followed. To break the pattern, Air Force special operations MC-130s airlanded Army Rangers in heavily armed 4-x-4 trucks to drive cross-country nightly to seize different airstrips to support the Little Bird raids.

Even as *Taliban* resistance crumbled across the country, some enemy forces remained dangerous. One of the largest battles of the Afghanistan campaign was an *al-Qaeda* prisoner uprising that began on 25 November and lasted four days. Three to four hundred of the more fanatic enemy fighters that surrendered near the Mazar-e-Sharif airfield had been interned in the prison area of the 18th-century fortress of Qala-i-Jangi, which had also served as Dostum's headquarters. While the Uzbek leader was away directing the siege of Konduz, the prisoners turned on their guards in a violent uprising. The prisoners seized a large arsenal of weapons and ammunition that included mortars and RPG launchers.[47] In the melee that

Figure 14. Loading nonstandard tactical vehicles aboard an MH-47E.

followed, the prisoners attacked two CIA officers inside the fortress. One escaped and radioed for help.[48] Nearby, the staff of the headquarters section, 3rd Battalion, 5th SFG, and a squad of British troops hastily formed an *ad hoc* rescue force. While local militia struggled to keep the fanatical prisoners inside the fortress, the Army Special Forces and British troops fought for the next three days to find the missing American. Special Forces ODA 533 and an infantry rifle platoon from the 10th Mountain Division were rushed by MH-47E helicopters from K2 to reinforce the 3rd Battalion staff.[49] While the rescue force directed airstrikes against the heavily armed prisoners on 26 November, an errant 2,000-pound American bomb hit near U.S. forward positions.[50] The awesome explosive blast destroyed an Afghan tank and its crew and wounded four British and five Americans soldiers. The explosion also caused a large breach in the fortress wall that almost turned the battle in favor of the *al-Qaeda*.[51]

The fortuitous arrival of Air Force AC-130 Spectre gunships the next night salvaged a very desperate situation. After another day of tough combat, the body of missing intelligence officer Michael Spann was recovered.[52] The last of the surviving prisoners gave up a day later when their underground bunker was flooded with water.[53] John Walker Lindh, a 19-year-old American citizen who had fought with the *Taliban* and *al-Qaeda*, was discovered among the twice-surrendered prisoners. U.S. Special Forces soldiers, alerted by a journalist, found Walker at the Sherbergan prison the following day. The 3rd Battalion, 5th SFG surgeon, with the help

Figure 15. U.S. Air Force AC-130 Spectre gunship firing at night.

of several Special Forces medics, saved Walker from dying of hypothermia.[54] The prisoner uprising at Qala-i-Jangi quelled, the focus of the JSOTF-North staff shifted back to operations in southern Afghanistan.[55]

At K2 Air Base, the JSOTF-North headquarters operated around the clock. Stronghold Freedom had been established in three weeks. The effort required 60 C-17 Globemaster III jet transport sorties to move hundreds of soldiers and more than 2,200 tons of equipment to the former Soviet fighter base.[56] Many of the staff officers had been detailed from other commands and services to augment the 5th SFG staff nucleus sufficiently to function as a major JTF headquarters responsible for fighting the war in Afghanistan. Reorganized by COL Mulholland for missions dictated by constantly evolving events, Task Force (TF) Dagger's staff managed the daily operations, field requirements, and base support normally distributed among three subordinate battalion headquarters and nine Special Forces company ODB teams. Stronghold Freedom was a newly created tent city that was much like a Gold Rush "boom town" in the middle of nowhere. But this modern military base had a major airport, field hospital, warehouse complex, staging area, ammunition dump, barracks, isolation facility, and worldwide communications center.

While directing Special Forces detachments in combat in Afghanistan, the staff also dealt with pressing local matters, ranging from vehicle accidents to VIP visits and USO entertainers to cleaning up toxic waste dating back to the Soviet era. While daily routine tasks became automatic, JSOTF-North was simultaneously making history. The long-range night helicopter insertions of Special Forces teams deep into Afghanistan and the airstrikes and refueling flights launched from K2 were the first U.S. combat operations ever staged from a former Soviet republic. Both at K2 in Uzbekistan and at their home bases in the United States, the 160th SOAR maintenance crews kept the critical MH-47E Chinooks flying. Activated for the first time in 30 years, Army National Guard (ARNG) D Company, 109th Aviation Battalion,

Figure 16. D Company, 109th Maintenance Battalion, ARNG, reinforces the 160th SOAR.

provided midlevel maintenance to sustain operational Night Stalker helicopters worldwide. This became critical when Operation ENDURING FREEDOM spread to the Philippines and 160th SOAR Chinooks were required to support antiterrorist missions there.[57]

In southern Afghanistan, two anti-*Taliban* Pashtun leaders finally emerged—Hamad Karzai and Gul Agha Sherzai. Advised and assisted by Special Forces teams, the two led their forces toward Kandahar, the "spiritual capital of the *Taliban* movement." Karzai, a Pashtun, spoke perfect English. On 8 October, Karzai returned to Afghanistan from Pakistan where he had been living in exile. The anti-*Taliban* political leader and two companions shared two motorcycles during the ride into Oruzgan Province north of Kandahar.[58] When Karzai returned to Pakistan a few weeks later, he talked with several American special operations officers, imparting the latest intelligence gathered on the southern provinces and suggested themes and specific products for PSYOP programs.

Figure 17. Hamad Karzai poses
with Special Forces soldiers.

Special Forces ODA 574 followed Karzai to Tarin Kowt, Afghanistan, on 14 November aboard four MH-60K Black Hawk helicopters from the 160th SOAR, which could operate better at the lower elevations 70 miles north of Kandahar. Although Karzai had only a few dozen fighters, his unexpected presence in Tarin Kowt so alarmed the *Taliban* leaders in Kandahar that they sent about 1,000 fighters in a 100-truck convoy to retake the town. At dawn on 17 November, from a ridge above the valley, ODA 574 directed flight after flight of Air Force and Navy jet fighters against the approaching *Taliban* convoy. The smart bombs produced devastating results on the line of trucks. But to their surprise, in the midst of destroying the entire *Taliban* convoy, the Special Forces team had to abandon its overwatch position to rally Karzai's Pashtun fighters who fled at the sight of the large *Taliban* force. Despite this unexpected problem, ODA 574 still managed to destroy some 30 trucks loaded with enemy fighters, which prompted an enemy retreat to the south.[59] The arrival of the first American conventional ground forces in Afghanistan further raised the pressure on the *Taliban* in Kandahar. On Thanksgiving Day, two U.S. Marine Corps infantry battalions were helicoptered into Objective Rhino, the undefended compound and dirt airstrip in the desert 50 miles southwest of Kandahar. On the night of 19 October, an Army Ranger task force had conducted a parachute assault on Objective Rhino to support attack helicopter raids against *al-Qaeda* targets.[60] The reconnaissance element for the U.S. Marine operation was a three-man U.S. Navy SEAL element.[61]

As the scale of the victory at Tarin Kowt became apparent to the local populace, Karzai's tiny coterie of supporters grew to more than 100 fighters in two weeks.[62] This victory, which gained more followers, prompted COL Mulholland to send a Special Forces lieutenant colonel as his senior military adviser just before Karzai's movement south toward Kandahar to begin negotiations for the city's surrender.[63] In their movement south, Karzai's Pashtun fighters and the Special Forces soldiers turned back a second major *Taliban* attack on 4 December at the Sayd-Alim-Kalay bridge, 40 miles north of the provincial capital. The same day, the Americans heard by radio that Karzai was the leading candidate to become prime minister of the Afghan Interim Authority (AIA).[64]

Karzai almost did not accept the nomination. The next morning, 5 December, a misguided 2,000-pound bomb struck the hilltop where the Special Forces team had gathered around the Pashtun leader. The Air Force airstrike controller inadvertently sent incorrect target map co-ordinates to a B-52 bomber orbiting overhead. The bomb wiped out ODA 574, killing three and wounding the other nine team members. At least 23 Pashtun soldiers died instantly. Several other Americans and numerous Afghans were wounded as well, some from being hurled through the air by the force of the blast. Karzai was injured but refused to be evacuated for medical treatment.[65] As U.S. Marine Corps helicopters at Camp Rhino (the name given to the compound on Objective Rhino) and Air Force special operations MH-53 Pave Low helicopters and MC-130 Combat Talons at Jacobabad, Pakistan, rushed in surgical teams to care for and evacuate the wounded, JSOTF-North dispatched ODB 570 and replacements for ODA 574 to the scene. That same day, the U.S. Air Force flew the most seriously wounded Americans to military hospitals in Germany, and the U.S. Marines ferried the Afghans to U.S. Navy ships for treatment.[66]

As Hamad Karzai, indifferent to his wounds, parlayed with Mullah Naqib to peacefully surrender Kandahar, Gul Agha Sherzai captured the *Taliban* capital. In early November, Sherzai had crossed the mountains from Pakistan into the Shin Narai Valley, southeast of Kandahar. Special Forces ODA 583 was inserted by 160th SOAR MH-47Es to join him on the night of 19 November. In a series of battles, CAS teams from ODA 583 directed the aerial bombardment of *Taliban* forces day and night. This enabled Sherzai's Pashtuns to seize the highway from Kandahar to Spin Boldak, thereby cutting off the primary *Taliban* supply line from Pakistan. These Pashtuns attacked up the southern avenue of approach to Kandahar. By 3 December, while Karzai's troops attacked the bridge at Sayd-Alim-Kalay 40 miles from Kandahar, Sherzai's 2,000-man force was probing the airport defenses just south of the city. As Sherzai returned in triumph to Kandahar, the streets were crowded with thousands of cheering Afghans who threw marigolds at the American pickup trucks and shouted "Thank you!" in English to the Special Forces soldiers accompanying the Pashtun leader. Sherzai, the provincial political leader before the *Taliban* forced him into exile, reoccupied his former office in the governor's palace at midday on 7 December. This rekindled the struggle for control with Karzai's supporter, Mullah Naqeebullah, but every major Afghan city and town had now been liberated from *Taliban* control.[67]

The U.S. Marines at Camp Rhino relocated a week later to the Kandahar airport, guided through the city to their new base by Pashtun and U.S. Special Forces troops. The U.S. Marine force preceded the headquarters of the recently constituted Joint Special Operations Task Force–South (JSOTF-South) (Task Force Kabar), commanded by U.S. Navy Commodore Bob Harward. Based on orders from the commander, SOCCENT, RADM Calland, Harward had formed JSOTF-South around the nucleus of his Naval Special Warfare Group One (NSWG-1) staff based in San Diego, California.[68] Unlike the 5th SFG that provided the core of the JSOTF-North headquarters and most of its combat forces, Harward's training command had no assigned combat units. SOCCENT assigned A Company, 1st Battalion, 5th SFG, to Harward. A-1-5 was specially trained and equipped as a mobile strike force. It was suited to conducting direct action (DA) missions in Afghanistan. The 81 Special Forces soldiers of A-1-5 and the 19 other service attachments finished training in Kuwait and joined their new task force on Masirah Island off the coast of Oman. There, they prepared for the special reconnaissance (SR) and direct action (DA) operations that were expected to start with the New Year.[69]

Figure 18. Masirah Island off the coast of Oman.

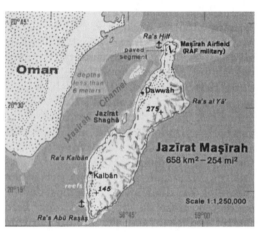

Figure 19. Masirah Airfield.

While the prisoner uprising at Qala-i-Jangi was being quelled and the Pashtun armies of Karzai and Sherzai were advancing on Kandahar from the north and south, allied aircraft began bombing the Tora Bora region 45 miles southwest of Jalalabad.[70] The Afghan resistance leaders claimed that Tora Bora contained the "last and strongest camp" of the *Taliban* army and *al-Qaeda* fighters.[71] Their estimates were that up to 1,200 enemy fighters from various parts of the country had congregated in the caves and tunnels there to rearm and regroup. CENTCOM headquarters directed COL Mulholland at JSOTF-North to send one Special Forces ODA to direct airstrikes for the Afghan militia units led by Commanders Hajji Mohammed Zaman and Hazrat Ali that would attack into that mountainous region.[72] SF ODA 572 was assigned that mission. After the aerial bombardment and Afghan militia ground battles in Tora Bora, other Special Forces teams climbed the rugged cliffs and escarpments searching for suspected cave openings spotted in aerial photographs. Afghan, British, and American Special Forces teams worked their way upward along narrow mountain trails to elevations as high as 15,000 feet above sea level where the air was thin and frostbite was a constant danger.[73] The allied air bombing and the ground searches continued through December into January.

American and allied Afghan forces managed to topple the *Taliban* government and most of its army in Afghanistan in two months.[74] In late September 2001, CENTCOM headquarters anticipated that the ground campaign would take two years.[75] By December, the nature of the UW campaign to destroy *al-Qaeda* and their *Taliban* sympathizers had changed.[76] CENTCOM and its anti-*Taliban* Afghan allies waged the initial phase of the war against enemy forces organized as conventional military units practicing orthodox tactics despite not having air superiority. This made them extremely vulnerable to conventional air attacks. The conflict took on the character of a true guerrilla war in December, as the surviving *Taliban* and *al-Qaeda* fighters scattered to distant mountain strongholds and cross-border sanctuaries and blended back into their neighborhoods in cities and towns across Afghanistan.[77]

The following soldier stories explain the ARSOF combat missions and duties in the early days of the UW campaign in Afghanistan. The essentially firsthand accounts are presented chronologically, adhering to the introductory presentation. These are the most representative stories that illustrate what was happening on the ground and in the air, and they have been cross-referenced for accuracy and completeness with headquarters records. They are intended to allow the reader to feel the danger, high stress, and determination of the young ARSOF soldiers as they endeavored to make everything work in combat as well as the vagaries associated with all warfare. One cannot help but be impressed by the élan and top-notch flying skills of the 160th SOAR pilots and the courage and bravery of the Rangers and Special Forces soldiers who strove to accomplish their missions against great odds.

Jumping Into the Dark: Seizing Rhino, 19 October 2001

At 1845Z (Zulu), 19 October 2001, Task Force 3/75 Ranger, with a regimental command and control element, conducted a night combat parachute assault to seize a remote desert landing strip (DLS) to destroy *Taliban* forces; gather intelligence; provide a casualty transload site for other simultaneous combat operations; establish a forward arming and refueling point (FARP) for rotary-wing aircraft; and assess the capabilities of the airstrip for future operations. Four Air Force special operations MC-130 Combat Talon aircraft dropped 199 Army Rangers at 800 feet above ground level (AGL) under zero illumination conditions to seize Objective Rhino.[78] This was the first Ranger combat parachute assault since Operation JUST CAUSE in Panama.

Objective Rhino, located southwest of Kandahar, Afghanistan, contained four separate objectives—Tin, Iron, Copper, and Cobalt. Air Force B-52 Stealth bombers had dropped 2,000-pound,

Figure 20. Shoulder scroll of the 3rd Battalion,
75th Ranger Regiment.

Figure 21. Receiving mission orders before departure.

Figure 22. 75th Rangers prepare for an airborne assault.

110

global positioning system (GPS)-guided bombs on Objective Tin before AC-130 Spectre gunships raked the target with heavy fire. Initial reports were that 11 enemy had been killed and nine were seen running away. The AC-130 aircrews had identified no targets on Iron. While they were unable to positively identify Copper from the air, they did fire on the buildings inside and the guard towers on the walls of Objective Cobalt.

A Company (-), 3rd Battalion, 75th Rangers, with an attached sniper team, had the mission to secure Objectives Tin and Iron and prevent enemy interdiction of Objective Cobalt and the landing strip. Specialist Four (SPC) Martin Pasquez (pseudonym) sensed how low the Combat Talon was flying when dust blew inside as the jump doors were lifted open. As the parachutists floated down in the darkness, SFC Ron Searcey (pseudonym) and his platoon used the fires on Objective Tin to orient themselves. Because airplanes and helicopters would be using the DLS, the Rangers had to bag their chutes and drop them clear of the strip. The Ranger task force was prepared for resistance, but only one enemy fighter appeared out of the darkness. Several Rangers of C Company swiftly shot him. Prior rehearsals paid off. The Rangers assembled quickly after the night drop, cleared Objective Iron, and established preplanned blocking positions to repel possible counterattacks.[79] The mission for the C Company platoons was to clear Objective Cobalt, the walled compound on Rhino. Although Spectre gunships had put devastating fire on the compound, damage was minimal. The thick concrete walls and building roofs (later discovered to be reinforced with rebar) had either absorbed the blasts or the cannon shells had punched through the roofs and ceilings leaving only holes. The guard towers were in the same condition. As the Rangers moved toward the walled compound, a loudspeaker team from the 9th POB broadcast tapes in three languages to encourage any remaining enemy fighters to surrender. Unbeknown to the Rangers, there was no one in the compound. Preassault fire had breached one wall, and that gap became the Ranger assault entry point into the compound. Well-rehearsed Ranger teams quickly moved to clear their assigned buildings and guard towers. Clearing the interiors of buildings proved difficult and took longer than anticipated. A number of rooms inside had locked steel doors that could be opened only with multiple shotgun blasts or explosive charges.[80]

Figure 23. Rangers preparing to seize Objective Rhino.

Figure 24. Parachute assault on Objective Rhino.

Fourteen minutes after C Company began clearing the compound, a Combat Talon landed with a medical team to treat those Rangers who had been injured on the jump. Six minutes later, the first flight of helicopters supporting another combat operation in the area flew in to be rearmed and refueled. Air Force special tactics squadron (STS) airmen were surveying the DLS to determine its capability to handle larger aircraft. As these activities were done, orbiting AC-130 Spectre gunships destroyed several enemy vehicles moving toward the airstrip and a group of people approaching on foot.

Figure 25. Rangers clearing Objective Cobalt.

112

Refueled and rearmed, the helicopters flew off as the Rangers who cleared Cobalt moved to board the MC-130s that had refueled the helicopters. TF 3/75 Ranger systematically drew in its combat elements, maintaining all-round security, to reload arriving MC-130 aircraft. After the final Combat Talon landed, the infrared airstrip markers were picked up, and TF 3/75 Ranger left Rhino 5 hours and 24 minutes after its parachute assault.[81]

Simultaneously with the parachute assault on Rhino, 26 Rangers from B Company, 3rd Battalion, 75th Rangers, and two Air Force STS airmen parachuted or airlanded on another airstrip, Objective Honda, to establish a support site for contingency operations related to Objective Rhino. As the second MH-60K helicopter flared on landing, the resulting "brownout" obscured the landing area, and the helicopter hit hard and tilted over on its side. Several soldiers aboard the aircraft were pinned under the Black Hawk wreckage. The mission quickly changed from supporting Rhino to rescuing the trapped soldiers and evacuating the friendly casualties. Unfortunately, two of the Rangers, Specialist Jonn Edmunds and Private First Class (PFC) Kristofor Stonesifer, were killed in the accident.[82]

True to their motto, "Rangers Lead the Way," the 3rd Battalion Rangers led the way in Afghanistan. Aboard MC-130s en route to Objectives Rhino and Honda, the Rangers, wearing their parachutes and loaded down with weapons and equipment, had recited the inspiring words of their creed. "Readily will I display the intestinal fortitude required to fight on to the Ranger objective and complete the mission."[83] Not only did they accomplish the mission but the Army Rangers also demonstrated that American military forces could strike swiftly, silently, and with deadly force day or night. They had shown the *Taliban* and *al-Qaeda* that there were no safe havens and that America could project its military power at will. CENTCOM commander GEN Franks said that the mission was an unequivocal success. "The objective was to prove . . . we will go anywhere we choose to go."[84] The *Taliban* and *al-Qaeda* learned that lesson on the night of 19 October. On 25 November, U.S. Marines occupied the site of the Ranger assault and designated their new facility Camp Rhino.[85]

Tactical PSYOP for Rhino

On 12 September 2001, Tactical PSYOP Detachment (TPD) 940, B Company, 9th POB, began target audience analysis for Afghanistan, specifically the *Taliban* regime, the Afghan populace, and the *al-Qaeda* network. Research continued until TPD 940 was sent to the 75th Ranger Regiment on 18 September, carrying its loudspeaker scripts that introduced forces, covered surrender appeals, and issued civilian noninterference warnings. After being briefed on Objective Rhino, TPD 940 decided to narrow its messages down to four. After several rehearsals with the Rangers, it departed for an initial staging base in the Middle East on 12 October, arriving there on the 14th.

For five days, TPD 940 conducted final planning, underwent several inspections, and participated in detailed rehearsals of actions on the objective. Inspections included personnel, weapons, ammunition, and combat equipment as well as the PSYOP product scripts and minidisc copies of the scripts in Urdu, Pashtun, and Arabic that would be used during the operation. The 9th POB Product Development Detachment (PDD) had also prepared leaflets that were to be left on the objective. They were to communicate America's resolve to stop terrorism and to let the enemy know that it had been there. Four of the most experienced PSYOP soldiers from TPD 940

Figure 26. 75th Ranger calling card.

were selected to make the parachute assault with the Ranger task force: SSG Jack Thomas, SGT Mario Perez, SGT Gene Ball, and Corporal (CPL) John MacGinnis (pseudonyms).[86]

On 19 October, the Ranger task force prepared for the parachute assault operation that night. Just before donning their parachutes, the Ranger commanders and sergeants major gave last-minute words of encouragement, and the 75th Ranger Regimental Chaplain invoked a blessing on the force. Everyone, wearing parachutes and full equipment, was packed aboard the MC-130 Combat Talon aircraft. Seated on the floor, the 4-hour flight was long, cold, and uneventful except for the occasional flare punctuating the darkness outside the paratroop doors. As TPD 940 flew to the objective, the soldiers' minds raced with possible scenarios of once they landed: "Would the drop zone be mined?" "How would they react to enemy contact?" What would they do if one of the team were wounded or killed?"

SSG Thomas described his recollections after jumping out of the MC-130 at 800 feet above the ground:

> It was completely black outside. . . . I could see one of the secondary objectives burning furiously from a bomb hit. . . . I heard sporadic fire coming from Rhino. . . . As I was descending, the last of the aircraft flew overhead, dropping its load of Rangers. Just as it passed over, flares started popping out of it, illuminating the night sky and the airfield below just in time to orient myself on the horizon and prepare to land. I hit the ground like a rock and promptly found myself entangled in parachute suspension lines and ¼-inch cotton webbing. I cut myself free, chambered a round in my weapon, activated my [night vision goggles] NVG, and scanned the immediate area for the enemy. Convinced that I was in no immediate danger, I gathered my chute and stuffed it into my kit bag, found a Ranger buddy, and moved to the assembly area.
>
> As we waited in the assembly area, my element leader spotted an unidentified person coming toward us from the vicinity of the compound. Several of us quickly acquired him and lased him with our PEQ-2s. Fire control was incredible as we watched and waited with lasers dancing all over the target until one found the glint tape arm band identifying him as a friendly Ranger. Once assembled, we moved toward our primary objective. [Tactical PSYOP Team]

TPT 943 (SGT Perez and CPL MacGinnis) was leading with TPT 941 (myself and SGT Ball) in trail. While moving toward the objective, gunfire erupted to our right rear flank. Our immediate response was to get down. Since we did not have a clear field of fire, we just stayed put. A lone Taliban had stumbled into a squad of Rangers guarding our right flank.

It was decided that another airstrike on the compound was necessary to ensure that no other enemy would walk into our formation by chance. Word was passed that an airstrike was imminent, so we lay flat on the ground, pulled security, and waited. The AC-130 Spectre gunship strike can only be described as impressive. I was awestruck because 500 meters from my location high-explosive shells were impacting on the compound. Once the strike was over, we moved to our initial broadcast position.

As the lead Ranger element moved toward the objective, SGT Ball and I set up our loud-speaker and began to broadcast our first message. It told anyone in the area that U.S. forces were present and that they needed to exit the buildings, stay away from the airfield, drop any weapons, and get down on the ground if they wanted to survive. We played the message for about 5 minutes. The broadcast resounded across the valley floor into the compound. There was no doubt that anyone in the area had fair warning. This done, we bounded forward to join the rest of the Ranger element at building #1, secured a room, and awaited orders.

We were told to assist in searching the building for any intelligence and weapons, and to be watchful for booby traps. We found a Soviet RPK machine gun with a belt of ammo in the feed tray, expended shell casings, belt links on the ground, a [rocket-propelled grenade] (RPG) launcher with 10 to 12 rounds nearby, and two AK-47 assault rifles. The rooms had articles of clothing strewn about, mattresses and bedding, and other personal effects. After collecting the weapons, we distributed about 400 leaflets in and around the building.

As we lifted off from the airfield to return to base, I proudly showed the machine gun on my back to those around me. We were all elated to have participated in and survived America's first ground strike against terrorism at Objective Rhino. I then got comfortable on the floor and went to sleep.[87]

The PSYOP broadcast team proved to be a combat multiplier for the Ranger task force deep in Afghanistan.

Showing American Power

"Good afternoon. Yesterday, U.S. military forces conducted ground operations in addition to our air operations in support of Operation Enduring Freedom. Under the direction of the President, . . . Special Operations Forces, including U.S. Army Rangers, deployed to Afghanistan. I have several video clips of yesterday's action to show you. You'll see troops exiting the C-130 aircraft and jumping onto the objective." These were the words of GEN Richard B. Myers, CJCS, at a press conference on 20 October 2001.[88] The events he referred to and the clips he showed were TF 3/75 Rangers parachuting onto a desert airstrip near Kandahar.

Seemingly unrelated to that press conference MAJ Walter Barstow (pseudonym) was ordered to report to a special operations command headquarters on 19 September. Although his primary specialty was military police, among his contemporaries, Barstow had several unique qualifications. This Nichols State University political science major was a master parachutist who had worked with the Rangers. With an alternate specialty of PSYOP, Barstow was waiting to assume command of C Company, 9th POB. Within a matter of hours, however, he and 14 members of the PDD were preparing for a new mission.[89]

Barstow had been briefed that his mission was to plan for PSYOP, to develop and produce

PSYOP products, and to distribute them throughout Afghanistan. To accomplish this, he reorganized the PDD around a core of PSYOP specialists from A Company and had two technicians, broadcasters, and their Digital Audio Production System from 3rd POB. Presciently, he brought computers capable of editing digital video. These assets gave him the ability to produce loudspeaker disks, a limited ability to print leaflets, and the ability to produce radio scripts for the Air Force EC-130 Commando Solo aircraft systems. Barstow was aboard an airplane bound for Masirah Island, Oman, on 10 October, knowing that the rest of the PDD would follow him two days later.

Like most Americans, Barstow and his team were immediately struck by the heat and humidity of Oman. Although they were personally uncomfortable living in those conditions, their greater concern was for their delicate, weather-sensitive equipment. The computers and printers had to be operated in an environmentally controlled work space. Once the PDD found a suitable place, installed and connected the environmental control unit, and tested its equipment, it could begin producing leaflets.

Within a week of arrival, the PDD team received a mission that was more sensitive than developing and printing PSYOP leaflets. Elements of 3rd Battalion, 75th Ranger Regiment, were to parachute onto a desert landing strip (DLS) near Kandahar to destroy *Taliban* forces and gather intelligence about the possible use of the strip for future operations. The media was constantly querying President Bush, Secretary of Defense Rumsfeld, and the CJCS about when American military ground forces would be committed in Afghanistan. The 3/75 Ranger raid became a golden opportunity not only to seize a military objective but also to demonstrate U.S. determination to root out and destroy *Taliban* and *al-Qaeda* forces. Barstow and the PDD were suddenly key players in that initiative.

Barstow learned what assets were available to film the Rangers on their objective. He found out that he would have the gun camera films from the AC-130 Spectres, Ranger combat cameramen, and videotapes from a Navy P-3C Orion command and control aircraft. The latter was of great interest because that aircraft had enhanced surveillance capability and could transmit real-time video imagery. This enabled Barstow and his PDD to capture the imagery and surveillance recordings and begin editing information immediately.[90]

Figure 27. U.S. Navy P-3C Orion aircraft.

Time was of the essence. Guidance from LTC Kim Battles (pseudonym), the special operations liaison officer in the Pentagon, was that the Secretary of Defense wanted film of the raid to be available for the major news networks to show during the Saturday news cycle on 20 October—the day after the planned Ranger raid. Because of the 9½-hour difference in time between Afghanistan and the east coast of the United States, Barstow knew he would have only a few hours to edit the videos and send a clip by satellite to the Pentagon for review. The edited version then had to be forwarded to the major networks to be incorporated into their broadcasts.[91]

As the video began to come in, Barstow realized he had about six hours of raw footage that had to be reduced to a 3-minute clip. He knew the Pentagon would then select segments to provide to the networks. The edited version had to clearly demonstrate American "boots on the ground" and to prove conclusively that those combat boots were on the ground in Afghanistan. Using their computer video editing capability, a combat cameraman and technicians from the PDD completed the task. Then, the communication section assigned it the highest dispatch priority and sent it to the Pentagon. LTC Battles received the video clip and rushed it to the Office of the Secretary of Defense (OSD) where it was carefully reviewed. On Saturday, 20 October, during his 12:10 p.m. news conference, CJCS GEN Myers showed the world what the U.S. Armed Forces had done the previous night in Afghanistan. The video soon was played on every major network and news channel across America.

The United States had sent a message to the *Taliban* and *al-Qaeda*. Myers told the assembled reporters: "One of the messages should be that we are capable of, at a time of our choosing, conducting the kind of operations we want to conduct." As MAJ Barstow and the soldiers of the 9th and 3rd POBs watched Myers' news conference, they had the satisfaction of knowing they had made a significant contribution in getting that message to the world. The United States was striking back.

"Look, We Have to Get the Special Forces Teams Into Afghanistan!"

After a week of aerial bombardment, Defense Secretary Rumsfeld ordered the next phase of the campaign against the *Taliban* and *al-Qaeda* in Afghanistan to begin. He wanted military forces on the ground in Afghanistan to collaborate with the Northern Alliance warlords and with those forces that were friendly to the coalition. It was imperative that Army Special Forces ODAs link up with allied Afghan forces to make the plan work. The primary means of infiltrating the ODAs was Army special operations helicopters flown by the airmen of the 160th SOAR. The Night Stalkers had trained to penetrate any environment in the world and in any weather to reach an objective on time to the standard of plus or minus 30 seconds. The rugged Hindu Kush Mountains in northeastern and central Afghanistan tested the endurance and mettle of the aircrews and the performance and capability limits of the aircraft.[92]

The precipitous granite-faced high-altitude mountain ranges created rapidly changing weather systems that were very difficult to forecast based on conventional computer models. There were times when the weather changed significantly by the hour. The terrain outside K2 rapidly soared from 6,000 feet to more than 16,000 feet mean sea level (MSL). Narrow mountainous valleys intensified and channelized the weather. Obscurations caused by precipitation and severe sandstorms that rose to more than 10,000 feet MSL forced helicopter pilots to fly in zero-visibility conditions for long hours.

The MH-47E Chinook could penetrate the obscured mountain ranges at these high altitudes. The MH-47E multimode radar (MMR) system permits pilots to fly in adverse weather with reduced visibility using its terrain following/terrain avoidance technology. The system cues the pilot to climb, descend, or turn to avoid obstacles and enables aviators to closely fly over and around rugged terrain approximately 300 feet above the ground using nap-of-the-earth (NOE) techniques, thereby evading enemy detection.

Imagine sitting very still in a chair with all four of your limbs fixed on a set of controls watching a 9-inch-square television screen 18 inches from your face. The pilot, often wearing NVG, is required to follow computer-generated directions that tell when to pull up on the controls, when to push down, and when to turn left or right. This procedure for terrain following requires continuous coordination between the pilot flying in response to computer cues and the second pilot, without NVG, who is navigating, announcing obstacles, and confirming the mission data via intercom. Then add simultaneously monitoring another small screen for forward-looking infrared radar (FLIR) that provides the pilots with limited situational awareness in obscured weather. This is not "seat-of-the-pants" flying.

The MH-60L Black Hawk Direct Action Penetrator (DAP) was designed to support the insertion of Army special operations teams deep in enemy territory to conduct SR and DA missions. Capable of providing armed escort as well as delivering a variety of ordnance, it has a sophisticated armament system, an integrated avionics suite that allows precise navigation, and a FLIR system that is superior to the MH-47E and enables the pilots to "see" through light obscurations. The DAP is not equipped with an MMR and must rely on tactical instrument flight to avoid mountainous terrain, essentially flying set altitudes above the highest terrain. Both aircraft can be refueled in the air. Knowing a little about the different capabilities of the two ARSOF aircraft and what was required to fly in zero visibility will help readers appreciate the flight demands on today's Night Stalkers.

Figure 28. 75th Rangers rehearsing a fast
rope infiltration from a 160th SOAR MH-60K.

Exact enemy locations were uncertain on the night of 19 October, but all knew that the antiaircraft artillery (AAA) threat was high. Without access to the bomb damage assessments from the air campaign, the 160th SOAR crews had little idea what percentage of the *Taliban's*

AAA had been destroyed during the first week of bombing. The attempt to infiltrate a Special Forces ODA into the Panjshir Valley on the night of 17 October had been unsuccessful because mountain obscurations had forced the two MH-47Es to turn around when they could not break out of the clouds at 10,000 feet MSL along the planned ingress course. Thus, the air mission for 19 October was to simultaneously infiltrate one ODA into Landing Zone (LZ) Elspeth to link up with Fahim Kahn and one ODA into LZ Albatross to link up with General Dostum. Politically, both warlords had to receive their Special Forces teams at the same time. On the night of 19 October, the infiltration missions of the two teams had to succeed according to the pressure being applied from senior leaders.[93]

Figure 29. Patriotism abounds at all hours.   Figure 30. High-mountain terrain obstructed the route.

With a timed separation, three consecutive flights of 160th SOAR helicopters lifted off from K2, Uzbekistan, in the darkness. The first sortie was a pair of MH-47Es followed by one MH-47E with two MH-60L DAPs, and the final sortie was a lone MH-47E carrying emergency fuel (the "fat cow") to serve as a forward arming and refueling point (FARP). Each flight of aircraft negotiated the obscured mountains of southeastern Uzbekistan. The Chinooks used their MMR, while the DAPs executed coordinated letdowns according to known terrain altitudes on their planned route that were cross-checked with the lead Chinook. Once each flight descended below the cloud layer, the aircraft rendezvoused with an Air Force special operations MC-130P tanker to refuel at approximately 3,000 feet MSL or 500 feet above the ground before crossing the Uzbekistan border. The single Chinook carrying the emergency fuel then broke off and flew to the southern border of Uzbekistan where it landed and waited for the other two flights to return.[94]

After refueling, the LZ Elspeth flight headed east and entered Afghanistan through Tajikistan. The visibility steadily decreased to near zero the farther south they flew because of a severe sandstorm in the high plains of northern Afghanistan. With Special Forces teams counting on them to get them to their LZ, the MH-47E helicopters separated and immediately began using the MMR to negotiate the terrain. Flying much the same route that had been unsuccessfully attempted two nights before, the flight of two climbed as it approached the mountain range and continued through the solid cloud layer. At 10,000 feet, the aircrews used the helicopter oxygen system to prevent hypoxia, a physiological condition resulting from a lack of oxygen in the blood that causes blackouts and, in extreme cases, death. Realizing the importance of the mission,

CPT John Gates (pseudonym), the air mission commander (AMC), said "Look, we have to get them in." CWO Arthur Solanis (pseudonym), the flight lead pilot, directed the aircraft to press onward. The rest of the ingress route was obscured in a blanket of clouds, and the crews relied on the helicopter's terrain-following radar.[95]

Figure 31. MH-47E clearing the "Bear" at night.

The route was planned to take advantage of narrow mountain passes. However, because clouds hid many of the mountain passes, the flight often had to estimate deviations to the course by relying on a paper map to locate alternate passes and avoid higher terrain. The flight of two MH-47Es had to climb to 16,500 feet, an unnerving altitude for any helicopter, to traverse the final ridgeline before entering the Panjshir Valley that was controlled by Northern Alliance forces. Once in the valley, the flight conducted a terrain-following letdown, relying solely on the aircrafts' computerized systems and radar to descend into clearer conditions.

When the MH-47Es hit the intended LZ, they had expected flashlights or fires marking the landing area but saw nothing. The two Chinooks cautiously landed and dropped off the ODA at 0300. Having seen a small group of Afghans approaching the Special Forces team, Solanis kept his crew chiefs on their miniguns and monitored his radios for an emergency evacuation call as they lifted off. None came as they orbited the landing area. Satisfied that the Special Forces had met their greeting party, Solanis turned the flight to its planned egress route.[96]

Again, they encountered the same conditions: marginal weather, mountain passes obscured, and poor visibility at even higher altitudes. At one point, the two helicopters flew up a narrow valley only to discover that they could not clear an obscured pass that approached 20,000 feet. Then, at that extreme high altitude where lift is severely reduced and winds are turbulent, the pilots of both aircraft had to execute a 180-degree hovering turn before retracing their entry path. The aviators faced a real predicament; they could look up and see the stars or down and barely see the ground, but they were unable to see anything directly in front of the aircraft. Solanis instructed the flight to revert to the original ingress route to negotiate the obscured mountain range. Predictably, the deviations caused the MH-47Es to burn more fuel than the pilots had planned. Then, to further complicate matters, while descending from the mountains, the flight again ran into dust storms in the flats of northern Afghanistan. Thus, by the time the two Chinooks crossed the border they were critically low on fuel, but the MC-130P tankers from the 9th Special Operations Squadron (SOS), true to their word, were waiting on station, and the flight refueled. Relying on the MMR a final time to negotiate the mountain range south of K2, the Night Stalker MH-47Es finally landed at the airfield after the more than eight grueling hours of flight—six hours of which was spent flying zero visibility in the clouds.[97]

The LZ Albatross flight of one MH-47E and two DAPs had a similar experience. After aerial refueling, CWO Alfred Mann (pseudonym), the flight lead in the Chinook, led the flight carefully around the populous town of Termiz, Uzbekistan, to fly southeast toward Tajikistan. Just beyond the Amu Darya River, the northern boundary between Uzbekistan and its neighbors, was potentially a high AAA threat area. Mann chose to avoid the area by deviating far to the east and then backtracking toward Mazar-e-Sharif to reach LZ Albatross undetected. But soon after penetrating Afghanistan, the flight of three encountered a severe sandstorm. The MH-47E crew began using its terrain-following radar to avoid obstacles.[98] The pair of MH-60L DAPs closed in on the lead Chinook, using the glow of its engine tail cones as reference points. The DAP pilots knew that as long as they stayed above the engine tail cones they would not fly into anything. Their main concern at this point was avoiding a collision with the other DAP.[99]

The flight pressed on. The pilots aboard the Chinook and the DAPs "white-knuckled" the flight controls and stayed intensely focused on the instrument panel and the little outside visibility that was available. The aircrew members and Special Forces team riding in the back of the MH-47E knew they were just along for the ride; their lives were in the hands of the pilots up front. The FLIR initially provided some comfort to the DAP pilots because it could "see" through the dust storm, but as the flight climbed to negotiate the mountains, the dust cloud was transformed into a solid white cloud. About 1½ hours into the flight, the DAPs, lacking a terrain-following radar capability, inadvertently lost sight of each other and the lead Chinook in the cloud blanket. The pilots on both DAPs executed their planned avoidance procedures and were able to climb clear and, with their aircraft infrared position lights illuminated, to regroup. The DAP pilots had pushed their aircraft capabilities to the extreme; the time had come to abort the escort mission and return to base. CWO Roger Charles (pseudonym), the DAP flight lead, explained his concerns to CPT Brian Jefferson (pseudonym), the AMC.[100] Both agreed that for safety reasons the two DAPs should break off. The formation separated; Charles led his flight on a return course as tactically as possible in limited visibility; Mann continued alone to insert the ODA.

The Chinook crew traversed *Taliban*-controlled areas around Mazar-e-Sharif and negotiated terrain in excess of 10,000 feet using the MMR. When they hit the valley that contained LZ Albatross, the pilots did a terrain-following radar letdown, breaking out of the clouds at about 500 feet above the ground. Despite the AAA threat, bad weather, and braving two hours of flying through enemy territory as a lone eagle, the Night Stalker MH-47E arrived at LZ Albatross on time. While the aircrew had been briefed to expect an LZ of loose gravel, the flaring of the big aircraft turned reality—4 inches of lightly packed dirt—into a brownout where a thick dust cloud enveloped the helicopter and prevented the pilots from seeing the ground. With Mann backing him up on the controls, CPT Jefferson continued the approach, relying on the hover symbology on the advanced avionics to land the helicopter at 0200. When the dust cleared, the MH-47E crew saw a group of Afghans approaching the helicopter carrying AK-47s and RPGs. They turned out to be Dostum's soldiers who had been guarding the LZ. The Special Forces team disembarked, gave the aircrew a "thumbs up" sign, and disappeared into the crowd.[101]

Mann adjusted his flight plan in the helicopter computer to egress and, confident that the Special Forces were secure, departed. The return route was almost a repeat of the entry—poor weather conditions, high terrain, and sandstorms. Without the burden of maintaining contact with the DAPs, the Chinook pilots returned at the best airspeed the aircraft could sustain, given the high altitudes. After crossing the Uzbekistan border, Mann met the MC-130P tanker at the right place and time, "hit the basket," and refueled for the final MMR leg to clear the mountain range southeast of K2. It had been a 5½-hour mission with 3½ grueling hours of flying blind in the clouds.[102]

Earlier, the DAP flight had crossed the border without incident, refueled, and returned to the airfield. The FARP Chinook lifted off from its location after all flights had crossed back into Uzbekistan and successfully refueled from the MC-130P tankers.

The Joint Special Operations Air Component–North (JSOAC-North) used the full spectrum of its air assets to complete the mission. The insertion of the two Special Forces ODAs deep into Afghanistan while TF 3/75 Rangers were parachute assaulting Objective Rhino had been accomplished by the highly trained, dedicated aircrews of the 160th SOAR and the 9th SOS. According to the Night Stalkers, the 9th SOS provided the best tanker support in theater. It was also a night of firsts for ARSOF aviation: MH-47Es served as the primary high-altitude, long-range insertion aircraft for the Special Forces teams going into combat; never before had Army helicopters flown in combat in zero-visibility conditions in obscured mountains that exceeded 16,000 feet in altitude for such long durations; and never before in Army rotary-wing aircraft history had an aircrew flown in combat more than two hours under oxygen. These 160th SOAR aircrews lived up to their motto, "Night Stalkers Don't Quit."

On Horseback With Dostum

Just after sunrise on 19 October 2001, in the Dari-a-Souf Valley in northern Afghanistan, CPT Mike Nash (pseudonym) waited for the man described in intelligence reports as a "ruthless warlord," who would likely be unreceptive to Americans, and who might even attempt to kill him at their first meeting.[103] General Rashid Dostum, commander of the largest armed faction in northern Afghanistan, was an ethnic Uzbek and former Soviet tank officer who had been fighting the *Taliban* in the canyons of the "valley of the river of caves" for years. Little else about him was known for certain.[104]

Nash and the 11 men of his Army Special Forces detachment, ODA 595, had arrived in the Dari-a-Souf Valley several hours earlier in the darkness, flown in aboard an MH-47E from the 160th SOAR. Relying on their MMR, the Night Stalker pilots flew the Special Forces soldiers over mountains higher than the Rockies through a night sandstorm that had forced the two MH-60L DAP escorts to abort and required an air refuel while flying at 110 knots just 300 feet above the ground. After two hours of NOE flying, weaving through narrow mountain valleys on a moonless night, the Chinook arrived at LZ Albatross, a small plowed field, at 0200, precisely on schedule. As arranged, a guide accompanied by his Afghan security guards awaited the team on the LZ. Emerging from the thick cloud of dust raised by the helicopter's downwash, the heavily robed Afghans appeared to one American like the "Sand People" from the movie "Star Wars." The guide led the Special Forces team into the darkness to a small mud-walled compound. There, the Special Forces soldiers formed a security perimeter with the Afghans around their new base.[105]

Then, Nash; his second in command, CWO Bill Phipps (pseudonym); and the team's senior NCO, MSG Pat Earnhardt (pseudonym) received a 3-hour intelligence update from the guide party. The sketchy personality profile of Dostum that Nash received in Uzbekistan was fleshed out by the guides who described the Uzbek warlord as a smart, pragmatic man who was eager for American Special Forces support. The meeting with Dostum had been set for 0800, but there was no sign of the Afghan general. At 0900, an advance guard of 30 Afghan horsemen galloped into the American base camp "armed to the teeth"—carrying AK-47 assault rifles, PK machine guns, and RPGs—and "looking pretty rough." Dostum and 20 more heavily armed riders trailed the security party. Halting by the Americans, Dostum jumped off his horse, strode up to the Special Forces soldiers, and welcomed each with a firm handshake.[106]

Figure 32. Dostum travels in a more traditional way.

Dostum, Nash, Phipps, and two of the guides, one of whom spoke Dari and served as translator, sat on a mound of carpets inside the walled compound. They drank a cup of hot *shai*—Afghan tea—before the general spread out his map and explained his long-term strategy and immediate campaign plan.[107] Nash sized up the Uzbek general. In the isolation facility (ISOFAC) tents at K2, the JSOTF-North staff had described Dostum to the Special Forces team as "frail," "crippled," and weak from diabetes. "This guy's healthy as an ox," thought Nash, "and much bigger than the average Afghan, maybe six foot one or two inches tall, about two hundred and thirty pounds, and definitely the man in charge." With close-cropped gray hair and a short beard, the deep-voiced Dostum looked Nash in the eye when he spoke. He shook hands frequently, in a confident, friendly way. Then, abruptly, the meeting was over. Dostum jumped up and announced that he wanted CPT Nash and three other Americans to accompany him on horseback to his command post several hours' ride to the west. They were to leave in 15 minutes. Their rucksacks would be delivered by mules later, he assured the Americans. Nash asked that two more Special Forces sergeants accompany the party, and the general relented. Nash quickly chose the men for his "split team" element. He took five NCOs: his intelligence specialist, a medic, two communications specialists, and a weapons sergeant—Al Mix, Barry Ball, Vinsong Ming, Paul Wannamaker, and Sol Kitts (pseudonyms). They hurriedly repacked their rucksacks so they would fit aboard their three donkeys. CWO Phipps and team sergeant, Earnhardt, stayed behind with the other half of the detachment—Sam Bagby, Wes Snow, Mark Exley, and Carey James (pseudonyms). They were to establish their base camp; organize the logistics of the Afghan-American force with Satar Hahn, Dostum's supply officer; and receive the resupply bundles being airdropped on the LZ that night. Then Dostum rode off toward Dehi, leaving behind 10 of his security guards to lead the Americans to his command post.[108]

123

Figure 33. Pack mules and rucksacks—
a good combination for ODA 595.

It was a pure coincidence that the Special Forces captain chosen to ride with Dostum was the best horseman in 5th SFG. The lean, sandy-haired Nash was raised in north central Kansas on his parents' cattle ranch and had competed in collegiate rodeo while he earned his degree in biology at Kansas State University. Initially, ODA 595 had been sent to Uzbekistan to accompany Army helicopters performing combat search-and-rescue (CSAR) operations in northern Afghanistan. Air Force special tactics personnel had arrived a week before the Army detachment, though, and were already on the job. Nash's original mission was

Figure 34. Mobility issues were overcome by an old-fashioned solution.

Figure 35. ODA 595's second echelon moves
to link up with Dostum's main body of fighters.

124

subsequently cancelled, and his men went to work putting up tents for the JSOTF-North head-quarters. The team was without a mission until, by chance, it was selected to support General Dostum's anti-*Taliban* force. The intelligence staffs had not discovered that Dostum's 2,000 troops were horse-mounted cavalrymen nor that Nash grew up as a cowboy.[109]

As the combined entourage moved up a narrow, rocky trail, Nash took measure of his team's mounts. They were "tough little mountain ponies," he noted, "like American mustangs from out West." The Afghan horses were all stallions that pushed, bumped, and bit each other if they got close. The primitive saddles were too small for the American soldiers, and the stir-rups were too short and nonadjustable. This forced the Special Forces soldiers to ride with their knees bent uncomfortably. The brass stirrups were also small and narrow; fine for the Afghans, but American combat boots stuck in them. The real danger, Nash realized, would be if anyone fell from his horse on the narrow mountain trails. He then issued the first of several

Figure 36. An American Special Forces soldier on his Afghan horse.

"Horse SOPs" to the men: "Keep your feet light in the stirrups," he ordered. "If any-one is thrown by his mount and has a foot caught in the stirrup and the horse doesn't stop immediately, the nearest man has to shoot the horse dead." "You'll be killed if you're dragged on this rocky ground," he warned his team. The SOPs were closely heeded. Although not as accomplished as Nash, Wannamaker had learned to ride as a boy in South Dakota. The other sergeants were all novices; several were first timers on horseback.[110]

ODA 595 Begins Bombing *Taliban* Defenses

The horseback ride to Dostum's command post was a journey back in time. When the Special Forces soldiers passed through the village of Dehi, CPT Nash felt like he was "riding through Biblical Jerusalem."[111] There were steep, barren brown mountains, the dirt trail, the mud huts, and not a single sign of modernity, save the muzzles of the Kalashnikov assault rifles poking out from underneath the bearded men's blanket-like robes. General Dostum had rallied some 300 fighters near Dehi, all rough-looking and well-armed *mujahideen* warriors. Their guides warned them about the village and its "hair-trigger reputation," advising them, "Don't hang out in Dehi." As they rode slowly down the street through the crowd of glaring onlook-ers, Nash told his team to assume the Special Forces version of a politician's "grip and grin." "Smile and wave with one hand," said the captain, "and grip your weapon tight with the other, ready to fire."[112]

On the ride to Dostum's mountain redoubt, Nash concluded that communicating with his new Afghan allies would not be easy. While Dostum proficiently spoke several dialects and languages, including Uzbek, Dari, Pashto, and Russian, Five-Nine-Five was lacking in that key area. The team had long prepared for operations in the Middle East; thus, most team members were schooled in Arabic and French. Nash knew enough Russian to converse at the "caveman level," and he was worried that he would not be able to talk with the Uzbek general that he was to support. The problem was alleviated in the afternoon when a middle-aged Afghan named Maqdoom came to the Dehi camp and introduced himself to Nash.[113] Maqdoom could speak passable English. He became the translator for Nash in the leaders' meetings.[114]

On 21 October, General Dostum led the Special Forces from his mountain command post to the front lines where Nash proposed to direct the aerial bombardment of the *Taliban* forces. Oddly, Nash observed, Dostum seemed very protective of him and his teammates. In addition to surrounding them with his personal bodyguards, Dostum would not allow the American soldiers any closer than 8 kilometers (km) from the *Taliban* front lines on a distant ridge. Nash's team used the global positioning satellite receiver to confirm their position, and then through the brownish haze plotted an azimuth and calculated the distance to a far-off enemy bunker. With this data, they plotted the map grid coordinates of the targeted bunker and radioed the coordinate numbers to a B-52 bomber high above.[115]

Figure 37. A middle-aged Afghan man.

The single B-52 bomber was flying 20-minute racetrack circuits in the sky 20,000 feet overhead, dropping a single smart bomb on each pass. The first two bombs impacted a mile west of the target. That was when Nash observed almost 100 *Taliban* fighters climb out of their trenches to watch the bomber as it left thin white oblong circles of contrail vapor overhead, ap-

126

parently oblivious to the danger. The third bomb came the closest, hitting only 200 yards from the bunker. Nash radioed adjustments to the B-52, but the next three bombs struck more than 2 miles farther away, in a different direction each time. Frustrated, Nash watched the *Taliban* troops disdainfully gather around the closest bomb crater. Disappointed with the results, Nash cancelled the B-52 bombing after the sixth pass.

General Dostum, however, was buoyant. Maqdoom, the translator, explained, "You made an aircraft appear and drop bombs. General Dostum is very happy."[116] Physical damage to the *Taliban* defenses was not as important to Dostum as the psychological impact the massive bombs had on the *Taliban* soldiers, the translator told Nash. Dostum's communications chief was able to tune in to the *Taliban*'s radio frequencies and, by listening to the chatter, gather intelligence. As the B-52 flew away, General Dostum picked up a walkie-talkie set to the enemy's frequency and announced to the *Taliban* commander across the gorge, "This is General Dostum speaking. I am here, and I have brought the Americans with me."[117]

Figure 38. JDAM strikes were a morale booster for Dostum.

Dostum was constantly on his satellite telephone. Riding at his side, CPT Nash heard him answer calls from journalists, national political leaders from Russia and Pakistan, and a U.S. Congressman. According to Maqdoom, the journalists repeatedly asked the general if American commandos had joined him. "No," he would reply, "the only foreigners in his camp were some aid workers assisting his own soldiers." This became an "in-house" joke between Dostum and ODA 595, with the general referring to the Special Forces soldiers as "humanitarian aid workers who were in Afghanistan to distribute 'lead' to the *Taliban*."[118]

Aerial Resupply From the Receiver

While in isolation at K2 preparing for its mission, ODA 595 had planned for a year-long stay in the Dari-a-Souf Valley.[119] All it would be able to carry with it on the helicopter into

Afghanistan was what it could carry in pockets and rucksacks. The other supplies the team would need to survive the winter, as well as organize and train the anti-*Taliban* resistance force with whom it would work, were packed in bundles for later parachute airdrops. These resupply bundles would be dropped, one or two at a time, from Air Force special operations MC-130 Combat Talon four-engine turboprop transports. The Air Force aircrews who were to deliver the resupply bundles had told Team ODA 595 in the ISOFAC, "All we need is a center point on your drop zone, and we'll drop the bundle within 100 meters." The drop altitude, they said, would only be 300 to 400 feet above the ground to ensure surface winds would not blow the parachute-supported bundle far from the center point. This was how the aircrews trained, and during joint exercises in the United States and the Middle East, the Special Forces detachment had witnessed bundle drops made with bulls-eye accuracy.[120]

The difficulty of flying through the deep valleys of the Hindu Kush at night dramatically altered these plans. On ODA 595's first full night inside Afghanistan, a medical bundle was to be delivered. As CWO Phipps waited on the drop zone, he noted that the Combat Talon made its approach at almost 1,500 feet above the valley floor. Needless to say, the bundle landed ½ mile away. Each subsequent night, Phipps watched the lumbering MC-130 transport fly the approach lower and lower, until the aircraft finally got down to an altitude of 800 feet, dropping that night's resupply bundles directly on the small riverbed drop zone. As they rapidly gained experience flying at night in the harrowing conditions common to Afghanistan, the Air Force Talons made "nothin' but net" parachute drops of resupply bundles onto drop zones no bigger than a tennis court.

After having to spend most of their initial days in Afghanistan on horseback, Nash wanted better saddles for the American team. He knew exactly what was needed—either the McClellan or the Australian saddle. These types were both lightweight, essential to prevent overloading the small Afghan stallions already burdened with about 75 pounds of blanket, saddle, feed, and bridles. The saddles that Nash wanted had adjustable stirrups. He specified that the McClellans must have saddle horns for the rider to hold onto to maintain balance while traversing the steep, winding trails. The canvas Australian saddle had a curved aluminum bar in front as part of its frame to serve that purpose. When Nash radioed his request by digital transmission, he also emphasized that he did not want the Western trail saddle. That saddle was fine for big American quarterhorses, but it was too large and heavy for the Afghan mountain ponies.[121] Three weeks later in mid-November, after ODA 595 had fought its way out of the Balkh Valley and into Mazar-e-Sharif, the team received two bundles with saddles by parachute drop. One set of saddles came from Fort Campbell, Kentucky, their home base, that the 5th SFG comptroller purchased. They were cordura nylon versions of the canvas Australian saddle, called "endurance riding saddles," and were quite adequate for the task Nash had in mind.[122]

The second set came from the 21st Theater Army Support Command in Germany, purchased from a local Western store.[123] "They were exactly what I said I didn't want," said Nash when he saw the heavy leather imitation Western trail saddles, well-ornamented with rows of nickel studs. At this point, it no longer mattered. Having defeated the *Taliban* and broken out onto the northern Afghanistan plain, the team had returned their horses and were now riding in small pickup trucks. Before leaving for Konduz, they turned the saddles over to the staff of the newly established Special Forces Forward Operating Base (FOB) 53.

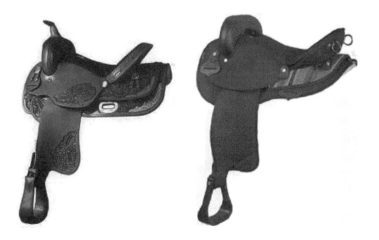

Figure 39. 40-pound Western leather saddle (left)
instead of requested 15-pound Cordura saddle (right).

Aerial Resupply by SOCEUR

Aerial resupply might appear simple to a casual observer, but combat experience from World War II, Korea, Vietnam, and even the humanitarian relief efforts of today have revealed how difficult the task can be. Weather and terrain do significantly impact aerial resupply because aircraft carry the loads, and most are delivered by parachute. Supporting the war efforts in Afghanistan by air from faraway supply bases several hours distant complicated the task for logisticians doing their best to meet the needs of the combat forces. The next vignette will discuss aerial resupply from the provider's perspective.

BG Les Fuller and his Special Operations Command, Europe (SOCEUR) managed aerial resupply for the Army Special Forces on the ground inside Afghanistan. When the 9/11 attacks occurred, Fuller and his staff were two weeks into a combined field exercise that had to be truncated so that participating American units could return to their bases in the United States. The U.S. European Command (EUCOM) ordered another operation in Bosnia-Herzegovina starting

Figure 40. GEN Holland and BG Fuller with COL Mulholland.

129

on 25 September to proceed. Thus, American special operations forces (SOF) deployed to Sarajevo under Fuller's direction where they helped police locate and arrest several terrorists, including suspected *al-Qaeda* members. The war on terrorism had begun for SOCEUR.[124]

When BG Fuller and his contingent returned to Stuttgart, he received orders to provide aerial resupply to SOF in Operation ENDURING FREEDOM. CENTCOM had tasked EUCOM to carry out this mission. SOCEUR got the mission and the authority to use $64 million of Title 10 funds to purchase the supplies that the Special Forces teams standing ready to enter Afghanistan would need. By 20 October, the day after the first Special Forces ODAs were infiltrated into Afghanistan, Fuller established a SOCEUR forward echelon at Incirlik Air Base, Turkey. This element soon grew to 250 personnel. Manpower for Incirlik came from the SOCEUR staff, including the J4 staff logistics officer, Air Force personnel from the 16th and 352nd Special Operations Wings (SOWs), the 5th SFG, and communications specialists from the SOCEUR signal detachment.[125] Fuller's deputy commander and chief of staff, both colonels, rotated the responsibility of commanding the SOCEUR element in Turkey monthly. To help with the logistics and aircraft coordination, Fuller sent two sergeants from C Company, 1st Battalion, 10th SFG, Stuttgart, to the CJSOTF-North base at K2, Uzbekistan.[126] The 21st Theater Army Support Command (TASCOM), U.S. Army, Europe (USAREUR), later sent part of the support battalion and parachute riggers from the 5th Quartermaster (QM) Company to Kaiserslautern, Germany, to assist with the steadily growing workload at Incirlik.[127]

The demand for aerial resupply grew every day. CENTCOM gave Fuller the JSOTF-North-generated list of 256 preplanned supply bundles that had to be assembled and prepared for parachute delivery at various dates over the next six months.[128] Fuller's number one priority, however, was to acquire and deliver red wheat and blankets to help America's new Afghan allies survive the coming winter in their mountain retreats. In Texas and Montana, Fuller's staff found the special red wheat that met CENTCOM's stipulated requirements and had the grain expeditiously flown to Ramstein, Germany, and then to Incirlik on scheduled C-5B Galaxy and C-17 Globemaster III jet transports.[129] In Turkey, the wheat and blankets were transloaded onto C-130 Hercules turboprop transports for the final leg to Afghanistan.[130] The red wheat and blanket drops went on for two weeks and stopped when Afghan Northern Alliance forces began a general offensive against the *Taliban*. However, the line of supply remained the same: items the Special Forces teams in Afghanistan requested were collected and packed at Kaiserslautern and Ramstein, flown by jet to Incirlik, then carried by tactical transports to their destinations. German parachute riggers helped the 5th QM Company (Air Delivery) [QM (AD)] and the USAR 421st QM (AD) Company from Fort Valley, Georgia, pack the non-lethal aid bundles.[131]

Figure 41. Units worked very long hours to support resupply demands.

Four U.S. Air Force MC-130 Combat Talon transports from the 16th SOW flew the first aerial resupply mission into Afghanistan on 22 October 2001. They took off from Incirlik at about 1500, local time, to arrive over their drop zones in darkness. The 14-hour round trip required two in-flight refuels. A Space Command representative at Incirlik provided digital maps to the pilots of the Combat Talons to help them program "way points" along their flight route. The drop altitude, the altitude at which the cargo was to be dropped by parachute, was typically 1,000 feet above the drop zone or lower for these aircrews. Visual contact or communications with someone on the ground was the requisite for all lethal aid drops.

SOCEUR did not conduct the high-altitude drops of the yellow-plastic-wrapped humanitarian rations (later blue wrapped) that were scattered for miles and that received considerable coverage in the international news. Conventional Air Force C-17 transport crews dropped their humanitarian rations 29,000 feet above the ground, beyond the range of any antiaircraft missile that the *Taliban* was thought to possess. Humanitarian aid could also be dropped without having communications with anyone on the ground.[132]

Problems arose constantly. Fuller, the senior Green Beret in Europe, was frustrated by Special Forces ODAs in Afghanistan sending urgent resupply requests without specifics. On any given morning, SOCEUR could receive messages demanding the impossible—delivery that same evening. The time just to transload cargo at Incirlik made these requests moot. Despite computer technology, all e-mail logistics requests had to be logged in to track the action until it was delivered and to provide strict accountability for those items purchased with Title 10 funds. SOCEUR also received pressing requests for special operations radios and night vision goggles (NVG), but none of those items were stocked in Europe and had to be ordered and transported from depots or stripped from units in the United States. This delayed fulfilling requests that Fuller knew from experience would be taken by the teams inside Afghanistan as "unresponsiveness" on the part of his command. He also felt that the Special Forces teams sometimes promised items to their Afghan allies that fell into the category of "unreasonable requests." In one instance that Fuller recalled, a team requested four all-terrain vehicles to be airdropped to them in Afghanistan in 18 hours. "These items were not available in Wal-Mart, let alone in Germany," said Fuller. "It's hard to get special ops items."[133]

Correspondingly, there were a number of problems on BG Fuller's end of the resupply pipeline. He had to call other general officers in Europe to get permission to include tobacco items and candy bars in resupply bundles. Fuller reminded them that EUCOM had turned down SOF requests from Somalia for tanks and AC-130 Spectre gunships before the debacle at Mogadishu. "Who are we to second-guess the requests from the soldiers on the ground?" asked BG Fuller. After initiating nightly video teleconferences (VTCs) with SOCCENT in Tampa, Fuller cancelled them after a month because they provided "nothing useful." That ended the direct coordination with SOCCENT. An early attempt to use high-velocity parachutes to drop critical gasoline and NVG padded with blankets and wheat was a total failure. All of the airdropped equipment and supplies "thundered in," and what was not destroyed was scattered everywhere. It also took some time before the 421st QM (AD) parachute riggers who assembled the bundles of supplies learned to make them "man-portable" from the drop zone. They repacked cold-weather clothing in duffel bags with handles and shoulder straps. Before the 21st TASCOM sent additional riggers to Germany and Turkey, SOCEUR was so short on manpower that Fuller observed "colonels and lieutenant colonels building pallets and packing ammunition bundles . . . it was truly a pick-up game." To Fuller, this demonstrated the "can-do" attitude prevalent in his command.[134]

A "Bump" and Missiles in the Abyss

The severe weather and high mountain terrain of northern Afghanistan tested the flying capabilities of the 160th SOAR pilots and the limitations of MH-47E Chinook helicopters during a critical resupply mission on the night of 23 October. A vast stationary front had settled along the Afghan-Uzbek border that thoroughly obscured the northeastern mountain ranges. The weather was horrible, and the terrain was extremely hazardous, which made the margin for flying errors miniscule, but the Special Forces team on the ground required special equipment, and "Night Stalkers Don't Quit." The detailed premission planning indicated that the potential for a mission abort existed at some time during the six-hour flight. But the 160th SOAR aircrews were mentally prepared for the long flight in the clouds at night in poor weather because they had been flying in these tough conditions for the past two weeks.

The flight of two MH-47E Chinooks lifted off in darkness from K2 Air Base without their MH-60L DAP escorts because the weather conditions in Afghanistan obscured the 8,000-foot "Bear," a steep mountain ridge just beyond K2. As they crossed into Afghanistan, the Chinooks once again encountered a sandstorm in the northern plains. Separated by several miles to avoid collision, the MH-47E pilots used their terrain-following radar along the same route toward the next mountain range. CW3 Arthur Solanis, the flight lead, noticed an image appear, disappear, and reappear on his radar screen before he determined that it was nonreflecting sand dunes—not a good sign.[135] As the flight began traversing the perilous mountain ridges, they relied solely on the aircraft systems as the "friendly" clouds masked them from enemy observation and potential antiaircraft fire.

The two Chinook crews had been flying in zero visibility for three hours when the lead aircraft reached the planned turnaround checkpoint. Solanis, the flight lead pilot, discussed the situation with CPT Gates (pseudonym), the air mission commander (AMC), and suggested that they proceed to LZ Albatross.[136] They had battled the environment to get this far, and the equipment aboard was said to be vital to the Special Forces ODA mission. Gates agreed, and Solanis radioed the trail Chinook, CW3 Derrick Donalds (pseudonym), of their decision to press on.[137]

As the flight continued toward LZ Albatross, the weather was slightly better than it had been earlier, but a dusty fog blanketed the valley containing the LZ. CW3 Donalds and his crew were able to visually close on the lead Chinook using their NVG and the FLIR since the fog was less dense at that altitude. The aircrew spotted the flashing infrared strobe that marked the LZ. As the lead Chinook made its approach to LZ Albatross, visibility was approaching a quarter of a mile. The lead MH-47E was to land while the second Chinook orbited overhead. Donalds slowed down and climbed a little above the lead Chinook to allow him space to maneuver in the narrow valley. Solanis told CW5 Brian Emerson (pseudonym), who was flying the cues generated by the radar, to overfly the objective so he could survey the area.[138] It was a tough LZ at the base of a horseshoe-shaped draw with steep terrain on all sides.

Solanis could see a strobe through his NVG when he took the controls to begin the

132

approach. He maintained sight with the ground, banking the helicopter to the right since he was in the right seat. As Solanis maneuvered in this attitude, the crew members in the back could distinguish the contrast colors of the terrain only by looking straight down. SSG Lee Clauden (pseudonym) shouted on the intercom to Solanis, "Hold your descent, sir!"[139] and immediately issued directives to climb "Up, up, up" as the distance between the Chinook and the "rising" terrain quickly evaporated. All four landing gear impacted simultaneously against the ground in a big bump!! Then the large helicopter "trampolined" off the sloping wall back into the mist. The Chinook attitude proved to be at exactly parallel to the terrain when it bounced off the ground. From above, CW3 Donalds saw both sets of helicopter rotor blades flex down, and a dust cloud puffed out from behind the Chinook. He knew they had just touched the ground.

Although startled, the pilots, with cool precision, held the lifting aircraft's attitude while quickly scanning multifunctional cockpit displays to gain situational awareness. The pilots confirmed that they were climbing and that the aircraft was clear of obstacles. The FLIR was still working but was locked in its last position, aimed at the LZ. Emerson quickly cycled the FLIR control and recovered full functions. The crew members in the back hung outside to confirm that all landing gear was still intact. No one had been injured during the bump and recovery. Once their beating hearts had slowed, CPT Gates and CWO Solanis decided that landing was too hazardous in these conditions. Solanis told Donalds that the flight was headed home. The two Chinooks reversed course, acquired separation, and headed into the obscured Hindu Kush Mountains, flying nap of the earth (NOE).

As the second helicopter had just cleared the final ridge at the edge of the northern plains and descended below the cloud layer at approximately 800 feet and while Solanis was focused on "a new city of lights" in the distance near the border, the crew in the back suddenly saw flashes in the clouds behind the trail Chinook. Donalds' aircrew also saw flashes, but they thought Air Force bombing was probably the reason. Later, Special Forces teams on the ground would report the flashes as antiaircraft artillery (AAA) fire. Then, as the two MH-47Es approached the border, Donalds reported a surface-to-air missile (SAM) launch at his 3 o'clock position. First he saw the booster motor flash and then the flight motor flash, but it exploded away from the helicopter. His right gunner also saw the flash. The automatic flare dispenser did not discharge because the missile never got close. But just seconds later, two volleys of flares were launched from Donalds' aircraft. The crews on both aircraft watched as the missiles exploded safely away from the Chinook. For the crews, it was a tense moment, but all were relieved when the flares worked as advertised. The flight crossed into Uzbekistan minutes later and returned to K2 Air Base without further incident.[140]

The Night Stalker pilots battled the environment for hours to arrive at their objective on time. Weather conditions compounded the landing risks posed by extreme terrain hazards that surrounded the LZ on three sides. Still, they persevered. The "icy cool" recovery from the bump experience demonstrated how good the 160th SOAR pilots were, but the "envelope had been pushed to the extreme" and further risk to the crew and aircraft was out of the question. It was not "life or limb" on the ground, and the air mission was only half over. They still had to deal with the terrain and weather systems, in reverse order, and the threat of AAA required constant vigilance by every crewman if they were to survive to fly tomorrow's SOF missions.

500 Afghans Can Die, But Not One American Can Be Injured

Figure 42. Bodyguards for the Special Forces team.

Rapport between General Dostum and his commanders and Special Forces ODA 595 improved with each bomb that was directed on the *Taliban*. Yet, CPT Nash had to improve the effectiveness of the bombing, and that meant getting closer to the enemy. Although he repeatedly insisted, the Uzbek general objected.[141] "Five hundred of my men can die," Dostum told Nash, "but not one American can even be injured or you will leave." Dostum was convinced that if any U.S. soldier was killed, the U.S. government would withdraw all Americans from Afghanistan.

Nash knew that Dostum had assigned his own bodyguards to protect the Special Forces troops but did not discover until later that the bodyguards were threatened with death should anything happen to the *Ameriki*. By continually pressing the matter at every meeting of commanders for two days, the general relented, having seen Nash under fire and been assured that the United States would not renege on its commitment to support him with soldiers.[142]

Figure 43. General Dostum sharing a meal with Special Forces personnel.

AAA = A Bad Night in the Hindu Kush

As the number of Special Forces ODAs being inserted in Afghanistan increased, the 160th SOAR aviators knew the enemy was becoming familiar with flight routes and how the helicopters operated. There were only so many avenues of approach through the mountain ranges, and these shrank considerably when the weather turned particularly bad. Enemy agents were known to be present along the borders, and the *Taliban* was known to have links with the Islamic Movement of Uzbekistan (IMU). Intelligence resources identified a pattern of increased activity along the border at the planned penetration points and times. To protect themselves, the Night Stalkers varied ingress routes across the border since they were never confident of the true threat picture. The intelligence section (S2) provided the best analysis based on the amount of data available. The weather remained as much a threat as the *Taliban* and *al-Qaeda* in October, but Special Forces ODAs had to be infiltrated and, once on the ground, resupplied. The adverse weather proved to be both a blessing and a curse.

The mission on the night of 28 October was to insert a two-man Air Force special tactics squadron (STS) team into LZ Albatross and to resupply the ODA operating in the area. The air mission required four aircraft: a pair of MH-60L DAPs to provide armed escort and a pair of MH-47E Chinooks to carry the personnel and cargo. While all aircrews were confident they could reach the border, anticipated weather in the Afghan northern plains posed a problem for the DAPs, which did not have terrain-following radar. The intelligence officer had reported no new AAA threats along the flight route.

The flight of four helicopters lifted off from K2 in typical fashion, gained separation to cross the "Bear" (the high mountain just outside of K2), and descended to refuel with the MC-130P tankers before crossing the border. As anticipated, the now familiar sandstorms in the northern Afghan plains were waiting for the helicopter flight. About halfway across the plains, or flats as the pilots referred to them, visibility dropped to almost zero/zero conditions, forcing the DAPs to turn back. CW4 Roger Charles (pseudonym), the DAP flight lead, told CW3 Solanis, the Chinook flight lead, that they would meet them on the egress route if the weather improved.[143] CPT Gates, the AMC, concurred.[144] CW3 Donalds, in the trailing Chinook, automatically picked up separation as they flew toward the Hindu Kush Mountains.[145] As the two approached the Hindu Kush, they passed in and out of scattered clouds, all the way up the mountainside. At 9,000 feet mean sea level (MSL) visibility cleared. The moon was full, and illumination was near 100 percent as they cleared the mountain ridge.

As Donalds descended below the clouds on the other side, the crew could see the lead Chinook about 1½ miles ahead. The flight of two flew parallel to a ridge on the right, and occasionally, the Chinook's reflection could be seen moving across the ground below. Suddenly, the crew chief manning a side minigun spotted a flashlight being switched on and off from a cave embedded in the mountainside. Farther down the ridge another flashlight switched on and off from another cave, with the beam shining down to the valley floor. The significance of the flashing lights had not registered with Donalds and his copilot, CW3 Jerry Tucker (pseudonym), until missiles streaked upward from the valley floor.[146] Tucker, flying in the left seat, reacted to the sight of antimissile flares being "popped" by the lead Chinook by releasing his flares. Then crew members in both helicopters saw two missiles explode between them. The pilots in each Chinook began executing radical evasive maneuvers, banked hard right, and climbed over a parallel ridgeline to escape the AAA threat. In the melee, Donalds and Tucker lost sight of the lead, which had a third missile fired at it before the helicopter cleared the danger area. As the two MH-47Es crossed into a big valley, the weather cleared, and the two helicopters linked up before landing at LZ Albatross.

CW5 Emerson, flying lead with Solanis, landed on the LZ. The STS team disembarked and was met by the Special Forces team that took the resupply bundle. Meanwhile, Donalds and Tucker, circling above, had two vital aircraft systems fail simultaneously—his multimode radar (MMR) and forward-looking infrared radar (FLIR). Reminded by the clouds hovering above the ridgeline that he had to fly through the same weather system to get home, Donalds explained his problems and improvised a plan. He would climb to an altitude that cleared the terrain, and Solanis, in the lead, would relay pertinent information en route, verifying clearance altitudes and updating weather conditions, much as the Chinooks had done for the DAPs. The lead lifted off LZ Albatross and headed toward the ridgeline with the trail helicopter picking up separation as the two Chinooks approached rising terrain and the cloud layer. Within minutes, the pilots of the second MH-47E were flying strictly with their instruments, deviating only when cued by the lead.

Solanis updated Donalds on his position and weather conditions. After several minutes, the two helicopters reached a clear space between a layer of scattered clouds above and broken below, several miles and terrain features offset from their ingress route. When Donalds, in the trail aircraft, was abeam the area of the missile shots, he jokingly remarked, "Well guys, if it makes you feel any better, we are in good guy land now and should have no more problems getting home." After descending below the clouds into a big valley illuminated by a full moon, Donalds saw muzzle flashes in the valley ahead near Solanis' helicopter.

Simultaneously, SSG Clauden, the flight engineer in the lead helicopter, saw flashes and yelled, "Triple A, Triple A, Break right, Break right!" into the intercom.[147] As the missile exploded behind the lead, the automatic countermeasures system instantly deployed flares. Instinctively, Clauden also manually launched additional flares, inadvertently silhouetting the second Chinook. Antiaircraft shells exploded all around his helicopter. Emerson and Solanis ordered the crew chiefs manning the two M-134 miniguns to "Return fire!" They did so, but the radical, abrupt turns Emerson executed to break contact rendered the fire very ineffective. The gunners were either looking up at the stars or the ground and most of the time were just hanging on for the ride. Emerson told Donalds that they were taking fire and were heading into the clouds for protection. As Emerson climbed, Clauden saw flashlights being illuminated, sequentially marking their flight path. Fortuitously, a saddle in the ridgeline appeared that enabled Emerson to accelerate out of the ambush valley into another that appeared to be uninhabited. In their frantic effort to break out of the AAA ambush zone, the pilots in the lead Chinook aircraft lost radio contact with Donalds in the trailing MH-47E.

Figure 44. MH-47E deploying flares during a AAA threat.

Within moments after Emerson was fired on, the trail Chinook began receiving fire. SSG Tom Dugan (pseudonym), the flight engineer, yelled, "Turn left, Turn left, Triple A, Triple A!"

into the intercom.[148] On the opposite side of the beleaguered Chinook, SSG Michael Bartley (pseudonym) yelled, "Hold your left! Hold your left! We're right next to a cliff!"[149] Donalds, a former AH-1 attack helicopter pilot, took the flight controls and began using his "Cobra flying skills," as the crew would later say, "bank-rocking" the helicopter hard in opposite directions to snake his way though the AAA ambush as his crew members called out the directions of the incoming rounds. The AAA rounds exploded in big flashes around the Chinook, causing the night vision goggles (NVG) to temporarily shut down. Realizing that he was caught in a cross-fire between a machine gun and AAA on opposing ridges, Donalds dove for the valley floor 2,000 feet below. As he pushed the yoke forward, he remembered that Soviet helicopter pilots tried the same tactic only to find the real ambush near the bottom of the valley. Soviet aircraft lacked the power to climb over the terrain while evading. But there were no other options because AAA and red tracers were encircling the aircraft.

The aircrew in the back had been thrown to the floor and could not return fire with the aircraft miniguns. The smell of burnt cordite filled the helicopter. When Solanis radioed from the lead, Donalds ignored the call as he responded to the instructions from the crewmen and continued evasive maneuvers. The *Taliban* forces easily shifted fire. It was obvious that they could see the big Chinook. Suddenly, a rocket-propelled grenade (RPG) shot straight up from the far ridge where they were headed. It missed and did not explode. As the ground raced toward them, Donalds eased his descent and slipped into the dark shadows of the terrain for cover, flying 20 to 30 feet off the ground. The enemy flashlights sequentially tracked the Chinook about a mile down the valley. Then, seeing the same saddle in the ridgeline by which Emerson had escaped, Donalds broke contact and escaped. The *Taliban* had the Chinook in their grasp for a full minute and a half before the big bird broke free. Afterward, one crew member remarked, "I didn't think a Chinook could fly like that!"

Figure 45. Night Stalker crew chief.

Solanis had just started turning back when Donalds radioed that he had made it through. Relieved, Solanis returned to the planned egress route, traversing the remaining mountains with Donalds following several minutes behind. As the two Chinooks raced over the northern flats, CPT Gates told the DAP flight lead, Charles, to turn around because they were flying as fast as possible and the MH-60Ls would not be able to keep pace laden with weapons. Eventually, the Chinooks passed the DAPs and "hit" the refuel MC-130P. All aircraft returned to K2 without any further problems.

The mission debrief was short. The crew handed the intelligence officer the FLIR tapes, and Clauden announced, "We're going to bed." Some just went off by themselves to reflect on the recent events, while others simply laughed; all had cheated death again. CW3 Donalds stated simply, "It was a bad night." The next day, the S2 told the Chinook crews that they had flown over a *Taliban* division headquarters that had relocated after fighting Northern Alliance forces. Amazingly, the current intelligence assessment of the battlefield was simply, no new threats. Regardless, the close calls under fire on 28 October strengthened crew cohesion and instilled greater confidence among the Night Stalkers.

Getting a Handle on the Air Threat

Once the Special Forces ODAs were on the ground, there was enough human intelligence (HUMINT) that CWO Jefferson's intelligence staff, 2nd Battalion, 160th SOAR, and the Joint Special Operations Air Component–North (JSOAC-North) could develop the *Taliban* order of battle down to company-level elements. This was critical to the Night Stalker aircrews. CENTCOM analysts had only identified brigade-level units. With the mobility of the *Taliban* AAA, it could split up elements rapidly to cover the limited air routes in and out of Afghanistan. The 2/160 SOAR order of battle assessment proved to be so well developed that the JSOTF-North, the Combined Air Operations Center, the Combined Force Air Component Command, SOCCENT, and CENTCOM used it. This order of battle later contributed to the success of the bombing campaign.[150] Additionally, the JSOAC intelligence staff functioned as the targeting cell until the JSOTF received an Air Force F-16 targeting officer. When everything was enemy or "red" in Afghanistan, there were few concerns, but once friendly or "blue" forces were on the ground, the targeting became more difficult.

Fostering Faith and Providing Solace

Some ARSOF warriors carried state-of-the-art weapon systems into battle, some flew sophisticated helicopters great distances in terrible weather, but for a small group of soldiers, the power of prayer was their weapon. CPT Mark Knapp (pseudonym) was the chaplain of 2nd Battalion, 160th SOAR, at K2. The Southern Baptist chaplain was everywhere—at air mission briefings, in the maintenance area during flight preparations, on the flight line for departures, at the flight line when the Night Stalkers returned, and he was available when the crews awakened.[151]

Before leaving Campbell Army Airfield, Fort Campbell, Kentucky, Knapp had prayed for the soldiers' protection aboard the C-17 Globemaster III and C-5 Galaxy transports and en route. At K2, he started building a ministerial team, locating first, Air Force Chaplain Daniel Cook (pseudonym) and a few days later, Chaplain (LTC) Mark Bojune (pseudonym), 5th SFG chaplain with whom he shared a chapel back at Fort Campbell.[152] The three chaplains acquired a 50-person tent and, with footlockers of Bibles, the Koran, a Jewish Prayer Book, Jewish scriptures, Spanish Bibles, and dehydrated grape juice, they began to offer religious services at Stronghold Freedom. Quickly, it became standing room only for most services.[153]

In the manly, chest-thumping world of special operations, with its competitiveness, aggressiveness, and sense of urgency, a dichotomy existed between the operational world and the spiritual world, and the two did not necessarily mix. The special operations soldiers conducted intense, precise planning and detailed mission rehearsals; missing the slightest detail could cost lives. According to Chaplain Knapp, "We told the operational world what God was doing as a result of time spent in prayer." The Special Forces teams and 160th SOAR aircrews survived the challenges of severe weather; rough, high-altitude mountainous terrain; and AAA nightly, and helicopter maintenance was nearly perfect.[154] The SOF commanders recognized their chaplains' important roles. An invocation opened each daily staff update. Knapp was added to the air mission briefing agenda to ensure that those seeking solace had an opportunity to pray. On the flight line, he rendered a departing prayer for protection and success, and afterward, he was available for those who wanted to give thanks, especially after the most harrowing flights. B Company's 1SG Dan Garrison (pseudonym) made it a point to know where Knapp was during the day to direct personnel.[155]

AAA Payback Time

By mid-November, the weather had improved slightly, enabling the MH-60L DAPs to perform their armed escort of the MH-47E Chinooks. No longer hindered by sandstorms, CW4 Charles, the flight lead, knew the DAPs posed a formidable threat to *Taliban* forces hiding in the darkness. These Night Stalkers could get up close and personal.[156] However, not all *Taliban* and *al-Qaeda* forces were dissuaded by the presence of the armed escorts and took shots at passing helicopter flights. Although the city of Mazar-e-Sharif fell to Northern Alliance forces on 9 November, sizable pockets of "hard-core" Chechen *al-Qaeda* fighters continued to resist. *Taliban* heavy weapons changed hands, sometimes daily, as Commander Usted Atta and General Dostum maneuvered to control the second largest city in Afghanistan. Caught in the middle by this jostling were the Special Forces ODAs assigned to each leader and the 160th SOAR DAP crews with a strong desire to destroy enemy targets, especially the *Taliban* AAA assets. The rules of engagement (ROE) were clear when heavy weapons belonged exclusively to *Taliban* and *al-Qaeda* forces. The problem was the forces of rival warlords using "captured" equipment to "fire up" American helicopters to cause trouble.

On the night of 13 November, while escorting a pair of MH-47E Chinooks to Deh Dadi airfield, the DAPs received antiaircraft fire and had a missile fired at them from the vicinity of a school compound on the outskirts of Mazar-e-Sharif. The pilots executed evasive maneuvers as the automatic countermeasure systems launched flares. Unable to positively identify the site from which the missile came, neither DAP returned fire. CW4 Charles diverted CWO Alfred Mann, the Chinook flight lead, away from the suspected danger area.[157] After completing the mission and returning to K2, the pilots, during their debrief, were told that Chechen fighters were suspected to be operating out of a school in Mazar-e-Sharif.

Three nights later, on another armed escort mission to Deh Dadi airfield, Charles alerted CWO Walter McCracken (pseudonym), in the other DAP, that he had spotted a group of vehicles along the east-west road leading into Mazar-e-Sharif.[158] The two MH-60Ls maneuvered for a closer look, weapons at the ready. As they drew near, the gun crews identified a halted, strungout convoy composed of armored personnel carriers, a few tanks, and about 15 people standing about in the vicinity of Chemtal, a small village 15 km west of the city. Since Mazar-e-Sharif had fallen, the ROE had become more restrictive. The DAPs could not engage threats unless fired on without the air mission commander's (AMC's) approval. The request was denied because ownership of the military equipment could not be determined. The DAPs simply diverted the Chinooks around the cluster of vehicles.[159]

As the flight closed on Chemtal, Charles spotted two Soviet ZPUs with quad-mounted 14.5mm machine guns used for air defense. They were in the open with people 500 meters away. This time, approval to engage was granted because the ZPUs posed a threat to aircraft; they fell within the ROE. The people 500 meters away made them "free game." Charles and McCracken coordinated their attack runs and destroyed the ZPUs with 2.75-inch rockets and 30mm chain guns—rapid-fire cannon capable of shooting 625 rounds of high-explosive 30mm ammunition per minute. The people scattered for cover when they heard the DAPs roaring in on the ZPUs. A final pass confirmed that the two ZPUs were ruined. Charles relayed the information to the Chinooks and to TF Dagger. The DAP aircrews felt that they had accomplished what they were sent to Afghanistan to do. After two months of frustration, the Night Stalkers had killed something. The rest of the mission was uneventful, but when the crews returned to K2, morale was very high.

Bastogne in Afghanistan

Students of American military history readily will recognize the name "Bastogne" as the site of the epic World War II battle where BG Tony McAuliffe and the 101st Airborne Division stood their ground against repeated German assaults during the Battle of the Bulge. In November 2001, B Company, 3rd Battalion, 75th Rangers, made the second combat parachute assault during Operation ENDURING FREEDOM. Like their airborne predecessors, these Army Rangers made a daring night jump to do what those "Screaming Eagles" would not have imagined—to seize a desert landing strip (DLS) to support forward arming and refueling point (FARP) operations to facilitate attack helicopter raids on *Taliban* and *al-Qaeda* objectives in Afghanistan.

Figure 46. 75th Rangers conducting long-range armed reconnaissance.

At 1800Z, 13 November 2001, with less than 24 hours' notice, one MC-130 Combat Talon dropped 32 Rangers and an eight-man Air Force special tactics squadron (STS) element led by CPT David Watson (pseudonym) onto DLS Bastogne southwest of Kandahar. The combat jump at 800 feet was made in pitch black darkness into an area without markings and without distinguishable landmarks. As soon as it landed, the Ranger assault unit bagged up its parachutes to preclude damage to arriving aircraft, assembled, and established security. Night combat jumps during World War II were characterized by paratroopers being scattered across the landscape. Assembling units, and sometimes just groups, of paratroopers was extremely slow. Technology, though, has progressed far beyond the "cricket" tin noisemakers 82nd and 101st Airborne Division soldiers used on D-day at Normandy. Using hand-held global positioning devices (about one per fire team of four to five soldiers), Rangers punched in the coordinates of the assembly area, and that single technological advancement enabled the troops to assemble, with parachutes, in about 45 minutes. The Air Force STS team verified that the strip was suitable for C-130 four-engine turboprop transports before placing the infrared landing lights down its length.

At 1915Z, the first MC-130 landed to quickly unload two helicopters and a mobile FARP. Fifteen minutes later, the second MC-130 landed and unloaded two more helicopters and another FARP. Less than 15 minutes after the second MC-130 landed, the four helicopters were airborne en route to their raid objectives. With the helicopters clear, the two MC-130s took off for an aerial refueling rendezvous. At 2100Z, the helicopters returned to rearm and refuel before departing on another raid. At 2222Z, the MC-130s began landing at DLS Bastogne to reload the FARPs and await the returning attack helicopters. After conducting their raids, the helicopters returned to Bastogne, were loaded onto awaiting airplanes, and the entire force, including the Rangers, was airborne by 2334Z.[160]

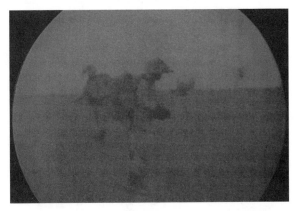

Figure 47. 75th Rangers awaiting MC-130s.

The parachute assault on Objective Bastogne demonstrated that airdropped Rangers could secure an airfield deep in enemy territory to support a FARP for attack helicopter raids. This capability provided American SOF commanders with another way to attack high-priority targets in areas where enemy forces might feel secure. The capacity to project surgical power anywhere and anytime the U.S. government decides is essential to America's global war on terrorism.

"Little Birds" of Prey

As part of the Joint Special Operations Task Force (JSOTF), the attack helicopter pilots and crews of B Company, 1st Battalion, 160th SOAR, were anxious to engage the *Taliban* and *al-Qaeda* forces on behalf of their nation. Their opportunity finally came early on the morning of 13 November. It was short notice, but the attack element was ready. CWO Joseph Morris (pseudonym), an AH-6 attack helicopter flight lead pilot, was told that the "Little Birds" would soon be part of the fight in Afghanistan.[161] About 0100, targets were identified, and the attack team went into action; the pilots and crew members developed courses of action, planned fuel and armament, and established flight requirements. Morris briefed their plan five hours later at 0600. With an approved plan, the "Little Bird" crews spent the next five hours coordinating final arrangements and preparing equipment, helicopters, and personal gear before bedding down.[162]

By 1730, four AH-6 attack helicopters and crews, two mobile FARPs, and the armament and refuel personnel were cross-loaded on two MC-130E Combat Talon transports. The four-engine turboprop engine aircraft is equipped to infiltrate, exfiltrate, and resupply SOF and equipment in hostile or denied territory.[163] The two MC-130Es departed at 1945 for a DLS that would be secured by Rangers. At 2345, the first Combat Talon landed and unloaded its cargo and was guided off the runway. Exactly 15 minutes later, the second MC-130E landed and was unloaded. By 0015, four heavily armed AH-6 "Little Birds" were en route to Objective Wolverine.

The zero-illumination condition stretched the limits of the night vision goggles (NVG) the special operations aviators routinely wore. The high desert vegetation provided little contrast. These flight conditions demanded precise navigation and intense concentration by the pilots under NVG to avoid flying into the ground. Despite these factors, Morris pressed his flight of four toward the target, a compound that resembled a vehicle maintenance park with stored equipment, vehicles, and some radar pieces. Morris located the target, and the two-ship attack teams made several runs, destroying the compound with rockets. Satisfied that the target was destroyed, Morris led the flight back to the DLS. At 0130, each attack team of two AH-6 helicopters landed at a separate rearm and refuel point operated by aircrew, fuel handlers, and armament specialists. Each pilot located the infrared chemlight that marked his landing point and landed in a heavy dust cloud. According to Morris, the pilots were happy to see that their helicopters were still upright when the dust cleared. Within 10 minutes, the four AH-6s departed with full loads of ammunition and fuel to raid Objective Raptor.

Figure 48. An AH-6 "Little Bird" armed for night raids.

Again, the flight of "Little Birds" traversed the barren terrain in total darkness to find its prey, another walled compound containing vehicles and equipment. The two-ship attack teams repeated the assault scenario, making several runs to destroy the objective. This time the rockets hit a fuel dump, and the compound was ablaze as the helicopters slipped away into the night. The four AH-6s arrived back at the DLS at 0315, and each team landed near its designated MC-130E. The "Little Bird" pilots shut down and, with the crew members, pushed their helicopters onto the Combat Talons. By 0400, both MC-130Es were airborne, en route to their staging base.

The Night Stalkers had demonstrated their ability to respond quickly and effectively, destroying enemy facilities hundreds of miles away at night in extremely tough flying conditions. Despite thousands of hours of combined flight experience, the Night Stalker attack pilots had to admit that it was extremely difficult under NVG to discern contrast on that barren high desert landscape in zero-illumination darkness. But these "Little Birds" of prey demonstrated another powerful long-range surgical strike capability unique to ARSOF.

High Desert Rat Patrol

"The Rat Patrol" was a popular television series that fictionalized the exploits of the Long-Range Desert Group (LRDG) fighting the Germans and Italians in North Africa during World War II. During Operation RELENTLESS STRIKE, A Company, 3rd Battalion, 75th Rangers, turned those fictionalized accounts into reality but with a new twist that the LRDG could never have imagined. The ARSOF are capable of striking suddenly in the most hostile environments after coming from the most unexpected locations. RELENTLESS STRIKE combined the lethal firepower of Army special operations attack helicopters with the desert mobility of Ranger forces. This joint mission required intense planning, close coordination and cooperation among several SOF elements, adaptability to a very harsh environment in winter, modification of established *modus operandi* to new combat situations, and great confidence in one another.

The mission of the attack helicopters was to strike critical targets within range of a desert landing strip (DLS) that had a forward arming and refueling point (FARP) to support further operations. Critical to the continuing mission was determining whether proposed landing strips would support the landing of MC-130 transports carrying the helicopters, FARP system, and personnel and securing the DLS areas during landings and takeoffs and while FARP operations were conducted. Reconnaissance revealed that the initial DLS (Anzio) would support the weight of the fully loaded MC-130, and the operation began.

On the nights of 16 and 17 November, MC-130s inserted six desert mobility vehicles (DMVs) and 48 Rangers and Air Force STS personnel led by CPT Chuck Seims (pseudonym) on DLS Anzio to provide security for the forthcoming attack helicopters and FARP.[164] After spending several hours carefully patrolling the area to ensure that their arrival had not prompted enemy responses, the Ranger force moved to the predetermined location for DLS Bulge to determine its suitability. Employing standard Ranger procedures, such as listening halts, bounding overwatch with the DMVs, and leader recons, the Rangers confirmed the second DLS. While Lieutenant Carter and SFC Bondurant (pseudonym) positioned the DMVs for all-around security on the proposed airstrip, the Air Force STS element assessed the area, verifying the dimensions; noting potential hazards and obstacles; and taking core samples of the "runway" area and determined that it was also suitable for MC-130 landings. Bondurant checked out the proposed "hide site," doing an on-the-ground reconnaissance. He found that their choice not only concealed the vehicles but also over-

Figure 49. 75th Ranger hide site.

Figure 50. 75th Ranger night movement under NVG.

looked DLS Bulge. The DMVs were moved into the hide site, and the Rangers proceeded to their tactical priorities—putting out local security, brushing away tire tracks, making radio contacts, setting up camouflage nets, and reviewing immediate action drills—before settling in for the night.

On 18 November, the Ranger task force was alerted to secure DLS Bulge for helicopter operations that night. After dark, the Rangers moved to the DLS to establish security around the strip while the STS, guarded by CPT Seims and 1SG Karl Maxey (pseudonym) in DMVs, set out the infrared landing lights along the length of the runway. At 1600Z, the MC-130s landed with their cargo of helicopters, the FARP, and a resupply bundle for the Rangers. The well-rehearsed helicopter crews quickly unloaded the helicopters, and the pilots took off minutes after the MC-130s landed. When the attack helicopters returned, they, like the Rangers, reported seeing heavy rocket fire in the distance. (The next day both groups were informed that they had witnessed a meteor shower.) After a second strike mission, the MC-130s returned to load the FARP and helicopters, and departed. The Rangers helped the STS retrieve the landing lights, swept the area of evidence, and returned to their hide site. Dismounted patrols maintained the security of the task force.[165]

The mission scenario was repeated the following night after ground patrols verified the absence of enemy forces in the area. Since it was to be a repeat operation from the same DLS, the Rangers established observation posts (OPs) farther out on higher ground to provide better early warning. According to CPT Seims, the Rangers were confident that "nothing could sneak up [on them]."[166] Again, STS laid out the landing lights, and the MC-130s with the helicopters and FARP aboard soon landed. The helicopters conducted their raid, returned to refuel and rearm, and conducted a second raid. These raids marked the end of Operation RELENTLESS STRIKE because the entire force was extracted that night. At 2045Z, 19 November 2001, MC-130s started landing. First the FARP and helicopters were taken out and then the Ranger task force with its DMVs. By 2221Z, 19 November, DLS Bulge was just another high desert area in the hinterlands of Afghanistan.[167]

While Special Forces teams, Army Rangers, and 160th SOAR helicopters, supported by Air Force special operations MC-130E Combat Talons, AC-130 Spectre gunships, MC-130P refuelers, and tactical teams were fighting *Taliban* and *al-Qaeda* forces in Afghanistan, JSOTF-North in Uzbekistan was directing operations and inserting other ARSOF units as combat multipliers on the battlefield. In the United States, the U.S. Army Special Operations Command

(USASOC), Fort Bragg, was mobilizing USAR and NG units to augment forces at home and overseas. In neighboring Pakistan, discussions were under way with Hamad Karzai, a Pashtun leader, to open a southern front against the *Taliban* and *al-Qaeda*. These vignettes demonstrate that the global war on terrorism was an ARSOF team effort.

The Great Communications Terminus

One of the staff elements most affected by the unique 5th SFG command and control arrangement was the communications section, which operated the signal base station for JSOTF-North. COL Mulholland anticipated that the task force would initially be supporting the forces of two major Afghan resistance leaders, expecting that a third leader would emerge later. Within weeks, however, more Special Forces ODAs had been committed to a variety of tribal chieftains and missions, without either a Special Forces company or Special Forces battalion as an intermediate headquarters, to share the responsibilities of "commanding and controlling" the Special Forces teams. MSG Don Sullivan (pseudonym), the 5th SFG communications chief in charge of the joint base station, only had four radio operators to communicate with one higher headquarters and three lower headquarters, as authorized by his table of organization and equipment.[168] By Special Forces doctrine, these three "out stations" normally would be the command posts of the 5th SFG's three battalions. Each of the battalion base stations, using its authorized number of radios, could talk to each of the three Special Forces company headquarters, led by majors and their staffs called Special Forces B Teams, in turn, would send and receive messages to and from the five or six Special Forces ODAs.[169]

Instead, by late November, Sullivan and his small section at the JSOTF-North terminus were receiving and transmitting to 47 different field stations 24 hours a day, 7 days a week. Without the normal hierarchical arrangement of headquarters to distribute responsibilities, the joint base station at K2 communicated with three lieutenant colonels (battalion commanders designated as "ODC team" leaders), six ODB elements, and 25 ODA SF teams. Many of them were subdivided into "split teams" to cover more territory and to operate in shifts to direct airstrikes around the clock. There were also Special Forces intelligence teams and CA and PSYOP units spread across Afghanistan that reported directly to JSOTF-North. Since this was 12 times as much communications support as MSG Sullivan's joint base station was manned and equipped to handle, the stress level "red-lined" in that element.[170]

For years, the signal community had postulated that in today's "information age" a "flat" command and control organization was possible. Digitized message traffic would eliminate the need for traditional three-layer communications. It also promised a faster, unfiltered flow of data between a senior leader and the elements of his command. Operations in Afghanistan, however, made this difficult. First, 5th SFG communications planning had been shared with the battalion and company communications sections. This complex and exacting task now fell solely to the officer and NCOIC of the 5th SFG signal center, which also served as the base station for JSTOF-North. Second, due to the unexpectedly rapid and fluid nature of the war with Special Forces teams and their Afghan allies almost constantly moving, JSOTF-North and its units had to rely almost solely on satellite radios for communications. The assigned satellite channels were the single point of convergence for all voice and data over-the-horizon radio traffic that was being transmitted on the 152 tactical satellite (TACSAT) radios in the 5th SFG.

Overhead, two U.S. military telecommunications satellites carried 54 channels of traffic, but almost all of them were already apportioned.[171] The President of the United States; the National Command Authorities; the JCS; and the various regional combatant commanders, intelligence services, and other national-level "customers" dominated most of the available channels. Even though Special Forces ODAs were in combat, MAJ Jacobi (pseudonym), the 5th SFG signal officer, and MSG Sullivan had to "vie for access" to the satellites.[172]

The four high-frequency (HF) satellite bands available to JSOTF-North permitted sufficient voice and data transmission if they were carefully administered. The task force J6 was usually allocated one wide-band channel, two narrow bands—one of those "on loan" from the U.S. Air Force—and a portion of the Demand-Assigned Multiple-Access (DAMA) band that digitally separated transmissions to permit simultaneous communication between stations. Still, Sullivan was very aware that the technology did not allow multiple messages to be "pushed" through one satellite channel ("pipe") at the same time, in parallel. He had to arrange for their transmission one after another, in series. Because of the enormous volume of satellite radio traffic, both the outgoing and incoming messages were backlogged. Sometimes as many as 200 digital messages sat in the electronic queue, waiting for a base station operator to record and forward the message to its addressee. The delays had the most serious impact on aerial resupply, especially on delivery times, drop zone locations, and supplies.[173]

Combine the communications backlog with the challenges and frustrations of SOCEUR and the comments from Special Forces ODAs in the field, and it should become evident that aerial resupply is not just a logistics function for ARSOF. It is a complicated process that involves other services, and there are distinct responsibilities at all levels, from the Special Forces teams, to the JSOTF commander, to the supporting theater commander. Fortunately, while air resupply has become the standard provisioning method for SOF since mid-World War II, the allies have enjoyed air superiority and not had to fight an enemy as well supplied with SAMs as the *mujahideen* were against the Soviets.

Resupply From 10,000 Feet

Inside shallow caves above the Balkh Valley just south of Boi-Becha, CPT Nash and Special Forces ODA 595, supporting General Dostum, were roused from sleep by the thunderous crashing of munitions bundles rolling down the mountainside around them.[174] At 0200, the night before the "big push" toward Mazar-e-Sharif, without notice to the Special Forces team, C-17 jet transports began dropping 32 parachute bundles of arms and ammunition onto the steep slopes surrounding the valley floor from 10,000 feet above ground level (AGL).

After the rain of bundles came an avalanche of broken bundles and crates, rocks, and boulders. When that stopped, the shouts of Afghan soldiers filled the night as they scurried about "collecting treasure." At dawn, ODA 595 surveyed the scene. More than two dozen bundles, each weighing 300 to 400 pounds, lay scattered among the rocks with parachutes draped on the valley slopes. Some of the ammunition bundles had burst, strewing mortar shells and hand grenades all over the ground. Across the narrow valley, SGT Bagby (pseudonym) saw three parachutes caught on high jagged outcroppings "like coat hooks," with their heavy bundles dangling in the air.

Figure 51. Unexpected, but welcome, resupply bundles.

CPT Nash realized that any major effort to collect the resupply arms and munitions would delay the offensive scheduled to begin in a few hours. For now, they would have to do without it, leaving troops behind to protect the site from scavenging locals. Later, General Dostum sent recovery parties back to collect the supplies that were strewn across the mountainside drop zone in time to support the fight through the Tangi Pass on 9 November.[175]

PSYOP = Hard, Steady Work

A year after graduating from high school in Seminary, Mississippi, SSG Logan Donovan (pseudonym), inspired by his older brother, an Army infantryman, joined the Army National Guard (ARNG). Mobilized as an electrician during Operation JUST CAUSE, Donovan repaired damaged buildings in Panama. His overseas duty convinced him to transfer to the Regular Army and acquire an entirely different skill—photo layout specialist. After serving in Germany and England, Donovan was assigned to the 3rd Psychological Operations Battalion (POB) at Fort Bragg.

In September 2001, SSG Donovan was in charge of a five-man squad that printed PSYOP leaflets. Within days of the 9/11 attacks, his team was alerted that it would be printing leaflets for distribution in Afghanistan. The battalion Heidelberg presses were soon running off thousands of leaflets. As each sheet of 12 leaflets rolled off the press, Logan's print squad transferred the sheets to a paper cutter that cut the sheets into individual leaflets. Then the squad boxed the leaflets for delivery. Many of these initial products advertised a $25 million reward for the capture of *al-Qaeda* leader Osama bin Laden.

Because the Heidelberg presses were large and permanently installed, the 4th Psychological Operations Group (POG), the parent headquarters of 3rd POB, had portable systems developed for rapid overseas movement to give field commanders an immediate print capability. The Modular Print System (MPS) consists of two smaller Heidelberg presses, a paper cutter, and two edit stations. Soldiers who

Figure 52. The Modular Print System (MPS) at Bagram Air Base.

Figure 53. Reward leaflet.

perform the edit function can process film as well as edit by computer. As the requirement for film processing has decreased, these soldiers generally use the computers to create an image that is fed to a pressmate printer. From the printer emerges a negative that can be transferred to an aluminum plate that is then affixed to the presses to print leaflets. The self-contained MPS has proven invaluable to overseas commanders for promulgating a PSYOP campaign.

Thus, SSG Donovan was not surprised when told in late October that his squad would deploy to Kuwait with the MPS to produce PSYOP leaflets to support Operation ENDURING FREEDOM. He knew his equipment was in top-notch shape because he made sure that his printer repair people (the "J6s") were available to deal with any press malfunctions.

On 12 November, Donovan and his squad joined the other four squads of 2nd Platoon, A Company, 3rd POB, aboard a C-17 Globemaster III for the flight to Kuwait. After two refueling stops, they arrived at Kuwait City International Airport. Awaiting buses took them to Camp Doha where they bedded down for the night.

The next morning, Donovan's squad opened the MPS shelters, inventoried the contents, and ran operational checks on all equipment so there would be no delay when the print missions became reality. Afterward, the soldiers explored their new home. They were impressed. It was not luxurious but certainly better than some places they had been. Latrines were in trailers that also had hot showers with running water. The food was good. The recreation center had a pool table and more than 200 VCR movies that they could check out. The movie theater on base had first-run movies, and other facilities had fast food. "All in all, not a bad place," said Donovan.

1LT Carol Clewell (pseudonym) organized her platoon into two shifts to conduct 24-hour operations. Two print squads worked a day shift of 12 hours—one squad per press—and two squads worked the 12-hour night shift. Periodically, the squads rotated shifts. The troops worked four days on and one day off because the work pace was steady. When radio broadcasts by the Air Force EC-130 Commando Solo aircraft became possible, Donovan's squad printed

Figure 54. CA personnel give
transistor radios to Afghans.

Figure 55. 4th POG leaflet with
radio broadcast frequencies.

handbills that ground units could distribute to villages. The handbills depicted a radio tower and had various frequencies for music and news. In conjunction, other PSYOP units working in the field distributed small transistor radios countrywide because the *Taliban* had made it a crime to possess a radio and few were available. There was only one maintenance problem. When the blade on the paper cutter broke, Donovan took it to Kuwait City and had a local machine shop fabricate a replacement.

In the rare periods when work slowed, 1LT Clewell encouraged her soldiers to visit Kuwait City. Very few had ever been in the Middle East, and she wanted to give them an opportunity to become familiar with the culture. After visiting other U.S. military bases in Kuwait, the troops unanimously agreed that the 2nd Platoon had the best facilities.

Even living in a good facility, the routine can sometimes get boring. Once printed and cut by the 2nd Platoon, the leaflets were packed, put on pallets, and flown to Diego Garcia. There, other 3rd Battalion soldiers would pack the leaflets into M129 leaflet bombs that B-52 Stratofortress bombers carried aloft and dropped over Afghanistan. At a preset altitude the two halves of the leaflet bomb separated, and the wind scattered the contents across the countryside. To ensure the pallets were not offloaded before reaching Diego Garcia, a 2nd Platoon soldier would go along as a "pallet rider." The first stop was always Bahrain where the soldier could stay in a hotel instead of a warehouse and experience a degree of Western culture. The soldier and pallet would then continue to Diego Garcia. SSG Donovan never had a problem getting volunteers to be "pallet riders."

While not as glamorous or exciting as other special operations missions, printing the PSYOP leaflets was critical to the air and ground campaign to topple the *Taliban* government and destroy the *al-Qaeda* in Afghanistan. Whether it was a leaflet offering a monetary reward, providing a radio listening frequency, extolling the new government, or warning about land mines, the 30 million leaflets 2nd Platoon, A Company, 3rd POB, printed were a significant contribution to the global war on terrorism. "It was hard, steady work," Donovan concluded, and then added proudly, "and we produced top-quality leaflets."[176]

A Supportive Populace

Less than two weeks after the 9/11 attacks, Fort Bragg soldiers, MAJ Jim McLemore (pseudonym) and SGT Charles Walters (pseudonym), were at Fort Campbell, Kentucky, attached to 5th SFG. Among the factors to be considered in planning military responses to the terrorist attacks was the human suffering of the long-oppressed Afghan people. McLemore and Walters, C Company, 96th Civil Affairs Battalion (CAB), were to be on the forefront of American action to establish a positive climate among a population that had been brutalized for years. Their actions, and those of other CA soldiers, could have a lasting impact not only on future American military activities but also on the future of a reconstituted democratic Afghan government. On 8 October, they were at K2 in support of JSOTF-North.

Figure 56. Diego Garcia in the Indian Ocean.

As the one active Army CA company regionally oriented toward the CENTCOM area of responsibility (AOR), the soldiers of C Company had no doubt that they would join Walters and McLemore overseas. That expectation was realized when Civil Affairs Team (CAT)-A32 deployed to K2 on 16 October, followed by CAT-A33 and CAT-B30 on 12 November and CAT-A34 and CAT-A36 on Christmas Eve.[177]

On 15 November, the Army component command of CENTCOM, ARCENT, directed JSOTF-North to send a CAT-A to Mazar-e-Sharif to establish a coalition humanitarian liaison cell (CHLC). Five days later, the newly created Combined Joint Civil-Military Operations Task Force (CJCMOTF) was given tactical control of C Company, 96th CAB. With that authority, the CJCMOTF directed that another CAT-A be sent to Bagram to establish a CHLC. Recognizing the importance of the two missions, MAJ John Bowman (pseudonym) split his company headquarters staff between the locations but left a CA liaison element at JSOTF-North. During the next months, the CA liaison team coordinated the delivery of 700 tons of red wheat as well as winter clothes and toys for children.[178]

Mazar-e-Sharif was critical to the flow of humanitarian aid. The airfield was the focal point for supplies coming into Afghanistan and the transload site to villages in need of aid. The city was also the road terminus for truck-transported supplies from Uzbekistan—a major objective that Secretary of State Colin Powell set. Bowman told CAT-A33 to make an area assessment to determine what support the people required and to determine how to facilitate the flow of humanitarian aid by nongovernment organizations (NGOs). CAT-A33 reached Mazar-e-Sharif on 27 November and, in the midst of its assessment, helped the Jordanians establish a major hospital. This hospital would provide free medical care to more than 8,000 people before the team left the city.[179]

Getting PSYOP on the Ground in Afghanistan

On the first of November, the 9th POB commander told SSG Jim O'Reilly (pseudonym) to get ready to go to Afghanistan to support the 5th SFG.[180] Twelve days later the Tennessee native and Tactical PSYOP Detachment (TPD) 930 were aboard a C-17 on the way to K2, Uzbekistan. As TPD 930 stepped off the airplane at K2 at about midnight on 14 November, the temperature was 45 degrees. CPT Mark Puller and SGT Harold Aspen (pseudonyms), the liaison officer and NCO from the JPOTF, bedded them down in the wood-floored chapel tent that first night.[181]

O'Reilly and his team leader, CPT Rick Harrison (pseudonym), were responsible not only for the 13-man TPD 930 but also for a nine-man PSYOP support element from the 3rd POB.[182] They were to operate the Deployable Print Production Center (DPPC) that could produce PSYOP products quickly at a forward base. Because neither PSYOP team had worked with 5th SFG before, O'Reilly and Harrison gave the JSOTF-North staff a briefing on the capabilities of their TPD and the DPPC. When Mazar-e-Sharif, the second largest city in Afghanistan, fell to Northern Alliance forces on 10 November, the PSYOP soldiers knew they would be going "in country" shortly.[183]

Have Tools Will Travel

The initial success of the war on terrorism depended heavily on the availability of ARSOF helicopters to infiltrate SOF deep into Afghanistan. Helicopter maintenance was key to operationally ready aircraft, and for that reason, the Army special operations aviation staff at the U.S. Army Special Operations Command (USASOC) sought assistance from the ARNG. D Company, 109th Aviation Battalion, was an aviation intermediate maintenance (AVIM) company that could provide maintenance expertise for various types and models of helicopters that were organic to the 160th SOAR. This unit seemed ideal to augment the Night Stalker maintenance team.

The AVIM company, predominantly filled by soldiers and airmen from Nebraska and Iowa, was commanded by MAJ Martin Jackson (pseudonym), a former Marine Corps CH-46 pilot and veteran of the Gulf war.[184] To preclude a delay in receiving the experienced mechanics that were urgently needed, the 160th SOAR assumed responsibility for all administrative requirements associated with activating the ARNG unit. With the support of Fort Campbell and the USAR mobilization command on post, the unit's required mobilization training was scheduled as time permitted. MAJ Jackson and LTC Edward Simpson (pseudonym), the 160th SOAR executive officer, worked closely to develop a plan that would capitalize on the backgrounds and experience of the factory-trained mechanics who normally worked on CH-47 Chinooks, UH-60 Black Hawks, and OH-58 Kiowas.[185] Although doctrine suggests that an AVIM company operate separately from its supported unit, Jackson and Simpson divided D Company's personnel into four maintenance contact teams that were assigned to the 1st, 2nd, and 3rd battalions and to the regiment's training company. This was a pioneering aviation maintenance concept.

All of the 109th contact teams quickly assimilated to the normal fast pace of the 160th SOAR's maintenance sections. Although each required some familiarization and training on the special operations helicopters, the 109th teams were filled with talent and years of experience—former contract mechanics from Lockheed Martin, Sikorsky, and Duncan Aviation—and quickly contributed to the maintenance effort. They promptly established credibility. Within a month, the 109th mechanics were working long hours and multiple shifts side by side with their 160th SOAR contemporaries. This teamwork enabled the 160th and 109th to complete helicopter phase maintenance in as little as 28 days, a remarkable feat. Both the ARNG and the 160th SOAR benefited from the relationship. The experienced ARNG mechanics shared their extensive knowledge with the regiment's younger mechanics, and the SOAR personnel, in turn, trained the 109th on the unique equipment common to ARSOF aircraft.

Figure 57. The 109th Aviation Maintenance Battalion (AVIM) provided quality support.

D Company personnel were also integrated into Green Platoon, the 160th SOAR's training and selection course. More than 60 soldiers from the unit completed the course during the first six months of activation. Successful completion of Green Platoon added to the ARNG members' credibility because it is a 160th SOAR requirement for deployment overseas. More than 27 mechanics from the 109th AVIM deployed overseas to Afghanistan, Korea, and the Philippines with the Night Stalkers. One outstanding graduate with a law enforcement background was selected to be a Green Platoon martial arts instructor.

This close working association with the 109th was unique in another respect. The ARNG unit brought 14 female mechanics to work with the 160th SOAR "maintainers." By regulation, women are precluded from being assigned to active duty special operations aviation units as mechanics or crew members. These 109th female helicopter mechanics enjoyed a wartime service experience beyond the reach of their active duty contemporaries.

The mutually beneficial assignment significantly contributed to the high operational readiness of the critically needed ARSOF helicopters in Afghanistan, the Philippines, and Korea. Success can be attributed to innovative organizational ideas; highly trained, competent professionals; specialized training; and a commitment to the highest standards of helicopter maintenance. While it was a groundbreaking effort, the 160th SOAR-D Company, 109th Aviation Battalion (ARNG), relationship was a "keeper" because it set the standard for future associations.

With PSYOP and CA units at K2 preparing to be coalition force multipliers in Afghanistan and an ARNG AVIM company working with the 160th SOAR to keep the ARSOF helicopters operationally ready, the JSOTF-North communications logjam was overlooked. More pressing issues faced TF Dagger. One major task was getting a Pashtun leader to open a second front in the south with an offensive.

Mr. President

MAJ Walter Barstow, C Company, 9th Psychological Operations Battalion (POB), knew he was to meet with an Afghan leader who had considerable influence on 12 November in Jacobabad, Pakistan. The PSYOP major was introduced to a fatherly looking man of medium build. Within seconds, Hamad Karzai, with his fingertips together, almost prayer-like, began articulating his views on the present state and future of Afghanistan in a clipped British accent. Then, the Pashtun Afghan switched to the American military PSYOP campaign to propagate anti-*Taliban* sentiment in his country. Karzai spoke passionately about the Afghan culture and the history of foreign invasion, periodically pausing for effect. Barstow listened attentively. After 30 minutes, the Pashtun ended his oratory, and the one-sided interview was over. At the time, Barstow had no idea that he had just met the man who would be named to head the interim government for Afghanistan in about a month.[186]

Figure 58. Hamad Karzai.

Karzai, who spoke six languages including English, was well aware of the power the media possessed. Barstow was unaware that the British Broadcasting Corporation (BBC) and Voice of America (VOA) had already interviewed Karzai several times. With a high illiteracy rate in Afghanistan, the Pashtun leader knew that radio broadcasts in various dialects would have a greater effect than leaflets. He had listened to the programs broadcast by the Air Force EC-130 Commando Solo aircraft and told MAJ Barstow that the music was very effective, but the BBC and VOA had better-quality programs. Karzai urged Barstow to make the messages more forceful. The people needed to be told what they should do about the *Taliban* and *al-Qaeda* who were still in their midst.

Karzai did not totally discount the value of leaflets and advised Barstow to keep them simple. He suggested using the national flag before the *Taliban* came to power as a symbol of traditional Afghanistan. He further told Barstow to stress themes that promoted a free country and the role of the people in its establishment. Education was critical to Afghanistan's future. In this regard, Karzai wanted something that stressed better education opportunities for all Afghans, including women, because it would have a positive appeal.

Karzai's insights into the various Afghan peoples were invaluable to Barstow. Writing furiously as the future leader "lectured," Barstow tried to capture every word. With the knowledge that the Afghan villagers were unhappy because American bombs sometimes killed innocent civilians, Karzai recommended that the information campaign stress that innocents were being killed only because the *Taliban* hid behind them. The broadcasts and leaflets ought to say, "Drive out the *Taliban* and the people will not be hurt," Karzai said. "Stress that the Americans have been invited and are not in Afghanistan as occupiers," he remarked and then added, "The people must be able to understand the distinction between the United States that is sending forces to help the country and the Soviets who sent forces to conquer the country."[187]

As Barstow flew back to Masirah Island, Oman, to implement the guidance, he pondered

Figure 59. Afghan leader with a PSYOP leaflet.

what Karzai had told him. His notes were turned into recommendations. Much of what Karzai espoused was transformed into leaflets and broadcasts.[188]

A Significant Meeting With an Unusual Man

Assisting with establishing JSOTF-North in Uzbekistan was just one of several major tasks for LTC Warren Richards. In late October 2001, COL Mike Findlay, commander, Special Operations Command, U.S. Joint Forces Command (SOCJFCOM), had told COL Mulholland that the "borrowed staff help" from SOCJFCOM was needed to support other overseas missions. The JSOTF-North commander asked, "Can I keep Richards for one more thing?" Findlay acquiesced. A few days later, Richards flew to Jacobabad, Pakistan, to meet a well-educated, articulate Afghan leader who wanted the *Taliban* out of his country.[189]

Hamad Karzai had been a diplomat for the *mujahideen* during the Russian occupation. Although he welcomed and supported the *Taliban* initially, Karzai quickly realized they had become "a proxy for a foreign power" and that "Osama bin Laden had embedded himself in the movement." After the *Taliban* murdered his father, Karzai emerged as a key Pashtun leader. According to Deputy Secretary of Defense Paul Wolfowitz, the CIA identified Karzai as "the most promising leader in the south."[190]

On 8 October 2001, Karzai, "armed only with a satellite phone," had entered Afghanistan on the back of a motorcycle from his refuge in Pakistan. His goal was to persuade fellow Pashtuns to rise up against the *Taliban*. When the *Taliban* surrounded him and his small group, Karzai put the phone to good use. The United States rushed in weapons, ammunition, and supplies. After collecting the airdropped equipment, Karzai and his 150 heavily armed fighters successfully escaped the *Taliban*. Wolfowitz made it clear that the United States would back his efforts to launch a front against the *Taliban* from the south and that he would have the backing of the American military. "When he [Karzai] goes back in," Wolfowitz said, "let's make sure he has the kind of support the Northern Alliance has with our Special Forces."[191]

By late October, the main American effort was still in the northern part of Afghanistan. Several Special Forces ODAs had been inserted and were supporting Northern Alliance leaders. Most of those leaders were Tajik, Uzbek, or Hazara. Karzai was a Pashtun from southern Afghanistan. Special Forces support to him would accomplish several goals. First, it would demonstrate that the United States was backing all Afghan tribes. This was in keeping with the ultimate goal of establishing an ethnically diverse national government. Second, Karzai and his forces could open another front against the *Taliban* and *al-Qaeda* in the south. Pressure on the enemy from several directions would hopefully hasten the collapse of armed resistance.[192]

Two Special Forces detachment commanders accompanied Richards. Their mission was to ascertain whether Karzai, an untested leader at this point in the war, was capable of assembling a military force and was willing to start offensive operations against the *Taliban* and *al-Qaeda*. Affirmation of these key factors would warrant inserting a Special Forces ODA to assist him and his forces. Six lieutenants accompanied Karzai to the meeting. Richards, the ODA team leaders, and representatives of other U.S. government elements talked with Karzai and his lieutenants for two days. Richards was also trying to determine the number of fighters that Karzai could rally and employ so he could recommend how many ODAs should be dedicated and whether a senior command element should work with Karzai. It became readily apparent, based on the number of fighters Karzai could promise, that only one Special Forces ODA would be necessary. Richards recommended that ODA 574, led by CPT Jason Amerine, be sent. On 14 November, ODA 574 was inserted near Tarin Kowt to support Karzai and his anti-*Taliban* force.

Interestingly, one of Karzai's lieutenants was a former *mujahideen* and *Taliban* soldier. As Richards was preparing to leave, the Pashtun, with a slight smile, turned to him and said (through an interpreter), "I have been fighting for almost 22 years in Afghanistan. I would have enjoyed meeting you on the battlefield." Richards looked him straight in the eye and calmly replied, "You would have lost." The Pashtun fighter laughed heartily and then presented Richards with an Afghan hat. The two soldiers parted, never having had to face one another in combat.[193]

The Battle of Tarin Kowt

"That was the turning point"—so spoke President of Afghanistan Hamad Karzai regarding the battle of Tarin Kowt.[194] Prussian military theorist Carl von Clausewitz postulated that war is the continuation of policy by other means.[195] That proved to be the case after the battle of Tarin Kowt.

Deputy Secretary of Defense Wolfowitz made it clear that when Karzai returned to Afghanistan, he would have the same level of Special Forces support that the United States was providing to the Northern Alliance leaders. After LTC Richards met with Karzai in late October 2001, he had recommended that ODA 574, commanded by CPT Amerine, be the Special Forces detachment that provided that support.[196]

When Amerine graduated from the U.S. Military Academy, West Point, New York, in 1993, he wanted to be a Special Forces officer. Since Army regulations precluded initial entry into Special Forces, he was an infantryman until he satisfied the prerequisites. After service in Panama; at Guantanamo Bay, Cuba; and in Korea, Amerine was accepted for Special Forces training and earned his Green Beret. The 5th SFG was his first assignment, and after a year on staff, he took command of ODA 574.[197]

ODA 574 was on a training mission in Kazakhstan on 9/11. A week later when the team returned to Fort Campbell, COL Mulholland told the detachment to get ready to conduct unconventional warfare (UW) operations with Northern Alliance forces in Afghanistan. After ODA 574 reached K2, the 5th SFG commander specified the mission: ODA 574 was to "link up with Hamad Karzai and his Pashtun fighters, and advise and assist his forces to destabilize and eliminate the *Taliban* regime" in the south. On the night of 14 November, four MH-60K helicopters inserted Amerine and his team into southern Afghanistan.[198]

As postulated by Clausewitz in *On War*, plans were interrupted by the friction of combat. Three of the helicopters landed at the correct landing zone (LZ) in Oruzgan Province, but the fourth was unable to set down because of insufficient space. Those Special Forces soldiers were landed about 2 miles from the rest of the team. Karzai and about 30 of his men met Amerine. "We knew we were among friends, but I was wondering what happened to the men on the fourth helicopter," Amerine said. After about an hour, the Pashtun tribesmen with Karzai had located them, loaded their gear on mules, and brought the soldiers to rejoin the ODA.[199]

Although Amerine, who had accompanied LTC Richards to Jacobabad, had met the Pashtun leader, there had been no time to build the rapport that would be critical to conducting a successful UW campaign. As Amerine put it, "We had to build trust, then go to war. I drank a lot of green tea with Hamad Karzai during late nights."

Drinking tea was not the only thing the Special Forces soldiers were doing. Karzai considered Tarin Kowt the "heart" of the *Taliban* movement because Mullah Omar and several key leaders lived in and around the city. Karzai believed that capturing Tarin Kowt would cause the Pashtuns in the region to align with him. As the Afghans made plans to attack the city, it quickly became apparent to ODA 574 that victory could be assured only if they blocked the southern approaches from Kandahar. The *Taliban* garrisons in Kandahar could easily overwhelm the Americans and the 200 Pashtuns with Karzai unless the Special Forces could block and repel a counterattack. The United States furnished arms and ammunition, and ODA 574 provided rudimentary tactical training while Karzai kept up a steady phone dialogue with other Pashtun leaders. When the citizens of Tarin Kowt revolted against the *Taliban* on 16 November, Karzai told Amerine that they needed to move into the city immediately.

Suddenly CPT Amerine was faced with a decision that might prove crucial to the outcome of the war. He quickly weighed the known and unknown factors. Karzai had a small, poorly trained Pashtun force. There were sizable *Taliban* garrisons nearby. The Pashtun leader wanted to move immediately. The Air Force and Navy could be called on to provide aerial fire support if the situation turned ugly. The unknown element was what kind of reception awaited them in Tarin Kowt. Amerine concluded that "We had to go in there and try to do what we could."

Assembling a convoy of pickup trucks, flatbed trucks, and any other vehicle that could move, the motley force of Pashtuns and Americans raced toward Tarin Kowt, arriving early in the evening on 16 November. The force was greeted with the news that about 80 to 100 vehicles with 500 to 1,000 *Taliban* were on the way from Kandahar to regain control of the city. Although Amerine was anxious to establish a defense, the Afghans, who had called for a council when Karzai arrived, were in no hurry. Despite his concern about the approaching *Taliban* force, Amerine politely ate beef stew, raisins, and bread before excusing himself to prepare for the coming fight.

After a quick survey of the terrain south of the city, ODA 574 and 30 to 50 Pashtun fighters assumed defensive positions on a ridge overlooking the main road from Kandahar. Their ridge position looked down into a valley with a pass at the far southern end. The *Taliban* would have to clear that chokepoint to reach the American-Pashtun defenses. "You could not have asked for better terrain," said Amerine. The Air Force tactical air controller radioed his headquarters that there was a strong possibility of a major battle and alerted them that both Air Force and Navy aircraft should be available based on the size of the Taliban force.

Shortly after dawn on 17 November, the lead *Taliban* trucks cleared the pass. Based on Amerine's order, "Well, smoke 'em," the close air support (CAS) team fixed the laser beam of the target designator on the lead vehicle, and the F-18's bomb unerringly followed the track to "kill" the first truck. The blast was deafening, even from a distance. The convoy stopped long enough to figure out how to bypass the wreck and continued onward as more bombs rained down on them. More trucks and *Taliban* soldiers were obliterated. Despite the awesome success being achieved, the Pashtun fighters panicked, abandoned their positions, ran down the backside of the ridge, jumped in their trucks, and took off toward Tarin Kowt, leaving the Americans alone. With the choice of defending the ridge by themselves or following the escaping Pashtuns, the American Special Forces team chose the latter. To ODA 574 "it felt like we were grabbing defeat from the jaws of victory."

Back in Tarin Kowt, CPT Amerine hurriedly explained the situation to Karzai, urging him to rally his men. The airborne command post reported that the *Taliban* convoy had reached Amerine's original position. Now he would have to find another site that was defensible; provide a measure of protection for the team and whatever Pashtuns accompanied it; and most important, offer good observation of the *Taliban* column. The Americans located another position south of town that was not as good as the previous site but was suitable, and it was the best they could find in the time available. Karzai got some of the Pashtun fighters moving, but it was a motley group. Old men with rifles came running to the position, as did curious children to see what was going on. While the CAS team was directing airstrikes, the kids were trying to pilfer their rucksacks.

Finally, the Americans got control of the situation and were able to concentrate on destroying the *Taliban* from the air. When a small enemy force managed to flank their position, the Afghans succeeded in driving them off. By 1030, the battle was over. Remnants of 30 trucks and about 300 dead *Taliban* littered the valley floor. The rest of the force withdrew to Kandahar.

That evening, local mullahs met with Karzai. They were respected as church leaders and for their literacy. Because of the influence they had in the area, their views would be crucial to ridding the country of the *Taliban*. If these mullahs expressed anti-American sentiments, it would have made Karzai's task even more difficult. What they did say was, "If the Americans had not been here, we all would have been killed." The *Taliban* would not have treated kindly those who had risen up against the regime and killed the mayor.

Not only was the battle to protect Tarin Kowt a decisive military success, it was also an overwhelming psychological and political victory. Had Karzai been defeated, the hopes that the U.S. government had for him as a southern Afghanistan war leader and future president would have been dashed. Instead, his stature increased immeasurably. His credibility among the regional leaders, with the leaders of the Northern Alliance, and with the U.S. government had been ensured. As Amerine said, "After the battle of Tarin Kowt, Hamad Karzai was a leader to be reckoned with [in Afghanistan]."

In the meantime, RADM Bert Calland, SOCCENT, had been dispatched to Mazar-e-Sharif following a summit meeting with CENTCOM commander GEN Tommy Franks, Fahim Khan, and COL Mulholland in Tajikistan. While the victor of Mazar-e-Sharif, General Rashid Dostum, concentrated on Konduz, one of the major battles of the war erupted at Qala-i-Jangi.

SOCCENT to Mazar-e-Sharif

GEN Franks, CENTCOM commander, called a summit meeting of his commanders with Fahim Khan in Tajikistan in early November. RADM Calland, SOCCENT, flew from his forward command post in Qatar, while COL Mulholland, JSOTF-North commander, flew from K2 on a Russian-built Mi-17 helicopter. With Dostum already on the offensive, they were meeting with Northern Alliance chief, Fahim Khan, to get him energized to start offensive operations with his forces. GEN Franks' priorities at Mazar-e-Sharif, as Calland recalled them, were to open the land bridge to Termez; get an airfield operational; and "Keep Dostum, Mohaqqeq, and Atta from killing each other."[200]

Taloqan was the key objective according to Fahim Khan who declared, "When Taloqan falls, all else will follow"—meaning Bagram and then Mazar-e-Sharif, in that order. Engineer Arath, Fahim Khan's primary aide and chief negotiator, wanted more airstrikes and other specific support in return for their promise to begin advancing on Bagram and Kabul by Thanksgiving.[201] After the discussions ended, RADM Calland ordered COL Mulholland to "send in three or four more ODAs to support Fahim Khan" while he, as directed by GEN Franks, assessed the situation in Afghanistan.[202]

Calland was flown into the old Soviet dirt airstrip at Deh Dadi aboard an MH-47E helicopter at night on 13 November. LTC Marc Bell (pseudonym) and some staff officers at Forward Operating Base (FOB) 53 met the admiral and took him to General Dostum's headquarters in the recently liberated Qala-i-Jangi fortress.[203] Calland missed Dostum and spent the night on a mattress on the floor, remembering that the departed *Taliban* troops had left piles of feces in rooms adjacent to his. The next day, Calland departed on an 8½-hour drive toward Konduz where Dostum was laying siege to the city and its *Taliban* defenders.[204]

Al-Qaeda Uprising—Qala-i-Jangi—24-29 November

When 300 *al-Qaeda* fighters surrendered just outside Mazar-e-Sharif on 24 November 2001, neither the anti-*Taliban* chiefs nor their American advisers anticipated an uprising that would become a major battle of the war in Afghanistan.[205] The mass surrender of the *al-Qaeda* seemed to be more good news for the two dozen U.S. Special Forces soldiers who staffed FOB 53.[206] They had established themselves in the five-story Turkish school that had been vacant for the past 4 years. Only the caretaker and a few instructors remained. While FOB 53 coordinated the consolidation of the newly liberated city among the supporters of Dostum, Mohaqqeq, and Atta, the general had led most of his troops against Konduz, the last *Taliban* stronghold in upper Afghanistan.[207] LTC Bell, FOB 53 commander, left with General Dostum on the morning of 24 November to monitor the encirclement of Konduz, a full day's drive to the east on a rough, rutted road across broken terrain. Dostum positioned his forces on the high ground overlooking the city and called for the capitulation of the disintegrating *Taliban* forces.[208]

Negotiating the surrender of the more than 300 *al-Qaeda* fighters near the Mazar-e-Sharif airfield the day before Dostum left for Konduz had been lengthy, violent, and tense. The spokesmen for the *al-Qaeda* at first tried to get safe passage to Kandahar in return for their submission.[209] At one point during the talks, a suicide bomber armed with a grenade killed himself and Dostum's chief of security, and wounded several of the anti-*Taliban* forces. Despite this incident, the warring parties reached an agreement by late afternoon, 23 November, and the *al-Qaeda* boarded trucks—most of which were their own, driven by their people—to be convoyed to a detention facility. On the way to the 18th-century fortress at Qala-i-Jangi, the convoy with the more than 300 *al-Qaeda* prisoners stopped in Mazar-e-Sharif, in front of a former *Taliban* militia barracks, opposite the Turkish school and FOB 53. Northern Alliance troops at the barracks looked over the *al-Qaeda* fighters for 10 minutes, and then the convoy continued to the old fortress, some 7 miles west of the city.[210] Non-Afghan prisoners were interned in the south compound of the fort and guarded by 100 local troops that Commander Fahkir led. Despite the *al-Qaeda* suicide attack to kill Dostum earlier, the guards conducted only occasional and cursory searches of the more than 300 *al-Qaeda* prisoners inside the fortress.[211]

Built of adobe-style mud bricks, Qala-i-Jangi was built on a 17th-century French design, and it dominated the landscape for miles in all directions.[212] More than 300 yards in diameter, the fortress was complete with moats, ramparts, scarps and counterscarps, parapets, and hundreds of firing ports atop walls that were 30 feet high and 45 feet thick. In the 20th century, the fortress had housed the Royal Afghan Army, the Soviet Red Army, anti-*Taliban* resistance, and the *Taliban*. General Dostum reclaimed it for use as his military headquarters once again on 10 November 2001, after having been driven out by the *Taliban* in 1997. The *Taliban* had left Qala-i-Jangi intact, abandoning huge stores of arms and munitions. Thus, rooms all over the fortress were piled high with World War I-era French rifles; World War II Russian submachine guns (called "burp guns"); and modern artillery rockets, mortars, and very effective rocket-propelled grenades (RPGs). Using the simple optical sight on an RPG, a person could shoot a powerful football-size explosive grenade at targets up to 300 meters with excellent accuracy. The Special Forces soldiers of FOB 53, essentially the headquarters staff of 3rd Battalion, 5th SFG, and CPT Mike Nash's ODA-595 briefly stayed inside the fortress before relocating to the cleaner, more spacious Turkish school on 21 November.[213] There, the Special Forces were less than a 10-minute drive from the Mazar-e Sharif airfield, which gave them access to a paved runway instead of the dusty airstrip at Deh Dadi south of the fortress.[214]

Trouble at the prison began to mushroom during the night of 24 November. FOB 53 received a report from Qala-i-Jangi that an *al-Qaeda* prisoner had killed himself and two guards with a concealed hand grenade. The next morning, the FOB learned of a second grenade suicide that killed three prisoners. At 1345, 25 November, the JSOTF-North at K2 radioed FOB 53 that an American had been killed at Qala-i-Jangi. The K2 message said that an American was wounded and another was trapped in the fortress by the prisoners. As the Special Forces soldiers soon discovered, the report was not completely accurate. The two Americans were identified later by CIA Director George Tenet as intelligence officers.[215] They were inside Qala-i-Jangi to interrogate the *al-Qaeda* prisoners.[216] At the Turkish school, a senior adviser to General Dostum arrived and "frantically pleaded" for immediate Special Forces assistance at the fortress. About the same time, RADM Calland returned to the FOB from Kodi Bar where

Figure 60. Preparations under way to reestablish control over the prison.

he had watched humanitarian aid supplies being delivered to a hospital. Calland remarked that he had heard explosions and gunfire coming from the direction of the huge fortress.[217]

Hiding inside the fortress headquarters in the north wall, one of the intelligence officers radioed to his chief that the *al-Qaeda* prisoners had exploded some sort of bomb, overpowered their guards, and seized control of the entire fortress (this was incorrect; they were only in the southern half, which was separated from the northern half by a 20-foot-high wall). The intelligence officer added that he last saw Mike Spann fighting hand to hand in a mob of *al-Qaeda* prisoners and did not believe that he was still alive. This alarming information was passed rapidly through channels, by secure telephone and radio, to FOB 53 at the Turkish school.[218] A German ARD-TV team filmed and recorded the intelligence officer's escape from the revolting prisoners and his satellite telephone reports to his superiors.[219]

The two senior Special Forces officers in FOB 53 knew that they had to rescue the Americans at Qala-i-Jangi. MAJ Kevin Sault (pseudonym), the executive officer, and MAJ Mario Magione (pseudonym), the operations officer, did a quick head count of available personnel. All of their Special Forces ODAs were a day's drive away at Konduz with LTC Bell and several members of the staff. FOB 53 also had to protect RADM Calland while he was in Afghanistan. The two officers decided that Sault would remain at the Turkish school to coordinate their efforts, and Magione would lead what soldiers he could assemble to the fortress to assess the situation there. The core of the rescue force became a vehicle-mounted squad of British troops with an attached U.S. Navy seaman who had been operating around Mazar-e-Sharif. Two Air Force intelligence officers, the Special Forces battalion surgeon, two Special Forces sergeants, the Afghan interpreter, and another American rounded out Magione's ad hoc force. Until the other scattered Special Forces personnel from the FOB returned to base, these men would serve as the medics, radiomen, and translators for the rescue attempt.[220]

The rescue force raced to the main gate of the Qala-i-Jangi fortress while steady gunfire and explosions filled the air. The 300 *al-Qaeda* prisoners had ransacked a large armory in the

160

southern compound and were as well, if not better, armed than the outnumbered anti-*Taliban* militia troops trying to contain them inside the fortress. The British detachment scaled the ramparts on the northeast corner, carrying two machine guns and ammunition, and began to pour fire into the mobs of armed *al-Qaeda* fighters in the south compound. Magione and a four-man team of Americans positioned themselves on the parapets to direct close air support (CAS) and aerial bombs against the buildings where the enemy was hiding. Inside the fortress, the militia troops struggled to contain the *al-Qaeda* in the southern compound. SFC Pete Bender (pseudonym) called the overhead Air Force airborne command post that controlled the fighters and bombers operating in Afghanistan. The command aircraft radioed Bender that the bombers sent to support FOB 53 were approaching at 20,000 feet. Because his troops and the Afghans were so close to the enemy, Magione demanded that the jets fly lower so they could actually see their targets rather than just drop their bombs toward a map coordinate. Twenty minutes later, a pair of F-18 fighters dropped down to 12,000 feet and in rapid succession dropped six 1,000-pound satellite-guided bombs into the south compound. Despite the blasts of the powerful joint direct-attack munitions (JDAMs), *al-Qaeda* fighters kept firing their captured assault rifles and launching rocket grenades into the north compound.[221]

The crew of a B-52 bomber orbiting overhead told SFC Bender it could not see the fortress that was now marked by a plume of thick black smoke from fires started by the last airstrikes. Magione waved off the bomber. Another pair of F-18s arrived, and Magione relayed a description of the target to the pilots through Bender. When the first bomb impacted in a field almost a mile north of the fortress, Magione put the airstrikes on hold so he could organize a search party to look for the missing Americans before the sun went down. As darkness gathered, Magione was worried about a possible attempt to break out at night when it would be impossible to distinguish Afghans from *al-Qaeda* and when the enemy could easily overwhelm their small rescue force. While the search party was stripping its equipment down to pistols and carbines, Magione decided to chance dropping another bomb. As the search party climbed over the the fortress wall, Magione heard the thundering explosion and saw the fireball of the bomb detonating on target. During the search of the marble-columned commander's residence, the rescue party found several Afghans hiding who described the escape of several Westerners. Magione assumed that this group of escapees included the American that he was seeking. What he did not know was that the one surviving American intelligence officer and the German film crew had escaped earlier over the roof of the headquarters, hailed a passing taxi van, and were riding to Mazar-e-Sharif when the American and British soldiers were driving to the fortress. The limited search complete, Magione assembled the entire rescue force by the main gate and ordered it to withdraw to the Turkish school to plan the next day's operations. Although the shooting subsided with the coming darkness, FOB 53 heard gunfire and explosions from the fortress throughout the night.[222]

On the morning of 26 November, RADM Calland granted permission to FOB 53 to continue its attempt to rescue the missing American. Reinforced by an infantry platoon from the 10th Mountain Division at K2 and additional Special Forces soldiers, Magione led the group back to the Qala-i-Jangi fortress to continue aerial bombardment in support of an Afghan ground assault.[223] Hundreds of Afghan militiamen, alerted to the prison uprising, were walking along roads toward Qala-i-Jangi. Some had captured small bands of *al-Qaeda* who had slipped out of the fortress in the night. The fugitive Arabs, Pakistanis, and Chechens proved easy to hunt down. The Afghan militia readily discerned them as "foreigners." Inside the fortress, *al-Qaeda* had set up 82mm mortars and were lobbing shells toward the ramparts as the American and British troops took up covered positions along the walls. As the volume and intensity of enemy fire steadily increased, Magione and a communications detachment led by CPT Pat Schroeder (pseudonym) prepared to guide in the first bomb run of the day.[224]

Magione and Schroeder selected the reinforced concrete "pink house" close to the center of the south compound as the first target and double-checked the coordinates from their Etrex Venture global positioning system (GPS) to fix their position and pinpoint the building. As an added safety measure, the rescue force laid out orange VS-17 marker panels to delineate its location to the aircraft. As he had done the day before, SFC Bender carefully described the targeted pink house to the F-18 pilot making the bomb run. The pilot replied, "Roger, I have a visual on the target," and confirmed his visual by reporting that he also saw the tall scarred trees next to the structure. Schroeder ordered the attack.

At 1051, the 2,000-pound bomb impacted. Magione stood up to spot the exact bomb strike in case corrections were required to bring the next bomb closer to the target. He discovered that the dust cloud from the blast was rising from the north side of the fortress, not the south compound. The JDAM missed its target by almost 200 yards and literally pulverized a section of the massive fortress wall. The blast had thrown a 35-ton battle tank that had climbed atop the wall into the air, tearing its gun turret completely off and killing the four Afghans inside. The explosive shock wave also blew down a lower wall on top of a 10th Mountain infantry squad that was hunkered down 50 feet from the point of impact. It pushed out from under the crumbled adobe wall like sand crabs coated in a powdery brown dust. Squad members were slightly injured, all having bloodshot eyes because their capillaries had been ruptured by the concussion.[225]

Two likewise injured British soldiers realized that American CPT Karl Latimer (pseudonym) had been blown over the wall by the blast. Despite their injuries, the two British soldiers ran through enemy gunfire to drag the unconscious captain back inside the fortress to cover. The other members of the rescue force, with the battalion surgeon, CPT Charles Moss (pseudonym), rallied to treat the five American and four British casualties. Based on "Doc" Moss' assessment of the seriousness of the injuries, Magione directed their immediate evacuation with the rest of the force heading back to the Turkish school. Latimer was so badly injured that MAJ Sault called JSOTF-North for a helicopter to get Latimer to a medical facility. An MH-47E was dispatched with a medical team to take him to K2. There, Latimer was put aboard a transport jet and flown to a U.S. military hospital in Europe.[226]

Repeated assaults by the Afghan militiamen on 26 November failed to break the *al-Qaeda* uprising. Commander Fahkir estimated that 50 of his troops had been killed and as many as 250 wounded in the fighting. When JSOTF-North told MAJ Sault that AC-130 Spectre gunships were available for aerial fire support that night, he said he wanted them to hit Qala-i-Jangi.[227] Magione, satisfied that his wounded men were in stable condition, organized another CAS team to return to the fortress. The major, four Special Forces sergeants, and an Air Force tactical air controller would direct the Spectre gunships at Qala-i-Jangi. They were accompanied by a heavily armed, mounted quick reaction force (QRF) of five Special Forces sergeants from ODA 534 and eight 10th Mountain infantrymen. The force arrived at Qala-i-Jangi just after sunset. After posting the QRF 1 km away, the CAS team went to meet Fahkir at the gaping breach in the north wall. When it got to the meeting site, Magione was alarmed to discover that because of the anticipated airstrikes that evening, all but a handful of the Afghan militia had left the fortress. Until the AC-130 arrived, his five-man team was the only thing between the *al-Qaeda* fighters in the south compound and the front gate. Air Force SGT Bobby Chesterfield (pseudonym) made a quick call to the inbound turboprop gunship on his tactical satellite (TACSAT) radio and learned that it was on schedule but was still two hours away. For an hour that seemed like an eternity, Magione and his team waited in the dark with mortar rounds exploding around them for the *al-Qaeda* breakout that never came.

To their great relief, the AC-130, Grim 12, arrived overhead an hour early, a little past 2200. Chesterfield described friendly and enemy positions to the AC-130's fire control officer and established targeting priorities. After the CAS team on the ground confirmed its exact location to the sensor operators on the Spectre gunship with special markers, Magione fired a hand-held parachute flare into the night sky to signal the remaining Afghan militia to leave the fortress. Five minutes later, Grim 12 began a punishing hour-long cannonade of the south compound, raining down hundreds of 40mm and 105mm high-explosive shells to create a carpet of yellow fire that enveloped the buildings and interior cells in which the *al-Qaeda* sought cover. An hour later, when Grim 12 ran out of ammunition, its sister gunship, Grim 11, arrived to orbit over the fortress and rake the *al-Qaeda* hideouts with cannon fire. At midnight, when Grim 11 reported that it was down to only four rounds of 105mm artillery, Chesterfield gave the gunship a new target—a long building just inside the wall that separated the south from the north compound where he suspected an *al-Qaeda* mortar was hidden. As the Spectre sequentially punched four 105mm rounds through the roof of the long shed, the third detonated a hidden munitions dump. Giant fireballs briefly blinded the low-light television camera on the gunship as a thunderous series of explosions followed, each more intense than the last. The blasts shook the entire fortress, hurling 100-pound artillery shells over the walls, and burning rockets shot off in all directions. With mud bricks, large dirt clods, rocks, and exploding ammunition showering down on top of them, Magione and his team ran from the fortress. They linked up with the QRF and drove back to Mazar-e-Sharif, wondering if any *al-Qaeda* had survived the Spectre assaults and exploding ammunition storage site. From the roof of the Turkish school nearly 10 miles away, FOB 53 watched the ammunition dump blaze fiercely all night.[228]

The FOB 53 troops on the roof of the Turkish school were joined by CPT Bill Gregg (pseudonym), commander, ODA 592. Five-Nine-Two had been alerted to go to Afghanistan just after news of the fratricidal bombing at Qala-i-Jangi reached JSOTF-North. Gregg was to command the QRF, and his Special Forces team would organize the 23 10th Mountain Division infantrymen and the guards at the Turkish school—27 Hazaran fighters with a Dari-speaking translator—into an effective fighting force. The FOB staff briefed Gregg on the situation at the fortress, the internal building layout, the terrain features, medical evacuation procedures, and various routes the QRF could use to and from Qala-i-Jangi. Afterward, when he had watched the AC-130 gunship detonate the ammunition dump and felt the explosive shock waves rumble through the building where he was standing, Gregg assumed his job was essentially over. No one inside the fortress, he thought, could have survived two hours of AC-130 gunfire and that final blast.[229]

On 27 November, day 3 of the uprising, additional reinforcements from Atta and Mohaqqeq arrived. The Afghan troops fought their way into the southern compound supported by

Figure 61. AC-130 20mm Gatling guns (Vulcan).

tank cannon fire and rapid-fire antiaircraft guns mounted on armored cars. Once inside, it was intense room-to-room fighting where the combatants were only yards apart. Their close proximity precluded the use of airstrikes. Clearing the southern compound was slow going.

On the morning of day 4, there were still a few pockets of die-hard *al-Qaeda* that, barricaded into rooms, were holding out. When an *al-Qaeda* fighter emerged from a doorway and approached the militia, seemingly to surrender, he killed himself using concealed hand grenades, wounding five Afghan soldiers. As the fighting continued, a squad of Afghans found the second American intelligence officer's body and carried it to the American-led rescue force in the northern compound. Mike Spann's remains would be flown to K2 that evening.

As the rotors of the MH-47E helicopter turned, 5th SFG Chaplain LTC Mark Bojune conducted a brief, solemn service.[230] After the American and British soldiers rendered honors to their fallen comrade, FOB 53 SGM Marvin Vandiver (pseudonym) produced an American flag that he had carried into Iraq during the Gulf war. Unable to drape it over the coffin because of the swirling rotor downwash, Vandiver asked the two escort officers to give the flag to Spann's family.[231]

The next day, 29 November, the last *al-Qaeda* fighters in Qala-i-Jangi surrendered. The day before, this group had retreated into the basement of the pink house. The reinforced concrete roof installed by Soviet army engineers proved too formidable for the AC-130 Spectre 105mm cannon to penetrate, and the building managed to escape any direct hit from the powerful JDAM bombs. The Afghan soldiers first tried to drive the *al-Qaeda* out by dropping grenades down the entry way, then by pouring burning diesel fuel inside. When these attempts did not prompt surrender, an ingenious fellow suggested pumping water from the fortress well down the stairs leading underground. This flooded the basement, forcing the *al-Qaeda* below to stand in several feet of freezing-cold water on a frosty November night. Hypothermia accomplished what explosions and fire could not, and the last holdouts, stupefied and numbed to impotence by the cold, gave up. These 86 were the only survivors of the more than 300 *al-Qaeda* who entered the fortress six days before.[232] Intelligence reports later revealed that the surrender may have been intended as a ploy to get the *al-Qaeda* fighters inside Mazar-e-Sharif to retake the district capital. If so, the *al-Qaeda* failed to anticipate their incarceration outside the city in the 18th-century fortress or that Afghan militia men, supported by American and British troops and airstrikes, would be able to contain and then break the prisoner revolt at Qala-i-Jangi.[233]

With the quelling of the *al-Qaeda* uprising at Qala-i-Jangi fortress, JSOTF-North shifted its focus back to General Dostum outside Konduz in the north and to the southern offensive where Hamad Karzai was working toward Kandahar from the north while Gul Agha Sherzai approached from the south. The question was who would get into the city first.

ODA 583 Meets Gul Agha Sherzai

Over the roar of the MC-130's turboprop engines, CPT Harry Sims (pseudonym) received his final mission guidance on the apron of the K2 runway in Uzbekistan on the night of 18 November 2001.[234] He and his team, ODA 583, were to fly to an airbase near Jacobabad, Pakistan, where he and two of his men would board a helicopter that would carry them into southern Afghanistan. During this leader reconnaissance, the rest of ODA 583 would wait in Jacobabad. "You might be on the ground in Afghanistan for only two or three days," said LTC Marcus Steinmann (pseudonym), the JSOTF-North Army forces commander. Sims was being inserted to meet Gul Agha Sherzai, the anti-*Taliban* Pashtun leader, and to evaluate his potential to rally sufficient following to begin offensive operations in southern Afghanistan. Sims had been told that Sherzai was a minor Pashtun figure with a few followers. Steinmann and LTC Matt Rhinehart (pseudonym), JSOTF-North operations officer, allowed that Sims and some of his ODA members might possibly stay longer "just to keep an eye on Sherzai."[235]

Sims was uncertain as to how his mission would unfold. Despite intense intelligence community efforts, personal backgrounds on Afghan leaders remained sketchy and sometimes contradictory. It was common that Hamad Karzai was confused with Gul Agha Sherzai in reports. Because the situation inside Afghanistan changed rapidly, the mission for ODA 583 changed several times. But CPT Sims was patient and determined that he would make his own

Figure 62. Gul Agha Sherzai.

opportunities once the Special Forces team was in the area of operations.[236]

At the intermediate staging base at Jacobabad, Sims met the four-man "pilot team" that would accompany him and SFCs Elias Sage and Stan Boyd (pseudonyms) aboard the Air Force MH-53 Pave Low helicopter into the Shin Narai Valley in southern Afghanistan, just across the border from Pakistan.[237] Both Sage, the intelligence sergeant, and Boyd, the communications sergeant, carried operational funds for mission needs. These needs could range from locally prepared meals to fuel for vehicles and electrical generators to construction material for bunkers or renting pack animals to carrying equipment in the mountainous terrain. One NCO was the class A agent who made purchases, and the other was the contracting officer who accounted for the funds used. Shortly after the MH-53 Pave Low helicopter lifted off, Sims fell asleep on the metal floor, awakening only after the aircraft touched down in Afghanistan just before midnight.[238]

Sherzai, accompanied by 20 fighters, personally met the Special Forces team on the landing zone (LZ). The Pashtun soldiers were surprised and seemed dismayed when the helicopter suddenly took off, leaving just three Special Forces soldiers and some other Americans behind. Lighting the way with his bright flashlight, Sherzai led the Americans to his base camp to meet his subcommanders. The news that Mazar-e-Sharif had fallen to the Northern Alliance had reached them, and Sims' pilot team was greeted warmly. Inside the command post, a mud-walled hut with a parachute for a roof, Sherzai politely asked for weapons, ammunition, food, and medicine for his Pashtun force.

At first light on 19 November, Sims and the pilot team fanned out through the valley to determine how large Sherzai's force might be. They counted at least 650 fighters and estimated there could be as many as 800. Sherzai claimed that he could call on another 400 to 600 from other locations. During a briefing at the JSOTF-North at K2, Sims had been told that there should be at least 500 anti-*Taliban* fighters in the Shin Narai for his entire ODA to be committed. He immediately radioed to have the rest of his men sent in.[239]

That evening, Sims reviewed the tenets of his assigned mission. As ordered, he had been infiltrated into Afghanistan and had linked up with Sherzai. Now he was supposed to "deny the area to *Taliban* and *al-Qaeda* forces by any means possible." Repeating "by any means possible" as he studied his aviator's map of the province, Sims reasoned that the best way to drive the enemy out of his area of operations was to seize the *Taliban* capital city of Kandahar. His terrain study, using the map, told the rest of the story, it seemed—the key to the city was the Kandahar Airport. His conclusion took only a few minutes. Sims explained his idea to Sage and Boyd, and to the other American advisers. "Let's see how much trouble we can cause," Sims said smiling. Everyone enthusiastically endorsed his plan.[240]

The next afternoon, on 20 November, Sherzai held a war council of his subcommanders. Earlier, Sims and an American adviser who had known Sherzai for several years rehearsed their proposed speech. At the council, the discussion moved one by one around the circle of a dozen Afghan chieftains seated on rugs in the mud hut headquarters. Then it was Sims' turn to talk to the leaders. Pausing regularly to allow the interpreter to translate his English into Pashto, Sims recounted that the *Taliban* had been defeated in northern Afghanistan and driven from Bagram, south of Kabul. He reminded Sherzai and his subcommanders that Karzai was fighting toward

Kandahar from the north and concluded by challenging Sherzai: "Do you want to sit here in the Shin Narai," asked Sims, "or do you want to be in Kandahar where you once were governor?"[241] This proposition got the Pashtun leader very excited.

Sims then spoke for 45 minutes without interruption. He detailed the phases of his bold plan that, sequentially accomplished, would lead Sherzai's forces to Kandahar. First, they would drive west from the Shan Narai Valley to Tahk-te-pol to block Highway 4 that linked Kandahar with Pakistan. Then they would advance north to the Arghastan Wadi to seize the bridge over the mile-wide dry riverbed. From there, they would attack and seize Kandahar Airport and the *al-Qaeda* training base at Tarnak Farms. Then, with Highway 4 blocked and the airport controlled by Sherzai, the city of Kandahar would fall. Sherzai listened intently and altered only one part of Sims' proposed plan—to approach the intermediate objective of Tahk-te-pol from the north, using a nearby mountain range for cover, rather than from the south. Sherzai then turned to his commanders and gave the order to march on the provincial capital.[242]

A day later, on 21 November, after JSOTF-North had cross-checked Sherzai's troop strength using other intelligence channels, the rest of ODA 583 was released to join Sims in Afghanistan. Eight members of Special Forces ODA 583 and an Air Force special tactics squadron (STS) were dispatched that night on an Air Force MH-53 helicopter. After an emergency landing at Quetta for engine trouble, the team was switched to another helicopter that dropped it in the darkness at the wrong LZ. By the time ODA 583 linked up with CPT Sims the next morning, Sherzai was already preparing to put his force in motion. Sims "split" the Special Forces A detachment into three close air support (CAS) teams of four men each to travel with the several troop columns. Then, they were off!

On the morning of 22 November, some 800 Pashtun warriors and Sims, with his 11 special operations soldiers, began the drive out of the Shin Narai Valley. Mounted in 100 vehicles— small Toyota pickups, large multiple-axle Ginga transport trucks, and farm tractors pulling trailers—the polyglot convoy slowly made its way west, bound for Kandahar.[243]

The Fight at Tahk-te-pol

The first objective in the Sims/Sherzai plan was to deny the *Taliban* the use of Highway 4.[244] The *Taliban* in Kandahar received most of its military supplies by truck convoy from Pakistan via Highway 4. The highway runs north through the mountains from Chaman, Pakistan, and crosses the Afghan border at Spin Boldak. From there, the single-lane paved road continues north, climbing to Tahk-te-pol, then climbs up again across more high desert before descending to the broad Arghastan wadi. There, the mile-long concrete bridge over the flat, shallow riverbed, which is dry except for occasional flooding in the rainy season, leads to the Kandahar Airport near the Tarnac Farms and then into Kandahar city. After two and one-half days of uncontested movement from the Shin Narai Valley, the 100 vehicles reached a bowl-shaped depression 5 miles east of the *Taliban* garrison at Tahk-te-pol late on 23 November.[245]

Sherzai, after consulting with Sims and his other advisers, decided to attempt to negotiate a *Taliban* surrender in the town. To provide some security for his delegation, Sherzai sent half of his 800 fighters to take up positions behind a low ridgeline 2 miles east of Tahk-te-pol. Sims went along, anticipating a fight. He brought seven of his team with him, split into two

167

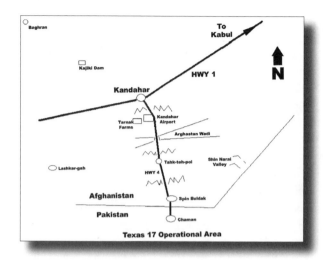

Figure 63. Location and importance.

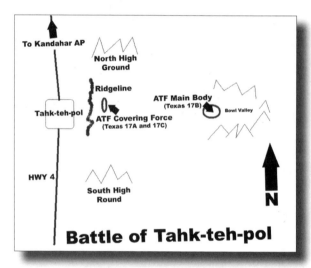

Figure 64. Deploying forces.

four-man CAS teams to accompany each of the Pashtun subcommanders who were leading the advance forces. The subcommanders shared the same name, so the Americans called them "Gulalai One" and "Gulalai Two." CPT Sims and Technical Sergeant (TSGT) Alan Kellogg (pseudonym), his Air Force airstrike controller, and SSGs Kim Joes and Stef Holman (pseudonyms) went with Gulalai One. SFC Sage followed Gulalai Two, with SFC Boyd and SSG Wally Czyrnyck and SSG Cory Loomis (pseudonyms). Sherzai remained behind in the bowl-shaped depression with the rest of his troops, the ODA 583 team sergeant, MSG Neal Nutting (pseudonym), and the remaining three Special Forces NCOs—SFC Chuck Fan, SSG Bobby Santiago, and SGT Gus Cornell (pseudonyms). Night fell. While the negotiations proceeded, the two Galalais noticed that *Taliban* elements were slipping out of Tahk-te-pol in pickup trucks, maneuvering around the Pashtun positions to surround them. The Pashtuns quickly moved to the top of the ridgeline for better observation. Sims told Kellogg to call for combat aircraft. At

168

the same time, Sims received the report that additional *Taliban* troops had driven around and beyond the Gulalais' covering elements and all but surrounded Sherzai and his men.[246]

At 2000, the *Taliban* negotiators rejected Sherzai's suggestion to surrender, and Sherzai's delegation fled from Tahk-te-pol. Almost simultaneously, *Taliban* soldiers attacked the Gulalais from the high ground to their north and south, and from Tahk-te-pol. Sims and Kellogg, who had moved to a better vantage point, began to call in airstrikes from the AC-130 gunship against targets they were able to spot in the darkness. Two air attacks silenced *Taliban* gunfire from the northern high ground, permitting the Pashtun negotiators to gain the protection of the Gulalais' position. The 400 Pashtun fighters and the two American CAS teams then withdrew to rejoin Sherzai in the bowl-shaped valley. Despite all the shooting in the two-hour gun battle, only six members of the Gulalais' advance force were slightly wounded.[247]

During the fight outside Tahk-te-pol, *Taliban* patrols had probed the defensive perimeter of Sherzai's main force. Firefights broke out in several locations, marked by tracers streaking through the dark in all directions. When the Gulalais' advance forces rejoined the main body at 2200, Sims sent his men to "circle the wagons" of Sherzai into a strong defensive perimeter. While the Special Forces sergeants set about doing this, CPT Sims and TSGT Kellogg, guarded by six Pashtuns, climbed to the highest ground on the north side facing Tahk-te-pol.

Shortly after getting in position, Sims and Kellogg spotted three groups of *Taliban* vehicles moving through the broken terrain to attack. In rapid succession, the Spectre gunship 105mm cannon blasted six enemy trucks, one of which was an ammunition carrier that exploded and burned brightly for 45 minutes like a huge bonfire in the night. The *Taliban* appeared to pull back about midnight, but Sherzai was sure that another wave of attacks would come just before dawn, so the Pashtuns and American Special Forces troops remained on full alert. At 0200, with the Spectre reporting no evidence of further enemy movement in the area, Sims and Kellogg left the observation post (OP) to return to Sherzai's headquarters. There, they found the ODA making plans for airstrikes to support a morning attack to seize Tahk-te-pol.[248]

Once the sun was fully up on 24 November, about 0900, Sherzai's troops began a three-pronged advance toward Tahk-te-pol. SFC Sage's CAS team advanced with the 350-man main assault force, only to discover that the *Taliban* had abandoned the town during the night, leaving the high desert cluttered with abandoned trucks and rapid-fire cannons. By 1300, the town had been completely occupied by Sherzai's Pashtuns and Highway 4, the key *Taliban* and *al-Qaeda* supply route between Pakistan and Kandahar, was blocked to traffic. Sims and ODA 583 had already begun to plan the next step to Kandahar—taking the bridge over the Arghastan wadi.

Fighting at Arghastan Bridge

Once Sherzai had occupied Tahk-te-pol on 24 November, CPT Sims and his Special Forces sergeants encouraged him and his subcommanders several times during the afternoon to take advantage of their success by continuing the offensive.[249] Late in the afternoon, Sims finally convinced Sherzai to send out strong security elements to establish vehicle checkpoints along Highway 4 to provide early warning of approaching threats and to interdict any *Taliban* vehicles heading to or from Kandahar. The Pashtuns drove 5 miles north from Tahk-te-pol to the Arghastan wadi and 5 miles south toward Spin Boldak to set up strongpoint roadblocks. Almost

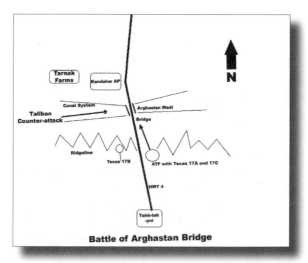

Figure 65. Battle of the Arghastan Bridge.

immediately, they captured a truck carrying Arab *al-Qaeda* fighters who had not heard about the previous day's battle.

The following day, however, the *Taliban* bombarded the northern security checkpoint at the Arghastan wadi with rocket artillery from the Kandahar Airport, seemingly in preparation for a counterattack.[250] Sims emphasized the danger to his thinly held forward line to Sherzai, and Sherzai sent 100 fighters to man defensive positions along a ridgeline several miles north of Tahk-te-pol. From that prominent position, Sherzai's 100 troops and a CAS team from ODA 583 overlooked the Arghastan wadi and could see, in the distance beyond, the Kandahar Airport. For the next seven days, the Special Forces CAS teams took turns directing a continuous stream of Air Force and Navy fighters and bombers against *Taliban* troops, vehicles, artillery, and Soviet tanks. Working 24-hour shifts, the CAS teams clobbered *Taliban* defenses around the airport to "soften them up" before Sherzai began his next attack.[251]

When the CAS team spotted the counterattacking Taliban forces seeking protection under the Arghastan Bridge from the airstrikes, the Special Forces spotters figured the enemy was thinking that the Americans would not destroy the bridge because they might need it. Thus, many sought protection from the concrete roadway. Aware that the Spectre's 105mm cannon could not destroy or drop the bridge, the CAS team directed the highly accurate AC-130's 40mm and 105mm fire into the wadi along the sides of the bridge span. Thousands of metal splinters from the high-explosive shells sprayed those sheltered underneath from both sides. The lethal fragments only chipped the concrete but killed the *Taliban* soldiers hiding between the abutments.[252]

The *Taliban* responded to the constant air attacks with volleys of shoulder-fired surface-to-air missiles (SAMs). The white smoke trails from the heat-seeking missiles reached up thousands of feet into the sky over Kandahar Airport and Tarnak Farms. Despite volleys of shoulder-fired SAMs and antiaircraft artillery (AAA) barrages from rapid-fire cannon and machine guns, no attacking U.S. aircraft were shot down.[253]

170

Figure 66. One of the major objectives of the southern offensive.

Now, with Sherzai's Pashtun forces threatening Kandahar Airport from the south, the progress of Karzai's Kandahar offensive from the north needs presentation. The size and composition of the two forces differed considerably, as did the aggressive spirit of their leaders. A Special Forces advisory team, headed by a 5th SFG battalion commander, was dispatched to support Karzai. Because capturing the *Taliban* capital, Kandahar, was the focus of both Pashtun leaders, the Special Forces teams had their hands full. Since a lot happened in a short time, the reader will be shifted back and forth between Karzai and Sherzai with the vignettes. Tenuous southern front conditions raised stress levels in JSOTF-North. Helicopter support for that region was coming primarily from Pakistan. This was a significant change.

Plans Versus Reality

On his laptop computer screen, MAJ Del Bennington (pseudonym), 2nd Battalion, 5th SFG, operations officer, at a Jordanian air base, read the order deploying his unit to Afghanistan in two weeks.[254] Transmitted on the secure Internet channel for classified message traffic, the order also specified that an advance headquarters element would go to K2, Uzbekistan, to plan the battalion movement to Bagram Airfield, Afghanistan, for combat operations. LTC Don Forsythe selected 14 of his staff to accompany him. They were Bennington and several others from operations, an intelligence team, Air Force meteorologists, and a communications section. MAJ Jeffrey Solis (pseudonym), the battalion executive officer, would remain behind with the battalion's main body to bring it forward when the JSOTF-North directed.[255]

The advance echelon (ADVON) flew to Uzbekistan on a commercial airline flight on 14 November in civilian clothes with their belongings and equipment in military backpacks and duffel bags. After arriving at the Tashkent Airport, they were bussed to K2. MAJ Stan Messinger (pseudonym), acting Army forces commander, JSOTF-North, met Forsythe and Bennington to explain a change in plans. The ADVON had been designated Special Operations Command and Control Element (SOCCE) 52.[256] Forsythe and SOCCE 52 were to be helicoptered into

171

the Tarin Kowt region of southern Afghanistan where they would serve as an advisory staff for Pashtun resistance leader Hamad Karzai. CPT Amerine and ODA 574 from the 3rd Battalion were about to leave Pakistan to join Karzai, about 70 miles north of Kandahar.[257]

An Air Force MC-130 Combat Talon transported the newly formed SOCCE 52 to Jacobabad, Pakistan. LTC Dan Herndon (pseudonym), deputy commander, Joint Special Operations Air Component Command–South (JSOAC-South), briefed Forsythe and his staff that they would enter enemy territory aboard MH-53 Pave Low helicopters. Before Herndon joined the Air Force and became a transport pilot, he had been an Army enlisted soldier and served in both Special Forces and Ranger units. Bennington thought that the SOCCE had a particularly strong collection of officers and sergeants. His primary assistant, CPT Douglas Bain (pseudonym), was a former A-team leader and was considered to be one of the best commanders in the battalion. The most experienced plans officer was CWO Tim Roswell (pseudonym). CPT Jack Loach and SSG Cody Prosser (pseudonyms) anchored the intelligence section. Two Army communicators, a meteorologist, and two tactical air control parties (TACPs) from the Air Force 19th SOS rounded out SOCCE 52.[258] They were also fortunate because they had several linguists on the team: SGM Rich Ryder (pseudonym) spoke Pashto (one of the few speakers in the 5th SFG); SSG "Charlie" Fazal (pseudonym) was a native Persian Farsi speaker; and SSG Nick Sands (pseudonym), a recent Special Forces school graduate, had been first in his modern Arabic language class.[259]

SOCCE 52 did not arrive in Afghanistan together. After meeting Hamad Karzai near Tarin Khot, CPT Amerine radioed back to Pakistan that "only three" more Americans would be welcome. Thus, Forsythe, Bennington, and Sands, who was a trained radio operator, made the cold three-hour flight by MH-53 Pave Low into Oruzgan Province. At 0300, 24 November, the MH-53 made a "controlled crash" on the landing zone (LZ). When the MH-53 helicopters hovered over the high desert LZs, the downwash from their rotors raised thick, blinding clouds of dust that enveloped the aircraft, creating a brownout condition. For the last several feet of the landing, the pilots could not see the ground—or anything else outside the cockpit—and could only maintain a steady rate of level descent until the helicopter landing gear bumped heavily onto the earth. Safely in Afghanistan, the three members of SOCCE 52 joined CPT Amerine and ODA 574. Over the next 10 days, they followed them and the slowly growing army of anti-*Taliban* Pashtuns marching toward Kandahar.[260] Forsythe and Bennington became the military advisers to Karzai. They also directed the operations of ODA 574 and ODA 583 with Sherzai south of Kandahar. Bennington focused on planning the details and coordinating the schemes of maneuver and air support for the two forces to prevent the converging militia armies from inadvertently attacking each other or having airstrikes directed against them.[261]

The Karzai Way to Kandahar

In late November 2001, Kandahar suddenly became the focus of attention. As the city that gave birth to the *Taliban* movement, it was most significant to those who supported the repressive regime and those who sought to free Afghanistan from these oppressors. The fall of Kandahar would have a tremendous psychological and political impact on the entire campaign. When LTC Forsythe, commander, 2nd Battalion, 5th SFG, arrived at K2 in mid-November, the chief operations officer (J3) of JSOTF-North, LTC Matt Rhinehart, directed him toward supporting Karzai near Tarin Kowt.[262]

Figure 67. Training new Karzai "recruits" for combat.

While CPT Amerine and ODA 574 were defeating the *Taliban* at the battle of Tarin Kowt north of Kandahar, CPT Harry Sims and ODA 583 were advancing on the city from the south. Forsythe sought to link up with Amerine and Karzai and assist in the move south. On 29 November at 0200, Forsythe and three members of his staff landed at Tarin Kowt where Amerine introduced him to Karzai. His "army" consisted of "25 to 30 well-meaning friends, farmers, shopkeepers. There was no army to speak of," said Forsythe.

Establishing rapport with a guerrilla leader is critical to advising an unconventional force. The Tarin Kowt region is known for its pomegranates, and there were thousands of trees about the camp. Forsythe told Karzai that his grandfather had a pomegranate tree in his backyard. They talked about their experiences as children climbing pomegranate trees and tasting the fruit. According to Forsythe, "That seemed to be the thing that broke the ice." Forsythe, Karzai, and Amerine then began to plan the advance on Kandahar in conjunction with Sherzai from the south. In the meantime, ODA 574 directed airstrikes against small groups of *Taliban* moving against them from Kandahar and coordinated airdrops of weapons, munitions, food, and humanitarian aid for the neighboring Afghan people.

To prepare for the move, Karzai sent four men to a village about halfway to Kandahar to reconnoiter the area. They reported no *Taliban*. On 30 November, the column of Pashtun trucks moved out but only went a short distance before Forsythe was called to the head of the column. The vehicles had stopped at a local gas station to refuel, and the attendant would not fill the vehicles because no one had any money. Finally, Karzai came forward and introduced himself and promised that he would come back to pay him if he would refuel the vehicles. That worked, and the convoy was on its way again.

There has been no U.S. military field manual written to describe the "tactical convoy" that the Afghans were conducting. Forsythe described it as something like "a cross between the Baja, California, off-road races and scenes from the movie, 'Mad Max.'" There was no order or semblance of security as local Afghans in Subaru and Toyota trucks joined the advance. All wanted to see Karzai. The trucks would race alongside the line of vehicles until they spotted him, pull alongside, wave, and shout a greeting. That would be replaced by another truck full of people racing alongside the future president of Afghanistan. The fact that no one wrecked was a miracle. Fortunately, the *Taliban* never threatened, but the Air Force was on call just in case. After about 30 miles, the convoy stopped for several days.

The new recruits had to be armed and fed. That meant an aerial resupply. Afterward, ODA 574 provided rudimentary training to the new volunteers who had never fired a weapon before. The training was simply how to load ammunition in a magazine, how to get a bullet in the chamber, where the trigger was, and that each knew "which end of the rifle the bullet came out of." The entire force, counting the Americans, numbered about 200. Having become increasingly concerned about the possibility of encountering enemy forces, Forsythe convinced Karzai to establish some control over the mob as they planned the next phase of the advance—attacking Sayd Alim Kalay, 15 miles north of Kandahar.

Returning to Sherzai and his Pastun forces south of the Arghastan Bridge, they were preparing to continue the offensive. Sherzai would attack the Kandahar Airport in the first days of December.

Charge to the Airport and Back Again

Facing only occasional rocket and artillery fire from the vicinity of the airport, about 100 of Sherzai's troops moved across the Arghastan Bridge on 2 December. CPT Sims stood alongside Sherzai on the bridge as he directed his fighters to take up defensive positions. As evening approached, Air Force aircraft spotted *Taliban* troops massing in the wadi to the west of the bridge. Their advance through a maze of canals had concealed them from Sherzai's forces but not hidden them from "overhead intelligence" satellites and aircraft that kept the battlefields under constant surveillance, reporting enemy movement. Hence, at nightfall, when the *Taliban* began a series of small counterattacks to recapture the Arghastan Bridge, Sherzai's Pashtuns were able to hold them off with the assistance of airstrikes directed by MSG Nutting's CAS team, observing from a ridgeline above the wadi.[263]

Figure 68. A U.S. Air Force A-10
Warthog CAS aircraft.

The next morning, 3 December, Sherzai and Sims talked about the day's operations to secure the bridge area to the entrances of the canal system, ½ mile away, by extending his defensive perimeter. At 0900, the security forces encountered *al-Qaeda* fighters guarding the canals, and a series of sharp firefights ensued. Sherzai quickly committed about 400 reinforcements to the attack, and this large force overran the *al-Qaeda* defenders so quickly that they captured heavy mortars in their firing positions. Special Forces medics Cory Loomis and Kim Joes treated the seriously wounded Afghans in the cover of the bridge.[264] Encouraged by this early success against the canal system, Sherzai pressed his advantage. At 1400, he sent 200

174

men up Highway 4 to seize the main entrance to Kandahar Airport that was a little over 2 miles away. CPT Sims dispatched SFC Sage and his CAS team with the assault force to keep him abreast of their progress and to direct airstrikes if needed. They were vitally needed when the Pashtun force was stopped by heavy machine gun and cannon fire just a few hundred yards from the airport main gate. More significantly, in their haste to reach the airport, the Pashtun commander had driven right past *Taliban* and *al-Qaeda* troops positioned near the highway who moved to surround the assault force. Under crackling fire, Sage and his CAS team made their way to the foremost line of Pashtuns. They started guiding airstrikes so that the bombs would impact directly in front of them to enable the Pashtuns to break contact with the dug-in enemy and withdraw south before they were trapped. The CAS team held the *Taliban* at bay with continuous airstrikes as the assault force retreated south.

By late afternoon, all of Sherzai's troops had reassembled back at the Arghastan Bridge. Sherzai, furious with the assault force commander, replaced him. ODA 574 knew that zealous haste almost cost Sherzai one-fourth of his Pashtun force and that Sage's CAS team had saved them. Nonetheless, the air attacks and heavy bombing had mauled the *Taliban*, which put the Arghastan Bridge firmly under Sherzai's control. The next attack on Kandahar Airport, Sims hoped, would be better planned and executed.[265]

While the back-and-forth fight across the Arghastan Wadi went on, *Taliban* forces moved up Highway 4 from Spin Boldak on the Pakistan border. They took cover in another wadi about 3 miles from Sherzai's security checkpoints south of Tahk-te-pol. On the day after the battle for the Arghastan Bridge ended, 5 December, the *Taliban* from Spin Boldak started bombarding the southern outposts with rockets and mortar fire. Sims sent Sage, SSG Czyrnyck, SFC Boyd, and a medic, SSG Loomis, by pickup truck to help the Pashtuns hold the line and to protect Sherzai's back while his troops recovered from the setback at the airport. They went into action as soon as they arrived. Sage's CAS team directed bombs on *Taliban* mortar positions and artillery pieces hidden in the wadi, achieving a direct hit on an antiaircraft gun. Sage then asked for permission to attack the bridge over the riverbed, reasoning that this would block the enemy from simply driving up Highway 4 to attack Sherzai from behind. The CAS team spotted *Taliban* soldiers and vehicles seeking cover under the bridge as they had at Arghastan. When Sims gave the OK, the bombs that blew down the span over the wadi also destroyed a mobile rocket launcher parked underneath and detonated a hidden ammunition truck. The fierce aerial bombardment shattered the *Taliban* counterattack force, and the CAS team watched the survivors retreat south toward Spin Boldak. With their southern flank secure, Sage and his CAS team returned to Arghastan to prepare for the assault on Kandahar.[266]

Attacking the Arghendab Bridge With Karzai

After the battles at Tarin Kowt and Patowek, Hamad Karzai's "Opposition Group," as CENTCOM referred to the anti-*Taliban* forces, advanced on Sayd-Alim-Kalay and the Arghendab Bridge. By 2 December, Karzai's Pashtun fighters had occupied the town, but they met sharp resistance when they tried to cross the bridge the following day. On 3 December, CPT Amerine and three other Special Forces soldiers from ODA 574 moved with the 60 Pashtuns in the advance force followed by the main body. Just after crossing the Arghendab Bridge, the advance came under fire from the village on the opposite side of the dry riverbed. When the Afghans began to retreat, Amerine ran forward and yelled for them to follow him. At the top of a slight ridge, he saw *Taliban* soldiers firing from buildings in the town. The American soldiers returned fire, killing several *Taliban* before joining the retreating Pashtuns on the other side of the bridge. If the advance were to continue, the bridge had to be seized. The soldiers quickly organized the Pashtuns into a defensive line for the night.

Shortly after dark, most of the Afghans suddenly jumped in their trucks and drove away, leaving only LTC Forsythe, ODA 574, and about 30 Afghans to defend the north side of the bridge. Then, approximately 100 *Taliban* counterattacked across the dry riverbed. Using the firepower and night vision capability of the AC-130 Spectre gunships to keep them alert for new threats, the Special Forces soldiers and Pashtuns drove back the attackers.

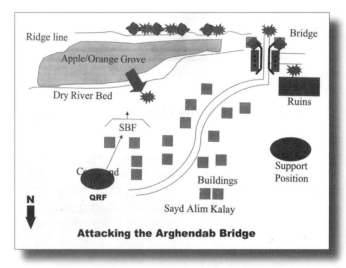

Figure 69. Actions at the Arghendab Bridge.

The next morning, 4 December, when Karzai brought the rest of his force to the forward position, Forsythe convinced him that they had to seize the bridge. MAJ Bennington "felt the pressure of time" because indications from the Bonn Conference were that Karzai would likely be named prime minister of the Afghan Interim Authority (AIA) and would be expected in Kabul in about two weeks. Amerine and half of his team with about 100 Pashtuns were the advance element in "the ruins," a crumbling set of mud walls 250 yards north of the bridge. Now very proficient at guiding bombs and directing close air support (CAS), Amerine's team used well-aimed aerial bombs to prevent enemy counterattacks across the two-lane concrete Arghendab Bridge. LTC Forsythe oversaw the fight from a knoll 200 yards behind the ruins with MSG Jefferson Davis, Five-Seven-Four team sergeant, and the rest of the Special Forces team and about 50 Pashtun fighters in the support position. Bennington and SSG Sands stayed at the "command post," a one-time Soviet mortar battery position on a prominent hilltop a little more than ¼ mile to the east of Forsythe. With them were their guides and a reserve force of about 70 Pashtuns positioned to move to wherever Karzai's lines were threatened by an enemy attack.[267]

During the back-and-forth fighting near Sayd-Alim-Kalay, a *Taliban* soldier had defected, bringing a hand-held radio with him. The defector was taken back to the command post where

Bennington and Sands heard the excited chatter on the radio still tuned to the *Taliban* frequency. They recognized that the crackling voices directing the enemy were speaking Arabic, not some Afghan dialect. "We're fighting *al-Qaeda*," realized Bennington, whose Arabic was rusty, but Sands, fresh from language school, clearly understood the orders being issued on the radio. "They're going to flank us on our left using the apple orchard for cover," announced Sands. Bennington radioed LTC Forsythe at the support position and recommended a plan to counter the enemy attack. He looked down toward the east side of the bridge above the wadi and saw the apple orchard the *Taliban* leader had described as the approach route that his soldiers should use to sneak down to the riverbed. "I'm going to take some guys down from my position," said Bennington, waving forward a quick-reaction squad of Karzai's Pashtuns, "and see what I can see."[268]

Bennington signaled for 12 Pashtun fighters to follow him, and with three guides, the group ran several hundred yards downhill toward the wadi. Long practiced in infantry tactics, Bennington quickly placed the riflemen and the machine gunner along the crest of the bank opposite the orchard by pointing out exactly where he wanted each to lie down. Moments later, about 30 *Taliban* soldiers emerged from the grove of leafless gray apple trees, slipped down into the dry riverbed, and started across. Taking careful aim at the approaching *Taliban* with his M-4 carbine, Bennington "triggered" the ambush by firing first. Instantly, his entire squad joined in, spraying the riverbed with bullets. The loud staccato of returning Russian-model PK machine gun fire and the "whoosh" and crash of rocket-propelled grenades (RPGs) could be heard over the Pashtun machine gun and rifle fire. With at least 10 of the enemy force wounded and down in the dry riverbed, the others turned and fled back to the cover of the apple orchard. The Pashtuns cheered out loud about their success. Bennington directed the senior Pashtun, a veteran fighter who the Americans had respectfully nicknamed "Sergeant Major," to keep the squad ready for another enemy attack. Then he ran back to Forsythe's location to report that the enemy assault had been repulsed. Forsythe realized that the *Taliban* might try a similar flanking maneuver on their right and dispatched American Special Forces soldiers with another band of 50 Pashtuns to the west side of the bridge. Both groups watched and waited for another attack, but the *Taliban* was content to harass them with small-arms fire for the rest of that day.[269]

Karzai's troops and the Special Forces soldiers were now firmly established on the north side of the wadi, controlling the approaches to the bridge with a glowing sense of having beaten the *Taliban* in the most intense close-in fighting of the offensive. During the battle, SSG Walter Madison (pseudonym), defending at the ruins, was shot through the shoulder.[270] Bennington reported their situation to JSOTF-North and that Madison had been wounded. The radio operator in the joint operations center responded with an order from "Marshal Eight-Five," COL Mulholland, the JTF commander. LTC Forsythe was to pull all of his men back ½ mile to the town of Sayd-Alim-Kalay.

Confused by the order to give up the position they had fought so hard to take and hold, MAJ Bennington asked for the message to be repeated a second, and then a third, time so that Sands and the guides could hear it as well. When Bennington delivered the order to Forsythe, he said, "I want verification," but, unaccountably, radio contact with the U.S. base at K2 had been lost. For the next 3½ hours, SOCCE 52 and ODA 574 were literally incommunicado. Unable to get the verification he wanted, Forsythe had no choice but to obey the last orders he had received.

He directed the American soldiers to abandon the positions by the bridge and pull back into the town to await the helicopters due that night with supplies, mail, and 12 more men, the rest of SOCCE 52. "We still have the initiative," said Forsythe. "We'll make plans for their next step in the morning."[271] That evening, Karzai was told on his cellular telephone that the next day the delegates of Afghan factions meeting in Bonn, Germany, would name him the interim leader of the new government of Afghanistan.[272] While the Karzai attack from the north was stalled at the Arghendab Bridge, Gul Agha Sherzai was determined to win the "race to Kandahar" from the south.

Who Dares, Wins

With Kandahar within striking distance, CPT Sims favored sending a large portion of Sherzai's growing force of Pashtuns away from the airport on a wide arc around the Tarnak Farms to approach the city from the west.[273] On 4 December, JSOTF-North radioed tactical guidance to Sims: "Don't go west. That course of action will stretch you too thin." His response was, "Well, let's get the marines in the fight." JSOTF-North replied that the marines were not at Objective Rhino for "direct combat." Sims was baffled. "Why were hundreds of Marines in the desert 80 miles from Kandahar if not to join in the fight?" he wondered. The operations center also expressed serious concerns about Sherzai and ODA 583 actually entering Kandahar and suggested that a better plan would be to surround the city. With Karzai and ODA 574 about 40 miles north of the last *Taliban*-held city in Afghanistan and pushing southward, JSOTF-North's final instructions to Sims were "Continue to develop the situation."[274]

Sherzai pushed his scout elements—small groups of pickup trucks carrying around 10 men each—around the outskirts of Kandahar. Then, Pashta, the older of Sherzai's two younger brothers, made a sizable reconnaissance in force with 10 trucks carrying 200 Pashtun troops toward the city. On the morning of 7 December, Sims was standing near the gate of Kandahar Airport with Sherzai when Pashta called him on his satellite telephone. Excitedly, the younger Pashta reported that he had entered the city meeting no *Taliban* resistance and was at the governor's palace. Sherzai turned to Sims and said (through the interpreter, Engineer Yosif), "I'm going to the palace, come with me!" Sims deliberately hesitated, knowing entry into the city was contrary to JSOTF-North directions, and said that he would have to get permission from his commander, LTC Forsythe. As Sims was trying to raise "Rambo 85" (Forsythe) by satellite radio for instructions, COL Mulholland came on the air and ordered Sims, "Don't go into Kandahar. We have reports that Sherzai's troops are looting the city, and the various factions are fighting each other. It's not safe." Impatient to return to his former seat of government, Sherzai did not wait for Sims to finish the radio conversation. He quickly gathered about 500 of his troops who mounted their trucks and sped away into the city with Sherzai in the lead vehicle. Four British soldiers in a four-wheel-drive truck followed the Afghans.[275]

Engineer Yosif drove back and found Sims 45 minutes later. "Sherzai invites you to his palace," implored the translator, "He asks why you're not there with him." As Yosif waited, Sims weighed the consequences of accepting Sherzai's invitation with COL Mulholland's reaction. Thinking quickly, he rationalized that the presence of U.S. Special Forces troops might deter interfactional fighting. The task force commander did not know that Sherzai was already in the governor's palace in Kandahar. Sims did not think that Mulholland or any of his staff in Uzbekistan knew the situation as well as he did, and so far, no one at JSOTF-North had second-guessed him on his decisions. Yosif said it was safe, and what was to be gained from joining Sherzai now was worth taking the risk. Sims had another motivation: he wanted his team, ODA 583, to be the first American soldiers into Kandahar. It took only a few moments before he yelled to Yosif, "Hell, yeah, we're coming!" Sims told four of his men to secure their base. As the rest of his team jumped into two sport utility vehicles, someone asked, "What did COL Mulholland say?" "That's not important now," answered Sims. "The situation is changing too rapidly."[276]

When they entered the former *Taliban* capital, Sims thought to himself, "So this is what it's like to liberate a city." As the Special Forces detachment drove its vehicles along dusty streets crowded with thousands of Afghans, the people were cheering, waving, and throwing marigolds at them. Sims heard occasional shouts of "Welcome!" and "Thank you!" in broken English coming from the crowd. Sims glanced at his watch and saw that it was nearly 1400.

Then it struck him. The date was 7 December—Pearl Harbor Day. That had been a surprise attack like 9/11, he thought, and thus, it seemed quite appropriate to ride into the enemy's capital in tribute to that "day of infamy" for Americans. When ODA 583 reached the governor's palace, Sims typed a message into his digital encrypting device to transmit to JSOTF-North: "We are in the governor's palace with Sherzai." It was 1500.[277]

Figure 70. The Kandahar welcoming committee.

Sims picked up his satellite radio and called JSOTF-North to make the same report, but personally, to the task force commander. LTC Mike Roberts (pseudonym), the JSOTF-North operations officer, answered for Mulholland.[278] "I'm in Kandahar," reported Sims. "Tell me why you went into the city," replied Roberts, calmly. In short, clipped phrases, Sims recounted the reasons that had run through his mind when Yosif presented Sherzai's invitation to him. He then described the buoyant crowds inside Kandahar, celebrating the fall of the *Taliban*. "Okay, sounds good," Roberts responded. To his relief, there had been no challenge to the decision. As he stood looking about the governor's palace, he recalled his original orders at the task force base in Uzbekistan three weeks before, telling him what he was to accomplish in Kandahar province: "Deny the area to *Taliban* and *al-Qaeda* forces by any means possible." A sense of satisfaction came over him. "I felt like I accomplished my mission," said Sims. Nineteen days after landing in the Shin Narai Valley, ODA 583 and Sherzai's Pashtun warriors had fought their way across high deserts and over mountains through thousands of enemy fighters to seize Kandahar, their objective, "by any means possible." This victory effectively ended the battle for Afghanistan.[279]

While ODA 583 and Sherzai's Pashtuns were fighting the *Taliban* on the southern outskirts of Kandahar, tragedy was about to strike the other Pashtun force converging on the city from the north. The news that Karzai had been selected to lead the AIA would be temporarily forgotten in the wake of a fratricide incident.

Death From Above

5 December 2001 was a day no member of ODA 574 would ever forget. Team members were busy sharing the contents of "care packages" from home that came with the resupply items on the helicopters that delivered the rest of SOCCE 52 to Sayd-Alim-Kalay the night before. In the

179

midst of this activity, the Special Forces soldiers had spotted several *Taliban* fighters on a ridge and around a cave nearby. The CAS team had already directed Air Force F-18s carrying bombs on the target while the tactical air control party (TACP) attached to ODA 574 talked to circling B-52 bombers. Suddenly, at 0930, "All hell broke loose." A joint direct-attack munition (JDAM) dropped from a B-52 impacted directly on a friendly position. In a split second, two Americans—MSG Davis, the ODA 583 team sergeant, and SFC Daniel Petithory—and at least six Afghans were dead; eight other Americans and perhaps 40 Afghans were wounded; and one American, SSG Prosser (pseudonym), was seriously wounded. CPT Amerine realized at once what had happened: "We were hit by our own bomb." Both of Amerine's eardrums had burst, and he was hit in the thigh by a bomb fragment. Karzai was injured by the shattered glass of a nearby window. Moments before, Davis had been sharing Rice Krispie treats from his wife's care package.[280]

Figure 71. A mission-ready JDAM.

The highly trained Special Forces soldiers reacted instinctively. The survivors hurriedly reconstituted a defense and applied first aid to the casualties. Luckily, the team had two medics and another soldier who was a former medic. Although one of the medics was injured, the trio did a quick triage of both American and Afghan casualties. They were all allies; they were all fighting for the same cause; they would have done the same. The intravenous kits all Special Forces soldiers carry were soon all in use. All Special Forces soldiers receive combat lifesaving training, and that basic skill ensured the survival of numerous wounded personnel.

Forsythe notified COL Mulholland of the disaster, and Mulholland alerted a quick-reaction force (QRF) in case the *Taliban* took advantage of the situation. Both Mulholland and Forsythe called for aerial medical evacuation. The nearest helicopters were at the U.S. Marine base at Camp Rhino, more than 100 miles southwest of Kandahar. U.S. Navy CH-53s in Pakistan responded the fastest. As medics on the ground sorted the casualties, the number kept rising. There was no question that the two helicopters would be loaded to capacity. After taking on the dead and wounded, the Navy helicopters lifted off for Rhino. Short of fuel, an Air Force CH-130P tanker met the flight and refueled them en route. Escorted by AH-1 Cobra gunships, two U.S. Marine CH-53 helicopters carrying ODB 570 and ODA 524 (dispatched from JSOTF-North) and SOCCE 540 personnel (with TF 58 at Rhino) arrived with doctors and Air Force pararescue medics. The U.S. Marine helicopters evacuated the wounded Afghans

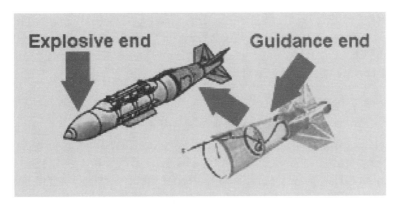

Figure 72. JDAM components.

to Rhino. Using the airstrip at Camp Rhino, an emergency surgical team treated the critically wounded Americans as they were flown to hospitals in the region. Some continued on to Germany and eventually to the United States.[281]

What went wrong? Initial indications revealed that the bomber received the wrong coordinates for the enemy position. A technological quirk in the global positioning system (GPS) the Air Force TACP was using required that the system be recalibrated after the batteries were changed. Otherwise, the GPS automatically displayed the map coordinates where the device was located. If the operator neglected to reenter the coordinates of the enemy position after changing batteries, he could inadvertently transmit his position as the target to the B-52 bomber circling overhead at 10,000 feet. Then ODA 574's location would automatically be entered in the JDAM homing mechanism, and the bomb would travel directly to where it was programmed—in this case, at friendly forces.[282]

Unfortunately, casualties from friendly fire (fratricide) are a fact of war. In World War II, GEN Lesley J. McNair was inadvertently killed by American bombs shortly before the breakout from Normandy. Almost a platoon of paratroopers from the 173rd Airborne Brigade, heavily engaged fighting the North Vietnamese at Dak To, were killed by American CAS when an errant bomb struck a command post. Like the JDAM bomb strike on ODA 574, such incidents are very difficult to accept. Despite the losses, the *Taliban* was defeated, the city of Kandahar was captured, and Karzai survived to become the interim president of a war-torn nation. President Bush spoke of the deaths and the soldiers' contributions: "And I want the families to know that they died for a noble and just cause, that the fight against terror is noble and just. And they defended freedom. And for that we are grateful."[283]

Figure 73. President George W. Bush.

181

Less than 48 hours after the fratricide incident at Sayd-Alim-Kalay involving Karzai's forces, ODA 574, SOCCE 52, Sherzai's Pashtuns, and ODA 583 entered the abandoned *Taliban* capital, Kandahar. The American plan for seizing the city in a coordinated assault involving the two Pashtun forces did not consider Afghan rivalry for power.

Another Reaction to Kandahar's Fall

Shortly before the JDAM struck ODA 574 as the U.S. soldiers were reading their mail and opening packages from home, Karzai was talking to a *Taliban* delegation in Kandahar on his telephone. For almost two weeks, Sherzai, advised by CPT Sims and ODA 583, had been steadily advancing on Kandahar from the south. From the north, Karzai had been moving toward the same city. As the birthplace of the *Taliban* movement, its fall would be significant in the war to establish a stable Afghanistan. As the two forces approached the city, it appeared imminent that resistance would soon collapse and a new era would begin. In CPT Amerine's opinion, "Taking Kandahar, as I saw it, was probably going to be the end of the war."[284]

After talking to the *Taliban* delegation by satellite phone, Karzai told reporters that he started "serious negotiations beginning this morning," and he hoped that the situation would be "resolved soon."[285] While Karzai was on the phone negotiating, LTC Forsythe was planning to coordinate the moves from south and north to "squeeze the *Taliban* between us."[286] His first move was to reoccupy the terrain approximately 700 meters from where the JDAM had struck. On 6 December, American Special Forces and Pashtun forces accomplished this without incident.

Karzai's efforts culminated in his agreement to meet with the *Taliban* delegation near Sayd-Alim-Kalay on 7 December. Concerned about the AIA president's safety, Forsythe advised Karzai to limit the *Taliban* delegation to a single vehicle. Karzai concurred. According to the Pashtun leader, the American presence was so intimidating to the *Taliban* delegates that they immediately surrendered. The terms of that surrender were somewhat unclear, however.[287]

"The *Taliban* have decided to surrender Kandahar, Helmand, and Zabul (provinces) to me, and in exchange, we have offered them amnesty," reported Karzai. This sweeping gesture, however, proved unacceptable to President Bush. According to Secretary of Defense Rumsfeld, any mutual agreement that granted amnesty to *Taliban* leader Mullah Omar would not be accepted. Furthermore, there were still *Taliban* and *al-Qaeda* dug in around the city. Sherzai and Sims faced a strong force and were about 2 miles from the city at the airport. Shortly after Karzai's meeting on 7 December, Sherzai entered Kandahar and occupied his old office in the governor's mansion.[288]

Figure 74. President Bush and Hamad Karzai.

When Karzai found out, he was furious. Mullah Naqueebullah, a senior *Taliban* military leader in Kandahar, had been negotiating his becoming the Kandahar governor in exchange for surrendering the *Taliban* military to Karzai. The mullah's issue was that Sherzai already occupied the mansion. LTC Forsythe convinced Karzai that a civil war over Kandahar was not in his or the country's best interest. The compromise with Naqueebullah was that Karzai would allow him to retain his title of mullah and his house in the city if he agreed to sever all political and military ties. Karzai, Forsythe, and the Special Forces soldiers of SOCCE 52 entered the city on 8 December. Three days later, Karzai agreed that Sherzai should be designated provincial governor, and Naqueebullah agreed to the compromise conditions.

Forsythe, Sims, and the rest of the Special Forces soldiers were still nervous about the arrangements. Consistent with Afghan tradition, many former *Taliban* suddenly were loyal to Karzai. Switching sides carried no stigma to these fighters. To the Americans, though, it was disconcerting. "One minute you're shooting at them, and the next minute they're your allies and friends," Forsythe remarked. An unanswered question was, where had all the *Taliban* leaders gone? Mullah Omar had disappeared from the city. The Americans had to conclude that during the negotiations the important *Taliban* leaders had fled. A few days later, Karzai officiated at the formal ceremony installing Sherzai as governor and then departed for Kabul to become interim president of Afghanistan.[289]

Amerine's prediction that the fall of Kandahar marked the end of the war proved wrong. Fighting continued. Nevertheless, two Afghan Pashtun forces with small advisory contingents of American Special Forces troops had liberated a major portion of their country. The Americans had accomplished the task without creating the impression that they were another foreign force bent on occupying the country. *Taliban* propaganda comparing the United States' actions with those of Great Britain or the Soviet Union would carry little weight. Coupled with the capture of Mazar-e-Sharif, Herat, Bagram, and Kabul in early November, the fall of Kandahar in December was a decisive victory in the war against terrorism.

As Northern Alliance forces, supported by the Special Forces ODAs, captured towns and cities in northern and central Afghanistan, Army civil affairs teams (CATs) followed close behind. These teams coordinated humanitarian assistance and reconstruction efforts, working closely with tactical PSYOP teams (TPTs). These "on-the-ground" tactical teams complemented the Air Force EC-130 Commando Solo airborne radio broadcasts and added emphasis to PSYOP messages being distributed in massive leaflet drops throughout the country. JSOTF-North directed all these efforts as part of the overarching unconventional warfare (UW) campaign.

CA and Humanitarian Relief

During its effort to rejuvenate old connections and establish new links to recent NGO arrivals, CPT Marty Cavanaugh (pseudonym) and CAT-A46, D Company, 96th Civil Affairs Battalion (CAB) learned that UNICEF had an inoculation campaign set up to begin in the area southeast of Herat in late November.[290] Concerned that the UNICEF inoculation teams would get caught up in Ismail Khan's offensive against the *Taliban* near Herat, MAJ DiJurnigan, chief, civil-military operations center (CMOC), Islamabad, after contacting Special Forces ODA 554, diplomatically suggested that the inoculation campaign be postponed. In another instance, when he received a call from an aircraft carrying humanitarian aid from Iran to Herat, DiJurnigan coordinated the landing instructions with ODA 554.

CAT-A46 spent most of its time recording, updating, and disseminating the multitude of humanitarian aid and assistance activity inside Afghanistan. Over time, more and more of the NGOs recognized and realized the benefits of coordinating with DiJurnigan and the CA team. However, many NGOs and private organizations were reluctant to work or cooperate with any organization that was overtly military like the CMOC. DiJurnigan, therefore, coined the title coalition humanitarian liaison cell (CHLC) to eliminate the word "military" from civil-military

Figure 75. Inventory and accountability were a
constant part of humanitarian aid.

operations center. The nondoctrinal CHLC, as well as its popular nickname, "Chiclet," became part of the CA legacy during the war in Afghanistan.

In October and November, while DiJurnigan coordinated humanitarian operations from Islamabad, elements of C Company, 96th CAB, deployed to Uzbekistan where they established CMOC-North at K2. With CAT-A46 capable of handling the requirements in Islamabad, DiJurnigan flew to Kabul in early December to imbed himself in the newly created Combined Joint Civil-Military Operations Task Force (CJCMOTF) to assist CMOC-North and CMOC-South with their information requests and serve as a voice for the 96th CAB teams in Afghanistan. Since many of the NGO personnel in Kabul had migrated there from Islamabad, this enhanced his value to the new headquarters. DiJurnigan was realistic about the CA role in the war: "The biggest issue was where do we [CA] fit into this particular conflict? That was always our biggest challenge—to find out where we could most effectively 'plug into' a longstanding humanitarian infrastructure." Secretary of Defense Rumsfeld commented on the role of the CA soldiers: "[They made] remarkable contributions. By demonstrating our concern for the welfare of the Afghan people through the delivery of humanitarian relief from the first days of the war, we showed the Afghan people that we were coming as a force of liberation, not a force of occupation."[291] And it all started in Pakistan.

CA Teams on the Ground

Decades of fighting had disrupted the Afghan economy, and the *Taliban* government institutions had not been functioning for some time. The Army CA teams were introduced as part of a massive effort to provide for the welfare of the people. At Mazar-e-Sharif, CAT-A33 helped a Jordanian medical team establish a hospital that provided care for about 8,000 people in 60 days.[292] Education was among the top civic-action priorities. The team assessed 15 schools in and around the city and submitted repair projects to CJCMOTF for funding. The CA soldiers helped deliver textbooks to local hospitals and a medical school. Because Mazar-e-Sharif was the second largest city in the country, it was to be a main food distribution center. CAT-A33 personnel arranged the construction of a large food storage warehouse at the airfield by the World Food Program.

The second critical site for the humanitarian relief effort was the airfield at Bagram. When it arrived on 23 November, CAT-A32's mission was to establish a distribution center to ship aid throughout Afghanistan. Thus, part of the headquarters staff of a CAT-B accompanied CAT-A32 to Bagram.[293] In the interim, MAJ Steve Small (pseudonym) and CAT-A32 arranged for the repair of two hangars that had been stripped of wiring. Four Soviet aircraft stored in one had to be man-handled out to make room for the rapidly arriving aid. They worked with several NGOs, including a European organization, to transport 40 injured children to Germany for treatment. SFC Charles Rogers (pseudonym), a former Special Forces medic on CAT-A32, described the scene of the wounded children as "heartbreaking." "I've got children of my own, and that's all I could think of when I was holding these kids," said Rogers. On 7 December, the first aircraft loaded with 945 bags of red wheat and 1,440 blankets arrived and was unloaded. Danger was ever present, and on 18 December, a U.S. soldier from another unit stepped on a mine near a hangar. Rogers administered first aid immediately and helped to stabilize the injured soldier until an ambulance with doctors arrived. That evening, CAT-A32 departed Bagram for K2 and was replaced by CAT-A41 from D Company, 96th CAB.[294]

Figure 76. CA collar insignia and the USACAPOC shoulder patch.

U.S. Army Field Manual (FM) 41-10, *Civil Affairs Operations*, defines civil-military operations as "the activities that . . . establish, maintain, influence, or exploit relations between military forces . . . and the civilian populace in a friendly, neutral, or hostile area of operations in order to facilitate military operations and consolidate and achieve U.S. objectives." ARSOF soldiers, in general, and CA soldiers, in particular, were often the first Americans that the Afghan people, especially in the cities, met as the *Taliban* regime collapsed. CA soldiers know that first impressions can determine whether the populace supports American military operations or views them as an invading, occupying army. The 96th CAB soldiers quickly won the Afghan people's support by appreciating their plight, meeting their basic needs, and shedding tears over their injured children. As one soldier said, "This is just an easy thing to do."[295]

Tactical PSYOP to Mazar-e-Sharif

Three weeks after Mazar-e-Sharif fell to General Rashid Dostum and a week after the *al-Qaeda* prisoner uprising at Qala-e-Jangi fortress, SSG Carl Dawkins (pseudonym) of Team 922, A Company, 9th POB, was the first PSYOP soldier to reach the town. After arriving by MH-47E, Dawkins unloaded his loudspeaker and Pashto and Dari tapes. He then met with the commander, Special Forces ODA 595, to determine what PSYOP would be most effective in the area. While becoming familiar with the city, Dawkins met an Afghan woman who had one of the airdropped American transistor radios. She told him that it was the first radio she had heard in seven years. Dawkins made it a point to request the delivery of more transistor radios. Five days later, SGT Charles Vargas (pseudonym) arrived with more batteries to power the portable loudspeaker. Finally, on 21 December, the third member of the team, PFC Paul Davis (pseudonym), joined Dawkins and Vargas at Mazar.

Although SSG O'Reilly (pseudonym), the detachment sergeant, could talk to his team by radio from K2, he had a responsibility to visit his soldiers in the field. Riding a resupply helicopter seemed to be the answer. When he did that the day after Christmas, the enemy threat at Mazar-e-Sharif was such that the helicopter did not shut down while the cargo was unloaded. On 5 January, O'Reilly tried again to deliver mail and Copenhagen tobacco to the team. This time, it turned into a night-long adventure when the aircraft commander suddenly told him that there was a change of mission—he and his team, with equipment, had to get on the helicopter. Four hours later they were in Kandahar for an "on-call" PSYOP loudspeaker mission. After sitting on the airfield with its engines running for several hours, the helicopter flew to Bagram with O'Reilly and TPT 922 aboard. By daylight, O'Reilly, TPT 922, and soldiers from the 19th SFG, who boarded in Bagram, were back at K2.[296]

While at Mazar-e-Sharif, SSG Dawkins had worked closely with ODA 595 and CAT-A33. The detachment sergeant, SSG O'Reilly, was most proud of that ARSOF integration at Mazar. The experience the Special Forces soldiers brought, together with that of the PSYOP soldiers, was not simply the sum of two parts. It had a synergistic effect. Together, they could tailor PSYOP products to assure the local populace that the United States was there to eliminate the *Taliban* and make their lives better. MAJ Barstow, commander, C Company, proudly commended his soldiers on that point: "The ability of attached forces to support the maneuver commander, to tailor psychological operations products that are as instantaneous as we can make them . . . is the beauty of what 9th PSYOP Battalion does." The humanitarian impact of providing food and information also paid great dividends. Particularly gratifying to O'Reilly was the work the PSYOP soldiers did to make the people aware of mines. Identified minefield boundaries were marked by rocks painted red on the side facing the minefield and white on the "safe" side. Barstow, O'Reilly, and the Special Forces commander focused their efforts on more prominently identifying minefields and distributing leaflets to warn the Afghan people about their presence. After returning to the United States, O'Reilly commented on his time in Afghanistan and the contributions of TPT 922. "It was a great thing," he concluded.[297]

Broadcast media proved very effective during the PSYOP campaign. More than 7,500 small battery-powered transistor radios were distributed both by airdrop and by TPTs with Special Forces ODAs. Simple leaflets told the Afghan people which numbered channels to tune to for American PSYOP-produced programs.[298] Initially, the EC-130 Commando Solo aircraft broadcast only 10 hours a day, but as soon as the Special Operations Media Systems–Broadcast (SOMS-B) radio stations were set up in Afghanistan, programs could be broadcast 24 hours a day. The Afghans queried said they liked the radio programs because they broadcast music, and for almost everyone, it was the first time they had been permitted to listen to music in six years. Changes to the selected music were made based on feedback provided by the PSYOP teams working with the Special Forces ODAs. Intelligence sources reported that the PSYOP campaign was a key factor in the surrender of Konduz. Other feedback indicated that the PSYOP leaflets and radio broadcasts were important contributors to the Afghan population withdrawing its support from the *Taliban*, especially from *al-Qaeda*.[299]

MAJ Henry Blackaby (pseudonym), commander of a psychological development company, 8th POB, recognized that leaflets and radio broadcasts were critical to Operation ENDURING FREEDOM; however, "The real heroes are the young troops who develop the products."[300] After World War II, GEN Dwight D. Eisenhower said, "The exact contribution of psychological warfare toward the final victory cannot, of course, be measured. . ., however, I am convinced that the expenditure of men and money in wielding the spoken and written word was an important contributing factor in undermining the enemy's will to resist."[301] There is no reason to believe that Eisenhower's assessment will be any less valid when the final history of Operation ENDURING FREEDOM is written.

Emergency Casualty Evacuation at K2

Army Special Operations Forces (ARSOF) operated with a concentrated focus during combat missions in central Asia. Garrison uniform and grooming standards were not mission-essential tasks. The ARSOF commanders established policies based on the missions being conducted and fully expected their soldiers to comply. Historically, when conventional forces collocate with special operations forces (SOF), an age-old clash of cultures occurs. Stronghold Freedom was no exception to this, but attitudes changed on 3 December.[302]

Base commander COL Albert Love left the K2 Air Base with five personnel—his driver, another soldier, two interpreters, and a DOD contractor—to attend a meeting with Uzbek officials. Not far from the compound, an Uzbek driving a dump truck inadvertently crossed the center lane and collided head on with the base commander's rented sport utility vehicle. Love received a severe head injury, lacerating most of his scalp, and the other five passengers had a variety of injuries, some critical.

Meanwhile, CWO Walter Striker (pseudonym), a 160th SOAR maintenance test pilot, had just returned from a midday test flight with a three-man crew.[303] They were the "day crew" that primarily did postmaintenance test flights and daily inspections on the helicopters. This procedure allowed night-mission crews to get up later in the day and make final preparations before the evening launches, thereby maximizing crew endurance and daylight maintenance time. As the crew was completing its postflight tasks, a soldier ran up and said, "Hey, we've got an accident out here. It's COL Love in his truck." Immediately, SGT Philip Svitak, the flight engineer, and Striker reacted, grabbed a crewman, and sent the runner for medical support. A doctor and several medics from the 274th Forward Surgical Team came running to the flight line with their emergency medical equipment. Company Commander CPT John Gates got an Air Force STS team for security and climbed into the copilot seat.[304] By then Striker had the MH-47E rotors turning.

Once everyone was aboard, Striker lifted off and found the accident site within 10 minutes. Careful not to create more problems with the downwash of the Chinook's rotors, Striker landed adjacent to the highway and dropped the ramp. Gates, the 274th medical team, and the Air Force STS team ran to the accident scene. Gates took charge of the accident site using the STS team to cordon off the area while the medical team administered first aid. The question

Figure 77. A casualty evacuation kit on an MH-47 Chinook.

of what to do with the injured Uzbeks from the dump truck was solved when another vehicle arrived to transport them to a local hospital. Since off-base security was always a concern, everyone worked quickly and remained vigilant. Soon, all the injured were carried or walked to the Chinook. They were back at the airfield 20 minutes after leaving. SSG Landon Falkerie (pseudonym), a 160th medic, met the Chinook and transported Love to the American field hospital.[305]

The Night Stalker maintenance crew displayed its ability to respond to any task. With limited information, it quickly gathered the medical and security personnel needed and raced to the rescue. COL Love underwent extensive surgery and fully recovered. After he presented Certificates of Appreciation to those involved in the emergency casualty evacuation, the ARSOF aviators noticed a change in the atmosphere around Stronghold Freedom.

Thus, the ARSOF preparation for combat and the war to topple the *Taliban* regime in Afghanistan was concluded. But the JSOTF unconventional warfare (UW) campaign was just beginning. The previous vignettes chronologically trace combat operations on the ground and in the air, primarily dominated by the 5th SFG ODAs supporting the anti-*Taliban* leaders in the north, northeast, and south; 160th SOAR aircrews inserting Special Forces teams, guard-

Figure 78. CA always fostering goodwill and demonstrating compassion.

ing insertions, and conducting surgical air raids requiring multiple aerial and ground refuels in extremely bad weather; and 75th Rangers assaulting airstrips to support follow-on operations. Throughout, PSYOP teams prepared leaflets, broadcasts, and a boots-on-the-ground video presented nationwide, and CA teams coordinated humanitarian relief to the Afghan populace. As the cities fell to anti-*Taliban* forces, tactical PSYOP teams (TPTs) and CA teams were attached to the Special Forces ODAs and a Coalition Joint Civil-Military Operations Command in Kabul. JSOTF-North at K2, Uzbekistan, commanded by a Special Forces colonel, developed the UW campaign plan, daily directed offensives in a constantly evolving operation, orchestrated Army and Air Force SOF assets into combat multipliers, and successfully fought the war to overthrow the *Taliban* in less than two months. Given the time involved, errors were made because combat priorities were constantly being triaged, but none proved to be mission stoppers.

Chapter 4 addresses ARSOF activities during the "transition period" between the fall of the *Taliban* regime in mid-December 2001 and Operation ANACONDA in February 2002. During this period, a second JSOTF for southern Afghanistan was established with control over coalition forces; the CJCMOTF expanded its role; an Army conventional brigade replaced the U.S. Marine force at Kandahar; the JSOAC-North headquarters relocated to a Persian Gulf base, taking the Air Force SOF elements with it; 19th SFG (ARNG) elements were committed in Afghanistan; the 3rd SFG was alerted to replace the 5th SFG; the 20th SFG (ARNG) was alerted for overseas movement; the 528th Special Operations Support Battalion (SOSB) was replaced by the 507th Corps Support Group from Europe; USAR CA and PSYOP units were alerted to replace 96th CAB and 4th POG units in theater; and the 160th SOAR rotated its Chinook helicopters to accomplish annual maintenance checks and introduced MH-60K Black Hawks to support ARSOF missions. The turbulence associated with transition was further complicated by the continuing mission to destroy *Taliban* and *al-Qaeda* forces and to support the Afghan Interim Authority (AIA) government.

Notes

1. Herman Melville (1819-1891) and Israel Potter (1855), *The Writings of Herman Melville,* Vol. 8, Harrison Hayford, Hershel Parker, and G. Thomas Tanselle, eds. (1982), chapter 10.

2. Geoffrey C. Lambert note to Charles Briscoe, 29 April 2003, Fort Bragg, North Carolina, at U.S. Army Special Operations Command (USASOC) Classified Archives, Fort Bragg, hererafter cited as Lambert note to Briscoe.

3. Central Intelligence Agency (CIA) Press Release, 11 April 2002. Jim Pavitt, Deputy Director of Operations, "Address to Duke University Law School Conference, 11 April 2002." "Teams of my paramilitary operations officers . . . were among the first on the ground in Afghanistan. . . . In those few days that it took us to get there after that terrible, terrible attack, my officers stood on Afghan soil, side by side with Afghan friends that we had developed over a long period of time. . . . We were there well before the 11th of September." <http://www.cia.gov/cia/public_affairs/speeches/pavitt_04262002.html>.

4. John F. Mulholland, 12 July 2002, Fort Campbell, Kentucky, interview with Charles Briscoe, transcripts and tapes, USASOC Classified Archives, Fort Bragg, hereafter cited as Mulholland interview.

5. LTC Warren Richards (pseudonym), 29 May 2002, Fort Bragg, interview with Richard Kiper et al., transcripts and tapes, USASOC Classified Archives, Fort Bragg, hereafter cited as W. Richards interview.

6. Mulholland interview, USASOC Classified Archives, Fort Bragg.

7. The term "Northern Alliance" was in widespread use at the time and appears in U.S. government publications that predate the 9/11 attacks. For example, see U.S. State Department, "Country Reports on Human Rights Practices 2000," 23 February 2001, <http://www.state.gov/g/drl/rls/hrrpt/2000/sa/721.htm>.

8. Najibullah was of Pashtun ethnicity. See Mark Fineman, "Afghan Leader Najibullah Forced to Resign by Rebels," *Los Angeles Times,* 17 April 1992, 2.

9. "The Battle for Mazar-e-Sharif," Information Paper, Department of the Army (DA), U.S. Army Center of Military History (CMH), 28 April 2002. See also Ahmed Rashid, *Taliban* (New Haven, CT: Yale University Press, 2000).

10. *FRONTLINE,* "Campaign Against Terror," 8 September 2002, <http://www.pbs.org/wgbh/pages/*Frontline*/shows/campaign/interviews/595.html>.

11. For reports on the cycle of massacres and reprisals in Afghanistan, see Ian Cobain, "Taliban's Child Victims Found in City of Blood," *London Times,* 13 November 2001, and David Rohde, "Executions of P.O.W.'s Cast Doubts on Alliance," *New York Times,* 13 November 2001. COL Mulholland ordered his Special Forces detachments to take what actions they could to prevent atrocities by their new Afghan allies and to report any atrocities they discovered. Mulholland letter to Kalev Sepp, 5 December 2002, Fort Campbell, USASOC Classified Archives, Fort Bragg.

12. CIA Press Release, 2 June 2002, A.B. Krongard, Executive Director of the CIA, "Remarks at the Conference on the 60th Anniversary of OSS, 7 June 2002." "[I]n an Afghan valley, a Special Forces team—among the first into the country and itself a proud successor to OSS—ran into a party of mysterious figures. From one of those figures, through darkness broken only by a flashlight, came the roar of an American voice: 'Hi! I'm Hal! Damn glad to meet you.' He was from CIA's Special Activities Division and had been scouting the ground, gathering information." <http://www.cia.gov/cia/public_affairs/speeches/ ossconference_06022002.html>.

13. Thomas E. Ricks and Vernon Loeb, "Special Forces Open Ground Campaign," *Washington Post,* 19 October 2001, 1; Greg Jaffe, "U.S. Offensive in Afghanistan Enters Riskier Phase of Commando Raids," *Wall Street Journal,* 22 October 2001, 1; Brad Knickerbocker, "US Strategy Moves to the Ground," *Christian Science Monitor,* 22 October 2001, 1; John Barry and Arian Campo-Flores, "The Warriors of the Night," *Newsweek,* 29 October 2001, 22; and Romesh Ratnesar, "The Ground War: Into the Fray," *Time,* 29 October 2001.

14. Thom Shanker and Steven Lee Myers, "Rumsfeld Says Attacks Seek to Help Rebels Advance," *New York Times,* 23 October 2001, 1.

15. Michael Smith, "US Special Forces Beat Retreat as Enemy 'Fought Back Like Maniacs,'" *London Daily Telegraph,* 26 October 2001.

16. Michael Janofsky, "2 Soldiers Remembered for Their Focus and Patriotism," *New York Times,* 23 October 2001.

17. Donatella Lorch, "The Green Berets Up Close," *Newsweek,* 14 January 2002. In this article, the author records that during ODA 534's preparations for its operations inside Afghanistan, the team requested a personality profile on General Atta Mohammed, the warlord it was to meet. Instead, it received a dossier on Mohammed Atta, one of the terrorist skyjackers who killed himself during the 9/11 suicide attack in New York. See also U.S. Army, "Narrative Justification for Award of the Presidential Unit Citation," Headquarters (HQ), 5th Special Forces Group

(SFG), Fort Campbell, n.d., and "The Battle for Mazar-e-Sharif," Information Paper, CMH, 28 April 2002.

18. The lieutenant colonels were the commanders of the 1st and 3rd Battalions, 5th SFG (at Bagram with Bismullah Khan and at Mazar-e-Sharif with General Rashid Dostum, respectively). U.S. Army, "Narrative Justification for Award of the Presidential Unit Citation," HQ, 5th SFG, Fort Campbell, n.d.

19. For one version of the story of Abdul Haq's death, see Robert D. Novak, "Abdul Haq's Last Hours," *Washington Post*, 1 November 2001, 35.

20. "Afghan War Chronology," Information Paper, CMH, 25 April 2002.

21. Carl Hooper (pseudonym), letter to Kalev Sepp, 5 December 2002, Fort Campbell, USASOC Classified Archives, Fort Bragg.

22. The Mi-17 and its earlier version, the Mi-8, are also known by the NATO reporting name "Hip." See Barbara Hall, "ODA 586, Northern Warriors," *The Drop* (Summer 2002), 15-17.

23. "The Battle for Mazar-e-Sharif," Information Paper, CMH, 28 April 2002.

24. "In the West, Gen. Ismail Khan, an alliance commander, has regained control of the city of Herat, and is again in position to be Iran's proxy." See David Rohde, "Warlords are Vying to Fill Vacuum Left by the *Taliban*," *New York Times*, 16 November 2001.

25. "During the first part of the Afghanistan campaign, the [21st Theater Army Support Command] was the sole supplier for U.S. military special operations teams and CIA special operating groups in Afghanistan, catering to every need and want made by military special operators or CIA agents in the field. They located and bought . . . specialized batteries, nonmilitary tactical gear, civilian camping gear, mountaineering clothing and special food. . . . By the time the conventional supply system took over, the [21st TASCOM] had bought and shipped nearly 2 million pounds of wheat and 93,000 blankets for humanitarian relief, along with the tons of equipment and supplies to keep the military operation going." See Dennis Steele, "Unconventional Logistics," *Army* (November 2002), 8-10; also, U.S. Central Command, Transcripts, "Informal Press Opportunity With Rear Admiral Craig Quigley, 30 October 2001." "We're providing weapons and ammunition to a variety of opposition groups in a variety of ways." <http://www.centcom.mil/news/transcripts/20011030.html>. For descriptions of some parachute supply drops, and misdrops, made to the CIA teams, see Evan Thomas, "A Street Fight," *Newsweek* (29 April 2002).

26. SOCEUR is pronounced "SOCK-yur."

27. Hamad Karzai, who later became the prime minister of the post-*Taliban* Interim Afghan Authority (AIA), described an early parachute drop: "[S]uddenly somebody rushed and said, 'There are planes.' So we came out and we saw the planes and they dropped parachutes. Half of them were exactly on the spot. The other half went just one mountain beyond." *FRONTLINE*, "Campaign Against Terror."

28. The color of the plastic wrapping of the food packets was soon changed from yellow to blue to avoid the chance of civilians confusing the food packets with yellow-painted explosive bomblets. See Steven Mufson, "U.S. Changing Color of Airdropped Food Packs," *Washington Post*, 2 November 2001, 21; Deborah Zabarenko, "U.S. Lesson: How to Tell Cluster Bombs From Food," *Washington Post*, 30 October 2001, 14.

29. Carla Anne Robbins and Neil King, Jr., "Powell Sees No Halt in Afghan Campaign During Muslim Holy Month of Ramadan," *Wall Street Journal*, 1 November 2001.

30. "The Battle for Mazar-e-Sharif," Information Paper, CMH, 28 April 2002.

31. Secretary of Defense Donald H. Rumsfeld describes his meeting at Karshi Kanabad (K2) with 5th SFG soldiers who had fought the battle for Mazar-e-Sharif in his essay, "Transforming the Military," *Foreign Affairs*, May/June 2002, 20-21. For more details about the three-week-long battle, see "The Liberation of Mazar-e-Sharif: 5th SFG Conducts UW in Afghanistan," *Special Warfare* (June 2002), 34-41.

32. Previously, there had been doubt that the Northern Alliance could achieve such success. For example, see Michael O'Hanlon, "At the Pace of the Offensive, the *Taliban* Will Survive the Winter," *Los Angeles Times*, 26 October 2002.

33. Civil Affairs Team Alpha 32 (CAT-A32) arrived in Bagram on 23 November 2001, and CAT-A33 arrived in Mazar-e-Sharif on 27 November 2001. "Operational Summary of Coalition Humanitarian Liaison Cell–Bagram (CHLC-B), Operation Enduring Freedom, Bagram Air Base, Afghanistan," 4 January 2002, C Company (-), 96th Civil Affairs Battalion (Airborne), 1; "Operational Summary of C Company, 96th Civil Affairs Battalion Deployment in Support of Operation Enduring Freedom (24 September 2001-31 March 2002)," 4 April 2002, C Company, 96th Civil Affairs Battalion (Airborne), 2, USASOC Classified Archives, Fort Bragg. See also Meg Laughlin, "The Army of Hope," *Herald-Leader*, 14 January 2002, and William Patterson, "Army Civil Affairs Builds Trust in Afghanistan," *Paraglide*, 3 January 2002.

34. U.S. Army, "Narrative Justification for Award of the Presidential Unit Citation," Headquarters, 5th SFG, Fort Campbell, Kentucky, n.d.

35. Thom Shanker, "The Stripes Are on Their Sleeves, Not Their Pants," *New York Times*, 13 January 2002.

36. Before the 9/11 attacks, CENTCOM normally oversaw 20,000-25,000 U.S. military personnel inside its geographic area of responsibility. See "Afghan War Chronology," Information Paper, CMH, 25 April 2002.

37. Scott Peterson, "Rebels Attempting First Big Gains," *Christian Science Monitor*, 9 November 2001, 1.

38. The U.S. Air Force title for airstrike controllers was tactical air control party (TACP). The Air Force sergeants in these units were called ETACs, for enlisted terminal attack controllers. However, Air Force special tactics airmen from other Air Force special operations units directed airstrikes as well. <http://www.globalsecurity.org/military/agency/usaf/tacp.htm>.

39. Susan B. Glasser and Molly Moore, "Rebel Forces Claim Key City of Herat, Seize Road to Kabul," *Washington Post*, 13 November 2001. "After missing the story of the fall of Mazar-e Sharif . . . reporters in the north were baffled to learn that the city of Herat had also quickly fallen. 'One day it was said to be a *Taliban* stronghold, and the next day Northern Alliance commander Ismail Khan was in power.'" Robert G. Kaiser, "Already, Too Many Pieces Are Missing," *Washington Post*, 23 December 2001, B1.

40. Keith B. Richburg and Molly Moore, "*Taliban* Flees Afghan Capital," *Washington Post*, 13 November 2001, 1.

41. Afghan Pashtun leader Haji Abdul Qadir occupied Jalalabad after the *Taliban* abandoned the town of 60,000 people. See Paul Wiseman, "Southern Tribes Help Fight *Taliban*," *USA Today*, 15 November 2001, 6, and Pamela Constable, "Two Rebel Groups Vie for Control of Key City," *Washington Post*, 16 November 2001, 26.

42. According to a sergeant from Special Forces A Detachment 595, during surrender negotiations, Dostum used a radio to allow the *Taliban* chieftain in Konduz, Mullah Fazl, to hear the voice of an American female weapons officer on board an AC-130 Spectre gunship. Dostum told his enemy counterpart that it was the voice of the "angel of death" who would come in the night and kill all the *Taliban* who did not surrender. *FRONTLINE,* "Campaign Against Terror."

43. "EC-130 'Commando Solo' psychological operations aircraft broadcast instructions to civilians to follow when U.S. troops arrive: 'Attention! People of Afghanistan, United States forces will be moving through your area,' according to transcripts released by the Pentagon. We are here for Osama bin Laden, al Qaeda and those who protect them! Please, for your own safety, stay off bridges and roadways, and do not interfere with our troops or military operations. If you do this, you will not be harmed.'" Ricks and Loeb, 1. See also David A. Fulghum and Robert Wall, "U.S. Stalks *Taliban* With New Air Scheme," *Aviation Week & Space Technology* (15 October 2001), and Michael R. Gordon and Steven Lee Myers, "*Taliban*'s Troops Hit as Allies Plan for Commando Raids," *New York Times*, 11 October 2001, 1.

44. Michael R. Gordon, "Afghans Block Britain's Plan for Big Force," *New York Times*, 20 November 2001; Michael R. Gordon, "Securing Base, U.S. Makes its Brawn Blend In," *New York Times*, 3 December 2001; Mulholland interview, USASOC Classified Archives, Fort Bragg.

45. According to Ambassador Richard Armitage, U.S. Deputy Secretary of State, Pakistan maintained its diplomatic ties to the *Taliban* only while the foreign aid workers inside Afghanistan remained in *Taliban* custody. *FRONTLINE,* "Campaign Against Terror."

46. Douglas Frantz, "Pakistan Ended Aid to *Taliban* Only Hesitantly," *New York Times*, 8 December 2001, 1; Vernon Loeb, "Pentagon Eyes Use of Tajikistan Air Base," *Washington Post*, 13 November 2001, 24.

47. Keith B. Richburg, "*Taliban* Prisoners Revolt," *Washington Post*, 26 November 2001, 1.

48. CIA Press Release, 28 November 2001. George J. Tenet, Director, CIA, "On the Death of a CIA Officer in Afghanistan." "[O]ne of our officers at the Central Intelligence Agency has died in the line of duty in Afghanistan. Johnny Micheal [correct spelling] 'Mike' Spann, who worked in the Directorate of Operations, was where he wanted to be: on the front lines serving his country. . . . Mike was in the fortress of Mazar-e Sharif where *Taliban* prisoners were being held. . . . Their prison uprising—which had murder as its goal—claimed many lives, among them that of a very brave American, whose body was recovered just hours ago." <http://www.cia.gov/public_affairs/press_release/archives/2001/prl11282001.html>. See also James Risen, "C.I.A. Names Agent Killed in Fortress," *New York Times*, 29 November 2001. Carlotta Gall, "An American is Said to be Killed During a Failed Prison Uprising," *New York Times*, 26 November 2001.

49. The rifle platoon was part of C Company, 1st Battalion, 87th Infantry Regiment, 10th Mountain Division.

50. Bay Fang, "Eyewitness: American 'Friendly Fire' Casualties," *USNews.com*, 26 November 2001.

51. Carlotta Gall, "Fight With Prisoners Rages at Northern Afghan Fort," *New York Times*, 27 November 2001, 1.

52. CIA, Press Release, 28 November 2001, 1, and "CIA Officer's Body Brought Home to Family," *Washington Post*, 3 December 2001, 13.

53. Carlotta Gall, "In Tunnels Full of Bodies, One of Them Keeps Firing," *New York Times*, 30 November 2001.

54. Christopher Marquis, "Before He Died, C.I.A. Man Interrogated U.S. Captive," *New York Times*, 7 December 2001; Jeff Gerth, "U.S. Detainee is Questioned, but His Fate is Still Unclear," *New York Times*, 10 December 2001; Daniel Klaidman and Michael Isikoff, "Walker's Brush With Bin Laden," *Newsweek*, 31 December 2001/7 January 2002; Mike Nash (pseudonym), Memorandum, "ODA 595, Operation Enduring Freedom," 19 March 2002, Fort Campbell; Mike Nash (pseudonym), 26 March 2002, Fort Campbell, interview with Kalev Sepp, transcript and tapes, USASOC Classified Archives, Fort Bragg, hereafter cited as Nash interview. See also *FRONTLINE*, "Campaign Against Terror."

55. Bradley Graham and Vernon Loeb, "Rebels' Gains Shift U.S. Focus to the South," *Washington Post*, 13 November 2001, 1.

56. U.S. Army, "Narrative Justification for Award of the Presidential Unit Citation," Headquarters, 5th SFG, Fort Campbell, n.d.

57. Mark Landler, "Philippines Offers U.S its Troops and Bases," *New York Times*, 3 October 2001; Richard C. Paddock, "U.S. Use of Bases in Philippines Renewed," *Los Angeles Times*, 18 December 2001.

58. *FRONTLINE*, "Campaign Against Terror."

59. Peter Finn, "Wounded Army Captain Details Teamwork Against *Taliban*," n.d., USASOC Classified Archives, Fort Bragg.

60. Thomas E. Ricks and Bob Woodward, "Marines Enter South Afghanistan," *Washington Post*, 26 November 2001, 1.

61. The SEAL reconnaissance element at Rhino came under attack by U.S. Marine Corps AH-1W Cobra attack helicopters leading the transport helicopters. The SEALs reported the attack on their surveillance position by the Cobras back to the JSOTF-South command post on Masirah Island, which relayed the "cease-fire" call through command channels to the Cobra helicopter crews. The SEALs did not suffer any casualties. Donald W. Richardson, 19 July 2002, Norfolk, Virginia, interview with Kalev Sepp, transcripts and tapes, USASOC Classified Archives, Fort Bragg. For a partial description of the reconnaissance mission, which incorrectly reports the SEALs as "the only U.S. force in . . . southwest Afghanistan" (Army Special Forces A Detachments 574 and 583 were already there), see James W. Crawley, "Navy's Silent Warriors Operated Alone, Deep in the Afghan Desert," *San Diego Union-Tribune*, 21 December 2001, p 1.

62. Willis Witter, "Afghan Leader Will Give *Taliban* a Chance to Flee," *Washington Times*, 4 December 2001, 1.

63. "Troops Inch Closer to Driving the *Taliban* From Kandahar," *USA Today*, 5 December 2001, 8.

64. Hamad Karzai's role in the future Afghan government was being debated at the Bonn conference. *FRONTLINE*, "Campaign Against Terror."

65. Norimitsu Onishi, "Interim Afghan Leader Discusses Kandahar's Surrender With *Taliban*," *New York Times*, 6 December 2001; John Pomfret, "For Incoming Chief, One More Close Call," *Washington Post*, 6 December 2001, 31; Vernon Loeb, "'Friendly Fire' Deaths Traced to Dead Battery," *Washington Post*, 24 March 2002, 21.

66. Tony Perry, "Marine Outpost Key Player in Treatment of Wounded Soldiers," *Los Angeles Times*, 7 December 2001.

67. U.S. Central Command, Transcripts, "GEN Franks' Testimony to the House Armed Services Committee, 27 February 2002." GEN Tommy Franks, Commander, CENTCOM: "Combining the resources and capabilities of the Defense Department, Central Intelligence Agency, and other agencies of the Federal government has produced results [in Afghanistan] no single entity could have achieved." <http://www.centcom.mil/news/transcripts/20020227.htm>.

68. A temporary combat designation for an officer in the U.S. Navy ranking above captain and below rear admiral. Thus, Commodore Bob Harward outranked COL John Mulholland in Afghanistan.

69. U.S. Army, "A-1/5th SFG(A) Operation Enduring Freedom Roll-Up, 15 December 01–15 February 02," A Company, 1st Battalion, 5th SFG, Fort Campbell, slide presentation, 8 July 2002, copy in classified files, USASOC Classified Archives, Fort Bragg.

70. Tora Bora means "black dust" in the local dialect.

71. Tim Weiner, "Afghan Says Fighters Are Ready to Attack Cave Complex," *New York Times*, 4 December 2001.

72. "The Course of Operation Enduring Freedom in Southern and Eastern Afghanistan," Information Paper, CMH, 26 April 2002; *FRONTLINE*, "Campaign Against Terror."

73. Michael Evans, "British Special Forces to Join Cave Assault," *London Times*, 3 December 2001.

74. For analytical overviews of the battle for Afghanistan, see Stephen Biddle, "Afghanistan and the Future of Conflict: Implications for Army and Defense Policy," paper, U.S. Army War College, Strategic Studies Institute, November 2002, <http://www.carlisle.army.mil/usassi/ssipubs/pubs2002/afghan/afghan.pdf>; Michael O'Hanlon, "A

Flawed Masterpiece: Assessing the Afghan Campaign," *Foreign Affairs* (May/June 2002), 47-63; Anthony Cordesman, "The Lessons of Afghanistan: A First Analysis," paper, Center for Strategic and International Studies, 12 August 2002, <http://www.csis.org/burke/sa/ lessonsofafghan.pdf>; Rebecca Grant, "An Air War Like No Other," *Air Force Magazine* (November 2002), <http://www.afa.org/magazine/Nov2002/1102airwar.asp>.

75. "[S]trategic analysts remain puzzled. Writing in the *Wall Street Journal* this week, Sir John Keegan, the British military historian, had this to say: 'The success of the bombers is nevertheless a surprise, even if not a wholly unpredictable one. What had been unpredictable is the resurgence of the Northern Alliance. Their ability to achieve practical superiority, against an enemy superior in numbers who had held them at bay for five years, could not have been foreseen and defies explanation. It is not due to superior weapons—there must have been a collapse of *Taliban* morale.'" R.W. Apple, Jr., "Pondering the Mystery of the *Taliban*'s Collapse," *New York Times*, 30 November 2001.

76. Michael R. Gordon, "Shifting Fronts, Rising Danger: The Afghanistan War Evolves," *New York Times*, 10 December 2001.

77. For a thorough analysis of the initial campaign, focusing on the combination of special operations forces, indigenous fighters, and precision-guided aerial bombing, see Biddle.

78. "Combat Operations Summary of Ranger Actions on OBJ Rhino, Southern Afghanistan on 19 October 2001" (Masirah Island, Oman: 3rd Battalion, 75th Ranger Regiment, 25 October 2001), 1; "The 75th Ranger Regiment: Combat Operations in Southern Afghanistan in support of Operation Enduring Freedom," briefing prepared by 75th Ranger Regiment, n.d., USASOC Classified Archives, Fort Bragg.

79. 1LT Kenneth Brown (pseudonym), SP4 Martin Pasquez (pseudonym), SFC Ron Searcey (pseudonym), SGT Thomas Evans (pseudonym), C Company, 3rd Battalion, 75th Ranger Regiment, interview with Richard Kiper, 28 March 2002, Fort Benning, Georgia, tape recording and notes, USASOC Classified Archives, Fort Bragg.

80. SSG James Turner (pseudonym), B Company, 9th Battalion, 4th Psychological Operations (PSYOP) Group, interview with Richard Kiper, 3 April 2002, Fort Bragg, tape recording and notes, USASOC Classified Archives, Fort Bragg; SFC Ron Searcey (pseudonym) and CPT Stanley Davis (pseudonym), C Company, 3rd Battalion, 75th Ranger Regiment, interview with Richard Kiper, 28 March 2002, Fort Benning, tape recording and notes, USASOC Classified Archives, Fort Bragg.

81. "Combat Operations Summary of Ranger Actions on OBJ Rhino," 1.

82. Janofsky.

83. CPT Sam Crevald (pseudonym), HHC, 3rd Battalion, 75th Ranger Regiment, interview with Richard Kiper, 28 March 2002, Fort Benning, tape recording and notes, USASOC Classified Archives, Fort Bragg; Ranger Creed, <www.benning.army.mil/rtb/ranger/rgrcreed.htm>.

84. *FRONTLINE*, "Campaign Against Terror."

85. Rowan Scarborough, "U.S. Grabs Airstrip Near Kandahar, Gains Fixed Base Inside Afghanistan," *Washington Times*, 27 November 2001, 1.

86. Jack Thomas, Mario Perez, Gene Ball, and John MacGinnis (pseudonyms), Operation ENDURING FREEDOM "Objective Rhino, the PSYOP Perspective," TPD 940, B Company, 9th PSYOP Battalion, n.d., USASOC Classified Archives, Fort Bragg.

87. Ibid.

88. "DoD News Briefing—GEN Myers," Defense Link, <www.defenselink.mil/news/Oct2001/t10202001_t1020jcs.html>.

89. Operation ENDURING FREEDOM, "Objective Rhino, the PSYOP Perspective," TPD 940, B Company, 9th POB, n.d., USASOC Classified Archives, Fort Bragg.

90. "Admiral (Rear Admiral Anthony Winns) Touts Role of Navy's P-3 Recon Aircraft in Afghanistan War," *P3 News*, <www.centerseat.net/p3news.htm>.

91. Kim Battles is a pseudonym.

92. James Brinks (pseudonym), commander, 2nd Battalion, 160th SOAR, interview with James Schroder, 27 March 2002, Fort Campbell, tape recording and notes, USASOC Classified Archives, Fort Bragg.

93. Alfred Mann (pseudonym), HHC, 2nd Battalion, 160th SOAR, interview with James Schroder, 25 March 2002, Fort Campbell, tape recording and notes, USASOC Classified Archives, Fort Bragg, hereafter cited as Mann interview.

94. Ibid.

95. John Gates (pseudonym) and Arthur Solanis (pseudonym) (hereafter cited as Solanis interview), B Company, 2nd Battalion, 160th SOAR, interview with James Schroder, 25 March 2002, Fort Campbell, tape recording and notes, USASOC Classified Archives, Fort Bragg.

96. Ibid.

97. Ibid.

98. Mann interview.

99. Roger Charles (pseudonym), D Company, 1st Battalion, 160th SOAR, interview with James Schroder, 18 April 2002, Fort Campbell, tape recording and notes, USASOC Classified Archives, Fort Bragg, hereafter cited as Charles interview.

100. Ibid.

101. Mann interview.

102. Ibid.

103. Dari-a-Souf, also spelled Darya-Suf, is pronounced "DAH-ree-ah SOOF." Mike Nash, Bill Phipps, Pat Earnhardt, Al Mix, Barry Ball, Vinsong Ming, Paul Wannamaker, Sol Kitts, Sam Bagby, Wes Snow, Mark Exley, and Carey James are pseudonyms.

104. Nash memorandum and Nash interview. See also *FRONTLINE*, "Campaign Against Terror."

105. Ibid.

106. Ibid.

107. Pronounced "shy."

108. Nash memorandum and Nash interview. See also *FRONTLINE*, "Campaign Against Terror."

109. Ibid.

110. Ibid.

111. Ibid.

112. Nash memorandum and Nash interview. See also *FRONTLINE*, "Campaign Against Terror."

113. Maqdoom is pronounced "mack-DOOM."

114. Nash memorandum and Nash interview. See also *FRONTLINE*, "Campaign Against Terror."

115. Ibid.

116. Ibid.

117. Ibid.

118. Nash memorandum and Nash interview.

119. Ibid.

120. Nash memorandum and Nash interview. See also *FRONTLINE*, "Campaign Against Terror."

121. Ibid.

122. According to MSG Pat Earnhardt (pseudonym), the detachment operations sergeant, the endurance riding saddles cost $300 each, compared to the top-of-the-line Australian saddles that went for $1,000 each. Nash memorandum and Nash interview. See also *FRONTLINE*, "Campaign Against Terror."

123. Dennis Steele, "Unconventional Logistics," *Army* (November 2002), 58.

124. Leslie L. Fuller, 15 April 2002, Fort Bragg, interview with Kalev Sepp, transcripts and tapes, USASOC Classified Archives, Fort Bragg, hereafter cited as Fuller interview.

125. SOCEUR was authorized 84 personnel, but with individual mobilization augmentees and reservists called to active duty from both the Army and Air Force, Fuller's headquarters numbered 120 personnel by the New Year. Fuller interview, tapes and notes in USASOC Classified Archives, Fort Bragg.

126. Ibid.

127. Ibid.

128. These resupply bundles are referred to inside Special Forces by their unclassified code name, "Marge Bundles," and are normally prepared for detachments in anticipation of long-term operations inside hostile territory.

129. Aircraft that travel on these routinely scheduled routes are called "channel flights." Later, the 16th Special Operations Wing moved several of its Talon I and II model aircraft to the former Soviet airfield at K2 where CJSOTF-North was headquartered. Fuller interview, tapes and notes in USASOC Classified Archives, Fort Bragg.

130. Fuller interview, tapes and notes in USASOC Classified Archives, Fort Bragg.

131. Ibid.

132. Ibid.

133. Ibid.

134. Ibid.

135. Solanis interview, tapes and notes in USASOC Classified Archives, Fort Bragg.

136. Ibid.

137. Ibid. Gates and Donalds are pseudonyms.

138. Ibid. Emerson is a pseudonym.

139. Ibid. Clauden is a pseudonym.

140. Derrick Donalds (pseudonym), B Company, 2nd Battalion, 160th SOAR, interview with Kalev Sepp, 17 April 2002, Fort Campbell, tape recording and notes, USASOC Classified Archives, Fort Bragg, hereafter cited as Donalds interview.

141. Mike Nash is a pseudonym.

142. Nash memorandum and Nash interview. See also *FRONTLINE*, "Campaign Against Terror."

143. Solanis interview.

144. Ibid.

145. Donalds interview.

146. Tucker is a pseudonym.

147. Lee Clauden (pseudonym), B Company, 2nd Battalion, 160th SOAR, interview with James Schroder, 27 March 2002, Fort Campbell, tape recording and notes, USASOC Classified Archives, Fort Bragg.

148. Tom Dugan (pseudonym), B Company, 2nd Battalion, 160th SOAR, interview with James Schroder, 26 March 2002, Fort Campbell, tape recording and notes, USASOC Classified Archives, Fort Bragg.

149. Michael Bartley (pseudonym), B Company, 2nd Battalion, 160th SOAR, interview with James Schroder, 27 March 2002, Fort Campbell, tape recording and notes, USASOC Classified Archives, Fort Bragg.

150. Mills interview, tapes and notes in USASOC Classified Archives, Fort Bragg.

151. Mark Knapp (pseudonym), chaplain, HHC, 2nd Battalion, 160th SOAR, interview with James Schroder, 26 April 2002, Fort Campbell, tape recording and notes, USASOC Classified Archives, Fort Bragg, hereafter cited as Knapp interview.

152. Pseudonyms.

153. Knapp interview.

154. Ibid.

155. Knapp interview; Garrison is a pseudonym.

156. Charles interview.

157. Ibid.; Mannis a pseudonym.

158. Charles interview; McCracken is a pseudonym.

159. Charles interview.

160. Headquarters, 3rd Battalion, 75th Ranger Regiment, memorandum for record, Subject: Combat Operations Summary of Ranger Actions on OBJ BASTOGNE, Southern Afghanistan on 13 November 2001, 17 November 2001, USASOC Classified Archives, Fort Bragg.

161. Morris is a pseudonym.

162. Joseph Morris (pseudonym), B Company, 1st Battalion, 160th SOAR, interview with Charles Briscoe, 18 April 2002, Fort Campbell, tape recording and notes, USASOC Classified Archives, Fort Bragg.

163. <http://www.af.mil/news/factsheets/MC_130E_H_Combat_Talon_I_II.html>.

164. CPT Chuck Seims (pseudonym), A Company, 3rd Battalion, 75th Ranger Regiment, interview with Richard Kiper, Fort Benning, 27 March 2002, tape recording and notes, USASOC Classified Archives, Fort Bragg.

165. CPT Chuck Seims, "Battle Summary for Relentless Strike 05," n.d., USASOC Classified Archives, Fort Bragg.

166. Headquarters, 75th Ranger Regiment, memorandum, Subject: Debrief Report A/3-75 Ranger Mission to Objectives ANZIO and BULGE, 21 November 2001, USASOC Classified Archives, Fort Bragg.

167. Seims, "Battle Summary."

168. Don Sullivan and Derrick Jacobi are pseudonyms.

169. Don Sullivan (pseudonym), 24 April 2002, Fort Campbell, interview with Kalev Sepp, transcripts and tapes, USASOC Classified Archives, Fort Bragg, hereafter cited as Sullivan interview.

170. Ibid.

171. The two satellites are each 20 years old and were designed to carry 30 channels each. Time and exposure have degraded their capacity from 60 to 54 channels. Sullivan interview, tapes and notes in USASOC Classified Archives, Fort Bragg.

172. Sullivan interview, tapes and notes in USASOC Classified Archives, Fort Bragg.

173. Ibid.

174. Boi-Becha is pronounced "BOY-buh-SHAY."

175. Nash memorandum and Nash interview, tapes and notes in USASOC Classified Archives, Fort Bragg. See also *FRONTLINE*, "Campaign Against Terror."

176. SSG Logan Donovan (pseudonym), A Company, 3rd PSYOP Battalion, interview with Kalev Sepp, 4 April 2002, Fort Bragg, tape recording and notes, USASOC Classified Archives, Fort Bragg; Carol Clewell is a pseudonym.

177. "Operational Summary of C Company, 96th Civil Affairs Battalion Deployment in Support of Operation ENDURING FREEDOM (24 September 2001–31 March 2002)," 4 April 2002, C Company, 96th Civil Affairs Battalion (Airborne), 2, USASOC Classified Archives, Fort Bragg.

178. MAJ John Bowman is a pseudonym. "C Co, 96th CA BN (A) CAT-A & B Activity Summary in Support of OEF," n.d., USASOC Classified Archives, Fort Bragg. CHLC is not a doctrinal term. It originated in the Afghanistan–Pakistan area as a term that does not use the word "military." The CHLC performs the functions of a civil-military operations center to interface between military civil affairs units, nongovernmental organizations, and international organizations. Although all of these organizations provide humanitarian assistance, several civilian organizations were uncomfortable coordinating the effort with military organizations. The term "CHLC" was created to address those sensibilities.

179. Ibid., 4; *FRONTLINE*, "Campaign Against Terror"; Gerry J. Gilmore, "Rumsfeld Praises Civil Affairs' Work in Afghanistan," American Forces Information Service, 20 August 2002. Mike Russell is a pseudonym.

180. SSG James O'Reilly (pseudonym), C Company, 9th PSYOP Battalion, interview with Kalev Sepp, 3 April 2002, Fort Bragg, tape recording and notes, USASOC Classified Archives, Fort Bragg, hereafter cited as O'Reilly interview. Mark Puller, Rick Harrison, Carl Dawkins, and Charles Vargas are pseudonyms.

181. O'Reilly interview.

182. Ibid.; Harrison is a pseudonym.

183. Ibid.

184. MAJ Martin Jackson (pseudonym), commander, D Company, 109th Aviation Battalion, interview with James Schroder and Charles Briscoe, 24 April 2002, Fort Campbell, tape recording and notes, USASOC Classified Archives, Fort Bragg.

185. LTC Edward Simpson is a pseudonym.

186. Major Walter Barstow (pseudonym), C Company, 9th PSYOP Battalion, interview with Kalev Sepp, 3 and 4 April 2002, Fort Bragg, tape recording and notes, USASOC Classified Archives, Fort Bragg.

187. Major Walter Barstow, "PSYOP Assessment—Mr. Hamad Karzai," 12 November 2001, USASOC Classified Archives, Fort Bragg.

188. Pamela Constable, "Assembly Elects Hamad Karzai as Transitional Head of State," *Washington Post*, 14 June 2002.

189. W. Richards interview.

190. Ahmed Rashid, "Hamad Karzai Moves From Lightweight to Heavyweight in Afghan Politics," *Eurasia Insight*, 12 December 2001, <www.eurasianet.org/departments/insight/articles/eav121001.shtml>; *FRONTLINE*, "Campaign Against Terror."

191. Ibid.

192. Lieutenant Colonel Jack Walters (pseudonym), U.S. Joint Forces Command, interview with Richard Kiper, 19 July 2002, Norfolk, tape recording and notes, USASOC Classified Archives, Fort Bragg.

193. W. Richards interview.

194. *FRONTLINE*, "Campaign Against Terror."

195. Carl von Clausewitz, *On War*, Michael Howard and Peter Paret, ed. and trans. (Princeton, NJ: Princeton University Press, 1976), 87.

196. W. Richards interview.

197. Tom Carhart, "In Afghanistan With CPT Jason Amerine '93," *Assembly* (March/April 2002), 54-55.

198. *FRONTLINE*, "Campaign Against Terror"; Hall.

199. Clausewitz, 580; Finn.

200. RADM Bert Calland, 3 May 2002, As Sayliyah, Qatar, interview with Matthew Dawson, tapes at USSOCOM Classified Archives, MacDill Air Force Base, Florida, hereafter cited as Calland interview.

201. Mulholland interview; "The Campaign Against Kandahar and Subsequent Events," information paper, CMH, 30 April 2002; "Engineer" is a form of address in Afghanistan, indicating the person's academic credentials in the same way "doctor" or "professor" is used.

202. Mulholland interview.

203. Marc Bell is a pseudonym; Calland interview, tapes and notes in USASOC Classified Archives, Fort Bragg.

204. Calland interview, tapes and notes in USASOC Classified Archives, Fort Bragg.

205. Pronounced "MAH-zar-ee-shar-EEF." Mario Magione, Kevin Sault, Marc Bell, Pete Bender, Pat Schroeder,

Karl Latimer, Bobby Chesterfield, Charles Moss, Bill Gregg, and Marvin Vandiver are pseudonyms. Mario Magione and Kevin Sault, 22-23 March 2002, Fort Campbell, interview with Kalev Sepp, transcripts and tapes, USASOC Classified Archives, Fort Bragg, hereafter cited as Magione and Sault interview.

206. Ibid.

207. Ibid. Initial reports indicated that there were 500 to 600 *al-Qaeda* fighters in this band, but at the time, no one took an accurate count. After the uprising, the sum of the number of surrendered fighters, counted precisely by American troops, and an approximate tally of *al-Qaeda* losses in the fortress totaled closer to 300.

208. Pronounced "KAHN-dooz."

209. The *Taliban* forces at Konduz included hundreds of Pakistanis urged by their mullahs to travel to Afghanistan to wage a *jihad* against the American "infidels" (non-Muslims) who the mullahs said had invaded Muslim territory. Magione and Sault interview, tapes and notes in USASOC Classified Archives, Fort Bragg.

210. Ibid.

211. LTC Bell told Calland that when he advised GEN Dostum at Konduz to order a thorough search of the prisoners, he refused. Calland felt Dostum's outlook was in accordance with the Afghan and Islamic traditions of hospitality and the granting of sanctuary, even for one's enemies. Calland interview, tapes and notes in USASOC Classified Archives, Fort Bragg.

212. Pronounced "KAHLA-ee-JAHN-guee." The fortress of Qala-i-Jangi had most recently been the head-quarters of the *Taliban's* 18th Division, which was defeated in the battles in the Bahlk Valley. Magione and Sault interview, tapes and notes in USASOC Classified Archives, Fort Bragg.

213. The Turkish school was also cleaner and better ventilated than the cell-like chambers inside the walls of Qala-i-Jangi. The arriving Americans discovered the floors of the fortress rooms covered with human feces the *Taliban* occupants left. The Special Forces medics told their commanders that as long as they stayed in the airless vaults, they were at risk for respiratory infections from fecal dust. Magione and Sault interview, tapes and notes in USASOC Classified Archives, Fort Bragg.

214. Ibid.

215. CIA Press Release, 28 November 2001.

216. CIA Press Release, 11 April 2002.

217. Calland interview, tapes and notes in USASOC Classified Archives, Fort Bragg; Magione and Sault interview, tapes and notes in USASOC Classified Archives, Fort Bragg.

218. Ibid.

219. Cable News Network, "CNN Presents: House of War: The Uprising at Mazar-e-Sharif," air date 3 August 2002, videotape, <http://www.cnn.com/CNN/Programs/presents/index.house.of.war.html>.

220. Magione and Sault interview, tapes and notes in USASOC Classified Archives, Fort Bragg.

221. JDAM is pronounced "JAY-dam." For details on the joint direct-attack munition (JDAM), GBU 31/31 1,000-pound (lb) and 2,000-lb bombs, see the U.S. Air Force fact sheet, <http://www.af.mil/news/factsheets/JDAM. html>. Magione and Sault interview, tapes and notes in USASOC Classified Archives, Fort Bragg.

222. Ibid.

223. The unit was 1st Platoon, C Company, 1st Battalion, 87th Infantry, 10th Mountain Division. Magione and Sault interview, tapes and notes in USASOC Classified Archives, Fort Bragg.

224. Ibid.

225. Ibid.

226. Calland interview, tapes and notes in USASOC Classified Archives, Fort Bragg.

227. Magione and Sault interview, tapes and notes in USASOC Classified Archives, Fort Bragg.

228. The AC-130 gunship is described at <http://www.af.mil/news/factsheets/AC_130H_U_Gunship.html>.

229. Magione and Sault interview, tapes and notes in USASOC Classified Archives, Fort Bragg; H.B.G., memorandum, "ODA 592, Operation Enduring Freedom," 6 March 2002, Fort Campbell, and 18 November 2002, Fort Campbell, telephonic interview with Kalev Sepp, memorandum and transcript, USASOC Classified Archives, Fort Bragg.

230. Mark Bojune (pseudonym), "The Beginning: Answered Prayers and Miracles," after-action notes, HHC, 5th SFG (Airborne), Fort Campbell, tape recording and notes, USASOC Classified Archives, Fort Bragg.

231. Magione and Sault interview, tapes and notes in USASOC Classified Archives, Fort Bragg.

232. Ibid.

233. The American, John Walker Lindh, was in this group of recaptured prisoners, but he did not identify himself until a day later when he was interred at Shebergan Prison, west of Mazar-e-Sharif; Magione and Sault inter-

view, tapes and notes in USASOC Classified Archives, Fort Bragg.

234. Harry Sims, Marcus Steinmann, Matt Rhinehart, Stan Boyd, and Elias Sage are pseudonyms.

235. Harry Sims (pseudonym), 27 March 2002, Fort Campbell, interview with Kalev Sepp, transcript and tapes, USASOC Classified Archives, Fort Bragg, hereafter cited as Sims interview.

236. Ibid.

237. Pronounced "SHIN-nah-RYE"; Ibid.

238. Sims interview, tapes and notes in USASOC Classified Archives, Fort Bragg.

239. Ibid.

240. Ibid.

241. Ibid.

242. Ibid.

243. Ibid.

244. Ibid.

245. Ibid.

246. Ibid.

247. Ibid.

248. Ibid.

249. Ibid.

250. Harry Sims, Neal Nutting, Elias Sage, Stan Boyd, Chuck Fan, Wally Czyrnyck, Stef Holman, Cory Loomis, Kim Joes, Bobby Santiago, Gus Cornell, and Alan Kellogg are pseudonyms; Ibid.

251. Harry Sims, memorandum, "ODA 583, Operation Enduring Freedom," 19 March 2002, Fort Campbell, hereafter cited as Sims memorandum; Sims interview, tapes and notes in USASOC Classified Archives, Fort Bragg.

252. Ibid.

253. Ibid.

254. MAJ Del Bennington, 25 March 2002, Fort Campbell, interview with Kalev Sepp, transcripts and tapes, USASOC Classified Archives, Fort Bragg, hereafter cited as Bennington interview.

255. Del Bennington, Don Forsythe, Nick Sands, Dan Herndon, Douglas Bain, Tim Roswell, Jack Loach, Rich Ryder, Charlie Fazal, Stan Messinger, Jeffrey Solis, and Walter Madison are pseudonyms.

256. Ibid.

257. SOCCE is pronounced "sock-SEE." Bennington recognized at the time that this organization and approach to unconventional warfare operations was not in accordance with established doctrine, which held that a Special Forces company headquarters, led by a major, was to perform this sort of mission. However, the staff began planning for its infiltration and follow-on operations immediately. Bennington interview, tapes and notes in USASOC Classified Archives, Fort Bragg.

258. Douglas Bain, 25 March 2002, Fort Campbell, interview with Kalev Sepp, transcripts and tapes, USASOC Classified Archives, Fort Bragg. TACP is pronounced "tack-PEA." The letters stand for tactical air control party, "A subordinate operational component of a tactical air control system designed to provide air liaison to land forces and for the control of aircraft," <http://www.dtic.mil/doctrine/jel/doddict/natoterm/t/01065.html>.

259. Bennington interview, tapes and notes in USASOC Classified Archives, Fort Bragg.

260. Ibid.

261. Del Bennington, letter to Kalev Sepp, 2 December 2002, Washington, DC, copy at USASOC Classified Archives, Fort Bragg, hereafter cited as Bennington letter.

262. LTC Don Forsythe (pseudonym), 2nd Battalion, 5th SFG, interview with Richard Kiper, 25 April 2002, Fort Campbell, tape recording and notes, USASOC Classified Archives, Fort Bragg, hereafter cited as Forsythe interview. Matt Rhinehart is a pseudonym.

263. Sims memorandum and Sims interview, tapes and notes in USASOC Classified Archives, Fort Bragg.

264. Ibid.

265. Ibid.

266. The U.S. Air Force 332nd Air Expeditionary Wing delivered most of the bombs in support of U.S. Army Special Forces operations in southern Afghanistan. The wing included B-52 bombers and F-15E and F-16 fighter bombers. The 391st Fighter Squadron ("Bold Tigers"), equipped with F-15E Strike Eagles, was part of the 332nd Air Wing during Operation ENDURING FREEDOM. One of the 391st's pilots, MAJ Jim Sisler, was the son of Medal of Honor recipient 1LT George K. Sisler, a 5th SFG officer during the Vietnam war. George Sisler received the Medal of Honor posthumously for heroism while directing airstrikes against enemy forces on 7 February 1967, when his

patrol was surrounded inside enemy territory in Laos. His son Jim painted the Special Forces regimental insignia on the nose of his F-15E fighter jet. Bennington letter, Sims memorandum, and Sims interview, tapes and notes in USASOC Classified Archives, Fort Bragg.

267. Bennington letter, USASOC Classified Archives, Fort Bragg.

268. Bennington interview, tapes and notes in USASOC Classified Archives, Fort Bragg.

269. Ibid.

270. SSG Walter Madison was evacuated by helicopter at 2230 that night from a pickup zone about 3 miles away. Bennington interview, tapes and notes in USASOC Classified Archives, Fort Bragg.

271. The 12 remaining members of Forsythe's battalion headquarters staff arrived by helicopter in the predawn darkness at 0430 on 5 December 2001. Later, Bennington heard that a satellite failure had interrupted all radio communications in JSOTF-North for more than 3 hours that afternoon and into the evening. Bennington interview, tapes and notes in USASOC Classified Archives, Fort Bragg.

272. Ibid.

273. Sims interview, tapes and notes in USASOC Classified Archives, Fort Bragg.

274. Ibid.

275. Ibid. See also ODA 583 (Texas 17), "Monograph, Operation Enduring Freedom, Southern Afghanistan Campaign (18 Nov 01 to 6 Feb 02)," n.d., copy at USASOC Classified Archives, Fort Bragg.

276. Sims interview, tapes and notes in USASOC Classified Archives, Fort Bragg.

277. Ibid.

278. Ibid.

279. Ibid.; Forsythe interview, tapes and notes in USASOC Classified Archives, Fort Bragg.

280. Ibid.

281. John Hendren and Maura Reynolds, "Afghanistan: Target Finder's Error Cost about 28 Lives to 'Friendly Fire,'" *Los Angeles Times*, 27 March 2002.

282. Michael A. Fletcher, "Victims Were Professional Soldiers," *Washington Post*, 6 December 2001, 28.

283. Hendren and Reynolds.

284. Forsythe interview, tapes and notes in USASOC Classified Archives, Fort Bragg; Finn.

285. Norimitsu Onishi, "Interim Afghan Leader Discusses Kandahar's Surrender With *Taliban*," *New York Times*, 6 December 2001; *FRONTLINE*, "Campaign Against Terror."

286. Forsythe interview, tapes and notes in USASOC Classified Archives, Fort Bragg.

287. Dallas Bronson (pseudonym), 2nd Battalion, 5th SFG, telephonic interview with Kalev Sepp and Richard Kiper, 5 December 2002, Fort Bragg, notes, USASOC Classified Archives, Fort Bragg.

288. Willis Witter, "*Taliban* Surrenders Stronghold," *Washington Times*, 7 December 2001, 1; Vernon Loeb and Bradley Graham, "Rumsfeld Says No Amnesty for *Taliban* Leader," *Washington Post*, 7 December 2001, 34.

289. Forsythe interview, tapes and notes in USASOC Classified Archives, Fort Bragg; *FRONTLINE*, "Campaign Against Terror"; David Rhode and Eric Schmitt, "*Taliban* Give Way in Final Province Where They Ruled," *New York Times*, 10 December 2001, 1.

290. Major Matt DiJurnigan (pseudonym), C Company, 96th Civil Affairs Battalion, interview with Richard Kiper, 4 November 2002, Fort Bragg, tape recording and notes, USASOC Classified Archives, Fort Bragg, hereafter cited as DiJurnigan interview.

291. Gilmore; Senate Armed Services Committee, *Testimony of U.S. Secretary of Defense Donald H. Rumsfeld*, 31 July 2002, <http://usembassy.state.gov/posts/pk1/wwwh02080201.html>.

292. DiJurnigan interview, 4; *FRONTLINE*, "Campaign Against Terror."

293. "Operational Summary, Coalition Humanitarian Liaison Cell–Bagram (CHLC-B), Operation ENDURING FREEDOM, Bagram Air Base, Afghanistan," 4 January 2002, C Company (-), 96th Civil Affairs Battalion (Airborne), 1; "Narrative Justification for the Meritorious Unit Citation," Company D, 96th Civil Affairs Battalion (Airborne), n.d., USASOC Classified Archives, Fort Bragg.

294. Ibid., 2-6; Gordon, "Securing Base, U.S. Makes Its Brawn Blend In"; Jon R. Anderson, "Soldiers Bring Joy and Hope to Kids in Afghanistan," *European Stars and Stripes*, 19 December 2001; MAJ Steve Small and SFC Charles Rogers are pseudonyms.

295. U.S. Army Field Manual 41-10, *Civil Affairs Operations* (Washington, DC: U.S. Government Printing Office, February 2000), 1-1; Anderson.

296. O'Reilly interview, tape recording and notes, USASOC Classified Archives, Fort Bragg. Mark Puller, Rick Harrison, Carl Dawkins, and Charles Vargas are pseudonyms.

297. Ibid.

298.   Keith B. Richburg and William Branigin, "U.S. Bombs Aid Rebels in North; Propaganda Campaign Intensifies," *Washington Post*, 8 November 2001, 13. Totals as of 17 October 2002 were 84,215,894 leaflets disseminated; 6,873:39 hours broadcast by SOMS-B and Commando Solo; 538 different radio scripts; and 7,670 radios distributed.

299.   Curtis interview, tapes and notes in USASOC Classified Archives, Fort Bragg.

300.   MAJ Henry Blackaby (pseudonym), Psychological Development Company, 8th Battalion, 4th Psychological Operations Group, interview by Richard Kiper, 17 April 2002, Fort Bragg, tape recording and notes, USASOC Classified Archives, Fort Bragg.

301.   Letter, General Dwight D. Eisenhower in Psychological Warfare Division, "Operations in Western European Campaign," October 1945, Record Group 319, National Archives, 1.

302.   SFC Kevin Easton (pseudonym), B Company, 2nd Battalion, 160th SOAR, interview with James Schroder, 26 March 2002, Fort Campbell, tape recording and notes, USASOC Classified Archives, Fort Bragg.

303.   Striker is a pseudonym.

304.   Gates is a pseudonym.

305.   Falkerie is a pseudonym.

Chapter 4

The Campaign in Transition
8 December 2001 - 28 February 2002

The art of war is simple enough.
Find out where your enemy is.
Get at him as soon as you can.
Strike him as hard as you can, and keep moving on.[1]

Three days after the *Taliban* defeat at Kandahar on 7 December 2001, 5th SFG soldiers conducted a brief ceremony at sunrise in Kabul, raising the American flag for the first time in 12 years at the U.S. Embassy.[2] The unofficial observance, which also honored the three Special Forces soldiers killed by friendly fire earlier that week during fighting that drove the *Taliban* out of the capital city, symbolized the end of the battle for Afghanistan.

Figure 1. American colors unfurled at the U.S. Embassy in Kabul.

The focus of the war had shifted to the eastern mountainous regions along the Pakistan border. While thousands of *Taliban* soldiers simply changed allegiance to the victorious side—a long-established Afghan tradition—and thousands more lay dead, there were thousands also retreating to redoubts and sanctuaries in eastern Afghanistan and western Pakistan.[3] In an effort to cut the escape routes and suspected safe havens, coalition air forces bombed the caves of Tora Bora, Special Forces teams assaulted *Taliban* leaders' residences, and Afghan soldiers—variously called the Anti-*Taliban* Forces, Opposition Group Forces, and the Afghan Military Forces (AMF)—advanced into the mountains to eliminate the enemy.[4]

The jagged, high mountain ranges of Tora Bora, about 45 miles southwest of Jalalabad on the Pakistan border, were reported to contain an elaborate maze of tunnels and caves that had been occupied as late as the *mujahideen* resistance. Intelligence staffs also believed that *al-Qaeda* leader Osama bin Laden, mastermind of the 9/11 attacks, and his chief lieutenants had retreated to this underground complex. American and British special operations units directed airstrikes on the dug-in *Taliban* fighters in support of the slowly advancing Afghan militia forces. Then, Special Forces detachments like ODA 561 began painstakingly methodical searches of dozens of possible hiding places in the mountains, earning them the unwanted reputation of the "cave experts."[5] Aerial photographs were used to guide Special Forces teams and their Afghan militia guards to suspected tunnel and cave openings in the mountainsides and craggy valleys. In most cases, the detachments found only shallow recesses that local goat herders used for temporary shelter and rock outcroppings. Occasionally, however, they found storage caches of weapons and ammunition, documents, and remains of enemy fighters killed by aerial bombs. Under pressure from the advancing Afghans and an intense bombing campaign—as many as 125 airstrikes per day—the enemy withdrew into the nearby snow-capped White Mountains, closer to Pakistan.[6]

Figure 2. Preparing for *al-Qaeda*.

By 17 December, despite numerous attempts by the Afghans to negotiate surrenders, the main body, estimated at 1,000 *Taliban* and *al-Qaeda* fighters, slipped away into the surrounding mountains and across the border.[7] The Special Forces teams did not find bin Laden, but the offensive netted some 60 *al-Qaeda* and *Taliban* prisoners.[8] U.S. forces flew the captives around the world to a newly constructed detention center at Guantanamo Bay (GTMO, pronounced Git-mo) on the island of Cuba. DOD referred to the captured enemy as "detainees" and named their facility "Camp X-Ray."[9]

In addition to the unconventional warfare (UW) missions conducted by COL Mulholland's Uzbekistan-based Task Force (TF) Dagger (JSOTF-North), Commodore Bob Harward's Joint Special Operations Task Force–South (JSOTF-South) carried out special reconnaissance (SR) and direct-action (DA) raids and searches from his new headquarters at the Kandahar Airport.[10] C Company, 112th Special Operations Signal Battalion (SOSB) installed the elaborate radio and satellite communications array the JSOTF-South staff needed to direct the missions as well as the connectivity for A Company, 1st Battalion, 5th SFG, and the 160th SOAR, relocated from K2 to Kandahar.

The 1,300 U.S. Marines and Navy Seabee engineers from the 15th and 26th Marine Expeditionary Units [MEUs that included TF 58 and TF 64 (Australians)], moved on 14 December

Figure 3. Under new management.

from Camp Rhino in the desert to the airport, making Kandahar the second coalition base inside Afghanistan. Bagram had been the first.[11] Eventually, the JSOTF-South command grew to more than 1,000 soldiers, sailors, and airmen and Special Forces units from four allied countries: New Zealand, Germany, Denmark, and Norway.[12] The task force staff also included a Turkish military liaison officer. The coalition special forces joined in the manhunt for bin Laden, Mullah Mohammed Omar, and other fugitive *al-Qaeda* and *Taliban* leaders.

On Christmas Eve 2001, A Company, 1st Battalion, 5th SFG (A-1-5), a 100-man SR and DA assault unit specially trained in urban warfare house-to-house fighting and long-range reconnaissance, left Masirah Island, Oman, and moved into Harward's base camp at Kandahar Airport. Over the next month, after extensive surveillance, the Special Forces company raided

Figure 4. Sand table for DA SSE raid preparations.

205

three suspected enemy hideouts in succession. The force was flown to its objectives on U.S. Air Force and U.S. Marine helicopters. The nighttime raids, called sensitive site exploitations (SSEs), netted more detainees as well as arms and munitions, documents, computers and discs, and pro-*Taliban* propaganda posters. At one site, several bags of processed heroin were found. Extremely sensitive to local customs and culture, the soldiers of A-1-5 conducted raids with such discipline that at one site, they removed their boots before entering a mosque to conduct a search. The mullah was so impressed that he told the villagers, "These men respect God." The surprise searches were executed so quickly that in three of four operations, only two shots were fired, both as warnings to prompt the surrender of Afghan sentries.[13]

Special Forces teams also established bases around the eastern Afghan border town of Khowst, in Paktia province, south of Kabul. On 4 January 2002, SFC Nate Chapman became the first American soldier killed by enemy fire in Afghanistan when his Special Forces element was ambushed near Khowst.[14] The soldiers of C-1-5 named the dirt runway at its camp "Chapman Airfield" in his memory. In the coming months, enemy forces assaulted the Special Forces camp at the airfield twice with rockets, mortar fire, and infantry. On 20 January, one of the two Marine Corps CH-53 Super Stallion helicopters carrying supplies to Chapman Airfield crashed into a snow-covered mountain near Kabul, killing two crewmen. Night Stalker aircrews from 2nd Battalion, 160th SOAR at Bagram scrambled to reach the site in less than 90 minutes and rescued the five U.S. Marine survivors.[15] Two Special Forces detachments from C Company, 2nd Battalion, 5th SFG, were sent to Zhob and Kohat, Pakistan, to advise and assist Pakistani army units in the search for *Taliban* and *al-Qaeda* on their side of the border adjacent to Khowst.[16] Despite U.S. diplomatic encouragement, the Pakistanis were reluctant to send their troops, accompanied by American Special Forces advisers, into the tenuously controlled "Federal Autonomous Tribal Areas" near Afghanistan, and the effort never came to fruition. A civil affairs team (CAT) from D Company, 96th Civil Affairs Battalion (CAB), had better success inside Pakistan monitoring and coordinating international relief efforts to aid Afghan refugees encamped near Islamabad, Quetta, and Peshawar.

The emerging concern of the Western powers was a possible major human disaster in Afghanistan, brought on by the shattered infrastructure, the return of a million refugees, and winter. CA and engineer units were quickly deployed into the theater of war to begin recovery and disaster relief operations. Humanitarian aid of every description, promised by the signatories of the 14 December 2001 Brussels Accord, had to be airlifted into the country, and with the aid came the multifarious agencies wanting to oversee distribution and application. They had to be supported and protected whether they wanted to be or not. This effort received additional impetus when the Afghan Interim Authority (AIA) was formally organized on 22 December and Hamad Karzai was sworn in as prime minister. Karzai understood that the relief efforts were essential to stabilizing Afghanistan against any *Taliban* resurgence or a new civil war among the ethnic warlords restored to power in various provinces.[17]

On Christmas Eve 2001, elements of the Coalition Joint Civil-Military Operations Task Force (CJCMOTF) arrived in Kabul. From a staff of six soldiers, the headquarters of BG David Kratzer grew in two months to more than 150, primarily USAR personnel.[18] A week before Kratzer's arrival, the International Security Assistance Force (ISAF), consisting of British Royal Marines initially in a peacekeeping role, was stood up in Kabul.[19] With the last large-scale fighting over in early December, the relief effort intensified and expanded throughout the country. The same day the *Taliban* deserted Kandahar, Special Forces engineers supervised and assisted the Afghans in completing the final repairs to the bomb-damaged runway at Mazar-e-Sharif. As soon as Air Force teams verified its suitability, international cargo airplanes began landing with humanitarian aid and a group of French engineers. An American Special Forces detachment accompanied a Jordanian field hospital and its staff. The Special Forces team had helped the Jordanian medical teams prepare for their mission to Afghanistan. This humanitarian aid task force eventually grew to 1,000 American and coalition soldiers and civilians. Only days later, the first overland relief convoy delivered supplies from Uzbekistan via the Friendship Bridge into Afghanistan.[20]

CAT-As, consisting of an officer and three Special Forces-qualified sergeants from the 96th CAB, managed most of the effort. The international media captured the highly qualified personnel, their positive attitudes, the wide variety of missions, and the unique contributions of the CAT-As. The American national press services and news networks focused on human interest feature stories as the teams treated children who had been injured by old Soviet-era mines, delivered food to refugee camps, arranged well digging, and began rebuilding schools and medical clinics—critical essentials for the Afghan communities.[21] The CATs also labored to find and apply the resources to repair the crumbling, war-damaged Afghan infrastructure—roads, bridges, and the vital Salang Tunnel through the Hindu Kush connecting northern and southern Afghanistan by a two-lane road.[22]

The number of U.S. military personnel in Afghanistan grew from the 130 SOF soldiers who waged the battles that defeated the *Taliban* in Afghanistan to almost 5,000 soldiers. Mechanics from the 528th SOSB who were trained to repair and service Army tactical vehicles applied their skills with ingenuity to keep the motley conglomeration of civilian Ginga trucks and Japanese-built pickups and other vehicles used by Special Forces elements and their Afghan allies running.

Figure 5. Afghan children.

207

Figure 6. The Camp Abel motor pool in Bagram.

Special Forces ODAs and ODBs from the ARNG 2nd Battalion, 19th SFG, and the 3rd SFG assumed the operational mission from departing 5th SFG teams in Uzbekistan and Afghanistan. The 2nd Battalion headquarters, 19th SFG, took control of the isolation facility (ISOFAC) and other Special Forces sites at Karshi Kanabad (K2). At Fort Bragg, B Company, 2nd Battalion, 3rd SFG trained for urban combat and long-range reconnaissance to assume the SSE mission from A-1-5 at Kandahar. 3rd Battalion, 75th Rangers, after the parachute assault on Bastogne in November, rotated its companies in and out of Afghanistan to support continuing operations theaterwide.

Conventional forces were on the move as well. Army infantry battalions from the 101st Airborne Division (Air Assault) from Fort Campbell arrived in mid-January 2002 to replace the U.S. Marines at Kandahar Airport. The 10th Mountain Division headquarters and a large contingent of infantrymen arrived at Bagram Airfield from Fort Drum, New York, between 13 and 21 February. On 22 February, an MH-47D Chinook helicopter company from the 3rd Battalion, 160th SOAR, arrived to replace the MH-47E Chinooks from the 2nd Battalion. The SOCCENT, RADM Bert Calland, assigned the 3rd Battalion, 3rd SFG to JSOTF-South at Kandahar. Although Commodore Harward, commander, JSOTF-South, initially planned to break up the unit and distribute its personnel to augment his staff sections and other units, Calland convinced him otherwise based on the merits of a forward operating base (FOB) and by committing his staff to support the headquarters. Thus, the "Third of the Third" became FOB 33, responsible for the command and control of its Special Forces companies and ODAs fighting in the Khowst region. Together with a group of joint staff officers and sergeants transferred from JSOTF-North at the end of February 2002, FOB 33 helped the predominantly Navy staff direct UW operations in southern Afghanistan.

The hunt for the leaders and supporters of the ousted *Taliban* government and the *al-Qaeda* terrorist organization continued. When A Company, 1st Battalion, 5th SFG, raided two enemy compounds simultaneously at Hazar Qadam on 23 January, it encountered sharp resistance. In the night gun battle that ensued, A Company fought from darkened room to darkened room wearing night-vision goggles (NVG) and using laser-sighted weapons, killing 16 enemy fighters and capturing 27.[23] In the days following the very successful night raid, local Afghans alleged that the defenders of both compounds had switched allegiance from the *Taliban* to the new AIA before the assault.[24] The international media, tired of humanitarian relief coverage, tried to expand the allegations into an exposé story. Secretary of Defense Donald Rumsfeld

208

settled the matter when he endorsed the soldiers' response to hostile fire—when fired on, the Special Forces soldiers fired back.[25]

The month before, a band of diehard *al-Qaeda* fighters barricaded themselves inside the Mir Wais Hospital in Kandahar, disrupting medical service to the population. The local women were particularly encumbered because the only gynecological facility in the Kandahar area was in the wing where the *al-Qaeda* fighters were holed up. A standoff had lasted for several weeks because sympathizers on the hospital staff smuggled food, water, and supplies to the diehards. With negotiations at a standstill, the commander, A Company, 3rd Battalion, 5th SFG, planned to end the deadlock with a DA assault. Just before dawn on 27 January, after training an Afghan force for weeks, Special Forces ODA 524 directly supported the hand-picked group of Pashtuns that stormed the hospital wing. After ODA 524 blasted a man-size opening through a wall with explosive charges, the Pashtun assault force was stopped by a fusillade of gunfire from the fortified room. A second assault team was hastily formed to attack down the hallway, throwing grenades. The six *al-Qaeda* fanatics who had sworn to "fight to the death rather than surrender" were killed, and the deadlock ended.[26]

During another night raid operation on 12 February, an aerial refuel rendezvous between two Air Force MC-130P tankers and three MH-47E Chinooks en route to their target ended in a miraculous high-mountain rescue mission. While the nighttime aerial refueling was under way, one of the two MC-130Ps crashed into the side of a snow-covered mountain almost 2 miles above sea level. Developing a rescue plan "on the fly," one Chinook landed in the deep snow immediately below the crash site while the other two MH-47Es finished refueling. Remarkably, although the four-turboprop MC-130P tanker plane had broken in half on impact and fuel had surrounded the smoking wreckage, all eight crew members survived. In complete darkness on a snow-capped peak, the Chinook pilots landed the assault force turned rescuers and took off to aerial refuel again, in turn, before flying the 9th Special Operations Squadron (SOS) airmen back to the base for medical treatment.[27]

With U.S. and coalition forces repairing and opening airfield runways across Afghanistan to supply flights, and fixing roads and replacing bridges for truck traffic, BG Lesley Fuller and the Special Operations Command, Europe (SOCEUR)-based support units began reducing parachute resupply drops. In the first 70 days of combat, personnel from SOCEUR units, the U.S. Army, Europe (USAREUR) 21st Theater Army Support Command (TASCOM), and the Air Force 16th and 352nd Special Operations Wings (SOWs) packed, parachute-rigged, and airdropped 1.8 million pounds of bundles that included most of the supply classes. During 135 combat air missions, the MC-130 Combat Talons dropped 1,347 containers. In those 70 days, only a single Talon could not fly as scheduled; however, its cargo was quickly transferred to a backup MC-130, and the airdrop mission was only 30 minutes behind schedule.[28]

The 5th SFG staff manning JSOTF-North at K2, Uzbekistan, prepared to transfer its missions, responsibilities, and remaining combat forces to JSOTF-South at Kandahar and return to the United States. The sequentially orchestrated transfer to maintain the Special Forces presence began at the end of February and continued into mid-March. In turn, the JSOTF-South headquarters at Kandahar, built around the Naval Special Warfare Group One (NSWG-1) staff, was also slated to close down on 30 March. It was to hand off the direction of operations

Figure 7. Post-mission discussions among ARSOF personnel.

to the arriving 3rd SFG headquarters that was building a new base camp at Bagram Air Base. Two hundred soldiers from the 3rd SFG and 100 soldiers from the ARNG 3rd Battalion, 20th SFG, were to staff the new Combined Joint Special Operations Task Force–Afghanistan (CJ-SOTF-A) headquarters.[29] As the 3rd SFG ODAs arrived, they were sent to replace the 5th SFG teams dispersed at sites across Afghanistan. As an example of what happened during the on-going transfer of responsibilities between JSOTFs, the changing character of the conflict, and the focus on supporting the AIA, Special Forces ODA 394 received new orders before it had carried out earlier ones, week after week.

Cued initially by intelligence reports from a Special Forces detachment in December 2001, the American and coalition military staffs began planning a brigade-size offensive operation against *Taliban* and *al-Qaeda* fighters that had regrouped in the rugged escarpments around the isolated Shah-i-Khot Valley.[30] Code-named Operation ANACONDA, the offensive sweep was intended to flush the *Taliban* and *al-Qaeda* fighters from their hiding places toward ambushes and blocking positions that would be established around the valley. Infantry battalions from the 10th Mountain Division and 101st Airborne Division, and U.S. and coalition SOF would support the main attack being made by several Afghan militia forces with American Special Forces advisers. After two weather-driven delays, the planned 48-hour operation started just after day-break on 2 March. The stubborn, very effective enemy defense of the Shah-i-Khot Valley took most American and Afghan commanders by surprise. Operation ANACONDA turned into two weeks of heavy bombing and hard fighting. U.S. Army, Navy, and Air Force SOF suffered the most killed-in-action (KIA) casualties—eight men killed by enemy and friendly fire and two MH-47E helicopters shot down in the high mountains.[31]

The entire character of the Afghanistan campaign continued to evolve, as had been the case since the Ranger parachute assault and the first Special Forces team insertions in Afghanistan on 19 October 2001. It rapidly became evident to the ARSOF commanders that the UW campaign in Afghanistan was not going to evolve neatly into a postconflict paradigm where peace-keeping forces oversaw nation-building projects. Rather, combat operations aimed at hunting down the surviving *Taliban* and *al-Qaeda* fighters would continue. Creating and training a new, multiethnic Afghan National Army (ANA) to prosecute this phase of the UW campaign fell to the 3rd SFG and a unit of French army mountain troops. The primary training site would be the bomb-cratered Kabul Military Academy and its grounds.[32] The Germans accepted the mission to train the national police force in the capital, and the British were to train Afghan national guard battalions to provide "internal security" for the new government.[33]

Once the major *Taliban* and *al-Qaeda* forces had been beaten in open combat and with the rest of them switching to guerrilla warfare, the U.S. Central Command (CENTCOM) placed a conventional Army corps commander (XVIII Airborne Corps) in charge of military operations in Afghanistan and sent in more infantry battalions to man the Kandahar and Bagram air bases. The CJSOTF-A and its assigned U.S. and coalition SOF were to support the conventional TF 180. American troop strength in Afghanistan reached 7,000, and the allied troops in the ISAF, manned by 18 nations, numbered almost 5,000.[34] The *loya jirga*—the grand national council of Afghanistan—was scheduled to convene in June 2002 to choose the new post-*Taliban* government. As infighting among the Afghan warlords grew in scope and intensity, coalition SR units reported that reorganized *Taliban* units had begun to reenter the country from Pakistan. Both posed threats to a successful convention of the *loya jirga*. The campaign to seal the military victory with political, social, and economic stability was a long way from concluding. This meant that the work of ARSOF in Afghanistan was far from over as well.

The following vignettes cover ground combat operations that were conducted to eliminate the remaining pockets of *Taliban* and *al-Qaeda* resistance; the key leaders who escaped during the final offensives; and the heavy demand for CA elements with increased emphasis on reconstruction, humanitarian relief, and infrastructure restoration to provide stability for the AIA. With units being replaced and joint headquarters being established as others were taken down, communications elements were fully employed, responding to constant changes and maintaining critical capabilities throughout. There were a lot of things happening but few as exciting as earlier combat segments.

Old Glory Flies Again in Kabul

After the fall of Kandahar, JSOTF-North Commander COL John Mulholland entered Afghanistan for the first time, having orchestrated the war from K2, Uzbekistan. His first task was to survey the abandoned U.S. Embassy in Kabul to determine, with State Department officials, when it could reopen. The survey team, escorted by Special Forces ODAs 550 and 575, drove through the city to the old embassy compound. There were bullet holes in the walls of the building, evidently the work of frustrated *Taliban*, but the interior was surprisingly unmolested. A Super Bowl 1979 poster was still tacked to the wall in one office, and copies of the embassy phone directories were found in desk drawers. Most amazing, however, was the embassy fleet of 1979 Volkswagen Jettas parked in the basement garage. All but two of them started. "It was kind of weird—like stepping into a 12-year time warp," said one soldier. Apparently, rumors of booby traps in the buildings and mines buried on the grounds, spread at the time the embassy was evacuated and perpetuated by the caretakers, had discouraged the *Taliban* from desecrating

Figure 8. Kabul sprawl and majestic mountains.

or plundering the buildings as it typically did when abandoning sites.[35]

Just before sunrise on Monday, 10 December 2001, Mulholland assembled the survey group and the ODAs in the crisp predawn air in front of the embassy for a brief ceremony before the U.S. Marines arrived from Camp Rhino to assume their traditional mission. CPT Mason Arquette (pseudonym), the joint operations center (JOC) link to K2, described the small, appropriate ceremony.[36] The 5th SFG commander, wearing his green beret and an Afghan tribal scarf around his neck, carefully unfolded a 3 x 5-foot Civil War style regimental "battle flag." Embroidered on the top red stripe of the American flag were "5th SFG (Airborne)" in white block letters, a parachutist badge next to the Special Forces shoulder patch, and the 5th SFG silver-bordered black flash worn on the green beret.[37]

Figure 9. U.S. Embassy cornerstone and a solemn ceremony.

As Arquette watched the flag being raised up the tall metal pole in front of the American Embassy, the sun was just breaking the horizon of the nearby mountains, and the white contrails of B-52 bombers circling several miles overhead could be seen. COL Mulholland called for a moment of silence "for our fallen comrades" who had been memorialized on the back of a map case: "In memory of Jefferson Davis, Dan Petithory, and Cody Prosser, ODA 574, killed in action" near Sayd-Alim-Kalay supporting Hamad Karzai three days before.[38] Then Mulholland spoke again, and the flag was lowered so the U.S. Marines could raise the embassy flag. Arquette lingered in the courtyard, surprised that he was so moved by the simple ceremony. Moments later, the fallen having been memorialized and America's presence having been restored at the embassy, the Special Forces soldiers silently departed to return to the war.[39]

Tora Bora

In early December 2001, when American and Afghan military operations were focused on Kandahar, the birthplace of the *Taliban*, intelligence sources began reporting that although significant *Taliban* and *al-Qaeda* forces remained near the city the leaders had already fled toward the White Mountains near the town of Tora Bora. There had been numerous reported sightings of Osama bin Laden in the area. Southwest of Jalalabad, the high mountain region offered not only excellent defensive terrain, but adjacent to the porous Pakistan border, there were also numerous escape routes. It was apparent to commanders at all levels that the Tora Bora region was the next logical military search objective.[40]

Afghan militia leader Hazrat Ali referred to Tora Bora as "the last center of al-Qaida in this country. It is the strongest center of al-Qaida, and now we want to take it and make it the weakest center of al-Qaida."[41] With its narrow defiles and innumerable natural caves in steep terrain topping 15,000 feet, the White Mountains were an ideal hideout for the remnants of the *Taliban* and *al-Qaeda* forces. Although American air power played a decisive role in the ground campaign during October, November, and early December, most of the targets had been in the high-altitude plains regions, not in the Hindu Kush. The predominantly mountainous terrain in the Tora Bora area limited its effectiveness. Military planners recognized that ground operations were essential to finding, then rooting out and destroying the enemy in the region.

Figure 10. Two northern Afghan leaders.

Hazrat Ali, who controlled the Afghan Military Forces (AMF) in the area, was quite anxious to launch an offensive into the mountains. Other American advisers with Ali had pushed him to launch an attack into the mountains. In mid-December, there were only limited American combat forces in Afghanistan—the U.S. Marines at Camp Rhino, southwest of Kandahar; several Special Forces ODAs scattered around the country supporting prominent AMF war leaders; and the SEALs at Kandahar. In June 2002, Deputy Secretary of Defense Paul Wolfowitz told Congress: "We deliberately did not plan an operation in Afghanistan based on putting in 100,000 or 150,000 American troops along the model of the Soviets." Thus, any major offensive into the White Mountains would have to be conducted by the Afghan forces.

This meant assigning a Special Forces team to Ali to advise him and to assist his ground operation with close air support (CAS). COL Mulholland, the JSOTF-North commander, was very skeptical and concerned about the plan. In his view, "This [was] a flawed concept. What [was being proposed was] a deliberate attack against an entrenched enemy in a mountain

213

stronghold, [an enemy that we knew was] going to fight to the death." Estimates of the *Taliban* and *al-Qaeda* numbers in the area varied from 500 to 3,000. Subsequent events established that they also had tanks. The 5th SFG commander knew that the Afghans did not have enough trained soldiers, heavy weapons, or logistics for such a large operation. Nevertheless, he realized that some key *Taliban* and *al-Qaeda* leaders might be in the region, and any operation had to be executed quickly. Mulholland tapped ODA 572 to support Ali.[42]

Figure 11. Cave searches locate weapons and munitions caches.

Figure 12. Mobile cave operations.

However, before the Special Forces team could be dispatched, Ali had loaded his forces into pickup trucks and moved into the mountains. With no logistics support or the means to arrange American air support, the probability of success was slim. Mulholland was concerned that Ali would launch a deliberate attack without the requisite preparation. On 4 December, CW3 Dwayne Torgelson (pseudonym) and ODA 572 arrived to support Ali. Torgelson divided his team into two CAS teams at Jalalabad before their mountain insertion by Air Force MH-53 helicopters. When the team became engaged in a firefight, an American reconnaissance element called for air support without knowing the location of all the friendly forces. Torgelson saw the potential for disaster and called off the airstrike. After ensuring that no friendly forces were in danger, both elements withdrew to safe distances, and a B-52 dropped its payload on the enemy positions.

When ODA 572 linked up with Hazrat Ali, the Afghan leader insisted that the CAS teams accompany his front-line soldiers into battle without understanding the difficulty of calling in airstrikes while under fire or the necessity to have a safety buffer zone between friendly forces and the impact area of the bombs. CAS strikes and the B-52 bombing were a part of a sustained air campaign that resumed on 1 December in support of the U.S. and Afghan effort to root out the *Taliban* and *al-Qaeda*. Special Forces teams that were on the ground to direct the air attacks made that campaign even more effective.[43]

Recognizing that there were serious coordination problems, JSOTF-North pulled ODA 572 back to Jalalabad until the situation could be sorted out between Ali, the American advisers, and the task force. Adding to the coordination problems was the fluid ground situation. Battle lines were shifting back and forth continuously, and Ali was concerned about the safety of the Special Forces soldiers. On 6 December, ODA 572 returned to Ali's forward command post and convinced him to provide it with a small security element. The next day it reentered the mountains and over the next several days occupied a series of advancing positions to provide CAS to the Afghan troops who were attacking caves and tunnels that were sites of resistance. Several groups of *Taliban* attempted to negotiate surrender with the Afghans, whose custom was to set the enemy free after surrendering. The Americans would not accept this practice because they wanted to ensure that those surrendering were not *Taliban* or *al-Qaeda* leaders and that they would not pose future threats by reverting back to fighting once released. The ODA 572 team sergeant, MSG Shannon Whitley (pseudonym) made it clear to the Afghans that "It's a complete unconditional surrender, and [they] are processed as prisoners." The Special Forces team was not going to allow *al-Qaeda* terrorists to escape by feigning surrender. Secretary of Defense Rumsfeld had been adamant about the unconditionality of enemy surrender: "This is not a drill where we're making deals."[44]

Airstrikes directed by ODA 572 supported the tough ground combat being waged by Ali's forces in the White Mountains. GEN Richard Myers, Chairman, Joint Chiefs of Staff (CJCS), said the mountainous fighting was "very tough." "The al-Qaida forces that we think are ensconced up there . . . are fighting for their lives," he told a television news reporter.[45]

On 20 December, SF ODA 561 elements arrived to assist ODA 572 as it searched caves and tunnels for intelligence documents, any indication of bin Laden's presence, and to take DNA samples from dead enemy bodies. When the rest of ODA 561 arrived, the two teams expanded their search areas to explore more enemy locations. Together, they found quantities of ammunition, heavy machine guns, documents, computer disks, maps, photographs, manuals, and videotapes. Unfortunately, local Afghans had already pillaged many of the caves. In most cases, the caves that intelligence photo analysts "spotted" proved to be shadows cast by overhanging rocks. To add to the frustration and sense of "chasing the proverbial wild goose," Afghan leaders charged the teams as much as $1,000 for meals and $300 for vehicle use. Despite this "price gouging," the two SF teams kept focused on accomplishing their mission.[46]

ODA 572 left the region on 17 January, followed by ODA 561 on 22 January. The two Special Forces teams returned to K2, Uzbekistan. Estimates of *al-Qaeda* killed by the Afghan commanders ranged from 200 to as high as 1,000. There were no signs of bin Laden or Mullah Omar. According to GEN Tommy Franks, commander, CENTCOM, we "simply don't know" where they are. SSG Jeremy Parsons (pseudonym) stated that finding bin Laden was not ODA 572's primary mission: "Our mission was to support General Ali's troops in getting rid of the pockets of resistance of *al-Qaeda* and *Taliban* and to go start the searches of the caves." Patently obvious was that many of these enemy fighters had escaped to Pakistan. The border was impossible to seal. Ali was not terribly concerned: "We're happy because we have expelled the foreigners."[47]

Despite the heavy coverage, the media treated the Tora Bora operation an "opportunity lost." Franks disagreed: "I look at Tora Bora as a favorable operation." There was no evidence found that proved bin Laden had been killed, but the *al-Qaeda* delaying operation had been disrupted. Many had been killed, and they had been dislocated. Special Forces ODA 572 and ODA 561 did exactly as tasked. They accompanied their Afghan allies into a mountainous complex containing well-prepared defenses and managed to dislodge the defenders. As "warrior diplomats," the teams had to balance support of military operations while ensuring that nothing they said or did would adversely affect the future of U.S.-Afghan relations. SSG Wallace Seifert (pseudonym) saw their mission as typical: "We were just there doing our job; just doing our job."[48]

While the Tora Bora operation was under way, the JSOTF-South and 101st Airborne Division's Rakkasan Brigade established themselves at Kandahar Airport. The 3rd Battalion, 3rd SFG, assigned to JSOTF-South would operate from that base. But it was the 5th Battalion, 19th SFG from the ARNG that would serve as the special operations liaison to the Combined Forces Land Component Command (CFLCC) headquarters at the air base.

One Army

In the aftermath of the 9/11 terrorist attacks, neither SSG Karl Kramer nor SSG Sylvester Largent (pseudonyms) had any idea that six months later they would be anywhere near Kandahar, Afghanistan.[49] Both were Special Forces soldiers in ODA 581, 5th Battalion, 19th SFG, ARNG, based in Colorado, and neither could imagine being deployed as part of the DOD response. Kramer continued working with the sheriff's department and Largent as a financial manager. Their daily routine suddenly changed on 30 November when their Special Forces company was alerted for possible overseas deployment.[50]

As the size of the active Army decreased, the role of the ARNG and USAR increased dramatically. Thousands of soldiers were mobilized for Operation DESERT STORM in 1991, and approximately 50,000 guardsmen have been mobilized for the war on terrorism.[51] These soldiers who train one weekend each month and two weeks in the summer have civilian jobs but must be prepared to be mobilized for state or federal missions. The active Army, and this is particularly true with its SOF, cannot perform all of its missions without the ARNG and USAR. The increased integration of these components has made the U.S. Army into a true "One Army."

Just days after the alert, the soldiers of B Company, 5th Battalion, 19th SFG, had reported to Fort Carson, Colorado, to be mobilized. By 5 December, the 5th Battalion personnel had joined the headquarters of the 2nd Battalion, 19th SFG, from West Virginia at Fort Knox, Kentucky, where they were mobilized again and then federalized. Deputy Commander, U.S. Army Special Forces Command (USASFC), COL David Burford elected to mobilize one Special Forces company from each of the three 19th SFG battalions to spread the combat experience throughout the ARNG. The 2nd Battalion from West Virginia would provide command and control.

216

After a week at Fort Knox, B Company, 5th Battalion, and the 2nd Battalion headquarters bussed to Fort Campbell, Kentucky, to prepare for overseas movement. Two other companies—one from the 1st Battalion in Utah and the other from the 2nd Battalion in West Virginia—joined them at Fort Campbell. Some of the units had previously trained together, while others had not. This further complicated the initial organizational decision because 2nd Battalion was unfamiliar with the state of training and equipment of the units from the 1st and 5th Battalions. To the dismay of everyone, there was only one Special Forces company from 5th SFG at Fort Campbell. The others had already deployed overseas, and the one left behind could do little to help the 19th SFG units because its equipment was palletized for movement. Although the 5th SFG rear detachment welcomed the guardsmen—even referring to them as the 4th Battalion, 5th SFG—there were few personnel available to assist them in preparing for overseas deployment. And no one could tell the 19th SFG personnel what their mission in Afghanistan might be.

Figure 13. The 19th SFG beret flash with Special Forces crest.

Nevertheless, the Special Forces ODAs worked to improve their small-unit tactical skills as well as their specific specialty skills. MSG Adam Fulkerson (pseudonym), 5th SFG signal detachment, recognized that the 19th SFG needed more training on newer-model radios.[52] He quickly arranged a hands-on familiarization program that would pay big dividends for the ARNG communications specialists.

This time, the ingenuity and innovativeness of the Special Forces soldiers to solicit training from outside sources, like the U.S. Army John F. Kennedy Special Warfare School, was constrained by 2nd Battalion's leaders because of memories of being mobilized, having been trained to standard by the active SFGs, and then not being deployed for Operation DESERT STORM. The priority was getting overseas. Outside assistance might give the impression that the ARNG Special Forces units were not operationally ready. They would prove themselves in theater. It was a "don't rock the boat mentality," said one Special Forces guardsman.

Figure 14. A 5/19th SFG soldier establishing communications in Afghanistan.

217

A significant problem was the lack of training ammunition to qualify personnel on their assigned weapons and refamiliarize them on hand grenades, light antitank weapons, M-203 grenade launchers, and crew-served weapons—the squad automatic weapon (SAW) and M-240 machine gun. Mobilization had happened so fast that there had been no time to forecast training ammunition requirements. Active component units that were familiar with installation range and ammunition procedures had forecasted and scheduled resources. The 19th SFG settled for "leftovers." For example, each ODA was allocated three hand grenades for familiarization. Despite the frustrations, the 19th SFG soldiers recognized that the 5th SFG rear could do little in the way of "sponsorship," especially when the Christmas holiday period descended on the post. In fact, the ARNG Special Forces had only praise for their active duty counterparts. "5th Special Forces Group set us up for success," declared SFC Kip Kupinski (pseudonym).

The 19th SFG ODAs began to deploy overseas in January 2002. By 17 February, all of B Company, 5th Battalion, had arrived at K2, Uzbekistan. LTC Don Forsythe, commander, 2nd Battalion, 5th SFG, told ODA 981 that part of the team would replace ODB 540 as the Special Operations Command and Control Element (SOCCE) for TF Rakkasan (3rd Brigade, 101st Airborne Division) headquarters at Kandahar Air Base. The other half of ODA 981 and B Company headquarters would go to Kandahar city. The other 19th SFG ODAs were assigned to serve as area support teams for 5th SFG ODAs preparing for and conducting combat operations in Afghanistan.[53]

The mission of the SOCCE at Kandahar Air Base was to coordinate special operations and activities with the ground force headquarters that controlled large numbers of conventional units operating nearby. The SOCCE also forwarded conventional force requests for assistance to the commanders, JSOTF-North and JSOTF-South.[54] With two infantry battalions working in and around Kandahar Air Base, a small SOCCE was the ideal organization to deconflict and coordinate the daily activities and long-range plans of conventional forces and SOF.

CPT Daniel Fitzgerald, commander, SF ODA 981, and two detachment members reached Kandahar Air Base on 26 February. Their immediate task was to meet with all forces in the area (American, coalition, and Afghan Military Force [AMF]) to ensure that everyone knew what friendly forces were where, what they were doing, and to prevent conflicts among the various simultaneous operations. Fitzgerald began with the 5th SFG liaison officer at the air base. SFC Kupinski went to the 3rd Brigade "Rakkasans," 101st Airborne Division tactical operations center (TOC), to discuss Special Forces and conventional operations. Because the Rakkasans were responsible for providing a quick-reaction force (QRF) to respond to field emergencies and medical evacuations—ambulances and helicopters—a close working relationship between the 19th SFG ODAs operating in and around Kandahar city, some 30 miles away, and the Rakkasans was imperative. Responsibility to coordinate with coalition forces belonged to SSG Jesus Martinez (pseudonym). Initially, the SOCCE had little contact with the AMF in separate encampments beyond the American defensive perimeter at the air base. At the air base, the SOCCE coordinated base operations and kept the 3rd Battalion, 3rd SFG, apprised of 19th SFG operations. Liaison with AMF forces was accomplished primarily by Army tactical CA and PSYOP units.[55]

On 1 March, the rest of ODA 981 arrived with the team equipment. Half of the ODA went to the city and half stayed at the airport to serve as the SOCCE. ODA 984 deployed to a compound owned by *Taliban* leader Mullah Omar outside of Kandahar city to supervise the destruction of collected arms caches, to coordinate firing ranges for coalition forces, and to identify helicopter landing zones (LZs) for future operations. The missions that B Company, 5th Battalion, 19th SFG, performed were neither glamorous nor the activities that filled adventure novels or combat action movies. They were, however, essential to the conduct of training and combat operations. In the military in a combat environment, "everyone singing off the same sheet of music" could mean the difference between life and death. In its SOCCE role, ODA 981 was the "maestro" of the military symphony at Kandahar. The fact that ODA 981 was an ARNG Special Forces detachment coordinating with conventional infantry battalions, another active Special Forces battalion, and the various coalition forces only demonstrated the viability of the "One Army" concept.

The Answer is Out There

C Company, 112th Signal Battalion, activated in July 2001 from assets within the battalion, hit the ground running. After several months of signal training exercises, evaluations, and unique equipment certifications, the company was deemed qualified to perform its wartime mission. Initially prepared to support another mission in a different part of the world, when the priorities changed, the company had five days to prepare to deploy to Afghanistan.

A nine-man signal advance echelon (ADVON) and its equipment traveled aboard a C-5A to Germany and then transloaded to a C-17 Globemaster III for the final leg to Kandahar Air Base, Afghanistan. The team was to establish communications between Forward Operating Base (FOB) 33, the 3rd Battalion, 3rd SFG, and various higher headquarters. While well trained to perform this mission, a myriad of problems impeded immediate success. "Doing what we have to do to get the job done" became the mantra for the C Company signal team members.[56]

Administrative troubles delayed the establishment of satellite communications (SATCOM) for four days. In the meantime, the signal team helped build the FOB. They set up tents, tore down the tents, and moved them to new locations. Even the simple task of getting their equipment to the desired location presented a challenge. An Air Force shortage of diesel fuel limited the use of their forklift to unloading aircraft. Since the SATCOM were "on hold," SSG Wilfred Chandler (pseudonym) traded some of the 85 gallons of diesel fuel for his generator to the Air Force forklift operator to get the team equipment from the flight line to FOB 33. This soon became the *modus operandi* for getting the mission accomplished.

As the communications bandwidth requirements quickly grew beyond those allocated before deployment, adjustments had to be made. C Company's mission had been expanded beyond the FOB to include coalition special operations units and the 3rd Battalion, 160th SOAR, forces located at the base. New bandwidth was granted, but it proved insufficient to satisfy the growing demand for secure and nonsecure Internet and telephone access. The number of computers threatened to exceed the capabilities of the local area network (LAN). The question was how to effectively connect more than 30 computers on the backside (from the router in the communications center to the end user) through two lines to the stepside (from the router to the communications van and satellite dish) for nonsecure Internet access.

Working collectively, the signal team members discovered a solution to this dilemma. SGT Dwayne Jackman (pseudonym), the technical control sergeant, said, "It has been a learning experience since we've been here." The team discovered the answer online at the Cisco website. Using the protocol instructions downloaded from the site, the team programmed the router to break down two Internet Protocol (IP) addresses into more than 50 sub-IP addresses for the backside computers, thereby accommodating the demand for nonsecure Internet access. This was the first time anyone in the 112th Signal Battalion had attempted this configuration, and it worked. Jackman had attended a Wave Tech Router course, but it in no way prepared him to program a router in this configuration. As he said, "I'm a satellite guy. Normally, a network user would receive a line from the local area network administrator to plug into his computer." Ingenuity helped the C Company signalers achieve success in their first wartime mission.

Figure 15. The 112th Signal Battalion successfully improvised at Kandahar Air Base.

SSG Thomas Barrington (pseudonym), the team sergeant, traded for an air-conditioning unit to keep the computer equipment and routers cool. Keeping the computer equipment clean and dust-free in the dusty environment of Kandahar prevented system failures and prolonged the service of the equipment. When materials or parts were either delayed in shipment or unavailable through the normal supply system, bartering with other signal elements and units at the airport ensured their communications center remained operational. After a few weeks, the team settled into a daily routine of maintaining equipment and solving minor technical problems. They functioned as a cohesive team and proved that they were capable of accomplishing anything they set out to do.

A New Twist on an Old Idea

Army CA units are active in peacetime as well as in war. A peacetime mission for the 96th Civil Affairs Battalion (CAB) is providing a Humanitarian Assistance Survey Team (HAST) to U.S. embassies abroad. The HAST prepares an assessment of humanitarian assistance requirements to the country team. The team has CA soldiers as well as specialists such as veterinarians, preventive medicine experts, and civil engineers.

MAJ John Bowman (pseudonym), commander, C Company, 96th CAB, recognized the value of the HAST concept in a hostile environment. By including preventive medicine specialists and engineers with skills other than those his soldiers already possessed, his CA teams could provide greater capabilities to the Combined Joint Civil-Military Operations Task Force (CJCMOTF) beyond what the CAT-As normally provided. Because the CJCMOTF forwarded civil infrastructure reports to the Department of State, Bowman put his concept into action on 9 December 2001.

Bamian, south of Kabul, and Konduz, east of Mazar-e-Sharif, had just been freed from *Taliban* control. The state of the populace in those cities and the condition of public utilities and services were virtually unknown. Bowman sent MAJ Jim McLemore and SFC Charles Walters (pseudonyms), who had deployed with 5th SFG, along with several specialists to conduct a thorough assessment of Bamian to expand the Special Forces ODAs' initial work.

Figure 16. Bamian Buddha site after the *Taliban* destroyed it on 11 March 2001.

Working closely with ODA 553, which had been the area since early November, enabled the HAST to expand its assessment to areas outside the city. Having been told that the *Taliban* had destroyed almost every village around Bamian as it withdrew, the HAST anticipated the worst. The Red Cross provided medical care in Bamian, but the hospital in nearby Yakawlang had been looted of its supplies. While some school buildings were generally intact, there was no money for teachers. The immediate need in the area was for clothing to survive the approaching winter. After completing their assessment and meeting with local officials to corroborate their findings and prioritize requirements, McLemore and Walters submitted their HAST report to CJCMOTF to coordinate expeditious assistance.[57]

On 19 December, another two-man HAST led by MAJ McLemore met with the Special Forces ODA at Taloqan to expand the humanitarian assessment there before going to Konduz. At Taloqan, the most critical requirement was to repair a bridge so that supplies could be delivered to the city. Konduz had a very large number of displaced persons living in camps outside the city and in makeshift shelters outside the camps. The quandary was who needed assistance. The camp numbers were relatively easy to estimate, but the team had to rely on local officials to provide the number of those living in makeshift shelters outside the camps. Since local officials usually exaggerated numbers, McLemore used his best judgment to estimate the approximate numbers—normally, one-fourth of the number provided. School repairs were needed in both Taloqan and Konduz. The HAST worked with a nongovernmental organization (NGO) to make the necessary repairs and submitted the other data to the CJCMOTF.[58]

The city of Herat in western Afghanistan was extremely sensitive because of its close proximity to Iran. On 3 January 2002, MAJ Bowman sent CAT-A34 with several attached specialists to Herat based on a report of 200,000 displaced persons in the area. CPT Chuck Allison (pseudonym) and CAT-A34 met with two NGOs to coordinate care for and the resettlement of the massive number of refugees. As was common in most other locations, the lack of medical care was a major concern. Two generators were needed to run the medical equipment at the hospital in Herat. Medical Civic Action Program teams were recommended to immunize the surrounding villages against disease. Half of the schools in the surrounding provinces needed repair and to support the emphasis on education, new facilities would have to be built. Problems soon surfaced in other areas.

Figure 17. Autoclaves inside Herat Hospital.

Figure 18. A typical classroom in a Bamian school.

Water was the most pressing need for farms near the city of Qal-e-yeh. During *Taliban* fighting to establish their dominance, the local irrigation canal had deteriorated badly and filled with silt. As a result, the farmers had no access to water and could not raise crops. On 11 February, local workers started to dredge 20 km of the canal. This initial effort was sufficient to raise interest at the U.S. Agency for International Development (USAID) to finish the remaining 150 km. This project had an immediate impact on the people near Herat because it revitalized 400 hectares of arable land in the district. The rapid start of the project established a direct connection between the arrival of American soldiers and improvement in the Afghan people's lives.[59]

Figure 19. CA teams examine the condition of a community well.

After completing its assessment of Bagram, CAT-A32 went to Konduz on 14 January 2002 to follow up on recommendations McLemore made. The team met with government officials to solicit their priorities in reestablishing local infrastructure and to advise them how to interact with the various humanitarian assistance organizations. Recommending how to operate within the confines of Afghan laws and culture proved critical to the NGOs. These efforts paid off when officials representing the NGOs met to coordinate local government projects

223

with organizations that were willing to do the work. After the ODA left, CAT-A32 provided situational awareness on the Konduz area to the commander, JSOTF-North.[60]

Between Bamian and Konduz, the CAT-As nominated approximately 90 projects for funding by the CJCMOTF. The little appreciated, mostly disregarded aspect of the proposed project process was the paperwork required. To submit projects for consideration and approved funding, the CAT-As had to solicit local contractors' assistance to develop the statements of work and cost estimates. Lacking experience in the contract proposal business where numerous persons/companies routinely solicit work in the United States and only one of several bidders receives the contract, it was easy for the CA teams working overseas in primitive field conditions to become frustrated with the system. In some cases, the teams were able to arrange with local NGOs to execute the projects.[61]

Figure 20. Impromptu "contract negotiations" with village leaders.

The CJCMOTF had been slated to operate from Dushanbe, Tajikistan, but the unexpected success of the campaign against the *Taliban* regime caused its relocation to Kabul. The need for a CA liaison cell in Tajikistan was still valid to assess the road system into Afghanistan and to coordinate humanitarian aid efforts, including one from Russia. Since the Red army blew the bridges over the Amu Darya as it withdrew in 1989, all traffic across the river had been by barge. CAT-A36 examined the three bridge sites and briefed the U.S. Ambassador. In January

Figure 21. Salang Tunnel and road conditions.

224

Figure 22. Friendship Bridge.

2002, the first land convoy of humanitarian aid crossed by barge at Dushanbe en route to Kabul. The convoy, guarded by Afghan forces, traversed the Salang Tunnel.[62]

The CAT-As of C Company, 96th CAB, provided a positive climate for military and diplomatic objectives in Afghanistan. Every day the CA soldiers dealt with "a multitude of inter-related issues, positions, and interests [that were] associated with the agendas of various groups or individuals" as cited in FM 41-10. They negotiated actual minefields and ethnic minefields of ancient tribal rivalries, jealousies, and competing interests. Sorting through that multitude of interrelated issues, CA soldiers never lost sight of their primary mission to "provide assistance to meet the life-sustaining needs of the civilian population." Mixing peacetime and wartime doctrine with innovation, initiative, expertise, and professionalism as seasoning, 96th CAB personnel did exactly what they were charged to do— to provide a positive climate to achieve U.S. national objectives.[63]

Figure 23. Making friends and influencing people.

Chokepoint

An essential element for any military operation is transportation. This not only includes the means by which soldiers and materiel move but also the routes by which they will travel to and from their destination. Since its completion in 1964, the Salang Tunnel, 39 miles north of

Bagram, has controlled north-south road movement in eastern Afghanistan. At 11,000 feet above sea level, the tunnel is the highest structure of its kind in the world. As key terrain in that region of the country, the Soviets and the *mujahideen* fought to control the tunnel in the 1980s. In 1997, Afghan resistance forces blocked the 1.6-mile-long tunnel to prevent the *Taliban* from reinforcing and resupplying their military units near Kabul and farther south. The Salang Tunnel was as critical in 2001 and 2002 as it had been since 1964.[64] The tunnel and the road had to be opened. Then tunnel traffic had to be controlled to support large-scale overland humanitarian relief coming south to Kabul. On 4 January 2002, MAJ Gary Jaffe (pseudonym), commander, D Company, 96th CAB, assigned CAT-A41 the mission to reconnoiter the tunnel and road leading to it.

All that MAJ Silas Greene (pseudonym) and CAT-A41 knew was that a Russian NGO had repaired one ventilation fan in the tunnel and a Scottish organization had cleared land mines from one lane inside the tunnel. Because of the bad weather, Greene planned a "top-to-bottom" recon, meaning the team would drive as fast as possible to its main objective—the tunnel—then turn around and do a detailed assessment of the road on the way back to the base in Bagram. The evaluation included damaged and destroyed bridges along the route, washed-out sections of road and resultant bypasses, major landslide areas, destroyed or broken culverts, variances in road width, major pothole hazards, and the extent of demining on the shoulders. Photographs and exact grid coordinates helped engineers determine what assets, heavy equipment, and materials were needed to repair the road and its structures. The first try got 4 km from the tunnel before snow and severe weather stopped the convoy. The team simply turned around and focused on the road survey back to Bagram.

"It was a horrendous road on the best of days." There were sections no more than 9 feet wide with no shoulder and, in others, a precipitous drop into a river valley far below. The team forded two washed-out areas. In several places, destroyed Russian military vehicles from the Soviet era had been pushed into large holes and rocks dumped on them to fill the gaps. As the winter weather became more severe, it became apparent that ground convoys were the only reliable way to deliver humanitarian assistance to the areas near Kabul. The necessity to clear the tunnel became more urgent. After a second attempt to reach the tunnel later in the month also failed, the Combined Forces Land Component Commander (CFLCC) funded the repairs on the road.[65] In the meantime, a collaborative effort by USAID, the French, the Russians, the Scots, and the Afghans opened the tunnel on 14 January to one lane of traffic, which required great care to negotiate.[66]

Although the priority mission for CAT-A41 was to assess the tunnel, the team pursued other tasks in the surrounding villages near Kabul and Bagram. In the village of Qarabagh near Bagram, MAJ Greene made a notable impression by participating in *buzkahsi* (translated "goat grabbing"), the national game of Afghanistan. Two teams on horseback fight to carry a headless calf across a line for points. It is a very brutal game in which the riders slam their horses against their opponents, then whipping and clawing, they try to take the carcass from the opposing team. Greene, a college animal science major who minored in equine management, was an expert horseman. While CAT-A41 was in Qarabagh, he played in several games, much to the Afghans' great delight.

Based on a report that an avalanche had trapped a Red Cross convoy in the Salang, the United Nations High Commissioner for Refugees (UNHCR) asked CAT-A41 to make a third attempt on 7 February. Forty-mile-an-hour winds, heavy driving snow, and approaching darkness precluded that effort. The following morning, a British helicopter flew SFC Bart Schuyler (pseudonym), the Special Forces medic on A41, to the snowed-in tunnel to assess the situation. Schuyler found four casualties—Afghans who had been asphyxiated by carbon monoxide poisoning while sleeping in their cars with the motors running. A British land mine-removal organization with heavy equipment eventually reached the tunnel and rescued numerous trapped Afghan travelers who had been patiently waiting their turn to use the single lane of traffic.[67] Increasing the flow of traffic grew even more important.

"60 Minutes II"

It was a newsworthy story from Afghanistan, said CBS's "60 Minutes II" producer Shawn Efran. With the military defeat of the main-force *Taliban* and *al-Qaeda* units, the difficult work of helping Afghans rebuild their country fell to small groups of U.S. special operations soldiers like CAT-A41.[68] These men were professional soldiers of the highest order, but wearing beards and local garb provided better access to the people they wanted to help. Their job was "nation building."

As characters in a news story, the four soldiers were "good copy." MAJ Greene led the team with energy and had excellent judgment. His urbane manner and articulate speech belied his background as a tank officer who had completed parachute and Ranger training. The effectiveness with which Greene led his team derived, in large part, from prior service in the U.S. Army 96th Civil Affairs Battalion (CAB), a special operations unit based in North Carolina. Greene became an expert horseman while pursuing an undergraduate degree in animal science at the University of Massachusetts at Amherst. The CA officer had just received a master's degree in national security studies at the Naval Post Graduate School, Monterey, California, and his thesis, coincidentally, was "Islamic Fundamentalism in Central Asia."[69]

CAT-A41 moved constantly in and around the town of Bagram to determine where U.S. resources could be applied. SFC Roger "Mac" McDonald (pseudonym), the team sergeant who had never quite lost his Queens accent, served as "front man" for the team. He made travel plans and meeting agendas for the constant sessions with local political and military leaders, and developed the security arrangements for each gathering. Everyone on the small team had to stay aware of his vulnerability and be constantly mindful of force protection because the team worked independently long distances from other American elements. The team expert on civil infrastructure was SFC Lyle Canberra (pseudonym), who surveyed and assessed water and sewage systems, aqueducts, wells, power grids, roads, and bridges. This Special Forces engineer also organized demining operations, as he had on other battlefields. SFC Schuyler was CAT-A41's medical specialist and, like McDonald and Canberra, was a veteran of Special Forces. He had also honed his skills on the edges of civilization throughout the world.[70]

CAT-A41 personnel were trained in foreign languages but not for Central Asia; it was regionally oriented toward Europe. MAJ Greene spoke French, McDonald spoke Polish, Schuyler spoke German and Spanish, and Canberra spoke Spanish and Portuguese. The projected CA effort in Afghanistan required as many teams as could be deployed. In any event, given the variety of Pashto, Dari, and Urdu dialects endemic to the numerous ethnic groups of Afghanistan, local translators were necessary for better communications.[71]

Shawn Efram, the "60 Minutes II" producer, brought his cameraman, Dave, and his sound man, Scott, to meet CAT-A41 in mid-January 2002 to do the background research and prepare the story. Their correspondent, Scott Pelley, would fly in later. As with any new team members, SFC McDonald and SFC Canberra gave the three "60 Minutes II" personnel some rudimentary weapons training and put them through basic security drills—immediate action responses to possible threat situations—for their self-defense, so they would not increase the already heavy security burden of the four-man CAT-A. SFC Schuyler taught basic first aid procedures for gunshot wounds and related trauma. Dave, the cameraman, was a former 82nd Airborne Division paratrooper. Both Dave and Scott, the sound man, fit in easily.[72]

When correspondent Scott Pelley joined CAT-A41 and his "60 Minutes II" crew a week later, MAJ Greene simply followed the team's normal busy schedule. On the day of the filming, the team was to revisit the Emergency Medical Clinic in Bagram. It was one of 23 clinics and a hospital supported by an Italian private volunteer organization. However, the Emergency Medical Clinic physician, Doctor Mohammed Atta, had not been paid in eight months. He had remained in his hometown, working through the Soviet and *Taliban* occupations, even when Bagram was a center of fighting. Dr. Atta was living "hand to mouth" in a bunker near the clinic and wanted to plant a garden on its roof.[73]

Just minutes after CAT-A41 and the "60 Minutes II" crew arrived, a mob of local children rushed in a badly injured 16-year-old boy who the doctor recognized. As the boy picked up a hand grenade, it detonated in his right hand. The little finger and parts of his ring finger and thumb were gone. The dorsal portion of his hand was degloved to the wrist—the skin was peeled back like a banana. He had a grenade fragment visible in his cheek, but most of the blood on his face was from his torn-up hand.[74]

CAT-A41 immediately went into action, forgetting completely the "60 Minutes II" crew who recorded the event. McDonald and Canberra took up security positions to hold back the gathering crowd of curious Afghans. SFC Schuyler knew he could do "*deminimus* activities"— on Greene's orders—to alleviate the immediate suffering of non-Americans. Schuyler followed Dr. Atta's lead in the treatment, serving as his primary medical assistant. MAJ Greene gathered some Afghans to help "push start" the worn-out "ambulance," a battered old Mitsubishi minivan with its back seats removed. Then, they loaded the boy into the running ambulance, and Dr. Atta jumped behind the wheel and headed to the hospital. Schuyler arranged for a U.S. Army surgeon to make a follow-up visit at the Italian-run hospital in Kabul and coordinated skin grafting and physical therapy. A few days later, Schuyler went to the hospital to check on the boy and was pleased to learn that there was no secondary infection. The boy's hand had been saved.[75]

The incident in the Bagram clinic was over in less than 20 minutes, and the "60 Minutes II" team caught all of it on tape. Correspondent Scott Pelley featured it in his story on CAT-A41, which was introduced nationwide as "Mission Impossible." But for Greene, McDonald, Schuyler, and Canberra, who comprised one of the 10 CA Alpha teams operating throughout the formerly *Taliban* nation, it was just another morning of another day trying to give Afghanistan "a good start" toward becoming a nation that would never again provide sanctuary for terrorists.[76]

The previous historical vignettes provided the Special Forces team perspectives on the Tora Bora operations and showed what the tactical CA teams were doing in the first months after the collapse of the *Taliban* regime. Despite the severe winter weather, helicopters supported the Army special operations elements that were spread throughout the country. The hunt for *Taliban* and *al-Qaeda* leaders continued, and the search fan spread along the Pakistan border areas. The next stories detail the hazards of helicopter operations and Special Forces teams conducting direct-action (DA) missions to eliminate *al-Qaeda* diehards and capture enemy leaders, weapons caches, and sensitive equipment.

High-Altitude Rescue of a Marine CH-53

For a downed aircrew or for isolated personnel, there was comfort in knowing that a procedure existed for extricating personnel from risky circumstances. Combat search and rescue (CSAR) was an imperative mission for the men of 2nd Battalion, 160th SOAR. The 160th was well prepared to perform the CSAR mission with its highly skilled flight medics, pilots, and crew members. The rapid response to a CSAR mission on a cold winter morning saved the lives of five marines whose helicopter had crashed in the mountains of eastern Afghanistan.

On 20 January, shortly after departing Bagram Air Base at 0800, one of two Marine Corps CH-53 Super Stallion heavy-lift helicopters carrying supplies to ARSOF troops operating in the vicinity of Khowst crashed into a remote snow-covered mountain about 40 miles south of Bagram.[77] The U.S. Marine helicopter pilots had flown similar routes earlier in the week and had received ineffective small-arms fire near the village of Azrow south of Bagram Air Base. This morning, the two Super Stallions were traversing the southern mountainous region approximately 200 feet above the ground. In the few moments when the crew chief in the lead helicopter made his interior compartment checks, the trail helicopter disappeared. All he saw to the rear was a billowing cloud of smoke rising behind a ridgeline. He passed this information to the pilot.[78]

CPT Alison Thompson (pseudonym), commander of the lead CH-53, quickly reversed course and flew toward the smoke while trying to contact the trail helicopter on the radio.[79] As Thompson crested the ridgeline, she saw the helicopter wreckage in the bottom of a valley that was surrounded by mountain ridges that soared more than 9,800 feet mean sea level (MSL). As CPT Thompson flew closer to the crash site, she could see scattered parts of the wreckage burning through the heavy black smoke. After circling several times and observing no movement, she assumed that the crew was dead. Thompson made a last effort to contact the aircraft by radio but received no reply. The U.S. Marine captain then tried to contact the orbiting Airborne Warning and Control System (AWACS) aircraft on four different radio frequencies. Again, she got no response. Uncomfortable with landing at such a high altitude, not knowing whether the other helicopter had been shot down, and uncertain of the ground threat, CPT Thompson made a final circle and flew back to Bagram for help.[80]

When this happened, Bagram Air Base was still a very immature military environment in the throes of expanding from a Special Forces field operating base (FOB) run by a Special Forces major, the "Khan of Bagram," into a conventional military base. Physical security was tenuous and the command relationships were still evolving. Virtually all the tactical operations centers (TOCs) got the word that a U.S. Marine helicopter had crashed and were examining courses of action. While the basic questions were being asked—what caused the crash, was it mechanical malfunction or due to hostile fire, were there any survivors—the number and variety of headquarters and yet-to-be-defined command and control relationships in the midst of transitions and relocations created more problems. Forward elements of JSOTF-North (TF Dagger), the newly formed JSOTF-South, units of the U.S. special operations task force, coalition special operations forces, and the 10th Mountain Division were all involved. The answers to the critical questions of CSAR, such as who had the authority to launch the rescue effort and who would provide the security force, were based on assumptions. Everyone wanted to do something now. Thus, concomitantly, the Joint Search and Rescue Center in Saudi Arabia launched Air Force HH-60 Pave Hawks and MH-53 Pave Lows simultaneously from different bases toward the crash site, but these helicopters were several hours away, and it was the height of winter in Afghanistan.

CPT Stan Rauch (pseudonym), the TF Dagger (Forward) operations officer, was attending a briefing at the TF Mountain TOC when he received a radio report that a U.S. Marine helicopter had crashed.[81] JSOTF-North at K2 had tasked the 160th SOAR to do the CSAR mission. Factoring the possible antiaircraft artillery (AAA) threat, the altitude of the crash site, and the weather conditions, Rauch debated the best solution to quickly execute the search-and-rescue mission. He went straight to "Motel 6"—a bombed-out three-story building at the airfield that served as the Night Stalker communal sleeping, eating, and planning area. The previous night's mission aircrews and medics were roused and alerted for the CSAR mission. Rauch brought CPT John Gates (pseudonym), the air mission commander (AMC), and CWO Christopher Gaines (pseudonym), the MH-47E lead pilot, to the special operations TOC where the staff was monitoring the situation.[82] Gates and Rauch provided a quick estimate of the situation: the CSAR could require the use of special insertion techniques, a potential enemy threat existed, and the circumstances dictated the use of special operations troops as a quick-reaction force (QRF) because they were familiar with high-risk recoveries. The commander of the special operations force agreed with the assessment and approved using his men as the QRF.[83]

Meanwhile, the 160th SOAR aircrews and medics had already started their well-established routine in preparation for a short-notice mission. The pilots and aircrew members rushed to the flight line to get the two MH-47E Chinook helicopters ready for immediate departure. Aircraft mooring ropes and engine intake covers were removed, the side miniguns and light machine guns were loaded, and the flight data was entered into the cockpit computer systems. The flight medics carried their emergency medical kits aboard and strapped everything down. These medics are intimately familiar with operating in and around the helicopters. As graduates of the Special Operations Combat Medic Course, they were trained in advanced trauma treatment and provided life-sustaining care to combat-injured personnel as they were transported to higher levels of medical care.

Working together, the medics and aircrew members reconfigured the helicopter interior with stanchion sets to accommodate litters on the left side of the aircraft. A Pro-Paq cardiac monitor, essential for monitoring vital signs in a noisy helicopter, and a medical bag with an assortment of medical supplies was placed immediately forward of the stanchion setup. Other medical life-support equipment included an oxygen bag and extra O$_2$ cylinder, emergency airway equipment and extra blankets, a hypothermia bag, a traction splint, and folded litters. CPT Kerry Regent (pseudonym), 2nd Battalion flight surgeon, and SFC Charles Lafayette (pseudonym), the senior flight medic, conducted final operational checks of their equipment to ensure that everything was functioning properly.[84] Forty minutes after being awakened from deep sleep, both MH-47Es were rigged, and the aircrews were ready to launch.

After CWO Gaines and CPT Gates discussed the *in extremis* plan (what to do in a worst-case scenario like an aircraft shoot-down) with the ground force, radio frequencies and call signs were confirmed, and the group headed to the flight line. By this time, 10th Mountain had sent its infantry QRF down to the flight line. The two groups converged at the ramps of the Chinooks as the helicopter blades began to rotate. Then a 5th SFG ODA arrived to act as the QRF. Neither was aware of the other being tasked to perform the mission. The issue was quickly resolved by the TF Bowie commander and CPT Gates. Orders were given to the pilots, and the Special Forces QRF boarded the helicopters. Just before liftoff, CPT Thompson, the U.S. Marine pilot, ran up to the lead helicopter. Realizing the benefits of having her accompany the mission, Gates invited her aboard. She quickly provided details and verified the location of the crash site on an aerial map.[85]

At 0950, 90 minutes after being alerted, the two MH-47Es departed the airfield. CPT Gates initially intended to fly to the coordinates of the crash site, identify the wreckage, assess the enemy situation, grab any survivors, and get out as quickly as possible. After talking with the AWACS, CWO Gaines was passed to the fighter aircraft en route to the site. Both the helicopters and the jet fighters arrived at the site almost simultaneously—for the MH-47Es that was just 17 minutes from Bagram. The fighter pilots observed no enemy in the area. As the Chinooks circled the site, the crew members spotted an SOS stamped out in the snow. Gates felt that the helicopter probably crashed because of mechanical problems but remained cautious. Since both helicopters were carrying identical mixes of medics and security forces, Gates directed the trail Chinook to land first while his helicopter remained aloft to coordinate with the MC-130P tankers, fighters, and Joint Search and Rescue Center (JSRC) in Saudi Arabia to recall the other CSAR assets.[86]

CWO Curtis Jameson (pseudonym) landed his helicopter 50 feet to the left of the crash site near the wrecked fuselage.[87] Manning the miniguns, the Chinook crew quickly scanned the wreckage site for any potential threat. The crash was horrible, and the area surrounding it looked like a mass casualty training exercise. The valley floor was covered with 2 feet of old snow. In stark contrast to the snow were grotesque charred and blackened chunks of the cabin. The broken rotor blades stuck up from the ground like obscene memorials. About 30 feet beyond was an unidentifiable section of the cockpit that had broken off on impact and had not caught on fire. Nothing of the wreckage was taller than 3 feet high.

The small group of survivors was spotted off to one side of the carnage. Marine CPT Douglas Glasgow (pseudonym) had dragged his copilot and three other crewmen out of the burning wreckage. As Glasgow got the living out, he gathered them in a tight circle. One deceased crewman was spotted some distance away from the aircraft; another was still wedged in the wreckage. Having done this, Glasgow stamped out SOS in the snow.[88]

The QRF rushed to secure the crash site. After a few minutes passed, in which the dazed marines stared at the rescue party and the aircrew stared at them, SFC Lafayette grabbed his aid bag and ran off to the Chinook to get things moving on the ground. A slightly dazed CPT Glasgow walked over to the aircraft and climbed the ramp. Dr. Regent directed him to a seat on the right side and began examining him. The four other survivors were brought aboard in litters. Each had a variety of injuries: one had a possible hip injury, one had chest injuries, another had a broken femur, and the last had lower back injuries. The "trauma room" aboard the MH-47E was put into operation. While the Pro-Paq provided vital signs, oxygen was administered, splints applied, and blankets wrapped about the injured men. Aircrew members stripped off some of their outer clothing to warm the patients. With the injured protected in the other aircraft, CWO Gaines landed. The QRF disembarked with the "jaws of life" and other tools to recover the dead crewman and increased the security around the helicopters.[89]

With the other Chinook on the ground and the fighter aircraft overhead, CWO Jameson lifted off to fly the five marine survivors back to Bagram at full speed. During the flight, Dr. Regent, Lafayette, and a QRF medic continued treating the injured. At the airfield, elements of the 244th Forward Surgical Team were standing by to receive the injured on the taxiway. Dr. Regent briefed the 244th surgeon on the condition of the patients as the medical response team hustled them into field medical emergency rooms and took over medical care.[90]

Meanwhile, CWO Gaines departed the crash site with the deceased marines. There was no joy awaiting his aircraft when it landed, only the mortuary team waiting on the taxiway. As the aircrews left the flight line, Jameson and Gaines realized that only 3 hours had elapsed since they were awakened in "Motel 6."[91]

According to a CENTCOM press release on 23 January 2002, FA-18s dropped precision-guided munitions on the remnants of the Marine Corps CH-53 to prevent pilfering and because it was unsalvageable. Although chastised by the JSRC in Saudi Arabia for not having the proper launch authority, five U.S. Marines were saved by the decisive actions of a valiant few who were closest to the crisis, could respond quickly with the right resources, and acted while others debated whether they had the authority to act. Those five marines were glad the Night Stalkers rescued them from the Afghan mountains in winter, especially since they had already been presumed killed in the crash.

Taking Down *al-Qaeda* at the Mir Wais Hospital

CPT Mel Pierce (pseudonym), with Special Forces ODA 524 and ODA 570, flew from K2 to Camp Rhino and boarded Marine Corps CH-53s to fly into Sayd-Alim-Kalay, north of Kandahar, to replace ODA 574. ODA 574 had fallen victim to a fratricidal bombing while supporting Hamad Karzai and his forces.[92] Two days later, Gul Agha Sherzai and his Pashtun forces drove into the "spiritual capital of the *Taliban* movement" from the south. Karzai and ODA 524 soon followed, entering the city from the north and occupying the former palace of Mullah Omar, the head of the *Taliban*, who had escaped.[93]

Pierce and his detachment executive officer, CWO Doug Anton (pseudonym), reflected on the current chain of command. Their 1st Battalion Special Forces ODA reported to an advanced operating base (AOB) of the 3rd Battalion, controlled by Forward Operating Base (FOB) 52, commanded by LTC Don Forsythe of 2nd Battalion. This was not an issue to ODA 524 because it was taking in the scope and suddenness of the military victory. The fall of the *Taliban* regime as a viable government had occurred exactly two months after the first U.S. Air Force bombs began to fall in Afghanistan. But there were still viable pockets of enemy resistance, and in mid-December, LTC Forsythe ordered Pierce and his team to go after the *al-Qaeda* diehards that had holed up inside the Mir Wais Hospital in downtown Kandahar.[94]

As *Taliban* and *al-Qaeda* resistance collapsed in Kandahar, first at the airport and then in the city, the leaders of both groups fled, and the able-bodied fighters abandoned the wounded as they withdrew. Local Afghan militia took a number of wounded *al-Qaeda* and *Taliban* to the Mir Wais Hospital for treatment. Nine of these "prisoners," thought to be Saudis and Yemenis, mutinied and barricaded themselves on the second floor of the southeast wing of the huge hospital complex. The medical facility occupied an entire city block and was surrounded by a high adobe mud wall. After days of negotiations, one of the *al-Qaeda* had surrendered and another killed himself using a hand greande. That left seven inside the hospital.[95]

The most compelling reason to remove the terrorists was because their presence prevented the Afghan women from gaining access to the obstetrics clinic. The female clinic was located on the ground floor of the wing where the armed diehards had barricaded themselves. To demonstrate his support for the women of the newly liberated city, Governor Sherzai wanted the *al-Qaeda* out. Forsythe directed CPT Pierce and ODA 524 to advise and train the Pashtun troops of Sherzai and Khan Mohammed on how to clear the building. Sherzai specified that the American Special Forces soldiers were not to enter the hospital.[96]

On 20 December, as ODA 524 moved into position to observe from the corners of the walled compound, one of the *al-Qaeda* spotted it and alerted the others. Negotiations proved fruitless. About 2000, after dark, a 15-man Pashtun force began firing at the windows of the barricaded rooms that drew heated counterfire. The exchange of fire went on for a quarter hour and then ceased. The Pashtuns never entered the hospital. Throughout the exchange, the diehards constantly yelled "*Jihad*! *Jihad*!"[97] The siege continued. After days of negotiations, two *al-Qaeda* had surrendered, one with a gangrenous leg and another had killed himself with a hand grenade. There were still six diehards inside. The American suggestion to "starve them out" failed when *Taliban* sympathizers among the hospital staff continued to smuggle food and drink to the holdouts.[98]

About 20 January 2002, CPT Pierce, CWO Anton, and the members of ODA 524 recruited 10 likely fighters from among Khan Mohammed's troops without revealing the purpose. Sherzai contributed 10 of his better warriors for the undisclosed mission. For more than a week, the team, knowing the *al-Qaeda* in more than 30 days had "bunkered themselves in quite well," trained the Afghans in urban warfare tactics and techniques that culminated in room-to-room fighting. Staying near Mullah Omar's palace, they built a mock "shooting house" of bamboo poles and target cloth to practice assault and room-clearing skills, repeatedly drilling the Pashtuns to "do everything by rote." "We didn't tell them what we were training them for because secrecy was essential, and besides, we thought they'd run," said Anton, the team's executive officer.[99]

On the evening of 27 January 2002, the Americans told the "Joes," as they had come to call the Afghans, that they were going to assault the Mir Wais Hospital in the morning. Shortly afterward, four of Khan Mohammed's men disappeared into the night. "Still, we had enough fighters," said CPT Pierce, "by taking the remaining six of Khan's 'Joes' and picking the best five of Sherzai's men for the attack." The ODA would ensure that the Afghan guards along the perimeter of the hospital let no one out. An American medical evacuation helicopter was standing by to assist if necessary.[100] An Air Force tactical air controller (TAC) and a special tactics airman were attached to ODA 524. Additional Special Forces medics and military ambulances were staged out of sight several blocks away. At 0505 on 28 January, the assembled force waited alertly in the cold, clear, predawn darkness.[101]

CPT Pierce and his Pashtun assault force climbed silently over the west wall of the hospital compound and carefully moved to the hallway connecting the north and south wings of the H-shaped main medical building. At the exterior doorway to the hallway, they clipped off the padlock with bolt cutters. Then, Pierce and his senior weapons sergeant, SSG Jim Hall (pseudonym), stealthily led the 11 Pashtun "Joes" into the attack position, a room off the bottom of the stairs that led to the southeast wing corridor. Right behind them was the demolition team—two Special Forces engineer sergeants and two explosive ordnance demolition (EOD) specialists—carrying high-explosive door-breaching charges. The Special Forces medics, SFC Robert Staunton (pseudonym), and SSG Robards (pseudonym) trailed the group. The breaching team and snipers occupied a room opposite the Joes at the bottom of the stairs while the medics set up in the first-floor lobby area.

At 0555, the American breachers and snipers moved silently upstairs. Trailing the demolition team, CWO Anton and SFC Jack Kittridge (pseudonym), armed with sniper rifles, turned in the opposite direction at the top of the stairs and moved to a room in the northeast wing, opposite the rooms that the six al-Qaeda had barricaded. Anton and Kittridge adjusted the sights on their weapons using a laser range finder to verify the distance across the open courtyard between the wings—65 meters exactly. Meanwhile, outside on the compound south wall, MSG Mike Huffman (pseudonym), ODA 524 team sergeant, and the Air Force TAC covered the southern side of the target with telescope-equipped M-4 carbines.[102]

The time had arrived to end the deadlock. The breaching team carefully placed its preshaped charges against the door that closed off the corridor to the al-Qaeda rooms. Then, the two Special Forces sergeants "tamped" (covered) the explosives with sandbags to protect the assault team. This tamping would direct most of the explosive force into the door area.[103] On CPT Pierce's signal, the demolition team detonated the explosive charges. Verification that a successful breach had been made delayed the "Joes'" assault through the man-sized hole. The al-Qaeda defenders had time to recover before the assaulters charged into the dark corridor. Two hand grenades exploded immediately, and then deafening and continuous gunfire resounded in the darkness. The Pashtun assaulters began screaming for the medics. The al-Qaeda, firing down the tiled hallway, retreated into a single room on the south side of the wing. When the firing died down, the American Special Forces soldiers dispatched Pashtuns to retrieve the wounded. The assault force retreated downstairs carrying their six wounded. The wounded were triaged, treated, and prepared for evacuation. The most seriously wounded were sent to Kandahar Air Base to the field surgical team.

Having abandoned the breach point, the remaining Pashtuns were unwilling to go back upstairs to prevent the al-Qaeda from escaping into another area of the hospital. SFC Staunton and SSG Robards moved to cover the opening while the ODA leaders sought guidance about the next assault. During the 3-hour gap between assaults, CW3 Carl Patterson (pseudonym) tried to "smoke them out" using a thermite grenade to ignite the bed sheeting scattered in the hallway.[104] The fire and acrid smoke spread throughout the enemy-held area, and movement was detected by the sniper team outside. When one of the *al-Qaeda* holdouts leaned out a window to gasp for air, MSG Huffman on the south wall killed him with a single shot. The number of effectives barricaded inside was reduced to five. CW2 Aaron (pseudonym), an Arabic speaker, futilely attempted to negotiate with the remaining holdouts.[105]

The Special Forces soldiers prepared for a second assault, but the few Pashtuns left showed little interest. A contingent of Kandahar police volunteered to clear the rooms after the Americans initiated the assault with a volley of hand grenades. SFC Staunton volunteered to launch the grenade assault overwatched by CW3 Mike Fontaine (pseudonym) and two others. CW3 Patterson got the police into position and orchestrated the attack. Grenades launched, the Afghan police rushed into the first room, discovered the *al-Qaeda*, and were driven out by a heavy volume of small-arms fire. They immediately exited the area and withdrew down the stairs. No amount of coaxing by CW3 Patterson could convince them to go back.

With no other recourse, SFC Staunton, covered by CW3 Fontaine, inched down the smokey corridor to the edge of the doorway where the *al-Qaeda* were barricaded.[106] Staunton's first attempt to get a grenade into the room was caught by an *al-Qaeda* fighter who tossed it back outside the room. Staunton and the other two American assaulters managed to reach cover in an adjacent room before it detonated. Having run out of grenades, the holdouts threw chunks of masonry into the corridor. In the murky area, the Americans initially thought that they were grenades and retreated into a room. After that, SFC Staunton allowed his grenades to "cook off" before throwing them low inside the room and through an air vent. After both had detonated, Staunton fired a 5.56mm magazine into the strongpoint, reloaded, and then charged into the room, shooting the remaining *al-Qaeda*. His two backup men ensured that all were dead.

When the firing stopped, the remaining Pashtun fighters and Kandahar police stormed into the corridor, firing their rifles into all the rooms, but the fight was already over. All six terrorists were dead. As they had publicly declared, the six *al-Qaeda* had fought to the death, the last two firing from behind the stacked bodies of their dead comrades. None of the Americans were injured. Before the combined American-Afghan force could depart the premises, the Mir Wais medical staff had already begun assessing what needed to be done to return the facility to full operation.[107] Almost seven hours after they had started, CPT Pierce reported that the hospital was clear of enemy fighters. The nearly 50-day siege had been ended by American Special Forces soldiers and Afghan militia. By mid-afternoon, U.S. Army CA tactical teams were en route to coordinate repairs at the Mir Wais Hospital.[108]

The Raid at Hazar Qadam

As the hunt for Osama bin Laden and the *al-Qaeda* leadership continued through winter 2001-2002, U.S. Central Command (CENTCOM) directed a discrete intelligence-gathering mission that required the long-range reconnaissance and surveillance and urban warfare close-quarters battle skills of A Company, 1st Battalion, 5th SFG (A-1-5).[109] This mission was referred to as a sensitive site exploitation (SSE), and it called for the focused search and recovery of enemy personnel, documents, manuals, monies, computers, communications equipment, explosives, weaponry, and related materials that might be of intelligence value.[110]

Figure 24. Ground mobility vehicles (GMVs) ready for action.

A-1-5, commanded by MAJ Jon West (pseudonym), was specifically trained, equipped, and organized for this type of mission. It was available to the CENTCOM commander for particularly difficult long-range reconnaissance and surveillance and direct-action (DA) missions—raids and surgical strikes—most often in urban or builtup areas. All unit members were highly trained in close-quarters, room-to-room fighting; long-range surveillance; and sniping.[111]

Since December 2001, A-1-5 had conducted three SSE missions with marked success. Surprise was so complete and execution so rapid that only two shots had been fired in all three missions—both as warning shots that prompted immediate surrenders. The company captured nine *al-Qaeda* suspects (detainees); destroyed several tons of weapons and ammunition; and made valuable intelligence finds, including satellite telephones, tape recordings. and encrypted electronic records.[112]

On 9 January 2002, the Combined Forces Land Component Command (CFLCC) of U.S. CENTCOM issued another SSE order to Commodore Robert Harward, commander, Joint Special Operations Task Force–South (JSOTF-South), then based at Kandahar Airport.[113] JSOTF-South was tasked to conduct an SSE of two suspected *al-Qaeda* compounds at Hazar Qadam near the town of Oruzgan, 166 km northeast of Kandahar in Oruzgan Province. The SSE mission, designated "AQ-048," was to kill or capture any *Taliban* or *al-Qaeda* personnel and collect material for intelligence analysis.[114]

The intelligence staff at CENTCOM identified the two target sites to the CFLCC. Each walled compound contained a collection of various-size buildings. The buildings were surrounded by orchards and farm fields, and the two sites were 1.5 km apart. When the photo interpreters suggested that there might be women and children in the compounds, a "kinetic strike" (aerial bombardment) was ruled out, and ground raids were directed. Because of the size and complexity of the two sites, target-designated AQ-048, Harward selected A-1-5 for the SSE mission and attached a New Zealand unit.[115]

West decided he would seize both sites simultaneously and divided his company into two assault forces. The New Zealand troops were designated the quick-reaction force (QRF). West would lead Special Forces ODAs 512, 513, and 514 in the assault of the western site, named Objective Kelly. The eastern compound, named Objective Brigid, would be the target for ODAs 511 and 516, led by the company operations officer, CWO Dwight Ashford (pseudonym). Each

Figure 25. A/1/5 SFG uses an "up" armored HMMWV GMV.

force would have radio operators, explosive ordnance demolition (EOD) experts, interpreters, and FBI agents attached. The FBI agents selected those detainees they wanted for questioning and assumed "chain of custody" for evidence collected to ensure admissibility in any subsequent legal proceedings. If necessary, they would also serve as government witnesses so that A-1-5 soldiers would not be required to return to the United States to testify in court (per *posse comitatus* rules).[116]

To avoid establishing operational patterns in their SSE missions, MAJ West arranged for night helicopters to infiltrate the assault forces into separate remote landing zones (LZs) that were several kilometers away from their objectives. The high mountain valley LZs were hidden from Hazar Qadam by intervening ridges that masked the sound of the helicopters as they flew nap-of-the-earth (NOE) routes that skimmed along the bottom of valleys and popped over passes. After landing, Ashford's mobile force, wearing night-vision goggles (NVG), would drive 6 km on a dirt road to Objective Brigid in two heavily armed high-mobility multipurpose wheeled vehicles (HMMWVs), or ground mobility vehicles (GMVs).[117] West's three Special Forces teams, also wearing NVG, would walk 5 km around a mountain peak to approach their target, Objective Kelly.[118]

The CFLCC wanted surveillance teams to have "eyes on the target" AQ-048 well ahead of the raids, in part, to confirm the presence of noncombatants (women and children) at the two sites. But three attempts by Marine Corps CH-46 helicopters to infiltrate a long-range reconnaissance element failed. The first attempt failed because of aircraft mechanical problems, the second failed because of heavy icing on the helicopter, and the third aborted on landing when the blowing snow whiteout obscured the LZ. During the 17 January video teleconference (VTC), the CENTCOM J3 restated his desire to execute the SSE mission AQ-048, and the CFLCC ordered the mission to proceed without preliminary surveillance of the target sites.[119]

Continuous changes because of helicopter availability and priorities delayed the mission until the night of 22 January. The Kelly force launched from Kandahar and landed at its offset

LZ. In the meantime, while flying to Kandahar to pick up the Brigid force, the Bagram-based helicopter pilots reported marginal weather near Hazar Qadam that was becoming worse. Based on their estimate, Commodore Harward, commander, JSOTF-South, decided to postpone the AQ-048 mission for 24 hours. Thus, under a bright moon with broken clouds and Fahrenheit temperatures in the low teens, the Kelly force marched back to its initial LZ for extraction, and the AC-130 Spectre gunship already en route to support the raid returned to Masirah Island, off the coast of Oman.[120]

The next night, the weather was clear, and the mission was launched again. This time, two Marine Corps CH-53s carried West's 45-man dismounted force to its insertion LZ.[121] Three MH-47Es from the 2nd Battalion, 160th SOAR, transported Ashford's mobile force. Two Chinooks carried a GMV and its driver inside while the third ferried the 26 soldiers who would ride the trucks to Objective Brigid.[122]

Figure 26. Elements of the Kelly force aboard a Marine Corps CH-53.

After a quiet tactical march and slow drive under NVG across terrain 7,000 feet above sea level at 17 degrees Fahrenheit, the two assault forces arrived at their preassault positions right on schedule. Maintaining close communications, the two forces simultaneously moved their security elements into position. A deep irrigation ditch just outside the wall of Brigid forced the assaulters to dismount and approach their entry points on foot. The vehicle drivers and gun teams aboard began hastily searching for a way to bypass or cross the deep ditch. To execute both "hits" simultaneously, CWO Ashford would assault without the backup heavy weapons from his GMVs. Understanding the situation, MAJ West proceeded.

Having received an "up" from all elements, signifying their readiness to attack, both assault leaders initiated their attacks according to a well-rehearsed sequence of commands: "Stand by . . . I have control. Five, four, three, two, one—Execute!" The three breaching charges on the three entry points were detonated on "Execute," and the assault elements positioned to the side of each entry point stormed into the compound. Within minutes, the assault teams at Kelly had physically overpowered two dozen enemy fighters in the 10 buildings on the compound. One enemy fighter, firing his weapon from a doorway, wounded SSG Jesse Wilcox (pseudonym) in the right foot. As the enemy fighter backed out of the building, spraying bullets into the darkness, a security team killed him. An enemy sentry was killed when he fired on the assaulters from outside the compound. These were the only two enemy fatalities at Objective Kelly.[123]

At Objective Brigid, a guard opened fire when he spotted Ashford's assault teams as they ran through the main gate of the compound to their breach points. His alarm shots started firefights as the assaulters fought their way across the courtyard and into the main building. Once inside, it was close-quarters combat from room to room, and the resistance was sharp. Having initially stunned the enemy fighters in the room with flash-bang grenades, the assaulters killed five enemy fighters as two escaped out windows. When MSG Albert Payle and SFC Jon Hsu (pseudonyms) burst into another room, an enemy fighter ran out right between them. Hsu spun about and pursued him, shooting him down before he could escape. Alone and wearing NVG, Payle faced three enemy fighters surrounding him in the darkened room. He quickly killed two of them with his M-4 carbine before the third jumped him from behind, clawing at his eyes. Payle, using combat jiu-jitsu, threw the enemy soldier over his shoulder, sharply snapping the man's head to one side. In the darkness, Payle felt the enemy fighter, even with a broken neck, still grasping at him. Payle drew his 9mm pistol and fired twice, finally finishing his opponent. As he started to move, Payle realized that his opponent was still hanging on him, his hand having been caught in his body armor during their struggle. Not all fought so violently or so stubbornly. In the next room, a single enemy fighter dropped his rifle when assaulters charged in and was readily subdued and flex-cuffed.[124]

In the courtyard, after killing several defenders, the outside assault team was under heavy rifle and machine gun fire from more enemy fighters hiding in a pile of rubble adjacent to the main building. Just as things were getting tense, the two heavily armed HMMWVs wheeled into the compound with their M-2 .50-caliber machine gun and MK-19 40mm grenade launcher.[125] This heavy firepower quickly silenced the enemy behind the rubble heap.

But the fighting was not over, even after Brigid was thought to have been secured. CWO Ashford's Pashto-speaking interpreter, Marine Corps CPL Colin Bermann (pseudonym), had come inside the main building to examine some documents. While Bermann was reading the papers with his small penlite, an enemy fighter, who was thought to be dead, quietly got up from the dirt floor and attacked Bermann with his bare hands. The surprised Bermann managed to shove his assailant away, and he and an assaulter killed him with their M-4 carbines.[126]

With the mission complete at Objective Brigid, Ashford sent a survey team to mark the nearby LZ before he radioed for the waiting helicopters to extract his force. The team reported back that the primary LZ was unusable and suggested the alternate site. However, the walled farmhouse next to it had not been checked, cleared, and secured. Ashford told ODA 516 to clear the building. The Special Forces team applied an explosive breaching charge to the wall and blew an entry way into the small yard. Inside the farmhouse, they found a family huddled together, frightened by the gunfire and explosions. The assaulters moved them into a windowless room for safety and continued to clear the area.

ODA 516's actions reflected the professionalism and character of the A-1-5 soldiers.

Minutes before, the detachment was fighting close quarters with the enemy in the freezing darkness. Then, a helmeted masked assaulter was patiently leading a little girl by her hand to her family. The unit's reputation had preceded it: The farmer's wife had been hysterical until the assaulters identified themselves as *Ameriki*. With that one word, the woman regained her composure and quietly guided her children to the safe area.[127]

At Objective Kelly, West knew the operation was a success, as defined by his orders. They had taken 27 detainees; confirmed 16 dead enemy fighters; seized radios and documents; and were about to demolish antiaircraft cannons, mortars, and other weapons and munitions.[128] The AC-130 Spectre gunships overhead that had covered their assault would cannonade the materiel the unit could not destroy. The entire operation had been completed in less than two hours, but MAJ West had an inkling of trouble.

Figure 27. Weapons captured during a Hazar Qadam raid.

As the Kelly force consolidated on its objective, an assaulter brought West a flag of the new Afghan Interim Authority (AIA) that he found during a search of the site. As the shooting died down at Objective Brigid, CWO Ashford radioed West that one of his assault force found an Afghan national flag inside the compound gate. West immediately radioed the JSOTF-South, requesting that CENTCOM provide confirmation that there were no "friendlies" at Hazar Qadam before he ordered the destruction of the captured arms and munitions. The reply was, "No, there are no 'friendlies' at that site." As it turned out, this was not quite correct.[129]

240

The intelligence that indicated Hazar Qadam (AQ-048) was a *Taliban* or *al-Qaeda* site proved to be dated. It seemed that the Afghan fighters at Hazar Qadam had crossed over to the new AIA government two weeks before the raid. Afghan officials had not reported this. Soon afterward, the *Washington Post* reported, "U.S. Was Misled in Deadly Raid."[130] Controversy was further exacerbated when the 24/7 news media published the unsubstantiated "eyewitness accounts" of Afghans who claimed to have been present during the attacks. They accused the American soldiers of atrocities against "unarmed farmers." Anti-American elements had easily duped the 24/7 international news media. The fabricated stories were all eventually disproved, but while the official investigation was still under way, the *New York Times* headlined the CENT-COM commander's remarks: "After January Raid, GEN Franks Promises to Do Better."[131]

For MAJ West and his men, there was no explanation for the obsolete intelligence at CENTCOM that directed the SSE on AQ-048. The fact that the Afghan men at Hazar Qadam stood and fought, while during all other A-1-5 SSE missions the men simply surrendered or fled, was established. And the fact that the women in the compound at Hazar Qadam, without being told, instinctively held out their hands to be flex-cuffed demonstrated that this group had known the American SSE procedure for *Taliban* and *al-Qaeda*. MAJ West felt no regrets about his company's actions at AQ-048. The Secretary of Defense personally defended A-1-5 after the raid: "It is no mistake at all," said Donald Rumsfeld, "if you're fired on, to fire back."[132] The rest, West knew, was to be expected when a foreign army was fighting a war in Afghanistan.[133]

The following special reconnaissance (SR) story explains the criticality of having "eyes on target" before conducting a direct-action (DA) mission. This had been done on all A-1-5 DA missions before Hazar Qadam. While difficult to accomplish successfully in the sparsely populated areas of Afghanistan, these SR teams showed how important their physical assessment was to the DA assault teams.

SR Eyes on Target

The possible sighting of Osama bin Laden at a safehouse near Shkin in early January 2002 prompted CENTCOM to order a DA mission against the complex. Since DA in Afghanistan was a CJSOTF-South mission, the task fell to A Company, 1st Battalion, 5th SFG, at Kandahar Airport. The confirmed presence of women and children ruled out a kinetic airstrike against the safehouse, an old Russian fort with outbuildings just 5.5 km from the Pakistani border. MAJ Jon West was ordered to send in an SR element on 8 January "to confirm or deny the presence of *al-Qaeda* leadership and facilitate direct action."[134]

Three surveillance and observation cells from Special Forces ODA 514 were to be inserted by MH-53M Pave Low IIIs that night. Two four-man cells were to be landed to the northwest and would move on foot to establish two separate observation posts (OPs). One three-man cell would be inserted west of the target and move on foot to set up an overwatch position south of the compound. While the Pave Lows inserted the soldiers at two LZs some 10 km north and south of the compound, there would be an AC-130 Spectre gunship overhead.

Wearing NVG, the foot movement to the OPs went slowly. Noise discipline was a major concern because sounds carried farther on the desolate terrain. The loose rocks made footing

Figure 28. ODA 514 conducts SR in mountains of southern Afghanistan.

unstable and a stealthy approach difficult. The steep terrain reduced the men to crawling on their hands and knees at times, and the lack of oxygen at altitude heightened fatigue. It took the three groups almost six hours to move the 3 to 4 km to their OPs.

Hide sites were established on the crests of very high, steep ridgelines well above the grass line on the edge of inaccessible cliff faces at elevations above 2,500 meters. The Special Forces soldiers wanted to be above the "natural lines of drift followed by local goat herders and the children that often trailed along behind, playing and exploring." Individual camouflage was a combination of civilian duck-hunting blinds and "yetti nets" tied to natural vegetation by strips of brown burlap with sticks used to break up the outlines. Brown-gray schemes blended well with the bushes and rocks.

Once the early morning fog cleared in the valley, the compiled reports from the SR cells provided a remarkable sense of activity in and around the target complex. A well-used road led to an excavation where the inhabitants appeared to be mining. There were four tractors, including one with a front loader used to dig irrigation ditches. Children played freely in and around the compound. Except for goat herders on the mountain slopes, most civilian activity was confined to the valleys and lower mountain slopes. Most people lived inside compounds just northwest of Shkin. Generally, the locals were asleep with their lights out by 2100. Virtually all living areas had dogs that barked at the slightest noise or light source at night. At one point, a young girl, following the sheep and goats up the mountain, came within 75 meters of the OP in the south, but the team was not compromised.

Despite the benign appearance of the target complex, the OPs witnessed military activity. It was the only compound in the area where the occupants carried weapons openly. A three- to four-man armed patrol roamed about the area during the day, leaving one armed sentry inside the compound. The men all wore similar white Arabic robes in contrast to the herders and farmers who wore traditional Afghan clothing with turbans and scarves. Sentries were regularly posted and relieved, and there was an actual formation inside the compound one day. One night, a four-vehicle convoy from the border patrolled around the compound before stopping for several hours 400 meters to the east. Every night, vehicle traffic back and forth across the border got heavy as soon as it got dark.

On 10 January, a weather front swept through, dumping 1½ inches of snow on the SR teams. Although the snow quickly melted, everyone was left wet and cold. After nearly 72 hours on the ground with most of their supplies gone, JSOTF-South had to either conduct the DA mission or replace the SR teams. CENTCOM believed that it was a likely meeting place for some of the key enemy leaders, and it did not want to jeopardize that opportunity by being premature with DA. The decision was to change out ODA 514 with ODA 515 the next evening.

The rotation took place at 2030, despite the MH-53M Pave Low III having difficulty finding the southern LZ marked by a chemlite "buzzsaw" until an infrared strobe light was used. Special Forces ODA 515 set up two OPs, one 7 km west of the target and the other 3.7 km south. It took the two groups almost three hours to reach their positions undetected.

On 12 January, SFC Rocky Salvadorini (pseudonym) had a kidney stone attack. When the valium that followed the ibuprofen produced no relief, SFC Slater (pseudonym), the team medic, started morphine to deal with the excruciating pain. This medical emergency threatened to compromise the target. MAJ West, company commander; CPT Bill Hall (pseudonym), battalion physician assistant; SFC Slater; and SFC Salvadorini "huddled" on Iridium telephones for a medical consultation. Despite the pain, the condition was not "life threatening." Salvadorini wanted to stay put. West agreed to keep him on the target another 24 hours until the DA strike; they had invested four days of SR on the target already. The opportunity came the next day.[135]

On 13 January, CENTCOM misinterpreted an ODA 515 report of 10 to 15 vehicles coming and going in the area around the target as a congregation at the target. The belief that this accumulation of vehicles signaled the arrival of a high-value target (HVT) prompted the order for a "kinetic" airstrike followed by a DA team to exploit the hit. The JSOTF-South staff scrambled to prepare as Commodore Harward looked at the new HVT target proposed by Tampa. It was the Shkin target. Harward called the chief of operations at CENTCOM to say that he had strong reservations about the "kinetic" airstrike because he had surveillance on the target for the past four days. No vehicles had congregated there, but there were definitely women and children on the target. The airstrike was canceled less than 30 minutes before it was to be executed. Having averted a near disaster, Harward ordered A Company, 1st Battalion, 5th SFG, to execute the DA mission. Ten days later, the lack of SR eyes on target on the Hazar Qadam complex caused a well-executed DA mission to get international media attention from action-starved correspondents in Afghanistan.

The Shkin compound proved to be an intelligence coup based on the value of seven detainees, the wealth of documents, and arms and munitions. Captured were eight RPGs with 30 rockets, 12 assault rifles, a complete 81mm mortar, .51-cal DshK heavy machine gun, Eastern bloc NVG, binoculars, bin Laden posters, identity cards and passports, heroin with syringes, photos and documents, and 200,000 Pakistani rupees as well as Afghan currency. The explosive ordnance demolition (EOD) team used 65 pounds of explosives to destroy the weapons and munitions. More important, there were 14 women and 17 children in the target complex that the day before had been marked for a "kinetic" airstrike.

Throughout the DA mission, the SR teams from ODA 515 provided overwatch and early warning as well as security. SFC Salvadorini was evacuated with the southern OP team when the assault teams left. The western OP stayed behind to observe responses to the DA mission. When they were compromised by curious villagers the next day, the Special Forces soldiers were exfiltrated to Jacobabad, Pakistan, by a Pave Low III that night. It was a major success for the SR teams that, despite a changeover of ODAs to extend the coverage, they were not compromised until after the DA mission had been completed, and their presence had prevented a disaster on 13 January.

While not as exciting as a Special Forces DA or SR mission, the experiences of a tactical PYSOP team (TPT) in the Kandahar area varied from emergency medical care to serving as a combat multiplier on a sensitive mission. TPT 911 was part of Tactical PSYOP Detachment (TPD) 910, A Company, 9th POB from Fort Bragg. It performed both of the following missions within two weeks of arriving in Afghanistan.

From EMT to Special Forces Force Multiplier

TPD 910 was alerted to deploy to Kandahar Air Base on 10 January 2002. The 8th POB, the PSYOP task force (JPOTF), provided an intelligence brief and a cultural and target audience overview as well as packages of PSYOP products on diskettes. TPD 910 (12 personnel), plus four augmentees from 3rd POB (a print specialist, electronic maintenance specialist, communications sergeant, and a graphic illustrator), departed Fort Bragg on 20 January. One TPT assistant team leader had a family emergency en route and was replaced by the electronic maintenance specialist.

When TPD 910 arrived at Kandahar Air Base on 24 January 2002, with its four HMMWVs, it was attached to the 3rd Brigade, 101st Airborne Division. TPT 913 (with driver/gunner = three personnel) described the facilities as quite primitive. It would be four weeks before showers were available. Latrines consisted of 55-gallon drums that were burned off daily by detailed troops. The single field mess served one hot meal a day, and it was just the basics. Meals, ready to eat (MREs) sufficed for the other meals. Bottled water was flown in. Having made arrangements with the local officials to hire interpreters, the TPTs started making rounds in their assigned sectors the second day in Afghanistan to gain support for the coalition forces. The teams attracted attention by simply playing Afghan music in the remote villages because most had no electricity. Initial broadcast efforts were directed toward mine awareness, support for the coalition forces, and keeping the Afghans away from the Kandahar Airport fence and the 101st Airborne Division perimeter defensive positions.

Figure 29. PSYOP leaflet warning about unexploded ordnance.

Within days, the local gunfire outside the camp was reduced. At first, the TPTs went afield with one vehicle to present the smallest possible "footprint," as recommended by TPT 930 that had supported the 5th SFG in November 2001. It distributed more than 100 portable radios in the various villages. The 101st Rakkasans created military information support team packages, combining military police, CA, counterintelligence, and PSYOP personnel. The Rakkasans envisioned such a support team assisting each battalion. The counterintelligence element was later dropped because the personnel proved counterproductive.

245

On Super Bowl Sunday, 4 February 2002, 12 days after TPT 913 arrived at Kandahar, SGT Mitchell Dennison, SP4 Dale Stevenson, SP4 Ike Monroe (pseudonyms), and an interpreter were driving to Kowantarkali when they encountered a young boy in the middle of the dirt road.[136] Dennison thought he should give him a copy of their mine-awareness flyer. The boy handed the flyer back. He immediately became frantic and spoke rapidly. The interpreter said that a man from the nearby village had just stepped on a land mine. Concerned about an ambush, Dennison reported the incident to the detachment before investigating. The PSYOP sergeant stopped the HMMWV alongside a dry field and carefully got out of the truck (the field had obviously been mined) as three Afghans drove the injured man up in a tractor.

The man was mangled, with visible chunks blown out of his thighs, calves, ankles, and wrists. He was obviously the victim of a mine. Monroe requested a medical evacuation helicopter, explaining the seriousness of the injury while Dennison began performing first aid,

Figure 30. PSYOP loudspeaker HMMWVs traveling in pairs.

Figure 31. Broadcasting music outside an Afghan village.

246

applying pressure bandages with field dressings from the combat lifesaver bag. It seemed that the Rakkasan medical evacuation helicopter was responding to an AMF soldier who had been shot near Kandahar, and the newly arrived aircrews were not familiar with the area.

"It was really, really bad. It was the first time I had ever been around so much blood in my life," said Dennison. Still, the sergeant believed that he could keep the man alive for 30 minutes, the time it should take a convoy with an ambulance to get there from the airfield. "Every time I applied a bandage and stopped the bleeding in one place, the locals would pull back the man's robe and show me a bigger wound to cover. After using all my field dressings, I began cutting off the bottom of the local villagers' robes to use as bandages. All in all, I used about 15 "ties" and all the splints on him because he was in bad shape. I tried to give him an IV, but he had bled out to the point that when I inserted the needle and missed his vein, he never bled when I pulled it out," Dennison said.

The man had already been waiting for more than half an hour when TPT 913 came along. "I couldn't give him water, so I wet part of my tee shirt to revive him while I worked on him. I talked with him and had the locals do the same, encouraging him. Throughout this effort, I was unarmed and surrounded by about 20 Afghans watching me work. I managed to stabilize him and keep him alive for almost an hour and a half, but it was 1 hour, 45 minutes before the convoy called from Shanendour, which was about 3 "clicks" (kilometers) away. Because none of the Rakkasans were familiar with the area, SSG Nolan Ward (pseudonym) from TPT 933 volunteered to lead the convoy into the village.

By the time the convoy with an ambulance and medics arrived, the man had already died. The locals said a prayer and took the body to the center of town. TPT 913 followed in its truck. "It made me feel really bad that the guy died, despite everyone reminding me that I was not a doctor. It was a pretty memorable experience for me, and one I'll never forget," said Dennison. "We helped the villagers dig the grave because he had to be buried by sundown according to custom, and we joined them in final prayers at the burial. All in all, this effort created great rapport with the local villagers. Until then, they had had very limited contact with Americans. Now, every time we return the people will remember what we did for them that day."

Figure 32. People long remember the good others do for them and for their children.

Before deploying to Kosovo, SGT, then PFC, Dennison attended the Combat Lifesaver Course at Fayetteville Tech as part of the company's overseas preparation training. A retired

Army Special Forces medic, SGM Jim Messenger, taught combat lifesaving. Basically, the course taught soldiers how to keep someone alive on the battlefield—the necessary steps to treat a casualty encountered in battle. Realizing that he needed more training, Dennison went through the course again. SGM Messenger said then, "Dennison, God forbid if you ever have to treat a casualty." Without the pressure of life and death it was easy to make a mistake on a dummy. TPT 913's experience caused TPD 910 to change its operating procedures because it showed that "anything could happen out there." With one man on the vehicle weapon, another operating the radio, and the third doing lifesaving, the TPT had been "maxed out." "There had been mines all over the place." From that day on, the 910 TPTs operated with two vehicles and more personnel.

Within days of SGT Dennison's combat lifesaving experience with an Afghan mine victim in a remote village, his TPT was tasked to support a Special Forces team conducting an HVT mission. Dennison and SPC Stevenson (pseudonym) rehearsed with the Special Forces team and coalition forces and then boarded helicopters for a night assault on a high-mountain target in the vicinity of Bagram. There was 1½ feet of snow on the ground when Stevenson began his message broadcasts to stop the firing in the village. As the helicopters left, they blew snow everywhere, creating a virtual snowstorm. The purpose for the mission was explained, and the villagers were told to stay inside until the search was complete. At daybreak, the loudspeaker script was changed to keep the curious villagers away while the Special Forces personnel accumulated the weapons, munitions, and equipment seized for removal. What could not be lifted out was prepared for destruction onsite. The broadcasted warnings ensured the safety of the villagers. That night, as the group was extracted, TPT 913 kept the villagers away from the LZ and was the last to board the helicopters. Afterward, the team praised the PSYOP soldiers for their professionalism and for demonstrating that they were truly force multipliers.

While the fight to eliminate the *Taliban* and *al-Qaeda* in Afghanistan continued, ARSOF was working with Pakistan. Pakistan had agreed to block its border against fleeing *Taliban* and *al-Qaeda* and had captured a quantity of the enemy fighters. As a border country, Pakistan had become the home of thousands of Afghan refugees. The following stories explain what Army Special Forces and CA soldiers were doing in that country to support America's war on global terrorism and the dilemma of military uniforms versus mufti in the combat zones.

Politics, War, and Rapport

Politically sensitive missions are common for Army Special Forces. On 7 December 2001, the JSOTF-North commander gave ODB 560 a mission that was extremely politically sensitive. Within days, the Detachment B commander, MAJ Mike Ryan (pseudonym), was in Islamabad, Pakistan, meeting with the CENTCOM liaison officer, BG Ronald Sams; Pakistani army plans officer MG Farooq Ahmad Khan; and U.S. Ambassador to Pakistan Wendy J. Chamberlin.[137]

ODB 560 arrived at K2, Uzbekistan, in late November. Three of MAJ Ryan's SF ODAs had flown directly from Jordan, and another had come from Kosovo where it had been engaged in other missions. As soon as they arrived, two Special Forces teams were assigned to be a quick-reaction force (QRF). Ryan was being briefed on yet another mission. Pakistan was concerned that *al-Qaeda* and *Taliban* fighters were fleeing across the border and was evaluating where to best stop the flow. President Pervez Musharraf requested U.S. support to assist an interdiction effort. Ryan's mission was to assess the situation: how serious were the Pakistanis about interdiction, what exactly did the Pakistanis want, and what was required to support their objectives? The Pakistanis said they intended to deploy Special Service Group forces into the Federally Administered Tribal Areas (FATAs) along the northwest border. Potentially, U.S. Army Special Forces would serve in a combined QRF to stop the exodus.

The FATA was created by the British to effect control of the region through the tribal leaders. Subsequent Pakistani control over the region after 1948 was tenuous at best because many of the leaders refused to acknowledge government authority over the tribes. The matter was so volatile that Pakistan's constitution specified that no act of parliament or court ruling applied in the FATA unless the president declared it to be and then only after consulting with the tribal leaders.[138] FATA tribal militia patrolled the northwest border, thus for Musharraf to deploy forces into the region would be an exceptionally delicate undertaking. Fortunately, Ryan and MSG Aaron Watson (pseudonym), from his team, had worked with the Pakistan Special Service Group previously and knew the unit capabilities as well as some of the soldiers. This experience proved immensely valuable because initial good rapport would enable the two forces to begin working together in harmony. With that potential difficulty erased, Ryan had to ensure that U.S. military actions did not exacerbate the political difficulties.

During the meeting with Ambassador Chamberlin, BG Sams, and MAJ Ryan, MG Farooq reminded the Americans that his government had requested U.S. military support in November 2001, and nothing had come of that request. Based on that rebuff, the Pakistani chief of military operations wanted an immediate commitment. As the discussion developed, it became evident to Ryan that what Farooq wanted was U.S. airlift to emplace the QRF as a blocking force. The Pakistanis did not have the requisite air support, and U.S. aircraft would cut the QRF's response time by half because the force was to be based at Zhob and Kohat. What Farooq outlined was feasible for Special Forces, and MAJ Ryan told this to COL Mulholland. Then, the JSOTF-North commander and BG Sams had to decide its viability and importance to the overall war effort. It was up to Ryan to determine whether the two proposed QRF locations had airfields and secure facilities for his soldiers.

Several trips to Zhob and Kohat convinced Ryan that the QRF could be based at those locations and that there was adequate space for his ODAs to train the Special Service Group. An Army helicopter pilot and an Air Force lieutenant colonel agreed that both airplanes and helicopters could safely operate from the airfields. Until the 160th SOAR's MH-47 Chinooks returned to the theater, Air Force MH-53 Pave Lows at Jacobabad, Pakistan, would be the QRF insertion helicopters. The 528th Special Operations Support Battalion (SOSB) would refuel at the two forward airfields.

Shortly before Christmas, two Special Forces ODAs deployed to Pakistan from K2 to support the mission. Ryan and his two teams immediately began a two-week training program for the Special Service Group. Training included loading and exiting aircraft, marksmanship, tactics, and using night-vision devices. Only the Pakistanis could order the QRF to be employed. Ryan ensured that procedures were established and how launching the QRF would be verified. He also worked with the group commanders to select ambush positions in the border region.

ODB 560 left Pakistan in early March. Although the QRF mission was never executed, this Special Forces detachment made significant contributions. Historically, relations between Pakistan and Afghanistan had been strained. As the only regional country to maintain relations with the *Taliban*, Pakistan's geographical location was important to the war effort. Musharraf's willingness to support the United States and the coalition nations against another Islamic border country posed potentially dire consequences for him, his country, and the war on terrorism. The political significance of having two Special Forces ODAs and one ODB in Pakistan, along with Army helicopters and Air Force airplanes and helicopters, cannot be minimized. Still, the major difference between Army and Air Force special operations is that Special Forces soldiers were training Pakistani soldiers in an area that was traditionally off limits to the Pakistani army. MAJ Ryan fully understood the issue. "You mess this up and the Pakistanis could tell the United States to leave," he said. The fact that American military forces remain in Pakistan is a tribute to the professionalism, diplomatic capabilities, and rapport-building skills that U.S. Army Special Forces soldiers brought to the battlefield.[139]

GTMO Bound

Ambassador Chamberlin had the challenging task of ensuring that President Musharraf remained committed to the war against the *Taliban* and *al-Qaeda* in neighboring Afghanistan. To assist the ambassador with the military aspects of the campaign, CENTCOM sent Air Force BG Ronald Sams with a liaison staff of 17 soldiers to Islamabad, one of whom was Army Special Forces LTC James Karnes (pseudonym). Their initial mission was to ensure that the flow of equipment and supplies from the United States to Pakistan that Musharraf had requested as quid pro quo for basing combat search and rescue (CSAR) forces in the country went uninterrupted. Sams and Karnes also coordinated U.S. airlift to support quick-reaction Pakistani military forces to block *Taliban* and *al-Qaeda* escaping across the mountainous border.[140]

However, in mid-December 2001, another sensitive mission became priority. Combat actions in Tora Bora led some 90 *al-Qaeda* fighters to flee Afghanistan and seek refuge in Pakistan. The *al-Qaeda* had been rounded up by Pakistani authorities and imprisoned. With the collapse of the *Taliban* regime, Pakistan wanted them out of the country. LTC Karnes got the mission. The impetus behind the rapid dispatch of the "political detainees" became suddenly apparent on 19 December when *al-Qaeda* prisoners at Parchinar overpowered their military guards. In the ensuing gun battle, several soldiers and some of the *al-Qaeda* were killed. Both sides had wounded personnel. In the ensuing melee, several of the *al-Qaeda* prisoners escaped. The Pakistani army soon recaptured most of them. Karnes, who had served with the 5th Special Forces in Vietnam, called the provost marshal at the Combined Forces Land Component Command (CFLCC) and told him a facility for enemy detainees had to be established immediately.[141]

At a Pentagon briefing on 27 December, Secretary of Defense Donald Rumsfeld announced that captured *al-Qaeda* and *Taliban* fighters would be transferred to a long-term facility—Camp X-Ray—at the American naval base at Guantanamo Bay, Cuba (GTMO, referred to as Git-Mo). That same day, two groups of 45 manacled, hooded detainees were loaded aboard MC-130 aircraft at Peshawar, Pakistan, and flown to a short-term holding facility guarded by marines and Army soldiers near Kandahar. LTC Karnes had a dedicated 15-person team that included an Army judge advocate, linguists, a military policeman, a Navy medic, and several U.S. Marines.

To establish custody and ensure security, all detainees were fingerprinted and photographed, and personal possessions were inventoried and bagged individually.

After watching the two MC-130s carrying the first group of detainees take off into the night bound for Kandahar, Afghanistan, Karnes flew to Kohat where Pakistani military were guarding more detainees. Between 31 December and 6 January 2002, Karnes orchestrated the secure movement of another 150 detainees to Kandahar. On the night of 5 January, after the four-engine turboprop MC-130 carrying 25 "bagged and tagged" (hooded, manacled, and identification tags attached) detainees was taxiing to the runway and the roaring noise of the aircraft receded in the distance, Karnes heard small-arms fire. As he glanced at the control tower, the lights inside abruptly went out. As Karnes entered the darkened tower, he heard, "Lieutenant Colonel *sahib*, they are shooting, get down." When he flicked his mini Mag Lite toward the voice, a Pakistani air force air traffic controller huddled under a table against the concrete wall said, "And please, *sahib*, turn off the light. They can see us." Obeying the request, Karnes turned and walked out into the darkness. Outside, FBI Special Agent Karen Williams (pseudonym), assisting the effort, asked if the small-arms fire was "friendly" or "hostile" and what caliber weapons were being used. Karnes responded, "When you're being shot at, it's hostile fire, and if you're hit, it doesn't matter what caliber weapon was used." When Williams asked if they should contact the aircraft, the Special Forces officer said, "No. If the aircrew thought they had been fired on, they might not come back, and we have one more detainee transfer mission from here and another two from Quetta. We want them to come back. Now, collect everyone up and we'll call it a night." The next morning, Karnes went to Quetta to arrange for the shipment of 15 ambulatory detainees and five on stretchers. They were sent to Kandahar on 8 and 10 January, accompanied by a medical team. To fill an aircraft load, Karnes picked up 16 detainees in Bagram and brought them to Kandahar.[142]

On 10 January 2002, the first group of 20 enemy detainees left Kandahar for Camp X-Ray. Three days later, another 30 shackled detainees were en route to Camp X-Ray.[143] The flights continued as long as American Special Forces troops scoured the countryside to kill or capture those seeking to continue their reign of terror in Afghanistan. For LTC Karnes, watching the enemy fighters deplane in Cuba on television was a satisfying moment. Although the detainee transfer was not a Special Forces mission, Karnes was proud to be the Special Forces soldier who had been given the mission and "made it happen" in Pakistan and Afghanistan.

CA Liaison Work

Soon after the attacks of 9/11, the tactical CA teams of the 96th Civil Affairs Battalion (CAB) began planning for possible missions in Afghanistan. Normally oriented toward Europe, CAT-A42, D Company, 96th CAB, knew very little about the country. Anticipating deployment to Afghanistan, the team immersed itself in regional studies focusing on the culture, religion, geography, politics, and economics of the region. Yet, when it did get alerted to deploy overseas, it was not to Afghanistan but to Pakistan. CAT-A42 leader CPT Barry Sanford, team sergeant SFC Sol Sorrenson, engineer SFC Forrest Kilbourne, and medic SFC Reggie Holloway (pseudonyms) immediately packed their equipment and, on 21 December 2001, departed for a country none of them had ever expected to visit.[144]

The United States had already initiated a massive humanitarian aid effort to help the Afghan people before CAT-A42 arrived in the region. The Air Force had been dropping aid by parachute since 7 October, but the ground tactical situation hindered overland distribution. By mid-November, as Northern Alliance forces liberated more of the country, aid began to flow in from Turkmenistan and Uzbekistan. Deputy Secretary of Defense Paul Wolfowitz was quite emphatic about the need to increase humanitarian aid in the face of the approaching winter. "It's a time to concentrate even more than we do anyway—which is a lot—on things like humanitarian operations." Two days before Christmas 2001, CAT-A42 arrived in Islamabad to do just that.[145]

In southern Afghanistan, offensive operations by Hamad Karzai, with the assistance of Special Forces ODA 574, were only beginning. How to get humanitarian assistance to the people in the southern and eastern parts of Afghanistan was the problem. Although there were many U.S. government, UN, and nongovernmental organizations (NGOs) in Pakistan with that goal, a willingness to coordinate efforts and cooperate for the common good was lacking. During their tenure in Islamabad, CAT-A46, working with MAJ Matt DiJurnigan (pseudonym), had made great strides to improve that cooperation, but more was required. CPT Sanford had worked CA in Bosnia and knew how critical it was to the overall effort to know exactly what the NGOs were doing and planning to do. CAT-A42 embedded itself in the coalition humanitarian liaison cell (CHLC) to help find a solution to the problem.

A continuous challenge was keeping abreast of what organizations were in Islamabad because all were looking to get into Afghanistan. The team finally obtained an updated list from the UN Humanitarian Information Center. That done, the real legwork was talking with every organization on the list. Education was a constant given because very few officials and representatives had any experience working with military CA units. The CAT-A carried a simple briefing that explained what capabilities the team possessed and how it could assist with the overall humanitarian aid mission. CPT Sanford took his medic, SFC Holloway, when he met with the NGOs in Quetta and Peshawar. Information collected during these visits was sent to CENTCOM in Tampa to D Company, 96th CAB, and when created, to the Combined Joint Civil-Military Operations Task Force (CJCMOTF) in Kabul. Thus, situational awareness was expanded for the ARSOF commands and units.

These efforts did pay off regularly. An NGO in Peshawar had 12 child victims of land mines who needed top-quality medical treatment. The question was whether the military could evacuate them to Germany. Although military aircraft were not available, Sanford and his men used their contacts to locate a charter air service that could do it. Within a week, the 12 children were on their way to a hospital in Germany and a better future. In another case, the Special Forces medic on a CAT-A working in Kandahar needed insulin for an Afghan child. Could CAT-A42 in Islamabad help? The team had to scramble because CPT Sanford was in Peshawar with another NGO. SFC Sorrenson tracked him down and explained the situation. Sanford bought the insulin at a local pharmacy with his own money, called the local Red Cross (Red Crescent) office to find an airplane going to Kandahar, delivered the medicine to the aircrew at the airport, and the next day, the CAT-A medic was injecting insulin into the child. Why did they do this? Because, as Sorrenson said, "We did anything humanitarianly possible for the Afghan people . . . whether or not we were supposed to be doing it."[146]

CJSOTF-West

Dexter "Dex" Yates (pseudonym), a retail broker and Special Forces master sergeant (MSG) in C Company, 3rd Battalion, 20th SFG, Florida ARNG, was going to vacation in southern Europe for a few weeks before doing a stint of active duty, when the 9/11 attacks interrupted his plans.[147] Since the president's declaration of war against global terrorism was made during the U.S. government's fiscal year (FY) changeover, ARNG funding was caught in limbo. Thus, without appropriate funding available for annual training, MSG Yates reported for duty with Special Operations Command Central (SOCCENT) in Tampa, working for several weeks for "points without pay." Service points counted toward a National Guardsman's total time in uniform, whether he received military pay or not.

On 4 January 2002, Yates finally received orders for paid active duty in the J3 plans section of SOCCENT. By then, SOCCENT had three Joint Special Operations Task Forces (JSOTFs) overseas supporting the campaign in Afghanistan: JSOTF-North at K2, Uzbekistan; CJSOTF-South in Kandahar, Afghanistan; and the CENTCOM crisis response element (CRE), Al Saliyah, Qatar.[148] Yates' specific mission was to help "stand up" a fourth task force for the Horn of Africa that would become CJSOTF-West.[149]

After several weeks of staff planning, coordination, and conferences, the SOCCENT staff directors announced that the planned CJSOTF-West was "not going to go"—the 3rd SFG, the intended main element of the Horn of Africa task force, had orders to relieve the 5th SFG in Afghanistan. Now without a specific staff assignment, MSG Yates volunteered to go overseas. "Send me to the smallest, most forward overseas element possible," he requested. Within a few weeks, Yates was at Al Saliyah to serve as a "utility infielder" in the J3 special operations section of SOCCENT's forward headquarters. Like most of his fellow Special Forces National Guardsmen, MSG Yates was willing to do whatever had to be done and serve wherever he was needed just to be part of the campaign to destroy the *Taliban* and *al-Qaeda*. Although Yates did not know it then, he would be much closer to the action in Afghanistan in a few months.[150]

End of Mission—Aerial Resupply in Afghanistan

As the anti-*Taliban* offensive gained momentum and expanded to the south, BG Lesley Fuller, the Special Operations Commander, Europe (SOCEUR) saw that "the action was moving faster than the supply cycle." Fuller considered moving his resupply transload operation from Incirlik, Turkey, to Baku, Azerbaijan, on the Caspian Sea to shorten the MC-130 flight routes and thus improve responsiveness. However, because the Horn of Africa was still a possible mission for the 3rd SFG, Incirlik could better support both theaters than Baku. The effectiveness of the resupply operations continued to improve as the three logistics staffs of the SOCEUR element in Turkey; JSOTF-North in Uzbekistan; and CENTCOM in Florida coordinated their requirements, priorities, and daily activities by routine video teleconferences (VTCs). Unique requests still continued to come in from the Special Forces teams in Afghanistan, asking for items like 12 Suunto digital watches for mountain climbers, 60 horse saddles and bridles, and bleach ("Who ordered the bleach?" Fuller wondered aloud).[151]

The Air Force MC-130 Combat Talons assigned to SOCEUR usually flew two to three missions every night, and each of the special operations turboprop transports was assigned to a single drop zone. Communications and coordination improved to the point that after resupply bundles packed by parachute riggers in Germany had been shipped to Turkey, the "customer" in the combat zone was called and queried. If events had overtaken the original requirements and changes were requested, the bundles could be reconfigured by the riggers at Incirlik before being loaded for parachute delivery in Afghanistan. Then, as the pace of war accelerated, more and more requirements were canceled just days after being requested. The unneeded supply and equipment bundles began to pile up in the SOCEUR hangars at Incirlik Air Base, bringing the resupply that had been overtaken by events to a head. Fuller's basic concept had been to "push" the supplies to the Special Forces units and not to demand perfection in administrative details. "Ask for what you think you might need," he told the teams, "and we can drop it wherever you want later."[152]

While the accelerated tempo of ground operations began to create problems for the SO-CEUR resupply operation, it also ended large-scale fighting in Afghanistan early. Once Kabul had been taken in mid-November 2001, aerial resupply missions fell to one a night. The need for aerial resupply was long over when CENTCOM ordered BG Fuller to cease aerial resupply operations to JSOTF-North on 14 January 2002. SOCEUR dropped bundles to the Army Special Forces units and their Afghan allies. While they did not directly support CA and PSYOP teams on the ground, they did so indirectly through the Special Forces regional command elements.[153]

Figure 33. Airdropped bundles created logistics challenges for the teams.

In the final tally, the SOCEUR headquarters, with U.S. Army, Europe (USAREUR) support and the 16th and 352nd Special Operations Wings (SOWs) flying MC-130 Combat Talons, delivered 1.8 million pounds of supplies in 70 days. The two SOWs flew 135 combat missions and dropped 1,347 containers. SOCEUR spent $59 million in supplies, materials, and parachutes to support the CENTCOM mission.[154] Army warrant officer supply specialists purchased and accounted for all the supplies in carefully maintained Operation ENDURING FREEDOM (OEF) mission property books. These records showed that 98 percent of all supplies SOCEUR Combat Talons delivered directly supported Special Forces teams and their missions.[155]

During those 70 days, only one MC-130 could not fly as scheduled. That Combat Talon had been taxiing to take off when it broke down, but its cargo was quickly transferred to another MC-130 that took off 37 minutes later. For BG Fuller, another resupply highlight came at Thanksgiving when turkey dinners with all the trimmings were packed in sealed thermal containers and airdropped to most Special Forces units in Afghanistan. The end of the aerial resupply mission for Afghanistan did not mean a break in activity for Fuller and his command.

OEF was a global mission that required SOCEUR attention in Europe, the Balkans, and Africa.[156]

"We're Going for Sure This Time"

When LTC Jack Sykes (pseudonym) took command of the Florida ARNG's 3rd Battalion, 20th SFG on 1 September 2001, he announced his intention to "get the battalion ready for war."[157] This was traditional "Hurricane Sykes"—the hard-charging Boynton Beach, Florida, policeman who earned his nickname by relentlessly emphasizing high standards of training and physical fitness. Sykes had earned his green beret by passing the same rigorous Special Forces assessment, selection, and qualification course that today's Regular Army soldiers and officers attend. After the United States was attacked, he knew he had to set aside his preparations to become a police chief and threw himself into ensuring that if called to active duty, his Special Forces battalion would be ready.[158]

The "Third of the Twentieth" already had a solid reputation as a competent, capable unit. Having shadowed the 3rd SFG during Operation TRADEWINDS in Guyana in 1999, the following year, the 3rd Battalion was the Special Forces component in the annual Latin American combined exercise. In August 2001 at the Joint Readiness Training Center (JRTC) in Louisiana, the chief evaluator for Special Forces units commended their performance.[159] Hence, it was not difficult for 20th SFG Commander COL Greg Champion to select Sykes' battalion to send to Afghanistan.[160]

LTC Sykes was directed to take his battalion command post and one Special Forces company to the mobilization center at Fort Bragg, North Carolina, for further training for eventual movement to the theater of war. His headquarters detachment and support company from Florida, a military intelligence detachment from Kentucky, and B Company from Virginia were selected because they were almost at full strength in personnel. Sykes still harbored "a burning memory" of the 20th SFG's mobilization for Operation DESERT STORM in 1991 when, after having had its operational readiness thoroughly evaluated, "we sat on our butts for months" and never deployed overseas. Sykes was determined this would not happen again. When the Third of the Twentieth arrived at Fort Bragg on 1 December 2001, they began live-fire weapons training right away.[161]

Coordinating personnel issues between three different state Adjutants General and the National Guard Bureau in Washington was an administrative nightmare. Processing security clearances, arranging medical examinations, and even issuing identification cards to soldiers' family members had the staff going crazy. The Kentucky ARNG put several soldiers on active duty and sent them to LTC Sykes, not to deploy overseas with his unit but to have the 3rd Battalion use its deployment priority to get them into military schools. Overweight and out-of-shape guardsmen who had not kept up a strict exercise regime during their off-duty time were transferred to other ARNG units. "If it hadn't been for 9/11," said SGM Jorgé Bustillo (pseudonym), "we might have tried to 'rehabilitate' them. But the urgency of the situation required their immediate transfer."[162] As was typical for most ARNG Special Forces units, the 3rd Battalion, 20th Special Forces was almost last on the priority list for new equipment purchases and issues in Florida. Hence, the Special Forces battalion received new body armor but not the new radios or laser sights for M-4 carbines to make them compatible with the Regular Army special operations units. When he discovered that B Company did not have the requisite large shipping containers necessary for transporting its unit equipment by air or sea, LTC Sykes had his nonmobilized units in Florida empty their containers—technically, the property of the state of Florida—and send them to Virginia.[163]

As Sykes and his staff worked their way through the gamut of problems, he received good news. The 3rd Battalion would be part of COL Mark Phelan's 3rd SFG, which would be the nucleus of a Combined Joint Special Operations Task Force (CJSOTF). When the two commanders met, however, Sykes was chagrined to learn that his unit would be used as individual staff augmentees in the CJSOTF headquarters. The additional staffing needed to operate and maintain CJSOTF-Afghanistan exceeded what 3rd SFG had assigned and what the higher headquarters could muster in support. Sykes would not serve as a battalion or forward operating base (FOB) commander as he had envisioned but would be the J5 future plans officer on the CJSOTF staff.

"Hurricane" took it in stride because, unlike 1991, he and his men were not going to be left behind while the rest of the Army went to fight. And who knew what would happen overseas? At the CJSOTF-Afghanistan, Bagram Air Base, one-third of the 300-person headquarters staff was ARNG Special Forces soldiers. Sykes was instrumental in rapidly integrating the numerous coalition special operations units into the CJSOTF, facilitating coalition access to information and coordinating combined combat operations throughout Afghanistan. The CJSOTF logistics chief strongly endorsed the National Guardsmen: "We couldn't run this place without the 'Third of the Twentieth.'"[164]

Be Prepared for SSE

In September 2001, B Company, 2nd Battalion, 3rd SFG, received the mission from CENTCOM to prepare to assume the sensitive site exploitation (SSE) from A Company, 1st Battalion, 5th SFG, by 1 February 2002. Although the date the mission was assigned was close to the date of the terrorist attacks on the United States, the timing was purely coincidental. While the SSE mission incorporated many of the tasks a Special Forces company would normally perform, there were additional essential tasks that required more personnel and specialized equipment and training.

B Company commander MAJ Dalton Carlisle (pseudonym) and his company sergeant major, SGM Geoff Beckwith (pseudonym), knew that their task was difficult.[165] First, they had to get more Special Forces soldiers to bring the company up to full strength. The 3rd SFG accomplished this by transferring soldiers with the requisite skills from other Special Forces companies. After training in basic skills during the SF qualification course, all Special Forces soldiers receive language and advanced skills training. The SSE mission required many of the advanced skills. Given the limited training time and criticality of the SSE mission, the U.S. Army John F. Kennedy Special Warfare Center and School (SWCS) accommodated an influx of soldiers from B-2-3 by temporarily shifting more instructors to the required courses. "That worked out very well," Carlisle said.

Next, the unit required mission-specific equipment, and to become proficient with the new items, it had to train with them; thus, the company needed them "yesterday." Acquiring these specialized items rapidly proved difficult. The contract purchasing process was slow. Funds to purchase the various items of equipment came from specific accounts. Unfamiliar with the complex process, Carlisle and Beckwith were confused and frustrated. The only thing certain was "the ball always seemed to roll back to them at the company." There were internal disconnects within the staff between those who validated the need for the equipment and those who procured the items. Then, LTC Julian McGinnis (pseudonym), the U.S. Army Special Forces Command (USASFC) logistics officer, got directly involved. "Although sheer willpower could not solve every problem, McGinnis solved most. Buy that man a six-pack," said SGM Beckwith.

Despite the Herculean efforts of McGinnis, it was just six days before deployment that the $753,000 arrived to buy the specialized equipment. In the midst of palletizing their equipment, determining aircraft load plans, and taking care of last-minute family issues, they had to focus on ordering critical equipment to perform the SSE mission overseas. Since there is no contracting officer on the Special Forces group or battalion staffs, the burden of problem resolution slid down to the lowest operational level that lacked personnel with the requisite experience or expertise.

Fortunately, both Carlisle and Beckwith had served in units with an SSE mission. The Special Forces company moved to Camp Mackall, North Carolina, to concentrate on the different mission profiles. The 160th SOAR provided an MH-60K Black Hawk to support the specialized training. Since the Night Stalker aircrew had extensive experience with the missions the company would perform, it shared planning skills, discussed tactics and techniques, and demonstrated ways to increase the probability of mission success. After several months of intense training, COL Phelan evaluated the company's operational readiness and declared the unit to be mission capable.

Having achieved the standards necessary to perform the SSE mission for CENTCOM, B Company flew to Qatar on 1 April. There, MAJ Carlisle and SGM Beckwith met with key staff from the SOCCENT crisis response element (CRE) and leaders of A Company, 1st Battalion, 5th SFG. CW3 Dwight Ashford (pseudonym), A-1-5's executive officer, had prepared a "smart book" of the most critical information that Carlisle and Beckwith needed to know based on his company's experience. After a week's overlap with A-1-5's leaders, Carlisle felt confident that his company could perform the SSE mission wherever CENTCOM needed its specialized skills. From then on, it would train, honing individual and collective skills, to be prepared to deploy into combat on short notice.[166]

Back in the United States, the "heavy lifting" for the PSYOP campaign continued. In the midst of high-priority requirements and short-fuse deadlines, an Army reservist had succeeded in making his unique talents available to the 4th Psychological Operations Group (POG), Fort Bragg. It took great personal initiative, perseverance, and the endorsement of the USAR command sergeant major to make it happen.

Native Pashto and Dari Speaker Seeking PSYOP Assignment

Akmed Astor (pseudonym) and his family escaped Soviet-occupied Kabul, Afghanistan, in 1983, first to Lahore, Pakistan, for about a year and then to Chicago, Illinois.[167] Kabul was his birthplace. His father, an Uzbek Herati from Heart in the northwest, worked for the British

Consul in Kabul and was the representative of the U.S. Library of Congress in Afghanistan. His mother, a Pashtun from Kandahar, had worked at the Bulgarian Embassy and the UN. After graduating from high school in Chicago in 1987, Astor joined the Army and served at Fort Campbell, Kentucky, and Grafenwoehr, Germany. He attended Chicago State University for two years, studying computer science, before rejoining the Army, again as a personnel records specialist. When Astor was levied for Korea in late 1997, he got reclassified as an interrogator; was schooled at Fort Huachuca, Arizona; and went to the JRTC, Fort Polk, for two years.

In October 2000, SGT Akmed Astor got out of the Army again but joined the USAR as a personnel records specialist. This led to the Active Guard Reserve Program and his assignment to the 99th Reserve Support Command (RSC), Pittsburgh, Pennsylvania, on Labor Day weekend just before the 9/11 attacks. Astor said, "As bad as I wanted to get out of deployments, I really wanted to help out in Afghanistan. So I called here [Fort Bragg] to the 8th Psychological Operations Battalion [POB] to find out if they needed help. Specialist (SPC) Mohammed Osterman (pseudonym) said that they needed a lot of help, especially with language, and since I had spent more time in Afghanistan than he, my knowledge of culture would be more current."[168]

SGT Astor talked with 99th RSC's leaders. They told him, "If you want to go, we're 100 percent behind you. We know what the Army needs at this time. We'll let you go." First, the 99th RSC had Astor attached to the 303rd PSYOP Company, Pittsburgh. By mid-December 2001, he was temporary duty (TDY) at 8th POB while the U.S. Army Reserve Command expedited his mobilization.

SGT Astor, born and raised in Afghanistan by a well-educated family, spoke Pashto, Dari, and Farsi and understood Urdu. He learned English at the French Center and Urdu from watching Hindi movies in Kabul. While the Afghans did not make films, 13 of the 15 theaters in the capital showed Indian movies. ARSOF and the PSYOP community were fortunate that Astor had been so persistent, especially because SPC Osterman left the service after fulfilling his enlistment in mid-January 2002.

Support for the Afghan Interim Authority (AIA), humanitarian reconstruction, and coalition forces seeking to eliminate the *Taliban* and *al-Qaeda* threat—the major PSYOP themes in December and January—were being heavily promulgated by radio broadcasts based on the advice of Hamad Karzai two months earlier in Pakistan. SGT Astor carefully balanced music selections between "fast dances" for the younger people and traditional classics that everyone enjoyed and provided introductions. For down south, the Special Operations Media Systems–Broadcast (SOMS-B) wanted more Pashto songs, and up north they wanted more Dari music. Then, specific requests came in from the SOMS-B. Astor went online to find the music and burned compact discs (CDs). One weekend, he copied the collections of his wife and sister—nearly 50 CDs.

The messages between the music had to be correct in both Dari and Pashto, the two major languages in Afghanistan. Since a Pashto message takes longer to read than one in Dari, there were fewer songs on the Pashto tapes. "It's a constant juggling match," said Astor. The messages solicited popular support for the legitimate government—the AIA warned the people to avoid interfering with the coalition forces; pushed the need for the *loya jirga*; gave specifics on humanitarian aid; and identified, by country, who was providing what to the Afghan people. The other topics were women's roles in government, the importance of education, and the reconstruction of girls' schools. One particularly good piece was a biography of female leader Sima Simar, a Hazzara (a minority group), that emphasized her important work in the government and stressed that women are as important in Afghan society as men and that they can make contributions. Then, they are told how to help. CENTCOM had already approved these scripts in English, but the final translations could not be in harsh language or offensive to a particular ethnic group. With seven other translators, supervision and careful review became mandatory for SGT Astor.

As Astor stated, "It wasn't that hard to counter the feeble *Taliban* and *al-Qaeda* PSYOP efforts." The *Taliban* and *al-Qaeda* psychological warfare consisted primarily of "night letters," a carry-over from the *mujahideen* anti-Soviet propaganda efforts. These zeroxed hand-written leaflets were delivered to doorsteps and glued on walls during the night. The message was basically, "Just like when the Russians were here, we fought a *jihad* against them. Now that the Americans are here, we have to do the same thing."[169]

The success of a special program based on the works of Ahmed Zahir, a popular folksinger who mixed modern Western musical instruments with traditional Afghan instruments, demonstrated how successful the 8th POB program was. Zahir, who was "as big as Elvis Presley in Afghanistan," had been killed by the communist regime. The idea for the program came from an online magazine article, "Afghan Music," written by a friend. With the author's permission and CENTCOM's approval, the 8th POB Product Development Company prepared a 75-minute, seven-part program in both Pashto and Dari. Even the narrated parts had Zahir's music in the background to emphasize the importance of his music contribution to the entire country. Feedback from overseas was positive, and CENTCOM wanted more products like the Zahir program to be developed. For a passionate admirer like Astor, it was literally "music to his ears," but further recognition was forthcoming.

The Command Sergeant Major of the USAR, CSM Ray Lackey, made a point of visiting SGT Astor at his work place when he visited Fort Bragg. Lackey told Astor, "I remember that when your paperwork came across my desk, the 8th POB had been asking for a reservist in Pittsburgh. I just wanted to meet you and find out what you are doing. I know that you had to 'jump through a lot of hoops' to get here, but I hear that you're doing a great job." Lackey then presented Astor with his coin.[170] This recognition was nice, but Astor was even prouder that his father had been selected to participate in the *loya jirga* in Kabul. Now both would be contributing to the betterment of Afghanistan.

SGT Astor summed it up appropriately: "Every place where the United States has conducted some type of military operation in favor of or against a government, you know good things have happened. We have seen good things happen, and I believe it will be the same for Afghanistan. The more we do for Afghanistan and the Afghan people, the more Americans will get out of it. The more you do good in the unstable countries of the Middle East the better. Good ties with Afghanistan and Pakistan will help improve relations with the other Middle Eastern countries."[171]

Returning to Afghanistan, the next collection of soldier stories will cover support to the AR-SOF combat forces; CA humanitarian, reconstruction, and food distribution efforts; an emergency air rescue mission; and Special Forces gearing up for SSE and Operation ANACONDA.

Keep on Trucking

The deployment of a maintenance support team (MST) from B Company, 528th Support Battalion, was as unique as some of their tasks while attached to Forward Operating Base (FOB) 33. Just getting to Afghanistan proved to be an adventure. The four-man team boarded a C-5A Galaxy jumbo cargo aircraft at Pope Air Force Base, North Carolina, that flew west to Travis Air Force Base, California. There, the aircraft was refueled, and a fresh aircrew resumed the flight to Guam. After a 24-hour layover in Guam, the C-5A flew to Diego Garcia in the Indian Ocean. At Diego Garcia, the four maintenance specialists were transferred to a C-17 Globemaster III and finally arrived at Kandahar just before daylight on a cold day in February.

The MST's primary mission was to provide vehicle and generator maintenance for the 3rd Battalion, 3rd SFG, at FOB 33 in Kandahar. This initially entailed repairing or replacing engines, transmissions, and major assemblies for the unit ground mobility vehicle (GMV), an armored version of the HMMWV. Needless to say, with mechanics "in town," the mission was expanded. Since the GMVs were in good shape, the team went to work on the various civilian pickup trucks and sport utility vehicles that the Special Forces had captured. Most of the Toyota Land Cruisers and small Japanese pickup trucks the ARSOF used throughout the country were old and in poor mechanical condition. The MST started doing basic vehicle maintenance—checking oil levels, filling radiators, servicing batteries, and tuning engines.[172]

SSG Jason Lafayette (pseudonym), the MST team sergeant, believed that since all diesel and gasoline engines work on the same basic principles, his mechanics could get the dilapidated vehicles running again and keep them functioning.[173] And they did but not without solving some major challenges. All the available reference manuals were written in Japanese, and replacement parts were nonexistent. American Toyota parts were incompatible with those found on captured *Taliban* vehicles. By using standard Army mechanic ingenuity, the team made a few "controlled substitutions," an Army maintenance term for cannibalizing, from other *Taliban* vehicles. As the Special Forces teams brought back more captured vehicles, the MST switched good parts for broken ones, replacing torn-off radiator shrouds and fans broken by the rough terrain conditions. The two major goals were to "make the decrepit vehicles last as long as possible and not to fail the guys down range." SPC Timothy Berdeau (pseudonym) spent four weeks at a desolate Special Forces team base keeping several all-terrain vehicles functioning with only his tools and a lot of imagination.[174]

The team's most significant accomplishment was a tactical modification to the GMV. The heavy-duty springs of the modified GMV posed a clearance problem for rapid infiltration and exfiltration of the truck using the MH-47E Chinook helicopter. SPC Berdeau and SGT Jack Felico (pseudonym), a mechanic from the 3rd Battalion, 3rd SFG, modified several GMVs for a special mission by adjusting the coil spring on the front end of the vehicle.[175] This lowered the GMV profile sufficiently to facilitate rapid helicopter loading and offloading, and could be readjusted on the ground afterward. The procedure had never been performed in an austere tactical environment and required great skill. It worked for the mission, and the truck drivers reported no problems with the temporary arrangement.

The 528th MST never failed to meet the demands imposed upon it. It was eager to be part of the ARSOF effort to find and destroy the *Taliban* and *al-Qaeda*. In the team's opinion, MSTs did not do anything special, but for the Special Forces teams in the field, MSTs were invaluable.

SSG Lafayette summed it up best, "Most of the time, mechanics do a whole lot of something with a whole lot of nothing."

Rescue at 10,000 Feet

Flexibility, dedication to mission, and reliability meant success to all special operations forces (SOF) in Afghanistan. The pilots and aircrews of the 9th Special Operations Squadron (SOS) demonstrated these traits since they arrived to support the combat search and rescue (CSAR) mission of the initial air campaign in northern Afghanistan. The MC-130P aircraft of the 9th SOS conducted aerial refueling support for the ARSOF helicopters of the 160th SOAR almost daily during the first three months of combat in Afghanistan. Given the high-altitude mountain chains along the Uzbekistan-Afghanistan border, the treacherous winter weather conditions and frequent sandstorms that reached 10,000 feet routinely, and the reduced lift associated with high altitudes in the region, the "Mother Hen" MC-130P refuelers that provided fuel as many as three times a night to the Night Stalker MH-47E and MH-60L helicopter flights often determined the success or failure of the long-range night infiltration missions in the near "zero-zero" weather conditions.

For a high-profile mission scheduled for 12 February, pre-mission planning revealed that this one, like most, was fuel dependent. This meant the 9th SOS MC-130P tankers were critical to executing the operation. For this particular mission, the aerial refueling track would be in the high northern mountains of Afghanistan. The MC-130P tankers were to refuel three MH-47E Chinooks that were supporting a Special Forces team conducting a direct-action (DA) mission. It was a short refuel track based on the location, and there was a 19-minute window allowed for refueling. The weather was typically marginal, and illumination was 0 percent; heavy snow had recently fallen, blanketing the mountains.

The flight of three Chinooks rendezvoused at the "refuel racetrack" that was supported by two MC-130P tankers, a primary tanker and a backup. The altitude of the racetrack was 9,500 feet mean sea level (MSL). Aerial refueling at this altitude was tough for two reasons: air turbulence was heavy and winds shifted radically around the high mountains, and the extreme altitude reduced aircraft performance for both the MC-130Ps and the MH-47Es, but the Army and Air Force aircrews were very experienced. CWO Alfred Mann (pseudonym), the flight lead, moved in to refuel off the left wing of the tanker, and CWO Jackson Ferrell (pseudonym) in the third Chinook crossed over to the right wing to receive gas. Both the first and third helicopters refueled without problems and backed off the tanker. Ferrell remained positioned on the right wing but was flying slightly above the tanker as the last Chinook approached to refuel.[176]

CWO Curtis Jameson (pseudonym) moved into the refuel approach "slot" after CWO Mann in the lead helicopter moved off. Jameson had just connected to the refuel basket as the MC-130P reached the end of the track. The 19-minute racetrack limitation required the tanker to turn in the direction of the helicopter ingress route. As the flight turned in the new direction, Jameson's MH-47E inadvertently disconnected from the tanker but quickly recovered and was reconnected after the turn. On the right wing of the MC-130P, Ferrell manipulated the aircraft navigation systems and caught a fleeting glimpse of terrain on his multimode radar screen.[177]

Suddenly, the tanker abruptly pulled up, causing a sine wave in the refueling hose. The sudden maneuver ripped the refueling basket off the helicopter refuel probe, and the MH-47E rotor

261

blades severed the gyrating hose, damaging the blades and causing the flight controls to vibrate slightly. Jameson was pulling the big Chinook upward as the MC-130P impacted on a mountain plateau at 9,800 feet MSL. Unbelievably, the skilled Air Force pilot, faced with an impossible situation, managed to wrench the MC-130P nose up in sufficient time to stall the airplane, pancaking the heavy aircraft onto the steep, heavily snow-covered mountain slope at approximately 80 knots. The MC-130P slid to a stop in the deep snow on an upward slope of a high plateau.

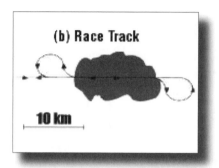

Figure 34. MC-130Ps fly a "racetrack" to remain available for refueling.

Luckily, the MC-130P struck the mountain at just the right angle and speed. The airplane fuselage cracked in half, sparing the lives of the crew aboard. CWO Mann flew over the top of the crashed tanker and pinpointed its position in his onboard navigation system. As he circled overhead, seven of the eight crew members emerged from the wrecked fuselage and signaled to him with flashlights. Mann acknowledged the signal with a white landing light and then moved to land about 200 feet down from the wreck. It was a very cautious, slow landing when he saw how deep the snow was. When the Chinook settled in on the 15-degree slope, the refuel probe was buried and virtually touched the ground.

The Special Forces soldiers aboard quickly exited the aircraft to begin wading through hip-deep snow toward the wrecked aircraft. The Air Force pilots had assembled everyone in the crew outside except the trapped flight engineer. The Special Forces team helped the airmen wade down the slope to their helicopter. The Chinook crew and flight medic quickly treated the injured and wrapped them in flight jackets, blankets, and sleeping bags taken from survival rucksacks—anything to warm the survivors. Having gotten most of the airmen aboard the MH-47E, the Special Forces team returned to the wreck to work feverishly to free the pinned flight engineer. The tanker was burning, hissing, and crackling as if it was about to explode at any minute. Aircraft fuel was everywhere inside and all around the broken MC-130P. Despite the physiological challenges associated with high-altitude work, the men persevered but were hampered by the lack of specialized rescue equipment. They had to be content with providing first aid.

Meanwhile, overhead, the aerial refuel mission continued with the backup MC-130P. CWO Jameson was low on fuel, and the second tanker quickly pulled into position. LTC James Brinks (pseudonym), the air mission commander (AMC), directed Ferrell, flying the trail helicopter and carrying the emergency refuel package—the "cow"—to return to Bagram Air Base. Because Jameson was carrying the CSAR package, as soon as he finished refueling, he was to fly to the mountaintop and land upslope from the wreckage. This would give the Special Forces team easier access to the wrecked aircraft. The CSAR package included two Air Force pararescue medics, a "jaws of life" mechanical device, and a large medical kit.[178]

Using the "jaws of life" device, the Special Forces team extracted the seriously injured flight engineer, loaded him aboard a Sked litter, and dragged him to the Chinook. After examining his injuries, a broken pelvis and probable internal injuries, the senior medic recommended an expeditious return to medical facilities. Mann and Brinks decided to abort the original mission and fly the injured airman back to Bagram as quickly as possible. Having spent so much time with engines running on the ground to keep the airman and his aircrew warm in the low teen Fahrenheit temperatures at high altitude, Mann had to refuel again from the MC-130P, closely monitoring the situation from above.

This rescue operation revealed the great trust and confidence shared within the SOF community. When the situation turned bad, the SOF team members responded quickly, never forgetting their responsibilities while capitalizing on their unique capabilities and high level of training. The lead Chinook immediately landed, the Special Forces team courageously rescued everyone from the crashed MC-130P tanker, the backup tanker automatically moved into the racetrack to refuel the helicopter with the CSAR package, and the force lived to fight again. Although altitude, the additional passengers, the condition of the injured airman, and lost hours of darkness prevented the flight from continuing its assigned mission, the orchestration of the recovery exemplified SOF skill, determination, and dedication.

Date Drop at Khowst

Ankle deep in mud, MAJ Silas Greene (pseudonym) stood on the edge of the Khowst airfield in the dark as a steady drizzle soaked the ground.[179] He was listening for the sound of three MC-130 transports that were to drop humanitarian aid bundles to his CA team. Greene had gotten a radio message earlier in the day, telling him that the CAT-A would receive drops of wheat and blankets starting that night and every night thereafter until further notice. The Air Force tactical combat controlers (CCTs) had already positioned dim marker lights on the drop zone, turned on homing beacons, and were speaking with pilots of the inbound aircraft on their high-band radios.[180] Because the rain had turned the dirt runway into mud, the CCTs requested that the transports drop the aid bundles alongside of the airstrip. When the MC-130s roared by overhead, unseen in the darkness, the parachute-delivered huge bundles landed one after another in a row, directly down the centerline of the runway. Greene was surprised to hear crashing as the bundles slammed into the ground rather than the dull thudding he expected from packages having been dropped by parachute.

As MAJ Greene walked the length of the airfield with his flashlight, he discovered the reason for the crashing sounds. All but one of the dozens of bundles exploded open on impact, spilling tons of wheat and scattering hundreds of blankets across the rain-soaked dirt strip for more than 1,000 yards. He discovered another surprise: tens of thousands of dates, wrapped in leaflets in a language that he did not recognize, had burst out of thin plastic containers, covering the soaking wheat like large pepper flakes. As Greene splashed through the puddles while enduring the drizzle, he saw that the recently repaired runway was now blocked by a half-mile-long stretch of canvas and nylon straps, cluttered mounds of broken cardboard boxes, tons of spilled wheat, wool blankets, paper leaflets, and sticky dates. It was a colossal mess.[181]

Having reported the disaster before going to bed, Greene was informed the next morning that the aid bundles had been specially packed by parachute riggers in Germany to deliberately break open on landing. This packing system had been devised for aerially dropping humanitarian aid into areas where no U.S. military personnel would be present to oversee the distribution of the aid to the local Afghans. The Containerized Delivery System used small parachutes designed to stabilize the bundles and keep them upright rather than to slow their descent. The shock of impact was to be absorbed by layers of honeycomb-shaped cardboard packed in the bottom of each bundle. It was obvious to MAJ Greene that no one had tested the bundles with these contents beforehand.

The dates caused Greene to recall a story about another "date drop" in November or December to one of the Special Forces ODAs in northern Afghanistan. Someone, somewhere in a PSYOP planning cell, probably based on Operation DESERT STORM experience, had convinced the "powers that be" that dates were a special treat in Central Asia, particularly on certain Muslim holy days. Thus, dates were packaged in small lidded plastic tubes, along with leaflets that read "A gift from the United States." As it turned out, the Afghans did not appreciate the airdropped dates, nor were they the delicacy that someone "in the rear" imagined them to be. At the time, Greene thought bemusedly that "maybe the Afghans were just regular guys." But he did remember—"No dates" for Afghans, at least until this drizzly February night in southeastern Afghanistan.[182]

Since the Khowst runway had been designated as an alternate airfield for the upcoming Operation ANACONDA that would begin in a few days, MAJ Greene had to get the mess cleared off immediately. At dawn the next day, CAT-A41 went to several of the local villages and hired 30 laborers at the going rate of 200 rupees a day, about $2.00 in U.S. currency. This pay was considered quite generous because almost no one was fully employed in the destitute province. In addition to the pay, Greene offered the workers all the wheat, blankets, and dates they could carry away. CAT-A41 and the Afghans worked for 14 hours straight, clearing the sodden mounds of wheat, blankets, and dates that "trashed" the runway. As the drizzling rain turned into a downpour, the trucks Greene used to carry off the debris got stuck in the mud. After the trucks were winched out, there were deep ruts criss-crossing the runway—another problem to solve when the rain stopped.

The local villagers did carry off a lot of the sodden "aid," including some of the wheat in wheelbarrows, although Greene thought that the rain would have ruined most of it. The villagers also took all the blankets and scrap canvas, but the dates were left behind. None of the local Pashtuns could read the leaflets that were packed with the dates. Greene soon discovered why. They were written in Tajik, which is spoken only in northeastern Afghanistan. The cleanup crew shoveled the sticky dates off the airstrip into piles. The piles turned into sticky globs in the rain. Finally, the "delicacies" ended up in a nearby dump.[183]

Three days later, when the rain stopped, Greene hired a local farmer to use his grader to make the strip usable for aircraft. He finished just before Operation ANACONDA kicked off. Afterward, MAJ Karl Jurgens (pseudonym), the 10th Mountain engineer who had helped Greene at the Salang Tunnel, brought a platoon of combat engineers to rebuild the airstrip. When MAJ Greene was leaving Afghanistan, he heard that wheat was growing alongside the Khowst runway.[184]

Figure 35. Recruiting "runway maintenance specialists" from the local population.

ODA 394: The Next Mission

The "fog and friction of war" so often referred to in military history and theory became reality for ODA 394 soon after the 12 Special Forces men landed in Afghanistan.[185] CPT Jed Samuels (pseudonym) received the first mission change from his battalion commander, LTC Terry Sanders (pseudonym), at the "Rose Garden," a former *Taliban* military training camp (Tarnac Farms) near Kandahar airport. ODA 394 deployed on 8 February 2002, with its four GMVs—armed HMMWV trucks—to conduct mounted special reconnaissance (SR) and direct-action (DA) missions in the desert.[186] As A Company, 1st Battalion, 5th SFG, left Afghanistan, C Company, 3rd Battalion, 3rd SFG, had been assigned sensitive site exploitation (SSE). MAJ Mickey Hensen directed SGM Rudy Madden and MSG Gregg Corr (pseudonyms) to start training the company in close-quarters battle (CQB) techniques to fight in buildings.[187]

This was not refresher training but entirely new training for the company and its Special Forces ODAs that lacked the specialized equipment to perform the mission. Samuels' team had to teach itself how to perform the advanced CQB tasks. CWO Max Gorley and MSG Ty McFadden (pseudonyms) built on to the company's two-day initial training program and modified its weapons, body armor, and personal carrying harnesses to fight in the mud-walled houses endemic to the villages of Afghanistan. The buildings had low ceilings and small windows. Exterior mud walls commonly surrounded a cluster of buildings. Thus, Americans tended to refer to them as compounds, but they were vastly different from compounds found in the Balkans and in Latin America. ODA 394 equipped itself with "hooligan tools"—sledge hammers and large crowbars to break down doors for entry. After almost two weeks of intense CQB training and rehearsals, ODA 394 was alerted for a mission. Instead of a building for which they had rehearsed for weeks, the mission was to search several square kilometers of mountainous terrain. Samuels' team was to be part of a coalition task force that would identify caves for destruction by aerial bombing. New Zealand, Canadian, Norwegian, and Danish units would participate with them.

But as the mission start time approached, ODA 394 and ODA 391 were designated to be the quick-reaction force (QRF) for the coalition. MAJ Hensen and his headquarters would be

265

the QRF command element. Leaving its vehicles behind, the QRF flew to Bagram Air Base, the abandoned Soviet airfield north of Kabul. Hensen and his men "froze their butts off" on the cement floor of a bombed-out hangar, waiting for orders.[188]

The next morning, SGM Madden asked the command sergeant major of the 10th Mountain Division, CSM Marc Lorenzo (pseudonym), if he could feed the Special Forces teams on QRF standby. Although all were unshaven, some sporting full beards, and wearing an assortment of jackets and pants, CSM Lorenzo said, "Of course. Come with me," and led them inside the hangar where he told the servers to give the Special Forces troops all they could eat for breakfast. Later, the QRF was stood down, and ODA 394 returned to Kandahar to prepare for a major new operation code-named ANACONDA.[189]

The preceding few stories, while not action-packed combat vignettes, reveal the ability of the ARSOF soldiers and airmen to adapt to the environment, adjust to new unfamiliar tasks determined to accomplish their missions, and respond with consummate professionalism to calamity. They also reflect innovative solutions, instinctual piloting reactions that come only with extensive experience, and basic humbleness. Although everyone tried to contribute and wanted to do the "right thing," mistakes were made.

In the next chapter, Army and coalition SOF and Afghan militias will be supporting American conventional units in the biggest battle of the war after the collapse of the *Taliban* regime. While Operation ANACONDA may have grown from a special operations concept, the operation was planned as a conventional force mission. Special Forces teams would advise and support the Afghan militia forces in the primary attack. As in any combat situation, events evolve and plans go to the winds when the first rounds are fired. Thus, the ARSOF fight on the mountain of Takur Ghar will distract and confuse many about Operation ANACONDA.

Notes

1. Ulysses Simpson Grant (1822-1885), quoted in Robert Debs Heinl, Jr., *Dictionary of Military and Naval Quotations* (Annapolis, MD: Naval Institute Press, 1966).

2. U.S. Marines arrived later that day, taking over guard of the U.S. Embassy from the Special Forces troops. The Marines raised an American flag at a formal ceremony 10 days later. Kit R. Roane, "For Special Forces, a Time to Remember," *U.S. News and World Report* (24 December 2001); Barry Bearak, "U.S. Prepares for Reopening of Embassy," *New York Times*, 11 December 2001; Kirk Spitzer, "U.S. Flag to Signal the Reopening of Mission in Kabul," *USA Today*, 17 December 2001, 2; Kevin Sullivan, "Embassy in Kabul Reopened by U.S.," *Washington Post*, 18 December 2001, 16.

3. According to news correspondent John F. Burns, from a single valley in northwest Pakistan, "10,000 to 15,000 [Pakistani] men marched off to Afghanistan to fight America in October, and 2,000 to 3,000 have not returned." John F. Burns, "*Jihad*'s Lost Battalions Mourned by Pakistani Kin," *New York Times*, 10 December 2001, 1.

4. Greg Jaffe and Michael M. Phillips, "Possible Bin Laden Hiding Places are Hit by Warplanes With Help From Commandos," *Wall Street Journal*, 4 December 2001; Rowan Scarborough and Bill Gertz, "U.S. Troops Join Bin Laden Search," *Washington Times*, 5 December 2001; Susan B. Glasser, "Al Qaeda Base Under Assault," *Washington Post*, 6 December 2001; Brian Knowlton, "All-Out Hunt for Bin Laden," *International Herald-Tribune*, 10 December 2001; Susan B. Glasser, "U.S. Attacks on Al Qaeda Intensify," *Washington Post*, 10 December 2001.

5. Stephen Farrell and Michael Evans, "SAS Searches 'Bin Laden' Cave System," *London Times*, 4 December 2001; Rowan Scarborough, "Caves in Tora Bora Survive," *Washington Times*, 19 December 2001, 1.

6. Susan B. Glasser, "Al Qaeda's Forces Flee Caves for Mountains," *Washington Post*, 11 December 2001; U.S. Army Center for Military History (CMH), "The Course of Operation ENDURING FREEDOM in Southern and Eastern Afghanistan," Information Paper, 26 April 2002.

7. For a journalistic assessment of the Tora Bora offensive written six months after the action, see Rod Nordland, Sami Yousafzai, and Babak Dehghanpisheh, "How Al Qaeda Slipped Away," *Newsweek* (19 August 2002). Michael O'Hanlon criticizes U.S military leaders' decisions during the fight for Tora Bora in "A Flawed Masterpiece: Assessing the Afghan Campaign," *Foreign Affairs* (May/June 2002), 54-58.

8. *FRONTLINE*, "Campaign Against Terror," air date 8 September 2002, <http://www.pbs.org/wgbh/pages/frontline/shows/campaign/etc/cron.html>; Michael R. Gordon with Eric Schmitt, "U.S. Putting Off Plans to Use G.I.'s in Afghan Caves," *New York Times*, 27 December 2001.

9. Esther Schrader, "POWs Will Go to Base in Cuba," *Los Angeles Times*, 28 December 2001, 1; "U.S. to Hold Detainees at Guantanamo Bay," *CNN.com*, 28 December 2001, <www.cnn.com/2001/US/12/27/ret.holding.detainees>; James Dao, "U.S. Begins First Airlift of Prisoners," *New York Times*, 11 January 2002, 1; Dave Moniz and Tom Squitieri, "U.S. Flies Second Batch of Afghan Prisoners to Cuba," *USA Today*, 14 January 2002, 8.

10. Mark Mazzetti, "How Special Ops Forces Are Hunting Al Qaeda," *U.S. News & World Report* (25 February 2002); Seth Hettena, "Navy SEALs Led Covert War Against Al-Qaida," *Ventura County (Calif.) Star*, 22 September 2002.

11. Carol Morello, "Marines Rebuilding Kandahar Airport," *Washington Post*, 21 December 2001, 31.

12. U.S. Navy, "TF-KBAR Coalition Conference (13-16 Aug 02) AAR (U)," Naval Special Warfare Group One, 26 August 2002, copy in U.S. Army Special Operations Command (USASOC) Classified Archives, Fort Bragg, North Carolina.

13. U.S. Army, "A-1/5th SFG(A) Operation Enduring Freedom Roll-Up, 15 December 01–15 February 02," A Company, 1st Battalion, 5th Special Forces Group (SFG), Fort Campbell, Kentucky, slide presentation, 8 July 2002, copy in USASOC Classified Archives, Fort Bragg.

14. SFC Nathan R. Chapman was a member of the 1st SFG based at Fort Lewis, Washington, and was on an assignment supporting the 5th SFG in Afghanistan. U.S. forces named the runway and its base "Chapman Field" in his memory. Gene Johnson, "Green Beret is Laid to Rest," *The Seattle Times*, 12 January 2002.

15. The quick-reaction force that flew to the crash site on board the MH-47 helicopters included U.S. Army Special Forces medics and a radio operator, and U.S. Navy special operations personnel. Steve Vogel and Marc Kaufman, "Helicopter Accident Kills 2 Marines in Afghanistan," *Washington Post*, 22 January 2002, 8; Tony Perry, "Pilots Helped Save Crew, Marines Say," *Los Angeles Times*, 23 January 2002.

16. Daniel Pearl and Scott Neuman, "U.S. May Beef Up Pakistan Border Force, Cutting Off Exit Route of *Taliban* Soldiers," *Wall Street Journal*, 4 December 2001; John Pomfret, "Fleeing Fighters Meet Some Resistance at Porous Border," *Washington Post*, 10 December 2001, 1; Willis Witter, "Pakistan Moves to Foil Escapes at Border," *Washington Times*, 11 December 2001; Douglas Frantz, "Pakistan Sends Troops to Border to Bar Bin Laden's Escape

From Tora Bora," *New York Times*, 12 December 2001; Arnaud de Borchgrave, "Holes Found in Pakistan's 'Sealed' Border," *Washington Times*, 18 December 2001.

17. Peter Foster, "Face-Saving Mission to Keep the Peace Among Warlords," *London Daily Telegraph*, 27 December 2001; Karen DeYoung, "$9 Billion Afghan Aid Outlined," *Washington Post*, 26 December 2001; Carlotta Gail, "As Afghans Return Home, Need for Food Intensifies," *New York Times*, 26 December 2001; Marc Kaufman, "Massive Food Delivery Averts Afghan Famine," *Washington Post*, 31 December 2001.

18. Scott Peterson, "Special Ops Tackle Aid Mission," *Christian Science Monitor*, 1 March 2002, 1, <http://www.csmonitor.com. 2002/0301/p01s03-wosc.html>; Greg Jaffe, "In Afghan Provinces, a Few GIs Struggle to Bring Aid and Order," *Wall Street Journal*, 28 February 2002, 1; CMH, "Afghan War Chronology," Information Paper, 25 April 2002.

19. Patrick E. Tyler, "Britain Ready to Lead Force for the U.N. After the War," *New York Times*, 12 December 2001; Carola Hoyos, Alexander Nicoll, and Hugh Williamson, "Germany Set to Contribute Up to 1,000 Troops," *London Financial Times*, 12 December 2001, 8; Betsy Pisik, "U.N. Planning Multinational Afghan Force," *Washington Times*, 14 December 2001; T.R. Reid, "Britain Pledges Up to 1,500 Peacekeepers for Afghanistan Force," *Washington Post*, 18 December 2001, 15; Richard Eden, "Britain Flies Out 300 More Soldiers," *London Daily Telegraph*, 27 December 2001.

20. William Patterson, "Civil Affairs Teams Re-Establish Afghan Relief," *ArmyLINK News*, 21 December 2001, <http://www.dtic.mil/armylink/news/Dec2001/a20011221 cateams.html>; CMH, "Afghan War Chronology."

21. CBS News, "60II: Mission Impossible," *CBSNews.com*, 6 February 2002, <http://www.cbsnews. com/stories/2002/02/06/60II/main328444.shtml>; Carol J. Williams, "Afghan Aid Handed Out, With Charges of Favoritism," *Los Angeles Times*, 11 December 2001; Liam Pleven, "U.S. Troops Help Restore Services," *Newsday. com*, 11 December 2001, <http://www.newsday.com/news/nationworld/world/ny-warmaza112505439 dec11. story>; David Zucchino, "Civil Affairs Troops Aim to Win Afghan Hearts, Minds," *Los Angeles Times*, 11 February 2002, <http://www.latimes.com/news/nationworld/world/la-021102civil.story>; Paul Purpura, "N.O. [New Orleans] Group Steadies Afghanistan," *New Orleans Times-Picayune*, 10 February 2002, 27.

22. "Russians Clear Explosives From Kabul, Afghan Tunnel Used by Soviet Troops," *Wall Street Journal.com*, 26 December 2001; Peter Graff, "For Needy Afghans, Light is Coming to End of Tunnel," *Philadelphia Enquirer*, 2 January 2002; "U.S. Aids Humanitarian Shipments," *Milwaukee Journal Sentinel*, 5 December 2001, <http://www. jsonline.com/news/attack/ap/dec01/ap-afghan-reclaimi 120501.asp>; Meg Laughlin, "The Army of Hope," *Herald-Leader* (Lexington, Kentucky), 14 January 2002.

23. Steve Vogel and Bradley Graham, "U.S. Forces Raid *Taliban* Compounds," *Washington Post*, 25 January 2002, 1; Eric Schmitt with Todd S. Purdum, "U.S. Forces Strike *Taliban* at Camps Near Kandahar, *New York Times*, 25 January 2002; John Hendren, "U.S. Raids Afghan Site, Seizes 27 *Taliban* Fighters," *Los Angeles Times*, 25 January 2002; Chip Cummins, "U.S. Troops Raid Two *Taliban* Compounds, Face Continued Resistance in Afghanistan," *Wall Street Journal*, 25 January 2002; U.S. Army, "A-1/5th SFG (A) Operation Enduring Freedom Roll-Up, 15 December 01-15 February 02," A Company, 1st Battalion, 5th SFG, Fort Campbell, slide presentation, 8 July 2002, copy in USASOC Classified Archives, Fort Bragg.

24. "Afghan Villagers Say Raid Claimed Innocent Victims," *Washington Post*, 28 January 2002, 13; Ellen Knickmeyer, "Afghan Officials Seek Release of Detainees Captured in U.S. Raid," *Boston Globe*, 29 January 2002, <http://www.boston.com/news/daily/29/attacks_afghanistan.htm>; "Afghans Protest Special Forces Raid," *Common Dreams*, 30 January 2002, <http://www.commondreams.org/headlines02/0130-03.htm>; "Pentagon Probes Whether Special Forces Raid Went Awry," *Washington Times*, 31 January 2001, 11; John Fullerton, "U.S. Was Mislead in Deadly Raid," *Washington Post*, 31 January 2001, 19; Vernon Loeb and Bradley Graham, "Rumsfeld Say U.S. Raid May Have Killed Allies," *Washington Post*, 5 February 2002, 9; Marc Kaufman and Peter Baker, "U.S. Mistakes Cost Innocent Lives, Afghan Leader Says," *Washington Post*, 6 February 2002, 1.

25. Eric Schmitt, "After January Raid, Gen. Franks Promises to Do Better," *New York Times*, 8 February 2002; Richard T. Cooper, "Rumsfeld Addresses 'Unfortunate' Attack," *Los Angeles Times*, 22 February 2002; U.S. Department of Defense, "DoD New Briefing—Secretary Rumsfeld and GEN Myers," *DefenseLINK*, 21 February 2002, <http://defenselink.mil/news/Feb2002/ t02212002_t0221sd.html>; Eric Schmitt, "Top General Defends Raid in Which 16 Afghans Died," *New York Times*, 26 February 2002. For an earlier example of confusion between friend and foe, see Amy Waldman, "Debate Over U.S. Raid on Convoy Exposes Fluid Loyalties in Area Shaken by War," *New York Times*, 28 December 2001.

26. Tyler Marshall, "U.S. Forces Storm Kandahar Hospital," *Los Angeles Times*, 28 January 2002, 1; Craig S. Smith, "Afghans Kill 6 Who Held Out Inside Hospital," *New York Times*, 29 January 2002, 1; Peter Maass, "A Bul-

letproof Mind," *The New York Times Magazine*, 10 November 2002, 52-57. The *ad hoc* organization of the 5th SFG units in JSOTF-North was evidenced at the Mir Wais Hospital take-down: ODA 524, from the 1st Battalion, took its orders from a company commander from the 3rd Battalion, who in turn reported to the lieutenant colonel commanding the 2nd Battalion.

27. Jonathan Ewing, "Accidents Kill One Soldier, Injure Eight Others in Afghanistan," *ArmyTimes.com*, 13 February 2002, Robert Wall, "War Drains U.S. Military's Aircraft and Munitions," *Aviation Week & Space Technology*, 18 February 2002, 31; CMH, "Afghan War Chronology."

28. Exclusive of SOCEUR's operations, the U.S. Air Force also air-dropped 2.4 million humanitarian rations over Afghanistan between 7 October and 17 December 2001. BG Leslie L. Fuller, 15 April 2002, Fort Bragg, interview with Kalev Sepp, transcripts and tapes at USASOC Classified Archives, Fort Bragg, hereafter referred to as Fuller interview.

29. During this transition period, JSOTF-South was officially redesignated as the "Combined Joint Special Operations Task Force-Afghanistan" (CJSOTF-A). The arriving 3rd SFG headquarters assumed the title from the departing task force. COL John F. Mulholland, 5th SFG, 5 December 2002, Fort Campbell, letter to Kalev Sepp, at USASOC Classified Archives, Fort Bragg.

30. COL John F. Mulholland, 12 July 2002, Fort Campbell, Kentucky, interview with C.H. Briscoe, transcripts and tapes at USASOC Classified Archives, Fort Bragg, hereafter cited as Mulholland interview.

31. U.S. Army, "Coalition Joint Task Force Mountain," Headquarters, 10th Mountain Division, Fort Drum, New York, slide presentation, 5 April 2002, copy in Classified Files, USASOC Classified Archives, Fort Bragg. A well-balanced journalistic overview of the battle is provided by Richard T. Cooper, "Fierce Fight in Afghan Valley Tests U.S. Soldiers and Strategy," *Los Angeles Times*, 24 March 2002, 1.

32. "U.S. General Advises Afghans on Raising Professional Army," *Washington Times*, 19 February 2002, 4; Vernon Loeb, "Franks Supports an Afghan Army," *Washington Post*, 26 February 2002, 16; Bill Gertz, "U.S. General Advocates Afghan Army as Stabilizing Force," *Washington Times*, 26 February 2002, 3; Tim Friend and Elliot Blair Smith, "U.S. Military to Lead Training for Afghanistan's New Army," *USA Today*, 27 February 2002, 9.

33. Philip Smucker, "Split Over British and US-Trained Armies," *London Daily Telegraph*, 26 February 2002; Michael Evans, "Germans Agree to Security Mission," *London Times*, 27 February 2002.

34. Michael Elliott, "The Battle Over Peacekeeping," *Time*, 4 March 2002, 31; Esther Schrader and Greg Miller, "Avowals Aside, U.S.' Afghan Role Has Become That of Peacekeeper," *Los Angeles Times*, 25 February 2002, 1.

35. Mason Arquette (pseudonym), 26 April 2002, Fort Campbell, interview with Kalev Sepp, transcripts and tapes at USASOC Classified Archives, Fort Bragg, hereafter referred to as Arquette interview.

36. Mason Arquette is a pseudonym.

37. Arquette interview, transcripts and tapes at USASOC Classified Archives, Fort Bragg.

38. Approximately 27 Afghan troops fighting alongside ODA 574 were also killed by the bomb blast.

39. Roane; Arquette interview, transcripts and tapes at USASOC Classified Archives, Fort Bragg.

40. Mulholland interview; Glasser, "Al Qaeda Aides Killed in Raids," *Washington Post*, 5 December 2001, 1. Tora Bora is actually the name of a village in a valley in the White Mountains region. In 1996 while in Jalalabad, bin Laden had used the nearby caves on Milawa Mountain. During the fighting the press used the term "Tora Bora" to define the area of the battle.

41. Glasser, "Reputed Bin Laden Hideout Targeted," *Washington Post*, 4 December 2001, 12.

42. Drew Brown, "Opportunity Lost in Tora Bora," *The Kansas City Star*, 13 October 2002, 1; Mulholland interview.

43. CMH, "The Course of Operation ENDURING FREEDOM in Southern and Eastern Afghanistan"; ODA 572, "Lessons Learned, Operation ENDURING FREEDOM," 12 March 2002, USASOC Classified Archives, Fort Bragg; Mulholland interview. Dwayne Torgelson is a pseudonym.

44. *FRONTLINE*: "Campaign Against Terror;" John Kifner and Eric Schmitt, "Fierce Al Qaeda Defense Seen As A Sign of Terror Leader's Proximity," *New York Times*, 14 December 2001, 1. Shannon Whitley is a pseudonym.

45. Glasser, "U.S. Attacks ON Al Qaeda Intensify," *Washington Post*, 10 December 2001, 1.

46. CPT Paul Douglas (pseudonym), ODA 561, 5th SFG, interview with Sepp, 25 April 2002, Fort Campbell, tape recording and notes, USASOC Classified Archives, Fort Bragg.

47. Molly Moore and Susan B. Glasser, "Remnants of Al Qaeda Flee Toward Pakistan," *Washington Post*, 17 December 2001, 1; Moore and Glasser, "Afghan Militias Claim Victory in Tora Bora," *Washington Post*, 18 December 2001, 1; *FRONTLINE*: "Campaign Against Terror." Jeremy Parsons is a pseudonym.

48. Brown, "Opportunity Lost in Tora Bora," 1; *FRONTLINE*: "Campaign Against Terror." Wallace Seifert is a pseudonym.

49. Karl Kramer (pseudonym) and Sylvester Largent (pseudonym), B Company, 5th Battalion, 19th SFG, interview with C.H. Briscoe and David Beech, 9 May 2002, Kandahar, Afghanistan, tape recording and notes, USASOC Classified Archives, Fort Bragg.

50. Ibid.

51. "History," *The Army National Guard*, at <www.arng.army.mil/history>.

52. Adam Fulkerson is a pseudonym.

53. Kip Kupinski and Don Forsythe are pseudonyms.

54. U.S. Army Field Manual (FM) 100-25, *Doctrine for Army Special Operations Forces* (Washington, DC: Department of the Army (DA), 1999), 4-14 and 5-15.

55. Daniel Fitzgerald, Adam Fulkerson, and Jesus Martinez are pseudonyms. "Rakkasan" is the nickname for the 187th Infantry Regiment that comprises the 3rd Brigade, 101st Airborne Division. During the occupation of Japan after World War II, the Japanese gave the regiment the name "Rakkasans" which loosely translates as "falling umbrellas."

56. Thomas Barrington, Wilfred Chandler, and Dwayne Jackman (all pseudonyms), C Company, 112th Signal Battalion, Fort Bragg, interview with James Schroder, 10 May 2002, Kandahar, Afghanistan, USASOC Classified Archives, Fort Bragg.

57. "Civil Affairs Humanitarian Assessment of Bamian Region, Hazarajat, Afghanistan, 09-18 Dec 01," C Company, 96th Civil Affairs (CA) Battalion, 28 December 01, USASOC Classified Archives, Fort Bragg; John Bowman, James McLemore, and Charles Walters are pseudonyms.

58. "Civil Affairs Humanitarian Assessment of Taloqan-Konduz, Afghanistan 19-25 Dec 01," C Company, 96th CA Battalion, 1 January 2002; "Operational Summary of C Company, 96th CA Battalion Deployment in Support of ENDURING FREEDOM (24 September 2001-31 March 2002," C Company, 96th CA Battalion (Airborne), 4 April 2002, 6, USASOC Classified Archives, Fort Bragg.

59. Ibid., 3-4; "Civil Affairs Humanitarian Assessment of Herat Region, Afghanistan 01-12 Jan 02," Company C, 96th CA Battalion, 12 January 2002, 1-2, USASOC Classified Archives, Fort Bragg. Chuck Allison is a pseudonym.

60. "Operational Summary of C Company," 4, USASOC Classified Archives, Fort Bragg.

61. Ibid., 6.

62. Ibid., 3; SFC Mark Patterson (pseudonym), CAT-A36 Team Sergeant, Company C, 96th CA Battalion, 1 October 2002, Fort Bragg, notes, USASOC Classified Archives, Fort Bragg; LTC John Olanski (pseudonym) and LTC Tim Marks (pseudonym), CJCMOTF, 30 September 2002, Fort Bragg, tape recording and notes, USASOC Classified Archives, Fort Bragg.

63. U.S. Army FM 41-10, *Civil Affairs Operations* (Washington, DC: Headquarters, DA, February 2000), 1-8, 1-9, 2-2.

64. Patrick Cockburn, "British Charity's Effort to Clear Tunnel Leads Way for Aid Projects," at <http://news.independent.co.uk/world/asia/_china/story.jsp?story=110493>.

65. Silas Greene (pseudonym), CAT-A41, 96th CA Battalion, interview with Sepp, 28 August 2002, Fort Bragg, tape recording and notes, USASOC Classified Archives, Fort Bragg, hereafter referred to as Greene interview. Gray Jaffe is a pseudonym.

66. U.S. Agency for International Development, "Central Asia Region—Complex Emergency Fact Sheet #43 (FY 2002), 14 January 2002; "Central Asia Region—Complex Emergency Fact Sheet #16 (FY 2002), 18 January 2002.

67. Bart Schuyler is a pseudonym. Marc Kaufman, "Hundreds Are Rescued After Afghan Avalanche," *Washington Post*, 8 February 2002, 18.

68. Silas Greene, Roger McDonald, Bart Schulyer, and Lyle Canberra are pseudonyms.

69. Greene interview, USASOC Classified Archives, Fort Bragg.

70. Silas Greene, Roger McDonald, and Bart Schulyer (pseudonyms), 5 April 2002, Fort Bragg, interview with Kalev Sepp, transcripts and tapes at USASOC Classified Archives, Fort Bragg.

71. Ibid.

72. Ibid.

73. Ibid.

74. Ibid.

75. Ibid.

76. Ibid.

77. CENTCOM update, <http://www.centcom.mil/operations/Enduring_Freedom/Updates/efupdatejan20. htm>.

78. Stan Rauch (pseudonym), HHC, 2nd Battalion, 160th Special Operations Aviation Regiment, interview with James Schroder, 25 April 2002, Fort Campbell, tape recording and notes, USASOC Classified Archives, Fort Bragg, hereafter referred to as Rauch interview.

79. Tony Perry, "Soil-Clogged Engines Blamed for Fatal Afghan Helicopter Crash," *The Los Angeles Times*, 7 August 2002.

80. Rauch interview, USASOC Classified Archives, Fort Bragg.

81. Pseudonym.

82. Pseudonyms.

83. Rauch interview, USASOC Classified Archives, Fort Bragg.

84. John Gates (pseudonym), Company B, 2nd Battalion, 160th Special Operations Aviation Regiment, interview with James Schroder, 25 March 2002, Fort Campbell, tape recording and notes, USASOC Classified Archives, Fort Bragg, hereafter referred to as Gates interview.

85. Pseudonym.

86. Charles Lafayette (pseudonym), HHC, 160th Special Operations Aviation Regiment, interview with James Schroder, 22 April 2002, Fort Campbell, tape recording and notes, USASOC Classified Archives, Fort Bragg.

87. Gates interview, USASOC Classified Archives, Fort Bragg.

88. Ibid.

89. Kerry Regent (pseudonym), HHC, 160th Special Operations Aviation Regiment, interview with Schroder, 25 April 2002, Fort Campbell, tape recording and notes, USASOC Classified Archives, Fort Bragg.

90. Gates interview.

91. Ibid.

92. Doug Anton, Mel Pierce, Don Forsyth, Jack Kittridge, Mike Huffman, and Jim Hall are pseudonyms.

93. Doug Anton, 11 July 2002, Fort Campbell, interview with Kalev Sepp, transcripts and tapes at USASOC Classified Archives, Fort Bragg, hereafter referred to as Anton interview.

94. Ibid.

95. B Company, 1st Battalion, 5th SFG After Action Report: Mir Wais Hospital dated 29 January 2002, provided by SFC Robert Staunton (pseudonym) in USASOC Classified Archives, Fort Bragg.

96. Anton interview, USASOC Classified Archives, Fort Bragg.

97. Ibid.

98. Ibid.

99. Ibid.; Khan Mohammed was the new military commander of Kandahar, serving under Sherzai, the returned governor of the city and province.

100. "Medevac" is the abbreviation for medical evacuation.

101. Anton interview, USASOC Classified Archives, Fort Bragg.

102. Ibid.; B Company, 1st Battalion, 5th SFG After Action Report: Mir Wais Hospital, dated 22 January 2002, USASOC Classified Archives, Fort Bragg.

103. Ibid.

104. CW3 Carl Patterson is a pseudonym.

105. CW2 Aaron is a pseudonym.

106. CW3 Fontaine is a pseudonym.

107. Anton learned that later, the two explosive ordnance specialists who helped blast through the corridor wall in the hospital were killed in a demolition accident while clearing mines and unexploded ordnance near Kandahar. Anton interview, USASOC Classified Archives, Fort Bragg.

108. COL Mulholland ordered the CA assessment after he received the "mission accomplished" report from A-524. Anton interview, USASOC Classified Archives, Fort Bragg.

109. Jon West and Dwight Ashford (pseudonyms), and ODA 516, 10-11 July 2002, Fort Campbell, interview with Kalev Sepp, USASOC Classified Archives, Fort Bragg, hereafter referred to as West and Ashford interview; Memorandum, "Narrative After-Action Report of Target AQ-048 (Hazar Qadam AQ Leadership Site)," 28 January 2002, copy at USASOC Classified Archives, Fort Bragg.

110. Jon West, Dwight Ashford, Jesse Wilcox, Albert Payle, Jon Hsu, Colin Bermann, and Sterling Jackson are pseudonyms.

111. Ibid.

112. Ibid.

113. CFLCC is pronounced "SIFF-lick."

114. West and Ashford interview, USASOC Classified Archives, Fort Bragg; Memorandum, "Narrative After-Action Report of Target AQ-048."

115. Ibid.

116. Ibid.

117. These modified trucks bristled with five M240 7.62mm machine guns and either an MK-19 40mm grenade launcher or an M-2 12.65mm (.50-caliber) heavy machine gun and carried 15 soldiers. They were benignly called ground mobility vehicles (GMVs).

118. West and Ashford interview, USASOC Classified Archives, Fort Bragg; Memorandum, "Narrative After-Action Report of Target AQ-048."

119. Ibid.

120. The company commander was not informed of the reason for the "mission abort" until his return to Kandahar, because at the landing zone, as per his plan, his force had not set up the satellite antenna needed to communicate with JSOTF-South at Kandahar. Jon West (pseudonym), 10-11 July 2002, Fort Campbell, interview with Kalev Sepp, transcripts and tapes at USASOC Classified Archives, Fort Bragg, hereafter referred to as West interview.

121. The two CH-53 helicopters came from the 26th Marine Expeditionary Unit.

122. This was the first and only mission where any element of A-1-5 flew in U.S. Army Special Operations Chinooks in Afghanistan.

123. West and Ashford interview, USASOC Classified Archives, Fort Bragg; Memorandum, "Narrative After-Action Report of Target AQ-048."

124. Ibid.

125. One of the two drivers was U.S. Navy BM1 Jackson Stirling (pseudonym), one of four Navy explosive ordnance disposal (EOD) specialists attached to West's company. West, Memorandum, "Narrative After-Action Report of Target AQ-048.

126. West and Ashford interview, USASOC Classified Archives, Fort Bragg; Memorandum, "Narrative After-Action Report of Target AQ-048."

127. Ibid.

128. Two other enemy fighters died of their wounds shortly afterward. Four of the detainees were found shackled in leg irons. West and Ashford interview.

129. West and Ashford interview, and Memorandum, "Narrative After-Action Report of Target AQ-048."

130. Fullerton, "U.S. Was Misled in Deadly Raid, Afghans Say," *Washington Post*, 31 January 2002.

131. Schmitt, "After January Raid, Gen. Franks Promises to Do Better," *New York Times*, 8 February 2002. COL Mulholland, 5th SFG commander, later commented on the trade-off between the security and surprise inherent to unilateral action, and the intelligence gained by including local Afghan forces in operations. Mulholland interview.

132. U.S. Department of Defense, "DoD New Briefing – Secretary Rumsfeld and Gen. Myers," *DefenseLINK* (21 February 2002), <http://defenselink.mil/news/Feb2002/t02212002_t0221sd.html>.

133. West interview, USASOC Classified Archives, Fort Bragg.

134. West and Ashford interview, USASOC Classified Archives, Fort Bragg; "AQ002 Overview" by Major David Crist, n.d., Kandahar, Afghanistan, tape recordings and notes at USASOC Classified Archives, Fort Bragg.

135. Ibid.; SFC Rocky Salvadorini is a pseudonym.

136. CPT Brian Acosta, SFC Steve Robinson, SGT Nolan Ward, SGT Mitchell Dennison, SP4 Ike Monroe, and SP4 Dale Stevenson (pseudonyms), TPD 910, A Company, 9th Psychological Operations (PSYOP) Battalion, interviews by C.H. Briscoe and James Schroder, 8 May 2002, Kandahar, Afghanistan, and SSG Morgan, 26 August 2002, Fort Bragg, tape recordings and notes, USASOC Classified Archives, Fort Bragg.

137. MAJ Mike Ryan (pseudonym), commander, C Company, 2nd Battalion, 5th SFG Operational Detachment Bravo 560, 5th SFG, interview by Richard Kiper, 26 April 2002, Fort Campbell, tape recording and notes, USASOC Classified Archives, Fort Bragg, hereafter referred to as Ryan interview.

138. Sultan Shahin, "Islamabad's plan to tame tribal areas," 15 November 2001, <www.jammu-kashmir.com/insights/insight20011201b.html>; *The Constitution of the Islamic Republic of Pakistan*, Part IX, Chapter 3: Tribal Areas, 12 April 1973, <www/[alostamo/prg/pakistan/constitution>.

139. Ryan interview, USASOC Classified Archives, Fort Bragg. Aaron Watson is a pseudonym.

140. "U.S. Ambassador to Pakistan on CNN," Washington File, U.S. Department of State, 7 November 2001, <http://usinfo.state.gov/topical/pol/terror/01110718.htm>; LTC James Karnes (pseudonym), U.S. Army John F. Kennedy Special Warfare Center and School (SWCS), interviews by Richard Kiper, 19 and 21 August 2001, Fort Bragg, tape recording, USASOC Classified Archives, Fort Bragg, hereafter referred to as Karnes interview; Edward

Cody and Kamran Khan, "Al Qaeda Prisoners Stage Revolt in Pakistan," *Washington Post*, 20 December 2001, 1.

141. Ibid.

142. Karnes interview, USASOC Classified Archives, Fort Bragg; Schrader, "POWs Will Go to Base in Cuba," *Los Angeles Times*, 28 December 2001, 1; "U.S. to hold detainees at Guantanamo Bay," <www.cnn.com/2001/US/12/27/ret.holding.detainees>.

143. Dao, 1; Moniz and Squitieri, 8.

144. CPT Barry Sanford (pseudonym), SFC Sol Sorrenson (pseudonym), SFC Forrest Kilbourne (pseudonym), and SGT Reginald Holloway (pseudonym), D Company, 96th CA Battalion, interview by Richard Kiper, 5 April 2002, Fort Bragg, tape recording and notes, USASOC Classified Archives, Fort Bragg, hereafter cited as Sanford interview.

145. "Fact Sheet: Humanitarian Aid to the Afghan People," U.S. Department of State International Information Programs, 9 October 2001, <http://usinfo.state.gov/topical/pol/terror/01100916.htm>; "The U.S. Commitment to the Afghan People," The White House, Office of the Press Secretary, 19 November 2001, <www.whitehouse.gov/news/releases/2001/11/print/20011110-4.html>.

146. Sanford interview, USASOC Classified Archives, Fort Bragg. Matt DiJurnigan is a pseudonym.

147. Dexter Yates is a pseudonym.

148. The crisis-response element (CRE) was pronounced "Kree."

149. Dexter Yates, 8 May 2002, Kabul, Afghanistan, interview with Kalev Sepp, transcripts and tapes at USASOC Classified Archives, Fort Bragg.

150. Ibid.

151. Twelve Suunto watches with built-in digital barometers were ordered by the deployed teams, because the U.S. Air Force Tactical Air Control Party (TACP) personnel needed to make barometric pressure readings when planning precision-guided bomb attacks. ODA 595 requested the saddles, which were purchased from a tack store in Germany. The saddles were delivered after the detachment obtained four-wheel-drive trucks, which they preferred for transportation. Fuller interview, USASOC Classified Archives, Fort Bragg.

152. Ibid.

153. Ibid.

154. Dennis Steele, "Unconventional Logistics," *Army*, November 2002, 8-10, and Fuller interview.

155. Fuller noted that these funds came out of EUCOM's budget, and were beginning to be reimbursed by CENTCOM six months later. Fuller interview. "During the first part of the Afghanistan campaign, the [21st Theater Army Support Command] was the sole supplier for U.S. military special operations teams and CIA special operating groups in Afghanistan, catering to every need and want made by military special operators or CIA agents in the field. They located and bought . . . specialized batteries, nonmilitary tactical gear, civilian camping gear, mountaineering clothing and special food. . . . By the time the conventional supply system took over, the [21st TASCOM] had bought and shipped nearly 2 million pounds of wheat and 93,000 blankets for humanitarian relief, along with the tons of equipment and supplies to keep the military operation going." Steele, 8-10.

156. Fuller interview, USASOC Classified Archives, Fort Bragg.

157. Jack Sykes (pseudonym), 8 May 2002, Bagram, Afghanistan, interview with Kalev Sepp, transcripts and tapes at USASOC Classified Archives, Fort Bragg, hereafter referred to as Sykes interview.

158. Ibid.

159. Until 9/11 changed their planning calendars, 3rd/20th SF was programmed to send one of its companies to Bosnia in 2002, and conduct Operation TRADEWINDS again in 2003. Jorge Bustillo, 8 May 2002, Bagram, Afghanistan, interview with Kalev Sepp, transcripts and tapes at USASOC Classified Archives, Fort Bragg, hereafter referred to as Bustillo interview.

160. Sykes interview, USASOC Classified Archives, Fort Bragg.

161. Ibid.

162. These transfers were not as difficult as might be anticipated. Other non-SF National Guard units, short of personnel and not under the same requirements for physical fitness, were eager to get new members. Also, many of the transferred soldiers left with invitations to rejoin their old unit when they could meet the physical testing standards again. Bustillo interview, USASOC Classified Archives, Fort Bragg.

163. Sykes interview, USASOC Classified Archives, Fort Bragg.

164. Justin Pine (pseudonym), 3rd SFG, 10 May 2002, Bagram, interview with Kalev Sepp, transcripts and tapes in USASOC Classified Archives, Fort Bragg.

165. MAJ Dalton Carlisle (pseudonym) and SGM Geoff Beckwith (pseudonym), B Company, 2nd Battalion, 3rd SFG, interview with Briscoe and Beach, 2 May 2002, Camp Snoopy, Qatar, tape recording and notes, USASOC

Classified Archives, Fort Bragg. Julian McGinnis and Dwight Ashford are pseudonyms.

166. Ibid.

167. Akmed Astor is a pseudonym. SGT Akmed Astor, 8th PSYOP Battalion, interview by SSG Patricia Johnston, 6 June 2002, Fort Bragg, tape recording and notes, USASOC Classified Archives, Fort Bragg, hereafter referred to as Astor interview.

168. Mohammed Osterman is a pseudonym.

169.

170. Ibid.

171. Ibid.

172. Jason Lafayette (pseudonym), MST, B Company, 528th Support Battalion, Special Operations Support Command, interview with James Schroder, 10 May 2002, Kandahar, Afghanistan, tape recording and notes, USASOC Classified Archives, Fort Bragg.

173. Ibid.

174. Ibid.

175. Ibid.

176. Alfred Mann and Jackson Ferrell are pseudonyms; Alfred Mann (pseudonym), HHC, 2nd Battalion, 160th Special Operations Aviation Regiment (Airborne), interview with James Schroder, 25 March 2002, Fort Campbell, tape recording and notes, USASOC Classified Archives, Fort Bragg.

177. Curtis Jameson is a pseudonym.

178. James Brinks is a pseudonym; Jackson Ferrell (pseudonym), B Company, 2nd Battalion, 160th Special Operations Aviation Regiment (Airborne), interview with James Schroder, 22 April 2002, Fort Campbell, tape recording and notes, USASOC Classified Archives, Fort Bragg.

179. Silas Greene and Karl Jurgens are pseudonyms. The Khowst airfield was a dirt runway almost 8,000 feet long built by the Red army during the Soviet war in Afghanistan. The U.S. forces named the runway Chapman Field in memory of SFC Nate Chapman, the first U.S. Special Forces soldier to be killed by hostile fire during the American expedition. P.W.B., 26 April 2002, Fort Campbell, interview with Kalev Sepp, transcripts and tapes at USASOC Classified Archives, Fort Bragg.

180. A U.S. Air Force Special Operations Combat Control Team (CCT) is "A team of Air Force personnel organized, trained, and equipped to conduct and support special operations. Under clandestine, covert, or low-visibility conditions, these teams establish and control air assault zones; assist aircraft by verbal control, positioning, and operating navigation aids; conduct limited offensive direct action and special reconnaissance operations; and assist in the insertion and extraction of special operations forces." <http://www.dtic.mil/doctrine/jel/doddict/data/s/04881.html>.

181. Greene interview, USASOC Classified Archives, Fort Bragg.

182. Ibid.

183. Ibid.

184. Ibid., and David A. Duffy, 8 July 2002, Fort Bragg, interview with Kalev Sepp, and 24 September 2002, Riyadh, Saudi Arabia, telephonic interview with Sepp, transcripts and tapes at USASOC Classified Archives, Fort Bragg.

185. Jed Samuels, Terry Sanders, Mickey Hensen, Rudy Madden, Gregg Corr, Max Gorley, Ty McFadden, Marc Lorenzo, Jason Thurman, Jake Millett, Jerry Rawlins, Stefan Morris, and Carl Hooper are pseudonyms. Samuels, et al., 10 May 2002, Bagram Air Base, Afghanistan, interview with Kalev Sepp, tape recording and notes, USASOC Classified Archives, Fort Bragg.

186. Ibid.

187. Ibid. Due to space constraints on transport aircraft, the team's vehicles arrived four days after the team had landed. The ODA personnel traveled on two different aircraft as well.

188. Ibid.

189. Ibid.

Chapter 5

The New War

It is not the critic who counts, not the man who points out how the strong man stumbled, or where the doer of deeds could have done better. The credit belongs to the man who is actually in the arena; whose face is marred by the dust and sweat and blood; who knows the great enthusiasms, the great devotions and spends himself in a worthy course; who at the best, knows in the end the triumph of high achievement, and who, at worst, if he fails, at least fails while daring greatly; so that his place shall never be with those cold and timid souls who know neither victory or defeat.[1]

This chapter explains the role of Army Special Operations Forces (ARSOF) during the transformation period of the war in Afghanistan. This period is marked by the U.S. resolve to help the Afghan Interim Authority (AIA) eliminate the remaining pockets of *Taliban* and *al-Qaeda* resistance, to widely distribute humanitarian assistance to the previously repressed citizens of Afghanistan, to organize and prioritize reconstruction efforts, and to shift the control of the war to conventional American forces. By late winter 2001, the U.S.-led coalition had driven the *Taliban* leaders from Kandahar and Kabul, destroyed *al-Qaeda* training camps, and installed Interim President Hamid Karzai. However, *Taliban* and *al-Qaeda* forces had not been totally eliminated; many escaped across the border into Pakistan, others retreated to sympathetic villages, and some simply switched sides.[2]

Responding to the changing face of the war, ARSOF conducted not only unconventional warfare (UW) missions but also foreign internal defense (FID) missions—like UW, an umbrella concept that covered a broad range of activities focused primarily on helping a host government address internal threats and their underlying causes.[3] And CENTCOM's Special Operations Command (SOCCENT) agreed to a rotation plan derived from special operations commanders in theater. Many of the ARSOF units had been in combat zones since the war started and needed a respite and a refit before conducting follow-on missions.

Figure 1. Marching was the "first step" in building a national army.

Figure 2. Equipment issue is the first, and sometimes last, official act for some Army recruits.

During this transition period, the elusive enemy in Afghanistan was sometimes difficult to identify. In this "Wild West" environment, carrying a weapon provided some measure of self-protection and symbolized manhood among the ethnic groups. Once the weapons were issued to many anti-*Taliban* fighters, they vanished into the night, not waiting for the payday that might never come. Groups of bandits roamed the countryside, terrorizing villagers and foreigners alike. More than a handful of journalists were either killed or wounded.[4] On 4 March 2002, Canadian journalist Kathleen Kenna was wounded when dissatisfied Afghan gunmen threw a grenade into the rented vehicle she was sharing with other media personnel. Fortunately for Ms. Kenna, 160th SOAR medic Kerry Zimmer (pseudonym) was at a Special Forces base area just a few kilometers east of Gardez.[5] Zimmer treated her wounds, and once she was stable, Special Forces soldiers arranged for Afghan security forces to accompany the journalists who wanted to attempt another trip into the city. As the group approached the city, the convoy came under mortar and small-arms fire. Everyone abandoned their vehicles until the shelling stopped, and then they returned to the Special Forces base. The SF soldiers offered a larger escort party, but the journalists declined and spent the night in their cars outside the compound in the cold.[6]

Special Forces soldiers routinely came under fire at their base areas. Despite the visible presence of paid Afghan security forces who conscientiously guarded the Americans, enemy fighters were undeterred and fired on soldiers at will. SF soldiers operating in and around the cities and in rural areas never forgot that Afghanistan was still "bad guy" country.

Impacting operations during this period were disputes over the spoils of war by anti-*Taliban* commanders; victorious warlords claimed many rewards, many of which were inconsistent with the newly formed AIA government's goals. Rewards went beyond war booty to control of humanitarian aid and reconstruction priorities. ARSOF commanders shifted their focus to another Special Forces mission, FID. The ODAs of the 5th SFG and 3rd Battalion, 3rd SFG, trained and equipped local tribal militias to provide the interim government with a viable defense force. That training convinced American conventional force leaders that the Afghan militias could have a major role in the upcoming ANACONDA operation.

The offensive into the Shah-i-Khot Valley quickly grew from a Special Forces initiative into a full-scale allied assault based on increased threat estimates. LTG P.T. Mikolashek, Combined Forces Land Component Commander (CFLCC), directed MG Franklin L. "Buster" Hagenbeck,

10th Mountain Division, to take control of the largest contingent of U.S. ground forces to date. COL Frank Wiercinski, 3rd Brigade "Rakkasans," 101st Airborne Division (Air Assault), would command Task Force (TF) Rakkasan, made up of about 1,500 soldiers from his 1st and 2nd Battalions, 187th Infantry, and from 1st Battalion, 87th Infantry, 10th Mountain Division.[7] Two hundred coalition soldiers from Australia, Canada, Denmark, France, Germany, and Norway would conduct reconnaissance.[8] Approximately 900 Afghans under several commanders supported by Special Forces ODAs were to participate.[9] Having worked with the key anti-*Taliban* leaders and their forces, Special Forces elements were critical to synchronizing the assaults of the unconventional Afghan militia forces with the conventional American units in the combined offensive.

Operation ANACONDA allowed sufficient overlap between the 5th SFG ODAs and the 3rd SFG teams to effect a smooth transition with local Afghan military forces and to appreciate the efforts of other ARSOF elements in the area. Before 3rd SFG assumed the CJSOTF mantle, LTC Terry Sanders (pseudonym), 3rd Battalion, 3rd SFG, was assigned to CJSOTF-South (TF Kabar) commanded by Commodore Robert Harward. The "Third of the Third" ODAs performed a variety of missions during ANACONDA while assuming the 5th SFG missions in southern Afghanistan. The 5th SFG returned to the United States at the conclusion of ANACONDA, and JSOTF-North (TF Dagger) at K2, Uzbekistan, stood down. There was a short period when CJSOTF-South (TF Kabar) served as the CJSOTF-Afghanistan, thus controlling all Army and coalition SOF in country. The 3rd Battalion, 3rd SFG teams continued to provide high-quality training and emergency medical care as they established good, solid rapport with the Afghan forces.

During the final stages of Operation ANACONDA, the 3rd SFG advance echelon (ADVON) worked feverishly to ensure that communications, automation, and infrastructure were established to assume the new CJSOTF-Afghanistan mission. During March 2002, 3rd SFG soldiers built the headquarters at Bagram with the assistance of contracted Afghan labor. COL Mark Phelan organized his operations, support, and signal centers for efficiency while fully integrating the coalition forces into the command, notably making a New Zealander his deputy commander.[10] Phelan continued the transition from UW to FID. Capitalizing on the coalition forces' capabilities to broaden the special reconnaissance (SR) aspect associated with identifying and confirming *Taliban* and *al-Qaeda* activity in the border provinces, Phelan expanded the hunt. However, the most important mission for the CJSOTF commander was to establish the Kabul Military Academy as a training center for the national Afghan army. A national army was a vital element of the AIA government plan for security and credibility.

Army National Guard (ARNG) Special Forces units entered Afghanistan in late February 2002, after a brief stay at K2. The Special Forces ODAs from the 5th Battalion, 19th SFG arrived in mid-February at K2 and were integrated into the Special Forces campaign plan, initially to replace rotating 5th SFG teams. On 1 March, ODAs from B Company, 5th Battalion, 19th SFG, replaced the 5th SFG Special Operations Command and Control Element (SOCCE) at Kandahar Airport, the location of the 3rd Brigade "Rakkasans," 101st Airborne Division. ODA 981 conducted operations in the surrounding areas, coordinated Special Forces activities with the 101st, and supported the Special Forces operating base in Kandahar. 19th SFG was initially assigned to JSOTF-South during March before coming under 3rd SFG at Bagram on 1 April 2002. Later in March, ODAs from the 2nd Battalion, 19th SFG arrived at K2 to assume control of the Special Forces facilities there. In late April 2002, ODA 923 and ODA 966 relocated to Bagram to conduct sensitive site exploitation (SSE) missions, reconnoiter landing zones (LZs) for future humanitarian support, and search for burial sites and weapons caches in the Tora Bora region.[11]

B Company, 3rd Battalion, 160th SOAR, at Kandahar Airport assumed the Chinook mission from 2nd Battalion, 160th SOAR, at the end of Operation ANACONDA, and by 31 March, it was task organized under the Joint Special Operations Air Component–South (JSOAC-South). Just after its arrival at Kandahar, the 3rd Battalion Night Stalkers were called to Bagram to assist with the rescue effort on Takur Ghar during Operation ANACONDA. Afterward, the combat losses of 2nd Battalion MH-47Es—one destroyed and two battle damaged—led to a joint effort by both Chinook units to meet the constant ARSOF aviation mission.

When JSOAC-South relocated its headquarters and Air Force special operations aircraft to Masirah Island, Oman, and Qatar, the 3rd Battalion, based at Kandahar, picked up most of the CJSOTF-Afghanistan missions in support of coalition forces that were split.[12] This was significantly different from the joint basing of JSOTF-North and the JSOAC at K2. Despite having to request air assets through the JSOAC on Masirah Island, the coalition units, more familiar with a very structured system, quickly adapted to the formal procedures and received ample support for their missions.[13]

The CA rotation plan brought many more Army reservists into the war for longer durations than the single active duty unit. The 489th CAB from Knoxville, Kentucky, eventually replaced the 96th CAB. Through the spring, soldiers from the 96th and 489th CABs increased local support, managed humanitarian efforts across Afghanistan, and effected well-coordinated handoffs between units. The CAT-A personnel, looking like relief workers with beards and in civilian clothing, negotiated with local Afghans on humanitarian projects that ranged from rebuilding schools to providing electric generators and digging wells to rebuilding agriculture irrigation canals. The civil-military goal was to identify projects that would have an immediate impact but would not compete with those projects the NGOs were working. The CA teams in the field, having unparalleled hands-on contact with ordinary Afghans, provided the catalyst necessary to stimulate national recovery. Military personnel wearing civilian clothing was a continuing "bone of contention" for many relief agencies, despite the absence of problems.[14]

PSYOP reservists also entered the war, and with the arrival of the 3rd SFG, COL Phelan stressed the integration of these force multipliers. Tactical PSYOP teams (TPTs) provided continuity in the region and shared assessments on the Afghan population's state of mind. While many ODA commanders, unfamiliar with PSYOP capabilities and their "value added," were reluctant to integrate the tactical elements with their teams because they had never trained together, eventually, they were won over. CPT Brian Acosta (pseudonym), PSYOP detachment commander, was able to integrate PSYOP objectives into the campaign plan, and Phelan pushed direct coordination with ODA commanders.[15]

During spring 2002, Special Operations Media Systems–Broadcast (SOMS-B) teams capitalized on the radio listening culture to influence the Afghan population's attitude toward U.S. and coalition forces. Through the work of CA teams that coordinated with Afghan radio stations in Khowst, Kabul, and Kandahar, messages and music tapes were accepted, integrated, and broadcast by local announcers. By 1 April, 66 soldiers of the 345th PSYOP Company

(Airborne), San Antonio, Texas, had assumed the tactical PSYOP efforts for noncombatant humanitarian and stability operations. In April, the SOMS-B was broadcasting health messages about endemic diseases to support CA medical awareness campaigns in Afghanistan.[16]

The Kabul Military Academy began training the first recruits for the Afghan National Army (ANA) on 1 May 2002. The mission of 1st Battalion, 3rd SFG was to train and organize an ethnically diverse national army. The ODAs from the First of the Third were to train nine 600-man infantry battalions and six 300-man border guard battalions within 10 months. The biggest challenge for the Special Forces, besides three distinct languages, no Afghan understanding of teamwork, and age-old tribal rivalries and hatred, was to reduce the inculcated tribal norms sufficiently to develop a national sense of unity. In the process, Special Forces troops worked to help Afghan recruits understand individual and unit relationships and responsibilities to a higher command and to embrace the lawful government of Afghanistan. When new recruits arrived without weapons or equipment, captured *Taliban* and *al-Qaeda* weapons were issued. Training ammunition for predominantly Soviet weapons came from the same source.

Figure 3. ANA officers course begins at Kabul Military Academy.

CJSOTF-Afghanistan took charge of Army special operations and coalition forces in Afghanistan on 31 March and pushed forward. As the war transitioned to its next phase, Phelan capitalized on CA and PSYOP units to help the interim government bring some stability to the country and humanitarian relief to the Afghan people. For as long as the United States remains committed to the Karzai government, ARSOF will continue to play a vital role in the stability of the region and present a powerful deterrent to enemy insurgency.

Army special operations soldier stories related to the developing fight in the Shah-i-Khot Valley will be chronologically integrated into the general narrative. In late January 2002, ODA 594, while conducting combat reconnaissance in the vicinity of Zurmat and Terghul Ghar Mountain in the Shah-i-Khot Valley, was warned by its Afghan security not to proceed any farther. The local villagers reported that groups of *Taliban* and *al-Qaeda* were concentrating in the valley. Based on ODA 594's report, JSOTF-North focused intelligence collection on the area. By mid-February, the K2 intelligence analysts had collected and studied data from a variety of sources, particularly human intelligence (HUMINT), to surmise that *al-Qaeda* were probably reorganizing, refitting, and preparing for a counteroffensive. Initial estimates were low—150 to 200 fighters.

Figure 4. Terrain models for officer tactical training.

The Shah-i-Khot Valley in Paktia Province encompasses an area of roughly 60 square miles between Gardez, Khowst, and Orgun. The valley begins near the flats of Gardez and runs in a southwesterly direction. To the east, a major mountain range, distinguished by steep ridges, caves, and deep ravines, rises to 12,000 feet above sea level. Shah-i-Khot—which means "place of the king"—has been a safe haven for Afghans for more than 2,000 years. The area contains a few main travel routes, traversing the valleys toward Pakistan, but numerous smaller goat paths that animal herders and smugglers used regularly offered additional avenues of escape for small groups. The towns of Serkhankheyl (Sair-khan-kell) and Marzak (Mar-zack), at the southern end of the valley, were thought to be harboring fugitive enemy fighters. The dominating terrain in the area consist-

Figure 5. Focused view of Paktia Province.

ed of a major ridgeline jutting west of the towns, Terghul Ghar, which the U.S. forces referred to as the "Whale" because it reminded many of the dominant terrain feature at the National Training Center (NTC), Fort Irwin, California. Takur Ghar, a high mountain peak south of the towns, offered an expansive westward view of the valley. The mountainous region was classic guerrilla terrain—easily defendable, controlled access, numerous routes of escape, and near a sympathetic border.

As the JSOTF-North staff continued to gather intelligence from all sources to develop the situation, the lessons learned from the Tora Bora operations were integrated into the analysis. As the threat estimate grew larger, COL John Mulholland, who had scrutinized the mountainous terrain, recognized that a deliberate attack against a well-entrenched enemy force exceeded the capabilities of his task force to plan and execute. Intelligence indicated that these gathering fighters would not follow the Tora Bora scenario.

Having discussed his concerns with MG Hagenbeck, commander, 10th Mountain Division, COL Mulholland arranged to brief the concept of the operation to LTG Mikolashek, the

CFLCC, at Bagram. Senior representatives from every joint and conventional headquarters in theater, as well as the coalition force commanders, attended the briefing. Mikolashek directed 10th Mountain Division to take the lead for planning and execution. JSOTF-North was to be heavily involved throughout. JSOTF-South was to develop the SR plan for the operation.

The center of gravity for planning became Bagram Air Base. COL Mulholland set up a small tactical operations center (TOC), JSOTF-North (Forward), next to the TF Mountain TOC. Almost simultaneously, LTC Terry Sanders, 3rd Battalion, 3rd SFG, charged with developing the SR mission for JSOTF-South, left Kandahar to establish a planning cell at Bagram.[17] SR teams were to maintain 24-hour surveillance of major escape routes and direct close air support (CAS) against escaping enemy forces as well as serve as early warning of reinforcing elements.[18] Coalition units from Australia, Denmark, France, Germany, and Norway totaled another 200 troops.[19] Army Special

Figure 6. Bagram Air Base becomes the "center of the universe."

Forces that had trained and equipped several Afghan forces would accompany about 900 fighters charged with launching the offensive operation.[20]

The urgency to get ANACONDA under way did not allow the intelligence picture to fully develop in the Shah-i-Khot. COL Mulholland consistently voiced his concerns that intelligence sources underestimated the strength and disposition of *al-Qaeda* and *Taliban* forces in the valley and nearby mountains. "I knew in my gut that there were more than a few hundred," said the 5th SFG commander.[21] It was most important to have eyes on the targets well in advance of the main assaults into the valley area. That was the purpose of well-positioned SR teams.

But precipitous terrain limited helicopter LZ choices, and a rash of bad weather delayed insertion of the SR teams until just two days before. Still, for more than a week, coalition planners joined CW3 Arthur Solanis (pseudonym), the 160th SOAR flight lead, in the "Coalition Café" to scour map sheets and photo imagery for LZs to insert more than 25 SR teams. The LZs had to be tenable, afford good reconnaissance, and cover the identified escape routes, or "ratlines," into Pakistan.[22] In retrospect, the most reliable intelligence picture came from earlier reconnaissance reports that ODA 594 had submitted.

Operation ANACONDA's main effort was to be TF Hammer, an Afghan force comprised of three local militias led by Commander Zia, being supported by LTC Carl Hooper (pseudonym)and two Special Forces ODAs.[23] Commander Lodi, an old *mujahideen* warrior, had appointed Zia as his successor to command his 500- to 600-man force that ODA 594 and ODA 372 had trained, organized, and equipped to conduct combat operations in the Gardez region. The Special Forces teams regarded Zia's own 300-plus Afghans as "Tier One Pashtuns" because of their willingness to learn and to be trained to follow directions, and because they had a strong desire to kill *al-Qaeda* and *Taliban* members. According to the American plan, Zia's forces were to move south from Gardez in a mounted formation and swing west to attack toward Terghul Ghar from west to east. Two other Afghan forces, labeled TF Anvil, would establish outer ring positions on the east and south to block escape routes into Pakistan. The 300 to 500 Afghan fighters of Zakim Khan from Orgun, supported by ODA 542 and ODA 381, would establish the southerly blocking positions. The 500 Afghan fighters of Kamel Khan from Khowst, supported by ODA 571 and ODA 392, would block on the eastern side of the outer ring.

To support the main Afghan attack from the west, U.S. light infantry forces from TF Rakkasan were to air assault into an inner ring of blocking positions on the eastern side of the valley floor. The objective was to hit the enemy (believed to be sequestered in Serkhankheyl and Marzak) with a swift and forceful attack, killing or capturing him, and to force the others to run into the blocking positions. As allied troops were massed at Bagram to support ANACONDA, the American force presence quadrupled in less than 10 days, thereby eliminating any element of surprise. The operation was to begin at dawn on 27 February, but heavy snowfall on the 26th delayed the start for two days.

Having established solid relationships with key anti-*Taliban* forces after living and fighting with them for months, Special Forces teams were critical to synchronizing the Afghan part of the combined offensive in the Shah-i-Khot Valley. The day before the operation began ODA 542 and ODA 381 had accompanied Zakim Khan's 300 to 500 Afghans from Orgun into their blocking positions in the Naka Valley. From the village of Zerok, Zakim Khan's forces conducted mounted reconnaissance patrols, established observation posts (OPs), and manned security checkpoints around the Naka Valley. On the same day in the east, ODA 571 and ODA 392 assisted Kamel Khan's movement from Khowst into the Shimal Valley.[24]

This basic summary of preparatory activities for Operation ANACONDA explains what was supposed to be happening. The next vignette will explain the Special Forces' role with the Afghan force; amplify the difficulties they encountered; and clarify some confusion about what the Americans expected, what support was promised, and what happened when conventional forces encountered resistance. The "fog of war" at the beginning of ANACONDA was almost impenetrable.

Entering the Valley

Special Forces ODA 372, along with the other detachments in 3rd Battalion, 3rd SFG, was preparing for a training exercise in Africa when the United States was attacked by terrorists on 9/11. There was speculation that it might be diverted to Afghanistan when the company headquarters moved to Kuwait in early December. But Three-Seven-Two stayed behind to provide future operations planners for the operations staff at battalion and to support the Special Forces teams overseas until just before Christmas.

CPT Mike McHenry (pseudonym), a former Armor officer turned Special Forces team leader, knew that to plan realistically for missions in Afghanistan he had to establish contact with the 5th SFG headquarters.[25] On 25 January, after flying into Kandahar where the 3rd Battalion's advance party was based, McHenry and ODA 372 flew to K2 to talk with the 5th SFG. Based on discussions with COL Mulholland, their mission was changed from future planning on 7 February to being inserted into the Gardez-Khowst area. The mission, based on six PowerPoint slides, was "to conduct clear and sweep operations, and be prepared to conduct security zone operations," and assist Hazara Afghan leader Commander Zia Lodin. They were assuming ODA 594's missions. Since "clear and sweep" is not a doctrinal term, McHenry was to determine its meaning. The team quickly realized that most of the information they needed would come from the team on the ground, ODA 594. By 17 February, all members of ODA 372 were together in Gardez.

Unbeknownst to McHenry and his team who were planning clear and sweep operations with Commander Zia's forces around Gardez, TF Mountain Commander MG Hagenbeck was planning Operation ANACONDA in the Shah-i-Khot Valley to the south. When ODA 372 and ODA 594 were told that their Afghan forces were to have key roles, another Pashtun leader, Commander Khoshkeyer, brought a company-size force to Gardez to join Zia. For seven days, the two Special Forces teams trained the Afghan forces in offensive tactical maneuvers, movement techniques, and basic first aid and then using 82mm mortars, conducted company live-fire exercises. Despite not having sights for their mortars, the Hazaras were able to place effective indirect fire rapidly using only their thumbs as aiming devices. The teams also made arrangements to supply the Afghan soldiers with cold-weather clothing and boots, new rifles, and much-needed ammunition.

A third Afghan force commanded by Zia Abdullah was based north of Gardez, but his questionable loyalties posed a dilemma. Animosity among Hazaras, Pashtuns, Zia Abdullah's men, and the Gardez shura made for a tense situation.[26] While Commander Khoshkeyer had agreed to be subordinate to Zia Lodin, the arrangements remained tenuous.

Command among the Afghans was not the only leadership issue. Which American was in charge of the forces? Although McHenry was senior to CPT Gary Towson (pseudonym) of ODA 594, neither team had been put in charge. To further compound the issue, the two Special Forces ODAs were from different SFGs. Because Towson had more experience in Afghanistan and had also established a close working relationship with Zia, the two captains mutually agreed that Towson should be in charge of operations. McHenry and ODA 372 concentrated on building rapport with Khoshkeyer. When LTC Hooper, commander, 2nd Battalion, 5th SFG, arrived, the command relationships were further obfuscated.[27]

In December 2001, ODA 594 had entered the northern end of Shah-i-Khot Valley near Gardez. Having been warned not to proceed farther by their Afghan security force, the Special Forces team was convinced that there were *Taliban* and *al-Qaeda* forces in the valley. After his arrival, Hooper had directed McHenry and Towson to develop a concept whereby the two teams could use their Afghan forces to attack the enemy. Conventional forces would be involved, but Hooper could not tell them the extent of that involvement, only that the Afghans were to be the main effort.

The plan presented to Hooper factored in the tense relations between the Afghan forces in Gardez. The combined force would leave Gardez together, moving west of the terrain feature known as the "Whale" and, at the town of Surki, swing north into the valley. An Afghan force under the command of CW2 Stanley Harriman (ODA 372) would place a blocking position on the northern pass into the valley. Three Special Forces soldiers from ODA 372 plus a few Afghans would establish an OP to bring close air support (CAS) onto the enemy. The main effort would be made by Zia and Khoshkeyer supported by most of the two ODAs. At the southern entrance of the valley, McHenry (ODA 372) would emplace the 82mm mortars to cover the main attack (Towson and ODA 594) toward the final objectives—four small villages in the valley. The forces of Zia Abdullah would establish checkpoints on roads leading into the area, guard the outer perimeter of the Gardez SF base, and reinforce Harriman at the northern blocking position.

283

Coalition forces and other Special Forces teams would establish long-range OPs in the mountains south of Surki, covering the potential escape corridors or ratlines. An Australian liaison officer would accompany McHenry (ODA 372) to keep the OPs abreast of the American and Afghan locations. American conventional infantry forces were to airland via helicopters behind the Afghan Military Forces (AMF). If the AMF encountered resistance beyond its capability, the conventional infantry force would pass through it to continue the attack and defeat the enemy. The American conventional forces would also exploit gains the AMF made. Hooper approved the concept.

In late February, CPTs McHenry and Towson flew to Bagram to be briefed on the special operations part of Operation ANACONDA. Both officers became concerned when they learned that TF Rakkasan troops would land just short of the main objectives rather than behind the Afghan force as they had suggested. Now the ODAs and Afghans would attack toward the American forces, engaging enemy forces between them. The possibility of a firefight between the forces was great. 101st Airborne and 10th Mountain soldiers had no means of identifying friendly Afghans from the enemy. According-

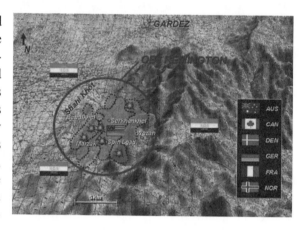

Figure 7. Coalition view of Operation ANACONDA.

ing to McHenry, the decision had been made, and no changes would be made. The operation used standing operating procedures (SOPs) of American conventional forces and followed the NTC timetable of events for a deliberate attack. Afghan forces were not attuned to this level of coordination and a very structured sequence of events. After the TF Mountain briefing, the two ODA commanders were concerned about the Afghan role in this combined operation. The AMF was still labeled as the main effort, but how the operation was to be executed (paragraph three of the five-paragraph Army standard operation order format) appeared contradictory. Both saw disaster looming on the horizon.

McHenry (ODA 372) and Towson (ODA 594) afterward returned to Gardez and briefed their teams and Commanders Zia and Khoshkeyer. Both Special Forces commanders knew they could do nothing to prevent the American conventional forces from firing on friendly Afghans during the heat of battle. They could, however, prevent the AMF from firing on the infantrymen of TF Rakkasan. Since most of the Afghans had never seen an American soldier wearing his standard combat gear—helmet, armored vest, load-bearing equipment, and rucksack—the two Special Forces commanders took advantage of the Army engineer squad collocated at their base. They had one of the combat engineers dress in his full combat gear and then took him around to all the Afghan encampments. They literally used the young American soldier as a "live training aid" to show the Afghans what a fully equipped conventional Army fighting man looked like. Satisfied that they had done all they could to prevent friendly casualties at their level, the soldiers prepared for the upcoming battle.

Field Expedient Triage

Early on the morning of 2 March, Commander Zia Loden's forces departed Gardez in a large column of 39 vehicles of various sizes and condition. CPT Towson understood that he was in command, although LTC Hooper accompanied the force. Although done under the cover of darkness, the moon was nearly full, providing 95-percent illumination. Still, the mounted column carrying 450 fighters experienced problems from the start. Concern for operations security (OPSEC) prevented the ODAs from reconnoitering the road before leaving. The American attempt to enforce vehicle light discipline failed completely; the Afghans were unfamiliar with and thoroughly uncomfortable driving at night with their headlights off. Concessions that every other truck could use lights were ignored. When a truck broke down, troops had to be crammed aboard other crowded vehicles.

Snow and rain had wreaked havoc on the unimproved dirt tracks that the column was forced to follow through rough terrain, skirting the valley to the west. The Afghan column was not a military convoy. "It was like trying to herd cats. If a truck slowed down, stopped, or got stuck in the mud, those behind would attempt to pass," said one Special Forces soldier.

In the midst of the controlled chaos, a large Ginga truck carrying 30 to 40 soldiers slid off the humped dirt track and tipped over, spilling troops everywhere. That element of the column halted, and the call went out for the Special Forces medics. Having few radios, the vehicles ahead continued off into the darkness. When SFC Bill Athens (pseudonym), the 3rd Battalion, 3rd SFG, senior medic traveling in the trail vehicle, finally reached the accident site, it looked like a surreal mass-casualty exercise.[28] There seemed to be about 30 or 40 Afghans laying around on the cold, wet ground moaning and groaning. Based on experience, Athens calculated that only 10 percent were really injured and required medical treatment.

As SFC Athens said later, "Totally bewildered by the scene but having a moment of brilliance, I grabbed the nearest interpreter and told him to yell as loud as he could, 'Anybody who is wounded, get on the other trucks now!!' There was a flurry of movement among the Afghan bodies on the ground as the 'wounded' leaped up and scrambled aboard the other trucks. When that group cleared out, I saw about 12 still lying on the ground. Having accomplished my 'field expedient triage,' we (the other medics and me) could focus on the seriously injured left on the ground."

Between the trucks stuck in the mud, broken-down vehicles, the wrecked Ginga truck, and vehicles diverted to carry injured soldiers back to Gardez, the mounted column evolved into a walking and rolling force that slowly moved toward its attack position. Now, with soldiers walking, for safety and to meet the established time to be in the attack position, the convoy turned on all headlights, thus alerting any *Taliban* or *al-Qaeda* sympathizers or the enemy force. At Surki, CW2 Harriman (ODA 372) and his force split off from the main body and headed northeast to the blocking position north of little Terghul Ghar ("Little Whale") mountain.

Disaster and Frustration

Disaster did not wait long before striking in the night. As the Harriman convoy moved northeast, an Air Force AC-130 Spectre gunship, circling above on station to provide CAS, mistakenly fired a 40mm cannon burst into the column. CW2 Harriman and two Afghans were killed instantly in the lead HMMWV.[29] Two other Americans and 13 Afghans were seriously wounded.[30] The surprise attack on the column was initially reported as an enemy mortar ambush. Fortunately for all concerned, frantic American calls after the initial barrage stopped the AC-130 from continuing its attack. Now the main column was delayed as McHenry and Towson tried to deal with the emergency. Medical evacuation was needed for the Harriman column. The CAS capability from the northern OP was now gone. Since the ODA commanders were separated in the now-divided main column, McHenry (ODA 372) and LTC Hooper thought Towson (ODA 594) had gone to the scene. He had not, and suddenly several Americans were giving orders to the disjointed column. The operation had quickly become very complicated amid the confusion.

After dealing with the Harriman convoy emergency, the column resumed its advance but was behind schedule. The Americans had coordinated 55 minutes of bombing preparation before the attack. That promise and CAS had been key to persuading the Afghans to participate. Expecting a massive allied bombing attack to clobber the enemy as the Americans had done against the *Taliban* in November and December, and then the *al-Qaeda* around Tora Bora, Commander Zia was surprised to observe and hear only seven explosions in the distance along the "Whale." The bombing preparation turned out to be seven smart bombs directed against specific targets. Despite the lack of preparation, Commanders Zia and Khoshkeyer pushed their advance forces into the assault. The Afghans had gone less than 200 meters when they were pummeled by heavy mortar fire. Now, having been promised extensive CAS, Zia angrily asked, "Where are the planes?" McHenry had no answer, and Zia had his advance elements withdraw, dragging their wounded with them. The main body remained poised near the tip of the "Whale," awaiting the promised CAS. As the discussion continued between the American officers and the Afghan commanders about air support, TF Rakkasan began helicopter assaulting infantrymen into LZs near the four towns at the far end of the Shah-i-Khot Valley. After a second Afghan assault got mortared, Apache helicopters arrived to attack the enemy mortars but were soon recalled because American ground troops, who landed unopposed initially, came under heavy mortar and small-arms fire when the helicopters departed. In the first minutes of the attack, LTC Hooper remembered thinking, "The boss [COL Mulholland] was absolutely right! We were facing a well-prepared, well dug-in, much larger force than expected."

The Special Forces officers realized that getting further CAS for the AMF would be slim as long as the Americans were engaged. Commanders Zia and Khoshkeyer pulled their forces back into covered positions to account for their soldiers since they had casualties. In a country where 80 percent of the people are illiterate, the ability to count is not a simple skill. What seemed like a routine task was, in reality, quite time consuming and difficult.

Zia's mortarmen, called "jundees" by ODA 594's SSG Cash Galtier (pseudonym) from Paducah, Kentucky, delivered counterbattery fire against suspected and known enemy positions with their six 82mm mortars. It was the only effective fire returned by Zia's Afghans on D-day of Operation ANACONDA. In another of the few bright moments of an otherwise dark day, ODA 594 was credited with destroying one enemy mortar position.[31] The arrival of a pair of AH-64 Apache attack helicopters from the 101st Airborne Division provided the most effective CAS for the Afghans during the campaign. Although not a preplanned mission or a specified task for these attack pilots, they diverted to Zia's location and put lethal fire on at least two *al-Qaeda* mortar positions on the western side of Terghul Ghar, the "Whale."

Because of the plight of TF Rakkasan, the ODAs and Afghans would get no further CAS. McHenry and Towson had to make a decision about the attack. Should they continue to advance into the valley with no air support where American soldiers were under fire? If they succeeded, how would they prevent the AMF from taking fire from American conventional elements? As they discussed the situation, the enemy mortar fire became more accurate. McHenry and Towson realized that the Afghan force was no longer the main effort. It was no longer a concern to TF Mountain, and advancing toward the American troops would be futile and only result in more casualties. LTC Hooper explained the situation to COL Mulholland who agreed to withdraw based on TF Rakkasan's continuing predicament. As the mortar fire continued, Zia's forces withdrew to Gardez, reaching the city by nightfall. Both Commander Zia and Commander Khoshkeyer lambasted the Special Forces officers for the weak bombing preparation, their resultant casualties, and the lack of CAS. They believed that they had been "hung out to dry," and the complete shift of CAS to the American effort reinforced that opinion.

Various news media reported that much of the heavy fighting involving conventional Army units was caused by the Afghans retreating in the face of mortar attacks. What was not mentioned was the very limited bombing preparation before the attack and the lack of CAS for the Afghan assault force that stayed under heavy mortar fire until it finally withdrew. There were other factors that influenced the intensity of the battle. Although Afghans had fought for years against the Soviets and then the *Taliban*, none of their "armies" could be likened to any army based on the Western model. One Special Forces officer made these comments about the Afghan performance in the early hours of Operation ANACONDA: "We can't expect the AMF to be like an American military force, but that makes them no less noble, no less brave, and no less willing to get out and engage our common enemy, and that's what the force has done."[32] The fact that this combined Afghan force remained cohesive in the confusion, attacked despite the lack of normal preparatory aerial bombardment, assaulted twice into enemy mortar fire, and withdrew only when CAS was unavailable is testimony to Special Forces ODA 594 and ODA 372 and the quality of the Afghan leadership.

Combat Multipliers

A major concern in combat is having enough infantrymen to perform an operation. This was especially relevant for TF Rakkasan, which planned to use PSYOP as a force multiplier. The infantry battalions reluctantly forfeited "shooter" seats on the initial CH-47D Chinook assaults for several three-man tactical PSYOP teams (TPTs). But the TPTs proved just how effective they could be in combat on two separate operations supporting the Rakkasans during Operation ANACONDA.

TPT 933 and CPT Acosta, commander, 910th TPD, boarded a 101st Airborne CH-47D Chinook on D-day, 2 March 2002, for Operation ANACONDA.[33] The two Chinooks and two MH-60 Black Hawks carried a 10th Mountain combat engineer platoon and the PSYOP team to a remote airfield to establish a forward arming and refueling point (FARP) called Texaco. It would also serve as an enemy prisoner of war (EPW) facility if necessary. The FARP, with a constant flow of helicopters, attracted curious Afghans like a magnet, especially since it was located next to a large village containing 30,000 residents and four other villages within a 5-mile radius. It did not take long before the curious villagers approached the airfield to see what was happening. As women and children drifted toward the combat forces, TPT 933 immediately went to work with its loudspeakers to broadcast messages of caution and explanation in their native language. Most villagers stopped, listened for a few minutes, and then headed away from the airfield. TPT 933 broadcast almost nonstop for the first 48 hours of ANACONDA.

The *modus operandi* was typical for Afghan loudspeaker missions. Engineer tape was strung around the perimeter as a "no cross" warning line and mine symbol placards attached to flap-like Tibetan prayer flags. The tape was well beyond hand grenade range and served as the first line of warning to divert the noncombatants. Phony minefields were created between the lines to lend further credence to the warning lines around the perimeter. This control measure was backed up by progressively more emphatic warnings being broadcast loudly to deter the curious Afghans and to keep them "out of harm's way." The TPT leaders had developed these specific transcripts from the standard warnings. Normally, from daylight to sunset, the teams would start the broadcast when anyone was spotted about 400 to 500 meters away. The people would stop, listen to the message, and then turn around.

Team leader, TPT 933, SGT Norman Wilcox (pseudonym) visited the provincial Afghan military commander, General Gul Haidar, to explain the team's purpose.[34] Haidar wanted to support the U.S. forces in any way he could and asked what Wilcox needed. The sergeant requested that the general meet with all the leaders from the surrounding villages to explain that U.S. forces were conducting dangerous military operations. Four hours later, the collected leaders were told that to keep their people safe, the villagers had to be kept away from the airfield to avoid being shot, especially at night. The village leaders were very happy about the Americans' presence, and they pledged their support.

General Haidar came back the next day and offered to provide a security force of a captain and 12 soldiers to help guard the FARP. CPT Acosta, SGT Wilcox, Haidar, and several Afghan Military Forces (AMF) soldiers reconnoitered the airfield and established six outer perimeter guard posts that were eventually occupied by 60 AMF soldiers. Afterward, the combat engineers and PSYOP personnel manned the inner security positions. By day 4 of Operation ANACONDA, civilian interference with FARP operations had ceased. The successful efforts of the PSYOP loudspeaker team contributed to the decision to extend the Texaco FARP beyond its original 48 hours to nine days.[35] While TPT 933 had the FARP mission, the other two PSYOP loudspeaker teams were attached to the 101st Airborne and 10th Mountain infantry battalions.

D-Day ANACONDA From the Viewpoint of Force Multipliers

SSG Jack Clinton (pseudonym) and his assistant team leader from TPT 912 had been attached to C Company, 1st Battalion, 87th Infantry, 10th Mountain Division, to broadcast "stay away" messages, warning the local populace not to approach the American blocking position. The team was carrying several broadcast theme scripts addressing civilian noninterference, support for the coalition forces, and mine awareness. However, when the first lift of the 1st Battalion, 87th Infantry, suffered 26 casualties just after landing, the second lift of helicopters carrying TPT 912 was held on the ground at Bagram. Eventually, all further lifts of the 10th Mountain were canceled, and TPT 912 joined CPT Acosta and TPT 933 at the Texaco FARP. This proved helpful because TF Mountain set up another short-duration FARP operation. TPT 912 broadcast for an hour while it was being set up. Never having to escalate to the second and third levels of warnings during ANACONDA validated the success of the PSYOP broadcasting effort.

TPT 913 was attached to C Company, 2nd Battalion, 187th Infantry, 101st Airborne Division, to broadcast "stay away" messages, warning the local populace not to approach the blocking position "somewhere in the mountains." After two rehearsals with C Company, weather delayed the start of the operation for two days. According to TPT 913 team leader SGT Mitchell Dennison (pseudonym), within three days, there were an additional 60 general purpose medium tents (general purpose medium tents can sleep 30 soldiers) and a second mess hall where previously there had only been a SOF and logistics center at Bagram. The American "signature" was very large. It had to be obvious to the local Afghans that a big operation was planned. The weather delay just added to the operations security (OPSEC) problem.[36]

Limited to two PSYOP personnel based on available helicopter seats, SGT Dennison and his assistant team leader, SPC Ike Monroe (pseudonym), carried 75- to 80-pound rucksacks when they boarded the CH-47D for a daylight insertion.[37] The weight of portable broadcast equipment, batteries for extended operations, and cold-weather gear "fell on deaf ears" among the Rakkasan leaders because the mission was only going to last two days. As the Chinook made its final approach to land, Dennison and Monroe looked out the window. It seemed like nothing was going on. Everyone ran off the helicopter and spread out in defensive positions until it lifted off. Since the LZ was on the high ground, they could see down into the valley in front of them. "It was like a scene out of a war movie. Although it was 4 'clicks' [kilometers] away, you could hear the loud, crazy gunfire and see tracers coming from the LZ where Charlie Company, 1/87 Infantry, was getting hit. All of a sudden some Apaches flew in from behind us and started firing Hellfire missiles right into the side of the mountains. We could see the Apaches taking ground fire. Obviously that was not the place to be so the company commander got everyone up, and we started moving out in a file up the first hill," said SGT Dennison.

As the lead elements of C Company crested a small pass about 500 meters from the LZ, two or three enemy soldiers opened up on the front of the column with rocket-propelled grenades (RPGs) and AK-47 rifles. "That was my first encounter with real fire coming at me. Being close to the company headquarters and right behind the lead platoon, we could hear the 'whizzes' of bullets going by, the distinct crack of the AK-47s, and the 'whooshes' of the RPGs," recalled Dennison. The fire seemed to be coming from a small village of about 10 mud houses. We got down while three Special Forces soldiers flanked the enemy forces. Using an M-240 machine gunner to lay down suppressive fire, the Special Forces team used .50-caliber sniper rifles to eliminate the threat. Suddenly, two Apaches came over, firing their machine guns, shooting at the Special Forces team. "That wasn't too cool," said Monroe, "and the radiomen in the Charlie Company headquarters stood up and started screaming and waving orange VS-17 panels. Although it was daylight, the Special Forces team was not dressed like us, so I could understand the mistake. It had been called in by a platoon behind us that did not know what was going on."

After the threat was eliminated, we moved to our blocking position and stayed there for several hours waiting. Although the soldiers had only walked about 1,500 meters from the LZ to the blocking position in the vicinity of several blownup mud houses, the 9,500- to 10,000-foot altitude left everyone short of breath. Dennison and Monroe realized then that there would be no need to broadcast because the locals had already left the area. With new orders, the infantry company loaded up and started "humping" through the mountains until 0100 or 0200. The soldiers watched the tracers of the attack helicopters working in the valley and the CAS being directed by the coalition reconnaissance teams before finally stopping to bed down for the night.

At daybreak on D+1, the infantrymen and the two PSYOP soldiers moved again for another 3 or 4 km until they reached an area where they began receiving mortar and small-arms fire from the surrounding three hills. This area was referred to as "Mortar Hill" by the Rakkasans. C Company was trying to link up with another Rakkasan company that was moving up a dry riverbed toward them. Afterward, it was discovered that the enemy had at least three mortar positions surrounding the hill and a truck-mounted .51-caliber DshK machine gun firing down the valley. The other Rakkasan unit sent a squad forward to effect a linkup with C Company.

The enemy mortared that infantry squad hard. The sergeant leading the squad had the chest plate blown completely out of his armored vest, and he was down with numerous shrapnel wounds all over his body. Other members of the squad were also wounded. As the Special Forces personnel dropped their rucksacks and moved down the ridge toward the mortar fire, six C Company personnel ran to assist the trapped squad with a Skedco (Sked Company) stretcher and drag the squad leader back for first aid and later medical evacuation.

Then the enemy forward observer shifted the mortar fire on C Company. The Special Forces team scrambled back up the ridge to cover. When the mortar fire started coming in, everyone dropped his or her rucksacks and headed for cover. "We sure didn't need our loudspeakers to talk to someone who was trying to kill us. From then on, we were strictly infantrymen," recalled Dennison. But the infantrymen were stuck for about 5 or 6 hours because they could not abandon the rucksacks with their cold-weather clothing and rations in them.

The Air Force enlisted tactical air controller (ETAC) was ready to call for CAS, but the enemy mortar forward observers had not been spotted. SPC Monroe grabbed some binoculars and climbed onto some boulders on the crest of the ridge. Monroe located a cave complex on one hillside with a stack of mortar rounds visible. He watched the enemy running out of a cave to fire mortars and then retreating inside afterward. Having pointed out the activity to the ETAC, SPC Monroe used the laser rangefinder to designate the target. The enemy got off three more rounds before a B-52 bomber carrying smart bombs came "on station" overhead. The enemy gunners hid during the bombing and survived to fire again. By the time an F-16 came on station, Monroe had better grid coordinates on the position, and the mortar was eliminated. The *al-Qaeda* used piles of stones and sticks as aiming points for their mortars. SPC Monroe's action, recommended for the Bronze Star for Valor by the company commander, permitted the company to be resupplied with water and rations. Since it was only supposed to be there for two days, the rations and water were gone by the third day.

The next morning (D+2), the two Rakkasan infantry companies moved down into the valley and assumed defensive positions on the high ground. The enemy had dug fighting trenches all over the area. SGT Dennison and SPC Monroe were put out on an observation post (OP) with a squad of infantrymen.[38] There was no longer a loudspeaker mission. There were only enemy soldiers out there; the civilians had abandoned the area. That night C Company went on 100-percent alert until an AC-130 Spectre gunship overhead eliminated 200 enemy troops moving toward them. Later, SGT Dennison's OP was pulled back when eight vehicles filled

290

with armed men were sighted heading for the company position. Again, the AC-130 Spectre gunship destroyed the vehicles, providing a terrific "light show" for the infantrymen. In the end, TPT 913, SGT Dennison, and SPC Monroe ended up being infantrymen for 11 days.

After returning to Kandahar, the entire TPT 913 was called to support Operation APACHE SNOW, the follow-on mission to ANACONDA. This time, Dennison, Monroe, and SPC Dale Stevenson (pseudonym) supported a 101st Airborne infantry company that was searching local villages.[39] The Rakkasan company surrounded a village and then sent in assault teams to deliberately search for weapons, munitions, and equipment. TPT 913 broadcast messages to explain what it was doing and warnings to keep away from the U.S. soldiers to ensure the villagers' safety. The infantrymen found some RPGs, AK-47 assault rifles, and large quantities of ammunition. The PSYOP soldiers demonstrated their value to the combat elements as force multipliers.

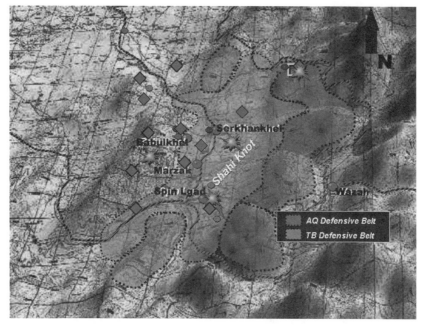

Figure 8. Objective Remington in the Shah-i-Khot Valley.

Figure 9. Babulkhel damage assessment.

Figure 10. Serkhankhal aftermath.

291

ARSOF in Direct Support

Working in a split-team configuration, combat-experienced ODA 563 supported the movement of TF Rakkasan infantry units during D-day operations as three Special Operations Team–Alphas (SOT-As) collected signal and voice intelligence to provide early warnings to the commanders at the blocking positions on Objective Remington. ODA 563 split teams eliminated a machine gun and grenade threat from a village near the LZ. SOT-A 502 and SOT-A 503 landed in respective blocking positions with the Rakkasans and immediately began collecting intelligence from Marzak, Zerkikheyl, and Serkhankheyl, the villages in the Shah-i-Khot Valley reportedly harboring *Taliban* and *al-Qaeda* fighters. SOT-A 506, caught in the cross-fire of small arms on landing, fought as infantrymen for 18 hours and directed CAS to cover the medical evacuation of casualties. When TF Mountain directed the unification of all 101st Airborne Division units and the exfiltration of 10th Mountain Division casualties, the Army SOT-As assisted ground commanders with consolidating and exfiltrating at the pickup zones (PZs). These operations drew heavy small-arms and mortar fire, and the SOF teams became embroiled in the firefights. As more Rakkasans were airlifted into the fight, these teams organized hasty fighting positions, engaged the enemy, called in CAS, and administered first aid for more than 30 hours until everyone was successfully exfiltrated by Chinook helicopters.[40]

Three tactical PSYOP loudspeaker teams were attached to the first TF Mountain infantry assault companies, and more than 1 million leaflets were dropped over the villages in and around the Shah-i-Khot Valley where *Taliban* and *al-Qaeda* fighters might seek refuge. On the second day, PSYOP leaflet bombs were dropped along possible escape routes (the ratlines) into Pakistan, encouraging surrender. Messages emphasized not supporting *Taliban* and *al-Qaeda* resistance and that the coalition forces were there to disarm the *Taliban*, not to occupy their country. Of the 10 million leaflets dropped over the Shah-i-Khot Valley during ANACONDA, only a few were found months later.[41]

Commander Zia Lodin regrouped his Pashtuns and returned to the vicinity of little Terghul Ghar Mountain ("Little Whale") the following night, a tribute to the professional rapport the Special Forces teams enjoyed with the tough Afghan fighters. ODA 594 and ODA 372 set up an OP on the "Little Whale" and vehicle checkpoints around Zurmat. LTC Carl Hooper wanted to get Zia back into the fight, especially after the first day fiasco. Returning to the fight significantly improved the morale of Zia's men, and they stayed for the rest of ANACONDA. More important, the CAS had increased in scope and duration by the next night. There was a vast difference from the nine smart bombs that had "prepared the battlefield" for an Afghan assault the day before. Now, Zia's men witnessed the awesome power of the coalition air munitions.

The massive CAS on the "Whale" encouraged Zia's forces to secure new vehicles and move closer to the battle. ODA 594 SSG Galtier and his jundees established mortar positions and began shelling suspected enemy positions on the "Whale." The Afghan forces manning outer blocking positions captured several enemy fighters attempting to escape the valley, and they were taken to Bagram and Kandahar for interrogation. But just as the Afghans were "warming up" for another "go" into the Shah-i-Khot, in the early morning of 4 March, American attention shifted to Takur Ghar mountain.

While some ARSOF elements had been given a role in ANACONDA from the start, oth-

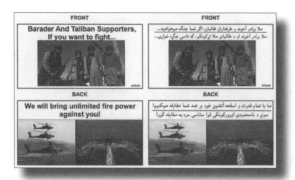
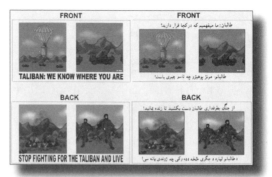
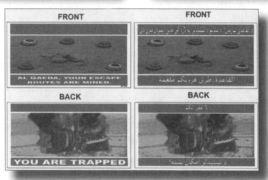

Figure 11. Millions of 4th POG leaflets emphasized
hopelessness and encouraged surrender.

ers continued with UW missions elsewhere. This was also a transition period for the 5th and 3rd SFGs, the mobilized 19th and 20th SFG elements from the ARNG, the 96th CAB to the USAR 489th CAB, the 4th POG battalions to the USAR 345th PSYOP Company (Airborne), the 3rd Battalion replacing the 2nd Battalion Chinooks of the 160th SOAR, a drawdown of JSOTF-North in Uzbekistan and JSOTF-South in Kandahar while the CJSOTF-Afghanistan was being stood up in Bagram, and the relocation of JSOAC-North. Within these changes, the ODAs were doing battle handoffs in the field, and missions changed rapidly in response to ANACONDA.

On Again-Off Again

Special Forces ODA 394 went through several mission changes in a span of days. After reorganizing, refitting, and rehearsing to conduct special reconnaissance (SR) from two mountaintop OPs bordering the Shah-i-Khot Valley in enemy-held territory for two days, the Special Forces team "stood down" to allow Danish and German troops to conduct the operation that they had planned. Back at the "Rose Garden," the disappointment of having three missions in succession canceled was wearing on the soldiers' morale. The biggest action of the war since their arrival in Afghanistan was about to begin—Operation ANACONDA—and they were sidelined, held in reserve at Kandahar. Then, on D-day of the operation, as they listened to the various American and allied commanders sending orders and information over the radio, it became apparent to them that "ANACONDA was not going the way the commanders thought it would." The raspy radio chatter indicated unexpectedly strong enemy resistance and numerous U.S. casualties from mortar and machine gun fire.[42]

Then ODA 394 received a terse message: "You have 1 hour to pack your rucksacks for a dismounted mission." Details would be provided later, but an aircraft was waiting to fly them back to Bagram Air Base where the C Company, 3rd Battalion, 3rd SFG, advanced operating base (AOB) had just been relocated. Several hours later that night, the Special Forces team was in the TF Mountain tactical operations center (TOC) for a grim intelligence briefing. Five AH-64 Apache attack helicopters had been badly shot up, and ODA 372 had taken casualties. CW2 Harriman, the team executive officer, had been killed when his Afghan truck convoy was attacked heading to the battle. 10th Mountain Division had 25 wounded who were still trapped near the landing zones (LZs) in the Shah-i-Khot Valley. "Not a good first day," commented one of the sergeants. The C-130 transport that carried the team to Bagram also had an empty metal coffin aboard for Harriman.

Figure 12. AH-64 Apache attack helicopter.

Now at Bagram with only their rucksacks, ODA 394 received another SR mission. It was to land at night by helicopter and climb to an observation site blanketed by 3 feet of snow, 10,400 feet above sea level. From the jagged escarpment, it could overwatch two trails ("rat-lines") that *Taliban* troops were thought to travel. Since the team had left almost all its equipment at Kandahar, it was pressed to borrow what it needed for the mission. Australian troops operating at Bagram were astounded at their lack of cold-weather survival clothing. "You blokes'll perish up there," they warned and generously provided snowshoes, walking poles, and camouflage overwhite clothing. Team medic, SFC Jason "J.D." Thurman (pseudonym), managed to get morphine auto injectors from the nurses at the Spanish military hospital. SSG Jake Millett (pseudonym) traded MREs to the Aussies for spare double-A and D-cell batteries.[43]

SSG Jerry Rawlins (pseudonym) particularly desired a Barrett M-82A1 .50-caliber sniper rifle. The vast open spaces in Afghanistan permitted the engagement of targets beyond 800 meters, the range of the Remington M-24 7.62mm rifles. Before leaving the United States, Rawlins had requested one of the "Barrett fifty cals" from joint operational stocks, but their entire inventory had already requisitioned. In exchange for some of his extra 7.62mm match-grade cartridges, the 10th Mountain Division reconnaissance platoon introduced Rawlins to the explosive ordnance demolition (EOD) detachment leader who had an extra Barrett to spare. Rawlins signed for the rifle and carried it into the ANA-CONDA battle.[44] By midnight, ODA 394 was as ready as it could be and settled down to rest before its insertion.[45]

At 0430, 15 hours before their SR insertion, LTC Sanders woke up medic SSG Stefan Morris (pseudonym). "Get the guys up. Repack your gear," the battalion commander said, "Your team is now part of the QRF for the downed helicopters" on Takur Ghar. Every available Australian, German, and American force at Bagram was urgently mustered to create a viable QRF. As the combined force was assembled, the team picked up rumors that an American had fallen out of a Chinook helicopter and that one, possibly more, of the Chinook cargo helicopters had been shot down by enemy ground fire.

About noon, ODA 394 was detached from the QRF. The original SR mission was back "on." Then, a few hours later, MSG McFadden (pseudonym) got word that their mission had been canceled. An estimated 200 enemy soldiers had been spotted in the vicinity of ODA 394's LZ. The area was bombed instead.[46]

But the ANACONDA operation had been adjusted. An unplanned second phase would accomplish the original mission of destroying *Taliban* and *al-Qaeda* who had escaped to mountain hideouts around the Shah-i-Khot Valley. ODA 394 would work with a seasoned 5th SFG team, ODA 594, out of Gardez, a 4½-hour drive away. While it would not be left behind when "the second push" of ANACONDA began, ODA 394 needed to get its equipment from Kandahar and return the borrowed gear at Bagram.

The team was elated. ODA 394 was going into combat. Its objective was the rocky massif, called the "Whale," west of the valley, and they would work with Pashtuns. For the first time since they had arrived in Afghanistan, their mission would not be changed.[47]

Although ODA 394 and other Special Forces teams were bumped from SR missions when they were assigned to coalition force teams, one American soldier serving an exchange assignment did participate.

With the Aussies

When Australia sent forces to fight alongside the other allied forces in Afghanistan, an American Special Forces soldier deployed with them. SFC Ray Lake (pseudonym) was the "Special Forces Exchange NCO" from 1st SFG to the Australian army at Perth. SFC Lake had been chosen by competitive selection for the highly popular posting and reported to his new unit for a 2-year tour on 13 August 2001.[48]

Well liked and respected by his Australian counterparts, the native Texan had served as a paratroop infantryman in Italy and a parachute rigger in Germany before qualifying for Special Forces. While assigned to the 1st SFG as an ODA communications sergeant, Lake had learned Thai and had been on training missions to Malaysia, Thailand, South Korea, and the Philippines.[49] By May 2002, Lake had participated in numerous combat operations with the Australians in Afghanistan and had the highest professional regard for the Aussie soldiers. He found them "less reliant on technology and more self-sufficient" than the Americans because of their nearly constant operational deployments.[50]

In particular, Lake thought the Australians were better at the very arduous special reconnaissance (SR) mission than any of the other coalition and U.S. units in Afghanistan. While SFC Lake could converse easily with his American friends about how much he was enjoying his time with the Australians, he never let slip a word about the details of what his unit was doing or what it had done, where it was, or where it was going in the future. This was just part of serving with the Australians.[51]

During Operation ANACONDA, the ARSOF supported TF Mountain with its conventional forces. The news media focused on that operation until an incident on the top of Takur Ghar, a mountain flanking the Shah-i-Khot, drew their attention. On the precipitous summit of that 10,000-foot mountain, special operations soldiers would fight for more than 17 hours to rescue, first, an SR team, and then an MH-47E Chinook crew whose helicopter was shot down delivering a Ranger QRF. Intense fighting during the rescue efforts would cost seven special operations servicemen their lives and leave even more wounded. The following vignette, the first of four in chronological sequence, covers the attempted night insertion of a special operations reconnaissance team on Takur Ghar during Operation ANACONDA.

Figure 13. Two-wheeled LZs became routine for 160th SOAR MH-47E pilots.

Forty-Five Seconds Too Long

Since late December 2001, the special operations aviators of 2nd Battalion, 160th SOAR, had been based at Bagram. By 3 March, they had inserted numerous coalition and U.S. reconnaissance teams into the Shah-i-Khot Valley in support of ANACONDA. Before this, the Night Stalkers, using MH-47E Chinooks, had done team insertions under the cover of darkness. The flights were routine with little enemy contact, but the helicopter LZs were at altitudes that ranged from 8,000 to 11,500 feet mean sea level (MSL) with limited space to land. The margin for error on the insertion was slim. The high altitudes of the LZs challenged aircraft performance and pilot skills to the maximum. Single-engine flight was never an option.

The SOAR air mission on the night of 3 March was not complicated: Two MH-47E Chinooks, radio call signs Razor 03 (Zero Three) and Razor 04 (Zero Four), were to infiltrate two special operations teams into two different LZs, one north of Objective Remington and the other south. The Night Stalkers flew their missions in pairs to provide emergency combat search and rescue (CSAR) in the event one aircraft had problems. Razor 03 planned to fly to the northern LZ with Razor 04, drop off Razor 04, and then proceed to the southern LZ. Razor 04 planned to land at the northern LZ, drop off its team, and then proceed north at a slow airspeed to allow Razor 03 to link up again. Once the two Chinooks had rejoined, they would return to Bagram Air Base and end the mission.

Razor 03 and Razor 04 departed the air base that night to fly to an offset location. The flight arrived at the pickup zone (PZ) without incident, loaded the two Special Forces teams, and departed on time. Intelligence indicated that flight routes and the LZs were relatively secure, but Nail 21, an Air Force AC-130 Spectre gunship, was to double-check each of the LZs before the insertions to confirm the assessment. When the flight was six minutes from the objective, Nail 21 diverted because of its proximity to a B-52 bomber airstrike, and it failed to get "eyes on the objective." In light of these factors, CWO Alfred Mann, the flight lead, and CPT Timothy Dickerson, the air mission commander (AMC) (pseudonyms), decided to return to the PZ since it was only a 15-minute flight to the objective and wait for the bombing operation to end. The flight of two Chinooks landed at the PZ and reduced their engines to ground idle to save fuel while they waited.[52]

Then an air assault by TF Rakkasan into Objective Remington further delayed the mission. The MH-47E Chinooks shut down. The delayed insertion was a problem for the ground force. They would not have sufficient time to climb to their observation position under the cover of darkness. Mako 20, the team leader, wanted to fly directly to the position. Mann calculated the performance figures and said that they could get in, but there was no guarantee that the LZ would be suitable for landing the team. The team leader had seen the imagery and was convinced that there were places to land.

As the Rakkasan air assault ended, the Chinook pilots began engine startup procedures. The right engine on Razor 03 exceeded its limits on startup. Mann knew that it was foolish to take an aircraft with a questionable engine to 10,000 feet MSL. He immediately shut down the helicopter while CPT Dickerson contacted the 160th SOAR operations center and requested a replacement aircraft. Coincidentally, two 160th SOAR Chinooks were in the forward arming and refueling point (FARP) called Texaco. Dickerson coordinated with the operations center for the Chinooks in the FARP to become replacement helicopters. Once the Chinooks arrived at the PZ, the pilots in Razor 03 and Razor 04 executed a "bump"—the pilots and aircrews swapped out aircraft because the aircraft were low on fuel.

Mann informed Mako 20, the ground force team leader, that "best case" they would get the team to the LZ by 0245. This would still allow an hour for movement under the cover of darkness. Mako 20 still wanted to go directly to the observation point (OP). At 0230, the two MH-47Es lifted off to fly directly to the position and execute the rest of the mission as briefed. When Nail 21, the AC-130 Spectre gunship flying overhead, reached its fuel limit, the CAS mission was passed to Nail 22. However, after Nail 22 cleared the new LZ/OP, it left the area for another tasking about six minutes before Razor 03 arrived at the LZ/OP.

During Razor 03's approach, the LZ/OP looked suitable, but as the Chinook began its flare to land, the aircrew, wearing night-vision goggles (NVG) and manning the miniguns, spotted footprints in the freshly fallen snow. As the aircraft hovered closer, they reported an unmanned .51-caliber DshK machine gun (in good shape) at the 1 o'clock position and military hardware all over the place. Then, they spotted a donkey tied to a tree at 3 o'clock. As they touched down, Mann informed Mako 20 that they were not alone.

As the team stood near the ramp hinge poised to exit the helicopter, SGT Jerald Curtis (pseudonym), the left door gunner, reported that he saw a man duck behind a berm at 9 o'clock.[53] Mann told Mako 20, who said his team was taking the hill. SGT Derrick MacKenzie (pseudonym), the aircrewman on the right side of the ramp, held the Special Forces team back while this information was relayed.[54] Just as he lowered his arm releasing the ground team to exit, an enemy soldier stood up and fired an RPG at the left side of the Chinook's fuselage. The RPG hit the left electrical compartment and knocked out all of the alternating current (AC) electrical power, something that had been considered impossible to do. The exploding round wounded Curtis, the left side M-134 minigunner, in the right leg. After the flaming projectile passed through the left side electrical panel, it crashed into the electrical compartment on the opposite side, knocking out the transformer rectifiers. With the transformer rectifiers destroyed, all of the multifunctional displays, the Advance Flight Control System (AFCS), radios, and aircraft mission equipment, including the 7.62mm miniguns, were inoperative. Electrical and insulation fires filled the cabin with smoke and obscured the vision of those in the back.

Small-arms fire slammed into the multimode radar pod, severing the No. 1 hydraulic servicing line that caused the No. 1 hydraulic system to fail. The RPG had also knocked out most of the intercommunication (intercom) system between the aircrew in the back and the pilots. The ground team stayed aboard the aircraft, and Mako 20 yelled, "Get us out of here!" MacKenzie, the only one whose intercom worked, told Mann, "Fire in the cabin! Rear ready! Pick it up! Pick it up! Go! Go! Go!" and began firing an M-60 machine gun mounted in the rear right cabin window. Mann grabbed the controls from CWO Jerry Tucker (pseudonym) and quickly pulled the heavy Chinook skyward without using the AFCS.[55]

The oil-soaked ramp was stuck in the down position because the hydraulics had been drained by small-arms fire damage. As Mann wrenched the helicopter off the ground, Petty Officer First Class (PO1) Neil Roberts slipped on the greasy floor and fell forward, tumbling toward the down ramp. SGT Paul Parcelli (pseudonym), the Chinook ramp gunner, lunged to arrest the heavily burdened SEAL and caught him.[56] MacKenzie, seeing the desperate, scrambling movement, rushed after the two of them. Parcelli and MacKenzie managed to get a hand on Roberts at the edge of the ramp, but the force of the accelerating helicopter provided enough momentum to break their tenuous holds during the takeoff. As the helicopter did its liftoff shudder about 5 feet off the ground, Roberts and Parcelli fell out of the helicopter. Parcelli, the aircrewman, tethered by his safety harness ("monkey strap"), stayed attached to the Chinook, but Roberts fell to the ground 5 to 6 feet below. As the big helicopter cleared the ridgeline, Parcelli dangled 3,000 feet above the ground in the dark.

Using his flashlight to illuminate the backup attitude indicator, one of the functioning flight instruments, Tucker called out airspeed, altitude, and directions to Mann. MacKenzie, the only crew member with a functioning intercom system, confirmed that both aircraft engines were running and told Mann that a man had fallen out of the helicopter at the LZ and that they had to go back. Then MacKenzie focused his attention on Parcelli, swinging below the helicopter ramp on his monkey strap and started to physically drag him back aboard as the lumbering Chinook took more small-arms fire.

Mann immediately decided to go back, fully aware that the two M-134 miniguns were inoperative and that they only had the rear M-60 machine gun and their individual M-4 carbines. Mann banked the helicopter to the right to come around and felt vibrations in the flight controls. Having pulled Parcelli back into the safety of the helicopter, MacKenzie turned around, only to be enveloped in a red haze of hydraulic fluid spraying from a severed line. It was obvious that the hydraulic systems were failing and the Chinook would soon be unflyable, which basically meant crashing in the mountains. MacKenzie checked the maintenance panel and verified that the hydraulic pressure for all three systems was zero. Aware of the gravity of the situation, he grabbed a quart can of hydraulic fluid, one of four that he kept near the pump, slammed a pour spout in, and dumped it into the hydraulic fill reservoir. He then quickly hand-pumped the life-saving liquid into the system. This maneuver temporarily restored cyclic control, but the cyclic controls would lock up again between each quart of fluid.

Mann realized that he could not fly the battle-damaged Chinook back to the LZ and that he had to land immediately to save those aboard. He identified a potential LZ and set the helicopter in a landing attitude.[57] The four quarts of fluid exhausted, the cyclic controls locked up 10 feet above the ground. Mann pressed down on the pedals to turn the nose, and he lowered the thrust. The aircraft hit the ground in a controlled crash. With the nose 15 degrees high and the right side 10 degrees high, the crew expected the helicopter to roll over. The pilots conducted an emergency shutdown, collected all sensitive items, and executed the emergency action plan. Mako 20 and his team exited the helicopter, established security, and used their radios to effect recovery. Minutes later Razor 04 arrived at the crash site.

"Leave no man behind" has become a tradition in SOF. Despite a severely damaged helicopter, the Night Stalker crew valiantly attempted to rescue Roberts. It was only when CWO Mann could no longer maneuver the unstable and virtually unarmed big helicopter that he was forced to abandon the rescue attempt. A combination of exceptional flying skills and quick-thinking, responsive aircrewmen enabled Mann to land the badly damaged aircraft without further casualties. It was a testimony to the dedication and courage of the "Night Stalkers" who, in the face of overwhelming odds, "Don't Quit!" The helicopter ambush on Takur Ghar mountain in the Shah-i-Khot Valley during the early morning hours of 4 March 2002 led to a chain of events that eventually ended with six special operations soldiers dead, more than a dozen wounded, and an incredible story of bravery and determination.

Never Leave a Fallen Comrade

Following the tradition of never leaving a fallen comrade behind, the actions that took place over 17 hours on Takur Ghar mountain demonstrated the valor, resolve, and honor of SOF soldiers. Facing heavy odds, two small elements of SOF warriors tried to rescue comrades captured by the enemy, only to find themselves in a fight for their lives in an uncompromising environment. It was intense combat in a frantic situation that cost six lives. This vignette chronicles the events after Razor 03 had force-landed and the first rescue attempt.

Figure 14. The impossible becomes inevitable.

Figure 15. The unlikely becomes fact.

Razor 04, the second MH-47E Chinook, had inserted its Special Forces reconnaissance team into Objective Ginger, an area occupied by infantry elements of TF Rakkasan. After departure, CWO Jackson Ferrell (pseudonym), the aircraft commander, flew the planned egress route to rendezvous with Razor 03, attempting to contact the other helicopter without success.[58] When Ferrell reached the flats surrounding Gardez, he radioed Grim 32, an AC-130 Spectre gunship that was overhead, to provide CAS. Grim 32 told Ferrell that Razor 03 had been forced to land because of enemy fire and passed the coordinates of his location. About 0330 local time, Razor 04 landed next to the battle-damaged MH-47E Chinook and extracted the crew and its ground force.

The ground force leader, Mako 20, and the 160th pilots quickly developed a plan to rescue PO Roberts from the mountaintop LZ/OP. CPT Timothy Dickerson, the air mission commander (AMC) of Razor flight, discussed the plan with the headquarters at Bagram Air Base and his pilots.[59] He decided to take the Razor 03 crew, including the wounded minigunner, SGT Curtis, back to the Special Forces base at Gardez before returning to the LZ/OP where Roberts fell out. Dickerson and Ferrell knew they would be returning to a hot LZ and did not want extra personnel aboard. While they were discussing the options on the ground by the damaged Razor 03 aircraft, Grim 32 warned Ferrell that enemy forces had gathered and were heading toward his location and recommended that he depart immediately. While the enemy was about 1,200 meters away, several Razor 03 crewmen were still in the damaged Chinook making a final sweep for sensitive items. When attempts to attract their attention using light guns were unsuccessful, Ferrell lifted off and hovered close by. This noisy maneuver got them out and aboard in a hurry. By 0340, Razor 04 was headed to Gardez, and Grim 32, the AC-130 Spectre gunship, had moved over the area where Roberts had fallen.

In the meantime, the 160th SOAR and the special operations TOCs were responding to the combat activity specifically involving their forces. Although separated by only 50 feet of space,

300

each had its own mission focus and separate concerns. The special operations leaders and staff officers in their TOC were trying to interpret the video display coming from an unmanned aerial vehicle (UAV) Predator flying above the Takur Ghar LZ/OP area when quick-reaction force (QRF) leader CPT Nathan Self, A Company, 1st Battalion, 75th Rangers, walked into the operations center.[60] Self discovered that there was a serious problem on the ground and realized his Ranger force would probably execute its QRF mission. Details were sketchy and somewhat confusing. Initially, Self believed his platoon would secure a downed helicopter in the Shah-i-Khot Valley. He collected the aerial imagery and started developing a plan with his squad leaders. It was 0400.

CWO Chris Gaines (pseudonym), the flight lead in Razor 01, had just returned from Gardez in the MH-47E Chinook that had the engine problem earlier in the night.[61] CPT John Gates (pseudonym), Commander, B Company, 2nd Battalion, told him to take his aircrew and "bump" to an airworthy Chinook and prepare to launch the QRF.[62] While Gaines' crew "prepped" the new aircraft, CWO Douglas Talbert (pseudonym) went to the 160th TOC to get details.[63] CPT Gates asked Talbert what he was doing in the TOC and told him to return to the flight line. Gates would relay information updates to the flight line.

The best "guestimate" of the situation was based on watching the UAV "Predator" video and piecing together radio transmissions from the 160th aircrews. Thus, special operations TOC officers thought that PO Roberts was alive but had been "joined" by several people and that Razor 03 had made a safe landing away from Takur Ghar. With this latest "guestimate," CPT Self marshaled his Ranger QRF and moved down to the flight line.

Outside the Special Forces camp at Gardez, Razor 04 landed to drop off the Razor 03 crew except for CPT Dickerson, who remained aboard as the AMC. CWO Ferrell and the ground force leader, Mako 20, listened to the confused reports on various radios but satisfied themselves that only Roberts was missing. Mako 20, unable to contact any of the special operations stations, had Ferrell relay information to Grim 32, the AC-130 Spectre gunship orbiting Takur Ghar. Grim 32 was told that all other U.S. forces were accounted for and that Roberts was properly marked; therefore, anyone surrounding him was the enemy. Grim 32 acknowledged and passed the information to the TOCs at Bagram.

As the special operations TOC tried to understand the images on the video monitors, CPT Dickerson briefed Ferrell and his crew on what to expect on the LZ/OP. Mako 20 and his five-man ground force was ready to go, but Razor 04 was now down to 3,000 pounds of fuel. Ferrell contacted Nail 22, another AC-130 Spectre, to tell Bagram that he needed to insert now or get fuel. Unfortunately, he did not have the coordinates for the 101st FARP, Texaco. With time of the essence and Texaco too far away for a round trip, Ferrell notified Grim 32 that he was departing immediately and needed preparatory fires on the LZ/OP to begin 5 miles out from his landing. The AC-130 Spectre gunship acknowledged and relayed the message. Razor 04 lifted off from Gardez at 0420 with the five-man ground force and an Air Force tactical air combat controller, TSGT John Chapman.

As Razor 04 approached Takur Ghar, Nail 22, the AC-130 Spectre gunship, had not been "cleared" to fire on the LZ/OP. Ferrell went into a holding pattern in a valley about a mile from the area, waiting for the preparatory fires to begin. Grim 32 reported that the request was denied because Nail 22 could not positively identify Roberts on the ground. CPT Dickerson decided to insert the team and headed inbound. Just as Razor 04 turned inbound, Dickerson was told to get the team on the ground. The special operations commanders knew that time was running out for Roberts. The only option was to land on the same LZ/OP where Razor 03 had taken intense fire. CWO Jacob Frost (pseudonym) stayed low, approaching horizontal to the LZ/OP, to use the terrain to mask the helicopter.[64] When Frost began his approach at 0455, the other pilots in front spotted an enemy soldier on the DshK .51 machine gun. There were muzzle flashes off the nose of the big Chinook. Frost continued flying inbound through a small saddle while Ferrell directed "forward and down, forward and down."

On final approach about 40 feet above the ground, the left side M-134 minigunner yelled "we're taking fire from 11 o'clock." Frost, concentrating on the landing, calmly asked, "Is it effective fire?" "Hell, yes!" was the answer as a stream of bullets smacked the left side of the helicopter, making distinct pinging sounds as they hit. "Then return fire!" About then, Ferrell and Dickerson saw muzzle flashes from the ridge of the mountaintop. Ferrell, backing up Frost on the controls, pushed the thrust down, and the Chinook landed in a white flurry of snow. As tracers flew overhead, the ground force disembarked, took up defensive positions off the ramp, and paused until the helicopter lifted off. The terrain masked the effectiveness of the enemy fire on the large helicopter. As Razor 04 crested the mountaintop, the left door gunner got off a short burst of 7.62mm fire with his M-134 minigun before it jammed. However, the right rear window gunner managed to deliver a long volley into the DshK with his M-60 machine gun.

Despite having lost radio contact with Mako 20 shortly after liftoff, Razor 04 entered a holding pattern about a mile away a little after 0500 in the event an emergency extraction was needed. When his fuel dropped below 1,000 pounds, the margin necessary to get back to Gardez, Ferrell departed. During the return flight, CPT Dickerson heard a radio transmission that said the QRF was 30 minutes away. Ferrell literally landed "on fumes" at the Gardez Special Forces base and, in his postflight inspection, discovered several bullet holes in the left fuel tank and a wire bundle that controlled the left engine.

Back on the mountaintop, the ground force, wearing NVG, split into two-man elements and moved toward the higher ground. The most prominent feature on the hilltop was a large rock formation and a tree. As TSGT Chapman approached the tree, he spotted two enemy personnel in a bunker under the tree. As Chapman and the team leader killed the enemy, they came under fire from another position 20 meters away. The airman was mortally wounded. The other two teams bounded forward through the snow, returned fire, and began throwing hand grenades at the enemy position to their front. Apparently outnumbered, caught in cross-fires, and with two men wounded, Mako 20 ordered his team to break contact. They glissaded 800 meters down the south side of the mountain. The natural sloping terrain of the escape route offered some protection, but another man was wounded in the process. Once sheltered from direct fire, the ground force contacted Grim 32, the AC-130 Spectre above, for fire support to cover their further withdrawal.[65]

Against All Odds

The scene at the Bagram flight line had become intense as the various special operations headquarters, all trying to stem the hemorrhaging situation of Takur Ghar—one soldier missing in action, one presumed dead, and three wounded; one downed MH-47E in hostile territory;

and one battle-damaged, out of fuel, Chinook at Gardez. Several QRF packages had been rapidly assembled and competed for the available aircraft. Now, the initial rescue force needed to be rescued and another soldier, presumed dead, had been left behind on the mountaintop. What happened to PO Roberts was still unknown. Two things were certain: there was a well-dug-in, well-armed enemy force on Takur Ghar that was ready to fight, and the hours of darkness were shrinking.

Rescue was the primary focus, but a myriad of questions abounded. Was there a need for an MH-47E with internal FARP ("fat cow")? How much fuel would each helicopter need? Who was the QRF? Who was the CSAR? What helicopters were actually launching? Would fast ropes be needed, and if so, where were the internal hardware and ropes? What was the plan? What was the situation on the mountain?

The 160th SOAR crews worked feverishly to prepare their aircraft. They started installing an internal fuel tank on Razor 02 to refuel the Chinook at Gardez, unaware that the battle-damaged aircraft was unflyable. In the end, the FARP mission was scrapped, but the partially configured tank was already aboard Razor 02. Crew members cross-loaded gear, reconfigured aircraft, and tried to identify which QRF was going.

CPT Self finally convinced the aviators that the Rangers were the QRF. CWO Talbert and Self discussed how many Rangers could be carried based on aircraft weight and QRF needs. Having planned for every contingency, Self had personnel identified by function and weapons and could adjust his numbers readily. But the Air Force CSAR team of enlisted tactical air controllers (ETACs) and pararescue personnel (PJs), with whom the Rangers had rehearsed the QRF mission, were away on another mission. Self acquired a 23rd Special Tactics Squadron (STS) CSAR crew that had worked with the 160th SOAR.

CPT Self's QRF package was reduced to one team of Rangers. Dissatisfied with this latest development, he got the Ranger battalion operations officer involved to get another team approved for a complete package. The second team would prove critical. While awaiting the final decision, Self briefed the new CSAR crew on order of exit and actions on the objective. When the senior special operations commander at Bagram became aware of the gyrations on the flight line, he directed that a Ranger QRF of two teams go and reduced the CSAR package to three men.

The SOAR crews were equally frustrated. CWOs Gaines and Talbert and SFC Charles Lafayette (pseudonym), the 160th senior medic, had bumped aircraft three times already and worked with a different crew each time.[66] Eventually, Razor 01 loaded nine Rangers with the attached Air Force ETAC and a three-man CSAR team, and Razor 02 loaded 13 Rangers aboard. Shortly after 0500, the flight left Bagram on its third mission of the night. Gardez, about 40 minutes away, was the clearance limit for the QRF. Since the commanders were now aware that Razor 04 had inserted the rest of Roberts' team on Takur Ghar, they decided that it was best to get the QRF closer to the situation than to delay its launch any longer.[67]

The QRF aboard Razor 01 did not have a clear threat picture of Takur Ghar as the two Chinooks raced toward Gardez. With daylight rapidly approaching, the AC-130 gunship was ordered off station (Air Force policy since Operation DESERT STORM). A missile launch during the night had been reported. This was very unfortunate because Grim 32, the AC-130, probably had the best situational awareness concerning Takur Ghar. When CWO Ferrell heard the Chinooks approaching Gardez, he tried to raise Gaines on the radio to advise him of the threat, but he failed to reach him. CPT Gates in the 160th TOC told Gaines to proceed directly to the mountaintop and to contact Matchbox, a Navy P-3 Orion, for further guidance because over-the-horizon communications were intermittent.[68] The time was 0540. Matchbox was an infrared search radar aircraft, not a command and control platform. When Gaines contacted Matchbox to confirm the LZ/OP coordinates in his aircraft navigation system and the location of Razor 03, he was told that there was movement on top of the mountain near the LZ/OP.

While inbound to Takur Ghar, the Razor flight passed over the downed Chinook, Razor 03. Surprised to discover the MH-47E only 4 miles away from their LZ/OP, Gaines questioned Matchbox on its LZ/OP coordinates. According to CWO Talbert, "the communications exchange was like pulling teeth." Matchbox repeated the same coordinates to confirm and passed on the location of a possible antiaircraft artillery (AAA) site nearby. Listening to additional radio traffic convinced Gaines, Talbert, and Self that their mission was either to reinforce or extract the rescue team on top of the mountain. They were unaware that the team had escaped down the backside (southern) of the mountain and that TSGT Chapman had been left behind.

CPT Self passed instructions over the Ranger platoon net to SSG Arin K. Canon (pseudonym), his squad leader on Razor 02. It was almost 0600. The snow-covered ground was now visible without the aid of NVG. The Rangers took off their NVG and stowed them. As the flight approached closer, they began receiving sporadic ineffective small-arms fire from the ground. Gaines instructed CWO Gary Corbin (pseudonym), the pilot flying Razor 01, "to keep the airspeed up and not to get too low" as they neared the mountain.[69] That is when Gaines told CWO Roger Oliver (pseudonym), who was flying Razor 02, to hold 2 miles from the LZ/OP.[70] Unknown to Gaines, Oliver was having radio problems and had received the message "broken." Following one-half mile behind Razor 01, Oliver entered a holding pattern, but as he did so, he lost sight of Razor 01. A few moments later, Oliver flew up to the next ridgeline and tried to contact Gaines, but by then Razor 01 was another ridgeline away.

CWO Gaines decided to make a pass to confirm the coordinates of the LZ/OP. As Razor 01 flew by the mountaintop LZ/OP, everyone aboard looked for the rescue team on the ground. The aircrew reported footprints in the snow, apparent bombed areas, and possible muzzle flashes coming from a boulder by the tree on the hilltop. Gaines reported enemy activity to Matchbox circling above and again questioned whether the hilltop was the right place to land; Matchbox acknowledged that it was.

CWOs Gaines, Talbert, and Corbin shared their concerns that the LZ/OP just did not feel right. Something was very wrong. The three highly experienced pilots all felt the "hair standing up on the back of their necks"; it was daylight and two very big, noisy helicopters were obviously being watched. Gaines did not like the situation at all. Based on his 20-plus years of flying experience, Gaines, a former Ranger, understood the tactical advantages of two forces of Rangers, but the situation on the ground was too sketchy to risk two aircraft landing in daylight. "Better one aircraft shot down than two," he thought. Gaines decided the situation warranted risking only one aircraft with a minimal ground force and sent Razor 02 back to Gardez to wait for instructions. He was unaware that Oliver had never received the LZ/OP coordinates. Gaines was also concerned about a midair collision if the small LZ/OP was hot.

With Gardez only 10 to 15 minutes away, Razor 02 could respond quickly if necessary.

As CWO Oliver in Razor 02 started to circle for the third time, he heard the faint order to return to Gardez and departed holding. This drew an instant reaction from SSG Canon aboard the MH-47E who argued emphatically the need to have both Ranger teams on the LZ/OP should anything happen. Corbin made another pass over the mountaintop, still unaware of the threat. There was no communication with the stranded rescue team. As the pilots talked about the bunker spotted during the first pass, Gaines gave the time warning for landing to CPT Self. Self shook SPC Marc A. Anderson, the machine gunner sitting next to him. Emotions were high among the Rangers; excitement filled the cabin. SPC Anderson leaned toward PFC David B. Gilliam, his assistant gunner, and said, "Today, I feel like a Ranger!"

Razor 01 was going in. Gaines and Corbin discussed the final approach path, and Gaines warned him to keep his airspeed up. At 0610, Razor 01 was coming in low and fast, using the terrain for cover instead of making a standard high approach to a pinnacle objective. SSG Donald Deese (pseudonym), the left door minigunner, gave a "thumbs up" sign to SGT Phil Svitak, the right gunner and flight engineer, and told the Ranger force to "get ready."[71] On short final, Corbin picked a landing site and thought, "Well, this is it, make it a good one." Gaines was backing him up on the flight controls because at 10,000 feet there was little room for error. SFC Lafayette was looking over SGT Svitak's shoulder until he said, "Doc, you better move back."

Suddenly, about 40 feet above the ground, bullets peppered the front cockpit and side windows. Corbin stayed locked on the approach, continuing to the landing. Unconsciously, he planned his abort path—straight over the top of the hill. As glass exploded around him, Corbin sounded off, "Taking fire at 2 o'clock!" as he felt several rounds hit his chest body armor hard and twisted his flight helmet to the left. As bullets raked the right side of the aircraft, Svitak opened up with his rapid-fire 7.62mm minigun. SGT Steve Larken (pseudonym) fired with the M-60 from the right rear window of the cabin.[72] Then it seemed that both gunners paused momentarily at the same time when a rocket-propelled grenade (RPG) hit the right engine. The big Chinook was 20 feet off the ground. Svitak, mortally wounded during the exchange of gunfire, slumped and fell back into the cabin.

Then the flight controls became sloppy. Corbin knew that he could not make the landing area, and the wounded Chinook did not have the power to abort. On his left, Gaines had been hit first in the left leg—a hot numbing pain—and then another round hit his flight helmet, slamming his head backward. At the same time, SSG Deese on the left minigun felt a sledgehammer hit his left leg. Looking down, he saw a spray of blood and instantly began sweeping his minigun left and right. Corbin wrestled with the controls and applied the remaining power to make a very firm but controlled landing. The landing impact threw everyone standing in the back to the floor. The right rear M-60 gunner, SGT Larken, wrenched his knee in the fall but quickly got up to drop the ramp. At 0610, with the Chinook receiving machine gun fire from three directions, the Ranger force exited into a hail of fire.[73]

The damaged aircraft seemed unstable, "almost like it was shuddering from the hard landing," so Corbin held the controls, knowing that the Rangers were exiting. Gaines reached up and pulled the engines to stop. He tapped Corbin on the arm, grabbed his M-4 carbine, released his emergency door, and because a bullet had shattered his femur, threw his body out of the open doorway into 2 feet of snow. Corbin stuck his M-4 out the shattered window and returned fire as smoke filled the cockpit from a fire in the power panel by his seat. Talbert, the AMC, released his seat harness, turned around, and saw total carnage in the back of the aircraft. He threw himself over the companionway seat, grabbed his M-4, and headed toward the ramp.

Once on the ground, the bus-sized target was no longer moving, and it was easier to hit. The wounded Deese fell into the radio rack when the helicopter landed hard. On the floor he tore the lanyard off his M-9 pistol and used it on his leg as a tourniquet. The heavy volume of enemy fire penetrating the fuselage turned the cabin soundproofing into confetti. Smoke was smoldering from the tracer bullets. Three rounds slammed into SFC Lafayette's flight helmet, stunning and rupturing blood vessels in an eye as it knocked him backward. Ranger SPC Anderson was mortally wounded midcabin, and the Air Force PJ, Senior Airman Jason Cunningham was working on him. SGT Larken retreated from the open ramp to find cover inside the Chinook. Then an RPG flew through the open right cabin door, striking the oxygen console hanging above the left window. Although the grenade did not explode, the impact sparks set the soundproofing on fire. With the Rangers off, SGT Bradley Walters (pseudonym), the tail gunner; CWO Talbert; and the other Air Force PJ, SSGT Kerry Miller (pseudonym), set up a defensive position on the ramp.[74]

The Ranger force exited the Chinook into a withering barrage of small-arms fire. SSG Raymond DePouli was the first Ranger off the ramp. Exiting, he was hammered in the back and spun around. The bullet hit his armor plate   inch above his exposed area. He quickly located the enemy fighter wreaking havoc from the 8 o'clock position and emptied a full magazine from his M-4 into him. SGT Joshua J. Walker exited the right side, immediately took several hits on his Kevlar helmet, but managed to empty his M-4 toward the bunker on the right. SPC Aaron Lancaster-Totten, an M-249 squad automatic weapon (SAW) gunner followed Walker into the knee-deep snow. PFC David B. Gilliam grabbed the fallen Anderson's M-240B heavy machine gun and high crawled out the ramp to the right. Air Force SSGT Kevin Vance, the ETAC, slipped off his rucksack carrying the radio and dropped it off the ramp. Thrown backward on landing, CPT Self scrambled over several downed men to reach the ramp. He discovered PFC Matthew A. Commons dead and saw SGT Bradley S. Crose, one of his team leaders, lying motionless, face down in the snow. Both had been killed while exiting. Self rolled off the ramp and processed the surreal scene. SPC Anthony R. Miceli, a SAW gunner, had had his M-249 shot out of his hands but was uninjured. He had picked up PFC Commons' M203 grenade-launcher rifle and was positioned on the left side for security.

Once the rotors had stopped, pilot Corbin released the emergency door, triggering a hail of fire. Several bullets had gone through his left palm, exiting the back of his wrist, and blood was spurting everywhere. He applied pressure with his right hand and attempted to escape back into the cabin. As the stunned SFC Lafayette realized that he was basically okay, he looked up to see Corbin with arterial blood spurting 2 feet into the air, trying to get out of the cockpit. Lafayette had just pulled him over the companionway seat when another RPG slammed into the cockpit, exploding shrapnel into Corbin's left leg. Lafayette immediately applied a tourniquet to Corbin's shattered wrist and packed the injury with bandages. When Lafayette's yelling provoked no response from Svitak, he moved over to him and checked for wounds and a pulse. Svitak was dead. Corbin hollered at Deese, asking if he was okay. Deese replied, "Take your helmet off and stop yelling!" Deese was pale but responsive and wanted to be left alone. Deese thought that Lafayette, the senior medic, "was in his element."

The fire inside had spread to nearby rucksacks. SFC Lafayette had to make a choice: either stand up and get shot at while putting out the fire or allow the fire to burn. Anytime someone moved inside, the enemy shot into the Chinook. CWO Larken could reach the rear extinguisher and tossed it to Lafayette. Lafayette stood up and extinguished the fire. Relieved not to have been hit, he crawled to Cunningham who was fixedly trying to revive SPC Anderson. The senior medic checked Anderson closely. Anderson was dead. There was nothing more they could do. He told Cunningham to get an IV started in CWO Corbin.

Outside the helicopter the battle raged. The enemy forces had shifted their fire to the Rangers once the helicopter engine noise ceased. Covered by the fire of SPC Lancaster, SGT Walker bounded forward through the snow to a small rock cropping on the right. CPT Self and Lancaster moved forward on the right side of the helicopter. On the left side down in the snow, Gaines looked underneath the Chinook and saw blood dripping from the cabin drain holes. Spotting a Ranger moving up the right side, he yelled over to him, "I might need a tourniquet." The Ranger replied, "Can you cover the left side for us right now?" Gaines said, "Yes" and pulled his leg around, twisting his kneeboard to use the elastic straps as a tourniquet. As he covered the left with his M-4, Gaines mentally prepared himself for a life without a leg. Bounding forward while the others provided suppressive fire, CPT Self, SPC Lancaster, and the ETAC, SSGT Vance, joined Walker at the rock cropping. In one of the fusillades of fire, Vance had forgotten his rucksack with the radio at the base of the ramp.

The Ranger force was being fired on from multiple sides. An enemy fighter popped up at the 4 o'clock position and launched an RPG that skipped off the ramp. SSG DePouli saw him, moved to the right side, and shot him in the head. Then DePouli and PFC Gilliam bounded to another rock pile farther to the right of the other Rangers. Beside the rock pile they discovered an enemy fighter riddled with bullets and simply pushed him out of the way. With five Rangers and the ETAC abreast, Self concentrated on the boulder position on top of the hill 50 meters away. The enemy threw hand grenades, wounding Lancaster in the calf, Self in the thigh, and Vance in the shoulder. Several Rangers tried throwing hand grenades in return, but thrown uphill, they all fell short, exploding in the snow.

While the Ranger force engaged the enemy position at the boulder, Air Force SSGT Gabe Brown from the combat control team (CCT) set up his radios behind a rock about 20 meters downhill from CPT Self. He feverishly worked to get CAS, but since his team did not normally support the Rangers, Brown had different radio frequencies. Thinking quickly, he contacted the AWACS aircraft using his line-of-sight radio, and the controller provided him the correct CAS frequencies. Twenty minutes had passed since they landed.

Having dealt with the problems inside the aircraft, the Chinook aircrew members moved outside. CWO Talbert and SSGT Miller, the Air Force PJ, crawled up the left side of the aircraft to retrieve the wounded CWO Gaines. Each man grabbed a shoulder of his survival vest and dragged him to the rear of the Chinook where there was a casualty collection point 5 feet beyond the ramp. Gaines disliked being strapped down on the litter while SSGT Miller, the Air Force PJ, tended to his leg.

Having attended to the aircrew, CWO Talbert and SGT Walters asked CPT Self what he wanted them to do next. Self told them to collect as much ammunition and M-203 grenades as possible. SGT Larken retrieved the 7.62mm ammunition from the minigun cans and magazines from the wounded. Scrounging around, he also found some hand grenades and built a cache near the ramp. The lack of oxygen at 10,000 feet altitude severely hampered everyone's movement. While the Rangers provided cover, CWO Talbert and SGT Walters "humped" ammunition and grenades to them. SGT Walker asked for the M-203 grenade-launcher rifle, and in the midst of the enemy fire, Walters ran it up to him. Walker tried bouncing the M-203 grenades off the boulder but ended up shooting over the hill. At one point, Talbert found it to be easier to roll across the snow than to run in it. Sometimes, he rolled two-thirds of the way and then tossed the ammunition to the closest Ranger. When Talbert asked one Ranger if he could throw him some M-203 grenades, he hurriedly said, "No, do not throw those!" After SGT Walters had carried a large cache of 7.62mm ammunition to PFC Gilliam, he stayed to be his assistant gunner.

Inside the helicopter, SFC Lafayette and Senior Airman Cunningham continued to tend the wounded. When Lafayette got ready to splint the minigunner's leg, he told him, "This is going to hurt." SSG Deese quickly realized just how much and asked for morphine. Lafayette regretfully said, "No, not at this altitude because it would slow down your heart rate." "Thanks," Deese thought. The two medics splinted his leg and strapped him on a rigid Skedco sled-like stretcher for evacuation. The wide ballistic resistant fuel tanks on the MH-47E offered some protection to the wounded lying on the floor. Having lost a lot of blood, CWO Corbin drifted in and out of consciousness. Since most of his medical supplies were shot up, Lafayette fixed a mask from the helicopter's portable oxygen system to Corbin's face to keep him lucid. The infusion of oxygen "snapped Corbin up quickly." The CWO aviator told SGT Larken to gather all the PRC-112 survival radios and try to contact someone on the search and rescue net. When he got no response, Larken left one radio on "beacon mode." The aircrewman thought, "Why do we always carry this survival radio if it doesn't work when it's needed?"

By now, most of the enemy fire had shifted to the Rangers outside. During a lull in the firing, PFC Gilliam tossed a set of "binoculars" to Self that he had found by his position; it was actually a set of NVG. Their appearance caused Self to wonder what other equipment the enemy had and to question whether the QRF had been landed in the wrong place. Before he had time to ponder these dilemmas, SSGT Brown, the Air Force CCT, called out that some F-15 fighters were inbound with "500 pounders." Since Vance, the Air Force ETAC, did not have his radios with him, he had to relay instructions to the fighters through Brown. Self talked with Vance about the 500-pound bombs and decided to try the 20mm guns first. Shortly before 0700, the two F-15 fighters arrived overhead. Vance called for a "dry run" and gave the approach heading to Brown. After the dry run, Vance told Brown to move the fighters farther to the west.

Just the presence of the two fighters provided some psychological relief, but CPT Self was worried about the small force being flanked. He told SSG DePouli to take SPC Miceli and check their right flank to see if the enemy could slip around that side. As the two Rangers began to descend along the ridge, the Rangers saw that the terrain dropped very precipitously on that side. Further exploration uncovered two living positions cut into the hill. DePouli told Self about the cliff and the positions. He then cleared the two positions, first firing into a blanket covering one. In them, he discovered a rucksack, a multiband inter/intra team radio (MBITR), and a bullet-holed helmet filled with blood. That report made Self wonder, "What is going on up here?" Leaving SPC Miceli to cover the right flank, SSG DePouli returned to his original position. When the two fighters made another pass, Vance aborted them before they started firing, pushing them even farther west. That done, the next series of strafing runs blasted the top of the mountain with 20mm cannon fire. CWO Talbert, behind the Chinook, thought the exploding 20mm rounds sounded like someone popping bubble wrap, only much louder.

Having discovered an MBITR on the mountain, SSG Brown pulled out his and raised the stranded special operations ground force. They told him where they were and their casualties but not why they were down below. When Self started to fit the pieces together, he incorrectly assumed that "We landed in the wrong place, but at least I know where the team is." Self had not been privy to Matchbox's LZ/OP confirmation. Meanwhile, Ranger SSG Canon, back at Gardez, was pushing to get his element on the mountain.

Joining the Fight on Takur Ghar

The communications problem that had kept the senior special operations commanders from acquiring situational awareness on the Takur Ghar problem continued into the following day. This prevented senior commanders from getting control of rescue efforts being launched from areas in "gray" communications zones. In the confusion at the tactical level, the senior operator on the ground making the most noise, with an incomplete situational picture as well, dominated decisions in this command and control "void." This was the environment awaiting Razor 02 when he landed at the Special Forces camp at Gardez with half of the Ranger QRF.

Razor 02 landed at Gardez at about 0625, about morning nautical twilight, to learn that Razor 01 had been shot down on the mountain. CWO Mann, flight lead of the disabled Razor 03, found CWO Oliver and gave him the map coordinates of the LZ/OP where he had landed and where PO1 Roberts had fallen. CPT Dickerson came aboard Razor 02 as the air mission commander (AMC) and briefed the crew on what to expect. This would be Dickerson's third time into the same LZ/OP. Then a special operations ground force officer climbed aboard with the Rangers because "his guys were trapped on the side of the mountain." Oliver contacted the special operations TOC in Bagram. They were ready to depart at 0640 but were instructed to "stand by." Twenty minutes later, Razor 02 lifted off from Gardez, heading for Takur Ghar mountain. Halfway to the LZ/OP, the stranded special operations ground team contacted Oliver on UHF and advised him that the LZ/OP was hot, that a CAS bombing run on the mountain was starting, and that he needed to hold. No information was provided concerning the downed MH-47E aircrew or the Ranger QRF. After Oliver received the team's location, he flew into an adjacent valley to wait for the bombing to end. After the CAS was completed, the ground force team vectored Razor 02 into the vicinity of its location. Encountering no enemy resistance, Oliver inserted the rest of the Ranger QRF and the lone special operations ground force officer within 300 meters of the ground force team and headed back to Gardez in search of fuel.[75]

Having heard the MH-47E initially approaching, CPT Self could not determine where the Chinook had landed. About 0800, SSG Canon called Self to tell him the bad news. The Rangers had landed but were closer to the ground force team than Razor 01 on the mountaintop. They would have to climb almost 2,000 feet up the mountain (from an 8,000-foot elevation to Self at about 10,000 feet) on a 70-degree slope and then traverse close to 800 meters, and the ground force officer wanted the Rangers "to help extract his guys." Canon questioned the priorities and relayed the message to CPT Self. Canon received an emphatic "No!" "You need to move out and climb up here. We are in contact and have casualties." Canon passed the information to the ground force officer who turned in the opposite direction and moved downhill to join his men.

For the Rangers, it was a daunting challenge, but the men on top needed reinforcement. Takur Ghar towered above them, heavily covered with snow—as it turned out, 3 feet deep in some places. Having no mountain-climbing equipment, the Rangers—carrying weapons, plenty of ammunition, and radios and all wearing 3-pound Kevlar helmets and body armor—surveyed the best route to the top. They did not feel like "the cavalry charging to the rescue." Looking up from the bottom, trying to pinpoint the Ranger location on the top, SGT Eric W. Stebner described the terrain features to Self to get his advice. Initially, Self thought they might be able to flank on the backside of the bunker, but when Stebner passed his grid coordinates, Self realized they were northeast of his position and recommended a different mountain pass. According to SSG Canon, "Just the grade of the ridge made it an unbearable walk, not including the altitude." The shale rock below the snow made climbing even more difficult as the Rangers slipped and fell, beating themselves up as they plodded and stumbled upward. Along the way, the Rangers shed some of their bulky winter clothing; they had dressed for comfort in the cold, not a horrendous mountain climb. Optimistically, SSG Canon estimated that the climb would take 45 minutes.[76]

Figure 16. The harsh terrain of Takur Ghar.

With no visual sign of the other Ranger force and no radio report, CPT Self moved down to SSGT Brown's location around 0900. Brown attempted to contact the special operations TOC in Bagram, but the radio operators there did not recognize his call sign and asked him to leave their net. Trying to reduce the confusion and to make things simple for TOC personnel to track

310

the situation on Takur Ghar, Self decided to limit radio traffic to one call sign, that assigned to the CCT, for the entire day. This contributed to erroneous conclusions in the TOCs and, hence, distorted the account of what transpired on the mountain. While Self and CWO Talbert were discussing an LZ for extraction, 82mm mortar rounds started exploding around the helicopter. Self recognized that the enemy observers were bracketing their position. He hoped that the aircrew did not fully realize how bad the situation was becoming. Getting concerned, Self called Canon for an update. "Another 45 minutes" was the reply. Self called back, explaining the latest enemy development and said, "You're moving too slow. Do you still have your back plates in?" When he was told, "Yes," Self gave them the choice to get rid of the heavy back protection. Removing the plates would reduce the individual burdens and facilitate mobility. SSG Canon passed the option to his men. Some launched the plates like Frisbees down the mountain, while others chose to keep them. The plates provided protection against 7.62mm bullets, and that was what the enemy was using.[77]

Concerned that a mortar round might hit the big helicopter, CWO Talbert recommended moving the wounded. He was not sure they could wait and see if the CAS could destroy the latest threat. SFC Lafayette recognized the imminent danger but pointed out that the battle-damaged MH-47E had withstood several RPGs and heavy machine gun fire up to this point. Directly exposing the wounded—putting them in the snow—could cause hypothermia, especially in the case of CWO Corbin who had lost a lot of blood. When another round hit a little closer, the two decided to move everyone to a small depression 20 meters behind the helicopter. First, Talbert, Lafayette, Senior Airman Cunningham, and SGT Walters manhandled CWO Gaines and then CWO Corbin in the Skedcos through the deep snow to the casualty holding area. The combination of altitude, steep snow-covered terrain, less oxygen, and plain physical exhaustion made the transfers especially laborious and difficult. As the tired Cunningham prepared to lift SSG Deese, he tripped and lost hold of the Skedco straps. The toboggan-like litter with Deese strapped aboard started sliding downhill like a one-man Olympic luge. In a frantic effort, Walters and Talbert lunged downhill after the runaway Skedco, just managing to grab hold of the straps as Deese crashed into CWO Gaines. Gaines had been the only obstacle between Deese and an 800-meter plunge down the mountain into the rocks below. Having witnessed the helplessness of someone on a litter, CWO Corbin used his good arm to cut his chest straps and loosened his leg straps. Lying on his back, Corbin watched a UAV "Predator" circling overhead and wished it were an AC-130 Spectre gunship since they had just been driven out of the shelter of the MH-47E by 82mm mortars.

As the mortar rounds got closer and closer, CPT Self decided to assault the position on the mountaintop and gain control. The assault team of Self, SSGT Vance, SGT Joshua J. Walker, and SSG DePouli would be supported by fire from PFC Gilliam's M-240B machine gun assisted by SGT Walters, the 160th crewman. Once briefed, the assaulters bounded up shooting while PFC Gilliam laid down suppressive fire. As they assaulted forward, CPT Self saw an enemy fighter stand up, shoot at them, and then duck back down behind a tree by a boulder about 30 meters away. The Ranger captain realized the enemy was well dug in and that it was a fortified position. "Bunker! Bunker! Bunker!" Self yelled. "Get Back! Get Back! Get Back!" The three Rangers and one airman broke contact and returned to their original positions. Then the mortar fire started up in earnest. They needed CAS badly.

Just as CPT Self told SSGT Vance to bring in the bombers, a pair of F-16 fighters came "on station" overhead. Self and Vance quickly devised a plan: Walk the 500-pound bombs from the backside to the bunker on top of the hill. To have bombs dropped "danger close" required the initials of the requestor. CPT Self was more than happy to do so, just to bring some air power to bear on the enemy positions. The first bomb exploded on the backside, sending debris into the bunker and downhill. A second bomb landed near the bunker, and the shooting stopped momentarily. Then the shooting from the bunker started again. What Self did not know was that the bunker system provided good cover and allowed plenty of movement. Since bombs were not doing the job, Self told Brown to find out if there was an armed UAV Predator in the area. Vance was reluctant to use an armed Predator because they carried Hellfire missiles, and he thought they were too close to the bunker. In the meantime, the mortar rounds were impacting closer and closer. Self believed that they were out of options.

CPT Self called for the missiles. The first Hellfire was long—hitting north of the mountain-top and sending debris toward the huddled ground force and the climbing Rangers. Ignoring the complaints from below, Self thought to himself, "Up here we're bringing in 500 pounders, and that missile wasn't even close to you." Despite the first shot miss, the Predator pilot convinced Self that he could hit the enemy bunker, and he did just that. The next missile was dead on and blew the nearby tree apart. Although they never received another shot from the bunker, Self was suspicious and decided to wait for reinforcements. Something had happened because the mortar fire had shifted; his men had to be getting closer.

Meanwhile, back at Bagram, the special operations headquarters was planning a deliberate extraction from Takur Ghar and was assembling resources. Two Chinooks loaded with more than 35 QRF personnel from various special operations task forces departed at 0830 for Gardez. Razor 54, the AMC for the extraction, was told to join Razor 02 at Texaco—a FARP located halfway between Bagram and Gardez—which, by coincidence, was approximately 50 nautical miles from the crash site on Takur Ghar. All three 160th aircraft were on the ground by 0900. They were joined by two AH-64 Apache gunships from the 101st Airborne Division. The flight leads, AMC, and QRF commanders began finalizing plans. As they were working at Gardez, the size of the mission grew.

As news of the two MH-47E shootdowns and soldiers trapped on Takur Ghar spread at Bagram, JSOTF-South (TF Kabar) and TF Mountain became involved to add to the command and control problems. Chinooks from the 7th Battalion, 101st Aviation Brigade, met an increased demand for fuel by ferrying more into FARP Texaco. When the JSOTF-South headquarters got the news early in the morning, the commanders prepared a plan to bring more SOF into the fight. MAJ Randal Schantz (pseudonym), B Company, 3rd Battalion, 160th SOAR, was alerted at 1030 to "be prepared to launch."[78] His company had just arrived in Afghanistan a week earlier. They set up camp at Kandahar, built up and tested their MH-47Ds, and conducted some preliminary mission planning. Their first mission would be to rescue their comrades from a mountaintop far to the north. While special operations unit commanders mobilized their troops for a rescue mission, Schantz roused his aircrews and started the mission preparations to fly the special operations troops to Bagram in four Chinooks.

Shortly after 1030, the second Ranger element was within sight of the Rangers on top. In an almost comical exchange, SSG DePouli on top and SSG Canon climbing upward, having talked on the radio, called and waved back and forth trying to confirm the other's identity. At one point, during a mortar barrage, SSG Canon tossed snow up in the air to confirm his identity to DePouli. Twenty minutes later, the two groups of Rangers linked up. CPT Self quickly descended to the rock cropping where SSGT Brown had set up his radios and issued a brief fragmentary order (FRAGO) to deal with the bunker above. He explained the layout of the bunker and his plan of assault. SPC Randy Pazder and SPC Omar Vela, the heavy machine gun team, moved up to Gilliam's M-240B position to add their guns to the fire support. They had carried the heaviest load up the mountain and had a brief chance to rest. In preparation for the assault, CWO Talbert and SGT Walters had collected more than 2,000 rounds of 7.62mm from the helicopter. SGTs Walker, Stebner, and Patrick George; SPC Jonas O. Polson and SPC Oscar J. Escano; and SSG Harper Wilmoth comprised the "fresh" assault element of two three-man Ranger teams.[79]

Instead of giving an assault-initiation signal, CPT Self simply said, "When ready, go!" With that, the two machine guns opened up with a steady stream of fire. The assault elements moved deliberately up the hill in the knee-deep snow, firing, maneuvering, and tossing hand grenades for 40 meters. When the aircrew yelled, "Slow down! You're going to run out of ammo," Self ignored the comments, knowing that his men were firing and maneuvering with precision and experience toward the objective. Within minutes, the Rangers reached the bunker by the large rock boulder. SGT Stebner reported finding the first American body, lying face down in the snow near the boulder. When SSG Wilmoth's team cleared the bunker, it found two dead enemy fighters and a second American amid the debris. With this "new" information, CPT Self was suspicious and a little confused: "What was the real story here? Had these two been captured and forced to call in an aircraft?" Self told SSGT Brown to ask the ground force below about them since they had not given him any information.

When SSGT Brown talked to Mako 20, the ground force leader, he confirmed that both Americans were part of his team. Finally, after more than 6 hours into the fight, Self had a complete picture. When the Rangers stopped firing, he sent SSG Canon to the bunker area to identify the two dead Americans. They were Roberts and Chapman. Having done that, Canon took a team and pushed down the saddle on the left side of the aircraft, found two more bunkers, and killed another enemy fighter. All around the top of the summit was a network of enemy positions that took advantage of the terrain to conceal movement, stock ammunition, and provide good cover from air attacks. Dead enemy fighters littered the entire ridgetop as well as RPGs, ammunition, and small arms.

By 1115, the Rangers controlled the key terrain. CPT Self and Air Force SSGT Miller walked along the summit looking for a helicopter pickup zone (PZ). SSGT Brown called the special operations TOC in Bagram to relay that the PZ on Takur Ghar was cold. Self started back down to the disabled helicopter to direct that the casualties be brought up to the mountaintop when the situation changed.

Just as Self dropped below the summit, an RPG exploded behind his head. As he scrambled back to get a look, Self saw tracers coming from a group of enemy fighters on a parallel ridgeline about 350 meters away, slightly below his position. SSGT Vance scrambled to get some CAS. SSG Stebner, SGT Larken from the aircrew, and two other Rangers carrying SSG

Deese in his Skedco "luge" were halfway up the ridge when the enemy firing started. At the command, "Take cover!" Deese in his "luge" was unceremoniously dropped in the snow as everyone dove for cover behind a rock outcropping. Left in the open, Deese was happy that he was not sliding down the mountain again but quickly grabbed a small bush nearby to anchor himself. Then he realized where he was and thought, "This is really bad." As SSG DePouli turned PFC Gilliam's M-240B machine gun downhill, SSG Stebner yelled to Deese from the rock outcropping, "Don't worry sergeant. We're coming to get you," as PFC Gilliam let loose a stream of machine gun fire. "You don't have to," replied Deese. Each time Stebner tried to retrieve him, bullets ricocheted closer to Deese. "Just leave me alone," Deese called back, feeling like a "bullet magnet." Stebner yelled back, "Shut up! I'm not going to leave you there." On his third try, Stebner managed to reach Deese and drag him into the cover of the outcropping. Meanwhile, the Rangers returned fire with their M-4 carbines and the machine gun, and launched rifle grenades at the enemy's location.

In the original casualty collection point, Airman Cunningham had just inserted an IV into CWO Corbin when the enemy opened up again. With nowhere to go, CWO Talbert, SFC Lafayette, and Airman Cunningham shot back. Lafayette thought, "I have to keep the enemy's head down to protect these patients." CWO Gaines yelled because Talbert was shooting about 18 inches from his head. The three men tried to move Gaines but needed more help. The enemy fighters would pop their heads up long enough to fire and then duck down. In the midst of the firefight, Talbert dashed to get some help from the Rangers. When he reached them, they said that CAS was inbound in a few minutes, and then an RPG flew over their heads and exploded near the helicopter.

The men in the casualty collection point were now "sitting ducks" for enemy fighters. SFC Lafayette remembered thinking that the RPG explosion was nothing compared to the 500-pound bombs. While crawling toward Cunningham, a burst of fire interrupted him. Lafayette turned around to shoot back. As he did so, he was hit twice in the abdomen. The impacting bullets "felt like a sledgehammer," hitting him in the lower stomach below his body armor. The medic looked at his watch; it was 1130. Senior Airman Cunningham, only 6 feet away, had also been hit in the fusillade of bullets. The round penetrated his pelvis area and triggered heavy bleeding. Cunningham was still lucid and told Lafayette that he was in unbelievable pain. The firing continued all around them. That was when the Rangers above and the wounded below yelled at Lafayette and Cunningham to quit moving.

CWO Gaines theorized, "If we all play dead, maybe they'll stop shooting at us." The absence of motion seemed to work as the enemy shifted its concentration of fire. Several minutes later, during a lull in the shooting, Lafayette mustered the courage to check himself. Being a medic, he knew that an abdominal wound was about the worst type to receive in this situation. He felt down and then looked; it was wet but not bleeding, possibly urine or snow. Lafayette felt a little better. During the firing, SGT Matthew LaFrenz, the Ranger medic, had low crawled to Cunningham and Lafayette and begun treating their wounds.

The Rangers continued to battle the enemy at long range. SPC Randy J. Pazder spotted and killed a foe that stayed exposed too long. Then, on a ridge to the east, they spotted another small group moving into position. SSG Canon sent SPC Vela to get more ammunition from the helicopter 150 meters away. As Vela rushed down through the snow to the helicopter, enemy fire erupted around him and he dove for cover behind a rock with SSG Stebner. Then Vela crawled over to SSG DePouli's position and quickly loaded 7.62 ammunition into the spare barrel bag and tossed it halfway to Canon, who retrieved the bag. Anticipating where the next fighter would emerge to shoot, SPC Pazder poured machine gun fire into the surrounding area. When Navy F-14 fighters arrived carrying 500-pound bombs, SSGT Vance tried to hit the reverse side of the summit ridge with the bombs.

The aerial munitions were dropped closer than expected. One 500-pounder landed about 75 meters from the Rangers, knocking SSG DePouli's helmet off. He called back to CPT Self and asked for a "heads up" next time. "Sure, no problem" was the reply.[80] CWO Talbert saw a piece of bomb shrapnel hit SGT Walker's helmet. The Ranger simply looked around as if to say, "What was that?" and started shooting again. About 1215, during a JDAM strike "danger close," Self heard a "whump, whump, whump" sound and then watched a baseball bat-sized chunk of metal fly end over end about 100 feet over his head. That was too close even for his initials. The JDAMs turned the tree- and snow-covered ridge into a massive dirt pile. As CWO Corbin looked skyward from his Skedco, he saw enemy bodies and debris being flung through the air above him. The Rangers cheered in unison when they saw three enemy fighters fly through the air, signifying the elimination of the current threat. Their cheers provided some comfort to the exposed casualties as well.

The Ranger medic, SGT LaFrenz, categorized the new casualties—the two medics, Lafayette and Cunningham—as urgent surgical, those with the most life-threatening injuries. He was very concerned about Cunningham. While he had controlled the external bleeding, he could not be certain if he had stopped any of the internal bleeding. SSGT Miller assisted LaFrenz in caring for the wounded and preparing them to be moved. The next big requirement was to get the casualties close to the new PZ.

Because of the high altitude and acute physical fatigue, it took four or five men to carry an injured man on a Skedco litter the 80 meters to the summit and required several stops along the way. CPT Self calculated that a good move took 10 to 15 minutes per casualty. Since there were now six litter-bound casualties and six bodies to move, it would take 2 to 3 hours to move everyone to the PZ. The Rangers, airmen, and Night Stalkers were worn out. As each man reached his physical limit, Self rotated tasks to provide a brief respite. At 1300, SSGT Vance made an urgent request to the special operations TOC in Bagram for immediate casualty evacuation. His call was acknowledged. He was told, "Stand by." The TOC requested the status of the PZ. As Vance replied "Cold," another mortar round hit in the area.

At FARP Texaco, the QRF commanders, helicopter flight leads, and AMC were still working on a deliberate evacuation plan. By 1330, a plan was ready, and the pilots and ground forces returned to the three Chinooks. At the same time, CPT Self made an urgent request for casualty evacuation, trying to negotiate an immediate extraction of the six wounded and a nighttime exfiltration of the remaining force if necessary. He told the special operations TOC that he had a good reverse slope PZ, protected from enemy fire, and emphasized his medic's opinion that the wounded might lose limbs or die if they were not evacuated before dark. The TOC replied that it understood the situation and that a 70-man QRF was standing by because intelligence reports indicated that the enemy leadership had called for reinforcements to converge on the Takur Ghar. Self did not want another 70 personnel crowded onto the mountain where there was no place for them to land.

A short time later, CPT Self sensed from radio traffic that the tone of the operation had changed. The special operations headquarters was prosecuting targets identified by long-range OPs manned by coalition troops and U.S. Special Forces. It was obvious that CAS was being called in on any enemy movement in the Shah-i-Khot Valley area. At 1430, with all three helicopters ready to launch on the 25-minute flight to Takur Ghar, the senior special operations commander at Bagram ordered Razor 54 to shutdown. The new extraction time was scheduled for 2015 local time.

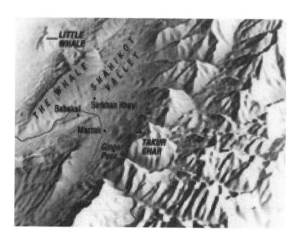

Figure 17. Mountains and "Whales."

The special operations soldiers on the top of Takur Ghar were not informed of the new extraction time. They continued to watch for the enemy and cared for the wounded men. CWO Talbert and SGT Walters rummaged inside the helicopter, stripping off the soundproof insulation to shelter the wounded and sharing the water and food they found aboard. Rangers provided security and helped to retrieve clothing, sleeping bags, and blankets, preparing for the drop in temperature as the sun dropped lower. SGT LaFrenz and SSGT Miller, the other Air Force PJ, made rounds of their patients every 15 minutes, monitoring vital signs and lucidity, changing dressings, and giving reassurance that help was on the way. LaFrenz was always positive. He repeatedly said, "Hey guys, they're going to come get us. We're going to be out of here soon." But the Night Stalkers knew differently. The rescue force would not come until after dark. As SSG Deese kept talking to keep everyone alert, SGT Larken stuffed IV bags inside his shirt to keep them warm for the wounded.

At 1520, SGT LaFrenz, the Ranger medic, called the TOC at Bagram, to explain that "medical conditions were getting worse." "Roger, we understand," was the reply. Ten minutes later, the TOC told CPT Self that the recovery would be at 2015. He realized that no one wanted to risk losing another helicopter, but he also felt that he had better situational awareness on Takur Ghar; the Rangers did control the summit. Self also understood that no one had gotten it right yet and that it was a "no-win" decision for the commanders at Bagram. Now, it would truly be a struggle for survival among the wounded.

Over the next 4 hours, the temperature slowly dropped with the sun, and a wind began to come up. During a quiet moment, SGT Stebner told SSG Wilmoth how strange it was to

316

be in such a beautiful place amid such dire conditions.[81] Darkness descended around 1700. The wounded men were bundled up with piles of clothing and soundproofing. While CWO Talbert was holding a pressure bandage on Senior Airman Cunningham, the PJ passed on his final wishes. A few minutes past 1730, Cunningham took a turn for the worst. LaFrenz and Miller immediately began emergency trauma care. SFC Lafayette began telling CWO Talbert what medical equipment to grab from his medical bag, giving its location and purpose. Talbert passed the equipment to LaFrenz or Miller as needed. After 30 minutes of trying everything and having exhausted his medical knowledge, LaFrenz angrily told CPT Self that Cunningham had died. It was 1800, and the helicopters were not due for more than 2 hours.

When the 3rd Battalion MH-47Ds arrived at Bagram at 1650, MAJ Schantz, the air mission commander (AMC), and his four aircrews were given an impromptu briefing. They were to carry another 59 Rangers to Texaco and depart in less than an hour. The death of Senior Airman Cunningham had been a crushing blow to the special operations commanders at Bagram and Texaco. Now an intimate sense of urgency filled everyone. CWO Charles Elkenback (pseudonym), 3/160th flight lead, pushed the four Chinooks to reach the deliberate extraction briefing at FARP Texaco.[82] While en route, Schantz was tasked to find and deliver an Air Force CCT to the Gardez airstrip, the site arranged for the medical transfer. The CCT was to control the helicopter flow for the surgical team that was aboard a specially equipped MC-130 Combat Talon aircraft. Schantz told Elkenback to fly to the FARP first and then to deliver the CCT to Gardez. Meanwhile, the key planners gathered at Texaco for a final update briefing.

The ground force recovery force, made up of CSAR teams and assault teams, needed a fourth Chinook. When the 3rd Battalion MH-47Ds arrived at 1850, CWO Daniel Henley (pseudonym), another flight lead, was tasked to support the recovery force.[83] Because the MH-47Ds had just arrived, CPT Brian Jefferson (pseudonym), Razor 54, the AMC, requested that the mission be "bumped" 30 minutes.[84] When approval was granted, Jefferson ran over to Henley's aircraft and briefed him on the scheme of maneuver, radio frequencies, and emergency contingencies.

The plan was not complex: Razor 02 would lead the flight to a release point where Razor 05 would separate and fly to the ground force's location on the south side of Takur Ghar. Razor 06 and Agile 03, Henley's Chinook, would hold at the release point until Razor 02 had cleared the Ranger PZ as "cold." Razor 02 would extract the critically wounded. Razor 05 would extract the KIA and noncritically wounded, and Agile 03 would pick up the remaining force on the ground. The two AH-64 Apache gunships would provide armed escort protection, along with two AC-130 Spectre gunships overhead. Each loaded helicopter would fly, in turn, to Gardez to transfer the wounded to the surgical team's MC-130 aircraft. The mixed flight of three MH-47Es, one MH-47D, and two AH-64 Apaches lifted off from Texaco at 1945.

CWO Talbert and CPT Self had discussed the best approach path, landing area, and the priority of evacuation for each helicopter. SSGT Brown relayed the flight information to the TOC, and it passed the information to the inbound Chinooks: "Inbound heading 090 degrees, landing heading 135 degrees, departure heading 270 degrees." The unmistakable sound of the Chinooks was the best sound CWO Corbin and the rest had heard all day, and many cheered. CPT Self radioed that the mountaintop was secure and that they needed help carrying the casualties. To his dismay and contrary to instructions, Razor 02 landed with its nose toward

317

the casualties instead of its tail. Informed of his mistake, CWO Oliver felt that he would cause more damage by repositioning. The CSAR and QRF elements exited the aircraft, assumed a kneeling position in a perimeter, and did not move or attempt to help. In the heavy downwash of the rotors, the Rangers, 160th crewmen, and airmen struggled to carry their casualties through 40 meters of knee-deep snow. The beleaguered men on the mountain were incensed. Physically exhausted, it took them 19 minutes to load their seriously wounded personnel, while a fresh recovery force watched. At one point, CWO Corbin fell completely out of his Skedco litter into the snow because of the steep slope of the terrain. Razor 02 left with 11 WIAs and the four-man CSAR team aboard.

The next two aircraft landed in the correct direction to facilitate loading. Once again, the QRF and CSAR exited the aircraft and set up a perimeter, and watched the men on the mountain stumbling down through the snow with the six KIAs. CWO Talbert recalled the feeling of relief once aboard the helicopter but also the uneasiness and vulnerability of waiting for what seemed like an eternity until the aircraft lifted off. Agile 03 swept the PZ and extracted the remaining Rangers and the third recovery force.

CWO Solanis, piloting Razor 05, knew that he was carrying too much fuel to land on the southern side of the mountain.[85] He remedied the problem by dumping fuel during the 25-minute flight to the PZ. Just before reaching the Shah-i-Khot Valley, Solanis achieved maximum landing weight for the altitude of the PZ. Having no communication with the ground force team, Razor 05 picked its way through the valley from the east. Luckily, the crew spotted a distant strobe light and picked up the laser designators from the team. Solanis knew that there were wounded among the ground force and that he needed to land as close as possible. CWO Derrick Donalds (pseudonym) went into a hover 80 feet above the team and descended straight down into a gorge with precipitous granite walls on three sides.[86] Fortunately, a small mound at the bottom of the gorge provided a raised landing area. SSG Greg Law (pseudonym), the flight engineer, verbally guided Donalds until the aft wheels touched down very close to the team.[87] With the front wheels off the ground, the ground force loaded aboard the hovering Chinook. Once aboard, Mako 20, the team leader, informed the crew that they had seen tracers fired at the helicopter, but the steep granite walls had masked the fires. Donalds eased the big helicopter straight up, then turned and picked his way back through the Shah-i-Khot Valley to Gardez.

Razor 05 arrived first at Gardez. The surgical team's MC-130 had taxied off the runway and was mired down in the mud. It was out of the mission. With three wounded aboard his aircraft, SGT Randal Kelley (pseudonym), a 160th medic, continued triaging the casualties.[88] When Razor 02 arrived with the very seriously wounded from the mountaintop, Kelley and the chief surgeon decided that the best course of action was to load the most critical casualties on a Chinook and fly them directly to Bagram. CWO Oliver and CPT Jefferson agreed and would use Razor 02 because it had the most fuel. The most critical were quickly loaded aboard Razor 02, and Oliver raced back to Bagram while SGT Kelley continued to work on his patients aboard Razor 05. By 2000, Razor 02 was delivering the critically wounded to the 274th Forward Surgical Team at the Bagram hospital pad.

Meanwhile, at Gardez, the less serious casualties were transferred to a British Chinook equipped with an operating room. The surgeons quickly stripped the wounded men, evaluated their conditions, sedated them, and began operating. Once the patients had been stabilized, the British Chinook flew them to Bagram and the 274th Forward Surgical Team. After Agile 03 delivered CPT Self and his Rangers to Bagram, the soldiers accounted for their sensitive equipment, cleaned weapons, and treated their injuries before going to bed.

In an effort to rescue Navy PO1 Roberts, a number of actions were taken that set in motion a rescue action that ultimately cost six more lives on Takur Ghar mountain. These combat actions demonstrated SOF's strong resolve to respond to comrades in peril on the battlefield. The extended fight was replete with examples of personal bravery under fire, valorous acts, self-sacrifice, and cool professionalism. While there were communications problems and situational awareness was lost at times, decisions at all levels were made with the best intentions and with the best information available at the time. What should not be forgotten is that the Night Stalkers and Rangers with special operations airmen accomplished their mission.

What began as an Operation ANACONDA supporting operation—inserting a special reconnaissance (SR) team on Takur Ghar in the Shah-i-Khot Valley—took public interest away from the main effort by conventional forces. The popular attention span drifted off shortly after the rescue was complete. In the meantime, the war against the *Taliban* and *al-Qaeda* holdouts was still being prosecuted in earnest by Army Special Forces teams working with Afghan Military Forces (AMF).

During 5 to 9 March 2002, offensive activities in ANACONDA hit a lull as the commanders adjusted plans for the next attack. TF Rakkasan, supported by coalition air power, deliberately swept across its objective area, clearing caves and fighting positions. COL John Mulholland, JSOTF-North commander at Bagram, asked LTC Carl Hooper whether armor or mechanized forces were needed to sweep around the "Whale." His affirmative response led to negotiations with the Afghan Interim Authority (AIA) for additional Afghan forces and tanks. Defense Minister Fahim Khan specifically chose General Gul Haidar to lead a 700-Tajik force from Kabul to Gardez. At JSOTF-North, there was considerable concern that Haidar's Tajiks and Commander Zia's Pashtuns would not cooperate and that the two groups might actually fight each other! The Special Forces leaders and other representatives worked out a basic strategy to unite the Tajik and Pashtun effort. The Americans would dictate the boundaries and concept of employment. At least that was what they planned. Reality was much different. ODA 394 was assigned to the operation on D+4 to replace the decimated ODA 372.

ODA 394 Climbs the "Whale"

During the second phase of ANACONDA, 3rd SFG CPT Jed Samuels (pseudonym) and ODA 394 were paired with a seasoned team from 5th SFG, ODA 594, known by their radio call sign of "Texas 14."[89] The two Special Forces teams and security elements left Bagram on 6 March 2002 in a small convoy of Hi-Lux and Toyota 4-Runner pickup trucks and sport utility vehicles driving 4½ hours to their new base just outside Gardez. To the soldiers of ODA 394, their camp "looked like an old West adobe fort, complete with towers." Inside the mud-walled compound there were already more than 100 coalition soldiers and their trucks. LTC Carl Hooper (pseudonym), 1st Battalion, 5th SFG, was the command and control element (radio call sign "Shark") of three Special Forces ODAs: 394, the combat-tested 594, and 372. There were also Australian troops; U.S. Army combat engineers; and

Figure 18. Typical Special Forces base camp area in Afghanistan.

other Special Forces elements with guides, vehicles, and gear jammed into the small fort.[90]

ODA 394's battalion commander, LTC Terry Sanders (pseudonym), originally told them that they had about 48 hours to plan and prepare before entering the combat zone.[91] But events had moved along at a faster pace. At about 2100 that evening, Samuels and his team sergeant, MSG Ty McFadden (pseudonym), received their mission orders from LTC Hooper on the second floor of a small hut inside the compound. Eight hours later, half of ODA 394 drove out of the crumbling fort to join the second Afghan offensive into the Shah-i-Khot Valley.

While half of the team headed toward the valley, SFC Jason "J.D." Thurman (pseudonym) and SFC Jules Arde (pseudonym), left at Bagram, headed toward Kandahar to collect the team equipment that was left behind. After hitching a ride aboard a C-130 transport going to Kandahar and collecting and loading the team's equipment, the two found themselves stranded. With everything happening up north, the two sergeants and their equipment were bumped off flight after flight by personnel and equipment having much higher priority for air movement. While they sat on the boxes of team gear by the runway, an Air Force airfield supervisor strode up and asked where they needed to go. As the three talked, Thurman and Arde realized that with their beards, mixed uniforms, and weaponry, they might pass as members of another special operations unit. Arde quickly fixed an unusual noise and flash suppressor to the muzzle of his M-4 carbine. It worked. The Air Force flight operations director made an assumption, and Thurman simply asked to go to Bagram. In short order, their equipment was loaded and they were airborne. At Bagram, their good luck lapsed.

ODA 394 had already left for Gardez. Their team boxes, lashed on an Air Force aluminum air-delivery platform, had been unloaded elsewhere in the night. A day later, SFCs Thurman and Arde finally found their team pallet in a distant part of the airfield appropriately called the "frustrated cargo" area. After acquiring additional cold-weather clothing for the ODA, they found room for their team boxes on a truck convoy bound for Gardez and climbed aboard.[92]

When half of ODA 394 left the Gardez compound on 7 March for the Shah-i-Khot Valley, CPT Samuels and MSG McFadden planned to rotate the split teams into and out of the battle every 48 hours, as they had heard other Special Forces teams had done when directing airstrikes. The "split 394 team" moved with ODA 594, ODA 372, and several hundred Pashtun

320

soldiers to "Checkpoint Charlie" where Samuels and SGT Stefan Morris (pseudonym), the medic, established a small command post with their Afghan translator and two sergeants from the other ODAs.[93] The main body of the group then dispersed to three forward positions.[94] McFadden, SSG Jerry Rawlins (pseudonym), and four members of ODA 372 went to Observation Post South (OP South), overlooking Tergul Ghar, that everyone called the "Whale" because of its close resemblance to the dominant terrain feature at the Army NTC in the Mojave Desert at Fort Irwin, California.[95] The Special Forces soldiers at OP South were accompanied by 15 Pashtuns, while another 15 guarded their trucks in the gully to their north.

Part of ODA 594, organized for 48-hour rotations like ODA 394, moved toward OP North on the northern knob of Tergul Ghar.[96] This rocky knoll on the "Whale" had been dubbed the "Guppy" by the Americans.[97] As 30 of Commander Zia's Pashtuns climbed the northern end of Terghul Ghar mountain, two pair of Marine Corps AH-1W Super Cobra attack helicopters flew in ahead, firing rocket-propelled antitank missiles into cave openings on the "Guppy."[98]

SSG Bernard Dubois (pseudonym), ODA 394, set up the mission support site, with several members of ODA 594, adjacent to the 82mm mortar position of SSG Cash Galtier (pseudonym) from ODA 594.[99] Dubois, a weapons specialist, was amazed by how proficient the Pashtun mortar crews were. He knew that ODA 594 had just managed a remarkable feat of training, turning several hundred "jundees," as they referred to the Pashtun tribesmen, from illiterate peasant village recruits into armed fighters in less than four weeks. But they were riflemen. The mortar is a fairly complex, crew-served weapon that requires close teamwork and trust. To fire it accurately requires advanced military skills, even for American soldiers.

Yet SSG Galtier had his "jundees" dropping mortar rounds and hitting enemy positions a mile and more to their front. The three Soviet-made 82mm mortars were fired without sights and fire-direction equipment. Galtier made his own plotting board and computed ballistic data sheets with appropriate explosive firing charges. The Paducah, Kentucky, native, known for his thick Southern drawl, did not have a translator while he was training his Afghan mortar teams. According to the ODA 594 team sergeant, "Galtier spoke 'Paducah' to his 'jundees,' and they understood."[100] Observing them in action was "truly amazing" to SSG Dubois.[101]

For the next 48 hours, B-1 and B-52 bombers bombed the "Whale" around the clock. The main ridgeline was a "free-fire zone," and American, British, and French warplanes that could not find targets anywhere else in Afghanistan flew to the Shah-i-Khot Valley and dropped their ordnance to avoid landing with it. "It literally looked like a fireworks display," said SGT Morris (ODA 394), who was 3 miles from the impact zone, "and when the 2,000-pounders [bombs] hit, they shook the checkpoint violently."

The constant bombing promoted surrenders and attracted the press. In the midst of the two days of bombing, a wounded *al-Qaeda* fighter, still carrying his rifle and barefoot in the freezing cold, walked to OP South and surrendered. He said he had been hit by the Pashtuns' mortar fire. The *al-Qaeda* prisoner was escorted back to Checkpoint Charlie where SGT Morris treated him. The combat medic was very impressed by how tough the prisoner was. "He had several 'through-and-through' mortar shrapnel wounds that I had to probe with my finger to see if the rib cage had been penetrated to make sure that no vital spot was hit," said Morris. "The guy didn't even flinch."[102] A teenager who identified himself as an *al-Qaeda* fighter also surrendered near OP South. All that he carried with him was a miniature copy of the Koran and a small radio.[103] When a group of journalists tried to enter the Shah-i-Khot Valley on the rutted road near Checkpoint Charlie, CPT Samuels and SGT Morris turned them back. The reporters were from all the major news services—BBC, CNN, ABC, CBS, and Reuters. Samuels noted that along with their hired guards all were wearing sidearms. "They said that they purchased them in Kandahar," Samuels recounted, "for self-protection."[104]

As CPT Samuels and MSG McFadden had planned, their split-team elements switched positions on 9 March. McFadden, SSG Rawlins, and SSG Dubois returned to Gardez, and WO Max Gorley (pseudonym) brought the other half of ODA 394 to the front lines. SSG Jake Millett and Air Force SSGT Damon Hulse (pseudonyms), the team enlisted tactical air controller (ETAC), went to OP South. CPT Samuels, WO Gorley, and SGT Morris stayed at Checkpoint Charlie. While the heavy bombing continued, the three Special Forces ODAs waited for the arrival of an additional Northern Alliance force from the Kabul area, supposedly with Russian-made tanks that were already a day late. In the outer Afghan ring of blocking positions, ODA 542 conducted a battle handoff with ODA 381 at the Orgun base on 9 March and redeployed.[105]

Gul Haidar finally arrived late on 8 March with about 600 Tajik fighters and four T-54 Russian tanks with 100mm guns. Although the tanks were early 1950s vintage, they were still effective combat machines. Six Russian BMP armored personnel carriers with small rapid-fire cannons mounted on top also accompanied the Tajik column. Although the BMP appeared to be a small tank, it could carry a squad of soldiers inside its armored hull. Intermixed in the column of vehicles were also several truck-mounted rocket launchers.[106]

Despite the fact that Commander Zia Lodin was Pashtun and General Gul Haidar was a Panshjir Valley Tajik—traditional enemies—they entered into negotiations. Under the very close scrutiny and supervision of the American Special Forces leaders and some senior representatives from the AIA ministries of defense and interior, the two rival Afghan leaders talked together for almost 4 hours. One of the success stories of Operation ANACONDA was the considerable amount of cooperation and mutual support that Zia and Haidar displayed for one another to develop an acceptable command relationship and general plan for attack. The rapport that the Special Forces teams enjoyed with Zia and Haidar did much to contribute to the success of the negotiations.

LTC Hooper explained the next phase of the ANACONDA plan to the three ODAs. Haidar's predominantly Tajik force would move to the northern end of the "Whale" while Zia's Pashtun fighters would maneuver around the western side of the ridge and position themselves at the southern end of the "Whale." At 0500 the next morning, the U.S. Air Force would drop a 15,000-pound "daisy cutter" bomb on top of the "Whale" to signal the start of the attack into the valley.[107] To better support the effort, CPT Samuels was to relocate part of ODA 394 to another observation position with a better view down the Shah-i-Khot. From that vantage point, it could direct close air support (CAS) for both the Pashtun and Tajik offensives into the valley when the attack started. That was the plan, anyway.

Controlling Gul Haidar proved to be impossible. While ODA 394 watched, bewildered, "the Gul's troops" moved to their assault line at the base of the "Whale" and then dismounted troops who began climbing the mountain. As evening approached, the Tajiks were climbing up the northern end as bombs were falling on the crest of the "Whale." Samuels reported that Haidar was "out of control." LTC Hooper issued new orders: ODA 394 was to join the Northern Alliance force on the "Whale" the next morning "to regain control." The split ODA was directed to form the Tajiks into a line, shoulder to shoulder, and sweep down the "Whale," clearing out any enemy that had survived the aerial bombardment. That night, "Gul's troops" built a huge bonfire on the northern crest of the "Whale." MSG McFadden thought that the Tajiks wanted to demonstrate their bravado and success. "It was like, 'See what we've done.'" At any rate, the act of defiance forced Hooper to cancel the "daisy cutter" bomb.[108]

Figure 19. General Haidar at rest.

Figure 20. General Haidar on the move.

ODA 394 was just reaching its new position with a contingent of Zia's Pashtuns when it received new orders by radio. As the sun went down, the small truck convoy turned around to head back to Checkpoint Charlie. The Special Forces soldiers had refrained from using their NVG to drive in the darkness because Zia's men had no goggles. They turned on their trucks' headlights. Worried that the lights would attract enemy, and possibly friendly, fire, ODA 394 stopped the convoy and managed to convince the "jundees" that only every other truck needed its lights on. This compromise worked haphazardly. At every opportunity, the "jundees" challenged the Americans and each other for convoy lead, despite the darkness, extremely bad road, and uncharted minefields. Among the Afghans, the "pole position" was a matter of prestige, and high-speed, reckless jockeying was a constant problem day or night. It did not matter. By the time ODA 394 got back to Checkpoint Charlie, the members were wondering how many other changes were in store for them tomorrow.[109]

When Tajik guides led the Americans up the northern slope of the "Whale" the next morning, Gul Haidar was not there. "The Gul" was in the valley below them with his armored vehicles. The infantry on the "Whale" was led by his second in command. CPT Samuels talked with him through a 46-year-old American citizen named Hafiz. This interpreter had been arrested during the Soviet occupation and imprisoned for a year before he escaped and walked across the southern mountains into Pakistan. Hafiz eventually immigrated to the United States, where he became an American citizen, living in Anaheim, California. He had worked as a driving instructor for the California Department of Motor Vehicles for 13 years when he agreed to be a translator for the U.S. military in Afghanistan. Hafiz was sent to K2 to join ODA 372. From Gardez, he saw action in the first phase of Operation ANACONDA. ODA 394 met Hafiz at Checkpoint Charlie as he helped manage the civilian traffic along the road. To MSG McFadden, Hafiz seemed "extremely sensitive, almost effeminate," and the Afghan-American scolded the Special Forces soldiers if they cursed in his presence. He was fluent in English, Pashto, and Farsi; "perceptive about men's characters"; and "physically very tough." While carrying a duffel bag, Hafiz easily stayed up with the team during the climb up and over the boulders on the north end of Tergul Ghar.[110]

After getting Gul's troops lined up abreast on the ridgeline, CPT Samuels had the Tajik commander begin the advance to clear the bare granite spine of the "Whale." "Ten steps from the start line," said Samuels, "Gul Haidar's men saw the three small hamlets, Babulkheyl, Zerikheyl, and Marzak, in the Shah-i-Khot Valley below them to the southeast. "They simply abandoned the line," he said, "and just ran off the mountain to steal stuff" from the villages, each of which consisted of no more than a dozen "bombed-out huts." Samuels tried to get the Gul to recall the marauding fighters to deal with the enemy on the mountain first. He reminded the robed leader that U.S. infantrymen across the valley were not expecting this rush of Afghans into the valley and might fire on them. Gul responded, "It does not matter if they are killed." Then, sensing Samuels' disapproval, Gul barked orders into his hand-held radio. Hafiz, the translator, leaned toward Samuels and McFadden and whispered, "He's telling his men that a few must come back so the Americans will see them, but the rest can keep going. These are very bad men."[111]

ODA 394 had been accompanied by 20 of Zia's Pashtuns who now guarded the Americans from Gul's Tajiks. The atmosphere became very tense as the Tajiks and Pashtuns traded insults about their tribes and provinces. "Zia's men were well paid and well disciplined, and they were very protective of us," said Samuels. They formed a circle around the Americans when the Tajiks and other Afghans came near.

The two groups could be distinguished in part by their uniforms. Gul's troops wore foreign-made green camouflage fatigues and caps. Only their commander wore traditional Afghan dress—a turban and long robe. When MSG McFadden was near the Tajiks, they reeked of burning hashish, which most smoked "all day long." Zia's Pashtuns wore American-made dark brown polyester fleece trousers with sage green nylon coats or olive drab canvas jackets. On their heads they wore either American black wool watch caps or the native Panjshir Valley hats. They were armed with newly issued Russian and Chinese assault rifles and machine guns, and wore ammunition magazine vests. The U.S. insulated boots, often too big for the Pashtuns' feet, were often replaced by light shoes or slippers, even in the freezing winter weather.

Having organized the Pashtuns along Western military lines, the leaders wore improvised rank insignia fashioned by their Special Forces trainers. ODA 594 and ODA 372 bought safety pins and buttons at a local market and in a formal ceremony in front of their newly formed platoons and companies, pinned the symbols of rank on the combat leaders: Platoon commanders, in charge of 40 to 50 fighters, wore one silver button on their collar; company commanders, who led three or four platoons, wore two; and Zia Lodin, the battalion commander with three companies numbering some 500 troops, displayed three gold buttons on a safety pin. "Zia's commanders were genuinely proud of those buttons," said one of the Special Forces advisers.[112]

These men also wore strips of reflective "glint tape" pinned to the tops of their caps and on one shoulder of their jackets. The sensor operators in the AC-130 Spectre gunships, prowling the night skies over Afghanistan, could see the glint tape readily. The glint wearers were friendlies.[113]

ODA 394 and its Pashtun platoon led the sweep southward down the "Whale." About 300 of Gul Haidar's "infantry" troops, having finished looting the three abandoned villages, trailed behind. They met no resistance, but at each promontory along the bomb-blasted ridge, the Tajik commander carefully stationed a few of his troops "to mark their territory," Samuels learned. When ODA 394 reached the south end of the massif about 1500, it formed a night defensive perimeter with their 20 loyal "jundees."[114]

Hafiz's warning about the Tajiks had not been taken seriously initially. SFC Arde was sitting on the slope checking his equipment when one of Gul's men walked straight up to him and cheerfully tried to chat with him in broken English. While Arde was distracted, several Special Forces teammates watched in amazement as another Tajik crept up behind him and silently, and very deftly, unlatched, twisted, and removed the flash suppressor from the muzzle of the M-4 carbine on his back. Earlier that day SFC Thurman and Air Force SSGT Millett were at the base of the "Whale" guarding their four pickups loaded with heavy equipment and had to chase away Gul Haidar's men who slipped aboard the trucks to rifle the team's gear. "It was like dealing with professional thieves," said Samuels.[115]

Once the Afghans supported by the Special Forces teams had cleared the "Whale," Gul Haidar's Soviet tank-led column entered the northern end of the Shah-i-Khot Valley. ODA 394, their Pashtun fighters, and Gul's foot soldiers along the peaks of the ridgeline watched them enter the valley. On the east side of the valley, several 101st Airborne infantry companies from TF Rakkasan still manned blocking positions where they had been since Operation ANACONDA started the week before. The green-painted T-54 battle tanks clanked down the dirt road at the base of the valley, sending up dark exhaust plumes from their ancient diesel engines. All of a sudden, to the amazement of the Special Forces soldiers, the Gul's tankers started firing their cannons at the American infantry soldiers guarding their flank.[116] On his radio, SSG Hulse heard another Air Force special tactics airman across the valley urgently trying to stop the tank fire.

Samuels yelled at the Tajik commander next to him that the Afghan tanks were shooting at Americans and that he had to stop them. The Special Forces soldiers were enraged by the Tajiks. "We were hoping," said Samuels, "that the 101st had Javelins [antitank missiles] and would fire back." Fortunately, the Rakkasan company commander under fire knew the tanks belonged to the anti-*Taliban* forces and had ordered his men to stay down under cover and hold their fire. "It was chaotic," remembered Samuels who quickly radioed MAJ Mike Hopkins (pseudonym), who was traveling with Gul's armored column, to call a "cease-fire." Only two tank rounds were fired at the U.S. troops before the Afghans stopped shooting, and they fell short. There were no American casualties, and the attack continued as the Soviet T-54 tanks traversed their cannons to the rear.[117]

During the advance down the valley, WO Gorley spotted several likely cave openings on the steep western slope of the "Whale." SSG Hulse called for CAS, got a pair of Marine AH-1 Super Cobra attack helicopters, and began the process of directing them to the targets. The craggy terrain and shadows made this difficult, but Gorley knew that there were no friendlies on that side of the mountain. As the slim gray Super Cobras circled to line up for their "rocket run," Gul Haidar's men ran to the Special Forces soldiers, yelling "No, no, stop the helicopters!" "Their people" were down below in the caves. Standing beside the Tajik second in command, MSG McFadden asked if any of his troops had moved down the slope. He replied, "Yes, we have a watering party down there." Having seen Gul's men wandering off in small groups during the day searching for loot, the Special Forces team sergeant could not be certain if the Tajik was lying or not. Rather than challenge the Afghan commander, McFadden told Gorley that there might be friendlies in the caves. Gorley said that it was not possible. He suspected that the Tajiks were afraid the helicopter rockets might destroy any booty the fleeing *Taliban* and *al-Qaeda* fighters might abandon. Frustrated but left with no choice, Gorley reluctantly had Hulse wave off the Super Cobras hovering near the ridge top waiting for clearance to fire.[118] As they banked to fly away, MSG McFadden saw one of the Marine pilots saluting him.[119]

Zia pushed north along his planned route and quickly secured Babulkheyl, Zerikheyl, and Marzak. Haidar attacked through scattered resistance and cleared Serkhankheyl within 90 minutes, meeting Zia's forces at Babulkheyl. There, Zia's Pashtuns stopped some of Haidar's men from entering the village because they were intent on looting. The situation became very tense—Tajiks were fighting in Pashtun territory—until the accompanying Special Forces teams defused it by separating the two forces.[120]

As luck would have it, ODA 394 had to spend the night on top of the "Whale." Perched at 9,000 feet above sea level at the end of a long day, the team redistributed their limited supply of water and rations. The "jundees" melted snow from the scattered patches on the mountain for drinking water. SSG Morris was particularly short. When he left Gardez four days earlier, he thought he would only be away for 48 hours. Instead of carrying a large rucksack, he elected to bring a "three-day assault pack," about the size of a student's book bag, and go with the clothes on his back. Unable to return to Gardez, Morris recalled the old soldier's joke, "Travel light, freeze at night." And he did that night on the "Whale." More serious was the situation with their Tajik allies. Angered by and distrustful of Gul Haidar's troops, Samuels told the commander to move his men several hundred yards north away from the detachment's overnight perimeter. For security against both the enemy and its allies, the team put out tripwires with flares attached to warn them of any unwanted intruders.[121]

Secretary of Defense Donald Rumsfeld stated that Operation ANACONDA had entered a "mopping-up" phase.[122] Early the next morning, 12 March, ODA 394 was alerted to prepare for the arrival of an American infantry battalion on top of the "Whale." The Special Forces team was to select and mark three helicopter landing zones (LZs) north of its overnight position on the ridge of the mountain. Then ODA 394 was to support the infantrymen for "24 to 48 hours." CPT Samuels sent WO Gorley with Air Force SSGT Hulse, Hafiz, and five Pashtuns to reconnoiter for LZs. Given the broken, rough terrain, it took an hour for the LZ party to reach the potential landing area. However, only two Chinooks would be able to land simultaneously. SSGT Hulse was to be the air traffic controller for the helicopters. An hour later, the party spotted three CH-47s enter the Shah-i-Khot Valley, but Hulse was unable to contact them on his radio. WO Gorley had "a ringside seat" as the three Chinooks flew by his LZs and, instead, landed in a cloud of dust 600 yards to his west where the valley floor met the base of the "Whale."[123]

As the first lift of medium-cargo helicopters flew off, Gorley could hear squad leaders shouting to their men in English to spread out and take cover—"very professionally done," he thought. Then he picked up a bright orange signal panel (VS-17), about the size of a small tablecloth, and waved it about until he could see the soldiers below him pointing up at him on the mountain. Having attracted their attention, Gorley walked down the slope with his arms out to his side, yelling, "Don't shoot, we're Americans!" "Don't worry, Yank," came the reply from the coalition point man. The lead element of the coalition battalion had arrived. They were soon joined by the rest of their battalion, the 2nd Brigade headquarters of the 10th Mountain Division, and an American infantry company. Gorley was told that the coalition forces were participating in Operation HARPOON, a cave-clearing mission on the "Whale" planned five days earlier. WO Gorley wondered why his Special Forces team had only been advised of this operation 2 hours earlier.[124]

The "24- to 48-hour" support of Operation HARPOON forces lasted six days. The coalition forces impressed the Special Forces soldiers. "They knew what they were doing," said Gorley, "and they went out and did it."[125] The caves they discovered and searched were mostly empty. It was the American infantry that had first contact with the enemy on a hilltop only 300 yards from ODA 394's first overnight position. When the U.S. infantrymen approached the cave, they followed an established procedure of firing two antitank rockets and a machine gun into the opening first. When they did, an enemy fighter "came running out of there, spraying [bullets] with an AK." He was instantly gunned down; the hail of bullets tore his head off.

The firing prompted several reactions. First, the shooting roused several of the American infantry heat casualties sitting on the ridgeline who got to their feet and started running toward the sound of the gunshots. The suddenly alert infantrymen were also surprised by the coincidental, unexpected arrival of a 30-truck Pashtun convoy with the vehicles displaying VS-17 orange panels led by Special Forces MAJ Mike Hopkins along the base of the "Whale." The American infantrymen—a "very aggressive" bunch, according to WO Gorley—instantly swung their weapons on the line of vehicles. Fortunately, from a vantage point on top, Gorley and COL Kevin Wilkerson, commander, 2nd Brigade, witnessed everything and with a few radio calls, defused the situation. In another nearby cave, ODA 372 discovered quantities of discarded ammunition and several dead *Taliban* fighters.[126]

East of the "Whale," droves of journalists began streaming into the Shah-i-Khot Valley. The leaders of the various Afghan militias arrived at 1400 on 12 March to be photographed and interviewed. In an agreement with the reporters, ODA 394 had made a creek bed a "no-camera zone" to isolate the Special Forces teams. The next day, ODA 394 discovered the validity of an agreement with the press when it saw satellite television clips of itself in the creek bed area, taken surreptitiously by the journalists.

On 12 March, the three Special Forces detachments still in the valley—ODAs 372, 394, and the newly arrived 395—met with the battalion commanders who had directed them during the Shah-i-Khot Valley combined operations to assess the results. All concurred that they needed to cease relations with Gul Haidar and his Tajiks and that all Afghan forces should withdraw back to Gardez. After the press conference, the Soviet T-54s led the "the Gul's" column out of the valley. Half of ODA 395 and 100 Pashtuns of Commander Zia Lodin were left guarding the entire Shah-i-Khot Valley. Only CPT Samuels, MSG McFadden, SSG Rawlins, and SGT Morris of ODA 394 stayed the night at Checkpoint Charlie; the rest of the team returned to the old fort at Gardez. As the sun set, they were keenly aware that suddenly there were only 10 Americans in the Shah-i-Khot where several thousand coalition and Afghan troops had maneuvered and fought for more than two weeks. For ODA 394, Operation ANACONDA was over.[127] On

15 March, the forces of Zakim Khan withdrew from its outer ring blocking positions, and ODA 571 conducted a battle handoff with ODA 392 for all operations at Khowst.[128] Two months of counterguerrilla warfare in the dun-colored Afghan mountains still lay ahead for the 3rd SFG teams. While Special Forces assisted and advised the AMF units in the continued search for *Taliban* and *al-Qaeda* resistance, civil affairs teams (CAT-As) expanded their efforts in the cities and towns of Afghanistan.

Integrating Civil Affairs

As the 3rd SFG prepared to assume the Afghanistan special operations mission from JSOTF-North and JSOTF-South, MAJ Ron Sutherland (pseudonym) brought several planners from E Company, 96th CAB, to join the group staff. Sutherland had built a solid relationship with 3rd SFG during several overseas exercises. The 3rd SFG knew how tactical CA teams could assist ODAs in accomplishing their missions. Although not involved in mission planning for the Special Forces teams, the CA company commander stayed attuned to where the teams would be operating. This enabled him to orient the preparations of his CAT-As toward those specific areas. Consequently, when the 3rd Battalion, 3rd SFG deployed to Kandahar, Afghanistan, CAT-A56 arrived with them on 7 February 2002.

During its first month in Afghanistan, CAT-A56 produced the CA annex to the 3rd Battalion, 3rd SFG plan for Operation ANACONDA. That accomplished, CPT Ken Harrison (pseudonym) moved his team to Gardez.[129] Using his infantry and military intelligence backgrounds, the team commander assessed the local situation from a tactical viewpoint and with an eye to providing information that could affect future operations. After ANACONDA ended, the CA soldiers thought that the Afghans in and around the Shah-i-Khot Valley would need food, blankets, firewood, and building supplies. Delivery was coordinated with the CJCMOTF staff in Kabul. CPT Harrison; his team sergeant, MSG Mike Ewell (pseudonym); and their engineer, SFC Karl Cantwell (pseudonym) went to Gardez with the Special Forces soldiers of ODB 390 to conduct a deliberate assessment. There, they discovered that the city was divided between two local warlords when rivals pointed weapons at them. That "no-win" situation caused the team to move to Khowst on 29 March.

Shortly after CAT-A56 arrived in Khowst, a 14-truck convoy carrying food arrived unexpectedly. At Khowst, the team arranged to meet with village officials to discuss supply distribution.

Figure 21. Humanitarian aid arrives.

Because culturally the Afghan women in the countryside did not appear in public meetings, the CA teams were forced to rely on the leaders for population figures. The continuing concern was that some leaders would inflate their numbers, receive extra food, and then use the "profits" as bargaining chips in the local political arena. CA teams could not prevent this problem because they could not be perceived as interfering in village or tribal government. While they were in Khowst, the tenuous nature of Afghan tribal relations became evident. The former Paktia province governor, Padsha Khan, attacked the Afghan Military Forces (AMF) at Gardez that were loyal to Taj Mohammad Wardak, who Hamid Karzai had appointed governor in February.[130]

About two weeks later, CAT-A56 returned to Gardez when the commander of ODB 390 felt the situation had calmed down. Although the team distributed food, their main project was to assess education needs. Their recommended projects included replacing windows in a girls' school, building desks, and replacing the fence around the school. They were submitted to the CJCMOTF staff for funding in mid-April. The 3rd Battalion commander had only praise for CAT-A56. "They had a focus on the right things," he said.[131]

In late April, the team received a new mission from the CJSOTF-Afghanistan. It was assigned to a combined task force (TF Jacana) made up of 19th SFG ODAs, AMF personnel, and the British Royal Marine Commandos. The combined task force was to assess the military situation in Paktia Province between Gardez and Khowst. The British Commandos did not understand CA and initially wanted to use CAT-A56 for PSYOP missions to pass out propaganda leaflets. CPT Harrison quickly educated the British on their mission capabilities. Then, after

learning that only two people in the village of 1,000 were literate, they worked with the leaders of Soran to distribute wheat and blankets to the population. Having demonstrated their capabilities to the satisfaction of the British, CAT-A56 became a "force multiplier" for the combined task force until mission completion on 10 May.[132]

Although the CA soldiers were convinced of the importance of their mission, they also felt great frustration. CAT-A56's team sergeant, MSG Ewell, saw the potential impact of quickly approved and funded projects as had CAT-A32 and the Humanitarian Assistance Survey Team (HAST) working at Bamian. As Ewell and SFC Cantwell explained, "It was extremely critical that the local Afghan people saw and made a direct connection between the arrival of American and Afghan soldiers who represented the Afghan Interim Authority (AIA) and very tangible help being provided to a village." After examining

Figure 22. Good wells are vital to life in Afghanistan.

329

schools or talking about the absence of wells with the villagers, they then expected you to do something about the problems. "When you leave and nothing gets done," Cantwell said, "that becomes a problem. High-visibility projects that have immediate impacts must be executed quickly to win the 'hearts and minds' of the people. Not doing that means lost opportunities."[133] MSG Ewell added, "If the people see Afghan soldiers with rifles protecting them and American soldiers getting wells dug and schools upgraded to help them, their attitudes toward both groups of soldiers will be positive. In effect, wells and schools provide security for all Americans because, in contrast to the Soviets, we are in Afghanistan to help the people build a future that includes a stable national government."[134]

The countrywide hunt for *al-Qaeda* and *Taliban* continued throughout Operation ANACONDA. Leaders and ranking staff personnel classified as high-value targets (HVTs) were always being sought. Arms, munitions, and equipment caches and the midlevel *Taliban* and *al-Qaeda* were the focus of sensitive site exploitation (SSE) missions conducted by Special Forces and SOF elements. The following vignette details a successful HVT and SSE mission executed on very short notice by ARSOF elements using Night Stalker Chinooks from two different battalions of the 160th SOAR.

Ambush at 80 Knots

This aviation mission during Operation ENDURING FREEDOM (OEF) showed that all the aviators in the 160th SOAR had been trained to the same high level of proficiency and shared a common aggressive flying spirit. During the Takur Ghar rescue operations on 4 March 2002 in which several MH-47E Chinook helicopters from the 2nd Battalion were damaged or forced down by enemy fire, the 160th SOAR used MH-47Ds from the 3rd Battalion to fulfill SOF air missions in Afghanistan. This practice would continue until the 2nd Battalion Chinooks rotated back to the United States.

On 16 March 2002, the 1st and 3rd Battalions were alerted for an HVT mission. The next day, Chinook helicopters from both units would carry a Special Forces element to intercept a convoy of *al-Qaeda* forces to either capture or destroy them. CWO Gary Black (pseudonym), the MH-47E flight lead who had served with the 3rd Battalion Chinook company, had overall responsibility for the mission.[135] He assembled all the helicopter crews and briefed the mission, diagramming the intercept procedure on butcher-block paper. Once he was sure that all aircrews understood their tasks and the emergency contingencies, Black released them to get some rest.

In the early morning hours of 17 March, the flight crews got a quick update brief, loaded the Special Forces element, and the combined flight departed with an MH-47E leading. Daylight came quickly for the Night Stalkers who use the dark to reduce the risk to aircraft and personnel. En route to the target area, the flight received continuous updates from a surveillance aircraft that routinely monitored activity on the battlefield.[136] As the flight raced toward the enemy convoy, the Special Forces element aboard the MH-47Ds wanted to remove the Plexiglas windows to allow them to fire if one of the Chinook's M-134 miniguns failed or jammed. The pilots agreed and the windows were jettisoned.

The *al-Qaeda* convoy of three trucks was driving in a dry stream bed (wadi) that served as a road, and a fourth vehicle trailed them about 2 miles behind in the same wadi. The Chinook pilots had expected to be able to spot the vehicles far enough away to plan their approaches to mask the insertion of the assault forces. However, 30-foot granite cliffs bordered the stream bed and prevented the aviators from spotting the convoy until they were almost on top of it. When the lead MH-47E responded to the last-minute sighting, it forced the trailing Chinooks to react very quickly to the situation.

CWO Black executed a gut-wrenching 90-degree right turn with a rapid deceleration to land his helicopter approximately 20 feet in front of the lead vehicle. The convoy was forced to stop. According to the rules of engagement (ROE), if the vehicle occupants pointed weapons at the helicopters, the door gunners could fire. When the convoy stopped, everyone jumped out of the trucks with their weapons aimed at the helicopters. The gunner on the left minigun opened fire from the lead Chinook, disintegrating truck doors and killing several enemy soldiers.

Black's maneuver forced CWO Charles Elkenback, flying the second helicopter, to bank hard to the left to avoid a collision.[137] As Elkenback banked the helicopter, SGT Christopher Eaton (pseudonym) on the right door minigun and SSG Greg Parker (pseudonym), the ramp gunner with an M-249, fired on the convoy.[138] As the other Chinooks moved into position to engage their assigned vehicles, the enemy fighters scrambled out of their trucks, firing at the helicopters as they attempted to run for cover in a nearby ravine. A hailstorm of gunfire from miniguns, M-4 carbines, and M-249 machine guns hit them as they tried to flee.

As CWO Mark Reagan (pseudonym) maneuvered to land his helicopter, SGT Roger Wilkerson (pseudonym), trying to follow his target simultaneously, only got off a short burst from his minigun before the ammunition belt broke and the gun jammed.[139] SSG Charles Martin (pseudonym), the flight medic and a former Ranger SAW gunner, immediately stepped into the open door with his M-4 carbine.[140] Firing semiautomatic, Martin killed the truck driver and then shot a second fighter as Wilkerson began to fire his M-4. As the aircrew and Special Forces element continued to fire from the window ports, the pilots quickly repositioned the big Chinook to a new spot just over the crest of a small hill. The new position masked the helicopter and gave the assault force a superb firing position overlooking all three trucks in the convoy.

In the meantime, CWO Elkenback and his crew spotted the fourth truck to the north in the same stream bed. They rapidly closed on the vehicle and forced it to stop by performing a 180-degree decelerating turn. SGT Shane Gerhing (pseudonym), mindful of the ROE, had the left minigun trained on the truck.[141] There was no place close to land, so Elkenback hovered the big Chinook close to the vehicle. A woman got out of the truck holding up a child; the other five people inside simply stared at the helicopter in amazement. Strict fire discipline was maintained as the assault element made a quick assessment. The Special Forces leader told the pilots to "abort," and Elkenback flew back to the main convoy.[142]

The ground force commander directed two Chinooks to perform an extensive search of the fourth vehicle. This time, one Chinook hovered in front of the stopped truck as the second helicopter landed nearby to unload the ground force. At the sight of the helicopters again, the Afghans got out of their vehicle, moved away from it, sat on the ground, and waited for the Special Forces team to search the vehicle. The two helicopters moved away while the search was being conducted. Afterward, they flew the team back to the convoy site.

As the ground force searched the area; secured and treated its wounded prisoners; and prepared the vehicles, weapons, and munitions for destruction, the helicopters were released to refuel from an MC-130P tanker flying nearby. After they had refueled, the Chinooks returned to exfiltrate the ground force. The HVT operation netted 18 enemy fighters—16 dead and two wounded prisoners—and the destruction of three vehicles, weapons, and munitions. The MH-47s suffered only minor battle damage, despite moderate enemy fire. The combined Chinook force from the 1st and 3rd Battalions, 160th SOAR, had performed a high-speed chase exceedingly well together in the best Night Stalker tradition.

As Operation ANACONDA wound down, SSE missions increased to locate arms and munitions that would support further *Taliban* and *al-Qaeda* resistance. The Shah-i-Khot Valley and surrounding mountains had to be painstakingly searched and battle-damage assessments submitted to the JSOTF. That mission fell to 3rd SFG ODA 372, ODA 395, and a group of 15 Pashtun fighters from Zia Lodin's forces.

Trail of Caches

By 13 March 2002, most U.S. and coalition soldiers and AMF personnel who had participated in Operation ANACONDA had left the Shah-i-Khot Valley. Commander Zia Lodin was not convinced that all *Taliban* and *al-Qaeda* forces that escaped ANACONDA had fled to Pakistan. Thus, he was concerned that the Afghan people would view the operation as a defeat, despite the acknowledgment that "a very few number of *al-Qaeda* may have escaped," made by MG Franklin L. Hagenbeck, the combined commander. The only real way to determine who or what remained in the valley was for someone to physically look. LTC Carl Hooper, therefore, ordered ODA 372, ODA 395, and 15 AMF soldiers to return to the valley. Their mission was to reconnoiter and search sites that possibly could hold sensitive material or supplies. Special Forces ODA 372 would again work with Pashtun Commander Khoshkeyer and his Afghans.[143]

Since CPT Mike McHenry (pseudonym) had gone to the United States to attend CW3 Harriman's funeral, MSG Jason Doolittle (pseudonym) was in charge, and SFC John Veringer (pseudonym) became acting team sergeant. Although Veringer had only been in Special Forces since 1999, his 18 years in the Army, plus combat experience in Operation DESERT STORM, prepared him well for the responsibility. Their immediate task was to rebuild rapport with the Pashtun leaders and soldiers that had been damaged during the first days of ANACONDA. Simply sharing a cup of tea with the Pashtun troops paid huge dividends. Suddenly, the American soldiers were treated like "rock stars." The Afghan fighters were anxious to meet them because it was obvious that the Special Forces soldiers cared about them.[144]

There appeared to be no enemy remaining in the valley, but the reconnaissance and search of the entire area was the mission. SF ODA 372 was looking for intelligence data, arms, ammunition, bodies of enemy fighters, and other evidence of destruction. On 14 March, the team conducted its first sensitive site exploitation (SSE) patrol. By the end of the day they had cleared seven buildings and found three footlockers filled with medical supplies, American money, passports, visas, drivers' licenses, and other documents. Having discovered so much in a single day, ODB 390 and 150 AMF soldiers arrived that evening to expand the effort and provide more security. The next day, MSG Doolittle and ODA 372 carried their materials back to Gardez.

Four days later, ODA 372 returned to the Shah-i-Khot. ODB 390 had established a base camp, and Commander Khoshkeyer had established his base near the village of Marzak. On 20 March, ODA 372 and half of ODA 395 conducted the first foot patrol into the valleys that led to Pakistan. They found nothing that day, but what they discovered the next morning sent chills up the spines of ODA 372. As they moved into a valley, they came across an abandoned Russian 12.7mm DshK machine gun that was pointed straight down the route that ODA 372 had planned to take into the Shah-i-Khot Valley that first day of Operation ANACONDA. They also found numerous Russian BM-12 rockets still set up on rocks, again pointed toward their route into the valley.

The SSE patrols continued for the next several days. Among the discoveries were truck-mounted Russian ZSU antiaircraft guns, some of which had been destroyed and some that were still functional; stockpiles of BM-12 rockets; and cave complexes that had sleeping areas, kitchens, offices, and communications bunkers. As the two ODAs carefully worked their way through the valleys leading to Pakistan, they noticed that the defenses between the Shah-i-Khot Valley and the Pakistan frontier appeared to be constructed in sequential belts. Each defensive line was covered by the next, all the way to the border. SSG Carey Robeson (pseudonym) had to admire the tactical sense of his enemy. "They were masters at using the terrain," he said.[145]

Contents in the caves varied from mundane food supplies to computer diskettes. Some caches contained only a few items, while others would best be described as "stores" that had mattresses; blankets; cold-weather items; and 50-kilogram bags of rice, flour, and sugar. Several caves had 5-foot-tall metal storage containers, almost like filing cabinets, filled with a variety of things. Munitions caches had 14.7mm and 23mm ammunition as well as rocket-propelled grenades (RPGs), Russian SA-7 surface-to-air missiles (SAMs), and recoilless antitank rifles. In one position, there was a functional 57mm antiaircraft weapon. Several caves contained computers with their hard drives still inside. Excitement coursed through the team when it found one computer disk labeled USS *Cole*. Within hours, that diskette was evacuated from the valley and was on its way to headquarters for analysis.

Figure 23. Destroyed DshK antiaircraft weapon system in the Shah-i-Khot Valley.

Figure 24. Cave caches produced a surprising variety of items.

Destroyed large cargo and pickup trucks, often with hundreds of mortar rounds scattered alongside, littered the trail avenues leading from the Shah-i-Khot. It was obvious that a sizable enemy force had used the valley as a major movement route between Pakistan and Afghanistan, as a well-concealed and covered storage and resupply point, and possibly as an alternate command post headquarters. GEN Tommy Franks, CENTCOM commander, had declared Operation ANACONDA "an unqualified success," and MG Hagenbeck told reporters that the Americans and Afghans had "rid the world of hundreds of trained killers who will now not slaughter innocent men, women, and children."[146]

The Special Forces soldiers of ODA 372 had killed few of the enemy, but they had collected valuable intelligence about *Taliban* and *al-Qaeda* operations in the Shah-i-Khot. And they had done something else of equal importance. They had developed close relationships with Afghan fighters who would continue to seek out and destroy enemy resistance. They had shown the AMF that America was on its side and that America was willing to fight with the AMF to free the nation.

On 18 March, Pentagon spokeswoman Torie Clarke declared, "Operation ANACONDA will end today." She reminded that the operation was designed to find and root out a relatively large pocket of *al-Qaeda* and *Taliban* fighters and was considered successful.[147] The cave searches revealed large caches of ammunition and arms, intelligence documents, and information that would be useful in future operations and in preventing future terrorist attacks. The total enemy killed varied from 800 to 1,500; the Afghan tradition of quickly burying the dead made identifying the actual count difficult.

In retrospect, allied forces faced a tough, dedicated enemy that had several months to prepare solid defenses. The *al-Qaeda* had well-fortified cave systems. On the "Whale," they used concrete to make solid bases for mortars and crew-served machine guns. The bunker systems in the high terrain were well outfitted and carefully concealed, taking advantage of the terrain. They afforded plenty of protection and had good interlocking fields of fire. The enemy fighters were acclimated to the altitude, terrain, and weather and were proficient with their rudimentary artillery systems.

Unlike the Tora Bora operation, the *al-Qaeda* and *Taliban* soldiers chose to stay and fight. The tough defenses and a willingness to "stand and fight" created some serious challenges for the allied forces during ANACONDA. Sometimes things just did not go as planned. The en-

Figure 25. Cave caches commonly were uncovered in sweeps of Shah-i-Khot Valley.

emy exercised its "right to vote" on all courses of action. However, in the end, the *Taliban* and *al-Qaeda* were defeated and pushed out of the Shah-i-Khot; the Pashtuns were able to reclaim their villages. The allied hunt went on for remaining pockets of enemy fighters.

In the midst of Operation ANACONDA, Joint Special Operations Task Force (JSOTF) headquarters; Special Forces groups (SFGs), battalions, and ODAs; CA and PSYOP tactical teams; 160th SOAR Chinook companies; and individual augmentees did mission "handoffs" throughout Afghanistan. ARSOF soldiers established a new CJSOTF-Afghanistan that had closer ties to the coalition forces, continued to rebuild the infrastructure of villages and towns, and prepared the facilities to train an "all Afghan" national military force in Kabul. This was all being done as the JSOTF was subordinated to support the conventional force commander of TF 180.

In mid-January 2002, COL Mark Phelan received orders to send one of his Special Forces battalion headquarters and a Special Forces company to Afghanistan to augment JSOTF-South at Kandahar. Phelan chose the 3rd Battalion, 3rd SFG, explaining that "Three Three had just finished Focus Relief [in Nigeria], and it was a well-seasoned battalion." He still believed that most of 3rd SFG was "going to the Horn of Africa." Two weeks later, however, CENTCOM canceled the deployment to Africa and directed Phelan to move the 3rd SFG to Afghanistan to assume the missions of both JSOTF-North and JSOTF-South. His new command would be called the Combined Joint Special Operations Task Force–Afghanistan (CJSOTF-Afghanistan) based at the Bagram Air Base. COL Phelan was to assume command of all U.S. and coalition SOF inside Afghanistan not later than the end of March 2002.[148]

The following vignettes explain what happened during the establishment of the new CJSOTF-Afghanistan at Bagram Air Base, the continued expansion of the CA mission, and the preparations in Kabul to train an "all Afghan" national military force. There were different challenges to be faced in Bagram versus K2, Uzbekistan. But the major requirement was that CJSOTF-Afghanistan would be operational not later than 1 April 2002.

Establishing CJSOTF-Afghanistan

After three months of preparation in North Carolina and Virginia for operations in the Horn of Africa, the 3rd SFG, in mid-January 2002, was ordered to deploy to Afghanistan.[149] In many ways, this change did not have much of an impact on the ongoing effort to transport the unit

335

overseas with its vehicles and equipment to establish a new CJSOTF headquarters in the global war on terrorism. The issues of different languages and cultures had to be considered, but the 5th SFG had not operated in Afghanistan before October 2001 either. Practically speaking, Afghanistan was just farther away than eastern Africa, near the extreme limits for high-frequency (HF) radio communications to the United States. What was significantly different in Afghanistan was the requirement for the 3rd SFG to replace two CJSOTFs conducting combat operations and to assume the mantle for coalition SOF while the nature of the war was changing.[150]

Setting up the new headquarters facility was the primary task of LTC Phillip Reese (pseudonym), deputy commanding officer, 3rd SFG. Reese was widely known inside ARSOF because the Plymouth, England, native had never lost his British accent. He had immigrated to the United States in 1975 and enlisted in the Army the next year. After service in Korea and graduation from Officer Candidate School, he became a U.S. citizen in 1982 and later joined the Special Forces. In mid-February 2002, Reese led an advance echelon (ADVON) of 14 3rd SFG soldiers to K2, Uzbekistan, and then to Bagram, Afghanistan, to survey likely sites for the joint command facility and support facilities. He returned to Bagram in late February with four men to begin work on the central layout of the joint operations center (JOC), the nerve center of the CJSOTF.

The idea had been conceptualized by COL Mark Phelan, commander, 3rd SFG. He developed and tested it over a six-year period that began when he was a battalion commander in the 5th SFG and Reese was his executive officer. Two internally framed tents, large enough to serve as airplane hangars, formed the central structure of the JOC.[151] This obviated the need to renovate any of the existing Soviet-era buildings at Bagram Air Base, which the 10th Mountain Division already occupied.[152]

Reese found a suitably large field to put in the JOC facility and the "tent city billets" for the troops that would be needed to support it. The field and the few decrepit concrete buildings on its borders were empty and unclaimed because they were seeded with buried mines, booby-trapped mines, and rockets left behind when the Soviet military withdrew from Afghanistan. MAJ James Pearl (pseudonym), 3rd SFG engineer, took on the task of getting the site cleared. First, a "Norwegian Flail," a tank that thrashed the ground with spinning chains, worked over the open field area, detonating mines every few seconds for several hours. Then two bulldozers—one from the Marine Corps and another contracted from a local Afghan—were used to clear off the top 12 inches of soil, moving away more buried mines. The bulldozing also created a protective dirt wall around the new base; unfortunately, a lot of unexploded ordnance (UXO) had been pushed into it. A grader leveled the field, followed by a roller to tamp the earth, which made a firm base for tents and vehicles.[153]

In the midst of clearing the field and cleaning out the long-abandoned, decrepit buildings, Reese and his team were approached by local Afghans who claimed the buildings and intended to reoccupy them when the Americans were finished. With only a few men, Pearl knew that it would be almost impossible to prevent the Afghans from sneaking back at night to establish their claim by "squatting" in the structures. In a flash of inspiration, SGM Rich Keogh (pseudonym), 3rd SFG operations sergeant major, suggested a simple scheme to keep the Afghans away until more of the 3rd SFG arrived and the camp construction was done. The Americans hammered 3-foot-long steel tent stakes around the perimeter and hung white cloth engineer tape with the universal minefield warning placards between them to mark the area as still "mined." Keogh added mounds of dirt to give further credence to the subterfuge of unexploded mines. When MAJ Pearl and his men left the site that evening, they were satisfied that the ruse would deter the Afghans.[154]

Early the next morning when MAJ Pearl returned to the JSOTF site, he found a team of Bosnians with their Alsatian "mine dogs" checking the field. Embarrassed, Pearl and Keogh quickly told the de-miner leader that the markers were a subterfuge. The Bosnian leader shook his head and informed them otherwise in broken English. Alsatian dogs were unusually skilled at sniffing out explosives, even underground wooden box types. The dogs were also trained to listen for the sound of air-vibrating trip wires. To signify a discovery, the dogs sat down near the suspected site. In their careful search of the new JSOTF base, the Bosnians and their dogs found even more UXO, including 122mm artillery shells, deeper in the soil. The Bosnian chief specifically pointed out that one of the 3-foot steel tent stakes driven by Pearl's team to mark the perimeter had just missed a buried Russian 107mm rocket by a fraction of an inch. The soldier who drove that stake visibly blanched.[155]

Now that their field was almost certainly clear of UXO, MAJ Pearl arranged the pouring of concrete for the slab foundations of the JOC tents. The local Afghan contractor assured him that he would be done in five days. The local construction crew used a miniscule cement mixer powered by a sputtering two-stoke engine. The crew moved the cement with wheelbarrows and laid all the rocks and reinforcing bars in the molds by hand. Five days stretched into 15, but the slabs were finally finished. The JOC tents were erected as the main body of the 3rd SFG headquarters arrived at Bagram. By the end of March, LTC Reese was able to tell COL Phelan that the JOC facility and staff would be ready for activation 24 hours ahead of the 1 April deadline. As the JSOTF-South headquarters at Kandahar Airport turned off its radios and literally struck its tents, CJSOTF-Afghanistan assumed operations at midnight 30 March 2002. Inside the JOC, staff officers and NCOs heard, over the constant low growl of generators powering their radios and computers, the crunching detonations of antipersonnel mines as the chains of the "Norwegian Flail" cleared other UXO fields around the air base.[156]

Communications continued to be the key to effective command and control, and ARSOF was no exception. The 3rd SFG communicators were determined to have the CJSOTF operational by its deadline. They wanted to capitalize on the lessons learned from the 5th SFG's experience at K2, Uzbekistan, with its teams operating all over Afghanistan.

Communications at Bagram

Until mid-February 2002, MSG Tony Santana (pseudonym) was not certain where the 3rd SFG would deploy.[157] This was important to him because distances between transmitting and receiving stations, as well as geographic locations, were critical to "making and maintaining communications." The 1st and 2nd Battalions, 3rd SFG had been preparing to deploy to the Horn of Africa to attack suspected terrorist bases in that region, but most of the 3rd Battalion had gone to Afghanistan. When it was confirmed that the 3rd SFG would replace the 5th SFG, but be stationed at Bagram, Santana prepared his communications plan.

MSG Santana knew that the 5th SFG relied heavily on single-channel, wide-band satellite communications. The system was very reliable, and the 5th SFG ODAs were constantly on the move as the anti-*Taliban* forces marched and rode hundreds of kilometers cross-country, capturing city after city. However, with the conclusion of this "maneuver phase" of the war, the Afghan Military Forces (AMF) had returned to their tribal provinces. The 3rd SFG faced a different military situation. Their ODAs would likely be more stationary, conducting operations locally from small bases throughout the country. Santana also knew that other SOF were still hunting for Osama bin Laden and his top lieutenants as well as *Taliban* leaders. Those missions would have top priority, and those units would be allocated most of the available satellite bandwidth. The group communications sergeant recommended relying on HF and extremely high-frequency (EHF) radio communications.[158]

During his three years as the NCOIC, 3rd SFG Communications Section, MSG Santana had been pushing the importance of good communications and pushing advanced training to improve the proficiency of all the communications sergeants from the Special Forces battalions to the individual ODAs. COL Phelan reinforced his efforts by regularly conducting long-range communications exercises. Even though their HF radios were only rated to 2,000 miles, the 3rd SFG communicators could "talk" reliably between Fort Bragg and virtually anywhere in Africa and the Persian Gulf, distances that ranged from 4,000 to 9,000 miles. This challenging and rigorous training would pay off in Afghanistan where the distances were shorter—it was no more than 700 miles from Bagram to any point in the country—but the high, 10,000-foot mountain ranges were a factor.

When the 3rd SFG communications section arrived at Bagram, Santana and the signal officer, MAJ Kent Willard (pseudonym), methodically emplaced their systems. Willard, Santana, and the radio men cleared debris away and had mines exploded in the areas they selected to erect their satellite dishes and antennas. They set up their tactical satellite (TACSAT) systems first because they were quickest and easiest to install. Iridium satellite telephones were initially used to coordinate establishment of their communications bases, but within weeks, the Iridiums were put aside to be used only for emergencies. Tents came next and then the "big pipes"—the large antenna dishes for the global telecommunications systems that linked the new CJSOTF at Bagram to U.S. military command posts around the world—were erected. The large size and weight of these systems required four days of work to put them in place properly. Finally, in conjunction with the group Information Management Section, they installed the computer local area network (LAN) and telephone lines and programmed the JSOTF headquarters' laptops and servers.[159] While establishing secure radio communications continues to be important, the computer automation part is equally critical on today's modern battlefield.

High Desert Automation Management

The digital information system that every American special operations unit and coalition element relied on for communications daily was run by a half-dozen soldiers and their captain from inside a dusty tent at Bagram. CPT Morris Washington (pseudonym) was in charge of six soldiers, technically designated "Seventy-Four Bravos" (74Bs), Systems Automation Specialists, but who acted simply as "loaders" and "fixers."[160] A year before, Washington had broken his back while serving in the 7th SFG and had been trained in automation management at Fort Gordon, Georgia, during his recovery. Having earned an undergraduate degree in accounting at the University of Central Florida, "working with numbers was no problem for him." Although Washington was now a "certified computer geek," he was happy to return to Special Forces as the head of the 3rd SFG's Information Management Section.[161]

Washington's principal task was to help the group commander manage the flow of all information inside the headquarters and to maintain the "technical arrangement" of equipment that made this possible. The demands of the job were heavy enough without the challenges of operating computer systems in Afghanistan's harsh climate. The micro-dust blown up by the windstorms on the northern Shomali plain would hang in the air like a faint khaki haze, and unprotected computer disks were unusable within 24 hours. The power for all computer systems came from generators that ran constantly, night and day. And there were soldiers whose sole duty was to ensure that their assigned generator never quit.[162]

The volume of message traffic in the CJSOTF headquarters was tremendous. Each day, between 500 and 1,000 messages were transmitted by the joint staff, and close to 90 percent of those were digital. The rest of the message traffic came on paper. To support this flow, Washington and his team of male and female technicians maintained two networks: one exclusively for the "secure," or classified, message traffic and a second one for more routine, nonsecure communications. The secure net connected 167 laptop computers to four 50-gigabyte servers. The smaller nonsecure net had two like-size servers to link 89 additional laptops and 10 laptops that were specifically dedicated to coalition force users. The computers were tied to switches by "backbone switches" to the servers and then to routers accessing communications satellites.[163]

Getting this system set up was a challenge because the young technicians, who Washington proudly called "the best soldiers in Special Forces Command," had not been permitted to train on the system before deploying. At Fort Campbell, like most military installations, civilian contract technicians operated the networks. Contractual specifications prevented the soldiers from doing any training on the installation computer networks, hence his team could not "train as they would fight." But overseas in the combat environment of Afghanistan, the 74Bs were loading software, managing the networks, configuring routers, and troubleshooting their systems, and Washington felt they were doing it "superbly" after a period of learning on the job and practical experience.[164]

The automation team's hardest job was managing the servers and fixing the scripting errors inherent in the new Web Interface Computer System that was intended to allow users simple access to organizational information like operation orders, intelligence summaries, and the like. The 5th SFG automators had similar problems that were only partly addressed by bringing a technical contractor to K2. The system worked while the technician was present, but after he left, it failed again. Washington worked with the Land Information Warfare Activity liaison officer to develop an "HTML starter page" to help solve the ongoing problems with the new web interface.[165]

Not all the automation team's troubles were as difficult to solve. Washington reported that "half of all our work orders dealt with untrained users." He smiled and added, "and that included sergeants major and colonels," the segment of the unit population that grew up before the desktop computer was common. His 74Bs would quickly find and fix these simple faults: "Usually a network or power cord was not plugged in." Big problems or small, Washington's automation team successfully dealt with the challenges of digital information management in wartime in as "computer-hostile" an environment as anyone could imagine. Inside CJSOTF-Afghanistan, the loaders and fixers of 3rd SFG made those electrons flow.[166]

While the 3rd SFG ADVON scrambled to establish the JOC, its communications and computer systems, and the support facilities for JSOTF-Afghanistan at Bagram Air Base to meet a 1 April deadline, a radio broadcast element of the 3rd Psychological Operations Battalion (POB), attached to the 8th POB, was preparing to assume the Air Force Commando Solo role in the country. It would use the rapidly deployable Special Operations Media System–Broadcast (SOMS-B) in its first combat mission. It was also part of the joint transition and battle handoffs that were taking place all over Afghanistan.

"Good Morrrrning, Afghannnnistan"

Everything about the new SOMS-B broadcasting as part of the global war on terrorism in Afghanistan would be a first, CPT Ben Crenshaw (pseudonym) discovered.[167] The tall, lean PSYOP officer led an eight-soldier operational detachment of the 8th POB at Fort Bragg. Since mid-September 2001, TPD 812 had been writing scripts for radio broadcasts to a variety of Afghan audiences. Kentucky born and of Scotch-Irish descent, Crenshaw had served in Bosnia as an artilleryman before studying Arabic. In early February 2002, Crenshaw was alerted that the Commando Solo airborne radio station flying over Central Asia would be replaced by the SOMS-B from the 3rd POB. Crenshaw was placed in charge of a 3rd POB element consisting of a SOMS-B platoon and a broadband satellite communications team. It would be the first "real-world" deployment of the SOMS-B station.

Figure 26. SOMS-B broadcasts the news.

Created and fielded after Operation DESERT STORM, the SOMS-B had not been used in a combat zone. "It was a real scramble," Crenshaw recalled, "to meet the operational deadline of 8 March 2002, the day before the Commando Solo EC-130 aircraft would cease operations. Commando Solo had been broadcasting 10 hours a day, every day, since November 2001.[168]

Not only did the SOMS-B team make the deadline but it also increased its broadcast time to 15 hours daily in less than a week of operation. CPT Crenshaw's detachment established two radio broadcast stations, one at Bagram Air Base in the center of the country and the other in the south at Kandahar Airport. They also scored another first when they boosted the SOMS-B's original design to broadcast a maximum of 18 hours a day using 6,000 watts of power to 24 hours a day at 10,000 watts. This accomplishment was not without problems. Adjustments were required because, although the SOMS-B easily performed beyond its design specifications, "it was wiping out all tactical communications" in the area around its Bagram antenna. Using a voltmeter solved the problem and "brought the signalers down from a very high hover," Crenshaw recalled.[169]

The SOMS-B was much more than an ordinary radio station. Being "frequency agile," it was not confined to a single channel and could broadcast on any frequency. The SOMS-B could serve as an AM, FM, shortwave, and television transmitter—any or all simultaneously—and broadcast different programs over the airwaves at the same time. Linked to the Digital Video Distribution System (DVDS), which can receive and transmit two programs concurrently, the SOMS-B could provide a secure video teleconferencing (VTC) capability with any other DVDS station in the world. For the SOMS-B team, this terminal was at Fort Bragg where the Joint Psychological Operations Task Force (JPOTF) was based, supporting its detachments in Afghanistan and around Central Asia. When Crenshaw managed to interview Afghan General Babazhan, he used the DVDS to transmit a videotape of the war leader's comments about education for Afghan women, rebuilding the Bagram valley, and destroying terrorism and his goal of a lasting peace. The interview was transmitted to the JPOTF at Fort Bragg moments later and then passed to CENTCOM in Tampa for approval to be disseminated across Afghanistan.[170]

The longer duration and increased power of the broadcasts did not guarantee the population was listening or that they were having an impact. CPT Crenshaw began pre- and posttesting in the neighboring communities, and the SOMS-B team ran "power surveys" two or three times a week to check signal strength. Tactical PSYOP teams (TPTs) canvassed Afghans face to face during their daily rounds of the villages and towns, but the best feedback came from three prominent local political leaders Crenshaw interviewed.

All were regular listeners of the SOMS-B station, and each Bagram politician provided several specific suggestions for improvement. They all objected to Hindi music in the daytime; it was considered much more appropriate in the evening. They thought that constant repetition of some of the messages and themes was tiring and pointed this out. They wanted more timely stories, especially international soccer scores and local news.[171] As a scriptwriter and Bagram radio station manager, Crenshaw appreciated their insightful comments.

Variety was the key ingredient in music and news. The SOMS-B team deployed with more than 100 compact discs (CDs) of Afghan music, purchased beforehand from a music store in an Afghan-American community in northern Virginia. Since they did not have an operational fund, the team depended on Fort Bragg for "fresh" music. Although Crenshaw transmitted script proofs over the DVDS in a matter of seconds, the approval process through the JPOTF and then through CENTCOM took another nine to 11 days. This meant "stale" news, which could have been improved with a decentralized script approval process for simple items such as sports scores and international news items. Dedicated interpreters for the SOMS-B detachments would support using news items from local sources. Instead, Crenshaw borrowed interpreters from the Army CA units nearby.[172]

Nonetheless, the popularity of the SOMS-B and the perseverance of the team paid off when they were invited to videotape a parade in the nearby town of Chair-Icar. Hamad Karzai, the newly appointed Prime Minister of the Afghan Interim Authority (AIA), was the guest of honor, and CPT Crenshaw, bearded and wearing an Afghan scarf around his neck, was invited to join Karzai and the leading citizens on the outdoor dais.

The colorful procession celebrating Afghanistan's emancipation from the Soviets went on for 2½ hours. Crenshaw was amazed and amused. "It was like a Soviet May Day parade, the Olympics' festive opening ceremony, and your hometown Fourth of July parade all together," he said. Tanks, armored cars, battalion-size units of AMF troops in various uniforms, school-children in their best clothes, local sports teams, and circus performers paraded before the distinguished guests on the reviewing stand. Crenshaw said the day was "the most exciting thing I've done in Afghanistan." "It was an honor," Crenshaw said, "to capture Karzai and his fellow Afghan leaders on video." After the excitement of the parade, CPT Crenshaw and his crew were back at the SOMS-B, broadcasting support for a new Afghanistan.[173]

As the PSYOP soldiers broadcast 24 hours a day from Bagram and Kandahar air bases, the tactical CA teams expanded their operations throughout Afghanistan. But, most significantly, a natural disaster served as the catalyst to clear the Salang Tunnel. CAT-A41 was the driving force behind that operation.

A Disaster Provides a Catalyst

A disastrous earthquake in the northern Afghan city of Nahrin on 25 March catalyzed action to clear the Salang Tunnel. The late winter catastrophe had leveled many of the typical mud-brick houses in the town and surrounding villages, and initial casualty estimates reported 2,000 dead. An American working in a French NGO told MAJ Silas Greene (pseudonym), the leader of CAT-A41, that humanitarian relief to the earthquake victims was hampered by the condition of the tunnel.[174] Not only was water still leaking from the ceiling to create large ice stalagmites akin to 6-foot-tall skiing moguls, but travelers also were stranded because their cars had run out of gas while they waited in the extreme cold. Groups were literally "camping out" in the tunnel because it offered some shelter. Even the open lane was severely restricted as a result of these conditions. To exacerbate the problem, a large truck had turned over inside the tunnel, blocking all traffic from moving in or out. Because sunlight never reached inside the tunnel, the roadway was heavily coated with ice. "It was basically a nightmare," Greene reported.

Greene and MAJ Keenan Jacobson (pseudonym), 10th Mountain Division staff engineer, had a solution to remove the overturned vehicle that blocked the tunnel. They loaded the back of a 5-ton cargo truck with sand and put chains aboard. Before leaving Bagram, CAT-A41 briefed the TF Mountain commander. MG Hagenbeck approved the mission, provided a security force, and arranged to have two Air Force A-10 Warthogs on standby.[175]

The convoy encountered backed-up traffic 10 km from the tunnel, and the closest they could get to the entrance with their vehicles was 2 km. At dark, when CAT-A41 reached the entrance on foot, it was met by clouds of blue exhaust fumes billowing from the tunnel. The Afghan truck drivers would not turn off their engines. The carbon monoxide danger was quite high. Weaving in and out and around traffic, inching by with millimeters of clearance, the vehicle convoy finally reached the tunnel at 1900. After carefully walking the tunnel length, the CA major calculated that the convoy could transit the tunnel, which it did. Then it set up for the night outside the north entrance. When the team got up early the next morning, it was told that another truck had gotten stuck in the tunnel during the night. The Americans set to work immediately. Enlisting some Afghans to spread sand, the soldiers used picks to crack the ice in the worst places, as the 5-ton truck dumped sand as it backed into the tunnel to the disabled vehicles. Eventually, both trucks were dragged out of the tunnel.

Normally, traffic alternated using the single lane—odd days for north to south traffic and even days for south to north traffic. But there was no Afghan authority figure to control the sequence to prevent traffic jams when the direction changed. MAJ Greene initially solved the problem by blocking one entrance with his 5-ton truck and used the security force to control the growing crowd. With these simple control measures, the Americans cleared the congestion from one end of the tunnel and then opened the road to traffic.

In the midst of clearing the traffic jam, CAT-A41 dealt with a Russian cameraman who, after demanding priority to drive through, attempted to run the American roadblock. When the security force surrounded his vehicle, the Russian backed off and eventually apologized for his behavior. A bona fide emergency was an Afghan with a compound leg fracture caught in the stalled traffic. SFC Bart Schuyler (pseudonym), the Special Forces medic on CAT-A41, splinted the Afghan's badly broken leg and escorted the vehicle in which the man was riding around the stalled traffic so that he could get to a hospital.

The assessment stressed several points: communications were imperative between the two entrances; someone with authority had to be placed at each entrance; and moveable barriers had to be constructed to prevent vehicles from ignoring the odd-even day system, at least until both lanes inside were cleared of broken-down vehicles and the tunnel road surface was repaired. More important, they needed a heavy vehicle with a tooth device on the front to break up and clear away the accumulated ice stalagmites and moguls that narrowed the tunnel to a single lane. Before leaving, the remaining sand was used to fill some of the holes in the road's surface. The CAT-A findings went to the 10th Mountain Division because it had the heavy engineer equipment to make the necessary repairs. "We told them what it was like," said MAJ Greene.

Fortunately, the weather cleared for several days and CH-47 helicopters were able to fly assistance from Bagram to Nahrin. En route back, the team had to deal with a large truck that had its front wheels off the edge of the road and was about to fall into the gorge. After several hours, Greene located a crane in a nearby village that was able to extricate the truck.

Opening the Salang Tunnel was important for several reasons. The route was critical to supporting the military commander's ground operations. The highway north from Kabul was the only road in eastern Afghanistan that reached from the capital to the northern cities and on to Uzbekistan and Tajikistan. The tunnel was key terrain and had to be controlled to facilitate moving military supplies for future operations against the *Taliban* and *al-Qaeda*. Because the tunnel was a critical link to the north, control of that point facilitated moving humanitarian assistance between distant points within the country as well as from countries to the north. Finally, the road and tunnel were essential for farmers and merchants to move their agricultural products to markets. Establishing a viable economy and reliable sources for food were foundational to Afghanistan's future stability.

Not only did CAT-A41 perform its humanitarian assistance responsibilities superbly, but also as MAJ Greene concluded, "This is one way we supported the military operations." The team's work was so significant that Secretary of Defense Rumsfeld called the TF Mountain commander because he wanted to personally thank the team that opened the tunnel. That telephone call symbolized the outstanding missions that CA soldiers performed. Although the work usually was done at the tactical level, it often had strategic implications. The accomplishment of this critical mission occurred as CJSOTF-Afghanistan assumed control of special operations in country.

The Communications Handoff

JSOTF-North turned off its radios on 1 March 2002, and MAJ Derrick Jacobi and MSG Don Sullivan (pseudonyms) passed their J6 staff communications responsibilities to JSOTF-South at Kandahar Airport.[176] Since the night of 18 October when the first Special Forces ODAs entered Afghanistan, the JSOTF-North joint base station had operated continuously for 135 days without interruption. In that period, the 5th SFG communications section processed 27,000 digital messages. At 1700, local time, on 30 March 2002, the CJSOTF-Afghanistan base station at Bagram went on the air, communicating with all special operations units inside Afghanistan. MSG Sullivan stayed at Bagram throughout March to work with his counterparts in the 3rd SFG, MAJ Kent Willard and MSG Tony Santana (pseudonyms), until their operations were successfully under way. He departed Afghanistan on the night of 30 March aboard an Air Force C-17 Globemaster III transport bound for Fort Campbell, Kentucky. MSG Sullivan earned the distinction of being the last member of the 5th SFG headquarters, who had not been transferred to other commands, to leave Afghanistan.[177]

Better Communications

MAJ Willard and MSG Santana organized their base communications station as the "hub," or master station, to "terminate traffic" for the four subordinate outstations: the 1st Battalion at Kabul; the 2nd and 3rd Battalions at Kandahar Airport; and the 2nd Battalion, 19th SFG, at K2 where JSOTF-North was originally headquartered. These unit stations, in turn, terminated traffic from their subordinate stations, which were near other cities and towns across Afghanistan. But they still needed to establish a portable secure radio link.

By the end of April, however, they had almost achieved their goal to have every station in the CJSOTF connected at their base with an EHF digital Single-Channel Antijam Man-Portable radio, called a SCAMPI. The SCAMPI had the range, power, and retransmission capability that gave the CJSOTF and all of its units the best communications capability possible, given the rugged mountainous terrain and harsh climate. To see the CJSOTF's complex, diverse communications work so well was very professionally satisfying to Santana. He had started out in the Army more than 20 years before as a radio operator, hauling a heavy battery-powered radio set in his backpack. "I enjoy making communications," Santana said, "but not carrying it."[178]

When JSOTF-North was formed at K2, Uzbekistan, the Joint Special Operations Air Component–North (JSOAC-North) had already established itself and collocated its Air Force and Army aircraft at the air base. JSOAC-South, with its Air Force assets, stayed in Pakistan when JSOTF-South was stood up at Kandahar. As the joint SOF mission changed from supported to supporting and the two JSOTFs handed off their missions to CJSOTF-Afghanistan, JSOAC-North command and control and Air Force assets left the country. This was a major change in *modus operandi* for the CJSOTF in Afghanistan supporting SOF operations throughout the country.

CJSOTF-Afghanistan and the Joint Air Component

Unlike the JSOTF-North commander, COL Mark Phelan did not have a JSOAC in the immediate vicinity of Bagram. With the dissolution of JSOTF-North, the JSOAC relocated to Masirah Island, off the coast of Oman, and came under the control of RADM Bert Calland's Special Operations Command Central (SOCCENT). The SOF Army air assets were based at Kandahar Airport—the 3rd Battalion, 160th SOAR MH-47D Chinooks. The Air Force SOF air assets were based out of Pakistan. LTC Phillip Reese, deputy commander, 3rd SFG, and chief of staff, Joint Operations Center (JOC), at Bagram, thought this to be a "novel approach" that good staff work would make viable.[179] As he saw the issue, the aircraft needed to support the 3rd SFG elements, and coalition troops did not need to be either at the task force or air component headquarters, or under his colonel's direct command. The CJSOTF staff just needed to communicate their aircraft requirements effectively. However, he did believe that the transport helicopters needed to be close to the troops who would ride in them and use them for support. What LTC Reese really needed were the JSOACC air planners with the expertise to integrate air and ground operations inside his JOC. In April 2002, when CJSOTF-Afghanistan took charge, that was not yet the case.[180]

When COL Phelan was told that his JSOACC would not be collocated with his own task force headquarters at Bagram but was based in Jacobabad, Pakistan, he was initially "very disappointed." He knew what support COL John Mulholland had available "within arm's reach" at K2. But, after meeting COL Joe Tinan, commander, JSOAC, Phelan felt better, and as combat operations proceeded, he became completely satisfied with the arrangement. "Joe Tinan and his Air Force crews supported every single request I made," said Phelan, "except for the bad weather days" when they could not fly. The Air Force even allowed an AC-130 Spectre gunship to fly during daylight hours at Phelan's request.[181] His only real concern was the Air Force MH-53 helicopters. Despite their excellent aircrews and avionics equipment, the "fifty-threes" were 50-year-old airframes, with very limited cargo-carrying capacity and high-altitude operational capabilities. Phelan's staff commented that "it took two of them to do what one [Army MH-47] Chinook did." But, as far as coordinating support with the air component, the CJSOTF-Afghanistan commander said, "I never had a problem, not one time."[182]

VTCs and operating time were two constants of the daily routine at CJSOTF-Afghanistan. Synchronizing watches before the big attack looked good in combat movies, but those players were not dealing with a four and one-half-hour time difference with the U.S. East Coast. VTC times were dictated by the senior commanders and staffs' normal working schedules in Tampa and Washington. Thus, overseas in combat zones, preparing for and implementing instructions to units in the field afterward naturally stretched commanders' "working days" early into the morning of the following day. In the special operations "nerve" centers in Afghanistan, 24/7— 24 hours a day, seven days a week—was reality.

CJSOTF-Afghanistan and "Zulu Time"

Synchronizing watches—working together on a common time zone reference—was essential to coordinating the operations of an international military coalition.[183] The global connectivity that instantaneous satellite-based communications provided; the distant location of the headquarters directing operations in Afghanistan; the odd four and one-half-hour time zone difference from Greenwich Mean Time (GMT) in Afghanistan; and the Air Force standard of running all of its worldwide operations on GMT, or Zulu Time in military parlance, compelled the CJSOTF at Bagram to follow suit.[184]

For LTC Reese, this meant that his day began on Afghanistan time but then quickly switched to Zulu Time. He rose at 0430 local time to read the latest situation reports in the JOC at 0500. By 0700, he had finished reading and was on his way to breakfast, after which he would switch his digital watch to Zulu Time. 0800 local time became 0430 Zulu, or zero-four-three-zero hours Zulu, or "Zee," Time. Then the deputy attended the daily commander's update briefing before his regular meeting with the JOC chief and officer in charge of current operations. Afterward, Reese met with the future operations staff officer to direct the formulation of operational concepts for projected missions and issue the necessary orders to the various staff to develop and execute them.

After verifying priorities with his principal staff officers, Reese attended his second commander's update of the day at 1100 Zulu (1730 local time) and "prepped" his boss, COL Phelan, for his 1200 Zulu meeting with the commanding general of JTF Mountain and the 1300 Zulu VTC with GEN Tommy Franks and his deputies at CENTCOM in Tampa. At 1400 Zulu (2030 local time), Reese attended a second VTC with a different echelon of staff officers in the United States to address unconventional warfare (UW) topics. The CJSOTF staff meeting followed to digest the information and guidance COL Phelan received in the VTCs. A late dinner afterward, and LTC Reese was ready to call it a day and return to local time, which now was 2300. For the CJSOTF chief of staff, Zulu Time and local time had something in common—in either zone, he had no time off.[185]

Command Guidance and VTCs

For mission guidance in Afghanistan, COL Mark Phelan received his orders from RADM Bert Calland, special operations commander for CENTCOM, and GEN Tommy Franks, the combatant commander of U.S. CENTCOM and the war campaign in Afghanistan. Phelan spoke with Calland three times before activating the new CJSOTF. The first and second meetings with Calland were at As Sayliyah, Qatar, during his trips into and out of Afghanistan on his survey of Bagram as the potential site for his task force headquarters. En route to take command in Bagram, Phelan had his third meeting, during which he laid out his plan for organizing and operating the CJSOTF-Afghanistan. "You are responsible for all SOF operations in Afghanistan," Calland told Phelan, and you are to "integrate the coalition units" into your campaign. MG Franklin Hagenbeck, commander, JTF Mountain, gave him similar instructions at Bagram Air Base.[186]

Although the 3rd SFG and CJSOTF-Afghanistan were under Calland's operational control at SOCCENT, COL Phelan received daily orders from MG Hagenbeck, who had tactical control over his special operations task force. "I had my guidance and I stayed on my azimuth," said Phelan. One of his first initiatives to fully integrate the coalition forces into his campaign plan was to make the senior officer from New Zealand his deputy commander. After two commanders' conferences with coalition leaders, Phelan arranged controlled access to intelligence for planning and integrated coalition staff officers into the JOC with dedicated computer terminals. These acts raised morale among the coalition forces as the foreign contingents finally joined the Americans on the combined team bench.

To ensure that he accomplished his assigned missions as expected, COL Phelan personally attended every Bagram VTC chaired by GEN Franks in Tampa, missing only one during his three-month tenure as CJSOTF commander. The VTCs were conducted daily in the JTF Mountain operations center, alongside the taxiway at Bagram Air Base. Phelan thought that it was most important to be part of the conferences because then "I heard exactly what the CINC [GEN Franks] said and I better understood what he wanted done."[187] From As Sayliyah, Calland directed CJSOTF-Afghanistan to develop a special reconnaissance (SR) plan for the continuing campaign against the remaining *Taliban* and *al-Qaeda*. But it was a verbal order with no details or guidance provided. MG Hagenbeck's staff gave all their orders to the CJSOTF in written form. Phelan felt that the two headquarters enjoyed a "great relationship" at Bagram.[188]

Creating an Afghan army that integrated all ethnic groups into a national military force was one of the primary missions assigned to the 3rd SFG before it left Fort Bragg. This foreign internal defense (FID) mission would be accomplished in conjunction with the UW campaign still being prosecuted throughout Afghanistan. The training mission was assigned to the 3rd Battalion, 3rd SFG, but the training facility it would use to accomplish this required extensive renovation and repairs.

Rebuilding the Kabul Military Academy

The challenge of rebuilding the dilapidated facilities at the Kabul Military Academy was assigned to a 1991 West Point graduate, MAJ Jeff Bosley (pseudonym).[189] He had a wealth of experience in engineer operations and reconstruction in underdeveloped and war-ravaged countries, based on his battalion deployments to Haiti, Somalia, and Bosnia and to "clean up" after Hurricane Andrew. Late on Friday afternoon, 25 January 2002, Bosley was in his office at the Seattle District Corps of Engineers when his commander called to tell him he would be a staff augmentee for U.S. CENTCOM for Operation ENDURING FREEDOM.

A week later, MAJ Bosley reported to Fort Benning, Georgia, for deployment to Camp Doha, Qatar, for a 30-day tour of duty with the facilities and construction staff (C7) of the Combined Forces Land Component Command (CFLCC). From there, Bosley was sent to Kabul, Afghanistan, for another 30 days with the Combined Joint Civil-Military Operations Task Force (CJCMOTF) in Afghanistan. When President George W. Bush announced that the U.S. military would begin training a new Afghan national army on 1 May 2002, Bosley got the job to prepare the site where this would be accomplished.[190]

"My mission," stated Bosley, "was to renovate and reconstruct the facilities at the Afghan National Army (ANA) training site." It would be the former Kabul Military Academy, built for the Afghan government by Czech and Russian engineers in 1956. The sprawling, well-ordered campus, set at the base of the mountains on the eastern edge of the capital city, had clearly once been the pride of the Royal Afghan Armed Forces. Finely etched marble tablets, still in place in the front courtyard, commemorated its opening. It had been a battleground during the civil war, and its firing ranges made it a target for coalition bombing during the campaign to oust the *Taliban* government. Portions of several of the three-story dormitories had been blasted away. Roofs had collapsed, and every window had been smashed. There were land mines and unexploded artillery shells scattered everywhere. Inside the once-grand auditorium, the tiered seats had been torn out, and the movie projection booth was ankle deep in 35mm movie film

Figure 27. The "scope of work" was immense.

that had been carefully cut into 3- and 4-inch strips by former *Taliban* occupants. Every wall in the complex was pockmarked by bullets and bomb fragments. "It looks like Godzilla walked through here," remarked a Special Forces sergeant during the initial survey.

MAJ Bosley first had to prepare a "scope of work" report, which became 25 pages long, describing what had to be done to make the academy a functional facility again.[191] This engineering "scope" document enabled Bosley to request initial funding to start work as soon as possible. The document was processed by the CJCMOTF before going to the CFLCC for approval to hire local contractors to begin the cleanup before reconstruction and renovation work could be started. Bosley had been appalled to discover that in almost every single one of the hundreds of rooms on the campus, the floors were covered with dried human feces, even on the top floors. In the latrines, piles of feces were 3 feet high on top of the toilets. It was a "cleanup nightmare" that would require more than 100 workers.

Bosley started with a cleaning contract for 200 workers at the rate of $3 per person per day to sweep out the buildings. As disgusting as the labor was, the opportunity to work for pay outweighed everything. The laborers went to work energetically, squatting and sweeping the crumbling waste up with small whisk brooms. It did not seem to bother anyone. They made a game of tossing chunks of rubble out of upper-story windows, cheering loudly when the mortar and brick pieces landed squarely on the litters below that another group of workers carried away to dump trucks. During the 10 days of cleaning, the laborers also filled in some of the bomb craters.[192]

Bosley's second priority was force protection for the Army engineer battalion, which would do the major construction work. This meant restoring water and electricity to the area. Special Forces engineers from the 3rd Battalion installed a temporary water system and began work on defensive bunkers and observation posts (OPs) around the perimeter of the academy. This perimeter would later be guarded by 101st Airborne Division infantry platoons that rotated up from Kandahar Airport. These infantry platoons received their force protection guidance from the Special Forces staff working at the academy.

At the end of April 2002, shortly before the first Afghan recruits were due to arrive for training, MAJ Bosley welcomed the 92nd Engineer Battalion from Fort Stewart, Georgia. This combat-heavy engineer unit had the major construction equipment that he needed to repair roads and move away debris as well as the technical specialists to install large generators and wire the complex for electricity. The 92nd had power and lights in the undamaged parts of the campus in time for the start of the first basic training course on 1 May 2002.

As MAJ Bosley walked the Kabul Military Academy grounds, now called the ANA Training Site, with LTC Kip Mantle (pseudonym), the 3rd Battalion, 3rd SFG commander in charge of the base, he discussed the next series of work projects. As the two officers made the tour, their conversation was regularly interrupted by "booms" as the British explosive ordnance demolition (EOD) teams blew up mines in the hills behind the academy. "There is three to five years of work still to be done, just to fix the bomb damage," advised Bosley. How much of that work might be his responsibility, Bosley was not sure. He was already 30 days past the end of his "only 30 days" tour in Kabul, and the job was far from over.[193]

Another View of the Kabul Military Academy Task

After several months in the SOCCENT forward command element in Qatar "making myself useful," as MSG "Dex" Yates (pseudonym), C Company, 3rd Battalion, 20th SFG, Florida ARNG, remembered his service there, an opportunity for some interesting work presented itself.[194] In early April 2002, MSG Yates accompanied a site survey team from the 1st Battalion, 3rd SFG, going to the Kabul Military Academy. They were to determine the suitability of the bomb-cratered academy as a training base for the post-*Taliban* regime Afghan defense forces. The survey was completed on 11 April, but when the team returned to Qatar, it was ordered to return immediately. "We were told the French wanted the Academy," recalled Yates, and the Americans rushed back to ensure it stayed under U.S. military control because President Bush had announced that training of the new Afghan army would begin 1 May 2002, barely two weeks away.[195]

By 14 April, the 3rd SFG team was back at the academy. MSG Yates provided a very graphic description of the task at hand: "No power, no water, just dirt, debris, dust, and feces." Two hundred Afghan laborers with two interpreters began to clear away the rubble of airstrikes and the filth left by the *Taliban* fighters. As work proceeded, Yates developed a personal relationship with the long-term custodian of the academy, COL Habib Rachman. The slight, bespectacled Pashtun had served in the pre-*Taliban* Afghan army for 13 years. He lived at the academy during the *Taliban* regime. Rachman had just completed basic training with the "1st Battalion of the Afghan National Guard." His battalion had been organized and trained by the British 2nd Parachute Battalion of the International Security Assistance Force (ISAF).[196] Rachman spoke enough English to converse with Yates, whose foreign languages were Greek and Spanish. As they came to know each other, they passed several evenings discussing the future of Afghanistan. Rachman was most concerned about balancing the ethnic makeup of the new national army.[197]

The outgoing Floridian enjoyed his relationship with Rachman. An English-language copy of the Koran, the Muslim holy book, provided by Yates, helped Rachman improve his English. Yates was proud of his positive interaction with the curious Afghan children who wanted to meet and speak to Americans. But a residual resentment and dislike toward the foreigners was still evident. While riding through Kabul aboard an armed reconnaissance truck one day in May, his convoy stopped at an intersection. A boy dressed in black wearing a black turban smiled up at Yates and asked, "You happy?" "Yeah," Yates replied cheerfully. "We'll soon see about that," responded the boy, who turned and melted into the crowd.[198]

ARSOF elements in the field continued to prosecute the UW campaign while simultaneously conducting foreign internal defense and development missions. The active Army 96th Civil Affairs Battalion (CAB) tactical teams had been replaced by the USAR 489th CAB from Knoxville, Tennessee, and 4th Psychological Operations Group (POG) tactical teams had been augmented by the 345th PSYOP Company (Airborne) from Dallas, Texas. The 19th SFG ODAs had assumed some missions originally assigned to 3rd Battalion, 3rd SFG, which rotated home to Fort Bragg in early May 2002.

"Chiclets" and PSYOP Teams in Kandahar

While deployed to Afghanistan, two coalition humanitarian liaison cells (CHLCs), called "Chiclets," of the 489th CAB, Knoxville, performed similar tasks but worked for different commands and coordinated programs with quite different populations. Getting troops into Afghanistan to do a "battle handoff" with the 96th CAB teams in the field and to sustain the momentum of the humanitarian effort already started was critical. Members of CHLC 6 lived out of their rucksacks for a month at Kandahar Airport while supporting the 101st Airborne Division's TF Rakkasan.

Initial meetings with the Afghan regional commander responsible for the outer perimeter security of Kandahar Airport enabled CHLC 6 to hire local interpreters and lease two pickup trucks to transport the team to outlying Afghan Military Force (AMF) camps and villages. With two Iridium telephones, MAJ Gregory Jernigan and SSG Eric Nolan (pseudonyms), both of whom were civilian law enforcement officers, established communications, and CHLC 6 was "in business" in less than a week.[199] Working in conjunction with local elders and government officials, the four- to six-man CHLCs were responsible for assessing humanitarian needs (water, food, shelter, clothing, and education), establishing priorities according to need, preparing specific contract requirements for projects, arranging food and clothing delivery, and overseeing humanitarian projects in progress.

Using common civilian transport and wearing civilian clothes and beards, the CHLC minimized the "footprint," or obvious presence, of their military connection. But the impact of their presence was significant. Within two weeks, 42 village elders had gathered at Kandahar

Figure 28. Local leaders help decide what comes next.

Airport. Some walked as far as 30 miles to meet Jernigan and to listen to his proposals. Since Afghanistan had been plagued by drought for seven years, all of his proposals—ranging from well-digging to irrigation projects—involved water. For the first time, the village leaders were being invited to share in prioritizing solutions. They were also seeing some response to requests for assistance, which was a radical change. In the past, the farther the villages were from Kandahar, the less prosperous they were. Distance reduced government interest.

While refining, validating, and updating the contract process, CHLC 6 used ARSOF and TF Rakkasan helicopters to begin distributing wheat, rice, dates, beans, and blankets to the 51 villages and towns around the airfield. Having visited most villages and talked with the elders, CHLC 6 and TPD 910, A Company, 9th POB, wanted to repay the hospitality of the villages. As a way of reciprocating, they established links with relatives in Palm Beach, Florida, and Knoxville, Tennessee, and with family support groups at Fort Campbell and Fort Bragg. They donated simple toys and school materials for the Afghan children. The stateside response was tremendous, and the actions of the families and the family support groups built strong bridges for the future.

Figure 29. One of America's favorite pastimes appeals to others as well.

Despite limited communications in outlying areas, "word of mouth" quickly spread the news that a small village without an internal water supply for more than 10 years had a new well. Staff engineers from the 489th CAB provided the necessary technical supervision and the experience to ensure that drilling went to the bottom of the aquifers—the critical part of reliable water sourcing. In Afghanistan, the CHLCs focused on basic necessities and sought to create positive impressions for future generations. Their mission was tough and demanding; it

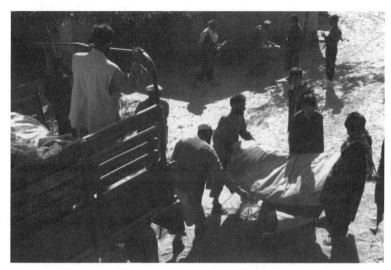
Figure 30. Deliveries were always a significant priority.

required consummate professionalism and a "can-do" attitude in the face of daily frustrations.

Meanwhile, in Kandahar, some 40 miles from the former Soviet airfield, the soldiers of CHLC 2 performed "hands-on" missions in a different way. CHLC 2 was an integral part of an ARSOF team built around a Special Forces company from the ARNG's 19th SFG. ARSOF integration had been prompted by rocket attacks, the deaths of a Special Forces medic and three members of an EOD team, and the wounding of a Special Forces lieutenant on patrol in the Kandahar market area.[200]

MAJ Harry Singletary, MAJ Gregory Mulligan, and CPT Terry Rounds (pseudonyms) emphasized that combat tactical skills became primary when CHLC 2 was to help defend the ARSOF team compound at night and when CHLC 2 was dispatched to clear suspected rocket-launch sites in a nearby apartment building.[201] However, during the day, CA missions (medical, food distribution, and education) took priority.

The CHLC 2 medical and education team, SPC John Harriman and SPC Arthur Walton (pseudonyms), dressed in civilian clothes to conceal their rank because the Afghans were very status conscious.[202] They concentrated on significant projects that would help residents and that would counter Iranian-sponsored anti-American propaganda. One of their dual-purpose projects was to get air conditioning to the building that housed the popular Afghan radio station.

The radio station project expanded communications to a population that was 75-percent illiterate. Because the antiquated Croatian radio equipment Iranian broadcasters used tended to overheat after 2 hours, air conditioning the Afghan station would allow them to dominate the local airways. Harriman also learned that employing locals who could "talk comfortably to the people and connect with them" as radio announcers was preferable to using U.S.-schooled Afghans. Employing locals also improved the station's credibility and expanded its listening audience. Both Harriman and Walton admitted that their toughest task was convincing nongovernmental organizations (NGOs) to shift from simple emergency actions to more complicated developmental projects that would yield long-term benefits.[203]

As CA projects, such as rebuilding the Mirawyse Hospital, were completed, the PSYOP team—Detachment 1-2 of the 345th PSYOP Company (Airborne) from Dallas, Texas—publicized the successes. However, when the 19th SFG Special Operations Command and Control Element (SOCCE) liaison team at Kandahar Airport discovered that Detachment 1-2 had an M-249 squad automatic weapon (SAW) and an M-203 grenade launcher with basic loads of ammunition, the Special Forces soldiers "reassigned and transported" the tactical PSYOP detachment to their advance operating base (AOB) in Kandahar. Within 48 hours, Detachment 1-2, with its SAW and M-203, was part of a Special Forces and Afghan vehicle-mounted task force en route to Nowzad to capture a noted *Taliban* leader. Because almost everyone in the village was illiterate, the assistant team leader, SGT Tim Elton (pseudonym), brought along several loudspeakers. The team sergeant, SSG Charles Milton (pseudonym), a veteran of Haiti, Bosnia, and Kosovo, was carrying the M-203. Milton, Elton, the SAW gunner, SPC Joshua Danner (pseudonym), and 12 other Americans were crammed into four small pickup trucks. Two hundred fifty Afghan soldiers were stuffed aboard 10 other trucks for the 18-hour cross-country trek. "It was a 'Rat Patrol' but twice as hairy. It was not a convoy—it was more like a herd racing across the high desert at night—like the Mel Gibson movie, 'Mad Max,'" remembered Milton.[204]

When the task force arrived, the entire village was totally dark; it had no electricity and no generator. Night visitors usually meant trouble, so an explanation was necessary to reassure the villagers that they were not in danger and to explain the "unexpected" intrusion. That was when Elton's loudspeakers were brought into play. Although the *Taliban* leader was not in the village, Detachment 1-2 demonstrated technical and tactical skills that made it a force multiplier. True ARSOF integration was achieved in the heart of Afghanistan.

Their Lucky Day

The 3rd Battalion, 3rd SFG had been ordered to prepare to deploy by mid-January 2002 to Kandahar, Afghanistan, for assignment to JSOTF-South. Special Forces ODB 390 arrived about 15 February. Three weeks later, MAJ Mitchell Harris (pseudonym) and his company headquarters moved first to Bagram and then, on 17 March, to Gardez where they set up an AOB. The ODB's missions were to resupply the ODAs that operated in its vicinity and, because the company had ground mobility vehicles (GMVs), or armored HMMWVs, to escort ARSOF convoys.[205]

On 8 April, three members of ODA 395 were in Gardez when three vehicles carrying AMF soldiers approached the town, responding to a report that a truck had run an AMF roadblock. As the lead Afghan vehicle approached a bridge, an individual jumped out of a taxi blocking the road, walked up to one of the trucks, and calmly dropped a hand grenade into the driver's lap, mortally wounding him. Two others then quickly ran out from under the bridge and threw several more grenades at the three AMF vehicles. Other individuals reportedly fired on the convoy with AK-47s. Five Afghans in the second truck and several more in the third truck were wounded by the grenades. The AMF soldiers fired on their attackers, killing two. At least one of the attackers fled into Gardez.

As soon as the Special Forces soldiers at the AOB heard about the attack, the ODB immediately deployed four GMVs from ODA 361 to protect the area around the headquarters. Three other GMVs with ODA 394 aboard moved to an overwatch position to protect AMF reinforcements being sent forward by local Afghan Commander Zia Lodin. Protected by the heavy weapons aboard ODA 394's GMVs, the AMF quickly cordoned off the area into which the assailants had fled and awaited the arrival of another 60 or 70 Afghan soldiers to conduct a house-to-house search. While this was happening, ODA 395 returned to the AOB. As ODA 394 provided overwatch, the Afghans swept through the area and captured three suspected attackers.[206]

SFC Fred Anderson (pseudonym) began preparing to receive the casualties at the AOB.[207] Four AMF soldiers with minor wounds walked to the base camp and were treated by the team medic. Soon, the seriously wounded casualties arrived, escorted by the medics from ODA 395, SSG James Atkinson and SSG Mike Davis (pseudonyms), who had gone to the scene. One Afghan had suffered a critical grenade wound on the right side of his head and had extensive shrapnel wounds along the right side of his body. Another had a serious abdominal wound with obvious internal bleeding. A third had a chest wound. Another had severe facial wounds. Several had extensive leg wounds. One had a broken leg, and others had sustained wounds to the shoulders and other extremities.

Two 20th SFG medics, who had stopped in Gardez en route to Orgun, delayed their departure to assist with the wounded. This raised the total to five 18Ds (Special Forces medics) treating the eight seriously wounded Afghans. The medics did a quick triage to separate the most critical and initially concentrated on them. Although the medics could detect no pulse in the individual with the abdominal wound, his heartbeat could be detected by stethoscope. They immediately administered blood expander and saline, and these measures probably saved his life. A surgically opened airway saved the life of the patient with the head wound. The third worst casualty was saved with an Asherman chest bandage that covered the half-inch hole in his chest. Then, as the most critical were brought under control, the medics began treating the other five seriously wounded Afghans.

A 101st Airborne UH-60 Black Hawk medical evacuation helicopter and an MH-47D Chinook helicopter arrived with the 3rd SFG flight surgeon and a flight medic aboard. The medics

Figure 31. Special Forces medics conduct triage of Afghan wounded.

Figure 32. Special Forces medics stabilize the wounded.

placed the three critically wounded on the Black Hawk and the two seriously wounded onboard the Chinook. Two 19th SFG soldiers accompanied them as security. Although neither of them was an 18D Special Forces medic, SFC Anderson, the ODB 390 senior medic, knew that they were competent, having had Special Forces training. He instructed them to watch the casualties, apply new dressings if needed, and ensure that the intravenous drip was flowing. At Bagram Air Base, the forward area surgical team took over the medical treatment. One Afghan with a serious leg injury had to have it amputated, but all 13 wounded men survived. As SFC Anderson said, "This was those Afghans' lucky day. There were five 18Ds in one place."[208]

In the harsh environment of Afghanistan, constantly working with AMF personnel whose reliability and capabilities varied greatly and doing most movement at night, sensitive items were occasionally lost. These were serious matters that impacted all ARSOF units in the field. But these things happen in war. Being prepared to deal with these mishaps enabled the field commanders to continue combat operations with minimal delays. The key to reducing the potential impact was rapidly notifying the headquarters.

Dealing With Cryptographic Compromise

Cryptographic keys—secret documents and electronic equipment that encoded radio communications—were lost on occasion during combat operations in Afghanistan.[209] One Special Forces ODA lost its communications security (COMSEC) material when the mule carrying the package ran off into the night. During an intense gun battle, *Taliban* forces got into the Special Forces vehicle park before they could be driven out. The team had no way of detecting whether the enemy fighters had sufficient time to extract electronic codes from the radios on the trucks in the brief period they were around them. A coalition force lost its "crypto" during a long night movement when a piece of equipment fell off its truck.[210]

As a veteran communications specialist, MSG Tony Santana (pseudonym), the 3rd SFG communications sergeant, actually expected accidental losses. "This could happen to any soldier in any unit in any theater," he said. "The most important thing was immediately reporting the COMSEC loss so that immediate actions could be taken to safeguard the larger communications systems from enemy "listening." The automatic response was much like quickly reporting the loss of a credit card to cancel the card before a thief could use it.

3rd SFG commander COL Mark Phelan had made all radio operators in the JSOTF headquarters rehearse the procedures involving what to do in the event they received a report of lost cryptographic keys. They would reencode their radios immediately by digitally transmitting new codes, a system called "over-the-air rekeying." To prevent an enemy from also getting the new keys on their radios, U.S. and coalition radios had been preloaded with unique electronic keys that were needed to receive the new cryptological codes. In this way, when an item of COMSEC was lost or suspected to have been compromised, the hundreds of radios connected to the JSOTF communications net could be reencoded in minutes.[211]

Special Forces ODAs daily reconnoitered and searched their areas of responsibility (AOR) for signs of continued *Taliban* and *al-Qaeda* activity. Unconventional warfare (UW) never ended in Afghanistan. Army National Guard (ARNG) Special Forces ODAs assumed many of the 5th SFG missions and operational sites during the transition that took place while Operation ANACONDA was ongoing in the Shah-i-Khot Valley.

Caves and Graves

Any doubt about the capabilities of the ARNG Special Forces units meeting active Special Forces standards was dispelled by ODA 923, 19th SFG from Utah. These guardsmen unhesitatingly exchanged their civilian clothes for desert camouflage uniforms (DCUs) when called to duty in December 2001. Exercises in Thailand, Korea, Tonga, and the Maldives in the previous two years had prepared the 19th SFG for special operations missions to support national objectives. Those objectives became crystal clear on the morning of 11 September 2001.

After a preparatory period at Fort Campbell, Kentucky, ODA 923 arrived in K2, Uzbekistan, in early March 2002. There it was made a quick-reaction force (QRF) for Pakistan to interdict *Taliban* and *al-Qaeda* fleeing Afghanistan—a mission that was never executed. On 25 April, the 2nd Battalion, 19th SFG sent the team to Bagram where CJSOTF-Afghanistan further assigned it to conduct and support cave searches in the Tora Bora region. The team was under the tactical control of TF Rakkasan of the 101st Airborne Division. Specifically, the team was to reconnoiter potential helicopter landing zones (LZs), determine the level of enemy activity in the region, and confirm suspected enemy cave sites.[212]

Jalalabad was a long way from the Utah drug store where CPT Kerry Barnes (pseudonym) worked as a pharmacist.[213] However, on 27 April, CPT Barnes was moving to Jalalabad to meet ODA 966 and its Afghan Military Forces (AMF) element. Because ODA 966 had established rapport with the Afghans, Barnes added six members of that team and 50 Afghans to his operation. On 30 April, the combined force began to move by truck.

Although the distance to the objective from Jalalabad was just 50 km, vehicles could only traverse the first 30 km. While the AMF leader, Commander Malek, sent a reconnaissance element to Alefkhel, the Special Forces soldiers enterprisingly contracted for 16 mules to move their equipment from Tangi Qolleh. The force left Tangi Qolleh at 0700 on 1 May and reached Alefkhel at 1100. At Alefkhel, the terrain was so steep and the trails so narrow that the mules could go no farther. Amazingly, the "hard scrabble" rough area was filled with wheat and poppy fields. Ironically, tents stenciled with large "UNHCR" letters sat in the poppy fields. The Special Forces teams contracted for porters from among the villagers.

The straight-line distance from Alefkhel to the proposed observation post (OP) was 2,500 meters to the west, but the elevation increased 1,500 meters in that short distance. After 1½ hours, the two teams had covered only 300 meters, straight-line distance. The lack of oxygen at that altitude and the elevation change made progress for the Americans slow. After climbing for 3½ hours, the Special Forces soldiers finally reached the OP site. From there, the teams could observe two ridges, and they discovered what appeared to be two large caves on each. They also located three potential helicopter LZ sites, but all required demolitions to make them usable. On 2 May, two Special Forces engineers arrived carrying explosives, and the next morning they began clearing the LZs.

ODAs 923 and 966 observed the caves and then, with the AMF, went to investigate the four sites. Two caves had been sealed by bombs. The third proved to be only the illusion of a cave caused by shadows from overhanging rocks. The fourth suspected cave turned out to be a fighting position with overhead cover and good fields of fire. Nearby were several bunkers that appeared to have been recently occupied.[214]

The ongoing search for Osama bin Laden required all reputed grave sites to be investigated. Village porters from Alefkhel reported that about 25 Arabs were buried in a mass grave nearby. The ODAs also found two graves on one of the ridges. Permission had to be obtained from the local elders to excavate the graves. In exchange for this permission, CPT Barnes, ODA 923, made arrangements with CA personnel to have more than 12,000 pounds of humanitarian assistance delivered to Alefkhel for further distribution to the outlying villages.

On 4 May 2002, American and Canadian conventional forces, accompanied by news reporters and a team of forensic experts, arrived at Alefkhel. The news media rushed to film the mounded mass grave because they would be denied access to the area once the forensic team began to exhume the bodies. Twenty-five bodies were found at the two sites. The forensic experts took DNA samples, and the bodies were reburied. The operation appeared on CNN and was reported in major newspapers.[215] On 7 May, CH-47 helicopters brought in the aid, and the village elders began to distribute it.

By truck, by mule, and by foot, ODAs 923 and 966 moved into the high mountainous objective area to accomplish their mission—"putting eyes on possible caves and locating landing zones," said CPT Barnes. In addition, after locating grave sites, they were culturally sensitive and politely sought permission to exhume the bodies for identification. The humanitarian aid arranged assisted a town of 2,000 inhabitants as well as those Afghans in smaller surrounding villages. Superior training, flexibility in solving issues, and dedication are the hallmarks of Special Forces soldiers. ODAs 923 and 966 clearly demonstrated that these attributes were common among ARNG Special Forces soldiers as well.

Vietnam-Style A Camp at Orgun-e

As his ODA loaded supplies aboard two CH-47 helicopters on the runway apron at Bagram Air Base, MSG Danny Woburn (pseudonym) explained the mission to the pilots.[216] The 101st Airborne Division Chinook pilots were flying Woburn and ODA 361 with supplies to Orgun-e, more than an hour south of Bagram. After unloading its equipment, the Special Forces team would then load several hundred boxes of Soviet 82mm mortar rounds recently abandoned by the *Taliban* into cargo nets to be evacuated out. These would be carried, or "slung," underneath the helicopters as "sling loads" to be delivered to the 1st Battalion, 3rd SFG at the Kabul Military Academy. There, they would be used by new recruits of the Afghan National Army (ANA) for mortar training.[217]

As they flew over Orgun-e, MSG Woburn told the B Company, 159th Aviation Regiment pilots to look for a large triangle of fortified entrenchments. As far as Woburn knew, in May 2002, his was the first purposefully built, fortified Special Forces A Camp in Afghanistan. The very large "fighting base camp" had been constructed by ODA 361 and named Camp Harriman in honor of CW3 Stanley Harriman who had been killed in action during Operation ANACONDA. The camp, based on plans used by Special Forces units in Vietnam more than 30 years before, was guarded by the 3rd Platoon, B Company, 3rd Battalion, 187th Infantry, 101st Airborne Division.[218] Three hundred AMF soldiers were based at Camp Harriman. ODA 361 advised them in their operations. The AMF elements served as "strike forces" to hunt down die-hard *Taliban* and *al-Qaeda* survivors.[219]

Although MSG Woburn and his team were very aggressive in accomplishing their UW and FID missions at Orgun-e, they often joked about the "noncombat actions" that they had carried out. During "Operation Tea Marathon," they had to sit for hours in a *jirga* drinking tea with local Afghan dignitaries, testing bladder capacities to the extreme, not wanting to offend their hosts. "Afterward, we would flee *en masse* to the nearest facilities. It was every man for himself then," laughed one sergeant.[220] On another mission, the Special Forces team hired a local guide to lead it to a village that did not appear on its maps. The guide led the team on a circuitous five-hour-long drive through the rugged countryside. When it arrived, Woburn checked his satellite global positioning system (GPS) device and discovered that it was only 6 miles from its point of origin. That experience became referred to as "Operation 'Century 21'" for all the real estate they saw during their wanderings. Good humor took the edge off the isolation in the hinterlands.[221]

A National Army for Afghanistan

Years of civil war left Afghanistan without a national army. Tribes and ethnic groups of *mujahideen* led by regional warlords had forced the Soviet withdrawal and then these warlords fought the Afghan army, fought among themselves, and finally fought the *Taliban* movement. Subsequently, beginning in October 2001, the few remaining dominant warlords, with American assistance, managed to drive out the *Taliban* regime by mid-December. The most successful of these war leaders and their "armies" became the dominant Afghan Military Forces (AMF) within the country. The Afghanistan Interim Authority (AIA) and the antiterrorist coalition recognized that the future security of Afghanistan could only be ensured by a well-trained army composed of all ethnic groups and tribes in Afghan society. In May 2002, President George W.

Bush pledged $2 million to interim Afghan leader Hamid Karzai to train and equip a national army for Afghanistan.[222]

To accomplish that task, soldiers from the 1st Battalion, 3rd SFG began to train the first battalion of recruits for an ethnically diverse Afghanistan National Army (ANA) on 1 May 2002. GEN Tommy Franks, commander, CENTCOM, emphasized the importance of that mission. "The national army of Afghanistan is going to be an essential element of their long-term security," he declared.[223] Military training is a basic Special Forces mission—one that soldiers do constantly to enable governments to protect their people from subversion or insurgency. The cross-cultural communications skills and regional expertise of Special Forces soldiers help them to organize and train host government forces to enhance the nation's security.

The 1st Battalion, 3rd SFG was given the mission to train the ANA in just 10 months. It was to organize and train nine 600-man infantry battalions and six 300-man border guard battalions. Afghan military cadre trained by Special Forces soldiers would then begin training additional forces. The objective, according to LTC Keith McDaniels (pseudonym), commander, 1st Battalion, was to build "a credible, capable force."[224]

ANA recruits were selected by provincial officials and sent to Kabul for training. Travel to Kabul was extremely difficult. Although transportation was a government responsibility, the U.S. and coalition forces intervened periodically to assist with movement to ensure that sufficient physically capable recruits were available to train. Birth certificates do not exist in Afghanistan. Verifying the age requirement was virtually impossible. There was no identification system in the country; therefore, the Special Forces soldiers had to devise methods to ensure that only those recruits who passed an initial medical screening would begin training.

Each recruit for the ANA was to bring an AK-47 rifle, four magazines, and extra clothing but few did. The AIA was responsible for basic recruit training equipment. Obtaining necessary gear proved to be a slow process. The Special Forces trainers adapted to the situation by using their personal equipment to teach basic infantry tasks such as camouflage, cover, and concealment. They also taught rudimentary soldier skills—discipline, marching, marksmanship, map reading, first aid, physical fitness, and small-unit tactics. Prospective officers received more leadership training after the first two weeks before assuming their positions in the infantry battalions. The training progressed to advanced skills like mortar firing and communications. The Afghans had no tradition of sergeants, or noncommissioned officers (NCOs), as intermediate-level leaders in the armed forces. Therefore, recruits/soldiers with leadership potential were identified early to receive additional leadership and management instruction after basic training to create an NCO corps. Compounding the difficulties of training were that most recruits were illiterate; the recruits spoke a mix of languages—Dari, Pashto, and Farsi; culturally, the concept of teamwork was foreign; and the recruits had come from tribal groups that had been fighting one another for centuries.

Tactical PSYOP teams (TPTs) assisted the Special Forces soldiers by teaching history, geography, and government classes covering the history of Afghanistan; its geography; the ethnicity of the various tribes; the concept of a national government; and free elections. Few recruits knew more than a few simple "facts" about any of these topics. All classes, formal and informal, emphasized national unity, identification, and ready recognition of AIA leaders and the legitimacy of the new government. Since many of the AIA leaders were unknown to the recruits, the Special Forces trainers emphasized the ability to recognize the leaders by physical appearance and then associate them by position. Critical to the success of the ANA and the nation was helping the recruits understand their individual and unit relationship to higher headquarters and to the government of Afghanistan—the "chain of command"—instead of traditional tribal hierarchal and oligarchic loyalties.[225]

This ANA training mission was what Special Forces units were created to do. Experience from previous training missions had prepared the 1st Battalion, 3rd SFG to operate from a "bare-base" facility and to train a local military force.[226] No other force in the U.S. military has the capability and flexibility to perform such an important political mission with such global implications. One member of the 3rd SFG company summed up the importance of the mission: "That we are here during this time is key to stabilizing Afghanistan for long-term growth and development."[227]

The preceding soldier vignettes illustrate the ARSOF combat operations and activities that took place in Afghanistan and Pakistan from mid-December 2001 through late May 2002, the established end date of this work. Transitions dominated the period. They influenced how the war to eliminate the remaining *Taliban* and *al-Qaeda* resistance was fought and how the United States and its allies sought to bring stability to Afghanistan. The fighting to drive the enemy from the Shah-i-Khot Valley dominated this period, and because this was the case, those stories fill a large part of this section. However, that does not mean this was the most important success of the total war. Not every story could be included. It is hoped that those provided will give readers a balanced picture of what Army special operations soldiers were doing in Afghanistan.

The final section contains observations and reflections on the preparations for the military deployments overseas; the combat operations directed from Uzbekistan to collapse the *Taliban* regime; the combat operations and activities directed from Afghanistan against the remaining *Taliban* and *al-Qaeda* forces; and the internal defense, reconstruction, humanitarian aid, and stability operations to support the AIA as elements of Operation ENDURING FREEDOM in Afghanistan from September 2001 to mid-May 2002. These are not proffered as lessons learned. They are objective observations and reflections from the ARSOF in Afghanistan writing team—all of whom are retired Army special operations soldiers. This is not intended to be a public relations piece, nor is it to be a critique. It is simply a presentation of how the ARSOF fought the war in Afghanistan. Thus, it is not "all sunshine and roses." There were minor mistakes made in achieving success in Afghanistan. Some ARSOF soldiers committed some valorous acts to ensure that success. None of the errors were ever "mission stoppers." The sacrifices ARSOF soldiers made contributed to the freedom provided to the Afghan people. These will always be remembered by Army special operations soldiers who preserve freedom and combat terrorism worldwide.

Notes

1. "Citizenship in a Republic," Speech at the Sorbonne, Paris, 23 April 1910, *The Works of Theodore Roosevelt*, Vol. XIII, 506-29.

2. Donald Rumsfeld, "Testimony as Delivered to the Senate Committee on Foreign Relations: The Situation in Afghanistan," June 26, 2002, Washington, DC, <http://www.defenselink.mil/speeches/2002/s20020626-depsecdef2.html>.

3. U.S. Army Field Manual (FM) 100-25, *Doctrine for Army Special Operations Forces*, U.S. Army John F. Kennedy Special Warfare Center and School (SWCS), Fort Bragg, North Carolina. August 1999, 2-4; COL John F. Mulholland, interview with C.H. Briscoe, 12 July 2002, Fort Campbell, Kentucky, transcripts and tapes at U.S. Army Special Operations Command (USASOC) Classified Archives, Fort Bragg.

4. Ann Scott Tyson, "Al Qaeda: Resilient and Organized," *Christian Science Monitor*, 7 March 2002, 2

5. Kerry Zimmer is a pseudonym.

6. Peter Baker, "These Guys Will Kill Anybody," *Washington Post*, 5 March 2002, 1; Jackson Ferrell (pseudonym), B Company, 2nd Battalion, 160th Special Operations Aviation Regiment interview with James Schroder, 22 April 2002, Fort Campbell, tapes at USASOC Classified Archives, Fort Bragg, hereafter referred to as Ferrell interview.

7. U.S. Army, "Coalition Joint Task Force Mountain," Headquarters, 10th Mountain Division, Fort Drum, New York, slide presentation, 5 April 2002, copy in USASOC Classified Archives, Fort Bragg.

8. Rowan Scarborough, "Enemy Forces Allowed to Regroup," *Washington Times*, 5 March 2002, 1.

9. John Hendren, "U.S. Took Time for This Afghan Raid," *Los Angeles Times*, 4 March 2002; Ann Scott Tyson, "US, Allies in a Riskier Kind of War," *Christian Science Monitor*, 5 March 2002, 1.

10. COL Mark Phelan, Commander, 3rd Special Forces Group (SFG), Fort Bragg, interview with C.H. Briscoe, 12 July 2002, Fort Campbell, transcripts and tapes at USASOC Classified Archives, Fort Bragg, hereafter referred to as Phelan interview.

11. Karl Kramer, 5th Battalion, 19th SFG, Co., interview with C.H. Briscoe, 9 May 2002, Kandahar, Afghanistan, tape recording USASOC Classified Archives, Fort Bragg.

12. MAJ Randall Schantz (pseudonym), commander, B Company, 3rd Battalion, 160th Special Operations Aviation Regiment, interview with James Schroder, 8 May 2002, Kandahar, Afghanistan, transcripts and tapes at USASOC Classified Archives, Fort Bragg, hereafter referred to as Schantz interview.

13. Phelan interview.

14. Silas Green (pseudonym), CAT A-41, 96th Civil Affairs (CA) Battalion, interview with Kalev Sepp, 28 August 2002, Fort Bragg, tape recording USASOC Classified Archives, Fort Bragg; Scott Peterson, "Special Ops Tackle Aid Mission, Afghanistan is a Laboratory for a New Kind of US Military Humanitarian Mission," *Christian Science Monitor*, 1 March 2002, 1.

15. Brian Acosta is a pseudonym.

16. Charles Burton (pseudonym), 8th Psychological Operations Battalion, interview with MAJ Teresa Johnson, 11 June 2002, tapes in USASOC Classified Archives, Fort Bragg, hereafter referred to as Burton interview.

17. Terry Sanders is a pseudonym.

18. "Coalition Joint Task Force Mountain."

19. Scarborough, 1.

20. John Hendren, "U.S. Took Time for This Afghan Raid," *Los Angeles Times*, 4 March 2002; Tyson, "US, Allies in a Riskier Kind of War," 1; .

21. Mulholland interview.

22. Arthur Solanis (pseudonym), B Company, 2nd Battalion, 160th Special Operations Aviation Regiment, interview with Jamee Schroder, 25 March 2002, Fort Campbell, tapes and transcripts in USASOC Classified Archives, Fort Bragg; Rumsfeld.

23. Carl Hooper is a pseudonym.

24. Drew Dice (pseudonym), commander, ODB 380, B Company, 3rd Battalion, 3rd SFG, interview with Kalev Sepp, 8 July 2002, tapes and transcripts in USASOC Classified Archives, Fort Bragg, hereafter referred to as Dice interview; Paul Blanchard (pseudonym), commander, ODB 530, C Company, 1st Battalion, 5th SFG, interview with Kalev Sepp, 26 April 2002, Fort Campbell, transcripts and tapes at USASOC Classified Archives, Fort Bragg, hereafter referred to as Blanchard interview.

25. CPT Mike McHenry (pseudonym), A Company, 3rd Battalion, 3rd SFG, interview with Richard Kiper, 31 October 2002, Fort Bragg, NC, tape recording and notes at USASOC Classified Archives, Fort Bragg, hereafter referred to as McHenry interview.

26. The *shura* is a council of elders that functions as the de facto government of many Afghan towns and villages.

27. Gary Towson and Carl Hooper are pseudonyms.

28. SFC Bill Athens [pseudonym], Headquarters and Support Company, 3rd Battalion, 3rd SFG, interview with C.H. Briscoe, 6 May 2002, Kandahar, Afghanistan, tape recording and notes, USASOC Classified Archives, Fort Bragg.

29. U.S. Central Command (CENTCOM) news release number 02-11-04, "Results of Investigation Into Death of U.S. Service Member," 8 November 2002.

30. On 8 November 2002 CENTCOM released a summary of the results of the investigation. It concluded that the AC-130 crew experienced "continuous problems with their navigation systems," and "misidentified ground reference points." McHenry states that he transmitted to the AC-130 the exact location of Harriman's convoy. According to McHenry, a crewman informed the Tactical Air Control Party (TACP) with the ODAs that the aircraft's computers were malfunctioning. Soon thereafter the crewman stated the computers were functioning and asked if friendly forces were at a specific grid location south of the main body. The TACP said no because there were no forces at the location. The AC-130 then fired into Harriman's vehicle. See "Results of Investigation Into Death of U.S. Service Member"; CW3 Sandy Belliard (pseudonym), ODA 594, 5th SFG, telephonic interview with Richard Kiper, 20 November 2002, Fort Bragg, NC, Memorandum For record, USASOC Classified Archives, Fort Bragg.

31. ODA 594 dispersed to four sites: O.P.-North (MSG DC, SSG J.C., SSG J.K., and U.S. Air Force Tech. SGT B.S.), the Mission Support Site and Mortar Position (CPT G.T., SFC J.S., and SSG C.G.), Checkpoint Charlie (SFC C.B.), and the old fort at Gardez (CWO S.B., U.S. Air Force MSG B.M., SFC M.G., and SSG G.S.). The team traveled in four armored Mercedes-Benz jeeps, donated by Norway when its peacekeeping force left Bosnia. The jeeps still had "SFOR" stenciling visible on the doors, and the operator's manuals were in Norwegian, which caused some difficulties for the American drivers. CPT G.T., Memorandum, "ODA 594, Operation ENDURING FREEDOM," 14 March 2002, Fort Campbell, USASOC Classified Archives, Fort Bragg.

32. Eric Schmitt and Thom Shanker, "Afghan's Retreat Forced Americans to Lead a Battle," *New York Times*, 10 March 2002, 1; Peter Baker and Pamela Constable, "Afghans Prepare for Final Assault," *Washington Post*, 12 March 2002, 1.

33. CPT Brian Acosta (pseudonym), 910 Tactical Psychological Operations (PSYOP) Detachment, A Company, 9th PSYOP Battalion, interview by James Schroder, 8 May 2002, Kandahar, Afghanistan, tapes and transcripts at USASOC Classified Archives, Fort Bragg, hereafter referred to as Acosta interview.

34. Norman Wilcox is a pseudonym.

35. Acosta interview.

36. SGT Mitchell Dennison (pseudonym), 910 Tactical PSYOP Detachment, A Company, 9th PSYOP Battalion, interview by James Schroder, 8 May 2002, Kandahar, Afghanistan, tapes and transcripts at USASOC Classified Archives, Fort Bragg.

37. SGT Mitchell Dennison (pseudonym) and SP4 Ike Monre (pseudonym), 910 Tactical PSYOP Detachment, A Company, 9th PSYOP Battalion, interview by James Schroder, 8 May 2002, Kandahar, Afghanistan, tapes and transcripts at USASOC Classified Archives, Fort Bragg.

38. Dennison are Monroe are pseudonyms.

39. SGT Mitchell Dennison (pseudonym), SP4 Ike Monroe, and SP4 Dale Stevenson (pseudonyms), 910 Tactical PSYOP Detachment, A Company, 9th PSYOP Battalion, interview by James Schroder, May 8, 2002, Kandahar, Afghanistan, tapes and transcripts in USASOC Classified Archives, Fort Bragg.

40. 5th SFG, "SOT-A Support to Operation Anaconda," n.d.; 5th SFG, "Lessons Learned Operation ENDURING FREEDOM: ODA 563," 20 May 2002, USASOC Classified Archives, Fort Bragg.

41. Burton interview.

42. Jed Samuels (pseudonym), et al., 10 May 2002, Bagram Air Base, Afghanistan, interview with Kalev Sepp, transcripts and tapes at USASOC Classified Archives, Fort Bragg, hereafter referred to as Samuels, et al., interview.

43. Ibid.

44. Ibid.

45. Rawlins never fired his Barrett during the ANACONDA battle. Because the *al-Qaeda* fighters often concealed their weapons beneath their robe-like coats, he was unable to positively identify any of the distant figures he spotted as "definitely enemy." Jerry Rawlins (pseudonym), et al., 10 May 2002, Bagram Air Base, Afghanistan, interview with Kalev Sepp, transcripts and tapes at USASOC Classified Archives, Fort Bragg.

46. Samuels, et al., interview.

47. Ibid.

48. Ibid.

49. Raymond W. Lake (pseudonym), 11 May 2002, Bagram, Afghanistan, interview with Kalev Sepp, transcripts at USASOC Classified Archives, Fort Bragg.

50. Ibid.

51. Ibid.

52. Ibid.

53. Mann and Dickerson are pseudonyms; Alfred Mann (pseudonym), HHC, 2nd Battalion, 160th Special Operations Aviation Regiment (Airborne), interview with James Schroder, 25 March 2002, Fort Campbell, tape recording and notes, USASOC Classified Archives, Fort Bragg.

54. Derrick Mackenzie is a pseudonym.

55. Derrick Mackenzie (pseudonym), A Company, 2nd Battalion, 160th Special Operations Aviation Regiment (Airborne), interview with James Schroder, 9 July 2002, Fort Campbell, tapes and transcripts at USASOC Classified Archives, Fort Bragg.

56. Paul Parcelli is a pseudonym.

57. Mann is a pseudonym.

58. Ferrell interview.

59. Timothy Dickerson (pseudonym), A Company, 2nd Battalion, 160th Special Operations Aviation Regiment (Airborne), interview with James Schroder, 9 July 2002, Fort Campbell, tape recording and notes, USASOC Classified Archives, Fort Bragg, hereafter referred to as Dickerson interview.

60. CPT Nathan Self, A Company, 1st Battalion (Ranger), 75th Infantry Regiment, interview with C.H. Briscoe, 19 September 2002, Fort Benning, Georgia, tape recording and notes, USASOC Classified Archives, Fort Bragg, hereafter referred to as Self interview.

61. Chris Gaines (pseudonym), HHC, 160th Special Operations Aviation Regiment (Airborne), interview with James Schroder, 9 July 2002, Fort Campbell, tape recording and notes, USASOC Classified Archives, Fort Bragg.

62. John Gates is a pseudonym.

63. Douglas Talbert (pseudonym), HHC, 2nd Battalion, 160th Special Operations Aviation Regiment (Airborne), interview with Schroder, 26 March 2002, Fort Campbell, tape recording and notes, USASOC Classified Archives, Fort Bragg.

64. Jacob Frost is a pseudonym.

65. Department of Defense Release, "Executive Summary of the Battle of Takur Ghar," 24 May 2002, <www.defenselink.mil/news/May2002/d20020524takurghar.pdf>.

66. Charles Lafayette is a pseudonym.

67. The accounts of this article are drawn from interviews with Self and the 160th personnel involved with the mission. Footnotes are annotated for specific interviews located at the USASOC Classified Archives, Fort Bragg.

68. Callsign Matchbox is a pseudonym.

69. Gary Corbin is a pseudonym.

70. Roger Oliver is a pseudonym.

71. Donald Deese (pseudonym), A Company, 2nd Battalion, 160th Special Operations Aviation Regiment (Airborne), interview with James Schroder, 9 July 2002, Fort Campbell, tape recording and notes, USASOC Classified Archives, Fort Bragg.

72. Steve Larken is a pseudonym.

73. Gary Corbin (pseudonym), B Company, 2nd Battalion, 160th Special Operations Aviation Regiment (Airborne), phone interview with James Schroder, 13 November 2002, tape recording and notes, USASOC Classified Archives, Fort Bragg.

74. Kerry Miller is a pseudonym.

75. Dickerson interview.

76. Self interview; Bradley Graham, "A Wintry Ordeal at 10,00 Feet," *Washington Post*, 25 May 2002, A01.

77. Self interview.

78. Schantz interview.

79. Names and minor accounts for the 2nd Ranger Squad are culled from the following reference: Bradley Graham, A01.

80. Graham, A01.

81. Ibid.

82. Charles Elkenback is a pseudonym.

83. Daniel Henley is a pseudonym.

84. Brian Jefferson is a pseudonym.

85. Solanis is a pseudonym.

86. Derrick Donalds (pseudonym), B Company, 2nd Battalion, 160th Special Operations Aviation Regiment, interview with Kalev Sepp, 17 April 2002, Fort Campbell, tape recording and notes, USASOC Classified Archives, Fort Bragg.

87. Greg Law is a pseudonym.

88. Randal Kelley is a pseudonym.

89. Jed Samuels, Terry Sanders, Max Gorley, Ty McFadden, Jason Thurman, Jake Millett, Jerry Rawlins, Stefan Morris, Carl Hooper, Jules Arde, Bernard Dubois, Damon Hulse, and Cash Galtier are pseudonyms.

90. Samuels, et al., interview.

91. Terry Sanders is a pseudonym.

92. In the same way, Thurman was later mistaken for a U.S. Navy SEAL and a U.S. Army colonel. Jason Thurman, et al., 10 May 2002, Bagram Air Base, Afghanistan, interview with Kalev Sepp, transcripts and tapes at USASOC Classified Archives, Fort Bragg.

93. The other two special forces noncommissioned officers were SSG B.G. of A-372, and SFC C.B. of A-594. CPT G.T., Memorandum, "ODA 594," USASOC Classified Archives, Fort Bragg.

94. Only ODA 394 members called this roadblock by the name "Checkpoint Charlie." Several weeks previously, ODA 594 had established a roadside guard post several miles north of the Shah-i-Khot which they designated "Checkpoint Charlie." The 5th SFG soldiers called the new roadblock manned by ODA 394 simply "the security site." CPT G.T., Memorandum "ODA 594," USASOC Classified Archives, Fort Bragg.

95. ODA 372 was dispersed to three sites: The "old fort" at Gardez (SFC J.V.A., SSG J.C., and SSG C.R.); Checkpoint Charlie (SSG B.G.); and O.P. South (MSG J.D., SFC B.A., SSG B.W., and U.S. Air Force SSG C.S.). This O.P. South, sited on Hilltop 2322 (height in meters above sea level), should not be confused with a previously named O.P. South, planned for use by ODA 372 before the change in operations. The team's executive officer, CWO Stanley L. Harriman, had been killed by fire from a U.S. Air Force AC-130 Spectre gunship on 2 March 2002, at the beginning of Operation ANACONDA. SSG. L.W. and SSG C.C., wounded alongside Harriman, had been evacuated to the U.S. medical facility at Landstuhl, Germany, and then on to the United States. A-372's team commander, CPT M.M., had returned to the United States to oversee Harriman's burial ceremony. J.V.A., 22 November 2002; Terry Sanders, 4 December 2002; and M.M., 6 December 2002; Fort Bragg, personal and telephonic interviews with Kalev Sepp, transcripts at USASOC Classified Archives, Fort Bragg.

96. CPT G.T., Memorandum, "ODA 594." G.T., the ODA 594 team leader, gained some notoriety because of his appearance and popularity with Afghan military commanders. A Japanese-American, G.T. acquired a strikingly Afghan-like appearance as his hair and beard grew out. G.T., 21 November 2002, Fort Campbell, telephonic interview with Kalev Sepp, transcripts at USASOC Classified Archives, Fort Bragg (hereafter referred to as G.T. interview).

97. The exact locations of the checkpoint, observation posts and mortar position, per Universal Transverse Mercator grid on the Sar Wahzeh 1:100,000 mapsheet (Ed. 2-DMA, Series U611, Sheet 2883), were: Checkpoint Charlie, 42SWB/099995; O.P. North, 42SWB/152970; O.P. South, 42SWB/123954; and the Mortar Position and Command/Mission Support Site, 42SWB/143977. Ty McFadden, et al., 10 May 2002, Bagram Air Base, Afghanistan, interview with Kalev Sepp, transcripts and tapes at USASOC Classified Archives, Fort Bragg, hereafter referred to as McFadden, et al., interview.

98. During their advance, the Pashtuns found the tough copper wire strands used to guide the missiles, called TOWs (pronounced "toes," for tube-launched, optically tracked, wire-guided missile), loosely strung for hundreds of yards across the slopes. However, none of them knew why the wires were there. When they pulled on one of them, an unexploded TOW missile detonated inside a cave in front of the band of fighters, and they stopped moving forward. Over his radio, G.T. explained what had happened, and soon the advance continued. G.T. interview.

99. ODA 594 dispersed to four sites. CPT G.T., Memorandum, "ODA 594."

100. D.C., 18 November 2002, Fort Campbell, telephonic interview with Kalev Sepp, transcript at USASOC Classified Archives, Fort Bragg.

101. B.D., et al., 10 May 2002, Bagram Air Base, Afghanistan, interview with Kalev Sepp, transcripts and tapes at USASOC Classified Archives, Fort Bragg.

102. Stefan Morris, et al., 10 May 2002, Bagram Air Base, Afghanistan, interview with Kalev Sepp, transcripts and tapes at USASOC Classified Archives, Fort Bragg.

103. McFadden, et al., interview.

104. For a description of the threat to journalists by various Afghan factions at the time, see Peter Baker, "'These Guys Will Kill Anybody,'" *Washington Post*, 5 March 2002, 1; Samuels, et al., interview.

105. Dice interview; Blanchard interview.

106. Barry Bearak, "Kabul Rushes 1,000 More Men to Join G.I.'s on Battle's Sixth Day," *New York Times*, 8 March 2002, 1; Samuels, et al., interview.

107. Samuels, et al., interview.

108. McFadden, et al., interview.

109. Ibid.

110. Ibid.

111. Samuels, et al., interview.

112. ODA 372 worked most closely with Commander Khoskhyar, a Pashtun from Gardez. Commander Rasul and Commander "Engineer" commanded the other two companies. J.V.A., 22 November 2002, Fort Bragg, interview with Kalev Sepp, transcripts and tapes at USASOC Classified Archives, Fort Bragg.

113. Max Gorley, et al., 10 May 2002, Bagram Air Base, Afghanistan, interview with Kalev Sepp, transcripts and tapes at USASOC Classified Archives, Fort Bragg, hereafter referred to as Gorley, et al., interview.

114. The locations of the overnight position, per Universal Transverse Mercator grid on the Sar Wahzeh 1:100,000 mapsheet (Ed. 2-DMA, Series U611, Sheet 2883), was 42SWB/155926. Samuels, et al., interview.

115. Samuels, et al., interview.

116. The Tajiks' tank crews reportedly fired at two tents they saw in the U.S. positions, which were not marked by orange panels as had been directed. The radio call sign of the U.S. commander whose troops came under fire was "Hard Rock Six." Carl Hooper (pseudonym), 10 December 2002, letter to Kalev Sepp, and Terry Sanders (pseudonym), 5 December 2002, letter to Kalev Sepp, Fort Bragg, in USASOC Classified Archives, Fort Bragg.

117. Samuels, et al., interview.

118. Gorley, et al., interview.

119. McFadden, et al., interview.

120. Jed Samuels (pseudonym), commander, ODA 394, 3rd Battalion, 3rd SFG, interview with Sepp, 10 May 2002, Bagram Air Base, Afghanistan, transcripts and tapes at USASOC Classified Archives, Fort Bragg; Kathy Gannon, "U.S., Allies Seize Shah-e-Kot Valley," *Associated Press*, 13 March 2002.

121. Stefan Morris, et al., 10 May 2002, Bagram Air Base, Afghanistan, interview with Kalev Sepp, transcripts and tapes at USASOC Classified Archives, Fort Bragg.

122. BG John Rosa, "DOD News Briefing," 12 March 2002, <http://www/defenselink.mil/news/Mar2002/t03122002_t0312asd.html>.

123. Gorley, et al., interview.

124. Ibid.

125. In contrast, the U.S. infantry company had just arrived in Afghanistan about a week before and had not yet adjusted to field conditions. The American riflemen wore all their heavy cold-weather clothing, even during the day when the temperatures warmed. When they moved to the top of Tergul-Ghar the morning after they landed, Gorley saw the young soldiers "dropping left and right from the heat. . . . All along the ridgeline, they've got a couple guys here getting I.V.'s [saline fluid given intravenously through a tube and needle], a couple guys there drinking I.V.'s, other guys with their feet up in the air, [others] pouring water on [soldiers]." Gorley and Hulse helped the unit's physician's assistant in administering first aid. Gorley, et al., interview.

126. Gorley, et al., interview.

127. After maneuvering with Zia's men southward along the west side of Tergul-Ghar, ODA 594 returned to Gardez and shortly afterward redeployed to the United States. Half of ODA 372 stayed in the Shah-i-Khot Valley for subsequent operations. Samuels, et al., interview.

128. Dice interview; Blanchard interview.

129. CPT Ken Harrison (pseudonym), CAT-A56 team leader, 96th CA Battalion, interview by Richard Kiper, 11 May 2002, Bagram, Afghanistan, tape recording and notes, USASOC Classified Archives, Fort Bragg; "25 killed as Afghan Rivals Fight," *Dawn, the Internet Edition*, 28 April 2002, <www.dawn.comj/2002/04/28/top11.htm>.

130. Ibid.

131. LTC Tom Sherman (pseudonym), 3rd Battalion, 3rd SFG, interview by Richard Kiper, 2 October 2002, Fort Bragg, notes, USASOC Classified Archives, Fort Bragg.

132. MAJ Don Barton (pseudonym), e-mail to Kiper, 3 October 2002, USASOC Classified Archives, Fort Bragg.

133. MSG Mike Ewell (pseudonym) and SFC Keith Cantwell (pseudonym), CAT-A56 team members, 96th CA Battalion, interview by Richard Kiper, 11 May 2002, Bagram, Afghanistan, tape recording and notes, USASOC Classified Archives, Fort Bragg.

134. Ibid.

135. Gary Black is a pseudonym.

136. Bill Gertz, "U.S. Attacks Afghan Convoy," *The Washington Times*, March 19, 2002, 6.

137. Charles Elkenback (pseudonym), B Company, 3rd Battalion, 160th Special Operations Aviation Regiment, interview with James Schroder, 8 May 2002, Kandahar, Afghanistan, tape recording and notes, USASOC Classified Archives, Fort Bragg, hereafter referred to as Elkenback interview.

138. Eaton and Parker are pseudonyms.

139. Roger Wilkerson is a pseudonym.

140. Charles Martin is a pseudonym.

141. Charles Martin (pseudonym), B Company, 3rd Battalion, 160th Special Operations Aviation Regiment, interview with James Schroder, 8 May 2002, Kandahar, Afghanistan, tapes and transcripts at USASOC Classified Archives, Fort Bragg.

142. Elkenback is a pseudonym.

143. Elkenback interview.

144. McHenry interview.

145. SFC John Veringer (pseudonym), ODA 372, 3rd SFG, interview with Richard Kiper, 31 October 2002, Fort Bragg, tape recording and notes, USASOC Classified Archives, Fort Bragg; Peter Baker and Susan B. Glasser, "U.S., Allied Forces Patrol Battle Zone, Pursue Survivors," *Washington Post*, 15 March 2002, 14. Jason Doolittle is a pseudonym.

146. Carey Robeson is a pseudonym.

147. Thomas E. Ricks and Vernon Loeb, "Commander: Largest Ground Offensive is Over," *Washington Post*, 19 March 2002, 16; Geoffrey Mohan and John Daniszewski, "Assault Set Back Al Qaeda, U.S. Sets," *Los Angeles Times*, 15 March 2002.

148. Jim Garamone, "Anaconda Ending; Defense Looks at Combat Air Patrols," *American Forces Information Service*, 18 March 2002, <http://www.defenselink.mil/news/Mar2002/n03182002_200203181.html>.

149. Phelan interview.

150. Phillip Reese, James Pearl, and Rich Keogh are pseudonyms.

151. Phillip Reese (pseudonym), 11 May 2002, Bagram, Afghanistan, interview with Kalev Sepp, transcripts and tapes at USASOC Classified Archives, Fort Bragg, hereafter referred to as Reese interview.

152. Each of the "circus tents," so called for their size, cost $137,000.

153. Reese interview.

154. Ibid.

155. Ibid.

156. Ibid.

157. Ibid.

158. Tony Santana and Kent Willard are pseudonyms.

159. Tony Santana (pseudonym), 6 May 2002, Bagram, Afghanistan, interview with Kalev Sepp, transcripts and tapes at USASOC Classified Archives, Fort Bragg, hereafter referred to as Santana interview.

160. Ibid.

161. Morris Washington is a pseudonym.

162. Morris Washington, 10 May 2002, Bagram, Afghanistan, interview with Kalev Sepp, transcripts and tapes at USASOC Classified Archives, Fort Bragg.

163. Ibid.

164. Ibid.

165. Ibid.

166. Ibid.

167. Ibid.

168. Ben Crenshaw is a pseudonym. Ben Crenshaw, 6 May 2002, Bagram Air Base, Afghanistan, interview with Kalev Sepp, transcripts and tapes at USASOC Classified Archives, Fort Bragg.

169. Ibid.

170. Ibid.

171. Ibid.

172. Ibid.

173. Ibid.

174. Silas Greene (pseudonym), CAT-A41, 96th CA Battalion, interview with Kalev Sepp, 28 August 2002,

Fort Bragg, tape recording and notes, USASOC Classified Archives, Fort Bragg. Gray Jaffe is a pseudonym.

175. Keenan Jacobson is a pseudonym. Dexter Filkins, "Toll in Thousands Feared as Quake Hits Afghan Town," *New York Times*, 27 March 2002, 1. By 28 March the death toll stood at 737. It was not expected to rise much beyond that. See Pamela Constable, "Quake Aid Sped To Afghans," *Washington Post*, 28 March 2002, 1.

176. Don Sullivan and Derrick Jacobi are pseudonyms.

177. Don Sullivan (pseudonym), 24 April 2002, Fort Campbell, interview with Kalev Sepp, transcripts and tape at USASOC Classified Archives, Fort Bragg.

178. Santana interview.

179. Phillip Reese is a pseudonym.

180. Reese interview.

181. An AC-130 was shot down at the Battle of Al Khafji in Saudi Arabia in 1990, during the Persian Gulf war, when it stayed over the battlefield after the sun came up. As a result, the large, slow-flying gunships were restricted to flying over hostile areas only at night. It was considered an extraordinary exception for the USAFSOC to deviate from its policy to support Phelan's task force.

182. Phelan interview.

183. Phillip Reese is a pseudonym.

184. The U.S. Armed Forces refers to all the world's time zones consecutively by letter designations, from A (Alpha) to Z (Zulu). Each letter of the alphabet is read with a unique phonetic pronunciation to aid understanding in radio communications: Alpha, Bravo, Charlie, Delta, etc.

185. Reese interview.

186. Phelan interview.

187. "CINC" (pronounced "sink") was verbal shorthand for commander in chief, the former title for the four-star theater commanders. The title had just been changed to "combatant commander," but the old term CINC remained in informal use. In 2002, commander in chief was reserved to refer only to the President of the United States. Phelan later reflected that his attendance at the daily VTCs "kept me from going out to visit the troops [of the CJSOTF, across Afghanistan], but . . . I felt very secure knowing I heard exactly what the CINC said." Phelan interview.

188. Phelan interview.

189. Jeff Bosley is a pseudonym.

190. Jeff Bosley, 11 May 2002, Kabul, Afghanistan, interview with Kalev Sepp, transcripts at USASOC Classified Archives, Fort Bragg.

191. Ibid.

192. Ibid.

193. Ibid.

194. Dexter Yates is a pseudonym.

195. Dexter Yates, 8 May 2002, Kabul, Afghanistan, interview with Kalev Sepp, transcripts and tapes at USASOC Classified Archives, Fort Bragg, hereafter referred to as Yates interview.

196. The British and Americans referred to these ISAF-trained units as the "First BANG," "Second BANG," etc. The Afghan national guard battalions were intended for internal security duties in Kabul.

197. Yates interview.

198. Ibid.

199. Gregory Jernigan and Eric Nolan are pseudonyms.

200. Gregory Mulligan and Terry Rounds (pseudonyms), CHLC-2, 489th CA Battalion, Knoxville, Tennessee, interview with C.H. Briscoe, 10 May 2002, Kandahar, Afghanistan, transcripts and tapes at USASOC Classified Archives, Fort Bragg.

201. Harry Singletary, Gregory Mulligan, and Terry Rounds are pseudonyms.

202. John Harriman and Arthur Walton are pseudonyms.

203. John Harriman and Arthur Walton (pseudonyms), CHLC-2, 489th CA Battalion, Knoxville, interview with C.H. Briscoe, 11 May 2002, Kandahar, Afghanistan, transcripts and tapes at USASOC Classified Archives, Fort Bragg.

204. SPC Joshua Danner, SGT Tim Elton, SSG Charles Milton (pseudonyms), 345th PSYOP Company, Dallas, Texas, interview with C.H. Briscoe, 12 May 2002, Kandahar, Afghanistan, transcripts and tapes at USASOC Classified Archives, Fort Bragg.

205. USASOC Crisis Response Cell Briefing, 15 February 2002, 2 March 2002, 17 March 2002 in USASOC Classified Archives, Fort Bragg.

206. Message, 082100Z APR 02, CDR AOB 390, Gardez, Afghanistan, to CDR FOB 33, Bagram, Afghanistan, subject: OPSUM GRENADE INCIDENT, in USASOC Classified Archives, Fort Bragg.

207. SFC Fred Anderson (pseudonym), C Company, 3rd Battalion, 3rd SFG, interview with Richard Kiper, 5 May 2002, Bagram, Afghanistan, tape recording and notes, USASOC Classified Archives, Fort Bragg, hereafter cited as Anderson interview. James Atkinson and Mike Davis are pseudonyms.

208. Anderson interview.

209. Santana interview.

210. Ibid.

211. Ibid.

212. MSG Andy Stewart (pseudonym), B Company, 1st Battalion, 19th SFG, interview with Richard Kiper, 10 May 2002, Bagram, Afghanistan, tape recording and notes, USASOC Classified Archives, Fort Bragg.

213. CPT Kerry Barnes (pseudonym), B Company, 1st Battalion, 19th SFG, interview with Richard Kiper, 10 May 2002, Bagram, Afghanistan, tape recording and notes, USASOC Classified Archives, Fort Bragg.

214. Ibid.

215. Ryan Chilcote, "Hunt for Bin Laden's Remains," <www.cnn.com>, 7 May 2002; Peter Baker, "Mass Grave is Discovered At Tora Bora," *Washington Post*, 8 May 2002, 16; Carlotta Gall, "Allies Exhume 23 Bodies Thought to be Qaeda Fighters," *Washington Post*, 8 May 2002.

216. Danny Woburn is a pseudonym.

217. Danny Woburn (pseudonym), 9 May 2002, Bagram, Afghanistan, interview with Kalev Sepp, transcripts at USASOC Classified Archives, Fort Bragg, hereafter referred to as Woburn interview.

218. See Thomas A. Jones, "On Camps," unpublished manuscript, 1992, held in the Marquat Library collection, SWCS, Fort Bragg.

219. Woburn interview.

220. A *jirga* is literally a circle and is often used to describe a meeting.

221. Woburn interview.

222. "U.S. to Help Equip Afghan Army," *Washington Post*, 3 May 2002, 5.

223. Laurie Goering, "Kabul Sees Army as Key to Peace," *Chicago Tribune*, 22 May 2002.

224. J.S. Newton, "New ranks emerge from dust," *Fayetteville Observer*, 2 June 2002, 1A. Keith McDaniels is a pseudonym.

225. MAJ Henry Deaver (pseudonym), CW4 David Carson (pseudonym), 1st Battalion, 3rd SFG, interview with Richard Kiper, Kabul, Afghanistan, 7 May 2002, tape recording and notes, USASOC Classified Archives, Fort Bragg, hereafter cited as Deaver interview.

226. CPT John Montgomery (pseudonym), MSG Charles Dunleavy (pseudonym), 1st Battalion, 3rd SFG, interview with Richard Kiper, Kabul, Afghanistan, 7 May 2002, tape recording and notes, USASOC Classified Archives, Fort Bragg.

227. Deaver interview.

Observations and Reflections

The presentation of observations and reflections follow the organizational chapters of the book, after the historical background of Afghanistan—preparation for war, ARSOF in the supported role (forcing the *Taliban* regime from power), the transition period, and ARSOF in the supporting role through mid-May 2002. To provide continuity for the reader, the sequence of observation and reflection discussions generally follow the standard five paragraphs of the Army field order:

* Situation—what is known about the enemy and what the enemy is most likely to do.
* Mission—what is to be accomplished by the allied forces in general terms.
* Execution—who will do what tasks and how things will be accomplished.
* Administration—including legal aspects, rules of engagement (ROE), and logistics (all types of support for the combat forces plus equipment accountability).
* Command and control—who is in charge of what and when that responsibility is to be transferred, including communications and how orders and plans will be issued.

The observations are based on official documents and interviews with participants at all levels, including coalition allies, and the reflections are situational assessments by active and retired ARSOF officers who participated in this operation's history. The overthrow of the *Taliban* government in Afghanistan represents the first success in America's global war on terrorism (GWOT).

The purpose of this book is to tell the general American public what the Army special operations soldiers did to drive the *Taliban* from power, to destroy *al-Qaeda* strongholds, and to support the organization of a democratic government in Afghanistan as part of the GWOT. Thus, the average American is the intended audience. It is not the purpose of this book to capture lessons learned, resolve special warfare doctrinal issues, create doctrine, or clarify definitions for ARSOF. The *Taliban* was driven from power by American captains, warrant officers, and sergeants on tactical teams and aircrews supporting Afghan forces. If ARSOF operations and how tactical teams were employed in Afghanistan create doctrinal debate, the appropriate venue to resolve these issues is the U.S. Army John F. Kennedy Special Warfare Center and School (SWCS). The chapter introductions and sanitized vignettes have been written so that readers with little or no military background can understand and appreciate the contributions a variety of ARSOF units made.

The historical vignettes selected tell the total ARSOF story. Many demonstrate tactical and technical skills and the determination and bravery of Army special operations soldiers and aviators. There was a conscious effort to ensure that the story included all ARSOF elements. Thus, to provide a representative sampling of the different ARSOF capabilities, operations, and activities within the security constraints, not all interviews became vignettes. This historical effort was not designed to be a definitive study. It is an "ARSOF snapshot" of the war from 11 September 2001 until mid-May 2002. Since the published word promotes analysis and provokes discussion, it is most appropriate that the first official account should come from an Army special operations organization because these forces spearheaded the unconventional warfare (UW) campaign that caused the collapse of the *Taliban* government and initiated the foreign internal defense (FID) and development campaign in Afghanistan.

The command decision to have professional historians with ARSOF experience capture the history of operations in Afghanistan indicated that the book was not intended to be a public relations piece. War and combat fighting have never been "all sunshine and roses." Just as campaign plans and orders tend to "go to the winds" once the fighting starts, reluctant and ill-prepared leaders were replaced, confusion and incomplete information were relegated to "fog of war," and perfect recollections from the headquarters as to what happened on the ground that often dominate after-the-battle reports have been cross-referenced with the tactical teams that were involved. When everything goes according to plan, most professional soldiers consider it to be an anomaly. And, since this book would be carefully read by the participants at all levels, the old sports adage, "It's easy to fool the fans, but you can't fool the players," was adopted to provide more than 95-percent objectivity.

Preparation for War

During the preparation for ground war from 12 September through 18 October 2001, the day before the insertion of U.S. troops into Afghanistan, the situation and anticipated *Taliban* and *al-Qaeda* reaction based on available intelligence was vague, incomplete, and associated with the *mujahideen* guerrilla tactics that caused Soviet forces to withdraw in 1989. Afghanistan was a "backwater" Muslim nation that merited little attention from the Department of State and official intelligence sources. The terrorist attacks on America prompted unity as well as unprecedented collaboration among U.S. intelligence agencies to coordinate efforts and integrate the mosaic of data and products. Topographical mapping that dated to the Soviet regime was modified and rapidly updated using current imagery.

To project significant American ARSOF combat power in Afghanistan required overseas basing in adjacent countries and U.S. Air Force tankers to refuel the troop-carrying helicopters and their armed escorts. To support the original conventional ground war plan that was to be initiated by an air campaign, the U.S. Central Command (CENTCOM), using its Special Operations Command, SOCCENT, made the 5th SFG the Joint Special Operations Task Force–North (JSOTF-North). JSOTF-North was to initiate the ground force offensive in mid-October 2001, in conjunction with another joint special operations headquarters. Army Special Forces ODAs were to support the anti-*Taliban* warlords, and other SOF would attack specific targets deep inside of Afghanistan.

Army Special Forces teams were to advise and support two identified anti-*Taliban* factions. These teams were to arrange the air delivery of arms, munitions, and supplies; advise the warlords on tactics and strategy; and support offensive operations by directing close air support (CAS). Army Rangers were to seize an airfield by parachute assault and attack a suspected *al-Qaeda* stronghold, Objective Rhino. From this airfield, 160th SOAR AH-6 attack helicopters attacked assigned targets and refueled and rearmed. At the same time, the MH-60L Direct-Action Penetrators (DAPs) and MH-47E helicopters were to insert Special Forces teams into Afghanistan. The air campaign initiated psychological operations (PSYOP) warfare with airdropped leaflet bombs.

Operations security (OPSEC) concerns affected mission preparation and planning at all levels. Compartmenting projects, imposing limited and special-access requirements to Secret materials and relationships, and issuing Top Secret plans from CENTCOM reduced access in the operational units and compelled tactical commanders at the colonel and below level to grant temporary access to information deemed critical to mission planning. The number of positions in an SFG that require Top Secret clearances are minimal, and it requires a final Secret clearance to technically grant access to Focal Point programs. The small intelligence sections at the tactical level faced an administrative nightmare. Conventional forces assigned as security forces at ARSOF forward operating bases (FOBs) had to be briefed, and the number of personnel with security clearances at the infantry rifle company level was miniscule. Despite the fact that only limited information flowed down to "junior leaders and soldiers," morale remained high—ARSOF soldiers knew they would be committed to the fight early, and CNN media coverage provided some information on the combat zone. The only question was when?

Based on unit strengths, operational readiness for overseas deployment, the ongoing worldwide commitments of active duty ARSOF, and the unknown duration of the war, U.S. Army Reserve (USAR) and Army National Guard (ARNG) units and individual personnel were mobilized to meet and sustain wartime requirements. These needs covered a wide variety of staff requirements in the United States and overseas headquarters to accelerate schooling and expand student capacities to train more ARSOF soldiers, to accommodate units' overseas rotations, and to mobilize the personnel and units for federal service. The higher headquarters (CENTCOM, SOCCENT, and USSOCOM) in Tampa and Fort Bragg (USASOC, USASFC, and USACAPOC) charged with mobilization filled their personnel staff augmentation needs first while the lower-level Joint Special Operations Task Forces (JSOTFs) deploying overseas to fight the war were filled last. The impact of this action was exacerbated when CENTCOM and SOCCENT elected to "direct the war" from Tampa. SOCCENT established a forward regional command and control cell (Joint Force Special Operations Component Commander [JF-SOCC]) at Doha, Qatar, and relegated command of the combat zone to the 5th SFG commander as JSOTF-North. The Special Operations Command, U.S. Joint Forces Command, Norfolk, Virginia, immediately conducted a "crash JSOTF course" for 5th SFG commanders and staff personnel. It also helped prepare the mission needs statement to specify joint as well as Army Staff personnel augmentation, automation, communications, and intelligence systems required as well as combat equipment and supplies. Because the "warfighting" JSOTF-North was given the lowest priority for staff augmentation, SOCJFCOM stripped personnel from its experienced joint staff to fill critical staff voids and coordinated with CENTCOM and USSOCOM for priority fills from the other services.

The mobilization and sponsorship of USAR and ARNG SOF units and personnel, while deemed critical to sustain a prolonged war against terrorism and support the rotation of active duty elements, were not well executed. Active component headquarters wanted Army Reserve mobilization groups to handle the physical requirements of mobilizing USAR and ARNG personnel and units. Unfortunately, the USAR mobilizers were activated after most ARSOF personnel and units had been. It was not uncommon for ARNG units to be mobilized twice before being federalized, especially the composite Special Forces units formed from the 19th and 20th SFGs that were spread throughout several states. Not only did this complicate state responsibilities for resourcing, it also created very disparate command chains. Active duty sponsors for USAR and ARNG units either had "their hands full" getting themselves deployed, or those elements left behind did not have the sufficient equipment and personnel assets to assist these units in preparing for overseas deployment. Having been mobilized and then not sent overseas during Operation DESERT STORM, the ARNG Special Forces units were so determined to be deployed that few issues were raised until they were in Afghanistan. One can ask most reservists or national guardsmen who were mobilized to elaborate on these problems.

A 5th Battalion, 19th SFG company of the Colorado ARNG was mobilized and trained at Fort Carson, Colorado, before being processed again for mobilization with the 2nd Battalion headquarters before federalization at Fort Knox, Kentucky. When the two Special Forces companies from the other battalions arrived at Fort Campbell, Kentucky, all personnel were again mobilized when they were attached to the 2nd Battalion, 19th SFG from West Virginia. When the 19th SFG units arrived, only one 5th SFG company was left at Fort Campbell. The company's equipment had already been palletized pending deployment. Concern that the 19th SFG units might not be considered operationally ready if mobile training assistance teams were requested from the SWCS precluded formal orientation on advanced radio and weapon systems common to active duty Special Forces units. Some very motivated NCOs at the ODA level took the initiative and arranged classes on PSC-5 radios and security devices.

The 489th CAB, Knoxville, Tennessee, mobilized at Fort Bragg to replace the 96th CAB, faced many of the same frustrations as the 19th SFG. In its case, OPSEC concerns limited unit access to daily operations and intelligence updates by the active duty forces. Individuals mobilized for ARSOF staff and instructor positions at the SWCS were processed by fellow reservists activated to conduct mobilization. Mandatory administrative processing and equipment issue that normally took less than 24 working hours were "compressed" into 10 working days. Individual service members were not available to "report" to their duty assignment until fully processed. Still, the individual guardsmen and reservists took it "all in stride" because they wanted to do their part to combat the terrorism that struck America on 9/11. They were not going to lose the opportunity to demonstrate their tactical proficiency and prove to the Active component that they were indeed force multipliers. Throughout the 2001 Christmas holiday period, the USAR conducted accelerated basic civil affairs (CA) officers classes as the first part of the SWCS "gear up." Once in-processed, the difficulty lay in getting the forces to the fight.

While more than two decades of planning had gone into a computerized, prioritized, and carefully timed flow of men, equipment, and supplies into the forward areas of combat zones by various U.S. Air Force and contract aircraft, the reality was that once the time-phased force deployment data (TPFDD) process started, regardless of whether it was tied to an obsolete or seriously modified plan, it was very difficult to alter by any of the military services. First, delays in negotiations for basing rights interrupted the flow as aircraft were held at intermediate bases throughout Europe, the Mediterranean, and the Middle East. Then, when access to Karshi Kanabad (K2), Uzbekistan, was limited to only Air Force C-17 Globemaster III cargo jets and C-130 Hercules turboprop aircraft, this created problems that rippled down to the lowest levels. The 2nd Battalion, 160th SOAR, which had always deployed its MH-47E Chinooks on C-5 Galaxy jumbo jets, had rapid helicopter buildup load plans with specially designed transmission stands and a four-wheeled lifter (SCAMP) to support rapid deployments. The 3rd

Battalion had shipped its MH-47Ds overseas aboard C-17s, but the 2nd Battalion had only done static load training with a C-17. Separating MH-47E transmissions and the SCAMP meant that an MH-47E could not be built up until the second C-17 carrying the other transmission or SCAMP arrived. With the MH-47Es broken down and the equipment palletized for C-5s, the arrival of C-17s at Campbell Army Airfield to transport the aircraft created quite a stir in the 160th SOAR. Aircraft loads had to be completely reconfigured and the helicopters broken down further. Since the 160th SOAR had been tasked to provide four MH-47Es as primary combat search and rescue (CSAR) for the air campaign in the north, only luck prevented a potential delay in the war.

Simultaneously, AH and MH-6s, MH-60Ls, and more MH-47Es from the 1st and 2nd Battalions were being prepared for deployment. Some scheduled departures were delayed while others were moved ahead. As the air movement of ARSOF elements began, the U.S. Secretaries of Defense and State were still coordinating diplomatic clearances for Uzbekistan and country overflight permissions. The resulting traffic jam caused by aircraft being held throughout the region awaiting clearance and the arrival of larger aircraft (Air Force C-5s, C-141s, and contracted civilian airplanes) to transload personnel, equipment, and supplies to C-17s and C-130s for entry into Uzbekistan grew worse each day. When landing clearance was granted, the TPFDD order was hopelessly torn apart as the disparate planeloads of personnel were disgorged at K2, and equipment and supplies had to be manually unloaded because K-loaders and forklifts had not arrived at the old Soviet air base in sufficient quantity. Confusion was rampant.

For the active duty units that regularly deploy overseas, the experienced air movement officers and NCOs "pushed the units out," and advance echelon (ADVON) parties of operations and logistics personnel in theater were used to dealing with these crises. It was a different story for the USAR and ARNG units whose commanders and staffs relied on "the system" to get their personnel, equipment, and supplies to the right place, together. These units lacked the practical experience and knowledge to cross-load personnel, equipment, and materiel to provide some operational capability in the event of problems as well as to function for extended periods without key equipment and supplies. When the 489th CAB headquarters arrived, it went to Kabul while its tactical teams were scattered throughout the country. This meant the small tactical civil affairs teams (CAT-As) lived out of their rucksacks for 30 days and contracted vehicles to accomplish their humanitarian missions in the villages of the desolate countryside.

At Fort Bragg, the major Army command (MACOM) and major subordinate command (MSC) staffs worked with the deploying units to validate statements of need based on personnel and equipment shortages. The USASOC headquarters looked first within the command to correct key personnel shortages and shortfalls in language capabilities. The MACOM staff reprioritized equipment on hand, worked with the Department of the Army staff to accelerate fielding of new systems, shifted outyear funds to accommodate war requirements, and appealed to USSOCOM and Department of the Army for critical unfunded and unprogrammed equipment needs as well as critical military occupational specialty (MOS) and linguist shortages.

Combat service support for the ARSOF deployed overseas was the responsibility of the Special Operations Support Command (SOSCOM). The 528th Special Operations Support Battalion (SOSB) provided initial logistics support at K2, while the 112th Signal Battalion furnished "long-haul" communications for JSOTF-North. The European signal detachment supported SOCEUR at Ramstein Air Base, Germany, and Incirlik, Turkey, as part of the aerial resupply mission. CENTCOM had operational command of ARSOF while SOCCENT had operational control of the USASOC forces.

Since most of the Army CA and PSYOP forces are in the USAR and two SFGs are in the ARNG, unit mobilizations and federalization for overseas deployment were approved. Although the USAR CA and PSYOP and ARNG Special Forces personnel had been mobilized as individuals for overseas duty before, this was the first time that large numbers of ARSOF units had been mobilized and deployed into combat overseas since the Vietnam war, although the 13th PSYOP Battalion was deployed during Operation DESERT STORM. The unit mobilizations required prior mobilization of USAR and ARNG personnel to fill the MACOM and MSC staffs involved in the process. The move to bring forces onboard was balanced with measures to prevent soldiers from leaving the service.

The "stop loss" program that froze retirements, enlistments, and resignations had four parts. The first part had the most impact on Active ARSOF components: Special Forces career management field (CMF) 18 and 180 series that also included senior enlisted personnel and aviation warrant officers (WOs) and CMF 150 series, with additional skill identifiers (ASIs) 4, 5, and 6 for 160th SOAR WO pilots and crew chiefs with a 67U MOS. The second captured ARSOF skills in the Active Army and USAR: functional area (FA) 39 PSYOP officers, USAR FA 38 CA officers, ARNG CMF 18 series and enlisted MOSs, WO UH-60 and CH-47 aviators, and 67U crew chiefs. The third iteration expanded the freeze to critically short conventional MOSs, and the fourth partially lifted some of the non-ARSOF specialties and added information management officers, artillery enlisted MOSs, explosive ordnance demolition (EOD) specialists, and unmanned aerial vehicle (UAV) operators. The EOD specialists worked closely with Special Forces personnel in Afghanistan, destroying weapon systems and stockpiled munitions in caches discovered after significant fights with *al-Qaeda* and *Taliban*.

The "stop loss" was an ARSOF "personnel Band-Aid fix" to deal with the immediate crisis affecting Special Forces and special operations aviators. Expanded recruiting was a long-term solution (two years or more) because the two-time volunteers (first time being airborne or parachute qualification) still had to qualify for Special Forces training (assessment and selection); complete the basic Special Forces qualification course; complete advanced skills training as communications, engineer, or medical specialists; and graduate from foreign language training before being fully qualified for assignment to an operational SFG. ARSOF aviators and aircrews undergo assessment and selection and several months' advanced training, and spend up to a year becoming fully mission qualified. Thus, "stop loss" assets moved through the personnel artery like an aneurysm, or air bubble, on the way to the heart of ARSOF—its highly trained people, not equipment.

While CENTCOM and SOCCENT tactically commanded and controlled the ARSOF forces, the responsibility for arranging the shipment of the units with equipment and basic logistics loads into the combat zone fell to the U.S. Special Operations Command (USSOCOM). USSOCOM arranged transportation through the Air Force Air Mobility Command based on

TPFDD schedules and deployment priorities and missions. CENTCOM approved the forces coming into its area of responsibility (AOR), and USSOCOM worked to ensure they arrived in theater on time and got where they belonged. The AOR war campaign plan was CENTCOM's responsibility, and the SOF annex addressed ARSOF missions in the theater.

SOCCENT was the only regional Special Operations Command (SOC) without assigned forces. As such, SOCCENT headquarters had the smallest staff and wartime augmentation from the services and was almost entirely Reserve personnel. Traditionally, command of regional SOCs rotate among the services. A Navy rear admiral (SEAL) commanded SOCCENT, and the key warfighting staff billets (deputy, chief of staff, and operations officer) were filled by Navy SEALs. There were few staff officers in the SOC who had prepared and issued warning orders and operation plans (OPLANs), let alone write a SOF campaign plan.

To fill the void and assist tactical units that were preparing to fight the war, USASOC, USACAPOC, 5th SFG, and the 4th POG sent teams of experienced operations and intelligence planners to Tampa to minimize the turbulence. They prepared multiple courses of action for presentation at CENTCOM and to the Joint Chiefs of Staff (JCS) and then wrote the necessary orders and messages to implement the decisions. The Joint Psychological Operations Task Force (JPOTF) headquarters was created at CENTCOM and staffed almost entirely by 4th POG personnel. This JTF headquarters was augmented predominantly with USAR and ARNG personnel.

ARSOF communications in the combat zone was the responsibility of the 112th Signal Battalion. SOCJFCOM, during its training of the 5th SFG to assume the role of the JSOTF in the combat zone, coordinated additional information systems requirements with the 112th. One responsibility was to operate all video teleconferences (VTCs). The Joint Communications Signal Element (JCSE) supported CENTCOM, SOCCENT, and the SOC forward command cell, the JFSOCC. Exactly where they operated and the condition of the site depended on the outcome of basing rights negotiated by the Department of State and DOD.

When permission was granted to use the former Soviet air base at K2, Uzbekistan, as an ARSOF logistics base and the headquarters for JSOTF-North and the Joint Special Operations Air Component (JSOAC), access was limited to C-17 Globemaster IIIs and C-130 Hercules cargo and smaller aircraft. When the TPFDD airflow bottlenecks were broken, K2 began receiving aircraft around the clock. Some of the chaos intrinsic to ADVONs "staking claims" to available real estate was an unsettled issue until COL John Mulholland, commander, 5th SFG, arrived to head JSOTF-North. To preclude any service squabbling, the 16th Special Operations Wing (SOW) commander became the deputy JSOTF commander.

The Army controlled JSOAC-North because the four MH-47Es and two MH-60L DAPs were the primary CSAR for the northern half of Afghanistan during the air campaign. JSOAC-South provided CSAR coverage of southern Afghanistan with four MH-53M helicopters from the 16th SOW. Each JSOAC had MC-130P aerial refueling aircraft assigned to support the helicopters as well as Air Force special tactics squadrons with combat control tactical and medical elements. The CSAR mission became subordinated to other tactical requirements after the ground war was launched, but it never went away.

Having dealt with the difficulties of getting an ARSOF headquarters operational in a "bare base environment," the 112th Signal Battalion and 528th SOSB were flexible and carried extra equipment and special supplies (plywood and 2 x 4 lumber proved invaluable). Getting the four MH-47E and two MH-60L helicopters "built up and tested" to meet the air campaign CSAR deadline required 24-hour maintenance operations until complete. The Night Stalker forklift operator worked with all elements to unload aircraft and relocate containers as the 160th SOAR bulk fuel team refueled all arriving Air Force and contract aircraft until Thanksgiving. It was a "beehive of activity" as all services and elements pitched in together to make K2 fully operational as quickly as possible.

As JSOTF-North "stood up" for operations, ARSOF tactical teams moved to FOBs in the region to prepare for the ground war. An integral part of the air campaign was distributing psychological warfare materials. Leaflet bombs were dropped on specific *Taliban* and *al-Qaeda* targets along with explosive munitions, and PSYOP messages were broadcast from aerial platforms. It was a well-coordinated joint effort.

When ARSOF forces were committed to Afghanistan, they were to be resupplied by air by the U.S. European Command (EUCOM) under the direction of COMSOCEUR. Transloading supplies and equipment began at Ramstein Air Base, Germany, before shipment to the forward supply base in Incirlik, Turkey. Logisticians and parachute riggers, American and German, prepared loads for airdropping throughout Afghanistan. SOCEUR controlled the MC-130H Combat Talons, while EUCOM controlled the C-17 Globemaster III aircraft until they entered the CENTCOM AOR when the JSOAC took charge in theater. Air Force C-17 aircraft, operating from a variety of bases, did the humanitarian relief airdrops, mostly high-altitude drops from above 30,000 feet mean sea level (MSL).

As soon as JSOAC-North had MH-47Es and MH-60Ls operationally ready to do the CSAR mission, pressure to demonstrate America's resolve to take the war to the *Taliban* and *al-Qaeda* intensified. ARSOF soldiers were anxious to respond to the 9/11 terrorist attacks. Weather along the Uzbekistan-Afghanistan border did not cooperate.

Driving the *Taliban* From Power: ARSOF in the Supported Role

When the air campaign began against key *Taliban* and *al-Qaeda* targets throughout Afghanistan, the initiation of the ground campaign to drive the *Taliban* from power and to seize or eliminate key *al-Qaeda* leaders was delayed by adverse weather in the northern mountains bordering the country. A primary consideration in launching a UW campaign was establishing relations with two principal anti-*Taliban* warlords while intelligence assets worked to clarify and update the enemy situation on the ground. The intelligence picture would remain unclear throughout the ground war in Afghanistan.

The multiple ARSOF missions on the night of 19 October 2001 demonstrated to the *al-Qaeda* and *Taliban* in Afghanistan that the United States could project awesome military power worldwide when and where its government decided and launch a UW campaign at the same time. The 75th Rangers conducted parachute and helicopter assaults into two separate areas to put "American combat boots on the ground" as other 160th SOAR helicopter crews inserted Special Forces ODAs to support anti-*Taliban* leaders and attack deep enemy targets. The Ranger airborne assault into central Afghanistan was the initial event in a well-orchestrated special operations ground and air attack on multiple targets. The rapid airfield seizure (Objective Rhino) was key to establishing a helicopter refueling and rearming site to support other Special Forces teams conducting direct-action (DA) assaults on key ground targets. With the completion of all missions, the deep-penetration assault force loaded all troops, equipment, and helicopters for return to their overseas launch bases. Army and Air Force SOF elements had demonstrated that American combat forces could successfully accomplish what they had tried and failed to do in Iran in spring 1980. A Ranger helicopter assault into Objective Honda secured an airstrip to serve as a CSAR base, forward arming and refueling point (FARP), and medical evacuation support site for Rhino operations. Unfortunately, that successful mission was clouded when an MH-60K Black Hawk helicopter carrying additional troops into the secured airfield crash-landed, killing two of the Rangers onboard.

While these operations were taking place, simultaneously, Special Forces ODA teams were inserted deep into northern Afghanistan by MH-47E helicopters to rendezvous with anti-*Taliban* leaders to organize forces for the UW campaign. MH-60L DAPs had protected the Chinooks. Extremely high mountainous terrain and the distance to the landing zones (LZs) dictated multiple aerial refuels during ingress and egress of Afghanistan. The "be prepared" mission for all 160th SOAR helicopter flight crews was to conduct self-CSAR and insert more ODAs to advise and assist other anti-*Taliban* leaders as they made known their willingness to join the fight. The unexpected offensive spirit of the first two anti-*Taliban* leaders, encouraged by U.S. military advice, assistance (money, arms, munitions, and supplies), and CAS, determined the pace of the unconventional war in Afghanistan.

With the start of the ground campaign, JSOTF-North essentially became the SOF tactical command post (CP) for CENTCOM and SOCCENT that had their main CPs in Tampa, with USSOCOM supporting. With this arrangement, the USASOC headquarters at Fort Bragg acted as the *de facto* Army special operations rear CP because it served as the major resourcing command for the ARSOF that constituted most of the SOF of JSOTF-North, the tactical SOF warfighting headquarters. Situational awareness was critical for all commands but more so for USASOC because that headquarters had to anticipate aviation maintenance issues, rapidly respond to combat losses—personnel and equipment—coordinate ARSOF-unique supply and equipment requirements, and recommend viable plans of action.

Twice daily VTCs between CENTCOM combatant commander GEN Tommy Franks; RADM Bert Calland, SOCCENT, Tampa; and COL John Mulholland, commander, JSOTF-North, K2, Uzbekistan, kept the main and *de facto* rear CPs abreast of the situation in the combat zone. Daily VTCs for primary staffs were interspersed between commanders' sessions. The 112th Signal Battalion proudly stated that it supported 14 VTCs per day. The contrast between the tactical CP overseas and the main CP in Tampa was stark, but computer systems linked all headquarters staffs, and electrons delivered orders to the combat elements in the field overseas.

Starting the ground war at the beginning of winter in Afghanistan brought the reality of high-altitude cold weather warfare to the forefront. This proved to be a challenge even for ARSOF units accustomed to operating at night wearing NVG and with experience in the western Rockies. Getting into Afghanistan by helicopter meant crossing mountain ranges above 17,000 feet MSL, flying in extremely variable weather (often zero/zero conditions), two or more aerial refuels in the frontier ranges to accomplish combat missions, responding to antiaircraft artillery (AAA) threats during ingress and egress, and no oxygen and limited heat for personnel riding in the cargo compartments of the MH-47E helicopters. The MH-47E Chinooks were the only SOF helicopters with the lift capability and avionics suitable to accommodate the high altitude and harsh weather conditions. The longer flight "legs" meant normal missions consistently exceeded 6 hours, many averaging 10 to 12 hours, depending on the launch and recovery locations. Another MH-47E helicopter was dedicated to carrying emergency fuel for mission aircraft.

Flying below 200 feet above ground level (AGL), "nap-of-the-earth" (NOE) ingress and egress routes, and wearing NVG in zero/zero conditions for those long hours placed tremendous stress on the MH-47E pilots. To minimize the effectiveness of the enemy AAA (guns and missiles) in the high mountains, the MH-47E pilots flew extremely narrow corridors between the mountains, which reduced left and right limits of error to 200 meters, causing the airmen to refer to the flight route as the "line of death." Larger-capacity portable oxygen systems were required for aircrews flying higher and longer than ever before. The variable weather conditions in and around the high mountains further complicated flying. The seldom-used fuel dumping capability enabled the MH-47Es to carry more weight and still clear the initial barrier of K2 mountain ranges, but it meant another aerial refuel before entering Afghanistan.

To add to the difficulty, Air Force weather forecasters at K2 invariably used the Kuwait computer-generated forecasting model until forced by the harsh weather realities to physically collect data and modify their predictions based on pilot reports of radical weather changes in flight. When climbing over the mountains (the "Bear" outside of K2) and descending down into the narrow "lines of death," it was not uncommon to experience heavy rain, then snow, and finally sleet conditions and face the same conditions again in reverse order negotiating a gradient of less than 1,500 feet wearing NVG. Aerial refueling in these conditions was especially harrowing for both parties at night because "refuel windows" were highly regulated to protect the Air Force C-130P supplier and the MH-47E and MH-60L customers. Knowing the criticality of an aerial refuel to the Army helicopters, the Air Force refuelers routinely went "above and beyond" to accomplish the mission.

With Air Force air weather teams on a 90-day rotation, each team tried to make the Kuwait computer model work for three weeks before reverting to "old-fashioned" weather-data collection and forecasting based on realities. Depending on the experience of the weather team, it required another three to four weeks before K2 forecasts were reliable enough for aircrews. Thus, half of each 90-day rotation was spent learning the regional weather phenomena of Afghanistan, and the learning sequence repeated itself with each new team rotating into the theater.

To add confusion, stateside Air Force weather forecasters using the same Kuwait computer-generated model promulgated generalized Afghanistan forecasts for their headquarters in the United States, which regularly caused bad weather reports in the combat zone to be questioned. Kabul, located on a high desert plateau, would be clear while the mountainous regions of southern Uzbekistan and northern Afghanistan would be "zeroed in" to cancel the flights. Since these missions had to be flown by helicopters and refuel airplanes, it was an "all or none" flying situation. The winter weather delayed the start of the ground war and then caused complaints when high-altitude airdrop missions were aborted.

Special Forces resupply doctrine proved to be woefully outdated. Adjustments to a fluid and rapidly changing battlefield and unique supply requirements—from saddles, tack, and feed for the animals used by American Special Forces personnel advising horse-mounted anti-*Taliban* guerrillas to Toyota 4-Runner vehicles for warlord commanders—challenged the SOCEUR logistics teams responding to JSOTF-North. Requests came primarily by electronic mail (e-mail), but they still had to be collated and tracked. Contracting became the primary way to do business quickly and efficiently. There were grave concerns that a hard, cold winter could cause famine throughout a country that had been plagued by a seven-year drought. Sometimes, delivering humanitarian aid was the priority. This disrupted the necessary arms, equipment, and supplies from being airdropped to build and maintain guerrilla forces. This required constant "deconflicting" and priority shifting between DOD and the U.S. Agency for International Development (USAID) to maintain the war against terrorism while helping the impoverished Afghan population.

The *Taliban* AAA threat caused the Air Force C-17s to airdrop humanitarian aid from much higher altitudes than normal. Thus, drops were consistently made between 17,000 to 20,000 feet AGL. This equated to 30,000 feet MSL, which reduced small, mountainous resupply drop zones (DZs) to postage stamp-size targets. Wind velocity and direction at drop altitude differed radically with ground-level conditions. Accordingly, complete loads were lost in the darkness, never seen by ground personnel, while others were dispersed over miles in the mountainous terrain. Unable to spend precious daylight hours searching for these scattered parachute loads, the advancing guerrilla forces abandoned the effort. Their priority was freeing the country from *Taliban* control and driving *al-Qaeda* from Afghanistan.

Despite the almost paranoid attention given to battlefield airspace control by JFACC since the Korean war and limiting CAS direction to specially trained Air Force personnel except in emergency situations, incidents of fratricide killed more ARSOF soldiers than enemy fire. Airspace control had been focused primarily on preventing midair collisions between combat jet aircraft. The collision part seemed to have been fixed; however, the almost *carte blanche* discretionary authority given to AC-130 Spectre gunships and day-flying jet fighters to engage visually acquired ground targets was a problem. This discretionary authority to engage targets without verification from ground elements led to the following "accidents": a 3rd SFG HMMWV being shot up by an AC-130 Spectre gunship before the start of Operation ANACONDA; the destruction of a crashed 160th SOAR MH-47E helicopter and the 3rd SFG HMMWV awaiting battlefield recovery; and an F-16 attack on Canadian soldiers training at Tarnac Farms less than 10 km from Kandahar Airport. The Ranger accounts of CAS on Takur Ghar revealed how poorly a jet pilot could discern ground targets at high speed and altitude. Incomplete passage of battlefield conditions (maintaining situational awareness) by rotating Air Force aircrews during mission handoffs between AC-130 Spectre gunships could have prevented one debacle. Ground force "boxed off-limits areas" marked on aircrew maps might have prevented the destruction of the crashed MH-47E helicopter and HMMWV and protected the Canadians training within 10 km of a major allied air base and cantonment area. Unfortunately, the MH-47E Chinook helicopter could have been repaired and returned to an ARSOF helicopter fleet whose airframes are as tightly managed as Air Force C-5 Galaxy jumbo transports.

ARSOF combat units had more attached Air Force CAS teams on the ground than ever before. There were extremely sophisticated airborne CAS control platforms monitoring activities above the battle areas. "Smart" munitions were delivered by manned and unmanned aircraft. Combat flight altitudes varied wildly between the DOD air services as well as AAA precautions whether or not the threats had been confirmed. C-17s continued to fly high altitudes and to land only at night in Afghanistan as late as May 2002, long after C-130s were conducting daylight operations and flying low-level profiles throughout the country.

CAS direction "rules" between the services also varied widely. Artillery was never a factor in this war as it was for eight years in Vietnam when Army, Marine Corps, and Navy SEAL junior enlisted personnel, sergeants, lieutenant platoon leaders, and two-year in-service captain company commanders managed to control CAS, naval gunfire, artillery, and mortars effectively in much more intense close combat with fewer per capita fratricide incidents. Instead of having just the Air Force involved in airspace management in today's battlefield environment where there are more helicopters than "fast movers" operating by day and especially at night, this should be a joint Army-Air Force-Navy-Marine Corps endeavor worked in close coordination with ground force commands. Pushing most of the CAS direction responsibility down to the lowest level—Air Force specialty teams—has not solved the fratricide nor do these "ground airmen" have any control over the discretionary authority given AC-130 Spectre gunships and "fast-mover" pilots to expend ordnance rather than land with it aboard. Responsibility for surface targets was also abnegated by ground forces that either brought no experienced field artillerymen (in the absence of artillery) to coordinate fire support and manage airspace or did not have assigned fire support officers (FSOs) like Army SF groups. If the Afghan war provided little else, it demonstrated that CAS fratricide has to be fixed at the services level, and the ARSOF ground forces, Special Forces, and SOF aviation have to have FSOs and get directly involved in battlefield airspace management.

Besides the heavy fighting, two significant things occurred during the Qala-i-Jangi prison uprising. The first was the outstanding crisis management performed by two majors in FOB 53, the battalion executive officer who directed the crisis action cell (CAC), and the battalion operations officer who led the QRFs. This model CAC operation would have been beneficial during the rescue efforts on Takur Ghar during Operation ANACONDA several months later. The second was the discovery of an American among the captured *Taliban* and *al-Qaeda* at Mazar-e-Sharif. This compounded the complex issue of the legal status of terrorists and detainees versus prisoners of war (POWs) protected by Geneva Conventions. As soon as John Walker Lindh was given medical treatment by FOB 53 medical personnel, custody was transferred to the U.S. Justice Department, and FBI agents removed him to the United States and charged him. The implications associated with *posse comitatus* to U.S. Armed Forces in war and appropriate responses should be addressed in all ARSOF courses.

The other issue that received international media attention, promulgated by the nongovernmental organizations (NGOs), was CA tactical teams wearing civilian clothes in Afghanistan and Pakistan. The GWOT has provided many challenges regarding understanding and applying the Law of Armed Conflict. ARSOF commanders and the military lawyers assigned to special operations tactical operations centers (TOCs) deal with many operational matters, including rules of engagement (ROE) and targeting conflicts. They also address issues involving combatant status and identification that did and will continue to require deliberate analysis on the nonlinear GWOT battlefield.

The experiences of ARSOF soldiers throughout Afghanistan demonstrated that the education and training the SWCS conducted was on target. The success of the UW campaign promulgated by Special Forces ODAs working with anti-*Taliban* resistance forces, assisted by PSYOP and CA teams and supported by the 160th SOAR, validated the individual selection process for ARSOF schooling. It also substantiated SWCS' qualification training, training assistance team concepts, unit training standards, and the 10-year investment the U.S. Army made to build ARSOF capabilities.

Flexibility, ingenuity, innovation, and current battlefield reality have to be applied to doctrinal issues and mandatory training. Topics to be addressed include aerial resupply for guerrilla support and humanitarian relief; DA missions in a variety of urban environments; doctrinally specified isolation periods for mission preparation; the necessity to compress air mission planning cycles; 528th SOSB forward support teams to serve as the interface with conventional logistics elements until all ARSOF elements redeploy; consistent attachment of tactical PSYOP and CA teams to Special Forces battalions to integrate force multipliers; contract officer representative training and operational funds management for all captains, warrant officers, and sergeants major in Special Forces, PSYOP, and CA; and a "how to be a staff battle captain in the battalion operations section" of the officer Special Forces qualification course, Special Forces warrant officer training, and CA officer courses. The issue of operational funds for CA tactical teams can be addressed doctrinally based on the experiences of these elements in Afghanistan.

Air mission planning times vary greatly between ARSOF and AFSOF elements. There is no flexibility in Air Force air mission planning. It has been "locked in concrete" while Army air mission planning can be compressed to accommodate crisis action. Consistency may be more applicable for peacetime training, but there has to be flexibility in combat. Instead of "living with the problem," this is a joint issue that affects conventional as well as ARSOF commands and the regional combatant commands.

The philosophy of "training as you will fight" should cause careful scrutiny of "lessons learned from the war in Afghanistan" to determine applicability. The Afghan unconventional war destroyed the long-proselytized World War II example of special operations personnel meeting indigenous resistance groups as "first" American encounters. The number of other American actors involved in a secret rendezvous with indigenous forces and those encountered all over the GWOT battlefield has vastly increased. Sorting out the players has become a game in itself. Daily fusion of intelligence and information from a myriad of sources is mandatory to reduce the confusion, improve management of assets, and quickly disseminate information to tactical units.

Coalition allies for the GWOT were politically vital, and several countries quickly dispatched their special operations forces to assist. Unfortunately, the allied responses outran the CENTCOM preparation to smoothly assimilate those welcome assets into the war. Thus, a collection of very frustrated, highly trained coalition special operations elements was relegated to Qatar bases while the CENTCOM and SOCCENT theater staffs worked employment options. One national element returned home while others used political clout to overcome the military inertia, and another flew directly into K2 to confront the JSOTF-North commander in Uzbekistan. The coalition part would not be fixed until CJSOTF-Afghanistan was organized at Bagram in late March 2002.

Command guidance and daily direction were given during unrecorded VTC sessions (to protect the privacy of senior officers ["back-channel" communications]). Computer systems were used to direct daily operations and produced electronic, paperless deployment orders; OPORDs; warning orders; and fragmentary orders (FRAGOs) that rarely included all five paragraphs of the standard OPORD. Acknowledgment was often simply an e-mail reply, and proposed courses of action or concepts of operations (CONOPS) were sent as attachments.

The sheer volume of official electronic message and order traffic, most of which is still classified, made traditional documentary cross-referencing impossible. The recorded interviews with leaders, staff, and soldiers could be readily cross-referenced and thus provided the best primary source material. The dilemma facing postwar analysts and historians will be the security classification of most material and the limited hard-copy documentation. While records management personnel pride themselves on having "harvested" vast quantities of official electronic traffic by downloading command and staff computer files, the limited screening beforehand and absence of cataloging afterward to facilitate keyword searches will frustrate the most dedicated researchers, even if they have the appropriate security clearances to access the stored files. Since the twice-daily VTC sessions were not recorded, senior commanders' specific guidance, as well as intent and involvement in daily operations, will be "best recollections" long after the event instead of documented fact.

Higher-headquarters battlefield situational awareness was often acquired from computer monitor views, a situation akin to the echelons of field commanders in helicopters orbiting above a battle site in Vietnam, trying to influence actions on the ground by listening to radio traffic. Downlinked video from UAVs provided situational awareness for many. Unfortunately, this was a very distorted reality at times because enlisted operators were remotely controlling the UAVs from various locations, some as far away as the United States. Neither JSOTF-North nor any of the TOCs in the combat zone controlled these assets. The video image provided a "soda straw" view of a very small section of the battle area that had attracted the attention of a UAV operator, often thousands of miles away. A bank of computer monitors in the TOCs was updated every few hours to reflect changes.

When the decision was made to expand the UW campaign into southern Afghanistan, SOCCENT decided to create another JSOTF in the south. The headquarters for JSOTF-South would be Naval Special Warfare Group One (NSWG-1), San Diego, California, and SOCJFCOM was tasked to train the Navy staff on JSOTF duties, responsibilities, and joint planning. The initial proposal to divide SOF responsibilities in Afghanistan along the latitude 30° line was countered by COL Mulholland. He proposed that JSOTF-South be responsible for all coalition SOF, DA, and special reconnaissance (SR) missions in the combat zone while JSOTF-North would retain the UW missions and take the FID mission to train the Afghan National Army (ANA), traditional Special Forces missions.

NSWG-1, a Navy west coast command, was minimally staffed primarily by SEAL officers. JSOTF-South received only a portion of its service staff augmentees. While SOCJFCOM trained the staff (almost entirely NSWG-1 personnel) at Qatar in November 2001, that joint command, having provided experienced joint staff augmentees to JSOTF-North from internal assets, made the same offer to the JSOTF-South commander. The offer was politely declined. JSOTF-South facilitated the deployment of coalition SOF elements into Afghanistan but did not correct the integrated employment problems. The JSOTF-South staff, minimal from the start, picked up a few of the JSOTF-North augmentees, but that did not make a dramatic change. Initially, only A Company, 1st Battalion, 5th SFG, and the coalition SOF units were allocated to JSOTF-South. SEAL platoons were informally detailed from the deployed Mediterranean Fleet assets. The MH-53M Pave Low IIIs controlled by JSOAC-South in Pakistan would support DA and SR missions. Interjecting a second JSOTF with minimal staffing and few forces into the combat zone as the *Taliban* regime collapsed was seen as politically driven to get the coalition SOF elements into the fighting during the final days of war.

Thus, JSOTF-South had a very short life during the transition period when the ARSOF changed from being the supported command to supporting the U.S. conventional forces. During this period, instead of proposing CONOPS for assigned missions in the standard five-paragraph field order format that included all critical elements of planning, ARSOF commanders had to present them to the JSOTF staff in PowerPoint "bullet" formats. When approved, these briefing slides served as the OPORD for assigned missions. The completeness of electronic OPORDs and FRAGOs degenerated another level at JSOTF-South and, more important, shifted the burden of joint staff coordination down to the combat tactical commander. This could be attributed to the lack of experienced joint staff officers in the new headquarters, the minimal staffing, and the fact that Navy officers and NCOs do not receive the DOD command and staff procedures training as part of their advanced professional education, training other service officers receive at the U.S. Army Command and General Staff College, the Armed Forces Staff College, the Air Staff College, and the Marine Corps Staff College.

Transition and Combat Operations

The fall of Kandahar and Kabul in November 2001 marked the collapse of the *Taliban* government and the disintegration of its fighting forces. While the organization of the Afghan Interim Authority (AIA) was taking place, JSOTF-North consolidated the stabilization effort by assigning UW to the three 5th SFG battalion commanders. The Special Operations Command and Control Elements (SOCCEs) were formed to better control operations by the various Alliance warlords and to reduce bypassed pockets of *Taliban* and *al-Qaeda* resistance around Tora Bora in eastern Afghanistan. A second Ranger parachute assault (Objective Bastogne) seized a remote airfield to support ARSOF attack helicopter operations. Destroying *al-Qaeda* leaders became a secondary mission for JSOTF-North under the new functional alignment directed by SOCCENT. That was to be the primary mission of the new JSOTF-South. The

ADVON of that headquarters relocated to Kandahar Air Base when Marine Corps forces at Objective Rhino moved there. The 10th Mountain Division left K2 for Bagram Air Base, south of Kabul. Just days after Hamid Karzai became interim prime minister, the Joint Civil-Military Operations Task Force (JCMOTF) was established in Kabul to direct and coordinate civil and humanitarian affairs in rebuilding Afghanistan. In mid-January 2002, TF Rakkasan from the 101st Airborne Division deployed to Kandahar Airport to replace the marines.

While ARSOF combat operations focused on the Tora Bora region, the amount of flux generated by mission shifts, the arrival of Army and departure of Marine Corps conventional forces, the formation of two new joint headquarters (JSOTF-South and the CJCMOTF) directing ARSOF forces, the arrival of TF Mountain and TF Bowie headquarters, and individual rotations were very significant. Add the euphoria and welcome respite that accompanied the surprisingly swift collapse of the *Taliban* regime to the focused effort to create an interim Afghan government, and there was sufficient disorder and distraction to allow *al-Qaeda* and *Taliban* resistance forces to regroup, reorganize, and get resupplied and time for key leaders to leave the country or move into the mountainous areas along Pakistan's uncontrolled frontier.

With a new interim Afghan government in power, Pakistan was anxious to get rid of suspected *Taliban* and *al-Qaeda*, to obtain the release of its nationals who had been detained as suspects in Afghanistan during the war, and to block escape routes for *al-Qaeda* and *Taliban* fighters. Special Forces ODAs advised and assisted in transferring detainees to and from Pakistan and trained military forces as QRF blocking elements. In the meantime, other ARSOF changes were being planned to further exacerbate the turbulence in the combat zone.

3rd SFG at Fort Bragg had been alerted to replace 5th SFG in the combat zone, and 19th and 20th SFG (ARNG) battalion staffs and ODAs were arriving in theater. Mobilized USAR CA and PSYOP units had been "earmarked" to replace Active Army forces in the theater. Since the 2nd Battalion, 160th SOAR MH-47Es had borne the brunt of the high-altitude missions in the mountains in north, east, and southwest Afghanistan for nearly three months, aircraft phase maintenance intervals dictated the rotation of these medium helicopters that had relocated from K2 to Bagram in January 2002. At Fort Campbell, B Company, 109th Aviation Maintenance Battalion (ARNG) from Iowa and Nebraska had been mobilized and integrated as intact platoons into the 160th SOAR maintenance companies to accelerate the phase inspections of the rotating helicopters. This ARNG aviation maintenance affiliation with the 160th SOAR during wartime proved to be a godsend and validated this practice for the future. The 3rd Battalion, 160th SOAR was tasked to assume the 2nd Battalion's mission. Ranger units were likewise rotating into Afghanistan from other regional bases. Forty-five-day overseas tours for some DOD services were common. SOCJFCOM's experienced joint staff personnel were released as soon as augmentees had been oriented.

In January 2002, A Company, 1st Battalion, 5th SFG, the primary JSOTF-South direct-action (DA) and special reconnaissance (SR) force conducted some very successful missions. Since JSOTF-South focused its DA efforts on middle-echelon *al-Qaeda* and *Taliban* leaders and staff, this larger group provided a very "target-rich" environment for A-1-5. However, since the supporting MH-53M helicopters were based at Shabaz Air Base outside of Jacobabad, Pakistan, missions could only be flown during hours of darkness. Because of the distances, this meant no mission rehearsals, less than 15 minutes to brief aircrews on target areas and LZs, and minimal loiter time awaiting the assault force's pickup to get them back to Kandahar and give the helicopters sufficient time to return to Pakistan during darkness. Since 5th SFG rarely trained with AFSOC MH-53M helicopters, both units suffered "growing pains" while performing high-stress, time-sensitive, violent DA missions. While the MH-53M flight crews did not have to contend with high mountains in the south, the winter snow and sleet conditions delayed the missions. Still, A-1-5 accomplished some of the most successful DA missions of the Afghan war.

Meanwhile, also in January 2002, the 3rd Battalion, 3rd SFG arrived at Kandahar Airport assigned to JSOTF-South. By mid-February 2002, headquarters site surveys of the Bagram Air Base had been completed by 3rd SFG ADVONs. Replacement MH-47Ds from 3rd Battalion, 160th SOAR had been built up at Kandahar. In the midst of the SR and DA missions being conducted by JSOTF-South, JSOTF-North elements continued to hunt *al-Qaeda* in the eastern areas of Afghanistan, and the regional SOCCEs advised and assisted the Afghan Military Force (AMF) leaders to stabilize their operational areas. In the midst of UW operations in the east and south and the arrivals and departures of personnel and units, planning was under way to conduct the largest combined operation in the war to date. One new PSYOP combat capability validated during this period was the Special Operations Media Systems–Broadcast (SOMS-B) that assumed the Air Force Commando Solo aerial broadcast mission. It then rapidly increased broadcast hours to 24/7 from both Bagram and Kandahar.

In late January 2002, ODA 594, on a ground reconnaissance mission, reported that its Alliance security forces were reluctant to enter the Shah-i-Khot Valley. The Afghans warned that there was a major enemy concentration in the valley. This got the interest of various commands. As intelligence reports began to escalate enemy force estimates as high as 800 to 1,000 *Taliban* and *al-Qaeda* fighters, the JSOTF-North commander recognized that Special Forces ODAs supporting the attack of AMF elements into the valley alone was not viable. Conventional and coalition forces would be needed in the well-defended area.

By mid-February 2002, TF Mountain was in charge of Operation ANACONDA. The modified OPLAN had offensive and defensive roles for the AMF and Special Forces elements. The main attack of Afghans supported by Special Forces would be into the southern end of the Shah-i-Khot Valley while another AMF moved into the northern end of the valley. Additional Afghan forces would form an outer ring of blocking positions (to prevent what happened during Tora Bora). U.S. and coalition SOF would perform SR. TF Rakkasan (headquarters, 2nd Brigade, 101st Airborne Division; 1st Battalion, 87th Infantry, 10th Mountain Division; and 1st and 2nd Battalions, 187th Infantry, 101st Airborne Division) would air assault into the valley as a show of force and occupy blocking positions near the three villages along the eastern side. Intelligence believed that concentrations of enemy fighters were in and around the valley villages. PSYOP loudspeaker teams were attached to TF Rakkasan to encourage the enemy to surrender and to keep "curious locals from getting too close to the show" at the helicopter FARP. The plan was to hit the *al-Qaeda* hard enough to kill or capture some in the valley and to squeeze the others against the blocking positions to be eliminated.

An aerial bombardment of the valley villages, the proposed helicopter LZs, and suspected enemy positions surrounding the area was to precede the main Afghan attack. This bombardment was expected by many to be equal to an intense 15- to 30-minute artillery and mortar barrage that would normally precede a deliberate attack. SR teams on high mountain ridges had snipers and could direct CAS. Other reconnaissance assets would be used to track "escapees" as they moved along natural avenues called "ratlines" to the Pakistan border. Since the allied forces planned to employ no artillery, Operation ANACONDA relied totally on aerial fire support from Air Force, Army, and Marine Corps aircraft. The U.S. conventional and Afghan forces had organic 60mm, 81mm, 82mm, and 120mm mortars with them.

During the planning for Operation ANACONDA, Army CA teams, previously introduced into Afghanistan from Uzbekistan and Pakistan in November 2001, operated out of Mazar-e-Sharif and Bagram to coordinate humanitarian relief and assistance countrywide. These CA teams were integral elements at the Special Forces base areas, sharing internal defense responsibilities, providing information gathered during their forays into the countryside, and working with the NGOs and USAID to store and distribute humanitarian assistance and identify critical infrastructure projects. These coalition humanitarian liaison cells (CHLCs, called "chicklets") assessed basic survival needs (water, food, and shelter) in remote villages that NGOs were reluctant to visit. After distributing humanitarian assistance supplies, the CA teams proceeded to community work projects such as wells, schools, and medical clinics. Opening the Salang Tunnel to improve land delivery of humanitarian aid from Uzbekistan was a priority project.

Weather delayed the start of Operation ANACONDA for two days. Having heard only seven of the explosions made by 48 JDAMs and two thermobaric bombs that were the battle-field preparation, AMF leader Commander Zia Lodin, charged with the main attack, had grave concerns, especially since elements of his column had already been attacked moving into position. More important, of the seven explosions that Commander Zia heard, none were seen between him and the suspected enemy positions. Nevertheless, Zia's Pashtun force moved into the attack. After advancing forward about 400 meters, the attacking Afghans were hit by heavy mortar fire just as lead elements of the 1st Battalion, 87th Infantry, 10th Mountain Division, and 2nd Battalion, 187th Infantry, 101st Airborne Division, air assaulted into their LZs. As 101st AH-64s responded to the calls for CAS, both American infantry units received mortar and ground fire that stopped their movement. The enemy proved to be better armed than anticipated and was quite willing to fight. Priority for CAS was shifted from the main attack to the American infantry under fire. Zia Lodin's 300 Alliance fighters were likewise halted by heavy mortar fire. When Special Forces requests for CAS were rebuffed, Zia Lodin withdrew his AMF forces from the valley. When the threat posed by the main attack from the south was removed, the *Taliban* and *al-Qaeda* concentrated on the American units who, by then, were calling for aeromedical evacuations.

ODA 563, operating as a SOCCE for TF Rakkasan, called in helicopter CAS while Air Force enlisted tactical air controllers (ETACs) directed F-15E and F-16 jet fighters and B-52s against suspected enemy positions. By the end of the first day, five of six AH-64 Apache attack helicopters from the 101st Airborne Division were nonoperational due to combat damage from RPGs, heavy machine guns, and ground fire. TF Mountain got Marine Corps AH-1W Super Cobra attack helicopters through JSOTF-South and more AH-64 Apaches from Kandahar. The military axiom that "no plan survives the first round" proved appropriate. TF Mountain sent 1st

Battalion, 187th Infantry, 101st Airborne Division, to reinforce and reorganize the effort on the second day as enemy positions were bombarded with CAS. A decision to position more Special Forces reconnaissance teams on high ridges overlooking the battle sites resulted in the fight on Takur Ghar on the third day of ANACONDA.

Inserting the SOF team on Takur Ghar was the third mission of the day for two 160th SOAR MH-47E aircrews. As the lead MH-47E landed on the LZ/OP, it found itself in the midst of bunkers and trenches and flanked by a heavy machine gun position. Then, the big helicopter was hit by a heavy fusillade of ground fire and RPGs. To break out of the killing zone, the pilot applied full power "to wrench the helicopter aloft." During that violent forceful maneuver, PO1 Roberts, a Navy SEAL poised to exit, tumbled out of the helicopter. Unable to return for the lost seaman because of severe hydraulic problems, the Night Stalker pilot managed to "hard-land" the badly damaged helicopter several kilometers away. The second MH-47E picked up the aircrew and SOF team and returned them to Gardez where a rescue party was hastily organized to recover the missing seaman. Going in just below the LZ/OP used by Razor 03, the second MH-47E, Razor 04, escaped a hot reception when it delivered the rest of the team. As the big helicopter lifted off, it was fired on, as was the rescue force. They fired and maneuvered uphill to the original LZ/OP. With one KIA and two WIA, the ground force broke contact and withdrew about a kilometer south to a protected position. Actions to this point in the scenario had been orchestrated by the SOF commander at Gardez. Poor radio communications between Bagram and Gardez, uncoordinated rescue efforts, and poor dissemination of crisis information between the TOCs hampered the acquisition of situational awareness as conditions deteriorated on Takur Ghar. Fortunately, the Ranger QRF was alerted, assembled, and prepared for commitment.

In the confused scramble to deploy a QRF, neither the Rangers nor the supporting 160th MH-47E aircrews were given updated information about the enemy threat on Takur Ghar or what had happened to the first rescue attempt. The AC-130 Spectre gunship overflying the action had the best situational awareness on what happened on the mountaintop, but it was ordered "off station" just before daybreak. Thus, Razor 01, with the first group of Rangers, landed "almost magnetically" in the "hot LZ" at daybreak. During the second landing on the hot LZ/OP, the MH-47E, Razor 01, was fatally disabled by a heavy fusillade of RPG and machine gun fire. Razor 02, carrying the rest of the QRF, was held up until the Gardez and Bagram TOCs could clarify the situation. With two crashed MH-47Es and another severely combat damaged (nonoperational) at Gardez, a risk assessment became critical based on the available ARSOF Chinooks and the necessity to reinforce stranded Rangers and Night Stalkers fighting on a snow-covered high Afghan mountain ridge.

The rest of the Ranger QRF would be inserted, and priority for CAS would be given to the Takur Ghar force to break up the enemy attacks. Razor 02 delivered the rest of the QRF well south of the hot LZ/OP. From 8,900 feet, the Rangers climbed more than 2 km in 2 to 3 feet of deep snow in 3½ hours to reach their comrades and the aircrew at 10,000 feet. The Ranger QRF cleared the ridge top and fought off an enemy counterattack. In all, the Ranger QRF and the Razor 01 aircrew suffered five KIAs and more than 10 WIAs. After assaulting an enemy bunker, the Rangers found the bodies of PO1 Roberts, who had fallen from the helicopter, and TSGT Chapman, an Air Force combat controller, killed during the first rescue attempt.

All told, the Rangers and Night Stalkers fought well, endured the worst to fulfill expectations, and succeeded in the toughest special operations mission of the war.

Situational awareness had been lost by the Bagram TOCs, and Gardez reports and UAV videos did little to recapture it. In the confusion, several command and control elements made plans to use the limited MH-47Es. This exacerbated the problem, and control of an escalating bad combat situation was lost. In the ensuing efforts by all to do the right thing, the communications problem was not fixed. Temporary establishment of a ground radio relay station was not factored into the equation. ANACONDA was taking place during the transitions of several headquarters and units. Aerial refueling was not part of the conventional plan because only SOF helicopters had this capability. The element that kept the situation at Qala-i-Jangi from turning into a debacle was a crisis-action cell directed by probably one of the most experienced officers in the battalion, the executive officer. A separate cell, for SOF emergencies only, composed of a handful of experienced ground and air operations officers led by a senior staff officer, could orchestrate and deconflict necessary crisis actions without the distraction of other ongoing combat actions. Finally, the reason for landing twice in the same hot LZ/OP can be attributed to a confused tactical situation on Takur Ghar; little time to coordinate alternate LZs with beleaguered, tired aircrews; the available LZs in the mountainous terrain near the battle site; and the absence of situational awareness after the AC-130 gunship departed. The fight on Takur Ghar showed "in flashing red lights" how few were the helicopters capable of all-weather, night operations in high mountainous terrain in the winter.

Operation ANACONDA revealed that conventional Army commanders had seriously underestimated the capabilities of the AMF and the contribution of CAS to the collapse of the Taliban regime. Special Forces-directed CAS had been critical to the successes Alliance forces achieved, and it was dedicated CAS that kept up the offensive initiative. The Taliban and al-Qaeda forces in and around the key Afghan cities could not defend effectively against unrelenting pressure made possible by the constant CAS preparation of the battlefield. When that did not happen on the opening day of ANACONDA, the Afghans attacked because their Special Forces advisers had never failed to produce air support. The realization that their priority for CAS had been lost once the American forces came under fire prompted AMF withdrawal.

Just moving AMF into assault positions was a complicated operation and a constant challenge. Alliance vehicle columns had little semblance of order. The fighters were packed, standing 40 to 50 deep in the open back of a Ginga truck. Dismounted for an attack, the fighters (wearing no body armor or helmets and carrying a variety of weapons and an assortment of ammunition) moved in groups of 30 to 50 in the general direction of an objective. There was no fire and maneuver and little coordination. Few Afghan fighters had ever seen a conventional armed U.S. soldier in full battle dress, and the reverse was likewise true. Yet, the Afghan and American forces, plus the coalition SR elements, were to fight a coordinated, conventional battle to destroy a determined *Taliban* and *al-Qaeda* force defending well-prepared positions in the mountains in winter. The fact that AMF fighting elements did not fight like a NATO military ally was clearly driven home the first day. Nevertheless, the enemy had been fixed, and his intention to fight had been established.

Throughout ANACONDA, transition continued among ARSOF units and headquarters. JSOTF-North and JSOTF-South established small tactical CPs in Bagram adjacent to the TF Mountain operations center. On day 2 of ANACONDA, with the Special Forces ODAs and Afghan forces involved in that operation, the base at Khowst was attacked. It would be CAT-A41 and the Alliance security force that drove off the enemy. The 528th SOSB rotated most of its elements in December 2001 when the transitions started. The absence of ARSOF-specific logistics support connectivity between the 5307th Theater Army Support Command (TASCOM) and the tactical ARSOF units still fighting the war in Afghanistan was felt immediately, especially since the turbulence occurred during the Christmas holidays at home. The need for 528th forward area support teams to provide that connectivity was reinforced. Interim ARSOF logistics assistance was deployed by USASOC to fill the gap afterward.

3rd SFG was building its base and the CJSOTF-Afghanistan command center to be able to assume control of U.S. and coalition SOF in Bagram by 1 April 2002. Like the other two JSOTFs, the shortage of staff augmentees caused COL Mark Phelan to assimilate 3rd Battalion, 20th SFG (ARNG), into the combined joint staff. 19th SFG (ARNG) ODAs moved from K2 into northern Afghanistan to work with 5th SFG teams before battle "handoffs." The 489th CAB and the 345th PSYOP Company (Airborne) were in the TPFDD pipeline to replace or augment elements of the 4th POG and 96th CAB. The MH-47Ds of 3rd Battalion, 160th SOAR, at Kandahar were pulled into the Takur Ghar rescue mission and supported ARSOF units until ANACONDA was terminated. As CJSOTF-Afghanistan became operational, JSOTF-North and 5th SFG turned over their responsibilities, first to the JSOTF-South, which, in turn, passed everything to CJSOTF-Afghanistan on 31 March 2002. In the meantime, the JMOTF in Kabul evolved into a CJMOTF headquarters with 150 personnel assigned.

The CJSOTF-Afghanistan Era Begins

With the establishment of CJSOTF-Afghanistan by COL Mark Phelan, commander, 3rd SFG, the coalition SOF were truly integrated with U.S. SOF. The ranking coalition SOF commander from New Zealand became the deputy commander of the CJSOTF. Because many of the coalition elements were based at Kandahar, liaison staffs were granted limited access to the integrated intelligence with certain constraints established by COL Phelan. Two commanders' conferences "ironed out" most problems, some dating to October 2001. By these actions, Phelan established professional rapport with the coalition SOF. But there was a price for the 3rd SFG.

Coalition forces had to use single-channel satellite communications, thus one-third of the SATCOM channels had to be dedicated to them. This left only two-thirds of the few allotted SATCOM channels to divide among the 3rd SFG field elements. The Special Forces ODAs used demand-assigned multiple-access channels based on assigned 15-minute block times. To make secure communications, several sequences of numbers had to be properly entered. This increased the opportunity for error. Despite Phelan's emphasis on high-frequency (HF) communications to avoid crowded satellite communications channels and priority traffic "bumping" that disrupted connections, the reduced clarity, additional weight, and time to set up antennas for HF made the system very unpopular among the moving ODAs. Thus, well before the morning and evening commanders' VTCs, field reports were required. As the numbers of ODAs in the field grew, it became a challenge to avoid the "logjams" and "hit the report windows" twice daily to complete transmissions.

A major change from the JSOTF-North *modus operandi* was the absence of a collocated JSOAC to facilitate coordination of ground and air for UW operations. With the disestablishment of JSOTF-North at K2, the JSOAC-North and its aircraft relocated to Masirah Island. The JSOAC-South at Jacobabad, Pakistan, relocated its headquarters to Masirah Island, leaving its Air Force SOF aircraft behind. The CJSOTF-Afghanistan staff was provided an Air Force JSOAC liaison officer to assist the predominantly SOF ground command. The 3rd Battalion, 160th SOAR's MH-47Ds remained based at Kandahar, the new location of 2nd Battalion, 3rd SFG, numerous coalition SOF elements, and most of the conventional forces, TF Rakkasan.

Limited SOF helicopters, uncertain weather conditions, and the need for the CJSOTF commander to be present for both daily commanders' VTCs virtually eliminated any senior Special Forces officer presence in the field with deployed ODAs and ODBs. Even the battalion commanders had a difficult time establishing or maintaining presence in the field due to wide dispersion of units countrywide. This meant centralized planning and decentralized execution with limited guidance, counseling, and mentoring of junior leaders. Careful assessment and selection and training of Special Forces personnel by the SWCS should emphasize this reality.

Although the international community was committed to training a "national" Afghan army and the central government promulgated the need for ethnic balance, the achievement of that goal was problematic. The provincial warlords were levied by the AIA to provide specific numbers of recruits from their tribal groups to receive national army training. Those drafted were also to bring their weapons. This proved to be a "hit or miss" requirement that was impossible to enforce. Primary loyalty, as it had been for hundreds of years, was to the tribe, not the nation, as the first-, second-, and third-world allied countries imagined. The recruit "washout" rate (medical problems and age) ranged between 25 and 30 percent. Each warlord was obligated to replace the losses with new draftees from his tribal group. Just as influence and money were used to avoid national service on both sides during the American Civil War, so it continues to be practiced in Afghanistan.

One of the most distinct observations was the MH-47E Chinook as the preeminent SOF long-range penetration helicopter for high-altitude, adverse-weather, and night operations. The MH-53M Pave Low III was conspicuously absent above 8,000 feet MSL. The assignment of primary CSAR for the air campaign in northern Afghanistan to the 160th SOAR was tacit acknowledgment that capabilities and airlift capacity of the MH-47E Chinook at altitude were superior to all other rotary-wing platforms. Air Force Pave Low IIIs were most active at lower altitudes in the southeastern part of Afghanistan. More significantly, the MH-47E Chinooks became the primary rotary-wing assault platform for all SOF. The MH-60L DAPs performed armed escort for MH-47E long-range, high-altitude penetrations. Multiple aerial refuels were a "given" for the combat operations launched into Afghanistan from bordering countries. Doing all of these tasks wearing NVG has been accepted as another "given" by ARSOF forces that must be highlighted when discussing SOF missions with the rest of the Army, DOD, and Congress. Collocating JSOTF-North, JSOAC-North, and Army and Air Force SOF air assets at K2 was key to collapsing *Taliban* power in Afghanistan in two months—the tactical battle commander had the necessary elements within arm's reach to direct combat operations. What he did not have, and what no other JSOTF commander had in the combat zone, was necessary staff augmentation. With 90 percent of the nationally mobilized personnel staff augmentees siphoned off by a multitude of stateside higher-level commands, the JSOTF-North and CJSOTF-Afghanistan commanders were compelled to meet their staffing requirements using Army National Guardsmen from the 19th and 20th SFGs. These were calculated risks.

These observations and reflections cover the prosecution of the war in Afghanistan from October 2001 to mid-May 2002. They are not intended to be lessons learned or criticisms of a successfully prosecuted UW campaign, nor are they provided to accord any single ARSOF the lion's share of credit. This was an unconventional war (collapsing the *Taliban* regime) in which ARSOF contributed to the success, and the situation in Afghanistan is far from being settled. Since this final chapter is based on nonattributable sources, I accept responsibility for these observations and reflections.—C.H. Briscoe

Glossary

AAA	antiaircraft artillery
ADVON	advance echelon
AFCS	Advance Flight Control System
AFSOC	Air Force Special Operations Command
AGL	above ground level
AIA	Afghan Interim Authority
AMC	air mission commander
AMF	Afghan Military Forces
ANA	Afghan National Army
AOB	advanced operating base
AOR	area of responsibility
ARCENT	U.S. Army Forces, U.S. Central Command
ARNG	Army National Guard
ARSOA	Army Special Operations Aviation
ARSOF	Army Special Operations Forces
ARSOTF	Army Special Operations Task Force
AT	antitank
ATV	all-terrain vehicle
AVIM	aviation intermediate maintenance
AWACS	Airborne Warning and Control System (E-3A aircraft)
BBC	British Broadcasting Corporation
C2	command and control
CA	civil affairs
CAB	civil affairs battalion
CAC	crisis-action cell
CAS	close air support
CAT	civil affairs team
CCT	combat control team
CENTCOM	U.S. Central Command
CFACC	Combined Forces Air Component Command
CFLCC	Combined Forces Land Component Command
	Combined Forces Land Component Commander
CHLC	coalition humanitarian liaison cell
	Coalition Humanitarian Liaison Center
CIA	Central Intelligence Agency
CJCMOTF	Combined Joint Civil-Military Operations Task Force
CJCS	Chief, Joint Chiefs of Staff
CJSOTF	Combined Joint Special Operations Task Force
CMOC	civil-military operations center
COMSEC	communications security

COMSOCCENT	Commander, Special Operations Command, Central Command
COMSOCEUR	Commander, Special Operations Command, Europe
CONOPS	concept of operations
CP	command post
CQB	close-quarters battle
CRE	crisis-response element
CSAR	combat search and rescue
DA	direct action
DAMA	Demand-Assigned Multiple Access
DAP	Direct-Action Penetrator (MH-60L)
DCU	desert camouflage uniform
DERF	Defense Emergency Response Fund
DLS	desert landing strip
DOD	Department of Defense
DPPC	Deployable Print Production Center
DVDS	Digital Video Distribution System
DZ	drop zone
EHF	extremely high frequency
EOD	explosive ordnance demolition
EPW	enemy prisoner of war
ETAC	enlisted tactical air controller
EUCOM	U.S. European Command
FARP	forward arming and refueling point
FAST	forward area support team
FATA	Federally Administered Tribal Area
FBI	Federal Bureau of Investigation
FID	foreign internal defense
FLIR	forward-looking infrared radar
FM	field manual
FOB	forward operating base
FRAGO	fragmentary order
FSO	fire support officer
FST	forward surgical team
FY	fiscal year
GMT	Greenwich Mean Time
GMV	ground mobility vehicle
GPS	global positioning system
GTMO	Guantanamo Bay, Cuba

HAST	Humanitarian Assistance Survey Team
HEMTT	heavy expanded mobility tactical truck
HMMWV	high-mobility multipurpose wheeled vehicle
HUMINT	human intelligence
HVT	high-value target
IMU	Islamic Movement of Uzbekistan
IP	Internet protocol
IR	infrared
IRF	Immediate Reaction Force
ISAF	International Security Assistance Force
ISB	initial staging base
ISOFAC	isolation facility
ISR	infrared search radar
IV	intravenous
JCS	Joint Chiefs of Staff
JCSE	Joint Communications Signal Element
JDAM	joint direct-attack munition
JFCOM	U.S. Joint Forces Command
JFSOCC	Joint Forces Special Operations Component Command
jihad	Islamic holy war
JOC	joint operations center
JPOTF	Joint Psychological Operations Task Force
JRTC	Joint Readiness Training Center
JSOAC	Joint Special Operations Air Component
JSOACC	Joint Special Operations Air Component Command
JSOTF	Joint Special Operations Task Force
JSRC	Joint Search and Rescue Center
JTF	joint task force
K2	Karshi Kanabad, Uzbekistan
KIA	killed in action
Koran (*Quran*)	Islamic holy book
LAN	local area network
LBE	load-bearing equipment
loya jirga	grand council
LRDG	Long-Range Desert Group
LZ	landing zone
MACOM	major Army command
madrasa	Islamic school
main CP	main command post

MBITR	multiband inter/intra team radio
MEU	Marine Expeditionary Unit
MIA	missing in action
MMR	multimode radar
MOS	military occupational specialty
MPS	Modular Print System
MRE	meal, ready to eat
MSC	major subordinate command
MSL	mean sea level
MST	maintenance support team
mujahideen	Afghani freedom fighters
NATO	North Atlantic Treaty Organization
NAVSPECWARCOM	Naval Special Warfare Command
NCO	noncommissioned officer
NCOIC	noncommissioned officer in charge
NGO	nongovernmental organization
NOE	nap-of-the-earth
NSWG	Naval Special Warfare Group
NTC	National Training Center
NVG	night-vision goggle(s)
ODA	Operational Detachment Alpha
OEF	Operation ENDURING FREEDOM
OJCS	Office of the Joint Chiefs of Staff
OP	observation point
	observation post
OPLAN	operation plan
OPORD	operation order
OPSEC	operations security
OSD	Office of the Secretary of Defense
OSS	Office of Strategic Services
PDD	Production Development Detachment
PJ	para-jumper/pararescue man
POB	psychological operations battalion
POG	psychological operations group
POW	prisoner of war
PR	personnel recovery
PSYOP	psychological operations
PZ	pickup zone
QRF	quick-reaction force
rear CP	rear command post

ROE	rules of engagement
RPG	rocket-propelled grenade
RSC	Reserve Support Command
SALT II	Strategic Arms Limitation Treaty II
SAM	surface-to-air missile
SATCOM	satellite communications
SAW	squad automatic weapon
SCAMPI	Single-Channel Antijam Man-Portable radio
SCIF	Secure Compartmented Information Facility
SEAL	sea-air-land (team), Navy
SEATO	Southeast Asia Treaty Organization
SFG	Special Forces group
SKEDCO	Sked Company
SOAR	special operations aviation regiment
SOCA team	special operations communication assemblage (team)
SOCCE	Special Operations Command and Control Element
SOCCENT	Special Operations Command Central
SOCEUR	Special Operations Command, Europe
SOCJFCOM	Special Operations Command, U.S. Joint Forces Command
SOF	Special Operations Forces
SOMS-B	Special Operations Media Systems–Broadcast
SOP	standing operating procedures
SOR	statement of requirements
SOS	special operations squadron
SOSB	special operations support battalion
SOW	special operations wing
SR	special reconnaissance
SSE	sensitive site exploitation
STS	special tactics squadron
SUV	sport utility vehicle
SWCS	U.S. Army John F. Kennedy Special Warfare Center and School
TACP	tactical air control party
	terminal attack control party
TACSAT	tactical satellite (radio)
TALCE	tanker airlift control element
Talib	religious student
Taliban	religious students
TASCOM	U.S. Army Theater Area Support Command
TDA	table of distribution and allowances
TOE	table of organization and equipment
TOC	tactical operations center
TPD	tactical PSYOP detachment

TPFDD	time-phased force deployment data
TPT	tactical PSYOP team
UAV	unmanned aerial vehicle
UHF	ultrahigh frequency
UN	United Nations
UNHCR	United Nations High Commissioner for Refugees
UNICEF	United Nations International Children's Emergency Fund
USAID	U.S. Agency for International Development
USAR	U.S. Army Reserve
USASFC	U.S. Army Special Forces Command
USASOC	U.S. Army Special Operations Command
USSOCOM	U.S. Special Operations Command
UW	unconventional warfare
UXO	unexploded ordnance
VOA	Voice of America
VTC	video teleconference
WIA	wounded in action

About the Contributors

Dr. Charles H. Briscoe has been compiling current Army special operations history in Kosovo, Afghanistan, and Iraq as the U.S. Army Special Operations Command Historian for three years. He is a retired airborne infantry and Special Forces officer who served overseas in the Dominican Republic, Vietnam, Germany, Italy, and Panama. Briscoe earned a Ph.D. in history from the University of South Carolina in 1996. He is the author of *La Fuerza Interamericana de Paz* (1999, 2000) and *Treinta Años Después* (2001). Briscoe teaches U.S. military and Latin American history at Campbell University.

Dr. Richard L. Kiper earned a Ph.D. in history at the University of Kansas. He previously served as an officer in Special Forces, airborne, and infantry units stateside and overseas. He also served on the Army Staff and as an instructor at the U.S. Military Academy (USMA), West Point, New York, and the U.S. Army Command and General Staff College, Fort Leavenworth, Kansas. Kiper is the author of *Major General John Alexander McClernand: Politician in Uniform*, which received the Fletcher Pratt Award for best nonfiction Civil War book in 1999. He edited *Dear Catherine, Dear Taylor: The Civil War Letters of a Union Soldier and His Wife*, published in 2002. Dr. Kiper teaches history at Kansas City, Kansas, Community College.

James A. Schroder earned an M.B.A. at Murray State University. A retired aviation chief warrant officer, he previously served seven years with the 160th Special Operations Aviation Regiment as an MH-47E Chinook pilot. He also served in military intelligence, Special Forces, and aviation units stateside and overseas, and earned two Air Medals piloting CH-47D Chinook helicopters in the Gulf war.

Dr. Kalev I. Sepp is on the defense analysis faculty, Naval Postgraduate School, Monterey, California. He was previously a consultant for the RAND Corporation. He holds a Ph.D. in American diplomatic history from Harvard University, a Master of Military Art and Science degree from the U.S. Army Command and General Staff College, and a B.A. in English from The Citadel. He was a U.S. Army Special Forces officer who served in Latin America and earned a Combat Infantryman Badge as a brigade adviser in the Salvadoran Civil War. Dr. Sepp also served in airborne, Ranger, artillery, and armored cavalry units and on General Staffs in the United States, Germany, and Korea. He also taught history at the USMA.

INDEX

"60 Minutes II": 227–28

*Aaron, Watson CW2: 235
ABC News: 23, 24–25
Abdur Rahman Khan: 5–6
AC-130 Spectre
    capabilities: 367n181
    friendly-fire incidents: 285–87, 362n30
    missions: 97, 111, 162–63, 168–69, 170, 176, 297–98, 301–03
*Acosta, CPT Brian: 278, 287–89
Aerial refuels: 79, 261–63
Aerial resupply: 100–101, 146, 174, 195n128, 209, 253–55, 379
Afghan Interim Authority: 240–41, 384
    and cooperation between ethnic militias: 322
    and planning for Operation ANACONDA: 319
    prime minister: 107, 176, 178
    PSYOP role in building support for: 62, 258–59
Afghan Interim Government: 17 (same as Afghan Interim Authority cited above)
Afghan Military Forces: 203
    command and control issues: 283, 286–87
    difficulties in movements of: 285
    equipment for: 283, 379
    killed by friendly fire: 180–81, 277, 386–88
    in Operation ANACONDA: 277, 282–87
    operations in the Tora Bora region: 213–14
    training for: 277, 280–81, 283, 390
Afghan National Army
    equipment for: 279, 359
    training: 211, 277, 279, 347–50, 358–60, 390
Afghan Revolutionary Council: 14–15
Afghanistan
    civil war of 1979: 9–10
    Communist Party of: 9
    demography: 33
    guerrilla resistance to Soviet occupation: 11–16
    lack of maps of: 53
    role of tribal ethnic groups in: 2–3, 276, 279, 322, 329–30
Ahmad Shah Durrani: 3
Air Expeditionary Wing, 332nd: 199n266
Air Mobility Command: 374–75
Air traffic control procedures: 66, 67
Airborne Division (Air Assault), 101st: 208, 210
    and CSAR at Takur Ghar: 312
    military information support teams: 245
    mission: 218
    PSYOP units attached to: 244–45
    Rakkasan Brigade: 216, 218, 245, 270n55, 277, 325, 350, 356
Aircraft. See also AC-130 Spectre; MH-47E Chinook; MH-60L Black Hawk.
    AH-6: 104, 141–43, 370

B-52 Stratofortress: 63, 96, 101, 126–27, 149, 180–81, 214–15
C-17 Globemaster: 46, 65–66, 67, 100–101, 105, 131, 146
CH-53 Super Stallion helicopter: 206, 229–32, 272n121
EC-130 Commando Solo: 46, 50, 63, 89n79, 103, 183, 186, 192n43, 340, 385
F-18: 161, 162
MC-130 Combat Talon: 47, 100, 109, 111, 128, 131, 140–41, 142–45, 209, 253–54, 263, 317, 318
MC-130P Combat Shadow tanker: 63, 83, 85, 96, 97–98, 135, 209, 261–63, 375–76
MH-47D Chinook: 208, 330–32, 372–73
MH-53 Pave Low helicopter: 345, 375–76, 384–85, 390
Mi-17 (Russian): 99
Albright, Madeleine: 21–22, 23–24
Alefkhel, Afghanistan: 356–57
Ali, Hazrat: 109, 213–16
Al-Jafr Air Base, Jordan: 58
*Allison, CPT Chuck: 222
al-Qaeda: 1–2
    in the Arghastan wadi: 174–75
    at the Arghendab Bridge: 176–77
    battle with at Mir Wais Hospital: 209, 232–35
    Chechens: 139
    encouraged to surrender: 292
    at Hazar Qadam: 235–41
    leaders of sought in Afghanistan: 205, 208–09, 210–11, 213–16, 330–32
    and Operation ANACONDA: 210
    in Pakistan: 204
    prisoner uprising at Qala-i-Jangi: 104, 158–65
    prisoners: 158–65, 198n207, n211, 204, 215, 233, 237, 240, 244, 250–51, 272n128, 321–22
    psychological warfare: 259
    PSYOP role in loss of public support for: 186–87
    and terrorist attacks on U.S. facilities abroad: 22–24
    in the Tora Bora: 203–04
    U.S. formation of a coalition to fight: 34–36
Amanullah: 6–7
Amerine, CPT Jason: 155–57, 172, 173, 175–76, 180, 182, 183
Amin, Hafizullah: 9, 10
Amu Darya River: 5, 6, 10
*Anderson, SFC Fred: 354–55
*Anderson, SFC Kevin: 74
Anderson, SPC Marc A.: 305, 306, 307
Anglo-Russian Convention: 5–6
Anti-Taliban Forces. See Afghan Military Forces.
*Anton, CWO Doug: 232–33, 234, 271n107
*Arde, SFC Jules, 320, 325

Arghastan Wadi/Bridge: 167, 169–71, 174, 175
Arghendab Bridge: 175–78
Armitage, Richard: 192n45
Army National Guard
    aviation battalions: 105–06
    aviation maintenance units: 43
    capabilities: 356–57
    equipment for: 255–56
    individual augmentees: 256, 371, 374
    logistical support for: 373
    mobilizations: 43, 44, 216–17, 255–56, 273n162, 371–72, 374
    stop-loss program: 374
    training: 217–18, 255–56
    units assigned to CJSOTF-A: 210
Army Special Operations Task Force
    background of: 38–39
    coordination with conventional units: 218
    need for ARNG and USAR personnel to perform missions: 216
    precombat activities: 46
    rotation plan: 275
    staffing for: 52
    stop-loss actions: 43
    training: 43–44, 371
*Arquette, CPT Mason: 78, 212
*Ashford, CWO Dwight: 236–37, 238–40, 257
*Aspen, SGT Harold: 151
Assistant Secretary of Defense for Special Operations and Low-Intensity Conflict: 49–50, 62
*Astor, SGT Akmed: 257–59
*Athens, SFC Bill: 285
*Atkinson, SFC Fred: 354
Atta, Mohammad: 77, 190n17
Atta, Commander Usted: 139
Auckland, Lord: 4
Auslev, Ruslan: 38
Australian forces: 34
    at Kandahar Airport: 204–05
    and Operation ANACONDA: 277, 281, 284, 294–96, 319–20
Aviation Battalion, 109th: 105–06, 151–53
Aviation maintenance units: 43, 44, 151–53, 384
Aviation Regiment, 159th: 358
Aviators, special operations, training for: 43

Babulkheyl, Afghanistan: 324, 326
Bacon, Ken: 44
*Bagby, Sam: 123, 146–47
Bagram, Afghanistan: 21, 25, 96, 101, 103, 191n33, 226, 227, 228
Bagram Airfield: 171
    19th SFG at: 277–78
    communications: 337–40
    humanitarian relief efforts at: 184–85
    operations at: 101, 208, 210, 229–30, 266, 335–37
    radio broadcasting from: 340–41
    and rescue of forces on Takur Ghar: 312, 317, 318–19

*Bain, CPT Douglas: 172
Balkh, Afghanistan: 4
Balkh Valley: 101–02
*Ball, SGT Barry: 123
*Ball, SGT Gene: 114–15
Bamian: 4, 23, 24, 99–100, 103, 221
Bank, COL Aaron: 38
*Barnes, CPT Kerry: 356, 357
*Barrington, SSG Thomas: 220
*Barstow, MAJ Walter: 115–17, 153–54, 186
*Bartley, SSG Michael: 137
Bastogne airstrip: 104
Battle Command Training Program: 44
*Battles, LTC Kim: 117
Baumann, Robert: 10
*Beckwith, SGM Geoff: 256–57
*Bell, LTC Marc: 88n69, 158, 198n211
*Bender, SFC Pete: 161, 162
*Bennington, MAJ Del: 90n118, 171–72, 176–78, 199n257, 200n271
*Bennington, MSG Jason: 77, 90n118
*Berdeau, SPC Timothy: 260
Berger, Sandy: 23–24
*Bermann, CPL Colin, USMC: 239
Bhutto, Benazir: 18–19, 25
bin Laden, Osama: 1, 23–24, 26–27, 33, 147, 241–42
    sought in the Tora Bora: 203–04, 205, 213, 215–16, 269n40
    and the Taliban: 22, 23–24, 25, 35
    and terrorist attacks on U.S. facilities abroad: 22–23
*Black, CWO Gary: 330, 331
*Blackaby, MAJ Henry: 187
Blair, Tony: 34
*Bojune, LTC Mark: 138, 164
*Bondurant, SFC: 143
*Bosley, MAJ Jeff: 347–49
Bosnian forces: 337
Boucher, Richard: 46
*Bowdler, MSG: 74
*Bowman, MAJ John: 150–51, 221, 222
*Boyd, SFC Stan: 166, 168, 175
Boykin, MG William G.: 88n40
*Bridgewater, ILT Michael: 73
*Brinks, LTC James: 71, 72, 78, 79, 82, 262–63
British forces: 211
    at Bagram: 103
    and Kabul Military Academy: 349
    and Qala-i-Jangi uprising: 104, 160–62
    with Sherzai: 178
British Royal Marines: 103, 206–07, 329
*Broderick, MAJ Steven: 74
Brown, LTG Bryan D.: 42, 53, 93
Brown, SSGT Gabe, USAF: 307, 308, 309, 310–11, 312–13, 317–18
Brussels Accord of 14 December 2001: 206
Brzezinski, Zbigniew: 11, 29n30
Burford, COL David: 216

Burns, John F.: 267*n3*
Bush, George W.: 1, 33, 34, 36–37, 38, 41, 44, 60, 85, 181, 182, 347, 349, 358–59
*Bustillo, SGM Jorgé: 255

Calland, RADM Albert M.: 41, 52, 53, 55–56, 57, 102, 158, 159–60, 161, 198*n211*, 208, 345, 346–47, 377
Camp Doha, Kuwait: 148
Camp Freedom, Uzbekistan: 68, 70–71, 72–73
Camp Mackall, North Carolina: 257
Camp Pickett, Virginia: 59
Camp Rhino: 107, 108, 113, 180–81
Camp X-Ray (Guantanamo Bay, Cuba): 250–51
Canadian forces: 265, 277, 357
*Canberra, SFC Lyle: 227, 228
Cannistraro, Vincent: 13
*Canon, SSG Arin K.: 304, 305, 309–10, 312–13, 314–15
*Cantwell, SFC Karl: 328, 329–30
*Carlisle, MAJ Dalton: 256–57
*Carr, SFC Brandon: 79
Carter, LT: 143
Carter, Jimmy: 10–11
Carter Doctrine: 11
Castro, Fidel: 11, 16
Casualties
    Afghan allies: 269*n38*, 285–86, 353–55
    allied at Qala-i-Jangi: 162
    British: 162
    from the earthquake: 342, 367*n175*
    enemy at Hazer Qadam: 239, 240
    friendly Afghan due to U.S. bombing errors: 162, 285–87
    friendly fire: 180–81, 285–87, 379–80
    helicopter crashes: 98
    Karzai, Hamad's forces: 180–81
    in Khowst: 206
    at Objective Honda: 113
    at Objective Rhino: 97
    Operation ANACONDA: 285–87, 289–90, 293–94, 302–03
    at Qala-i-Jangi: 162, 164
    Rangers: 98
    at Takur Ghar: 293–94, 302–19, 387
    Taliban: 157
*Cavanaugh, CPT Marty: 61, 183
Cave clearing operations: 203–04, 327, 333, 334, 356–57
CBS: 227–28
Central Intelligence Agency: 191*n25*
    logistical support for: 273*n155*
    officers attacked at Qala-i-Jangi prison: 104, 192*n48*
    Special Activities Division: 190*n12*, 193*n67*
Chamberlin, Wendy J.: 248, 249, 250
Champion, COL Gregory: 255
*Chandler, SSG Wilfred: 219
Chaplains: 138–39

Chapman, TSGT John: 301, 302, 304, 387–88
Chapman, SFC Nate: 206, 267*n14*, 274*n179*, 313
Charikar, Afghanistan: 4
*Charles, CW4 Roger: 82–84, 121, 135, 137–38, 139–40
*Chase, MSG Morton: 88*n54*
Chemtal, Afghanistan: 140
*Chesterfield, SGT Bobby, USAF: 163
*Childs, CPT: 70
China: 5, 10
Christopher, Warren: 11
Civil Affairs Battalion, 96th
    and Afghan refugees: 206
    CAT-As: 207, 328
    coordination with nongovernmental organizations: 183–84
    and humanitarian aid: 207, 220–25, 278
    at Karshi Kanabad: 45, 150
    liaison element at JSOTF-North: 150
    liaison officer to CENTCOM: 60, 61
    missions: 220–21, 225, 251–52, 271*n108*
    and reconstruction of Mazar-e-Sharif: 102, 150–51
Civil Affairs Battalion, 489th: 278, 350–52, 372, 373
Civil affairs teams: 373
    A32: 150, 184–85, 191*n33*, 223–24
    A33: 150–51, 184, 186, 191*n33*
    A34: 150, 222
    A36: 150, 224–25
    A41: 184, 226–28, 264, 342–44
    A42: 251–52
    A46: 61, 183–84, 252
    A56: 328–30
    B30: 150
Civil affairs units
    command and control of: 79
    mobilization of: 43, 44
    planning for humanitarian aid missions: 46, 150
    role of: 41
Civil-military operations center, Islamabad: 183–84
Civil-Military Operations Center-North: 184
Civil-military operations centers: 60–61
Civilian noninterference warnings: 113–14
Clarke, Torie: 334
*Clauden, SSG Lee: 133, 136, 138
Clausewitz, Carl von: 37–38, 155, 156
*Clewell, 1LT Carol: 148–49
Clinton, Bill: 23, 25
*Clinton, SSG Jack: 288–89
Close air support
    for Afghan Military Forces: 285–87, 292, 387, 388
    failures of in Operation ANACONDA: 285–87, 311–12
    guided by forces with General Dostum: 95
    guided by forces with General F. Khan: 96
    guided by ODA 555: 96
    guided by ODA 595: 96
    guided by Special Forces soldiers on horseback: 95
    for ODA 583: 167–69, 170, 174–75

Operation ANACONDA: 285–87, 289, 292, 311–12,
313–14, 315, 316, 322, 325–26, 386–88
problems with: 379–80
provided by the 101st Airborne Division: 286–87
and the Qala-i-Jangi uprising: 161–63
in support of Karzai: 176
in support of Sherzai: 167–69, 170, 174–75
at Takur Ghar: 311–12, 313–14, 315, 316
at Tarin Kowt: 157
Coalition forces: 103
communications support for: 338
integration with U.S. forces: 41, 346–47, 382, 383
and JSOTF-South: 41
morale: 346
PSYOP support for: 50
Coalition humanitarian liaison cell: 183–84, 197n178,
252
at Bagram: 150
in Kandahar: 350–53
at Mazar-e-Sharif: 150–51, 184
in Pakistan: 252
Cohen, William: 23
Cold War: 7, 8, 9
*Colter, CPT Paul: 51
Combat search and air rescue operations
Air Force teams: 303
aircraft for: 375, 376
command and control of: 45–46, 70, 229–30, 303,
309, 312, 316–17
communications support for: 75–76
for a MC-130P aircraft: 261–63
at Takur Ghar crash: 299–319
training for: 72, 230
Combined Joint Civil-Military Operations Task Force:
206–07, 347, 348, 384
and funding for civil affairs projects: 184, 329
and humanitarian aid: 221, 222, 224, 252
tactical control of the 96th CAB: 150, 184
Combined Joint Special Operations Task Force-
Afghanistan: 269n29, 277, 278, 279, 293,
335–37, 389–91
command and control: 346–47
communications: 337–40, 344, 389–90
forces assigned to: 210
integration of coalition forces: 346–47, 382, 389
and the Joint Air Component: 345, 390
mission: 211
synchronized time for: 345–46
Combined Joint Special Operations Task Force-South:
241, 256, 389
Combined Joint Special Operations Task Force-West:
253
Command and control issues: 374
Afghan militias: 322–23
air support: 375
at Bagram Air Base: 229–30
for CSAR operations: 45–46, 70, 229–30, 303, 309,
312, 316–17
at Karshi Kanabad: 67, 74–75, 373–74

of ODAs: 145
Operation ANACONDA: 283–84, 286
PSYOP units: 50, 79, 151
quick reaction forces: 265–66, 303
Commons, PFC Matthew A.: 306
Communications
at Bagram: 337–40, 344
equipment: 56, 81, 219
integration of Air Force and 112th Signal Battalion
systems: 75–76
JSOTFBNorth problems with: 55, 56–57, 75–76,
80–82
lost cryptographic materials: 355–56
problems on Takur Ghar: 304–05, 307, 308–09,
310–11, 318
signal base station for JSOTF-North: 145–46, 375,
377
standard deployment packages: 81
tactical satellite: 81, 145–46, 196n171
training: 217, 220
training exercises: 81, 338, 339
Computers
for coalition forces: 346, 389
hardware: 53, 56
helicopters: 118
local area networks: 53, 55, 56, 219–20, 338
need for environmentally controlled work space:
116, 339
personal: 81
power for: 339
Web Interface Computer System: 339
*Cook, Chaplain Daniel, USAF: 138
*Corbin, CWO Gary: 304–07, 308, 311, 314, 315,
317–18
*Cornell, SGT Gus: 168
*Corr, MSG Gregg: 265
*Crenshaw, CPT Ben: 340–42
Crose, SGT Bradley S.: 306
Cuba: 11
Cunningham, Senior Airman Jason: 306, 307, 308,
311, 314, 315, 317
*Curtis, SGT Jerald: 298, 300
*Czyrnyck, SSG Wally: 168, 175

Danish forces: 205, 265, 277, 281, 293
Daoud Khan: 7–8, 9
Dari-a-Souf Valley: 95, 96, 101, 122–28
Davis, MSG Jefferson: 176, 180, 212
*Davis, SSG Mike: 354
*Davis, PFC Paul: 186
Dawkins, SSG Carl: 185–86
Declaration of War Against the Americans Occupying
the Land of the Two Holy Places, by Osama bin
Laden: 23
*Deese, SSG Donald: 305, 306–07, 308, 311, 313–14,
316
Defense Emergency Response Fund: 42
Defense Intelligence Agency: 77
Deh Dadi airfield: 139–40, 158

Dehi, Afghanistan: 123, 125–26
Demining operations: 227
*Dennison, SGT Mitchell: 246–48, 289–91
Department of the Army, stop loss actions: 43
Deployable Print Production Center: 151
DePouli, SSG Raymond: 306, 307, 308–09, 311, 312–13, 314–15
Desert landing strips
   Anzio: 143
   Bastogne: 140–41
   Bulge: 143–44
   Objective Rhino: 109–13
   security for: 142–45
*Dickerson, CPT Timothy: 297, 300, 301–02, 309
Diemer, COL Manuel: 51, 52
*DiJurnigan, MAJ Matt: 60, 61, 183–84, 252
Disraeli, Benjamin: 5
*Donalds, CW3 Derrick: 132–33, 135–36, 137–38, 318
*Donovan, SSG Logan: 147, 148–49
Donovan, MG William J.: 38
*Doolittle, MSG Jason: 332
Dost Mohammad Khan: 4–5
Dostum, General Rashid: 17–18, 19, 21, 22, 26, 59, 77, 95, 192n42, 198n211
   5th SFG liaison officers with: 59–60
   and battle for Mazar-e-Sharif: 101–02
   and bombing of Taliban forces: 126–27, 134, 139
   campaign planning with: 123–25
   coordination with Atta: 98
   early ARSOF contact with: 82, 83–85
   ODA 595 coordination with: 96, 119–27, 134, 146–47
   offensive against Konduz: 158
   and Qala-i-Jangi uprising: 159–60
   rivalry with Fahim Khan: 98
   security forces: 123, 134
   Special Forces advisors to: 98
*Dubois, SSG Bernard: 321, 322
Dubs, Adolph: 9
*Dugan, SSG Tom: 136–37
Dupree, Louis: 3, 6
Durand, Mortimer: 5
Durand Line: 5, 7

*Earnhardt, MSG Pat: 122–23, 195n122
Earthquakes: 342
*Eaton, SGT Christopher: 331
Edmunds, Specialist Jonn: 113
Educational facilities: 184, 329–30
Efran, Shawn: 227–28
Eisenhower, GEN Dwight D.: 187
*Elkenback, CWO Charles: 317, 331
*Emerson, CW5 Brian: 132–33, 135, 136, 137
Engineer Battalion, 92nd: 349
Engineers, Special Forces, at Mazar-e-Sharif: 102
Escano, SPC Oscar J.: 313
*Ewell, MSG Mike: 328, 329–30
Exercise BRIGHT STAR: 57–58

Exercise EARLY VICTOR: 58
*Exley, SSG Mark: 123

Fahkir, Commander, 159, 161, 162–63
*Falkerie, SSG Landon: 188
*Fan, SFC Chuck: 168
Farah: 12
Farooq, MG Ahmad Khan: 248, 249
*Fazal, SSG Charlie: 172
Federal Bureau of Investigation: 237, 251
*Felico, SGT Jack: 260
*Ferrell, CWO Jackson: 261, 262–63, 300, 301–02, 304
Fighter Squadron, 391st: 199n266
Findlay, COL Michael: 51, 53, 55–56, 57, 154
*Fitzgerald, CPT Daniel: 218
*Fontaine, CW3 Mike: 235
Force protection
   for civil affairs units: 227, 228
   at crash sites: 232
   at Gardez: 353–54
   at Kabul Military Academy: 348
   at Kandahar: 352
   at Karshi Kanabad: 66, 74
   at Landing Zone Albatross: 83–84
   provided by Afghan security guards: 122, 126, 134, 276, 288, 324, 325
   at the Salang Tunnel: 342, 343
Foreign internal defense mission: 275, 276
*Forsythe, LTC Don: 58, 88n69, 171–72, 173, 174, 176–77, 178, 180, 182–83, 200n271, 218, 232–33
Fort Bragg, North Carolina: 39, 40, 55–56, 58–59, 62, 98, 103, 208, 255, 341, 372, 373, 377
Fort Campbell, Kentucky: 52–54, 56, 63, 90n110, 128, 138, 151, 217, 339, 356, 372
Fort Carson, Colorado: 216, 372
Fort Irwin, California: 44
Fort Knox, Kentucky: 216–17
Fort Leavenworth, Kansas: 44
Fort Polk, Louisiana: 44
Fort Stewart, Georgia: 349
Forward arming and refueling points
   at DLS Bastogne: 140–41
   at DLS Bulge: 144
   at Karshi Kanabad: 68
   MH-47E Chinooks used as: 119
   mobile: 140–41, 142–45, 377
   in Operation ANACONDA: 287–89, 312, 315, 317
Forward Operating Bases
   33: 208, 219–20, 260–61
   53: 159–65
Forward Surgical Teams
   244th: 232
   274th: 187–88, 318, 319
Franks, GEN Tommy: 38, 41, 50, 51, 113, 158, 193n67, 215–16, 334, 346–47, 359, 377
Fratricide
   during the Qala-i-Jangi uprising: 104
   ODA 574: 107

Fratricide–*Continued*
  Pashtun soldiers with Karzai: 107
  at Sayd-Alim-Kalay: 180–82
French forces: 211, 277, 281
Friendly-fire incidents: 162, 193*n61*, 379–80
  efforts to prevent: 284, 287
  in Operation ANACONDA: 285–87, 289–90,
    362*n30*
  at Sayd-Alim-Kalay: 180–82
*Frost, CWO Jacob: 302
*Fulkerson, MSG Adam: 217
Fuller, BG Lesley: 100, 129–30, 131–32, 195*n125*,
  209, 253–55, 273*n155*

*Gaines, CWO Christopher: 230, 231, 232, 301, 303,
  304–06, 307, 311, 314
*Galtier, SSG Cash: 286, 292, 321
Gardez, Afghanistan: 282–83, 285, 287, 300, 303–05,
  309, 312, 317, 318–19, 320, 322, 326,
  327–28, 332, 353
*Garrison, 1SG Dan: 139
*Garvey, CWO Vincent: 52
*Gates, CPT John: 119–20, 132–33, 135, 137–38,
  187–88, 230, 231, 301, 304
Genghis Khan: 2
George, SGT Patrick: 313
*Gerhing, SGT Shane: 331
German forces: 205, 277, 281, 293, 295
Germany: 7, 211
Ghazni: 4, 19
Gilliam, PFC David B.: 305, 306, 307, 308, 311, 313,
  314
*Glasgow, CPT Douglas, USMC: 231–32
Global positioning system: 101–02, 126–27, 141,
  162, 181
Golts, Aleksandr: 38
Goodman, Capt Randy, USN: 53–54, 59
Gorbachev, Mikhail: 16
*Gorley, CWO Max: 265, 322, 325–28, 365*n125*
Goryeev, General Makmut: 38
Grave sites, investigation of: 357
Great Britain
  forces for Afghanistan operations: 34, 103, 104,
    160–62, 178, 206–07, 211, 329, 349
  historical role in Afghanistan: 4–6, 7
  and humanitarian aid: 60, 61
Green Beret (as official Special Forces headgear):
  38–39
*Greene, MAJ Silas: 226, 227, 228, 263–64, 342–44
*Gregg, CPT Bill: 163
Grim 32: 300, 301–02, 303–04
Gromov, LTG Boris: 38
Guantanamo Bay, Cuba: 204, 250–51

Habibullah Khan: 6
Hafiz: 323–24, 325, 326
Hagenbeck, MG Franklin L.: 276–77, 280–81, 283,
  332, 334, 342, 346–47
Hahn, Satar: 123

Haidar, General Gul: 288, 319, 322–23, 324–28
*Hall, CPT Bill: 243
*Hall, SSG Jim: 234
*Halstedt, LTC Sam: 48, 49–50
Haq, Abdul: 16–17, 29*n46*, 98–99
*Harriman, SPC John: 352
Harriman, CW2 Stanley: 283, 285–86, 294, 332, 358,
  362*n30*, 364*n95*
*Harris, MAJ Mitchell: 353
*Harrison, CPT Ken: 328, 329
*Harrison, CPT Rick: 151
Harward, Commodore Robert, USN: 108, 193*n68*,
  204, 208, 236, 238, 243–44, 277
Hazaras: 20, 22, 30*n55, n61*, 99–100
Hazar Qadam, Afghanistan: 208, 235–41
Hekmatyar, Gulbuddin: 11, 14, 16–18, 21, 30*n58*
Helicopters. *See also* Aircraft; MH-47E; MH-60L.
  antiaircraft threat to: 99, 118–19, 120–21, 138,
    139
  buildup of at Karshi Kanabad: 71–72, 372–73, 376
  fired on: 133, 135, 136–38, 139
  in the high mountains: 78–79, 96, 99, 117–22,
    132–33
  lack of adequate intelligence for: 82
  maintenance of: 151–53, 376
  night infiltrations: 78–79, 96
  visibility problems: 82, 83, 84–85, 117, 118,
    119–20, 132
  weather problems: 78–79, 82, 83, 84–85, 96,
    118–19, 132–33
*Henderson, MAJ Mark: 71
*Henley, CWO Daniel: 317
*Hensen, MAJ Mickey: 265–66
Herat, Afghanistan: 2–3, 4, 5, 6, 9, 12–13, 14, 17, 18,
  20, 22, 100, 183, 192*n39*, 222–23
*Hernandez, CPT Carlos: 77
*Herndon, LTC Dan: 172
High value target missions: 330–32
Highway 4, effort to block *Taliban* use of: 167–69,
  174–75
Hindu Kush mountain range: 53–54, 99, 117, 134,
  135, 213
Holland, GEN Charles R.: 93
*Holloway, SFC Reggie: 251, 252
*Holman, SSG Stef: 168
*Holmes, SSG Celeste: 73
*Hooper, LTC Carl: 53, 88*n69*, 281–82, 283, 284,
  285, 286, 287, 292, 319–20, 323, 332
*Hopkins, MAJ Mike: 325, 327
Horn of Africa, preparation for operations in: 58–59,
  253
Horses
  saddles for: 125, 128, 195*n122*, 273*n151*
  used with General Dostum's forces: 96, 123–25,
    128
Hospitals: 151, 184, 207, 222, 228, 232–35
*Hsu, SFC Jon: 239
*Huffman, MSG Mike: 234, 235
*Hulse, SSGT Damon, USAF: 322, 325–26, 364*n125*

Humanitarian aid
  to Afghan refugees: 206
  airdrop operations: 46, 100–101, 206–07, 252, 263–64, 269*n28*, 376, 379
  at Bagram: 184–85
  blankets: 130, 185, 263–64, 273*n155*, 329
  CMOC role in: 60–61
  coordination of nongovernmental organizations' efforts: 183–84, 185, 206–07, 222, 223–24, 252, 278, 386
  to earthquake victims: 342, 343–44
  food: 130, 131, 150, 184–85, 191*n28*, 263–64, 273*n155*, 329, 351
  funding for: 223, 224, 273*n155*, 329–30
  in the Kandahar area: 173, 351
  at Khowst: 263–64, 328–30
  at Mazar-e-Sharif: 102, 150–51, 184
  needs assessment: 220–22, 223–24, 328–30, 350–51, 386
  organization of: 60–61, 150–51, 185, 191*n25*, 350–51, 386
  overland deliveries of: 252
  planning for: 41, 46, 60–61, 221, 278, 350–51
  SOCEUR's role in delivery of: 130
  toys: 150, 351
  used as a bribe: 357
  water-related: 351–52
  winter clothes: 150, 221, 351
Humanitarian Assistance Survey Teams: 220–21, 222

Immunizations: 222
Incirlik Air Base, Turkey: 66, 100, 130, 131, 254
India: 4, 5–6, 7, 9
Infantry, 87th: 74, 192*n49*, 198*n223*, 277, 288
Infantry Regiment, 187th: 270*n55*, 277, 289, 358
Infrastructure repair: 102, 209, 225–27
Intelligence
  based on video from unmanned aerial vehicles: 382
  failures of in Operation ANACONDA: 281, 285, 297–98
  failures of regarding Dostum: 123, 125
  failures of with respect to Afghan leaders: 165–66
  general inadequacy of: 370, 376, 382
  incomplete threat information: 82, 281
  limitations of regarding threat picture for aviators: 134–35, 138
  limited access to: 371, 372
  regarding enemy forces on Takur Ghar: 302–03
  from satellites and aircraft in the Arghastan wadi: 174
Intelligence operations
  at Hazar Qadam: 235–41
  JSOTF-North: 77–78, 79
  Operation ANACONDA: 281–82
  in the Shah-i-Khot Valley: 279–80, 281, 296
  near Shkin: 241–44
International Islamic Front for Holy War Against Jews and Crusaders: 23
International Security Assistance Force: 206–07, 211, 349, 367*n196*

Iran
  and history of Afghanistan: 8, 9, 11, 12, 14, 28*n15*
  and response to 9/11: 34
  and the *Taliban*: 18, 20, 21, 22, 24, 30*n55, n58, n61*
Islamabad, Pakistan: 252
Islamic Alliance for the Liberation of Afghanistan: 11
Islamic fundamentalists and the *Taliban*: 17–18, 19–20
Islamic Martyrs Brigade: 30*n58*
Islamic Movement of Uzbekistan: 26, 64, 134
Islamic Society of Afghanistan: 12–13, 16
Islamic Unity of Afghan: 16–17
Izvestia: 16

Jaamat-e-Islami militia, supported by ODA 534: 98
*Jackman, SGT Dwayne: 220
*Jackson, MAJ Martin: 151
Jacobabad, Pakistan: 345
*Jacobi, MAJ Derrick: 74, 75–76, 146, 344
*Jacobson, MAJ Keenan: 342
*Jaffe, MAJ Gary: 226
Jalalabad, Afghanistan: 4, 6, 12, 17, 19, 21, 192*n41*, 214–15
*James, SSG Carey: 123
*Jameson, CWO Curtis: 231, 232, 261–63
*Jefferson, CPT Brian: 121, 317, 318
*Jefferson, CWO Erick: 79, 138
*Jernigan, MAJ Gregory: 350–51
Jihad, calls for against the Soviets: 11
*Joes, SSG Kim: 168, 174
Joint Chiefs of Staff: 7, 40–41
Joint Combined Exchange Training: 44
Joint Communications Signal Element: 375
Joint direct-attack munitions: 180–81
Joint Psychological Operations Task Force
  mission: 41, 48–49, 244, 375
  precombat activities: 47–50, 62, 63
  Product Development Company: 46
Joint Readiness Training Center: 43–44
Joint Search and Rescue Center, Saudi Arabia: 230, 231, 232
Joint Special Operations Air Component: 71–72, 79, 81, 82, 122, 138, 278, 375
Joint Special Operations Air Component Command: 46, 172
Joint Special Operations Task Force-North
  civil affairs liaison element at: 150
  command and control issues: 74–75, 79–80, 371
  and command and control of CSAR operations: 45–46, 53, 68, 70–71
  command and control of PSYOP units: 50
  communications responsibilities: 56–57, 70, 75–76, 80–82, 90*n110*, 145–46, 373–74
  intelligence operations: 77–78
  and planning for Operation ANACONDA: 319
  and planning of aviation operations: 79
  problems getting established: 41, 53–54, 70–71, 74–75, 78, 79–80

Joint Special Operations Task Force-North–*Continued*
 responsibility for planning: 57
 role of: 41
 staffing for: 51–52, 53, 55–56, 57, 60, 78, 79–80,
  105, 371
 standup of: 41–42, 54–57, 70–71, 75–76, 77–78
 tactical guidance on battle for Kandahar: 178–79
 training for staff of: 53, 55, 56–57, 79–80
Joint Special Operations Task Force-South: 269*n29*
 command and control issues: 208, 277
 communications: 204, 272*n120*
 forces assigned to: 204–05, 208, 382–83
 foreign forces assigned to: 41, 204–05
 mission: 41, 204, 383–84
 move to Kandahar: 108, 209–10, 385
Joint Task Force Mountain: 346–47
Jomini, Antoine Henri de: 72
Jordan: 58, 102, 151, 171, 184, 207
Journalists: 276, 322, 327, 357
*Jurgens, MAJ Karl: 264

Kabul, Afghanistan: 4, 5, 6
 as base for humanitarian operations: 224–25, 226
 as base for peacekeeping operations: 206–07
 and the Soviet occupation: 12–13, 16, 17
 and the *Taliban*: 17–18, 19–21, 25
 U.S. embassy in: 211–12
Kabul International Airport: 10
Kabul Military Academy: 211, 277, 279, 347–50, 358
Kahlili, General Kareem: 99
Kaiserslautern, Germany: 130
Kandahar, Afghanistan: 2–3, 4, 5, 6, 7, 8
 fall of: 178–79, 182–83
 Mir Wais Hospital: 209, 232–35
 planning the offensive against: 166–67, 173, 178
 and resistance to the Soviet occupation: 11–13, 14,
  16, 17
 and the *Taliban*: 18, 19, 20, 25, 106–08, 156
Kandahar Airport: 166–67, 170–71, 174–75, 178
 JSOTF-South stationed at: 204–06, 209–10, 218
 radio broadcasting from: 340–41
Karimov, Islam: 26, 65
Karmal, Babrak: 10, 12, 14–15, 16
*Karnes, LTC James: 250–51
Karp, Aaron: 29*n38*
Karshi Kanabad, Uzbekistan
 advance echelon coordination with Uzbeks: 64–66
 aircraft based at: 195*n129*, 373
 base operations responsibilities: 79–80
 civil affairs function at: 184
 command and control issues at: 67, 74–75, 375
 communications support at: 81–82, 373–74
 construction of base at: 53
 development of: 105, 373
 food service: 73
 force protection at: 66, 74
 forces based at: 44–45, 102, 208
 fueling operations: 68
 isolation facility: 74

logistics support: 72–73, 373–74
 real estate management: 74
Karzai, Hamad: 18, 106, 191*n27*, 342
 and battle at Tarin Kowt: 106–07
 and the battle for Kandahar: 172–74, 182–83
 guidance on U.S. PSYOP activities: 153–54
 and humanitarian aid: 206
 injured by U.S. fire: 180
 intelligence gathered by in Oruzgan Province: 106
 as leader of Pashtun efforts in the south to oust the
  Taliban: 154–58
 ODA 574 assigned to support: 155–58, 172, 173,
  175–78
 as prime minister of the Afghan Interim Authority:
  176, 178, 182–83, 193*n64*
 sudden loyalty of former *Taliban* to: 183
 wounded by U.S. forces: 107
Kasymov, General: 65, 74
Keegan, John: 194*n75*
*Kelley, SGT Randal: 318
*Kellogg, TSGT Alan: 168–69
Kenna, Kathleen: 276
*Keogh, SGM Rich: 336–37
Khan, General Bismullah: 98
Khan, Burillah: 98
Khan, General Daoud: 99
Khan, Fahim: 77, 95, 119, 319
 5th SFG liaison officers with: 59–60
 and ODA 555: 96
 rivalry with Dostum: 98
 summit meeting on Northern Alliance campaign:
  158
Khan, Ismail: 12–13, 17–18, 19, 20, 77, 100, 183,
  191*n24*, 192*n39*
Khan, Kamel: 281–82
Khan, Padsha: 329
Khan, Zakim: 281–82, 328
Khoshkeyer, Commander: 283, 284, 286, 287, 332–
  33, 365*n112*
Khowst, Afghanistan: 13, 14, 17, 274*n179*
 civil affairs with units based in: 328–29
 date drop at: 263–64
 Special Forces bases in: 206, 208
*Kilbourne, SFC Forrest: 251
*Killinger, MAJ Kyle: 66
Kim, by Rudyard Kipling: 4
Kipling, Rudyard: 4
Kisner, COL Frank: 68, 72, 74, 75, 85
*Kittridge, SFC Jack: 234
*Kitts, SGT Sol: 123
*Knapp, CPT Mark: 138, 139
Kohat, Pakistan: 249
Konar Province: 12, 14
Konduz, Afghanistan: 21, 158, 186–87, 192*n42*,
  198*n209*, *n211*, 221–22, 223–24
*Kramer, SSG Karl: 216
Kratzer, BG David: 206–07
*Kupinski, SFC Kip: 218
Kuwait: 102, 108, 148

Lackey, CSM Ray: 259
*Lafayette, SFC Charles: 231, 232, 303, 305, 306–07,
    308, 311, 314, 315, 317
*Lafayette, SSG Jason: 260–61
LaFrenz, SGT Matthew: 314, 315, 316–17
*Lake, SFC Ray: 295–96
Lambert, MG Geoffrey: 50–51, 52, 53, 88n40, 93
Lancaster-Totten, SPC Aaron: 306, 307
Land Information Warfare Activity: 339
Landing zones
    Albatross: 83–85, 119, 120–22, 132–33, 135–39
    desert: 109–13, 140–41, 142–45
    Elspeth: 119–20
    markers for: 113, 120, 132–33, 140–41, 142, 144
Language difficulties: 125–26, 227, 258–59
*Largent, SSG Sylvester: 216
*Larken, SGT Steve: 305, 306, 307, 308, 313–14, 316
*Latimer, CPT Karl: 162
*Law, SSG Greg: 318
Leaflets: 63, 89n79, 103, 147–49, 186–87, 292
    dropped in leaflet bombs: 103, 149, 292, 370, 376
    encouraging surrender: 292
    guidance from Karzai regarding: 153–54
    used at Mazar-e-Sharif: 102
    used at Objective Rhino: 113–14, 115
    used in Operation ANACONDA: 292
    warning about minefields: 186
Lindh, John Walker: 104–05, 198n233, 380
Linguists: 172, 373
Lisinenko, Lieutenant Igor: 35
Literacy: 8, 9, 14, 15, 286, 329, 352, 359
*Loach, CPT Jack: 172
Lodi, Commander: 281–82
Logistics support
    aerial resupply by SOCEUR: 129–32
    planning for: 41–42
    resupply of ODA 595 in the Dari-a-Souf Valley:
        127–28
    and SOCEUR: 41–42, 273n155, 374
*Loomis, SSG Cory: 168, 174, 175
Looting by Afghan militias: 324–26
*Lorenzo, CSM Marc: 266
Loudspeaker broadcasts: 288
    at Mazar-e-Sharif: 185–86
    at Objective Rhino: 111, 113–15
Love, COL Albert: 187–88
Loya jirga: 3, 7, 9, 11, 14, 211

MacDill Air Force Base, Florida: 47–50
*MacGinnis, CPL John: 114–15
*MacKenzie, SGT Derrick: 298–99
Macnaghten, William: 4
*Madden, SGM Rudy: 265–66
*Madison, SSG Walter: 177, 200n270
*Magione, MAJ Mario: 160, 161–65
*Mahoney, MAJ Charles: 72
Maintenance support teams: 260–61
Mako 20: 297–98, 299, 300, 301, 302, 313, 318
Malek, Commander: 356–57

Malik, General Abdul: 21
*Mann, CWO Alfred: 120–21, 139, 261–63, 297–99, 309
*Mantle, LTC Kip: 349
Maps: 53, 88n54, 370
Maqdoom: 126, 127
Marine Expeditionary Unit, 26th: 272n121
Marine Expeditionary Units: 204–05
Marion, BG Francis: 38
*Marks, CPT Steve: 76
*Martin, SSG Charles: 331
*Martinez, SSG Jesus: 218
Marzak, Afghanistan: 282, 292, 324, 326, 333
Masirah Island, Oman: 108, 116, 205, 278, 345
Massoud, Ahmad Shah: 12, 13, 14, 16–17, 18, 19–21,
    24, 25, 26, 29n35, 95
*Masterson, 1SG Martin: 76
*Matteson, LTC Darrin: 51
*Matthews, SSG Timothy: 73
*Maxey, 1SG Karl: 144
Mazar-e-Sharif, Afghanistan: 6, 12–13
    fight for control of: 139
    humanitarian relief efforts in: 102, 150–51, 184
    ODA 595 operations at: 101–03
    PSYOP in: 185–87, 191n33
    Qala-i-Jangi prison uprising: 158–65
    struggle for political control of: 101–02
    and the Taliban: 21, 22
Mazari, Abdul: 20
McClure, BG Robert: 38
*McCracken, CWO Walter: 139–40
*McDaniels, LTC Keith: 359
*McDonald, SFC Roger: 227, 228
*McFadden, MSG Ty: 263, 295, 320–21, 322, 323–
    24, 325–26, 327
McGhee, COL Phillip: 42
*McGinnis, LTC Julian: 257
*McHenry, CPT Mike: 282–84, 286, 287, 332,
    362n30
*McKellar, MAJ Wes: 70
*McLemore, MAJ Jim: 150, 221–22, 223
Medical care for Afghans: 222, 234, 246–47, 277,
    285, 343, 354–55
Medical Civil Action Program teams: 222
Medical evacuation: 107, 112–13, 162, 180–81, 187–
    88, 200n270, 234, 286, 315–19, 354–55
*Mercado, MAJ Victor, USAF: 70
Messenger, SGM Jim: 248
*Messinger, MAJ Stan: 171–72
Meyer, GEN Edward: 39
MH-47D Chinook: 208, 330–32, 372–73
MH-47E Chinooks
    attacks on: 296–99, 303–09
    buildup of at Karshi Kanabad: 71–72, 372–73
    capabilities: 99, 118, 132, 378, 390
    crashes of: 299, 301–09, 387–88
    CSAR operations: 209, 230–32, 262–63, 267n15
    maintenance of: 105–06
    missions: 47, 83, 85, 95, 119–22, 132–33, 135,
        301–09, 330–32, 370, 375, 376, 377

MH-47E Chinooks–*Continued*
  navigation: 119–20, 121, 132–33, 135–36
  Operation ANACONDA: 296
  refueling needs: 79, 119
  shot at: 135–39
MH-60L Defensive Armed Penetrators Black Hawks
  buildup of at Karshi Kanabad: 71–72
  capabilities: 82, 118, 121, 139
  crashes: 113
  missions: 82–85, 95, 103, 119, 135, 139–40, 370, 375–76
  navigation: 119, 121, 135
  refueling needs: 79
Miceli, SPC Anthony R.: 306, 308–09
Mikolashek, LTG P. T.: 276–77, 280–81
Military history detachments: 44
*Millender, Lt Cdr: 65, 66
Miller, SSGT Kerry, USAF: 306, 307, 313, 315, 316–17
Millet, SGT Jake: 294, 322, 325
*Mills, CPT Jason: 79
Mine clearing operations: 337
Minefield awareness: 186, 245, 246
*Ming, SGT Vinsong: 123
Mir Wais Hospital, Kandahar: 209, 232–35, 269n26
*Mix, SGT Al: 123
Modular Print System: 147–48
Mohammed, General Atta, and battle for Mazar-e-Sharif: 101, 102
Mohammed, Khan: 233–34, 271n99
Mohaqqeq, General Mohammed: 99–100, 102
Mojadeddi, Sibghatollah: 17–18
*Monroe, SP4 Ike: 246, 289–91
*Morris, CWO Joseph: 141–42
*Morris, SSG Stefan: 295, 321–22, 326, 327
*Moss, CPT Charles: 162
Mountain Division, 10th: 74
  at Bagram Airfield: 208, 384
  Operation ANACONDA: 201, 280–82, 284, 287–89
  at Qala-i-Jangi: 161–63, 192n49
  Quick Reaction Force: 231
  and the Salang Tunnel: 343–44
Mujahideen: 11–16, 18
Mulholland, COL John: 51, 52, 53–54, 75, 190n11, 211–12, 271n108, 272n131, 375, 377, 382–83
  and advisor for Karzai: 107
  and assignment of advisors to Afghan resistance leaders: 98
  liaison officers assigned to the Northern Alliance: 59–60
  and medical evacuations: 180–81
  planning for insertion of ARSOF into Afghanistan: 88n69
  and planning for OperationANACONDA: 280–81, 286, 287, 319
  planning for operations in the Tora Bora region: 213–14
  and reorganization of JSOTF-North: 105

responsibility for planning: 57
  and staffing of JSOTF-North: 79–80, 88n52, 89n70
  summit meeting on Northern Alliance campaign: 158
  and taking of Kandahar: 178–79
*Mulligan, MAJ Gregory: 352
Musharraf, General Pervez: 25–26, 34–35, 249, 250
Myers, GEN Richard B.: 115, 117, 215

Nadir, Shar: 3
Nahrin, Afghanistan: 342, 343–44
Nail 21: 297
Nail 22: 297, 301–02
Najibullah, Mohammad: 16–17, 21, 95, 190n8
Naka Valley: 282
Naqid, Mullah: 107
Naqeebullah, Mullah: 108, 182–83
*Nash, CPT Mike: 122–28, 134, 146–47, 159
National Security Council: 7, 8
National Training Center, ARSOF training at: 43–44
Naval Special Warfare Group One: 41, 57, 108, 209–10, 382–83
New York Times: 241
New Zealand, forces for Afghanistan operations: 34, 205, 236–37, 265, 346, 389
Night Stalkers. *See* Special Operations Aviation Regiment, 160th.
Night vision cameras: 97–98
Night vision goggles: 137, 142, 143, 176, 208, 237, 238, 241–42
*Nolan, SSG Eric: 350
Nongovernmental organizations relief efforts in Afghanistan: 60–61, 102, 183–84, 185, 206, 252, 352
North Atlantic Treaty Organization: 34
Northern Alliance: 21, 35–36, 59–60, 77, 82–85, 88n69, 93, 95, 98, 190n7, 191n32, 194n75, 377
Norwegian forces: 205, 265, 277, 281
*Nutting, MSG Neal: 168, 174

Objective Bastogne: 140–41
Objective Honda: 113
Objective Raptor: 142–43
Objective Rhino: 97–98, 107, 109–17, 370, 377
Objective Wolverine: 142
Office of the Joint Chiefs of Staff: 49–50
*Oliver, CWO Roger: 304–05, 309, 318
Oman: 72–73, 102, 116, 205, 278
Omar, Mohammad: 18
Omar, Mullah: 11, 20, 22, 23, 24, 25, 26, 30n57, 35, 156, 182, 183, 205, 215, 219
Operation ANACONDA: 210, 277–84, 319–23, 333–35, 385–89
Operation ENDURING FREEDOM: 40, 42, 50
Operation HARPOON: 327
Operation NOBLE EAGLE: 42
Operation RELENTLESS STRIKE: 144

Operational detachment As
  aerial resupply of: 131, 135, 146–47
  close-air-support teams: 101–02
  command and control of: 145, 232–33
  for initial parachute assault: 47, 376–77
  integration of PSYOP teams: 278
  missions: 231–32, 370
  sent to Northern Alliance leaders: 119, 377
  training for: 217–18
  used to direct tactical airstrikes and guide smart
    bombs: 101
Operation Detachment As (units)
  361: 353, 358
  372: 281–84, 287, 292, 294, 319–21, 324, 327,
    332–33, 334, 364n95, 365n112, n127
  381: 281–82, 322
  391: 365–66
  392: 282, 328
  394: 210, 265–66, 293–95, 319–28, 353–54, 364n94
  395: 327, 332, 333, 353–54
  511: 236–37
  512: 236–37
  513: 236–37
  514: 236–37, 241–43
  515: 243–44
  516: 236–37, 239–40
  524: 180–81, 209, 232–35, 269n26
  534: 98, 101, 162–63, 190n17
  542: 281–82, 322
  550: 211–12
  553: 99–100, 221
  554: 100, 183
  555: 96, 99, 101
  561: 216–17
  563: 292, 386–87
  570: 232
  571: 282, 328
  572: 109, 214–16
  574: 106–07, 155–58, 172–78, 180–81, 212, 232,
    252, 269n38
  575: 211–12
  581: 216
  583: 107, 165–71, 172, 173, 174–75, 178–79
  585: 98
  586: 99
  592: 163
  594: 99, 279, 281–84, 286–87, 292, 295, 319–28,
    362n31, 364n94, n96, n99, 365n127, 385
  595: 96, 101–03, 119–28, 134, 146–47, 159, 185–
    86, 192n42, 273n151
  923: 277–78, 356–57
  966: 277–78, 356–57
  981: 218–19, 277
  984: 219
Operational Detachments Bs (units)
  390: 328, 329, 332–33, 353
  560: 248–50
  570: 107, 180–81
  580: 74

Opposition Group Forces. See Afghan Military Forces.
Ordnance units: 44
*O'Reilly, SSG Jim: 151, 186
Oruzgan Province: 106, 156, 172, 236
*Osterman, SPC Mohammed: 258

Pace, Frank: 62
Pact of Neutrality and Nonaggression (with Russia): 6, 7
Pakistan
  Afghan refugees in: 16–17, 206
  al-Qaeda prisoners in: 250–51, 384
  blocking of escape routes to: 281–82, 283, 384
  diplomatic relations with the Taliban: 103, 192n45
  Federal Autonomous Tribal Areas: 206, 249
  forces sent by mullahs to reinforce the Taliban:
    199n209
  historical relationship with Afghanistan: 5, 7, 8, 9,
    10, 11, 16–17
  humanitarian aid organizations in: 252
  jihad brigade from: 98–99, 267n3
  and resistance to the Soviets in Afghanistan: 13, 14,
    16–17
  and the search for Taliban and al-Qaeda in border
    areas: 206, 248–50
  Special Service Group: 249–50
  supply line to the Taliban: 107–08, 167–69
  and the Taliban: 18–19, 20, 21, 22, 24–26, 34
  U.S. Embassy in: 60–61
  U.S. relations with: 7, 8, 9, 34–35, 248–50
Pakistani army
  American advisors to: 206
  U.S. air support to: 249
  U.S. combined operations with: 249–50
  U.S. training for: 249–50
Paktia Province: 10, 14, 279–80, 329–30
Panjshir Valley: 12–13, 14, 16, 120
Parachute assaults: 47, 97–98, 103–04, 107, 109–13,
    140–41
*Parcelli, SGT Paul: 298–99
*Parker, SSG Greg: 331
Parker, COL Richard, USAF: 74
*Parsons, SSG Jeremy: 215
*Parsons, SSG Mark: 73
Party of Islam: 11–12, 13, 14, 16
Pashtun tribes
  and Afghan history: 3, 4, 5, 6, 7, 8, 11
  anti-Taliban leaders: 94–95, 106, 154–58, 165–67
  in battle with the Taliban: 106–07, 167–71
  Karzai role in enlisting in the U.S. efforts against
    the Taliban: 153–55
  killed by U.S. airstrikes: 107
  ODA 574 assigned to support: 155–58
  and Operation ANACONDA: 280–83, 319–28,
    364n98, 365n112, 386
  operations at Mir Wais Hospital: 209, 233–35
  and rise of the Taliban: 17, 18, 30n61
  and sensitive site exploitation missions: 332–35
  training for: 281–82, 283, 321
  U.S. efforts to form an alliance with: 35–36

*Pasquez, SPC Martin: 111
*Patterson, CW3 Carl: 234–35
*Pavitt, Jim: 190*n3*
*Payle, MSG Albert: 239
Pazder, SPC Randy: 313, 314–15
Peacekeeping operations: 206
*Pearl, MAJ James: 336–37
Pelley, Scott: 228
People's Democratic Party of Afghanistan: 9, 10, 16
*Perez, SGT Mario: 114–15
Persia: 2–3, 4–5, 28*n15*
Persian Safavid Empire: 2–3
Peshawar region: 4, 16–17, 19
Petithory, SFC Daniel: 180, 212
Phelan, COL Mark: 58–59, 256, 257, 277, 278, 279, 335, 336, 337, 338, 345, 346–47, 356, 367*n187*, 389
*Phipps, CWO Bill: 122–23, 128
Pickering, Thomas: 25–26
*Pierce, CPT Mel: 232–35
*Polson, SPC Jonas O.: 313
Powell, Colin: 33, 34–36, 44–45, 150–51
Pravda: 10
Prisoners: 158–65, 198*n207, n211*, 204, 215, 233, 237, 240, 244, 250–51, 272*n128*, 321–22
Prosser, SSG Cody: 172, 180, 212
Psychological operations: 41
  approval for: 49–50, 62, 259, 341
  funding for: 50
  leaflets. *See* Leaflets.
  in Mazar-e-Sharif: 102, 185–87
  planning for: 62–64, 278
  precombat activities: 47–50, 62, 376
  radio programs. *See* Radio broadcasts.
  units: 43, 44, 50, 62
Psychological operations battalions
  3rd: 98, 116–17, 147–49
  8th: 46, 48–49, 50, 62, 63, 244, 258–59, 340–41
  9th: 39, 111, 113–17, 186, 244, 351
Psychological Operations Company, 345th: 278–79
Psychological Operations Group, 4th: 45, 62–64, 147–48, 375
*Puller, CPT Mark: 151

Qadir, Abdul: 17, 192*n41*
Qal-e-yeh, Afghanistan: 223
Qala-i-Jangi, prisoner uprising at: 104–05, 158–65, 198*n207, n211, n212, n213*, 380
Qalat, history of: 4
Qarabagh, Afghanistan: 226
Qatar: 58, 253, 278, 382
Quartermaster Companies
  5th: 130
  421st: 130, 131–32
Quartermaster units: 44
Quick reaction forces
  aircraft for: 249, 250
  combined U.S. and Pakistani: 249–50
  command and control of: 265–66, 303

ODB 560 as: 248–50
for Operation ANACONDA: 295, 301
for rescue on Takur Ghar: 295, 301, 303–19, 387–88

Rabbani, Burhannudin: 17–18, 19, 21
Rachman, COL Habib: 349–50
Radio broadcasts: 62, 63, 278
  of Afghan music: 103, 186–87, 245, 258–59, 278–79, 341
  aircraft used for: 63, 116, 186, 248, 376, 384
  broadband satellite communications teams: 340–41
  guidance from Karzai regarding: 153–54, 258–59
  in Kandahar: 352
  keep-away messages: 288–89, 291
  leaflets advertising: 148–49, 186
  medical awareness campaigns: 279
  mine awareness: 245
  in Operation ANACONDA: 288
  precombat: 46, 89*n79*, 103, 192*n43*, 245, 248, 376
  used in Mazar-e-Sharif: 102
Radios distributed in Afghanistan: 89*n79*, 149, 185–86, 245
Ramstein, Germany: 130, 376
RAND studies: 11–12
Ranger Infantry Regiment, 75th: 47, 88*n63*, 104, 107
  1st Battalion: 301, 303–19
  3rd Battalion: 97–98, 109–13, 140–41, 143–45, 208, 370, 376–77
Rashid, Ahmed: 19
Rasmussen, COL Dave: 55–56
*Rauch, CPT Stan: 230
*Rawlins, SSG Jerry: 294–95, 321, 322, 327, 362*n45*
Razor 01: 303, 309
Razor 02: 303, 304–05, 309, 317–18
Razor 03: 296–303, 304
Razor 04: 296–97, 299, 300, 301–02, 303
Razor 54: 312, 316, 317
*Reagan, CWO Mark: 331
*Reese, LTC Phillip: 336, 337, 345, 346
Refugees: 206, 221–22
*Regent, CPT Kerry: 231, 232
Reserve Special Operations Command, U.S. Army: 39
*Rhinehart, LTC Matt: 51, 88*n40*, 165, 172
Rice, Condoleeza: 37
*Richards, LTC Warren: 54–55, 57, 75, 78, 79, 154, 155
Richardson, Bill: 22
Roadblocks: 169–70, 285, 288–89, 364*n94*, 384–85
*Robards, SSG: 234–35
*Roberts, LTC Mike: 179
Roberts, P01 Neil: 298–99, 300, 301–02, 303, 309, 313, 319
*Robeson, SSG Carey: 333
*Rogers, SFC Charles: 185
Rogers, MAJ Robert: 38
*Roswell, CWO Tim: 172
*Rounds, CPT Terry: 352

Rules of engagement
   high value target missions: 331
   for SOAR DAP crews: 139
Rumsfeld, Donald: 33, 35, 36, 38, 40, 46, 65, 67, 98,
   102, 117, 182, 184, 191*n31*, 208–09, 215, 241,
   250–51, 326, 344
Russia, historical role in Afghanistan: 4–6, 7, 28*n15*
*Ryan, MAJ Mike: 248–50
*Ryder, SGM Rich: 172

*Sage, SFC Elias: 166, 168, 169, 175
Salang Pass Tunnel: 7, 10, 207, 225–27, 342–44, 386
*Salvadorini, SFC Rocky: 243, 244
Sams, BG Ronald: 60, 248, 249, 250
*Samuels, CPT Jed: 265, 319–25, 326, 327
*Sanders, LTC Terry: 265, 277, 281, 295, 320
*Sands, SSG Nick: 172, 176–78
*Sanford, CPT Barry: 251, 252
*Santana, MSG Tony: 337–38, 344, 356
*Santiago, SSG Bobby: 168
Saudi Arabia: 21, 22, 24–25, 34, 230
*Sault, MAJ Kevin: 160, 162
Sayd-Alim-Kalay: 174, 179–81, 182
Sayd-Alim-Kalay bridge: 107, 175–77
*Schantz, MAJ Randal: 312, 317
Schools: 221, 222
*Schroeder, CPT Pat: 162
*Schuyler, SFC Bart: 227, 228, 343
*Searcey, SFC Ron: 111
Secure Compartmental Information Facility (SCIF):
   81
Security classification of information: 57
*Seifert, SSG Wallace: 216
*Seims, CPT Chuck: 143, 144
Self, CPT Nathan: 301, 303, 304, 305, 306, 307–13,
   315–19
Sensitive site exploitations
   Pashtun forces used for: 332–33
   in the Shah-i-Khot Valley: 332–35
   in southern Afghanistan: 206, 208, 235–41, 256–
      57, 265–66
   specialized equipment for: 256–57, 265
Serkhankheyl, Afghanistan: 282, 292, 326
Shah-i-Khot Valley: 210, 276–77, 279–80, 281–82,
   283, 286, 292, 294, 320–28, 332–35, 365*n127*,
   385–86
Sharif, Nawaz: 25
Shariff, General: 96
*Shaw, LTC Richard, USAF: 74
Sheberghan: 22
Shelton, General Henry: 23–24, 36
Sher Ali Khan: 5
*Sherman, CWO Will: 52
Sherzai, Gul Agha: 106, 107–08, 167–71, 271*n99*
   and the battle for Kandahar: 173, 174–75, 178–79,
      182–83
   and Mir Wais Hospital: 233
   ODA 583 support for: 165–69, 173, 174–75,
      178–79

Sherzai, Pashta: 178
Shi'a Muslims: 20, 30*n55, n61*
Shimal Valley: 282
Shin Narai Valley: 166, 167
Shkin, Afghanistan: 241–44
Shomali Plains: 96, 98
Shuja Mirza, Shah: 4
Sicily: 66
*Simpson, LTC Edward: 151
*Sims, CPT Harry: 165–70, 173, 174–75, 178–79,
   182–83
SCAMPI: 79, 81, 82, 90*n128*, 344
*Singletary, MAJ Harry: 352
Sisler, 1LT George K.: 199*n266*
Sisler, MAJ Jim: 199*n266*
*Slater, SFC: 243
*Small, MAJ Steve: 185
*Snow, SSG Wes: 123
*Solanis, CW3 Arthur: 120, 132–33, 135–36, 137–38,
   281, 318
*Solis, MAJ Jeffrey: 58, 171
Somalia: 59
Soran, Afghanistan: 329
*Sorrenson, SFC Sol: 251, 252
Spain: 66, 67
Spann, Johnny Michael: 104, 160, 164, 192*n48*
Special Forces Group, 3rd: 39, 58–59, 335–37,
   384
   2nd Battalion: 256
   3rd Battalion: 208, 211, 260–61, 265–66, 267, 279,
      280–83
   at Bagram Air Base: 210, 335–37
   as CJSOTF-Afghanistan: 277, 335–37
   Information Management Section: 338–40
   integration of civil affairs: 328–30
   and Kabul Military Academy: 349–50
   mission: 359–60, 385
   preparation for role in Afghanistan: 41–42
   surveillance and reconnaissance: 280–81
   training for: 59
Special Forces Group, 5th: 39, 45, 47, 88*n69*, 105,
   209
   1st Battalion: 108, 204, 235–44
   2nd Battalion: 57–58, 171–74, 206
   3rd Battalion: 159–60, 209
   and assignment of ODA 574 to support Karzai:
      155–56
   base operations responsibilities at Karshi Kanabad:
      79–80
   command and control issues: 45–46, 60, 79–80,
      145
   handicaps: 41
   mission: 41, 55, 370, 384–85
   ODA as Quick Reaction Force: 231–32
   operations at Hazar Qadam: 208–09
   preparation for role in Afghanistan: 41–42, 52–54,
      90*n110*
   problems adjusting to role as JSOTF-N: 52–54, 57,
      78, 79

Special Forces Group, 5th–*Continued*
  PSYOP liaison offices with: 63
  role as ARSOTF: 52–54
  training for: 53, 55, 56–57, 79, 371, 375
Special Forces Group, 19th: 218, 277–78, 371–72
  1st Battalion: 217
  2nd Battalion: 208, 216–19
  5th Battalion: 216, 277
  mission: 218–19, 277–78, 329–30, 352, 356
Special Forces Group, 20th: 79, 210, 255–56,
    273n159, 354, 371–72
Special Forces Groups, mobilization of ARNG units:
    44, 371–72
Special Operations Aviation Regiment, 160th: 39
  1st Battalion: 141–43, 370
  2nd Battalion: 96–97, 206, 296–99, 370
  3rd Battalion: 88n63, 208
  aborted missions: 132–33
  aircraft used: 330, 372–73
  ARNG units assigned to: 151–53
  CSAR mission: 46, 70–71, 206, 229–32, 296–99
  and delivery of forces to fight with the Northern
      Alliance: 117–22
  FARP units: 68
  helicopter buildup at Karshi Kanabad: 45, 71–72
  incompleteness of threat picture for: 134–35
  at Kandahar: 204
  maintenance teams: 105–06
  and operations in the Hindu Kush Mountains:
      117–22
  parachute assaults: 47, 96, 141–43, 370
  rules of engagement: 139–40
  training: 43
Special Operations Command, 1st: 39
Special Operations Command, Europe: 41, 100–101,
    129–32, 195n125, 209, 253–54
Special Operations Command, U.S. Joint Forces
    Command: 41–42, 53, 55–56, 57, 90n108, 371,
    375, 382–83, 384
Special Operations Command and Control Elements:
    218–19, 383–84
  52: 171–72, 177–78, 182–83, 199n257
  540: 180–81, 218
Special Operations Command, Central: 40–41, 58–59,
    70–71, 275
  coordination with SOCEUR on resupply of forces:
      131–32
  and planning for the SOF campaign: 50–51, 53, 56,
      57, 370
  staffing of: 56, 57, 375
Special Operations Communication Assemblage
    teams: 81, 82, 279
Special Operations Media Systems' Broadcast radio
    stations: 186–87, 258–59, 278–79, 340–41, 385
Special Operations Signal Battalion, 112th: 39, 45,
    55, 70, 75–76, 80–82, 204, 219–20, 373–74, 375,
    376, 377
Special Operations Squadrons
  6th: 88n63

9th: 68, 85, 120, 122, 209, 261–63
19th: 172
Special Operations Support Battalion, 528th: 39, 44,
    45, 68, 72–73, 207, 249, 260–61, 373–74, 376,
    389
Special Operations Wings
  16th: 68, 131, 195n129, 209, 254, 375–76
  352nd: 209, 254
Special reconnaissance searches: 204, 205–06,
    235–41
Special Tactics Squadron, 23rd: 303
Special tactics squadron teams (Air Force): 135,
    140–41, 143, 144, 167, 187–88, 192n38
Spin Boldak, Afghanistan: 19, 167, 169–70, 175
Stanhagen, COL Eric: 51
*Stark, SSG Michael: 83
*Staunton, SFC Robert: 234–35
Stebner, SGT Eric W.: 310, 313–15, 316–17
*Steinmann, LTC Marcus: 51–52, 165
*Stevenson, SP4 Dale: 246, 248, 291
Steverson, SFC Douglas: 68
*Stirling, BM1 Jackson, USN: 272n125
Stonesifer, PFC Kristofor: 113
Straw, Jack: 34
*Striker, CWO Walter: 187–88
Stronghold Freedom. *See* Karshi Kanabad,
    Uzbekistan.
Sudan: 23
*Sullivan, MSG Don: 75–76, 90n110, 145–46, 344
Sun Tzu: 47
Sunni Muslims: 2, 30n61
*Sutherland, MAJ Ron: 328
Svitak, SGT Philip: 187, 305, 306
*Sykes, LTC Jack: 255–56

Tactical air control parties: 172, 180–81, 199n258,
    273n151
Tactical PSYOP Detachments
  812: 340
  910: 244–45, 248, 287–88, 351
  930: 151, 245
  940: 113–15
  941: 114–15
  943: 114–15
Tactical PSYOP Teams: 278, 287–89, 359–60
  912: 288–89
  913: 244–45, 246, 247, 248, 289–91
  922: 102
  933: 287–88
Tahk-te-pol, Afghanistan: 167–69
Tajikistan: 224–25
Tajiks: 16, 17–18, 20, 365n116
  ODA 394 in support of: 322–28
  ODA 534 assigned to work with: 98
Takur Ghar: 280, 295, 296, 299–300, 302–13, 387
*Talbert, CWO Douglas: 301, 303, 304–06, 307–09,
    311, 313, 314, 315, 316–17, 318
Taliban
  airstrikes against: 101, 174–75

Taliban–Continued
   antiaircraft artillery: 133, 135–39, 170–71
   battle with Karzai's forces: 106–07
   bombing of in the Dari-a-Souf Valley: 126–27, 134
   defectors: 176–77
   and effort to re-take Tarin Kowt: 156–58
   encouraged to surrender: 292
   entrenched in Pakistan: 203
   entrenched in the Tora Bora: 203–04
   force concentrations in Kandahar: 156, 170
   Karzai guidance on turning the people against: 153
   Karzai negotiations with: 182–83
   at Konduz: 192n42, 198n211
   leaders of sought in southern Afghanistan: 205,
      208–09, 210–11, 213–16
   morale: 194n75
   Northern Alliance resistance against: 94
   and Operation ANACONDA: 210
   order of battle: 138
   Pakistani: 198n207
   Pashtuns enlisted in the fight against: 154–55
   prisoners: 204, 215
   PSYOP role in loss of public support for: 186–87
   relations with bin Laden: 22, 23–24, 25, 35
   relations with foreign governments: 18–19, 20, 21,
      22, 24–26, 34
   road to power in Afghanistan: 18–20
   sudden loyalty to Karzai: 183, 203
   supply line to Pakistan: 107–08, 167–69
   U.S. efforts to form a coalition against: 35–36
   withdrawal from Kandahar: 178–79, 182–83
Taloqan, Afghanistan: 158, 221–22
Tampa, Florida: 40
Taraki, Nur Mohammed: 9, 10
Targeting lasers: 101
Tarin Kowt, Afghanistan: 106–07, 155–58, 172–73
Tarnak Farms: 178, 265
   al-Qaeda training base at: 167, 170
Task Force 3/75 Ranger, and Objective Rhino: 109–
   15, 116–17
Task Force 180: 211
Task Force Dagger. *See* Joint Special Operations Task
   Force-North.
Task Force Kabar. *See* Joint Special Operations Task
   Force-South.
Task Force Mountain: 280–82, 284, 287, 292, 294,
   296, 312, 385, 386–87
Task Force Rakkasan: 277, 384
   and cave searches in the Tora Bora region: 356–58
   and humanitarian aid: 350, 351
   and Operation ANACONDA: 282, 284, 286, 287,
      292, 385–87
Tenet, George: 26, 36, 159
Terghul Ghar (the "Whale"): 280, 321, 322–23
Terrain
   and crash on Takur Ghar: 302, 308–09, 311, 313,
     315
   and defense of Tarin Kowt: 156–57
   descriptions of: 33, 53–54

   and direct action operations: 241–42
   and helicopter operations: 78–79, 83, 96
   and intelligence operations: 281
   role in Afghan history: 2
   and the Soviet occupation of Afghanistan: 12
   in the Tora Bora region: 213, 357
Texas 14. *See* ODA 594.
Theater Army Support Commands
   21st: 128, 130, 131–32, 191n25, 209, 273n155,
     389
*Thomas, SSG Jack: 114–15
*Thompson, CPT Alison: 229, 231
*Thurman, SFC Jason: 294, 320, 325, 364n92
Tinan, COL Joe: 345
Tora Bora region: 108–09, 193n70, 203–04, 213–16,
   269n40, 356–58, 383–84
*Torgelson, CW3 Dwayne: 214
*Towson, CPT Gary: 283–84, 285, 286, 287
Training
   3rd SFG: 59
   19th SFG: 217
   Afghan militias: 174, 276, 277, 281–82, 283, 321,
     367n196
   Afghan National Army: 211, 277, 279, 347–50,
     358–60
   ARNG units: 217–18, 255–56, 371–72
   ARSOF: 43–44, 374, 381
   aviation mechanics: 152
   civil affairs officers: 43, 372
   communications support: 81, 217, 338, 339, 372
   for CSAR missions: 230
   with foreign militaries: 44, 102
   JSOTF staffs: 53, 55, 56–57, 79–80, 90n108, 371,
     375, 382–83
   lack of ammunition for: 218
   language: 43
   Pakistani forces: 249–50
   Pashtun forces: 156, 233
   psychological operations: 43
   for sensitive site exploitation: 256–57, 265
   special operations aviators: 43
   at the U.S. Army John F. Kennedy Special Warfare
     Center and School: 39, 43, 256–57, 372, 381
Transportation units: 44
Treaty of Gandamak: 5
Treaty of Rawalpindi (1919): 6
*Tucker, CW3 Jerry: 135–36, 298–99
Turkey: 66, 67, 205
Turkmenistan: 252

Under Secretary of Defense for Policy: 49–50, 62
UNICEF: 183
Union of Soviet Socialist Republics
   invasion and occupation of Afghanistan: 10–16
   military advisors in Afghanistan: 7, 9–10, 16
United Arab Emirates: 34, 102
United Islamic and National Front for the Salvation of
    Afghanistan (Northern Alliance): 21. *See
    also* Northern Alliance.

United Nations
   humanitarian relief efforts: 60–61, 252
   Joint Logistics Cell: 60–61
   response to 9/11: 34, 35, 36
   and the *Taliban*: 21, 22, 24
United Nations Charter: 10
United Nations General Assembly: 11
United Nations High Commissioner for Refugees:
   226–27
United Nations Security Council: 22, 26
United States
   and the Cold War: 7, 8, 9
   and efforts to capture bin Laden: 23–24, 25–26
   Embassy in Afghanistan: 267*n2*
   goals for the conflict in Afghanistan: 35–36
   reaction to Soviet invasion of Afghanistan: 10–11
   relations with Pakistan: 7, 8, 9, 34–35
   support for Hekmatyar: 17
   and the *Taliban*: 21–22
   terrorist attacks on facilities abroad: 22–24
U.S. Agency for International Development: 223,
   226, 386
U.S. Air Force personnel
   pararescue medics: 180–81
   special tactics airmen: 101, 103–04, 112
U.S. Army Field Manual 41–10, *Civil Affairs
   Operations*: 185
U.S. Army John F. Kennedy Special Warfare Center
   and School: 39, 43, 256–57, 372, 381
U.S. Army Recruiting Command: 43
U.S. Army Reserve
   civil affairs units: 43, 278
   logistical support for: 373
   mobilizations: 43, 44, 50, 216, 371–72, 374, 384
   PSYOP personnel mobilized: 62, 278
   PSYOP units: 43
   quartermaster units: 130
U.S. Army Reserve Special Operations Command: 39
U.S. Army Special Operations Command: 39, 40, 42,
   44, 377
U.S. Central Command: 40–41, 192*n36*
   Combined Forces Land Component Command:
     236, 237, 250–51, 347, 348
   command and control issues: 373–74
   funding for resupply efforts: 273*n155*
   intelligence information provided to JSOTF: 79
   JPOTF: 48–49, 62, 63
   liaison to U.S. Embassy in Pakistan: 60–61
   and logistics support for Operation ENDURING
     FREEDOM: 129–30, 374–75
   and operations in the Horn of Africa: 59
   operations security: 371
   planning for unconventional warfare in Afghanistan:
     93–95, 109, 211, 370–71
   and precombat PSYOP activities: 47–50
   reconnaissance and surveillance and direct action
     operations: 235–41, 243–44
   response to 9/11: 40–42
U.S. European Command: 40, 41, 129–30, 273*n155*

U.S. Marine Corps
   engineers at Kandahar Airport: 204–05
   forces at Kandahar: 108
   and guarding of the U.S. Embassy: 267*n2*
   helicopter crash: 206, 229–32
   infantry battalions: 107
   and medical evacuation: 180–81
U.S. Navy
   and medical evacuation: 180–81
   Seabee engineers at Kandahar Airport: 204–05
U.S. Navy Sea-Air-Land (SEAL) teams: 54, 56, 107,
   193*n61*
U.S. Special Operations Command: 40, 54–55,
   374–75
Uzbekistan: 5, 10, 26
   humanitarian aid based in: 207, 252
   U.S. and coalition forces based in: 44–45, 64–66, 74,
     102. *See also* Karshi Kanabad, Uzbekistan.
Uzbeks: 2–3, 17–18, 22

Vance, SSGT Kevin: 306, 307, 308–09, 311–12,
   313–14, 315
*Vandiver, SGM Marvin: 164
*Vargas, SGT Charles: 186
Vela, SPC Omar: 313, 314–15
*Veringer, SFC John: 332
*Victoro, SGM Manuel: 74
Video teleconferences: 56, 76, 341, 345–47, 375, 377,
   382
Videotapes of action at Objective Rhino: 98, 116–17
Volckmann, COL Russell: 38

Walker, SGT Joshua J.: 306, 307, 308, 311, 313,
   315
*Walters, SGT Bradley: 306, 307–08, 311, 313,
   316
*Walters, SGT Charles: 150, 221
*Walters, LTC Jack: 56, 57, 79–80
*Walton, SPC Arthur: 352
*Wannamaker, SGT Paul: 123, 125
*Ward, SSG Nolan: 247
Wardak, Taj Mohammad: 329
*Washington, CPT Morris: 338–39
*Washington, 2LT Tom: 82
Washington Post: 38, 40, 241
Water for farming: 223
*Watson, MSG Aaron: 249
*Watson, CPT David: 140–41
Weather
   dust storms: 82, 96
   in the high mountains: 117–18, 119–20, 132–33,
     376, 377–78
   and intelligence operations: 281
   and need for humanitarian aid: 46
   and Operation ANACONDA: 282, 285
   problems forecasting: 378–79
   problems with rain at Karshi Kanabad: 77–78,
     376
   sandstorms: 66, 82, 83, 84–85, 117, 119–20

*West, MAJ Jon: 236–41, 243
*West, CPT Paul, USAF: 65–66
"Whale," the. *See* Terghul Ghar.
White, Thomas: 38
White Mountains: 204, 213, 215–16, 269*n40*
*Whitley, MSG Shannon: 215
Wiercinski, COL Frank: 277
*Wilcox, SSG Jesse: 239
*Wilcox, SGT Norman: 288
Wilkerson, COL Kevin: 327
*Wilkerson, SGT Roger: 331
*Willard, MAJ Kent: 338, 344
*Willet, SSG James: 64–65, 66
*Williams, Karen: 251
Wilmoth, SSG Harper: 313, 316–17
*Woburn, MSG Danny: 358
Wolfowitz, Paul: 33, 154, 155, 213, 252
Women
    aviation mechanics: 152
    broadcasts promoting the roles of: 259

role of: 7–8, 9, 15
    and the *Taliban*: 18, 19, 21–22
World Food Program: 184

*Yates, MSG Dexter: 253, 349–50
Yemen: 102
Yosif: 178–79
Yousuf, Muhammad: 8–9

Zahir, Ahmed: 259
Zahir Shah, Muhammad: 7, 8, 9
Zaman, Hajji Mohammed: 109
Zerkikheyl, Afghanistan: 292, 324, 326
Zhob, Pakistan: 249
Zia Abdullah, Commander: 283
Zia Lodin, Commander: 281–83, 284–85, 286–87,
    292, 321, 322, 323, 324, 326, 327, 332, 353–54,
    365*n 127*, 386
Zia ul-Haq: 16–17
*Zimmer, Kerry: 276